MW00992473

HANDBOOK OF VIOLENCE RISK ASSESSMENT

International Perspectives on Forensic Mental Health

A Routledge Book Series
Edited by Ronald Roesch and Stephen Hart,
Simon Fraser University

The goal of this series is to improve the quality of health care services in forensic settings by providing a forum for discussing issues related to policy, administration, clinical practice, and research. The series will cover topics such as mental health law; the organization and administration of forensic services for people with mental disorder; the development, implementation and evaluation of treatment programs for mental disorder in civil and criminal justice settings; the assessment and management of violence risk, including risk for sexual violence and family violence; and staff selection, training, and development in forensic systems. The book series will consider proposals for both monographs and edited works on these and similar topics, with special consideration given to proposals that promote best practice and are relevant to international audiences.

RANDY K. OTTO AND KEVIN S. DOUGLAS, EDITORS

HANDBOOK OF VIOLENCE RISK ASSESSMENT

New York London

Routledge
Taylor & Francis Group
270 Madison Avenue
New York, NY 10016

Routledge
Taylor & Francis Group
2 Park Square
Milton Park, Abingdon
Oxon OX14 4RN

Routledge is an imprint of Taylor & Francis Group, an Informa business

Printed in the United States of America on acid-free paper
10 9 8 7 6 5 4 3 2 1

International Standard Book Number-13: 978-0-415-96214-8 (Hardcover)

Library of Congress Cataloging-in-Publication Data

Handbook of violence risk assessment / edited by Randy K. Otto, Kevin Douglas.
p. cm. -- (International perspectives on forensic mental health: a Routledge book series)
Includes bibliographical references and index.
ISBN 978-0-415-96214-8 (hardback : alk. paper)
1. Violence. 2. Violence--Forecasting. 3. Risk assessment. I. Otto, Randy K. II. Douglas, Kevin S.
[DNLM: 1. Forensic psychiatry.]

HM1116.H363 2009
363.32'12--dc22 2009010308

Visit the Taylor & Francis Web site at
http://www.taylorandfrancis.com

and the Routledge Web site at
http://www.routledge.com

Contents

Contributors vii

Introduction and Overview ix

1 Violence Risk Assessment Tools: Overview and Critical Analysis 1
KIRK HEILBRUN, KENTO YASUHARA, and SANJAY SHAH

2 The Use of Measures of Psychopathy in Violence Risk Assessment 19
DAVID DEMATTEO, JOHN F. EDENS, and ALLISON HART

Part I Child and Juvenile Risk

3 Gender-Specific Childhood Risk Assessment Tools: Early Assessment Risk Lists for Boys (EARL-20B) and Girls (EARL-21G) 43
LEENA K. AUGIMERI, PIA ENEBRINK, MARGARET WALSH, and DEPENG JIANG

4 Structured Assessment of Violence Risk in Youth (SAVRY) 63
RANDY BORUM, HENNY LODEWIJKS, PATRICK A. BARTEL, and ADELLE E. FORTH

5 Youth Level of Service/Case Management Inventory 81
ROBERT D. HOGE

Part II Adult Risk

6 The Violence Risk Appraisal Guide and Sex Offender Risk Appraisal Guide for Violence Risk Assessment and the Ontario Domestic Assault Risk Assessment and Domestic Violence Risk Appraisal Guide for Wife Assault Risk Assessment 99
MARNIE E. RICE, GRANT T. HARRIS, and N. ZOE HILTON

7 Two Treatment- and Change-Oriented Risk Assessment Tools: The Violence Risk Scale and Violence Risk Scale–Sexual Offender Version 121
STEPHEN C. P. WONG and MARK E. OLVER

8 Historical-Clinical-Risk Management-20 (HCR-20) Violence Risk Assessment Scheme: Rationale, Application, and Empirical Overview 147
KEVIN S. DOUGLAS and KIM A. REEVES

9 The Classification of Violence Risk 187
JOHN MONAHAN

10 The Level of Service (LS) Assessment of Adults and Older Adolescents 199
D. A. ANDREWS, JAMES BONTA, and J. STEPHEN WORMITH

11 The Spousal Assault Risk Assessment Guide (SARA) 227
P. RANDALL KROPP and ANDREA GIBAS

12 Static-99: An Actuarial Tool to Assess Risk of Sexual and Violent Recidivism Among Sexual Offenders 251
DANA ANDERSON and R. KARL HANSON

13 Structured Professional Judgment Guidelines for Sexual Violence Risk Assessment: The Sexual Violence Risk-20 (SVR-20) and Risk for Sexual Violence Protocol (RSVP) 269
STEPHEN D. HART and DOUGLAS P. BOER

Author Index 295

Subject Index 305

Contributors

Dana Anderson, Ph.D.
Private Practice
Barrie, Ontario
Canada

Don A. Andrews, Ph.D.
Department of Psychology
Carleton University
Ottawa, Ontario
Canada

Leena K. Augimeri, Ph.D.
Centre for Children Committing Offenses
Child Development Institute
Toronto, Ontario
Canada

Patrick A. Bartel
Youth Forensic Psychiatric Services of British Columbia
Vancouver, British Columbia
Canada

Douglas P. Boer, Ph.D.
Department of Psychology
University of Waikato
Hamiton, New Zealand

James Bonta
Public Safety Canada
Ottawa, Ontario
Canada

Randy Borum, Ph.D.
Department of Mental Health Law and Policy
Florida Mental Health Institute
University of South Florida
Tampa, Florida

David DeMatteo, J.D., Ph.D.
Department of Psychology
Drexel University
Philadelphia, Pennsylvania

Kevin S. Douglas, LL.B., Ph.D.
Department of Psychology
Simon Fraser University
Burnaby, British Columbia
Canada

John F. Edens, Ph.D.
Department of Psychology
Texas A&M University
College Station, Texas

Pia Enebrink, Ph.D.
Department of Clinical Neuroscience
Karolinska Institute
Stockholm, Sweden

Adelle E. Forth, Ph.D.
Department of Mental Health Law and Policy
Florida Mental Health Institute
University of South Florida
Tampa, Florida

Andrea Gibas
Department of Psychology
Simon Fraser University
Burnaby, British Columbia
Canada

R. Karl Hanson, Ph.D.
Corrections Research
Public Safety Canada
Ottawa, Ontario
Canada

Grant T. Harris, Ph.D.
Research Department
Mental Health Centre Penetanguishene
Penetanguishene, Ontario
Canada

Allison Hart, M.S.
Department of Psychology
Drexel University
Philadelphia, Pennsylvania

Stephen D. Hart, Ph.D.
Department of Psychology
Simon Fraser University
Burnaby, British Columbia
Canada

Kirk Heilbrun, Ph.D.
Department of Psychology
Drexel University
Philadelphia, Pennsylvania

N. Zoe Hilton, Ph.D.
Research Department
Mental Health Centre Penetanguishene
Penetanguishene, Ontario
Canada

Robert D. Hoge, Ph.D.
Department of Psychology
Carleton University
Ottawa, Ontario
Canada

Depeng Jiang, Ph.D.
Applied Health Research Centre
St. Michael Hospital
York University
Toronto, Ontario
Canada

P. Randall Kropp, Ph.D.
British Columbia Forensic Psychiatric Services Commission
Vancouver, British Columbia
Canada

Henny Lodewijks
Rentray (Juvenile Correctional and Treatment Facility)
Eefde, The Netherlands

John Monahan, Ph.D.
School of Law
University of Virginia
Charlottesville, Virginia

Mark E. Olver, Ph.D.
Department of Psychology
University of Saskatchewan
Saskatoon, Saskatchewan
Canada

Randy K. Otto, Ph.D.
Department of Mental Health Law and Policy
Florida Mental Health Institute
University of South Florida
Tampa, Florida

Kim A. Reeves
Department of Psychology
Simon Fraser University
Burnaby, British Columbia
Canada

Marnie E. Rice, Ph.D.
Research Department
Mental Health Centre Penetanguishene
Penetanguishene, Ontario
Canada

Sanjay Shah
Department of Psychology
Drexel University
Philadelphia, Pennsylvania

Margaret Walsh, B.A.
Centre for Children Committing Offenses
Child Development Institute
Toronto, Ontario
Canada

Stephen C. P. Wong, Ph.D.
Department of Psychology
University of Saskatchewan
Saskatoon, Saskatchewan
Canada

J. Stephen Wormith
Department of Psychology
University of Saskatchewan
Saskatoon, Saskatchewan
Canada

Kento Yasuhara
Department of Psychology
Drexel University
Philadelphia, Pennsylvania

Introduction and Overview

Risk for violence to others is relevant in a variety of legal (for example, civil commitment, criminal sentencing, parole decisions, and disposition in delinquency proceedings) and clinical contexts (for example, case management of and decision making regarding clients who pose a risk of harm to others). Consequently, accurate assessment of violence risk is of concern to legal, correctional, and mental health professionals alike. Monahan's 1981 monograph, *The Clinical Prediction of Violent Behavior*, which documented the limited ability of mental health professionals to identify persons who are at greater and lesser risk for violence, stimulated considerable research on the prevalence of violence among different groups of persons and systematic assessment of risk for violence. As a result, the field is now in a very different place than it was three decades ago. We know much more about how common violent behavior is in different settings and among different groups, and our ability to identify persons at greater and lesser risk for violence has improved significantly. It is this latter issue—assessment of violence risk—that is the focus of this book.

In the past 30 years, a large number of violence risk assessment tools have been developed for use with a variety of populations. However, psychologists, psychiatrists, correctional personnel, attorneys, and judges typically have to access a variety of publications in order to learn more about the development and potential utility of these tools. As such, we saw the value in consolidating what is known about contemporary risk assessment instruments into a single volume. We invited the authors of the most frequently used violence risk assessment tools to prepare chapters for this volume, which we conceptualize as a handbook or reference guide.

The book begins with two introductory chapters. First, Heilbrun, Yasuhara, and Shah provide an "overview and critical analysis" of contemporary risk assessment instruments. They discuss six key considerations for potential users of violence risk assessment instruments: (1) context, (2) purpose, (3) population, (4) parameters, (5) approach, and (6) applicability. They also provide an analysis of the current state of the research, broadly speaking, as it applies to the two main approaches to risk assessment—*actuarial* and *structured professional judgment* (SPJ).

Second, DeMatteo, Edens, and Hart review research regarding psychopathy and its relevance to understanding and making decisions about violence risk. Although measures of psychopathy are not risk assessment instruments per se, such measures (most commonly measures from the Hare family of psychopathy instruments) are most often used in risk assessment. As such, inclusion of a chapter focusing on the uses and misuses of such measures was warranted.

The remainder of the book focuses on risk assessment instruments. In order to facilitate a comparison of the various measures, authors whose chapters focus on a particular tool(s) were provided with a chapter template. Although there is as one might expect some variability. Each chapter begins with an overview of the instrument(s), its development, and populations with which it can be used, followed by a discussion of the research regarding its reliability and validity. The chapters then outline the limitations of the instruments and the areas for future research. Finally, a case study is provided so that the reader can see how each tool might be used clinically.

Although there were a variety of ways that we could have grouped these tools, we simply chose to section them according to the age(s) of the population with which they might be used. In the "Child and Juvenile Risk" section, Augimeri, Enebrink, Walsh, and Jiang describe two structured professional judgment tools that they developed for use with preadolescent populations—the Early Assessment Risk List for Boys (EARL-20B) and the Early Assessment Risk List for Girls (EARL-21G). Borum, Lodewijks, Bartel, and Forth summarize the literature regarding the Structured Assessment for Violence Risk in Youth (SAVRY), another SPJ instrument. Hoge then reviews what is known about the rationally derived through actuarially applied Youth Level of Service/Case Management Inventory (YLS/CMI).

The "Adult Risk" section includes chapters devoted to tools that are designed to inform judgments about three kinds of violence risk: (1) general violence, (2) domestic violence, and (3) sexual violence. Rice, Harris, and Hilton devote a chapter to summarizing the body of research examining the utility of two well-known actuarial tools—the Violence Risk Appraisal Guide (VRAG) and the Sex Offender Risk Appraisal Guide (SORAG), as well as two actuarial instruments that were more recently developed, the Ontario Domestic Assault Risk Assessment (ODARA) and the Domestic Violence Risk Appraisal Guide (DVRAG). Wong and Olver's chapter then focuses on the Violence Risk Scale (VRS) and the Violence Risk Scale–Sexual Offender Version (VRS-SO). Douglas and Reeves then provide an overview of an SPJ instrument, the Historical-Clinical-Risk Management 20 (HCR-20). Next, Monahan describes the development of the Classification of Violence Risk (COVR), an actuarial instrument. Andrews, Bonta, and Wormith summarize research examining the development and utility of two rationally derived measures—the Level of Service Inventory–Revised (LSI-R) and the Level of Service/Case Management Inventory (LS/CMI). Kropp and Gibas review research examining the development and utility of the SPJ tool that is to be used in domestic violence contexts—the Spousal Assault Risk Assessment (SARA). This section concludes with two chapters devoted to risk assessment tools designed for use with sex offenders: Anderson and Hanson's chapter describing the Static-99 (and its predecessor, the Rapid Risk Assessment for Sex Offender Risk, or RRASOR), the Sex Offender Needs Assessment Rating (SONAR), the Stable-2000 and 2007, and the Acute-2000 and 2007; and Hart and Boer's chapter detailing two SPJ tools—the Sexual Violence Risk-20 (SVR-20) and the Risk for Sexual Violence Protocol (RSVP).

Chapter authors took their tasks seriously, and provided very careful and useful summaries of their respective instruments. We are confident that readers will agree, and find the chapters of great use in determining whether and how to use the instruments covered in this book.

Kevin S. Douglas

Randy K. Otto

1
Violence Risk Assessment Tools
Overview and Critical Analysis

KIRK HEILBRUN, KENTO YASUHARA, and SANJAY SHAH

The problems presented by violence in contemporary society have been an important consideration for many decades. As the law has turned to the behavioral and medical sciences to improve the prospects for accurately appraising and managing the risk of violent behavior, the past twenty years in particular have witnessed the development of specialized tools for the prediction and management of certain kinds of serious violence and criminal offending. This book will offer a description of some of the tools that have been developed for specific purposes in legal contexts.

The present chapter will provide a context in which the specific tools described in subsequent chapters can be considered. There are six important considerations applicable to risk assessment tools that will be addressed in the first section: context, purpose, population, parameters, approach, and applicability. Subsequent sections of the chapter will focus on approaches to risk assessment, the major features of each approach, the strengths and weaknesses of each approach, and their respective states of validation. The present chapter will not provide an in-depth review of the validation data relevant to specific tools. That will be covered in the respective chapter on each of the specialized risk assessment tools included in this book.

Context

The first consideration in conducting a violence risk assessment involves the broad context in which this appraisal is being conducted. The context influences the nature of the decision to be made, who is responsible for that decision, and the consequences that can result from differing appraisals. There are four important (and different) contexts in which a risk assessment is likely to be conducted: legal, clinical, school/workplace, and threats to protectees. Each will be described briefly. *Legal contexts* are those in which a legal (or quasi-legal) decision-maker must render a decision in the course of litigation or administrative tribunal. Such contexts may be in the domain of criminal, civil, or child/family proceedings (see, e.g., Melton, Petrila, Poythress & Slobogin, 2007). Decisions in this context may involve initial commitment or sentencing, release from incarceration or secure hospitalization, or steps that may be associated with a planned release (such as community notification or postsentence civil commitment for sexual offenders). *Clinical contexts* involve circumstances under which interventions are delivered to reduce the risk of violence or offending in the broader context of a treatment relationship. This context is sufficiently broad to include interventions in secure settings (e.g., jails, prisons, forensic hospitals) as well as those delivered using some leverage (e.g., to individuals on parole, probation, diversion from prosecution, or juvenile home-based placement) and others using no leverage at all (e.g., psychotherapy delivered on a voluntary basis to individuals in the community, in a jurisdiction in which there is a settled *Tarasoff*-type obligation to warn or protect). *School/workplace contexts* encompass threats of harm to others that are typically not yet a part of formal legal proceedings, in which both the seriousness of the threat and the nature of the indicated risk-reduction strategies are important parts of the overall appraisal. Assessment in these settings is typically conducted in response to the concerns raised by the actions of specific individuals, rather than in a broader process involving all individuals in the setting. Finally, *threats to protectees* also involve the dual issues of threat seriousness and risk management. However, they differ because they occur outside a specific environment and are directed toward specific individuals (those under the protection of the Secret Service or Federal Marshalls, for example) or the kind of broader targets involved in domestic or international terrorism. Included as well in this category are threats involving potential harm to a domestic partner, where there is typically a specified victim and the initial appraisal is made by police who are called to the scene.

The subsequent chapters in this book are devoted to different specialized risk assessment tools that are almost entirely applicable in legal contexts. Accordingly, that will also be the focus of discussion in this chapter. It should be noted that a number of specialized measures referenced in this chapter and described further in this book would be appropriate for use in *clinical* and *threats to protectees* contexts, as these have been described in the present section.

Purpose

One of the important influences on contemporary conceptions of risk assessment is the risk/needs/responsivity (RNR) model described by Canadian researchers (Andrews & Bonta, 2006; Andrews, Bonta, & Hoge, 1990; Andrews, Bonta, & Wormith, 2006). This involves the appraisal of three related domains. *Risk* refers to the probability that the examinee will engage in a certain kind of behavior in the future, typically either violence/violent offending, or criminal offending of any kind, with higher-risk individuals receiving more intensive intervention and management services. This kind of risk classification has typically employed static risk factors, which do not change through planned intervention, although some tools (for example, the Level of Service Inventory [LSI] measures) (see Andrews & Bonta, 2001; Andrews, Bonta & Wormith, 2004) use both static risk factors and risk-relevant needs. *Needs* are variables describing deficits which are related to the probability of such targeted outcomes; they are composed of dynamic risk factors (called *criminogenic* needs in the RNR model) or protective factors that have the potential to change through such planned intervention. *Responsivity* refers to the extent to which an individual is likely to respond to intervention(s) designed to reduce the probability of the targeted outcome behavior.

A comparable distinction involving risk assessment in legal contexts has been made between prediction and risk management (Heilbrun, 1997), in which it was observed that some legal decisions are best informed by a prediction of whether the individual will reoffend or otherwise behave violently. Perhaps the most frequent example of such a decision involves civil commitment, in which the court or other decision-maker must decide whether the likelihood that the individual will harm others (or self) is sufficient to justify involuntary hospitalization. There is a limited risk management component to this decision, although future decisions regarding such individuals (such as release from hospitalization) must consider risk management to a much greater extent. If the risk is sufficiently high, the court will presumably grant the petition for civil commitment. If not, the petition is likely to be denied (or granted on grounds other than risk to harm others). But under neither circumstance would the court be particularly concerned with a specific approach to lowering the violence risk. By contrast, when the court maintains jurisdiction over the individual following the decision—for example, when the defendant is diverted to a mental health court or committed as *not guilty by reason of insanity*—then both the level of risk and the nature of the risk-relevant needs can help inform the court's decision.

Specialized risk assessment tools are designed to provide information that is either particular to the question of prediction, or that addresses both risk and needs (with associated implications for intervention). This will be discussed in greater detail subsequently in this chapter. To our knowledge, there are no specialized tools that focus only on risk reduction. However, there is a technique (anamnestic assessment) derived from applied behavior analysis that promotes the informed selection of risk-relevant needs based on the individual's history. Such an approach can also be used with risk-needs tools, in a manner to be discussed later in this chapter.

Populations

One of the important considerations in risk assessment involves the population to which the individual being assessed actually belongs. There are important differences in base rates of violence, risk factors and protective factors, and risk-relevant interventions for differing populations. In addition, specialized tools are typically derived and validated to apply to a single population (for example, juvenile offenders) or related populations (adult offenders or insanity acquittees, sex offenders), but not across widely discrepant populations.

There are four considerations in delineating a population for risk assessment purposes. These are age, gender, mental health status, and location. *Age* typically refers to three distinct groups: (1) preadolescent children, (2) adolescents, and (3) adults. *Gender* is important because a specialized tool may not be validated for females, or may use different norms. The *mental health status* of a population refers to whether it is selected through assessment, intervention, or legal action as having a number of individuals with mental health problems. Since offender and mental health problems are among the populations to which risk assessment is most often applied, it is particularly important to distinguish mental health populations without formal criminal involvement at the relevant time (for example, those who are civilly committed) from general offender populations in which mental health problems are not part of the selection criteria. This can become more complex when considering populations such as defendants acquitted as Not Guilty by Reason of Insanity, which by definition include both mental health and offending among the selection criteria. Finally, the variable of *location* refers to the setting from which the population is drawn. Offending populations can be drawn from the community (for example, those on probation or parole) or from an incarceration setting. School and work are examples of settings with populations that are typically not offenders. There can again be increased complexity when the risk appraisal seeks to assess individuals in one setting but considers their risk for violence or offending in another—as when individuals in prison are appraised for their risk of violence in the community following release. The consideration of these four variables—age, gender, mental health status, and setting—allows the identification of a population with sufficient specificity to determine whether a given risk assessment tool should be used. This choice is straightforward when the examinee is part of a specific population for which a particular tool was developed (for example, a sexual violence risk tool for an individual convicted of a sexual offense).

Parameters

The next important consideration in risk assessment involves what is being predicted, with what frequency of outcome, at what probability or category of risk, in what setting, over what period of time, and the nature of the risk factors and protective factors involved in the appraisal. It is important to specify, in the beginning, what outcome(s) will be predicted. Typically the broader the class of outcomes, the higher the base rate will be; the impact of base rates is discussed elsewhere in this chapter. It is also necessary to consider how this outcome will be measured. Common approaches to measuring outcomes such as violent behavior or violent offending include: (1) self-report, (2) the report of collateral observers, and (3) official records (for example, rearrest, rehospitalization). In the context of noncriminal community violence in the United States, the most sensitive of these measures is self-report, with collateral observation second and official records a distant third (Monahan et al., 2001; Steadman et al., 1998), but this may vary widely across jurisdictions, countries, and contexts, depending on whether the individual has a strong incentive to deny or minimize self-report, whether she or he is seen regularly by a collateral observer, and the extent to which official records are likely to reflect the occurrence of such behavior.

Next we consider the specific parameters of the behavior itself. Are we targeting serious violence only, or is more minor aggression considered as well, or only a specific type of violence (e.g., sexual reoffending)? Are verbal threats included? What of behavior (such as arson) that may be directed at property, but has the potential to harm other persons? It is also important to indicate whether the appraisal would consider a single act of the behavior as a "yes," or whether the specified outcome encompasses possible multiple acts of the behavior. In addition, there is an outcome period of time that the appraisal must designate. For some risk assessment, the relevant outcome period might be quite short—perhaps no longer than 24 to 48 hours. Intermediate outcome periods often used in community and correctional outcome research in the last decade tend to range from 6 to 12 months. Much longer periods, up to 5 to 10 years, have been used in the development of some specialized tools and were more typical of violence research in the 1980s and 1990s.

Location is a particularly important aspect of context in risk assessment. There is a substantial difference between the appraisal of violence risk in a structured setting such as a juvenile placement, prison, or hospital versus risk in the community when the examinee is living at home. The degree of structure associated with the former means greater monitoring by staff, clearer expectations and less tolerance for deviation from these expectations, the absence of drugs and alcohol (presumably), and the provision in some instances of interventions to lower violence risk. There is also a much higher probability of being detected and suffering adverse consequences in response to violent behavior displayed in a structured setting. In the community, by contrast, there is a wider range of circumstances encountered in daily living. An individual may be at work or in school, which itself may be the specific context in which violence risk is assessed. Such an individual may be living in a setting with others who may be targets for violence, particularly when domestic tensions are exacerbated by substance use and weapons are readily accessible. But location is a very important parameter in risk assessment; it contributes to the situational influences on violent behavior that have been investigated less extensively than have personal variables (Silver, 2001; Steadman, 1982). Fortunately, that is changing. Recent investigators have pursued the measurement of situational influences on violence in hospitals (Ogloff & Dafferns, 2006) and prisons (Cooke, Wozniak, & Johnstone, 2008) through the development of specialized tools that may both prove useful when validated and influence the development of comparable tools for measuring community violence risk.

The next parameter involves the manner in which risk level is to be conveyed. There are currently differences in the structure of specialized tools that center on whether a risk assessment should provide a quantitative estimate of the probability of future violence, or a categorical appraisal that seeks to distinguish lower- from higher-risk individuals without using a specific number. The substance of these differences will be discussed in this chapter. However, it is fair to say that one of the shared purposes of contemporary risk assessment tools involves providing some appraisal of relative risk. By contrast, there is a process that can also be employed in risk appraisal that seeks only to identify risk factors and protective factors applicable to the individual being assessed. This process, sometimes termed "anamnestic" (meaning recollection or account of one's history) assessment, will also be discussed in this chapter.

Finally, the important parameters in risk assessment include the identification of risk factors, which are associated with increased risk of violent outcome, and protective factors, associated with a decrease in risk. Specialized risk assessment tools have selected the risk and protective factors that are most relevant and empirically related to outcome for their populations of use. They vary in how they select these factors; some do so from a specific dataset or meta-analysis, while others use the broader empirical literature to identify important, recurring influences.

Approach

For the purposes of this chapter, three approaches to risk assessment will be described: actuarial,* structured professional judgment (SPJ), and anamnestic. The use of unstructured clinical judgment will not be discussed, for several reasons. First, there is a 50+ year history of research comparing the accuracy of unstructured clinical judgment with actuarial approaches, with a consistent, modest advantage in predictive accuracy observed for the latter (see meta-analyses conducted by Ægosdóttir et al., 2006; Grove et al., 2000). In the area of violence prediction, Mossman's (1994) meta-analysis indicated that clinical predictions were more accurate than chance (AUC = .67) but less accurate than the mean area under the curve (AUC) for all studies (.78), for cross-validated discriminant function predictions (.71), or for behavior-based predictions (.78). Second, it seems clear that much of the progress that has been made during the last two decades in developing risk assessment approaches that are more accurate and scientifically supported has resulted from the use of greater structure, both in the selection of risk factors and the way in which they are rated and combined. Unstructured clinical judgment by itself is no longer a useful or necessary approach to appraising violence risk. (When there are no applicable structured measures available, evaluators should at least "structure" their risk appraisals by focusing on known risk factors for the target outcome, derived from the scientific literature, the individual's history, or both.) However, in the context of a risk assessment conducted as part of broader forensic assessment, clinical judgment does facilitate important aspects of data gathering such as interviewing of the individual and third parties, identifying and reviewing relevant records, interpreting all data, and reasoning toward conclusions (Heilbrun, 2009).

Actuarial assessment is "a formal method" that "uses an equation, a formula, a graph, or an actuarial table to arrive at a probability, or expected value, of some outcome" (Grove & Meehl, 1996, p. 294). It uses predictor variables that can be quantified, either through classification (for example, gender) or rating, with a high degree of reliability. The predictors, and the weights assigned to them, are validated against the outcome that is being predicted through empirical research. Both the risk factors and their weights are typically derived through empirical research as well, from a single dataset or larger meta-analysis. So it is the objective, mechanistic, reproducible combination of predictive factors, selected and validated through empirical research against known outcomes, that is the *sine qua non* of actuarial assessment.

Structured professional judgment involves the presentation of specified risk factors, which are usually derived from a broad review of the literature rather than from a specific data set. Risk factors are well operationalized so their applicability can be coded (usually as no, possible, or yes) reliably. Evaluators complete an SPJ tool by rating all the specified factors, using interview, collateral interviews, records, and other sources of information. Then, when rating overall risk,

* The "adjusted actuarial" debate addresses whether the results of actuarial risk assessment should be modified in light of other considerations. As noted elsewhere (Heilbrun, in press), this can involve either "adjusting" the score or the final risk level yielded by the actuarial tool at the scoring stage, or adjusting their meaning at the interpretation stage. Changing a score or risk level at the scoring stage is extremely problematic. Actuarial tools were designed and validated to be used with an established algorithm. Changing this (for whatever reason) would raise questions about the meaning of the adjusted score. It would substitute clinical judgment for the actuarial algorithm, reducing accuracy over multiple cases. If the evaluator is not clear about doing this, the result may appear actuarial when it is something different. For these reasons, adjusting actuarial results at the scoring stage should not be done. At the interpretation stage, however, the actuarial tool may be one of multiple sources of information contributing to the final conclusion. In forensic mental health assessment, no single source of information is considered definitive, and final opinions result from integration across sources (Heilbrun, 2001). But actuarial measures provide valuable data concerning future violence risk, so deviation from their conclusions should involve (1) noting the actuarial results, (2) describing the deviation, (3) noting the information contributing to the different opinion, and (4) describing the logic underlying the evaluator's reasoning.

evaluators are asked to consider the presence of the risk factors and the anticipated intensity of management, treatment, or supervision needs in reaching an overall conclusion about risk. This is done by having the evaluator draw this conclusion, however, rather than having the rated risk factors combined in a predetermined fashion using an established formula, as is done in actuarial assessment. This procedure makes it more feasible to use risk factors that are dynamic (potentially changeable through planned intervention) as contrasted with the static (unchanging through planned intervention), largely historical risk factors that constitute the large majority of the risk factors used in actuarial assessment.

There are several respects in which actuarial and SPJ risk assessment approaches are similar. Both employ variables that have been selected for their empirical relationship to the outcome of violence (although actuarial measures tend to rely more on variables drawn from a single data set, while SPJ approaches have tended to use variables for which there appears to be broad empirical support in the literature). Both specify the variables to be considered, and both require that these variables be sufficiently well operationalized so they can be coded or rated reliably.

These approaches differ as well in some important respects. Actuarial approaches combine their risk factors into a predictive score, which has been cross-validated against known outcomes in the validation phase of developing an actuarial risk assessment tool. SPJ approaches do not combine risk factors in a predetermined fashion, instead leaving it to the judgment of the user as to whether the individual is (for example) high, moderate, or low risk. The respective accuracy of both approaches will be discussed later in this chapter.

The third approach might better be characterized as a process than a specialized tool.* Anamnestic assessment (Melton et al., 2007) uses applied behavior analytic strategies to gather detailed information from individuals regarding their history of violence. For each prior violent event, the individual is questioned in detail concerning the preceding and subsequent thoughts, feelings, and behaviors, the act itself, those involved, and relevant details (for example, whether drugs or alcohol were ingested, by whom, and at what level; whether weapons were involved, and their source; how victims were targeted; where and when the event occurred; and other relevant details). The goal of this process is not to derive an estimate of future violence risk. Rather, the evaluator can use this procedure to identify risk factors and protective factors that recur across violent acts. Such information can help make more accurate ratings on such factors if a formal risk assessment tool is used. It can also help to identify risk-relevant intervention targets—dynamic risk factors that are present during different violent acts may, if improved through targeted intervention, reduce that individual's risk of future violence.

Applicability

The value of a specialized risk assessment tool will depend upon its applicability. This section has outlined several important considerations in judging the applicability of a given tool. To what extent are the nature of the evaluation and the attributes of the specialized tool congruent? Such congruence should be judged according to context, purpose, populations, and parameters. The information needed to make this decision should be included in the manual of the specialized tool—one reason that it is important to have such a manual when using a specialized tool in practice (AERA, APA, & NCME, 1999; Heilbrun, Rogers & Otto, 2002). Since this book offers chapters describing specialized tools focusing on children, adolescents, and adults, in juvenile, criminal and civil litigation, it will be clear that these tools are congruent with the kind of risk

* Anamnestic assessment is described here as a distinct kind of risk assessment. However, it is a useful complement to other aspects of risk appraisal in any evaluation. In effect, it provides a way of individualizing the risk assessment that is substantively valuable and also allows the risk assessment to appear more valid—both important considerations in forensic mental health assessment.

assessment described in their respective chapters. The issue of congruence, and the decision whether to use a given tool, can become more complex when the context is not very similar to that described in the chapter in which the tool is discussed.

Approaches to Risk Assessment

In this section, we will offer a more detailed discussion of the characteristics of each of the major approaches to risk assessment described previously—actuarial, structured professional judgment, and anamnestic. It is useful to distinguish two major goals in risk assessment: prediction/classification, and risk reduction (Heilbrun, 1997). Some legal decisions call for expert evaluations that are strongly focused on the question of prediction. Examples include civil commitment and end-of-sentence sexual offender commitment. In these instances, the legal decision-maker is concerned with whether the risk of violent behavior or future sexual offending is sufficiently high to justify a decision restricting individual liberty on public safety grounds—but the court will not retain jurisdiction and make subsequent decisions based on whether this risk has been decreased. By contrast, a legal decision to involuntarily hospitalize a defendant found Not Guilty by Reason of Insanity may indeed involve the retention of such jurisdiction—so the court might be informed by accurate information concerning both risk level and risk reduction potential.

Table 1.1 summarizes three important questions in risk assessment, and the extent to which each of these questions is typically addressed by actuarial, SPJ, and anamnestic assessment. The strength of actuarial assessment, using a tool that is appropriately derived and cross-validated, is in facilitating a quantitative estimate of risk level. This is a two-edged sword. Because of the inextricably quantitative nature of actuarial risk assessment, actuarial tools lend themselves to research that calculates accuracy using relatively sophisticated measures such as sensitivity, specificity, and area under the curve in receiver operating characteristic (ROC) analysis, as well as 95% confidence intervals of the risk categories. This is important in promoting empirically supported practice. However, actuarial tools that are not sound—derived on relatively small samples, not well validated, and/or having wide confidence intervals that make it difficult to meaningfully distinguish between risk categories—may advertise more than they can deliver. SPJ tools typically have one section that functions much like an actuarial measure of risk, providing several risk factors which can be scored and summed to yield an overall risk measure for research purposes. In practice, evaluators are encouraged to consider all risk factors but draw their conclusion concerning risk based on their own judgment rather than this sum. The juxtaposition of these two practices raises a philosophical question ("How accurate do we want to be?") and a practical question ("How accurate is it feasible to be?") regarding the prediction of violence. In the next section, the evidence regarding the relative accuracy of each approach will

Table 1.1 Approaches and Important Questions in Risk Assessment

Question/Approach	Prediction/ Classification	Reflects Change in Risk Status	Provides Information for Risk Reduction Intervention Planning
Actuarial	Yes	Variable	Limited
Structured professional judgment	Yes	Yes	Yes
Anamnestic	No	Limited	Yes

Source: Bonta, J., Law, M., & Hanson, K. (1998). The prediction of criminal and violent recidivism among mentally disordered offenders: A meta-analysis. *Psychological Bulletin*, 124, 123–142. (Reprinted with permission.)

be discussed. But it should also be noted that the third approach, anamnestic assessment, is not well suited at all for drawing an informed conclusion about the risk for future violence.

When an individual's risk is being considered over a period of time, this often reflects an interest in how that risk might have changed. Skeem and colleagues (2006) have distinguished between risk status (relatively unchanging aspects of violence risk) and risk state (aspects of risk that do change, even over short periods of time). If there are interventions being delivered with the goal of making the person less likely to behave violently, it is important to appraise the impact of such interventions through considering how overall risk may have changed. Some actuarial tools (e.g., the Level of Service/Case Management Inventory, the Violence Risk Scale) do this, because they incorporate dynamic risk factors and hence provide a different overall "risk score" as the dynamic variables change. Other actuarial tools (e.g., the Classification of Violence Risk, the Violence Risk Appraisal Guide) do not; they are designed to provide a stable estimate of the individual's risk that focuses on risk status.

SPJ tools are designed to appraise risk needs as well as risk status, so they typically do offer a way of estimating change in risk status. They do so in the same manner that they provide the risk estimate: the evaluator considers the applicable risk factors, including the dynamic factors, and whether there is a perceived change in the necessary intensity of intervention or management, or the configuration of risk factors to be addressed, and judges whether the overall risk has changed as a result. The question of how accurately any risk tools gauge the *change* in overall violence risk is an almost entirely unresearched question, however (Heilbrun, Douglas, & Yasuhara, 2009).

Anamnestic approaches can descriptively convey previous and current changes in risk-relevant needs through linkage with an intervention plan designed to address the specific risk factors identified in the initial assessment. When individualized risk factors are reduced in number and intensity through treatment, it is reasonable to assume that risk has been reduced. But how much, and for how long, and related questions have not yet been answered through research.

Actuarial measures that accurately estimate risk do provide some information relevant to intervention-planning by distinguishing between higher- and lower-risk individuals, applying the risk/needs/responsivity notion that higher risk individuals are appropriate for more intensive interventions over a longer period of time (Andrews & Bonta, 2006). Actuarial measures do not offer specific treatment targets unless dynamic risk factors are assessed. However, they may also be used in creative ways to design interventions based on both risk and needs, assuming risk-relevant needs can be measured in another way (see, e.g., Quinsey, Harris, Rice & Cormier, 1998, 2005). For example, assessing risk through an actuarial measure and risk-relevant needs through a separate measure, or through anamnestic assessment, could identify at least four categories of risk-needs (high risk/high needs, high risk/low needs, low risk/high needs, and low risk/low needs) with associated needs for intervention and monitoring that differ considerably across categories.

Actuarial, Structured Professional Judgment, and Anamnestic Approaches to Risk Assessment: States of Validation

In this section, we will highlight important trends in the empirical literature relevant to actuarial and structured professional judgment approaches to risk assessment. In addition, we will review studies that offer an empirical comparison of the performance of tools of each type. There are no empirical studies on anamnestic risk assessment to be reviewed, but we will offer brief comments on the validation status of this approach.

Actuarial Approaches to Violence Risk Assessment. The empirical literature in this area features a number of meta-analyses conducted during the last decade. These are in addition to the meta-analytic studies noted earlier citing a consistent, modest advantage in accuracy for actuarial relative to clinical prediction over 50 years of research (Ægosdóttir et al., 2006; Grove et al., 2000), and the Mossman (1994) meta-analysis indicating that clinical predictions were more accurate than chance (AUC = .67) but significantly (although only modestly) less accurate than cross-validated discriminant function predictions (AUC = .71).

An important meta-analysis conducted about a decade ago (Bonta, Law, & Hanson, 1998) considered studies of mentally disordered offenders and used outcomes of any kind of criminal recidivism (general offending) and crimes against persons (violent offending). As may be seen in Table 1.2, there are a number of indications for support of predictors that could be incorporated into actuarial prediction. These include historical variables (criminal history, juvenile delinquency, hospital admissions, violence, escape), personality variables (antisocial personality), and substance abuse. The positive predictor with the largest recidivism effect size for violent recidivism was objective risk assessment, supporting the accuracy of approaches using predictors that can be scored reliably.

Table 1.2 Predictors of General and Violent Recidivism Among Mentally Disordered Offenders

	General		Violent	
Positive Predictors	**Recidivism Effect Size**	**N**	**Recidivism Effect Size**	**N**
Objective risk assessment	0.39	1,295	0.30	2,186
Adult criminal history	0.23	4,312	0.14	2,163
Juvenile delinquency	0.22	4,312	0.20	985
Antisocial personality	0.18	1,736	0.18	1,634
Nonviolent criminal history	0.18	2,910	0.13	1,108
Institutional adjustment	0.13	627	0.14	711
Hospital admissions	0.12	1,874	0.17	948
Poor living arrangements	0.12	396	NR	
Gender (male)	0.11	1,936	NR	
Substance abuse (any)	0.11	2,345	0.08	2,013
Family problems	0.10	730	0.19	1,481
Escape history	0.10	646	NR	
Violent history	0.10	2,240	0.16	2,878
Drug abuse	0.09	1,050	NR	
Marital status (single)	0.07	987	0.13	1,068
Negative Predictors				
Mentally disordered offender	−0.19	3,009	−0.10	2,866
Homicide index offense	−0.17	1,147	NR	
Age	−0.15	3,170	−0.18	1,519
Violent index	−0.14	905	−0.04	2,241
Violent index (broadly defined)	−0.10	3,240	0.08	1,950
Sex offense	−0.08	2,371	0.04	1,636
Not guilty by reason of insanity	−0.07	1,761	−0.07	1,208
Psychosis	−0.05	2,733	−0.04	1,208
Mood disorder	−0.04	1,856	0.01	1,520
Treatment history	−0.03	3,747	NR	
Offense seriousness	−0.01	1,368	0.06	1,879

Source: Bonta, J., Law, M., & Hanson, K. (1998). The prediction of criminal and violent recidivism among mentally disordered offenders: A meta-analysis. *Psychological Bulletin*, 124, 123–142. (Reprinted with permission.)

Consistent with the observed predictive strength of both historical variables and antisocial personality functioning, the construct of psychopathy has been associated with violent offending in the community. In one meta-analysis (Gendreau, Goggin, & Smith, 2002), investigators compared the Psychopathy Checklist–Revised (PCL-R) (Hare, 1991, 2003) with the Level of Service Inventory–Revised (LSI-R) (Andrews & Bonta, 2001) in their respective associations with both general and violent recidivism. Using over 50 studies, they found a slight difference in favor of the LSI-R for strength of association with violent recidivism (effect sizes of .26 for the LSI-R and .21 for the PCL-R, a difference the authors suggest is significant using fail-safe calculations). Fail-safe analyses indicated that there would need to be 37 additional PCL-R studies with the maximum observed effect size, or 22 LSI-R effect sizes of 0, in order for their predictive performance to be equal. Both specialized tools performed well, but this comparison is consistent with the tendency to use the PCL-R as a benchmark against which other tools are compared. (It might also be noted that there is some judgment required to rate certain items on each of these tools, but the items are combined through numerical scores and the total score considered as the indicator of risk—so each qualifies as an "actuarial" tool in this respect. It is also somewhat ironic that the PCL-R has come to be considered by some as a benchmark for the performance of risk assessment tools; it was not developed as a risk assessment measure, but as a way of assessing a specific personality disorder.)

Two meta-analyses have been conducted addressing the predictive validity of the PCL-R (Hare, 1991) for violent criminal recidivism. In the first, Walters (2003) described the capacities of the PCL-R and the Lifestyle Criminality Screening Form (LCSF)* (Walters, White, & Denney, 1991) to predict both general and violent criminal recidivism among offenders. Both tools were effective in predicting criminal recidivism (AUC values were .665 for the PCL-R and .673 for the LCSF), although these levels of accuracy were not significantly different.

The second meta-analysis (Leistico, Salekin, DeCoster, & Rogers, 2008) considered the relationship between the PCL measures and antisocial conduct, including criminal recidivism. Using 95 published studies providing a merged data set with over 15,000 participants, they observed a significant relationship between both Factor 1 and Factor 2 scores and the outcome of interest (recidivism risk). Factor 2 effect sizes were significantly larger than those for Factor 1. Effect sizes were also moderated by participant characteristics, including gender, race, and setting (correctional vs. hospital facility). This does potentially limit the use of the PCL-R in some settings, and for some people.

These four meta-analyses provided considerable evidence for the utility of the actuarial prediction of violent behavior, including criminal recidivism. Additional evidence comes from the MacArthur Risk Assessment Study (Monahan et al., 2001; Steadman et al., 1998), the largest and best-designed study to date of violent behavior in the community committed by those who had been discharged from inpatient mental health treatment facilities. The original MacArthur data were combined with additional validation data (Monahan, Steadman, Robbins et al., 2005) to yield an actuarial tool (the Classification of Violence Risk, or COVR) (Monahan, Steadman, Appelbaum et al., 2005) that is demonstrably effective in predicting serious acts of violence in the community committed by individuals with mental disorders. There was some shrinkage in the accuracy rates from derivation sample (AUC = .88) to the cross-validation sample (AUC = .63 to .70, depending on the definition and measurement of outcomes). This kind of shrinkage is typical of actuarial measures when moving from derivation to cross-validation samples.

Moving from meta-analysis to single cases, there has been recent debate concerning the applicability of actuarial measures to prediction in single cases. Hart, Michie, and Cooke (2007) have

* The LCSF is a procedure that uses only information from the file to rate an individual's irresponsibility, self-indulgence, interpersonal intrusiveness, and social rule-breaking.

argued that wide confidence intervals and consequently overlapping categories of risk classification limit the accuracy associated with applying actuarial prediction to a single case. These points have not met with universal agreement within the field (see, e.g., Harris & Rice, 2007; Mossman, 2007). It is important that an actuarial tool be derived and validated on large samples, both to increase its generalizability and to ensure that the confidence intervals are narrow and the risk categories do not overlap. However, the assertion that actuarial tools are not useful when applied to individual cases because confidence intervals are necessarily very wide in the individual case remains controversial (see Heilbrun, Douglas, & Yasuhara, 2009, for a fuller discussion).

One of the active debates in the field over the years has involved the way in which actuarial weighting and scoring can miss certain influences that may apply in the individual case. Apparently the first study of the impact of "clinical overrides" of actuarial risk levels—the "adjusted actuarial" procedure—was recently conducted (Gore, 2008). The investigator considered the accuracy of the actuarial versus "adjusted actuarial" conclusions in 383 cases in which there had been a clinical override of the Minnesota Sex Offender Screening Tool–Revised (MnSOST-R) (Epperson et al., 2003) risk level. The clinical adjustment did not yield increased accuracy, but it also did not lower the overall accuracy substantially. MnSOST-R actuarial levels were more accurate than the adjusted levels, but the difference was not statistically significant. In addition, the direction of the adjustment was not related to measured predictive accuracy.

In addition, the process of weighting predictors in the course of actuarial assessment has been considered in another study. Using 10 well-established risk factors for violent criminal recidivism from the Historical-Clinical-Risk Management 20 (HCR-20), the investigators (Grann & Langstrom, 2007) considered the impact of four different weighting schemes in applying these predictors to 404 former forensic psychiatric examinees in Sweden. These weighting approaches included Nuffield's method, bivariate and multivariate logistic regression, and an artificial neural network procedure. Upon cross-validation, they reported that simpler weighting techniques did not increase predictive accuracy over an unweighted approach. In addition, more complex weighting procedures were associated with significant shrinkage.

The findings of these two studies (Gore, 2008; Grann & Langstrom, 2007) may suggest that the use of empirically validated risk factors in prediction yields an increase in accuracy over unstructured judgment, but there may be limits to the increases in accuracy that can be achieved through the specific weighting and combination of predictors that are typically present in actuarial prediction (a point made nearly 30 years ago by Dawes, 1979). On this point, another study (Kroner, Mills, & Reddon, 2005) compared the predictive accuracy of three widely recognized actuarial tools (the PCL-R, LSI-R, and the Violence Risk Appraisal Guide, VRAG), another approach using "General Statistical Information on Recidivism," and four additional instruments that had been constructed through randomly selecting items from the total pool of original items. Intriguingly, none of the three actuarial tools or the fourth using general statistical information on recidivism was more accurate in predicting postrelease failure than the four randomly generated instruments. The investigators argued that the development of better risk theory, yielding the capacity to test hypotheses and explain behavior, is necessary to advance the process of risk assessment in the criminal justice and mental health fields. A related explanation—that there is a ceiling on the predictive accuracy that can be obtained using any approach that incorporates empirically supported risk factors, regardless of how these factors are weighted or combined—will be discussed in more detail later in this chapter.

Structured Professional Judgment Approaches to Violence Risk Assessment. Structured professional judgment is an approach to risk assessment that began to be used in the 1990s. It is more recent that actuarial risk assessment, and also less oriented toward quantifying conclusions. Rather than yielding a final numerical score, SPJ tools typically call for a risk judgment of low, moderate, or high. Assuming that an SPJ tool uses risk factors whose rating can be quantified, it is possible to study that tool by using these risk factors in an actuarial sense—by obtaining a "total score" and relating that score to observed outcome. However, it is important to test SPJ tools in the way it is recommended they be used. Rather than relying on specific weights for predictors that would be derived using an actuarial approach, the SPJ approach uses risk factors that have support in the broad empirical literature; it also makes the general assumption that a greater number of risk factors will result in a higher risk (Douglas & Kropp, 2002). Research on the relationship between final risk judgments and outcomes is most meaningful in testing this approach. That is what we will describe in this section.

We have located 12 published studies and one dissertation (McGowan, 2007) addressing the relationship between final SPJ risk judgments and violence. Of these 13 studies, 11 have yielded findings to the effect that SPJ judgments are significantly predictive of violent recidivism (Catchpole & Gretton, 2003; de Vogel & de Ruiter, 2005, 2006; de Vogel et al., 2004; Douglas, Ogloff, & Hart, 2003; Douglas, Yeomans, & Boer, 2005; Enebrink Langstrom, & Gumpert, 2006; Kropp & Hart, 2000; McGowan, 2007; Meyers & Schmidt, 2008; Welsh et al., 2008). Two additional studies (Sjöstedt & Långström, 2002; Viljoen et al., 2008) did not support the predictive validity of SPJ judgments. In the first of these two studies (Sjöstedt & Långström), none of the three actuarial and one SPJ measures predicted the outcome of violence. In addition, five studies have assessed whether the SPJ "final judgment" adds incremental predictive accuracy to the use of the tool elements combined in an actuarial fashion. In all five (de Vogel & de Ruiter, 2006; Douglas et al., 2003, 2005; Enebrink et al., 2006; Kropp & Hart, 2000), such incremental validity was observed.

Taken together, these studies (all conducted during the last decade) provide strong evidence that structured professional judgment is an efficacious approach to risk assessment. But how does it compare to actuarial assessment? In certain respects this is not a meaningful question, because actuarial and structured professional judgment share several important features. Both use risk factors that are specified *a priori* and can be rated reliably. In both *data selection* and *data coding*; therefore, these approaches are quite similar.* It is in *data combination* that they diverge. Actuarial approaches combine data according to an established formula derived and validated on specific data sets; SPJ approaches call for the combination of data into a professional judgment that is "structured" through provision of risk factors (obtained from the broader literature but typically not from any specific dataset) that can be rated reliably.

Accordingly, we might attribute observed differences between actuarial and SPJ approaches to their divergence in data combination, because they are similar in data selection and data coding. With that in mind, we now review studies that have compared these approaches.

Actuarial Versus Structured Professional Judgment Approaches to Violence Risk Assessment. We have located four studies that compare actuarial with structured professional judgment approaches. Invariably these studies compare the results of using a specific actuarial tool with those obtained using another specific SPJ tool. It is often difficult or impossible to separate the variability attributable to the tool from the broader method (actuarial vs. SPJ) variability. Nonetheless, the tools used in these studies are among those that are recognized measures of risk assessment—they do not compare poor actuarial tools with strong SPJ tools, or vice versa.

* Indeed, in some respects the risk factors used by actuarial and SPJ tools are identical. For example, the HCR-20 (a structured professional judgment tool) and the Violence Risk Appraisal Guide (an actuarial measure) both include the individual's score on the Psychopathy Checklist–Revised edition (which itself is sometimes used as a risk assessment measure).

Douglas and colleagues (2005) compared the respective predictive validities of an SPJ measure (the HCR-20) and several actuarial measures (the Violence Risk Appraisal Guide and the Hare Psychopathy Checklist–Revised and the Hare Psychopathy Checklist–Revised: Screening Version, PCL:SV), among others. Several indices were related to violent recidivism with large effect sizes. These included HCR-20 structured risk judgments, VRAG scores, and behavioral scales of psychopathy measures. These findings are consistent with strong predictive performance by actuarial measures, but not with a noteworthy advantage to such measures. The HCR-20 structured risk judgments were also strongly related to violent outcomes.

A similar comparison between the HCR-20 and two actuarial measures (the Level of Service Inventory–Revised and the Psychopathy Checklist–Revised) was conducted on offenders in Germany (Dahle, 2006). The investigator noted only minor differences in predictive accuracy among these measures. As with the Douglas et al. (2005) study, the observation was that all measures performed reasonably well, but without noteworthy advantage to any particular measure. It is worth noting that, in the latter study, direct entry of variables into the regression equation resulted in significance of both the VRAG score and HCR summary risk rating, while stepwise entry yielded significance for only the HCR summary risk ratings.

In another comparison of an actuarial measure (the Static-99) with an SPJ measure (the Sexual Violence Risk-20 [SVR-20]), de Vogel and colleagues (2004) did observe significantly better predictive performance of the latter. Using file information to complete these measures on 122 sexual offenders admitted to a Dutch forensic psychiatric hospital between 1974 and 1996, they tracked recidivism over an average outcome period of nearly 12 years. Base rates of reconvictions over this period were 39% (sexual offenses), 46% (nonsexual violent offenses), and 74% (any offenses). Predictive validity for the SVR-20 was good for both the total score (AUC = .80) and the final risk judgment (AUC = .83), and reasonably good but significantly lower for the Static-99 total score (AUC = .71) and risk categories (AUC = .66).

Finally, a study with adolescents (Catchpole & Gretton, 2003) compared two actuarial approaches—the Youth Level of Service/Case Management Inventory (YLC/CMI) (Hoge & Andrews, 2002) and the Psychopathy Checklist: Youth Version (PCL:YV) (Forth, Kosson, & Hare, 2003)—with the Structured Assessment of Violence Risk in Youth (SAVRY) (Borum, Bartel, & Forth, 2003). A total of 133 participants were obtained from consecutive referrals from youth court judges. The YLS/CMI ratings were completed by probation officers; the PCL:YV and the SAVRY were coded using file data. Follow-up periods ranged from 7 to 61 months, with a mean of 35.8 months. Violent recidivism was among the outcomes measured. For such violent recidivism, the SAVRY (AUC = .81) was most accurate predictively, followed by the PCL:YV (AUC = .73) and the YLS/CMI (AUC = .64).

This is clearly a small number of studies on which to base any conclusion about the relative predictive accuracy of actuarial measures versus SPJ approaches using a "final judgment" as the risk classification. Accordingly, such conclusions must be drawn tentatively. But to date, evidence suggests that actuarial and SPJ approaches are at least comparable in predictive accuracy for violent outcomes. This is an important observation, as this book will feature descriptions of both SPJ and actuarial risk assessment tools.

Anamnestic Approaches to Violence Risk Assessment. The anamnestic approach to risk assessment does not lend itself easily to research on predictive accuracy. Indeed, the identification of risk factors, particularly those that are subject to change and hence targets for intervention, by using the individual's own history of violence is much better suited to risk management. But focusing the risk assessment at least in part on the individual's own history of violence will remain an important part of the risk assessment process when it is part of a broader legal decision. Three considerations are worth noting in this respect. First, the assumption of some relationship between the number of risk factors present and the overall risk level has some support from SPJ studies that allow the evaluator to make a final judgment in light of the number and intensity of observed risk factors. Final judgments made in this context seem about as accurate predictively as actuarial conclusions. Second, the process of "individualizing" the evaluation of forensic mental health assessment (FMHA) is quite important as a broad principle in forensic assessment, including risk assessment done in forensic contexts (Heilbrun, in press). Third, there are occasionally "broken leg exceptions" that involve a substantial difference in the individual's personal attributes or situation that distinguish their present from most of their history. One of the best ways to learn about such exceptions is through obtaining detailed information about a person's history of violent behavior and the circumstances surrounding each event.

Although it would be difficult, it is certainly feasible to investigate the extent to which anamnestic risk assessment is accurate in identifying level of risk and relevant treatment targets, and leads to intervention-planning that is more effective in reducing risk. Such research would be similar to a "clinical trial" in which one approach (using anamnestic risk assessment) was compared with others (e.g., a standard risk assessment tool, "usual practice" by a treatment team, and perhaps some combinations). The added demand to deliver interventions makes this a more challenging study than the typical "administer tool, observe outcome" design of a prediction study, but this is true for any investigation of risk reduction, and it would be important to use the anamnestic approach for what it should do best (identify treatment targets to reduce risk) as well as what it may do (help inform an accurate conclusion about risk level).

Conclusion

The development of specialized assessment tools provides one of the best avenues to promote empirically informed best practice. Toward that end, the various chapters in this book will describe particular risk assessment tools that have been developed and validated for some of the various purposes and populations described in this chapter. This introductory chapter has provided a context within which the development of such tools can be viewed.

References

Ægosdóttir, S., White, M. J., Spengler, P. M., Maugherman, L. A., Cook, R. S., Nichols, C. N., Lampropoulos, G. K., Walker, B. S., Cohen, G., & Rush, J. D. (2006). The meta-analysis of clinical judgment project: Fifty-six years of accumulated research on clinical versus statistical prediction. *Counseling Psychologist, 34*, 341–382.

AERA (American Educational Research Association), APA (American Psychological Association), & NCME (National Council on Measurement in Education) (1999). *Standards for educational and psychological testing* (2nd ed.). Washington, DC: American Educational Research Association.

Andrews, D., & Bonta, J. (2001). *Level of Service Inventory–Revised (LSI-R): User's manual.* Toronto: Multi-Health Systems.

Andrews, D., & Bonta, J. (2006). *The psychology of criminal conduct* (4th ed.). Newark, NJ: Lexis Nexis/Mathew Bender.

Andrews, D., Bonta, J, & Hoge, R. (1990). Classification for effective rehabilitation: Rediscovering psychology. *Criminal Justice and Behavior, 17*, 19–52.

Andrews, D., Bonta, J., & Wormith, J. S. (2004). *Level of Service/Case Management Inventory (LS/CMI): An offender assessment system user's manual.* Tonawanda, NY: Multi-Health Systems.

Andrews, D., Bonta, J., & Wormith, J. S. (2006). Recent past and near future of risk and/or need assessment. *Crime and Delinquency, 52*, 7–27.

Bonta, J., Law, M., & Hanson, K. (1998). The prediction of criminal and violent recidivism among mentally disordered offenders: A meta-analysis. *Psychological Bulletin, 124*, 123–142.

Borum, R., Bartel, P., & Forth, A. (2002). *Manual for the Structured Assessment of Violence Risk in Youth. Consultation version.* Tampa: University of South Florida, Florida Mental Health Institute.

Catchpole, R. E. H., & Gretton, H. M. (2003). The predictive validity of risk assessment with violent young offenders: A 1-year examination of criminal outcome. *Criminal Justice and Behavior, 30*, 688–708.

Cooke, D., Wozniak, E., & Johnstone, L. (2008). Casting light on prison violence in Scotland: Evaluating the impact of situational risk factors. *Criminal Justice and Behavior, 35,* 1065–1078.

Daffern, M., & Howells, K. (2007).The prediction of imminent aggression and self-harm in personality disordered patients of a high security hospital using the HCR-20 Clinical Scale and the Dynamic Appraisal of Situational Aggression. *International Journal of Forensic Mental Health, 6,* 137–144.

Dahle, K. P. (2006). Strengths and limitations of actuarial prediction of criminal reoffence in a German prison sample: A comparative study of LSI-R, HCR-20 and PCL-R. *International Journal of Law and Psychiatry, 29,* 341–442.

Dawes, R. (1979). The robust beauty of improper linear models. *American Psychologist, 34,* 571–582.

de Vogel, V., & de Ruiter, C. (2005). The HCR-20 in personality disordered female offenders: A comparison with a matched sample of males. *Clinical Psychology and Psychotherapy, 21,* 226–240.

de Vogel, V., & de Ruiter, C. (2006). Structured professional judgment of violence risk in forensic clinical practice: A prospective study into the predictive validity of the Dutch HCR-20. *Psychology, Crime & Law, 12,* 321–336.

de Vogel, V., de Ruiter, C., van Beek, D., & Mead, G. (2004). Predictive validity of the SVR-20 and Static-99 in a Dutch sample of treated sex offenders. *Law and Human Behavior, 28,* 235–251.

Douglas, K. S., & Kropp, P. R. (2002). A prevention-based paradigm for violence risk assessment: Clinical and research applications. *Criminal Justice and Behavior, 29,* 617–658.

Douglas, K., & Ogloff, J. (2003). The impact of confidence on the accuracy of structured professional and actuarial violence risk judgments in a sample of forensic psychiatric patients. *Law and Human Behavior, 27,* 573–587.

Douglas, K. S., Ogloff, J., & Hart, S. (2003). Evaluation of a model of violence risk assessment among forensic psychiatric patients. *Psychiatric Services, 54,* 1372–1379.

Douglas, K., Yeomans, M., & Boer, D. (2005). Comparative validity analysis of multiple measures of violence risk in a sample of criminal offenders. *Criminal Justice and Behavior, 32,* 479–510.

Enebrink, P., Langstrom, N., & Gumpert, C. (2006). Predicting aggressive and disruptive behavior in referred 6 to 12-year-old boys: Prospective validation of the EARL-20B Risk/Needs Checklist. *Assessment, 13,* 356–367.

Epperson, D., Kaul, J., Huot, S., Goldman, R., & Alexander, W. (2003). *Minnesota Sex Offender Screening Tool-Revised (MnSOST-R) technical paper: Development, validation, and recommended risk level cut scores.* Currently unpublished manuscript retrieved March 20, 2009 from http://www.psychology.iastate.edu/~dle/TechUpdatePaper12-03.pdf.

Forth, A., Kosson, D., & Hare, R. (2003). *The Psychopathy Checklist: Youth Version.* Toronto, Ontario, Canada: Multi-Health Systems.

Gendreau, P., Goggin, C., & Smith, P. (2002). Is the PCL-R really the "unparalleled" measure of offender risk? A lesson in knowledge cumulation. *Criminal Justice and Behavior, 29,* 397–426.

Gore, K. (2008). Adjusted actuarial assessment of sex offenders: The impact of clinical overrides on predictive accuracy. *Dissertation Abstracts International: Section B: The Sciences and Engineering, 68*(7-B), 4824.

Grann, M., & Langstrom, N. (2007). Actuarial assessment of violence risk: To weigh or not to weigh. *Criminal Justice and Behavior, 34,* 22–36.

Grann, M., & Wedin, I. (2002). Risk factors for recidivism among spousal assault and spousal homicide offenders. *Psychology, Crime & Law, 8,* 5–23.

Grann, M., Belfrage, H., & Tengstrom, A. (2000). Actuarial assessment of risk for violence: Predictive validity of the VRAG and the historical part of the HCR-20. *Criminal Justice and Behavior, 27,* 97–114.

Grove, W., Zald, D., Lebow, B., Snitz, B., & Nelson, C. (2000). Clinical versus mechanical prediction: A meta-analysis. *Psychological Assessment, 12,* 19–30.

Grove, W., & Meehl, P. (1996). Comparative efficiency of informal (subjective, impressionistic) and formal (mechanical, algorithmic) prediction procedures: The clinical–statistical controversy. *Psychology, Public Policy, and Law, 2,* 293–323.

Hanson, R., Morton, K., & Harris, A. (2003). Sexual offender recidivism risk: What we know and what we need to know. *Annals of the New York Academy of Sciences, 989,* 154–166.

Hare, R. (1991, 2003). *The Hare Psychopathy Checklist–Revised.* Toronto, Ontario, Canada: Multi-Health Systems.

Harris, G. T., & Rice, M. E. (2007). Characterizing the value of actuarial violence risk assessments. *Criminal Justice and Behavior, 34,* 1638–1658.

Harris, G., Rice, M., & Cormier, C. (2002). Prospective replication of the Violence Risk Appraisal Guide in predicting violent recidivism among forensic patients. *Law and Human Behavior, 26,* 377–394.

Harris, P. (2006). What community supervision officers need to know about actuarial risk assessment and clinical judgment. *Federal Probation, 70,* 8–14.

Hart, S., Michie, C., & Cooke, D. (2007). Precision of actuarial risk assessment instruments: Evaluating the "margins of error" of group versus individual predictions of violence. *British Journal of Psychiatry, 190* (suppl. 49), s60–s65.

Heilbrun, K. (1997). Prediction versus management models relevant to risk assessment: The importance of legal context. *Law and Human Behavior*, 21, 347–359.

Heilbrun, K. (2001). *Principles of forensic mental health assessment.* New York: Kluwer Academic/Plenum.

Heilbrun, K. (2009). *Evaluation for risk of violence in adults.* New York: Oxford University Press.

Heilbrun, K., Douglas, K., & Yasuhara, K. (2009). Violence risk assessment: Core controversies. In J. Skeem, K. Douglas, & S. Lilienfeld (Eds.), *Psychological science in the courtroom: Controversies and consensus* (pp. 333–357). New York: Guilford Press.

Heilbrun, K., Rogers, R., & Otto, R. (2002). Forensic assessment: Current status and future directions. In J. Ogloff (Ed.), *Psychology and law: Reviewing the discipline* (pp. 120–147). New York: Kluwer Academic/ Plenum Press.

Hoge, R., & Andrews, D. (2002). *The Youth Level of Service/Case Management Inventory manual and scoring key.* Toronto, Ontario, Canada: Multi-Health Systems.

Kroner, D., Mills, J., & Reddon, J. (2005). A Coffee Can, factor analysis, and prediction of antisocial behavior: The structure of criminal risk. *International Journal of Law and Psychiatry, 28,* 360–374.

Kropp, P. R., & Hart, S. D. (2000). The Spousal Assault Risk Assessment (SARA) Guide: Reliability and validity in adult male offenders. *Law and Human Behavior, 24,* 101–118.

Kropp, P., Hart, S., & Lyon, D. (2002). Risk assessment of stalkers: Some problems and possible solutions. *Criminal Justice and Behavior, 29,* 590–616.

Leistico, A., Salekin, R., DeCoster, J., & Rogers, R. (2008). A large-scale meta-analysis relating the Hare measures of psychopathy to antisocial conduct. *Law and Human Behavior, 32,* 28–45.

Marczyk, G., Heilbrun, K., Lander, T., DeMatteo, D. (2003). Predicting juvenile recidivism with the PCL:YV, MAYSI, and YLS/CMI. *International Journal of Forensic Mental Health, 2,* 7–18.

McGowan, M. (2007). The predictive validity of violence risk assessment within educational settings. *Dissertation Abstracts International: Section A: Humanities and Social Sciences, 68*(3-A), 876.

Melton, G., Petrila, J., Poythress, N., & Slobogin, C. (2007). *Psychological evaluations for the courts: A handbook for mental health professionals and lawyers* (3rd ed.). New York: Guilford.

Meyers, J., & Schmidt, F. (2008). Predictive validity of the Structured Assessment for Violence Risk in Youth (SAVRY) with juvenile offenders. *Criminal Justice and Behavior, 35,* 344–355.

Monahan, J., Steadman, H., Silver, E., Appelbaum, P., Robbins, P. C., Mulvey, E., Roth, L., Grisso, T., & Banks, S. (2001). *Rethinking risk assessment: The MacArthur study of mental disorder and violence.* New York: Oxford University Press.

Monahan, J., Steadman, H., Appelbaum, P., Grisso, T., Mulvey, E., Roth, L., Robbins, P., Banks, S., & Silver, E. (2005). *Classification of Violence Risk: Professional manual.* Lutz, FL: Psychological Assessment Resources.

Monahan, J., Steadman, H., Robbins, P. C., Appelbaum, P., Banks, S., Grisso, T., Heilbrun, K., Mulvey, E., Roth, L., & Silver, E. (2005). Prospective validation of the multiple iterative classification tree model of violence risk assessment. *Psychiatric Services, 56,* 810–815.

Mossman, D. (1994). Assessing predictions of violence: Being accurate about accuracy. *Journal of Consulting and Clinical Psychology, 62,* 783–792.

Mossman, D. (2007). Avoiding errors about "margins of error." *British Journal of Psychiatry, 191,* 561.

Ogloff, J., & Daffern, M. (2006). The Dynamic Appraisal of Situational Aggression: An instrument to assess risk for imminent aggression in psychiatric inpatients. *Behavioral Sciences & the Law, 24,* 799–813.

Quinsey, V., Harris, G., Rice, M., & Cormier, C. (1998). *Violent offenders: Appraising and managing risk.* Washington, DC: American Psychological Association.

Quinsey, V., Harris, G., Rice, M., & Cormier, C. (2005). *Violent offenders: Appraising and managing risk* (2nd ed.). Washington, DC: American Psychological Association.

Silver, E. (2001). *Mental illness and violence: The importance of neighborhood context.* El Paso, TX: LFB Scholarly Publishing.

Sjöstedt, G., & Långström, N. (2002). Assessment of risk for criminal recidivism among rapists: A comparison of four different measures. *Psychology, Crime and Law, 8,* 25–40.

Skeem, J., Schubert, C., Odgers, C., Mulvey, E., Gardner, W., & Lidz, W. (2006). Psychiatric symptoms and community violence among high-risk patients: A test of the relationship at the weekly level. *Journal of Consulting and Clinical Psychology, 74,* 967–979.

Steadman, H. (1982). A situational approach to violence. *International Journal of Law and Psychiatry, 5,* 171–186.

Steadman, H., Mulvey, E., Monahan, J., Robbins, P. C., Appelbaum, P., Grisso, T., Roth, L., & Silver, E. (1998). Violence by people discharged from acute psychiatric facilities and by others in the same neighborhoods. *Archives of General Psychiatry, 55,* 393–401.

Viljoen, J. L., Scalora, M., Cuadra, L., Bader, S., Chávez, V., Ullman, D., & Lawrence, L. (2008). Assessing risk for violence in adolescents who have sexually offended: A comparison of the J-SOAP-II, J-SORRAT-II, and SAVRY. *Criminal Justice and Behavior, 35,* 5–23.

Walters, G. (2003). Predicting criminal justice outcomes with the Psychopathy Checklist and Lifestyle Criminality Screening Form: A meta-analytic comparison. *Behavioral Sciences & the Law, 21,* 89–102.

Walters, G., White, T., & Denney, D. (1991). The Lifestyle Criminality Screening Form: Preliminary data. *Criminal Justice and Behavior, 18,* 406–418.

Welsh, J. Schmidt, F., McKinnon, L., Chattha, H., & Meyers, J. (2008). A comparative study of adolescent risk assessment instruments: Predictive and incremental validity. *Assessment, 15,* 104–115.

2
The Use of Measures of Psychopathy in Violence Risk Assessment

DAVID DEMATTEO, JOHN F. EDENS, and ALLISON HART

Introduction and Description of the Psychopathy Checklist (PCL) Measures

The term "psychopath" (and related terms such as "sociopath" and "antisocial personality") has a long history of being used to inform perceptions of violence risk or "dangerousness" in western civilization. Although historically psychopathy has been a somewhat muddled descriptor of a variety of symptoms and behaviors (see Millon, Simonsen, & Birket-Smith, 1998, for a historical review of the construct), present-day conceptualizations of psychopathy began to gel with the 1941 publication of Hervey Cleckley's seminal work, *The Mask of Sanity.* Other works around that time, such as Karpman's (1946, 1948) descriptions of "idiopathic" versus "symptomatic" or secondary subtypes of psychopathy, were also influential in shaping modern-day conceptualizations of psychopathy. Of particular note in relation to violence risk assessment, Cleckley's original collection of case studies included numerous examples of psychopaths engaging in various forms of socially deviant behavior, and in fact, Cleckley incorporated "*inadequately motivated* antisocial behavior" (emphasis added) as one of the 16 core criteria for diagnosing the disorder. Although Cleckley's vivid descriptions of the (oftentimes peculiar and seemingly pointless) antisocial conduct of psychopathic patients were for the purpose of illustrating his theory about the disorder, from a more applied or pragmatic perspective they also highlighted the frequently destructive impact that this disorder had on others and society—as well as to the individuals identified as psychopathic.

The changing conceptualizations of psychopathy are reflected in the terminology used in the various iterations of the American Psychiatric Association's *Diagnostic and Statistical Manual of Mental Disorders* (DSM). Although the first two DSMs reflected Cleckley's conceptualization of the disorder, termed "sociopathic personality disturbance" in the first DSM (American Psychiatric Association [APA], 1952) and "personality disturbance, antisocial type" in DSM-II (APA, 1968), the diagnosis of psychopathy eventually moved away from the personality traits evident in Cleckley's criteria and toward more criminological (behaviorally based) traits. With the publication of the DSM-III (APA, 1980), the disorder was renamed "antisocial personality disorder." Subsequent editions of the DSM made minor changes to the diagnostic criteria and included a statement that the disorder includes features "commonly included in traditional conceptions of psychopathy" (APA, 2000, p. 703) (see Lilienfeld, 1994, for an overview).

Perhaps in part because of dissatisfaction with the more recent (and behaviorally based) DSM conceptualizations of what constitutes a psychopath, since the 1980s the construct of psychopathy has been operationalized—at least among research psychologists—primarily using instruments developed by Robert Hare and his colleagues. These instruments include the Psychopathy Checklist (PCL) (Hare, 1980), the Psychopathy Checklist–Revised (PCL-R) (Hare, 1991, 2003), and the Psychopathy Checklist: Screening Version (PCL:SV) (Hart, Cox, & Hare, 1995). Additionally, an instrument with highly similar item content domains, the Psychopathy

Checklist: Youth Version (PCL:YV) (Forth, Kosson, & Hare, 2003), was developed specifically for use with adolescents.

In contrast to recent DSM formulations of Antisocial Personality Disorder (APD), these instruments (hereafter referred to collectively as the "PCL" unless otherwise noted) place greater diagnostic emphasis on characteristics that are not, at least overtly, tied to criminality and antisocial conduct, such as affective (e.g., callousness), interpersonal (e.g., grandiosity), and behavioral (e.g., irresponsibility) features thought by many to be more representative of the disorder. The amount of research conducted on the PCL-R in particular is voluminous, and there is substantial empirical evidence that the PCL-R operationalizes a construct of considerable importance to the criminal justice system, although there continue to be significant debates (e.g., Skeem & Cooke, in press) concerning the extent to which the PCL-R adequately operationalizes the core features of psychopathy in the tradition of Cleckley (1941) and others (e.g., Lykken, 1995). Due to space limitations, this chapter will focus primarily on PCL research that is relevant to violence risk assessment (for broader reviews, see Hare, 2003; Patrick, 2007; Skeem & Cooke, in press).

PCL-R and PCL:SV

Descriptively, the PCL-R is a 20-item construct rating scale used in research and clinical settings (including forensic) for the assessment of psychopathy among adults. The standard administration procedure involves a combination of a semistructured psychosocial interview and a review of file/collateral data, although scoring the PCL-R without the interview is common in research settings. The PCL:SV is a 12-item tool derived from the 20-item PCL-R. Research suggests that PCL:SV Total scores are highly correlated with PCL-R Total scores, at least when used with forensic/correctional samples and scored based on the same information sources (Guy & Douglas, 2006). Examiners rate each PCL item on a 3-point scale based on the degree to which the personality/behavior of the examinee matches the item description in the manual—0 (item does not apply to the individual), 1 (item applies to a certain extent), or 2 (item applies)—which results in scores ranging from 0 to 40 for the PCL-R (and 0 to 24 for the PCL:SV). Although the PCL-R was normed on criminal offender and forensic psychiatric samples, it has been used with other populations, including community samples (DeMatteo, Heilbrun, & Marczyk, 2005, 2006; Forth, Brown, Hart, & Hare, 1996; Ishikawa, Raine, Lencz, Birhle, & Lacasse, 2001). Moreover, a small but growing body of research suggests that the descriptive properties and correlates of the PCL-R are similar for male and female offenders (see Book, Clark, Forth, & Hare, 2006, and Hare, 2003, for reviews of relevant research). Finally, research suggests that PCL-R scores are not unduly influenced by the race or ethnicity of the individual being examined (Cooke, Kosson, & Michie, 2001; Skeem, Edens, Camp, & Colwell, 2004; see Hare, 2003, for a review), although this statement needs to be qualified, because the available research is limited and most studies have only examined differences between Caucasian and African American individuals.

Early exploratory factor analyses of the PCL (Harpur, Hakstian, & Hare, 1988; Harpur, Hare, & Hakstian, 1989) consistently resulted in a two-factor solution, with Factor 1 primarily reflecting the fundamental interpersonal and affective characteristics of psychopathy in the tradition of Cleckley (1941) and others, and Factor 2 primarily reflecting antisocial and socially deviant characteristics commonly seen among many criminal offenders. The factor structure of the PCL-R has been the subject of considerable debate in recent years, with confirmatory factor analyses questioning the validity of the two-factor model, and research teams instead proposing three-factor (Cooke & Michie, 2001; Hall, Benning, & Patrick, 2004) and four-factor models (Forth et al., 2003; Neumann, Kosson, & Salekin, 2007; Vitacco, Rogers, Neumann, Harrison, & Vincent, 2005). In early work on this issue, Cooke and Michie (2001) proposed a hierarchical three-factor model—reflecting interpersonal, affective, and lifestyle features of psychopathy—based on the results of a confirmatory factor analysis of 13 items from the PCL-R. Recent studies have replicated this three-factor model (Cooke, Michie, Hart, & Clark, 2004; Cooke, Michie, & Skeem, 2007; Weaver, Meyer, Van Nort, & Tristan, 2006), although some researchers (Hare, 2003; Hare & Neumann, 2005; Vitacco, Neumann, & Jackson, 2005) argue for the existence of a four-factor model of PCL psychopathy that retains item content explicitly tied to criminal history variables.

Proponents of the three-factor model argue that criminal behavior is "causally downstream" in relation to the core features of the disorder and that numerous factors other than psychopathy may cause such conduct (Cooke et al., 2004). Advocates of the four-factor model, in contrast, assert that criminal and antisocial behavior are part of the "core" of the construct of psychopathy. As recently noted by Edens, Skeem, and Kennealy (2009) and Skeem and Cooke (in press), the ultimate relevance of a history of antisocial conduct to the core construct of psychopathy cannot be determined by cross-sectional factor-analytic methods, which simply examine patterns of relationships among variables rather than their causal relevance to the disorder itself. Given the potential importance of this distinction for interpreting elevations on this scale as it relates to the construct of psychopathy, we will return to this issue later in this chapter.

Although the legal system may be primarily interested in psychopathy as a categorical construct (that is, an offender is or is not a psychopath) because of the need to make discrete placement decisions, there is no naturally occurring diagnostic cutoff for categorizing individuals as "psychopaths" per se, given that almost all recent taxometric studies indicate that PCL scores represent an underlying dimensional construct rather than a latent taxon (Edens, Marcus, Lilienfeld, & Poythress, 2006; Guay, Ruscio, Hare, & Knight, 2007; Walters, Duncan, & Mitchell-Perez, 2007; Walters, Gray et al., 2007). However, PCL Total scores of 30 and above oftentimes are used to categorize examinees into somewhat arbitrary "psychopath/nonpsychopath" groups. There is also precedent for using lower cutoff scores in some research settings, including Total scores of 29 (Serin, 1996), 28 (Serin, 1991), and 25 (Harris, Rice, & Cormier, 1991; Harris, Rice, & Quinsey, 1993).

PCL:YV

The PCL:YV is similar to the PCL-R in terms of number of items (20), administration procedures (semistructured interview and review of collateral information), scoring procedures (0, 1, 2), and range of total scores (0–40). The authors of the PCL:YV (Forth et al., 2003, p. 2) assert that "the PCL:YV is a downward extension of the PCL-R" to adolescents because it assesses similar content domains (interpersonal, affective, antisocial, and behavioral features). Importantly, however, the authors revised some of the PCL-R items to make the PCL:YV content "more appropriate for use with adolescents" (Forth et al., 2003, p. 2). For example, some of the items from the PCL-R, including "parasitic lifestyle" and "many short-term marital relationships," were modified on the PCL:YV to permit the assessment of these characteristics among adolescents.

The PCL:YV can be used with adolescents ranging in age from 12 to 18 years, inclusive, in applied and research contexts. Although early research suggested that the four-factor model of psychopathy developed with respect to the PCL-R is also a good fit with the PCL:YV (Forth et al., 2003; Vitacco, Rogers et al., 2005), recent research has yielded more equivocal results. Jones, Cauffman, Miller, and Mulvey (2006) used a large sample of juvenile offenders to examine the fit of various underlying factor structures, and they concluded that the three- and four-factor models provided a similar fit. Similar results were obtained by Neumann, Kosson, Forth, and Hare (2006). Importantly, the PCL:YV provides a dimensional measure of psychopathy, and the PCL:YV manual does not provide categorical diagnostic cut scores. The authors stated that providing diagnostic cut scores for the PCL:YV would be premature until there is "solid empirical data on the stability of psychopathic traits from adolescence into adulthood" (Forth et al., 2003. p. 2).

As Hare (2003) has noted, the PCL measures are not intended to be risk assessment measures (see Hemphill & Hare, 2004). Rather, they purport to measure the construct of psychopathy, which just happens to bear implications for certain risk assessment purposes. Such a caveat notwithstanding, it is clear that one of the reasons, if not *the* reason, is that there is so much applied interest in the psychopathy construct in general and the PCL measures in particular (see DeMatteo & Edens, 2006; Edens & Vincent, 2008) is because these measures have been demonstrated to be *prospectively* associated with various forms of antisocial conduct, such as general and violent recidivism among released offenders (Edens, Campbell, & Weir, 2007; Leistico, Salekin, DeCosta, & Rogers, 2008). (Additional discussion on this point is provided later in this chapter.) The PCL measures are also used to inform clinical judgments concerning violence risk in various U.S. and Canadian court cases (DeMatteo & Edens, 2006; Walsh & Walsh, 2006). For example, experts have been called by the prosecution in U.S. capital murder trials to testify regarding the PCL in cases in which "future dangerousness" aggravating factors are to be considered by juries during sentencing phases. In Canada, the PCL measures are widely used to inform risk assessments in their federal penal system, and they may be used to help justify indeterminate commitment in some contexts (Gagnon, Douglas, & DeMatteo, 2007). Finally, the United Kingdom recently implemented a policy initiative to reduce the violence risk among offenders determined to have a "dangerous and severe personality disorder" (DSPD), which can be diagnosed based in part on an elevated PCL-R score (Maden & Tyrer, 2003).

As can be discerned from subsequent chapters within this text, aside from being used to inform clinical judgments of violence risk, the PCL-R has been incorporated into two actuarial risk assessment instruments: the Violence Risk Appraisal Guide (VRAG) (Harris et al., 1993; Quinsey, Harris, Rice, & Cormier, 2006) and the Sex Offender Risk Appraisal Guide (SORAG) (Quinsey et al., 2006); and three structured professional judgment instruments: Historical-Clinical-Risk-20 (HCR-20) (Webster, Douglas, Eaves, & Hart, 1997); Sexual Violence Risk-20 (SVR-20) (Boer, Hart, Kropp, & Webster, 1997); and Risk for Sexual Violence Protocol (RSVP) (Hart et al., 2003). Of note, some large-scale studies and meta-analyses have suggested that PCL measures *in isolation* may function as well as or better than more elaborate risk assessment instruments such as the VRAG and HCR-20 (Cooke, Michie, & Ryan, 2001; Edens, Skeem, & Douglas, 2006; Edens et al., 2007; Kroner & Mills, 2001), although other research (Douglas, Ogloff, Nicholls, & Grant, 1999; Gendreau, Coggin, & Smith, 2002; Glover, Nicholson, Hemmati, Bernfeld, & Quinsey, 2002) suggests that these risk instruments may improve on the predictive validity of the PCL measures alone.

This state of affairs may not be entirely surprising, given that PCL conceptualizations of psychopathy are heavily weighted toward a history of social deviance and criminality (see Cooke et al., 2007; Skeem & Cooke, in press), which would be expected to be modestly to moderately predictive of future criminal behavior. Although the PCL was clearly informed by the "personality" criteria for psychopathy espoused by Cleckley and others (but see Rogers, 1995, for an alternate perspective), it places considerable weight on criminal and other socially deviant behaviors, as evidenced by ongoing debates concerning the theoretical and etiological significance of the "Antisocial" facet identified in some (Forth et al., 2003; Vitacco, Rogers et al., 2005) but not all (Cooke & Michie, 2001) factor analyses of the PCL measures. These debates largely focus on the question of whether antisocial conduct/criminality is a core component of the disorder or whether it is simply "causally downstream" as a natural consequence of psychopathic traits that predispose one to engage in such acts. Although such debates may seem academic, they are of considerable pragmatic importance. For example, if the Antisocial facet is not part of the "core" of the *construct* of psychopathy, and if the predictive validity of the PCL *measures* is primarily the result of their operationalization of "generic" social deviance (that is, propensities toward antisocial behavior not specific to the psychopathy construct), then a strong argument could be made that it is not "psychopathy" per se that is important for violence risk assessment purposes (Edens et al., 2009; Skeem & Cooke, in press).

That being said, however, in applied settings it does not appear that examiners are concerned with debates regarding the construct of psychopathy. Instead, they are more focused on the applied utility of the PCL measures as currently constituted, particularly the PCL Total scores. This issue should not be glossed over, because attributions of psychopathic traits, particularly Factor 1 traits, to adult and juvenile offenders can have a pronounced impact on how they are viewed in terms of perceptions of dangerousness and attitudes concerning legal dispositions (see Edens et al., 2009, for an overview of mock jury and other studies relevant to the stigmatizing effects of psychopathy). If these traits are less central to identifying "higher-risk" individuals, then examiners should eschew focusing on them when interpreting the results of their risk assessment data. We address this issue in greater detail later.

From an applied perspective, a key question is who should be considered competent to administer and score the PCL measures. In other words, what specific qualifications, training, and experience are needed before an examiner is considered "qualified" to use these measures in applied settings? As recently noted by Edens and Petrila (2006), the issue of what constitutes "adequate" training on the PCL measures is a complicated question that raises general ethical issues regarding examiner competence and certification and legal questions regarding the credentialing of expert witnesses. According to the American Psychological Association's (2002) "Ethical Principles of Psychologists and Code of Conduct," "competence" is based on relevant "education, training, supervised experience, consultation, study, or professional experience" (p. 1063). Importantly, the ethics code does not provide guidelines regarding what constitutes minimum thresholds in these areas. For example, it is not clear how much "education" or "supervised experience" is sufficient for one to be considered competent to administer the PCL, although being able to cite reliability statistics for one's own training ratings in relation to expert examiner ratings would provide some general assurances in this regard.

The PCL-R manual (Hare, 2003) suggests minimum qualifications needed to use the PCL in clinical contexts, including possession of an advanced degree (in social, medical, or behavioral sciences), and completion of graduate courses in psychometrics and psychopathology. Importantly, Hare (2003) also asserts that he has "no professional or legal authority to determine who can and cannot use the PCL-R, or to provide judgments about the adequacy of specific clinicians and their assessments" (p. 16). Despite this declaration, Edens and Petrila (2006) noted that the suggested qualifications listed in the manual appear to be given considerable weight when evaluating examiner competence to administer, score, and interpret the instrument.

Although it may seem self-evident that competence to administer, score, and interpret the results of the PCL-R should be a prerequisite to its use in applied (and research) contexts, there is a growing corpus of anecdotal and empirical evidence suggesting that some examiners provide highly suspect PCL ratings in judicial contexts (see, e.g., DeMatteo & Edens, 2006; Edens, 2001, 2006; Edens & Vincent, 2008; Hare, 1998; Walsh & Walsh, 2006; see also Murrie, Boccaccini, Johnson, & Janke, 2008). Whether these PCL ratings reflect questionable competence or some other, more pernicious, influence (for example, bias, partisanship) is unclear—although the data reported by Murrie et al. (described below) certainly raise the specter of allegiance effects being at play.

In terms of the extensiveness of prior training, the PCL-R and PCL:YV manuals indicate that training workshops are offered by Darkstone Research Group. They acknowledge that completion of the workshops indicates that a clinician has received formal PCL training, but that the workshops are not the only way in which qualified clinicians can prepare themselves to conduct competent PCL-R assessments. For example, some facilities have developed in-house training programs. The manuals also note that most clinicians who participate in these training programs should not have difficulty conducting reliable PCL assessments. We are not aware of any published research examining the efficacy of any particular PCL training program, although it is clear from published studies that several research labs have training programs that produce highly reliable psychopathy scores, based on measures of inter-rater reliability.

Method of and Rationale for the Development of the PCL Measures

The second edition of the PCL-R manual (Hare, 2003) reports psychometric data for large samples of criminal offenders and forensic psychiatric patients. In the following sections, we review the evidence concerning the reliability and validity of the PCL measures, focusing mostly on the PCL-R and PCL:YV.

Reliability

The manual for the second edition of the PCL-R presents classical test theory indices of reliability based on several large samples of criminal offenders and forensic psychiatric patients (Hare, 2003). In terms of North American samples, PCL-R data were obtained from 6,500+ male and female criminal offenders and 1,200+ male forensic psychiatric patients using the standard administration procedure, and from 2,500+ male criminal offenders and 400+ male forensic psychiatric patients using the file-review-only administration procedure. Additional psychometric data were derived from European samples of male criminal offenders and male forensic psychiatric patients. The normative data are discussed in following sections (see Book et al., 2006, for a review of the psychometric properties of the PCL measures).

Internal Consistency. The second edition of the PCL-R manual (Hare, 2003) reports corrected item-total correlations (*r*) based on the standard administration procedure for pooled samples of male criminal offenders, male forensic psychiatric patients, and female criminal offenders. The mean corrected item-total correlation was .45 for male criminal offenders, .38 for male forensic psychiatric patients, and .40 for female criminal offenders. Overall, virtually all of the item-total correlations were at least .30. Similar item-total correlations were obtained when using the file-review-only administration procedure. Specifically, the mean corrected item-total correlations were .45 for male criminal offenders and .51 for male forensic psychiatric patients.

Other measures of internal consistency were generally high (Hare, 2003). For the pooled samples using the standard administration procedure, Cronbach's alphas were .85 for male criminal offenders, .81 for male forensic psychiatric patients, and .82 for female criminal offenders, yielding a mean of .84 across the pooled samples. For the pooled samples using the standard administration procedure, mean inter-item correlation coefficients were .23 for male criminal offenders, .19 for male forensic psychiatric patients, and .19 for female criminal offenders, yielding a mean of .22 across the pooled samples. When using the file-review-only administration procedure, the mean Cronbach's alpha coefficient (.87) and inter-item correlation (.25) were slightly higher than with the standard administration. Mean inter-item correlations of .20 or greater indicate that the items measure similar content (Nunnally & Bernstein, 1994).

Less research has examined the internal consistency of the PCL:YV, but the available research suggests it is psychometrically sound in this regard. The PCL:YV manual (Forth et al., 2003) presents measures of internal consistency for several samples, including institutionalized ($N = 1{,}676$), probation ($N = 550$), and clinic/community ($N = 160$). Cronbach's alphas were .85 for institutionalized samples, .87 for probation samples, and .94 for clinic/community samples. These values are comparable to those reported for the PCL-R. Mean inter-item correlations were reported as .23 among institutionalized samples, .25 among probation samples, and .43 among clinic/community samples. In more recent research, Campbell, Pulos, Hogan, and Murry (2005) examined the internal consistency of the PCL:YV by reviewing published and unpublished studies. They calculated a mean Cronbach's alpha of .85 based on $k = 18$ reliability estimates.

Although the PCL measures demonstrate relatively high levels of internal consistency, we should highlight that such results do not lead to the conclusion that high scorers on the PCL measures represent a homogeneous group (Edens et al., 2009). In contrast, a growing body of research suggests considerable heterogeneity among individuals who obtain high scores on these instruments. Several recent studies have cluster-analyzed PCL scores and other theoretically important variables and demonstrated the existence of variants or subtypes of psychopathy (for a recent review, see Poythress & Skeem, 2006; see also Skeem, Johansson, Andershed, Kerr, & Louden, 2007). Although an extensive review of these data is not possible here, suffice it to say that all "psychopaths" are not "alike" (see, e.g., Karpman, 1948; Lykken, 1995). Unfortunately, the implications of these putative subtypes for risk assessment purposes are largely unstudied (although for informed speculation, see Skeem, Poythress, Edens, Lilienfeld, & Cale, 2003).

Inter-Rater Reliability. Many research studies report high levels of rater agreement for PCL-R scores using either the standard administration procedure or file-review-only administration procedure (Hare, 2003). Inter-rater reliability is typically measured using intraclass correlations coefficients (ICCs) for a single rating (ICC_1) and for the average of two independent ratings (ICC_2). According to the manual for the second edition of the PCL-R (Hare, 2003), the pooled ICC for male criminal offenders was .86 for a single rating (ICC_1) and .92 for the average of two ratings (ICC_2). For the male forensic psychiatric patients, ICC_1 was .88, and ICC_2 was .93. Finally, for the female criminal offenders, ICC_1 was .94, and ICC_2 was .97.

Although many studies have examined inter-rater reliability for PCL-R scores, only a handful of studies have examined inter-rater agreement among real-world practicing clinicians (see Murrie, Boccaccini, Johnson et al., 2008, for a review). In an early study, Gacono and Hutton (1994) reported strong inter-rater agreement among 31 staff members at a forensic hospital who had undergone comprehensive PCL-R training. In more recent research, Kroner and Mills (2001) and Porter, Woodworth, Earle, Drugge, and Boer (2003) found ICC values greater than .90 among practicing correctional psychologists compared to each other and to trained research coders.

In most studies that have examined inter-rater agreement among clinicians administering the PCL, the clinicians review the same collateral information and observe the same interview of the individual. Although this approach is reasonable for training purposes in research contexts, it arguably does not accurately reflect what takes place in real-world clinical practice (see Murrie et al., 2008, for a discussion of this issue). According to Murrie, Boccaccini, Johnson et al. (2008), only two studies have examined levels of inter-rater agreement for interviews conducted by different raters at different times. In an early study that examined test–retest values for the PCL-R, Alterman, Cacciola, and Rutherford (1993) reported correlations of .85 and .89 between scores at baseline and scores obtained 1 month later in a sample of 88 clients receiving substance abuse treatment. In a later study, Rutherford, Cacciola, Alterman, McKay, and Cook (1999) obtained a 2-year test–retest reliability value of .60 (ICC) for PCL-R Total scores among 200 male patients receiving services in a methadone clinic. Based on this small body of research, Murrie, Boccaccini, Johnson et al. (2008) concluded that the PCL-R test–retest values appear to be lower than the inter-rater agreement values of ICCs greater than .85 reported in the research literature for research assistants and clinicians.

The studies discussed above are informative, but they do not address the reliability of PCL scores in legal cases, which arguably could introduce systematic and/or random error into the assessment. Murrie, Boccaccini, Johnson et al. (2008), however, recently compared PCL-R scores provided by opposing clinicians in a real-world adversarial context. They identified 23 sexually violent predator civil commitment trials in Texas in which opposing clinicians (that is, one for prosecution and one for defense) reported PCL-R Total scores for the same individual. They found that differences in PCL-R Total scores from opposing clinicians were typically in a direction that supported the party who retained their services: average state expert ratings were 26 (*sd* = 8.48), while average respondent expert ratings were 18 (*sd* = 6.62). Given that PCL scores range from 0 to 40 in theory, and 6 to 38 in practice with male criminal offenders (Hare, 2003, p. 25), an average disparity of 8 points is remarkable and troubling. Further, the score differences were greater in magnitude than would be expected given the PCL-R's standard error of measurement (SEM) (i.e., standard deviation of observed scores if the true score is held constant). The PCL-R manual reports SEMs for male offenders of 2.9 for single ratings and 2.0 for the average of two ratings using the standard administration (Hare, 2003). The ICC for absolute agreement for the PCL-R Total score from a single rater was .39 in this study, which is well below values reported in previous research and the PCL-R manual. After ruling out other potential explanations, Murrie et al. concluded that the results raise concerns about the role of "partisan allegiance" among forensic clinicians in terms of influencing PCL-R scores in adversarial contexts.

Importantly, concerns about real-world inter-rater reliability in forensic contexts are not limited to the PCL-R. There is preliminary evidence that inter-rater reliability may be less than ideal for other commonly used forensic measures, including the STATIC-99 and Minnesota Sex Offender Screening Tool–Revised (MnSOST-R) (see Murrie, Boccaccini, Turner, & Meeks, 2008). Nevertheless, the results of the Murrie, Boccaccini, Johnson et al. (2008) study highlight the subjective nature of the PCL-R scoring criteria (at least for some of the items), which can result in disparate PCL-R scores when used in real-world settings.

The initial inter-rater reliability estimates for the PCL:YV were established on a relatively small sample of institutionalized (*n* = 103), probation (*n* = 63), and clinic/community (*n* = 25) participants (Forth et al., 2003). The ICCs for two independent raters were quite high, with ICC values of .96 for institutionalized and clinic/community samples, and .95 for probation samples. In more recent research, Campbell et al. (2005) calculated a mean estimate of inter-rater reliability based on their review of published and unpublished research studies examining PCL scores among youth. They calculated a mean ICC estimate (based on PCL ratings made by two or more independent raters) of .91. This value is similar to the mean value obtained with the normative samples during the validation of the PCL:YV, and it supports the proposition that the PCL:YV demonstrates good inter-rater reliability in research settings. Although we are not aware of a study comparable to that of Murrie et al. (2008) in relation to possible examiner allegiance effects on the PCL:YV, there are anecdotal accounts of significant discrepancies that raise similar concerns regarding its use in litigation (Edens & Vincent, 2008).

Validity

There is a well-developed body of research suggesting that the PCL-R's construct validity is supported by convergent/divergent correlations with theoretically relevant variables (see Patrick, 2006, for an overview). Given the strong correlation between the PCL and PCL-R, evidence for the validity of the former is applicable to the latter. Although space limitations preclude a full discussion of the PCL-R's validity, suffice it to say that PCL-R scores are related to a variety of clinical, self-report, and demographic variables (see Book et al., 2006, and Hare, 2003, for reviews). In terms of clinical assessment instruments, PCL-R scores are strongly related to DSM diagnoses of Antisocial Personality Disorder (APD) (Hart & Hare, 1989), prototypicality ratings of APD (Hart & Hare, 1989), and APD symptom counts (Hildebrand & de Ruiter, 2005).

PCL-R scores are correlated to varying degrees with several self-report measures of personality and psychopathology (see Hare, 2003, for a review). For example, PCL-R Total scores are positively correlated with the Psychopathic Deviate (Pd) and Hypomania (Ma) scales of the

Minnesota Multiphasic Personality Inventory, and negatively correlated with the Masculinity–Femininity (Mf) and Social Introversion (Si) scales. PCL-R Total scores are positively correlated with the Antisocial, Narcissistic, Passive–Aggressive, Paranoid, and Substance Dependence scales of the Millon Clinical Multiaxial Inventory-II, and negatively correlated with the Dependent, Somatoform, Anxiety, and Dysthymic scales. PCL-R Total and Factor 2 scores have meaningful correlations with the Personality Assessment Inventory (PAI) scales, whereas correlations between Factor 1 and the PAI scales are small. Finally, PCL-R scores are positively correlated with the dimension of Negative Emotionality and negatively correlated with the dimension of Constraint from the Multidimensional Personality Questionnaire. PCL-R scores are also correlated with several self-report measures of psychopathy, including the Psychopathic Personality Inventory, Interpersonal Measure of Psychopathy, and Levenson's Self-Report Psychopathy Scale (Hare, 2003).

The PCL-R is unrelated, or weakly and inconsistently related, to other variables, such as anxiety, depression, and suicide (see Hare, 2003, for a review). Some of these findings are theoretically troubling, as the lack of association with anxiety in particular runs counter to historical conceptualizations of psychopathy (Cleckley, 1941). These inconsistencies may be attributable to PCL Total scores including both the "old" Factors 1 and 2 items, given that these factors have shown preferential correlates with important constructs such as anxiety. They may also stem from the existence of etiologically distinct psychopathy subtypes among which the PCL-R *in isolation* is unable to differentiate (Poythress & Skeem, 2006).

Predictive Validity

Although the forms of validity discussed above are important, the ability of the PCL measures to predict antisocial behavior takes precedence in any discussion of violence risk assessment. The predictive validity of the PCL measures has been examined in a growing number of studies and several large meta-analyses, and researchers have begun to take a more sophisticated look at the ability of these measures to predict various outcomes, including general recidivism, violent recidivism, sexual recidivism, institutional misconduct, and institutional violence. The predictive validity of the PCL measures has been examined among several populations. As noted previously, although the PCL measures are not purported to be risk assessment measures per se, they have been demonstrated to be prospectively associated with several forms of antisocial and violent behavior (see, e.g., Edens et al., 2007; Gendreau et al., 2002; Guy, Edens, Anthony, & Douglas, 2005; Leistico et al., 2008; Walters, 2003a, 2003b). Besides presenting the key findings related to the predictive validity of the PCL measures, our discussion will examine the role of moderator variables, notably gender and race/ethnicity, whenever such analyses were included in a study. Although such analyses are informative, research regarding the potential moderating effects of gender and race/ethnicity is still in a nascent state, which makes it difficult to draw firm conclusions at this time.

Community Recidivism. Several large meta-analyses have examined the ability of the PCL measures to predict criminal recidivism in the community (see Douglas, Vincent, & Edens, 2006, for a recent review of this literature). A few caveats are worth mentioning before proceeding. Although some studies distinguish between types of recidivism (e.g., general vs. violent vs. sexual), other studies simply measure *any* recidivism. Further, the metric used to quantify recidivism varies by study, with some using dichotomous statistical measures (e.g., chi-square, Phi) and others using more sophisticated statistical techniques that incorporate time at risk prior to reoffending (e.g., survival or Cox regression). Finally, although the studies discussed below focus primarily on recidivism in the community, they often included findings on institutional recidivism, which makes it difficult to neatly categorize some of the studies.

Two early meta-analyses examined the relationship between psychopathy and criminal recidivism. Salekin, Rogers, and Sewell (1996) meta-analyzed 18 predictive and postdictive studies that investigated the relationship between the PCL or PCL-R (and the PCL: SV in one study) and nonviolent and violent recidivism. They obtained moderate to strong effect sizes, and concluded that the PCL measures are reliable predictors of both nonviolent and violent recidivism. In the other meta-analysis, Hemphill, Hare, and Wong (1998) examined 10 studies that used either the PCL or PCL-R to predict general and violent community recidivism. They found that Factor 2 was more predictive of general recidivism than Factor 1, but that neither Factor 1 nor Factor 2 was more strongly correlated than the other with violent recidivism.

More recent meta-analyses used larger samples of studies to examine the relationship between psychopathy as measured by the PCL-R and criminal recidivism. For example, Gendreau et al. (2002) compared PCL-R Total scores and scores on the Level of Service Inventory–Revised (LSI-R) (Andrews & Bonta, 1995), which is an index of risk for recidivism within correctional samples, in terms of ability to predict general and violent recidivism in the community. They reported a weighted effect size (Phi coefficient) for the PCL-R of .23 for general recidivism (based on 30 studies) and .21 for violent recidivism (based on 26 studies). In another meta-analysis, Walters (2003b) relied on 50 effect size estimates from 42 studies that prospectively assessed the relationship between PCL and PCL-R Factor scores and community recidivism (general, violent, and sexual). He found that Factor 2 is moderately predictive of community recidivism ($r = .29$; $k = 34$), whereas Factor 1 is less robustly associated with these outcome measures ($r = .18$; $k = 34$). This study will be discussed again later in this chapter.

The ability of the PCL measures to predict criminal recidivism among youthful offenders has received more limited attention from researchers (Campbell, Porter, & Santor, 2004; Corrado, Vincent, Hart, & Cohen, 2004; Edens & Cahill, 2007; Gretton, Hare, & Catchpole, 2004). In a widely cited study, Gretton et al. (2004) reported general, violent, and sexual recidivism data among a sample of 157 Canadian adolescent male offenders followed over a 10-year period. Results revealed that PCL:YV Total scores were not related to general or sexual recidivism, but were predictive of violent recidivism, with a point-biserial correlation coefficient of .32. In addition, Factor 2 was significantly correlated with nonviolent recidivism ($r_{pb} = .33$).

To summarize this growing body of literature, Edens et al. (2007) recently meta-analyzed recidivism data for the PCL measures across 21 nonoverlapping samples of male and female juvenile offenders. Results revealed that psychopathy was significantly associated with both general and violent recidivism, with weighted mean correlation coefficients of .24 ($n = 2{,}787$) and .25 ($n = 2{,}067$), respectively. Psychopathy was not, however, associated with sexual recidivism, although Edens et al. (2007) noted that the base rate for sexual offending was quite low across studies. Despite the positive effect sizes, homogeneity statistics indicated that the effects for violent recidivism were too heterogeneous to aggregate in a meaningful manner, indicating that the relationship between PCL scores and violence across studies was too diverse to be explainable simply by chance variability. Of some concern, moderator analyses revealed that a large proportion of the variability among the effect sizes was attributable to the percentage of Caucasian participants in each sample, with studies composed of higher proportions of non-Caucasian participants reporting lower effect sizes than the more ethnically homogeneous (i.e., primarily Caucasian) samples. These results counsel against making generalizations about the relationship between psychopathy and criminality among minority youth, at least until more research is conducted that addresses this issue. Also, effects for studies including female juveniles were generally weak and nonsignificant.

In a study completed subsequent to (and not included in) the Edens et al. (2007) meta-analysis, Edens and Cahill (2007) reported 10-year general recidivism (any misdemeanor or felony conviction), felony recidivism (violent and nonviolent convictions), and violent recidivism data for a sample of 75 multiethnic male offenders who had been administered the PCL:YV in 1996 when they were, on average, 16 years old. Overall, results revealed that a large portion of the sample (84%) had been reconvicted for at least one misdemeanor or felony offense during the lengthy follow-up period, with the reconviction rate for violent offenses being 32%. Unlike the 10-year follow-up data of Gretton et al. (2004), prospective statistical analyses revealed that neither the PCL:YV Total scores nor either Factor score significantly predicted any form of reconviction during the follow-up period. Edens and Cahill (2007) also conducted a series of logistic regression analyses to examine the effect of ethnic group membership (Caucasian, African American, and Hispanic). The results of these analyses did not provide any evidence that ethnicity directly predicted recidivism or moderated the relationship between PCL:YV scores and any type of recidivism.

Finally, a recent meta-analysis by Leistico et al. (2008) examined effect sizes from 95 nonoverlapping studies ($N = 15{,}826$) to study the relationship between the PCL measures and antisocial conduct, which was broadly defined to include both recidivism and institutional infractions. Overall, they found that PCL Total scores, Factor 1 scores, and Factor 2 scores were moderately associated with increased antisocial conduct, with mean weighted effect sizes (Hedges' d) of .55, .38, and .60, respectively. Consistent with prior meta-analyses, Factor 2 had a stronger relationship with antisocial conduct than Factor 1. Leistico et al. (2008) conducted moderator analyses to examine the influence of several variables, including gender and race/ethnicity. They found that effect sizes were significantly moderated by several variables, including the country in which the study was conducted, the racial and gender composition of the sample, institutional setting, type of information used to score the PCL, and the independence of psychopathy and transgression assessments. Leistico et al. (2008) concluded that predictions of antisocial conduct based on PCL measures should be "interpreted more cautiously for members of minority ethnic groups, males, and prisoners than for Caucasians, females, and psychiatric patients" (p. 40).

Institutional Misconduct. The ability of the PCL measures to predict general and violent recidivism in the community is seemingly well established, although the aggregated magnitude of this relationship is modest to moderate, and the variability of the strength of this relationship across studies is of some concern. The ability of these measures to predict institutional disciplinary infractions and violence, however, arguably has been a greater source of controversy. Over the past 20 years, many studies have examined the relationship between the PCL measures and institutional misbehavior, with outcome measures ranging from nonviolent infractions to serious physical violence. Importantly, from a methodological standpoint, many early studies provided postdictive or concurrent evidence rather than predictive evidence regarding the relationship between the PCL-R and institutional misconduct, which raises questions about the true relationship between this instrument and institutional misbehavior.

Fortunately, in recent years, the ability of the PCL measures to *predict* institutional misconduct among correctional populations has received a considerable amount of attention from researchers (see, e.g., Cunningham & Reidy, 2002; Edens, Buffington-Vollum, Keilen, Roskamp, & Anthony, 2005; Edens, Petrila, & Buffington-Vollum, 2001; Guy et al., 2005; Walters, 2003a, 2003b; Walters, Duncan, & Geyer, 2003). Overall, there is mixed empirical evidence regarding the relationship between the PCL measures and various forms of institutional misconduct, particularly violent acts. Most of the studies that examined this issue reported nonsignificant or small-to-moderate correlations between the PCL measures and various types of institutional misconduct. Given the large body of literature regarding the ability of the PCL measures to predict institutional misconduct, we will focus mostly on meta-analytic studies.

Two meta-analyses by Walters (2003a, 2003b) warrant attention in this discussion. In a meta-analysis of $k = 14$ studies, Walters (2003a) reported a moderate association ($r = .27$) between psychopathy, as measured by PCL-R total scores, and several measures of institutional adjustment.

He did not, however, report analyses related to violent institutional misconduct in prison. In a subsequent meta-analysis, Walters (2003b) examined the ability of the PCL and PCL-R Factor scores to predict institutional adjustment and community recidivism among forensic patients and prison inmates. Walters (2003b) relied on 50 effect size estimates obtained from 42 studies that prospectively assessed the relationship between PCL and PCL-R Factor scores and institutional adjustment (violent and nonviolent), community recidivism (general, violent, and sexual), or both. He reported that PCL-R Factor 2 is moderately predictive of institutional adjustment (r = .27; k = 16) and community recidivism (r = .29; k = 34), both broadly defined, whereas Factor 1 is less robustly associated with these outcome measures, with correlation coefficients of .18 (k = 16) for institutional adjustment and .18 (k = 34) for community recidivism. In other analyses, Walters (2003b) reported mean correlation coefficients of .12 for Factor 1 and .22 for Factor 2 with respect to violent infractions, which included verbal aggression, hostility, property destruction, fighting, and assault.

In a recent comprehensive meta-analysis that included published and unpublished studies examining the PCL measures, Guy et al. (2005) coded 273 effect sizes to examine the relationship between several PCL measures (PCL, PCL-R, PCL:SV) and various types of institutional misconduct in civil psychiatric, forensic psychiatric, and correctional facilities. They reported separate results for PCL Total scores and Factor scores. Overall, the mean weighted effect sizes for PCL Total, Factor 1, and Factor 2 scores were highly heterogeneous and weakest for physically violent institutional misconduct (r_w = .17, .15, and .14, respectively). For PCL Total scores, they reported weighted average correlation coefficients of .29 (k = 38 studies) for any institutional misconduct and .21 (k = 12 studies) for nonaggressive institutional misconduct. Finally, moderator analyses revealed that the effect sizes for physically violent institutional misconduct were smaller in U.S. prison samples (r_w = .11) than in non-U.S. prison samples (r_w = .23). Guy et al. (2005) also examined whether having a sample composed mostly of Caucasian participants acted as a moderator, and the results were not significant, but approaching significance, in several analyses. They concluded that these results raise serious questions about the use of the PCL measures to predict violence among U.S. prison samples. More recent studies published since the completion of this meta-analysis generally have reported similarly weak effects in relation to the prediction of violence (McDermott, Edens, Quanbeck, Busse, & Scott, 2008).

Several studies have specifically examined the ability of the PCL measures, typically either the PCL-R or PCL:YV, to predict institutional misconduct among youthful samples (Edens & Campbell, 2007; Edens, Skeem, Cruise, & Cauffman, 2001; Forth & Mailloux, 2000; Vincent & Hart, 2002). Earlier narrative reviews appear to support the predictive validity of the PCL measures in relation to outcome measures such as adjustment to incarceration or detention among youthful offenders (Edens, Skeem et al., 2001; Forth & Mailloux, 2000; Vincent & Hart, 2002). For example, Edens, Skeem et al. (2001) concluded that the correlation between psychopathy and institutional aggression among youths was approximately .30. It should be noted, however, that this figure was derived from a review of only three prospective studies available at that time.

The first meta-analytic investigation of the relationship between psychopathy among adolescents and institutional misconduct was published by Edens and Campbell in 2007. They meta-analyzed effect sizes for three types of institutional misconduct—total misconduct, aggressive behavior, and physically violent behavior—across 15 nonoverlapping data sets from 13 studies (N = 1,310). Edens and Campbell (2007) used a hierarchical coding scheme to reflect the increasingly severe forms of institutional misconduct reported in the various studies. The "total misconduct" outcome category included all forms of institutional misconduct. The "aggressive behavior" outcome category, which captured a more narrow range of institutional misconduct, included verbal aggression, physical aggression, and (in some studies) destruction of property. Finally, the "physically violent behavior" outcome category was limited to overt acts capable of causing physical harm to another person. Edens and Campbell (2007) reported weighted mean correlation coefficients of .24 (k = 15; n = 1,310) for total misconduct, .25 (k = 14; n = 1,188) for aggressive misconduct, and .28 (k = 10; n = 1,001) for physically violent misconduct. Importantly, they noted that there was considerable heterogeneity among effect sizes for both aggressive and physically violent misconduct. Based on these results, they concluded that the relationship between psychopathy among adolescents and various measures of institutional misconduct may be "considerably less robust and somewhat weaker" than what was suggested by some of the earlier narrative reviews (Edens & Campbell, 2007, p. 23).

Incremental Validity

Even though the PCL measures are not risk assessment instruments per se, a large body of research suggests that they are prospectively associated with various forms of antisocial conduct, such as general and violent recidivism among released offenders. Given these well-established findings, a logical next question is whether the PCL measures add appreciably to what clinicians and researchers can obtain from empirically established risk factors or from other measures routinely administered as part of violence risk assessment evaluations. Along these lines, several researchers have recently addressed the question of whether there is anything unique about the predictive utility of psychopathy once other risk factors and risk assessment instruments are taken into account (see Douglas et al., 2006, for a brief review).

Psychopathy Versus Other Risk Factors. In earlier research, Hemphill et al. (1998) reviewed several studies that compared the predictive utility of the PCL-R to other risk factors, including demographic variables, criminal history variables, and personality disorders. They concluded that the PCL-R was more strongly predictive of violence than the other risk factors, and that it also added incrementally to these other risk factors. A subsequent study also supported the incremental validity of the PCL-R. Tengström, Hodgins, Grann, Langström, and Kullgren (2004) concluded that the PCL-R retains its predictive utility after other risk factors are controlled, including demographic variables, substance abuse, and criminal history.

In a more comprehensive examination of the incremental validity of psychopathy, Skeem and Mulvey (2001) conducted incremental predictive analyses, comparing the PCL:SV to several established risk factors, and propensity score analyses, in which nonspecific antisocial behavior was removed from the estimate of the relationship between psychopathy and violence. These analyses were conducted on a large data set from the MacArthur Violence Risk Assessment Study (Monahan et al., 2001), which examined 134 risk factors among 1,136 patients admitted to acute civil psychiatric inpatient facilities. In the MacArthur Study, the PCL:SV was administered to roughly 750 participants during the first or second follow-up interview, which were 10 and 20 weeks postdischarge. Skeem and Mulvey (2001) used hierarchical logistic regression analyses to determine that the PCL:SV added to the model fit produced by 15 covariates alone. Based on propensity score analyses that held constant the nonspecific psychopathy-related variance, the correlation between the PCL:SV and violence was reduced from .26 to .12. Skeem and Mulvey (2001) concluded that the .14 reduction in the correlation coefficient represented the "unique" variance of psychopathy in terms of predicting violence (Skeem & Mulvey, 2001). Importantly, because the PCL:SV was administered during the follow-up interviews, it is possible that the first violent act was actually postdictive to the PCL:SV assessment. Nevertheless, this study provides important data regarding the unique variance of psychopathy in predicting violence. By controlling for 15 other variables that are theoretically or empirically related to psychopathy and violence, Skeem and Mulvey (2001) conducted a highly conservative test of the incremental validity of the PCL:SV.

In a more recent study, Walters, Knight, Grann, and Dahle (2008) examined the incremental validity of the four facet scores of the PCL-R and PCL:SV among six forensic/correctional samples. The average follow-up time periods for the six samples ranged from 20 weeks to 10 years, and outcomes included both general and violent recidivism. The results revealed that Facet 4 (Antisocial) demonstrated incremental validity relative to Facets 1 (Interpersonal), 2 (Affective), and 3 (Lifestyle), whereas Facets 1, 2, and 3 demonstrated minimal incremental validity relative to Facet 4. In 11 of the 11 analyses conducted, Facet 4 contributed unique variance to predictions of recidivism above and beyond Facets 1, 2, and 3, while Facets 1, 2, and 3 added unique variance to recidivism predictions above and beyond Facet 4 in only 2 of the 11 analyses. Walters et al. (2008) concluded that the antisocial component of the PCL measures is a robust predictor of recidivism, and that the interpersonal, affective, and lifestyle components "add little to predictions of recidivism beyond what is available from the antisocial component" (p. 402). Finally, Walters et al. (2008) noted that the demonstrated superiority of Factor 2 in prior studies is more a function of Facet 4 than Facet 3.

Psychopathy Versus Risk Assessment Measures. Several researchers have compared the PCL measures to validated risk assessment instruments to gauge the incremental predictive validity of psychopathy. In a recent study, Edens, Skeem, and Douglas (2006) examined the incremental validity of a modified VRAG and the PCL:SV in a sample of 695 civil psychiatric patients from the MacArthur Violence Risk Assessment Study. Based on ROC analyses, the AUC for the VRAG, independent of the PCL:SV, was .58, whereas the AUC for the PCL:SV, independent of the VRAG, was .75. The authors obtained similar AUC values, .57 and .73, respectively, using data derived from the 50-week follow-up. Based on these results, they concluded that, although the VRAG has a strong bivariate relationship with community violence, the VRAG was unable to improve on the predictive validity of the PCL:SV alone. They also noted that the VRAG items accounted for little or no variance in violent outcomes beyond the PCL:SV, whereas the PCL:SV continued to account for a large amount of variance after controlling for the VRAG.

In another study examining the incremental validity of the PCL, Walters (2006) meta-analyzed 27 pairs of effect sizes from 22 prospective studies that used at least one risk assessment measure—HCR-20; Lifestyle Criminality Screening Form (LCSF) (Walters, White, & Denney, 1991), LSI-R, PCL, and VRAG—and at least one self-report measure. The PCL was used in over half of the studies examined. Overall, risk-appraisal procedures demonstrated an advantage over self-report procedures in terms of predicting recidivism. However, when the meta-analysis was limited to studies using content-relevant self-report predictors, which Walters (2006) defined as surveys and inventories developed specifically for criminal offender and antisocial populations with item content that features criminal offending and antisocial behavior, risk assessment measures and self-report measures produced comparable results. In 19 of the 36 self-report/risk-appraisal contrasts (53%), the risk-appraisal procedures demonstrated incremental validity, and in 20 of the 36 self-report/risk-appraisal contrasts (56%), the self-report procedures demonstrated incremental validity.

Not all studies, however, support the incremental validity of the PCL in terms of predicting violence. In several studies, Douglas and colleagues found that the HCR-20 (with the psychopathy item removed) added incrementally to the PCL measures in multivariate analyses, but that the converse was not true (Douglas, Ogloff, & Hart, 2003; Douglas et al., 1999; Douglas, Yeomans, & Boer, 2005). In more recent research, Doyle and Dolan (2006) compared the incremental validity of the HCR-20 and PCL:SV, among other measures, in a sample of patients discharged from mental health services. They found that the HCR-20 was the most robust predictor of community violence, with the clinical and risk management items adding significant incremental validity to the assessment of risk (beyond more static risk factors contained in the historical scale of the HCR-20) (Doyle & Dolan, 2006).

One meta-analysis compared the predictive utility of the PCL:YV to the Youth Level of Service/Case Management Inventory (YLS/CMI) (Hoge & Andrews, 2002), which is a measure designed to assess risk level among juvenile offenders (Edens et al., 2007). Their analysis was based on five published studies comparing psychopathy to the YLS/CMI. All five studies examined general recidivism (combined n = 799), and four of the studies also examined violent recidivism (combined n = 727). Results revealed that the measures performed comparably. For general recidivism, the weighted mean effect size was .27 for the PCL:YV Total scores and .25 for the YLS/CMI. For violent recidivism, the weighted mean effect size was .24 for the PCL:YV Total scores and .21 for the YLS/CMI. Unfortunately, due to the analyses reported in the five studies, Edens et al. (2007) were not able to directly address the question of whether either measure demonstrated any incremental validity over the other in terms of predicting recidivism. However, based on the high average intercorrelation ($r_w = .77$) in the three studies that reported associations between the measures, Edens et al. (2007) concluded that it "seems unlikely that the measures were accounting for much if any unique variance in these outcomes" (p. 68).

In a more recent study, Dolan and Rennie (2008) examined the predictive and incremental validity of the Structured Assessment of Violence Risk in Youth (SAVRY) and the PCL:YV in 99 male adolescents who were assessed in custody and then followed for 12 months postrelease. The base rates for violent and general recidivism were 38.4% and 70.7%, respectively. Results revealed that the SAVRY was a modest, but better, predictor of both types of recidivism than the PCL:YV.

Finally, Douglas, Epstein, and Poythress (2008) examined the incremental validity of the PCL:YV, Antisocial Process Screening Device (APSD) (Frick & Hare, 2001), and Childhood Psychopathy Scale (CPS) (Lynam, 1997) in terms of predicting criminal recidivism among 83 delinquent youth. The predictive validity of the self-report measures (i.e., APSD, CPS) was better than the predictive validity of the PCL:YV. Moreover, incremental validity analyses revealed that all of the predictive effects for the measures of psychopathic features disappeared when relevant covariates, such as substance use, conduct disorder, young age, and past property crime, were entered into multivariate predictive models. Importantly, it should be noted that the PCL:YV did not make it into the incremental stage of analyses.

Before concluding this section, one other study deserves comment. In a 2005 study using the MacArthur data set described above, Skeem, Miller, Mulvey, Tiemann, and Monahan compared the incremental statistical utility of the Five Factor Model of personality, measured by the Neuroticism Extraversion Openness–Five Factor Inventory (NEO-FFI) (Costa & McCrae, 1992), and the PCL:SV for modeling the relationship with violence among 769 civil psychiatric patients. Although the NEO-FFI is not a risk assessment measure, this study provided additional data regarding the predictive validity of the PCL:SV. Skeem et al. (2005) found that, after controlling for previous misbehavior, the NEO-FFI and PCL: SV shared much of their violence postdictive variance. After controlling for previous misbehavior and NEO-FFI scores, the PCL:SV modestly increased one's ability to postdict violence. The authors noted that the overlap in postdictive variance was attributable to the violence-related constructs tapped by antagonism (on the NEO-FFI) and PCL:SV Factor 2. Moreover, Skeem et al. (2005) noted that each measure supplied some unique postdictive variance, with the NEO-FFI contributing neuroticism and the PCL:SV contributing some Factor 1 features, most notably conning-manipulative traits.

Conclusion

Recent research suggests that the PCL-R is being used with increasing regularity by forensic mental health professionals in U.S. and Canadian courts, primarily to assess risk of future violence (DeMatteo & Edens, 2006; Gagnon et al., 2007; Walsh & Walsh, 2006). Given that the appropriateness of any measure used in a forensic context is primarily dependent on the extent to which the measure meaningfully addresses the referral question, the ability of the PCL measures to reliably predict future violence has obvious importance in violence risk assessment contexts. In short, the validity of the PCL measures in violence risk assessments depends upon the extent to which inferences that are drawn from the measures are empirically defensible.

This chapter reviewed the most recent literature regarding the utility of the PCL measures in violence risk assessments. We hope this chapter clearly conveyed the notion that the ability of the PCL measures to predict violent behavior depends on a variety of factors. Key factors in this regard include the type of behavior being predicted (e.g., general vs. violent vs. sexual recidivism), the context in which the offender is or will be located (e.g., correctional facility vs. community), and the time frame for the prediction (e.g., 1 year postrelease vs. 10 years postrelease). Further, as illustrated by some of the studies previously discussed, one must consider demographic variables, such as age, gender, and race/ethnicity, when determining whether the PCL measures have been shown to be valid predictors of violent behavior. Given these considerations, it is clear that the referral question must possess a sufficient level of specificity to determine whether it is appropriate to use the PCL as part of a violence risk assessment (see DeMatteo & Edens, 2006; Edens, 2006). A circumscribed referral question might concern the possibility of violent behavior in an adult male criminal offender being released from incarceration into the community. Because existing research with the PCL can inform this type of an evaluation, there would be no significant concerns regarding the relevance and probative value of using the PCL as part of a more comprehensive assessment in this context.

There are a variety of factors one must consider when determining whether the PCL is a valid predictor of future violence, so it is difficult to provide a summary of the research that holds true across all conditions. With that said, the research reviewed in this chapter suggests that the PCL has a modest to at best moderate relationship with future community violence, and a weak to modest relationship with future institutional violence. Importantly, most of the meta-analyses reviewed in this chapter evidenced considerable heterogeneity among effect sizes. Therefore, any discussion of "average" effect sizes may be misleading. As such, even if the research is considered in the most favorable light, experts should not blindly rely on these meta-analyses as establishing that the PCL is a reliable and valid predictor of future violence.

Our review of the existing research also highlights some gaps and shortcomings in our current knowledge regarding the relationship between the PCL and future violence. In addition to simply needing more studies that examine the predictive validity of the PCL (which would bolster the results of future meta-analyses), researchers should study more ethnically and racially diverse samples. This is particularly important given that racial/ethnic diversity has been shown to moderate the relationship between the PCL and recidivism in some of the meta-analyses discussed in this chapter. More research with girls and women is also sorely needed and would add to our limited body of knowledge. Longer-term follow-up studies, particularly with juvenile offenders, would also be helpful in examining the ability of the PCL to make long-term predictions of violence.

Although some may consider the PCL to be the "gold standard" of psychopathy measures, clinicians should look past the rhetoric and ask pragmatic questions about the utility of the PCL in specific contexts. Concluding that a measure is "valid," without specifying the contexts in which it is valid, should be avoided, because validity is not a static property of a measure. Rather, it is a question of the accuracy of the inferences that may be drawn from a measure in specific contexts (Messick, 1995; see DeMatteo & Edens, 2006).

The research reviewed in this chapter can be used to provide guidance to evaluators who may consider using the PCL measures in clinical practice. As with all measures, the decision to use the PCL in a case warrants close scrutiny, and evaluators should be able to defend its application, relevance, and implications in each context in which it is used (see Hare, 2003). The PCL should be considered valid only when it is used in contexts in which inferences drawn from the PCL results are empirically defensible. This highlights the importance of having a well-defined and circumscribed referral question. As previously noted, using the PCL-R with an incarcerated adult male offender to predict community violence would permit an evaluator to draw meaningful and empirically defensible inferences relevant to the referral question. By contrast, using the PCL-R to predict institutional violence would place one on shakier ground, given the demonstrated weak to modest relationship between the PCL and future institutional violence.

Importantly, limiting the use of the PCL to contexts in which it has demonstrated probative value is consistent with several provisions of the revised ethical guidelines and code of conduct promulgated by the American Psychological Association in 2002 (see Edens & Petrila, 2006, for a discussion of legal and ethical issues associated with the assessment of psychopathy). For example, Standard 9.02(a) states: "Psychologists administer, adapt, score, interpret, or use assessment techniques, interviews, tests, or instruments in a manner and for purposes that are appropriate in light of the research on or evidence of the usefulness and proper application of the techniques" (p. 1071). As another example, Standard 9.02(b) states: "Psychologists use assessment instruments whose validity and reliability have been established for use with members of the population tested" (p. 1071).

Moreover, we would argue that risk assessments should not rely solely on the results of the PCL (which, as noted, is not a risk assessment instrument per se); rather, the PCL, if used, should be part of a more comprehensive risk assessment battery. This could mean using an actuarial measure (i.e., VRAG, SORAG) or structured professional judgment instrument (i.e., HCR-20, SVR-20, RSVP) that incorporates the PCL-R, or using the PCL-R along with other measures that provide risk-relevant data. As with almost any type of forensic mental health assessment, an evaluator's conclusions in the context of a risk assessment are more defensible when they are based on multiple sources of data, including multiple testing procedures (see Bonta, 2002; Conroy & Murrie, 2007; Heilbrun, Marczyk, & DeMatteo, 2002).

References

Alterman, A. I., Cacciola, J. S., & Rutherford, M. J. (1993). Reliability of the Revised Psychopathy Checklist in substance abuse patients. *Psychological Assessment, 5,* 442–448.

American Psychiatric Association. (1952). *Diagnostic and statistical manual of mental disorders.* Washington, DC: American Psychiatric Association.

American Psychiatric Association. (1968). *Diagnostic and statistical manual of mental disorders* (2nd ed.). Washington, DC: American Psychiatric Association.

American Psychiatric Association. (1980). *Diagnostic and statistical manual of mental disorders* (3rd ed.). Washington, DC: American Psychiatric Association.

American Psychiatric Association. (2000). *Diagnostic and statistical manual of mental disorders* (4th ed.)—Text revision. Washington, DC: American Psychiatric Association.

American Psychological Association. (2002). Ethical principles of psychologists and code of conduct. *American Psychologist, 57,* 1060–1073.

Andrews, D. A., & Bonta, J. (1995). *The Level of Service Inventory–Revised (LSI-R).* Toronto, ON, Canada: Multi-Health Systems.

Boer, D. P., Hart, S. D., Kropp, P. R., & Webster, C. D. (1997). *Manual for the Sexual Violence Risk-20: Professional guidelines for assessing risk of sexual violence.* Vancouver, British Columbia: British Columbia Institute on Family Violence and Mental Health, Law, & Policy Institute, Simon Fraser University.

Bonta, J. (2002). Offender risk assessment: Guidelines for selection and use. *Criminal Justice and Behavior, 29,* 355–379.

Book, A. S., Clark, H. J., Forth, A. E., & Hare, R. D. (2006). The Psychopathy Checklist–Revised and the Psychopathy Checklist: Youth Version. In R. P. Archer (Ed.), *Forensic uses of clinical assessment instruments* (pp. 147–179). Mahwah, NJ: Erlbaum.

Campbell, M. A., Porter, S., & Santor, D. (2004). Psychopathic traits in adolescent offenders: An evaluation of criminal history, clinical, and psychosocial correlates. *Behavioral Sciences and the Law, 22,* 23–47.

Campbell, J. S., Pulos, S., Hogan, M., & Murry, F. (2005). Reliability generalization of the Psychopathy Checklist applied in youthful samples. *Educational and Psychological Measurement, 65,* 639–656.

Cleckley, H. (1941). *The mask of sanity.* St. Louis, MO: Mosby.

Conroy, M. A., & Murrie, D. C. (2007). *Forensic assessment of violence risk: A guide for risk assessment and risk management.* Hoboken, NJ: John Wiley & Sons, Inc.

Cooke, D. J., Kosson, D. S., & Michie, C. (2001). Psychopathy and ethnicity: Structural, item and test generalizability of the Psychopathy Checklist Revised (PCL-R) in Caucasian and African-American participants. *Psychological Assessment, 13,* 531–542.

Cooke, D. J., & Michie, C. (2001). Refining the construct of psychopathy: Towards a hierarchical model. *Psychological Assessment, 13,* 171–188.

Cooke, D. J., Michie, C., Hart, S. D., & Clark, D. (2004). Reconstructing psychopathy: Clarifying the significance of antisocial and socially deviant behavior in the diagnosis of psychopathic personality disorder. *Journal of Personality Disorders, 18,* 337–357.

Cooke, D. J., Michie, C., & Ryan, J. (2001). *Evaluating risk for violence: A preliminary study of the HCR-20, PCL-R and VRAG.* Report prepared for the Scottish Prison Service.

Cooke, D. J., Michie, C., & Skeem, J. (2007). Understanding the structure of the Psychopathy Checklist–Revised. *British Journal of Psychiatry, 190* (suppl. 49), s39–s50.

Corrado, R. R., Vincent, G. M., Hart, S. D., & Cohen, I. M. (2004). Predictive validity of the Psychopathy Checklist: Youth Version for general and violent recidivism. *Behavioral Sciences and the Law, 22,* 5–22.

Costa, P. T., & McCrae, R. R. (1992). *Revised NEO Personality Inventory (NEO-PI-R) and NEO Five-Factor Inventory (NEO-FFI) professional manual.* Odessa, FL: Psychological Assessment Resources.

Cunningham, M. D., & Reidy, T. J. (2002). Violence risk assessment at federal capital sentencing: Individualization, generalization, relevance, and scientific standards. *Criminal Justice and Behavior, 29,* 512–537.

DeMatteo, D., & Edens, J. F. (2006). The role and relevance of the Psychopathy Checklist–Revised in court: A case law survey of U.S. courts (1991–2004). *Psychology, Public Policy, and Law, 12,* 214–241.

DeMatteo, D., Heilbrun, K., & Marczyk, G. (2005). Psychopathy, risk of violence, and protective factors in a noninstitutionalized and noncriminal sample. *International Journal of Forensic Mental Health, 4,* 147–157.

DeMatteo, D., Heilbrun, K., & Marczyk, G. (2006). An empirical investigation of psychopathy in a noninstitutionalized and noncriminal sample. *Behavioral Sciences and the Law, 24,* 133–146.

Dolan, M. C., & Rennie, C. E. (2008). The Structured Assessment of Violence Risk in Youth as a predictor of recidivism in a United Kingdom cohort of adolescent offenders with conduct disorder. *Psychological Assessment, 20,* 35–46.

Douglas, K. S., Epstein, M. E., & Poythress, N. G. (2008). Criminal recidivism among juvenile offenders: Testing the incremental and predictive validity of three measures of psychopathic features. *Law and Human Behavior, 32,* 423–438.

Douglas, K. S., Ogloff, J. R. P., & Hart, S. D. (2003). Evaluation of a model of violence risk assessment among forensic psychiatric patients. *Psychiatric Services, 54,* 1372–1379.

Douglas, K. S., Ogloff, J. R. P., Nicholls, T. L. & Grant, I. (1999). Assessing risk for violence among psychiatric patients: The HCR-20 violence risk assessment scheme and the Psychopathy Checklist: Screening Version. *Journal of Consulting and Clinical Psychology, 67,* 917–930.

Douglas, K. S., Vincent, G. M., & Edens, J. F. (2006). Risk for criminal recidivism: The role of psychopathy. In C. J. Patrick (Ed.), *Handbook of psychopathy* (pp. 533–554). New York: Guilford Press.

Douglas, K. S., Yeomans, M. & Boer, D. P. (2005). Comparative validity analysis of multiple measures of violence risk in a sample of criminal offenders. *Criminal Justice and Behavior, 32,* 479–510.

Doyle, M., & Dolan, M. (2006). Predicting community violence from patients discharged from mental health services. *British Journal of Psychiatry, 189,* 520–526.

Edens, J. F. (2001). Misuses of the Hare Psychopathy Checklist–Revised in court: Two case examples. *Journal of Interpersonal Violence, 16,* 1082–1093.

Edens, J. F. (2006). Unresolved controversies concerning psychopathy: Implications for clinical and forensic decision-making. *Professional Psychology: Research & Practice, 37,* 59–65.

Edens, J. F., Buffington-Vollum, J. K., Keilen, A., Roskamp, P., & Anthony, C. (2005). Predictions of future dangerousness in capital murder trials: Is it time to "disinvent the wheel?" *Law and Human Behavior, 29,* 55–86.

Edens, F. F., & Cahill, M. A. (2007). Psychopathy in adolescence and criminal recidivism in young adulthood: Longitudinal results from a multi-ethnic sample of youthful offenders. *Assessment, 14,* 57–64.

Edens, J. F., & Campbell, J. S. (2007). Identifying youths at risk for institutional misconduct: A meta-analytic investigation of the Psychopathy Checklist measures. *Psychological Services, 4,* 13–27.

Edens, J. F., Campbell, J. S., & Weir, J. M. (2007). Youth psychopathy and criminal recidivism: A meta-analysis of the Psychopathy Checklist measures. *Law and Human Behavior, 31,* 53–75.

Edens, J. F., Marcus, D. K., Lilienfeld, S. O., & Poythress, N. G. (2006). Psychopathic, not psychopath: Taxometric evidence for the dimensional structure of psychopathy. *Journal of Abnormal Psychology, 115,* 131–144.

Edens, J., F., & Petrila, J. (2006). Legal and ethical issues in the assessment and treatment of psychopathy. In C. Patrick (Ed.), *Handbook of psychopathy* (pp. 573–588). New York: Guilford Press.

Edens, J. F., Petrila, J., & Buffington-Vollum, J. K. (2001). Psychopathy and the death penalty: Can the Psychopathy Checklist–Revised identify offenders who represent "a continuing threat to society?" *Journal of Psychiatry and Law, 29,* 433–481.

Edens, J. F., Skeem, J. L., Cruise, K. R., & Cauffman, E. (2001). Assessment of "juvenile psychopathy" and its association with violence: A critical review. *Behavioral Sciences and the Law, 19,* 53–80.

Edens, J. F., Skeem, J. L., & Douglas, K. S. (2006). Incremental validity analyses of the Violence Risk Appraisal Guide and the Psychopathy Checklist: Screening Version in a civil psychiatric sample. *Assessment, 13,* 368–374.

Edens, J. F., Skeem, J. L., & Kennealy, P. (2009). The Psychopathy Checklist (PCL) in the courtroom: Consensus and controversies. In J. L. Skeem, K. S. Douglas, & S. O. Lilienfeld (Eds.), *Psychological science in the courtroom: Controversies and consensus* (pp. 175–201). New York: Guilford Press.

Edens, J. F., & Vincent, G. M. (2008). Juvenile psychopathy: A clinical construct in need of restraint? *Journal of Forensic Psychology Practice, 8,* 186–197.

Forth, A. E., Brown, S. L., Hart, S. D., & Hare, R. D. (1996). The assessment of psychopathy in male and female noncriminals: Reliability and validity. *Personality and Individual Differences, 20,* 531–543.

Forth, A. E., Kosson, D. S., & Hare, R. D. (2003). *The Psychopathy Checklist: Youth Version.* Toronto, Ontario: Multi-Health Systems.

Forth, A. E., & Mailloux, D. L. (2000). Psychopathy in youth: What do we know? In C. B. Gacono (Ed.), *The clinical and forensic assessment of psychopathy: A practitioner's guide* (pp. 25–54). Mahwah, NJ: Erlbaum.

Frick, P. J., & Hare, R. D. (2001). *The Antisocial Process Screening Device.* Toronto: Multi-Health Systems.

Gacono, C., & Hutton, H. (1994). Suggestions for the clinical and forensic use of the Hare Psychopathy Checklist–Revised (PCL-R). *International Journal of Law and Psychiatry, 17,* 303–317.

Gagnon, N., Douglas, K., & DeMatteo, D. (2007, June). *The introduction of the Psychopathy Checklist–Revised in Canadian courts: Uses and misuses.* Paper presented at the 7th Annual Conference of the International Association of Forensic Mental Health Services, Montreal, QC, Canada.

Gendreau, P., Coggin, C., & Smith, P. (2002). Is the PCL-R really the "unparalleled" measure of offender risk? A lesson in knowledge cumulation. *Criminal Justice and Behavior, 29,* 397–426.

Glover, A. J. J., Nicholson, D. E., Hemmati, T., Bernfeld, G. A., & Quinsey, V. L. (2002). A comparison of predictors of general and violent recidivism among high risk federal offenders. *Criminal Justice and Behavior, 29,* 235–249.

Gretton, H., Hare, R., & Catchpole, R. (2004). Psychopathy and offending from adolescence to adulthood. *Journal of Consulting and Clinical Psychology, 72,* 636–645.

Guay, J., Ruscio, J., Hare, R., & Knight, R. A. (2007). A taxometric analysis of the latent structure of psychopathy: Evidence for dimensionality. *Journal of Abnormal Psychology, 116,* 701–716.

Guy, L. S., & Douglas, K. S. (2006). Examining the utility of the PCL: SV as a screening measure: Using competing factor models of psychopathy. *Psychological Assessment, 18,* 225–230.

Guy, L. S., Edens, J. F., Anthony, C., & Douglas, K. S. (2005). Does psychopathy predict institutional misconduct among adults? A meta-analytic investigation. *Journal of Consulting and Clinical Psychology, 73,* 1056–1064.

Hall, J. R., Benning, S. D., & Patrick, C. J. (2004). Criterion-related validity of the three-factor model of psychopathy: Personality, behavior, and adaptive functioning. *Assessment, 11,* 4–16.

Hare, R. D. (1980). A research scale for the assessment of psychopathy in criminal populations. *Personality and Individual Differences, 1,* 111–119.

Hare, R. D. (1991). *The Hare Psychopathy Checklist–Revised manual.* North Tonawanda, NY: Multi-Health Systems.

Hare, R. D. (1998). The Hare PCL-R: Some issues concerning its use and misuse. *Legal & Criminological Psychology, 3,* 99–119.

Hare, R. D. (2003). *The Hare Psychopathy Checklist–Revised manual* (2nd ed.). North Tonawanda, NY: Multi-Health Systems.

Hare, R. D., & Neumann, C. S. (2005). The structure of psychopathy. *Current Psychiatry Reports, 7,* 57–64.

Harpur, T. J., Hakstian, A. R., & Hare, R. D. (1988). Factor structure of the Psychopathy Checklist. *Journal of Consulting and Clinical Psychology, 56,* 741–747.

Harpur, T. J., Hare, R. D., & Hakstian, A. R. (1989). Two-factor conceptualization of psychopathy: Construct validity and assessment implications. *Psychological Assessment, 1,* 6–17.

Harris, G. T., Rice, M. E., & Cormier, C. A. (1991). Psychopathy and violent recidivism. *Law and Human Behavior, 15,* 625–637.

Harris, G. T., Rice, M. E., & Quinsey, V. L. (1993). Violent recidivism of mentally disordered offenders: The development of a statistical prediction instrument. *Criminal Justice and Behavior, 20,* 315–335.

Hart, S. D., Cox, D. N., & Hare, R. D. (1995). *The Hare PCL: Screening Version.* North Tonawanda, NY: Multi-Health Systems.

Hart, S. D., & Hare, R. D. (1989). Discriminant validity of the Psychopathy Checklist in a forensic psychiatric population. *Psychological Assessment: A Journal of Consulting and Clinical Psychology, 1,* 211–218.

Hart, S. D., Kropp, P. R., Laws, D. R., Klaver, J., Logan, C., & Watt, K. A. (2003). *The Risk for Sexual Violence Protocol (RSVP): Structured professional guidelines for assessing risk of sexual violence.* Burnaby, British Columbia: Mental Health, Law, and Policy Institute, Simon Fraser University; Pacific Psychological Assessment Corporation; and the British Columbia Institute Against Family Violence.

Heilbrun, K., Marczyk, G. R., & DeMatteo, D. (2002). *Forensic mental health assessment: A casebook.* New York: Oxford University Press.

Hemphill, J. F., & Hare R. D. (2004). Some misconceptions about the Hare PCL-R and risk assessment: A reply to Gendreau, Goggin, and Smith. *Criminal Justice and Behavior, 31,* 203–243.

Hemphill, J. F., Hare, R. D., & Wong, S. (1998). Psychopathy and recidivism: A review. *Legal and Criminological Psychology, 3,* 141–172.

Hildebrand, M., & de Ruiter, C. (2005). PCL-R psychopathy and its relation to DSM-IV Axis I and Axis II disorders in a sample of male forensic psychiatric patients in the Netherlands. *International Journal of Law and Psychiatry, 27,* 233–248.

Hoge, R., & Andrews, D. (2002). *Youth Level of Service/Case Management Inventory.* Toronto, ON, Canada: Multi-Health Systems.

Ishikawa, S. S., Raine, A., Lencz, T., Bihrle, S., & Lacasse, L. (2001). Autonomic stress reactivity and executive functions in successful and unsuccessful criminal psychopaths from the community. *Journal of Abnormal Psychology, 110,* 423–432.

Jones, S., Cauffman, E., Miller, J. D., & Mulvey, E. (2006). Investigating different factor structures of the Psychopathy Checklist: Youth Version: Confirmatory factor analytic findings. *Psychological Assessment, 18,* 33–48.

Karpman, B. (1946). A yardstick for measuring psychopathy. *Federal Probation, 10,* 26–31.

Karpman, B. (1948). The myth of the psychopathic personality. *American Journal of Psychiatry, 104,* 523–534.

Kroner, D. G., & Mills, J. F. (2001). The accuracy of five risk appraisal instruments in predicting institutional misconduct and new convictions. *Criminal Justice and Behavior, 28,* 471–489.

Leistico, A. M., Salekin, R. T., DeCosta, J., & Rogers, R. (2008). A large-scale meta-analysis relating the Hare measures of psychopathy to antisocial conduct. *Law and Human Behavior, 32,* 28–45.

Lilienfeld, S. O. (1994). Conceptual problems in the assessment of psychopathy. *Clinical Psychology Review, 14,* 17–38.

Lykken, D. T. (1995). *The antisocial personalities.* Hillsdale, NJ: Erlbaum.

Lynam, D. R. (1997). Pursuing the psychopath: Capturing the fledgling psychopath in a nomological net. *Journal of Abnormal Psychology, 106,* 425–438.

Maden, T., & Tyrer, P. (2003). Dangerous and severe personality disorders: A new personality concept from the United Kingdom. *Journal of Personality Disorders, 17,* 489–496.

McDermott, B. E., Edens, J. F., Quanbeck, C. E., Busse, D., & Scott, C. L. (2008). Examining the role of static and dynamic risk factors in the prediction of inpatient violence: Variable- and person-focused analyses. *Law and Human Behavior, 32,* 325–338.

Messick, S. (1995). Validity of psychological assessment: Validation of inferences from persons' responses and performances as scientific inquiry into score meaning. *American Psychologist, 50,* 741–749.
Millon, T., Simonsen, E., & Birket-Smith, M. (1998). Historical conceptions of psychopathy in the United States and Europe. In T. Millon, E. Simonsen, M. Birket-Smith, & R. D. Davis (Eds.), *Psychopathy: Antisocial, criminal, and violent behavior* (pp. 3–31). New York: Guilford Press.
Monahan, J., Steadman, H. J., Silver, E., Appelbaum, P. S., Robbins, P. C., Mulvey, E. P., Roth, L. H., Grisso, T., & Banks, S. (2001). *Rethinking risk assessment: The MacArthur study of mental disorder and violence.* New York: Oxford University Press.
Murrie, D. C., Boccaccini, M. T., Johnson, J. T., & Janke, C. (2008). Does interrater (dis)agreement on Psychopathy Checklist Scores in sexually violent predator trials suggest partisan allegiance in forensic evaluations? *Law and Human Behavior, 32,* 352–362.
Murrie, D., Boccaccini, M., Turner, D., & Meeks, M. (2008, March). *Does evaluator (dis)agreement on actuarial risk measures suggest adversarial allegiance?* Paper presented at the 2008 Annual Conference of the American Psychology-Law Society, Jacksonville, FL.
Neumann, C. S., Kosson, D. S., Forth, A. E., & Hare, R. D. (2006). Factor structure of the Hare Psychopathy Checklist: Youth Version (PCL:YV) in incarcerated adolescents. *Psychological Assessment, 18,* 142–154.
Neumann, C. S., Kosson, D. S., & Salekin. R. T. (2007). Exploratory and confirmatory factor analysis of the psychopathy construct: Methodological and conceptual issues. In H. Herve and J. C. Yuille (Eds.), *The psychopath: Theory, research, and practice* (pp. 79–104). Mahwah, NJ: Erlbaum.
Nunnally, J., & Bernstein, I. (1994). *Psychometric theory.* New York: McGraw-Hill.
Patrick, C. J. (Ed.) (2006). *Handbook of psychopathy.* New York: Guilford Press.
Porter, S., Woodworth, M., Earle, J., Drugge, J., & Boer, D. P. (2003). Characteristics of violent behavior exhibited during sexual homicides by psychopathic and non-psychopathic murderers. *Law and Human Behavior, 27,* 459–470.
Poythress, N., & Skeem, J. L. (2006). Disaggregating psychopathy: Where and how to look for variants. In C. Patrick (Ed.) *Handbook of psychopathy* (pp. 172–192). New York: Guilford Press.
Quinsey, V. L., Harris, G. T., Rice, M. E., & Cormier, C. A. (2006). *Violent offenders: Appraising and managing risk* (2nd ed.). Washington, DC: American Psychological Association.
Rogers, R. (1995). Psychopathy Checklist (PCL). In R. Rogers (Ed.) *Diagnostic and structured interviewing: A handbook for psychologists* (pp. 229–243). Odessa, FL: Psychological Assessment Resources.
Rutherford, M., Cacciola, J. S., Alterman, A. I., McKay, J. R., & Cook, T. G. (1999). The 2-year test-retest reliability of the Psychopathy Checklist–Revised in methadone patients. *Assessment, 6,* 285–291.
Salekin, R. T., Rogers, R., & Sewell, K. (1996). A review and meta-analysis of the Psychopathy Checklist and Psychopathy Checklist–Revised: Predictive validity of dangerousness. *Clinical psychology: Science and practice, 3,* 203–215.
Serin, R. C. (1991). Psychopathy and violence in criminals. *Journal of Interpersonal Violence, 6,* 423–431.
Serin, R. C. (1996). Violent recidivism in criminal psychopaths. *Law and Human Behavior, 20,* 207–217.
Skeem, J. L., & Cooke, D. J. (in press). Is antisocial behavior essential to psychopathy? Conceptual directions for resolving the debate. *Psychological Assessment.*
Skeem, J. L., Edens, J. F., Camp, J., & Colwell, L. H. (2004). Are there racial differences in levels of psychopathy? A meta-analysis. *Law and Human Behavior, 28,* 505–527.
Skeem, J. L., Johansson, P., Andershed, H., Kerr, M., & Louden, J. (2007). Two subtypes of psychopathic violent offenders that parallel primary and secondary variants. *Journal of Abnormal Psychology, 116,* 395–409.
Skeem, J. L., Miller, J. D., Mulvey, E. P., Tiemann, J., & Monahan, J. (2005). Using a five-factor lens to explore the relationship between personality traits and violence in psychiatric patients. *Journal of Consulting and Clinical Psychology, 73,* 454–465.
Skeem, J. L., & Mulvey, E. P. (2001). Psychopathy and community violence among civil psychiatric patients: Results from the MacArthur Violence Risk Assessment study. *Journal of Consulting and Clinical Psychology, 69,* 358–374.
Skeem, J. L., Poythress, N. G., Edens, J. F., Lilienfeld, S. O., & Cale, E. (2003). Psychopathic personality or personalities? Exploring potential variants of psychopathy and their implications for risk assessment. *Aggression and Violent Behavior, 8,* 513–546.
Tengström, A., Hodgins, S., Grann, M., Langström, N., & Kullgren, G. (2004). Schizophrenia and criminal offending: The role of psychopathy and substance use disorders. *Criminal Justice and Behavior, 31,* 367–391.

Vincent, G. M., & Hart, S. D. (2002). Psychopathy in childhood and adolescence: Implications for the assessment and management of multi-problem youths. In R. R. Corrado, R. Roesch, S. D. Hart, & J. K. Gierowski (Eds.), *Multi-problem violent youth: A foundation for comparative research on needs, interventions, and outcomes* (pp. 150–163). Washington, DC: IOS Press.

Vitacco, M. J., Neumann, C. S., & Jackson, R. L. (2005). Testing a four-factor model of psychopathy and its association with ethnicity, gender, intelligence, and violence. *Journal of Consulting and Clinical Psychology, 73,* 466–476.

Vitacco, M. J., Rogers, R., Neumann, C. S., Harrison, K., & Vincent, G. (2005). A comparison of factor models on the PCL-R with mentally disordered offenders: The development of a four-factor model. *Criminal Justice and Behavior, 32,* 526–545.

Walsh, T., & Walsh, Z. (2006). The evidentiary introduction of Psychopathy Checklist–Revised assessed psychopathy in U.S. courts: Extent and appropriateness. *Law and Human Behavior, 30,* 493–507.

Walters, G. D. (2003a). Predicting criminal justice outcomes with the Psychopathy Checklist and Lifestyle Criminality Screening Form: A meta-analytic comparison. *Behavioral Sciences and the Law, 21,* 89–102.

Walters, G. D. (2003b). Predicting institutional adjustment and recidivism with the Psychopathy Checklist factor scores: A meta-analysis. *Law and Human Behavior, 27,* 541–558.

Walters, G. D. (2006). Risk-appraisal versus self-report in the prediction of criminal justice outcomes. *Criminal Justice and Behavior, 33,* 279–304.

Walters, G. D., Duncan, S. A., & Geyer, M. D. (2003). Predicting disciplinary adjustment in inmates undergoing forensic evaluation: A direct comparison of the PCL-R and the PAI. *Journal of Forensic Psychiatry and Psychology, 14,* 382–393.

Walters, G. D., Duncan, S. A., & Mitchell-Perez, K. (2007). The latent structure of psychopathy: A taxometric analysis of the Psychopathy Checklist–Revised in a heterogeneous sample of male prison inmates. *Assessment, 14,* 270–278.

Walters, G. D., Gray, N. S., Jackson, R. L., Sewell, K. W., Rogers, R., Taylor, J., & Snowden, R. J. (2007). A taxometric analysis of the Psychopathy Checklist: Screening Version: Further evidence of dimensionality. *Psychological Assessment, 19,* 330–339.

Walters, G. D., Knight, R. A., Grann, M. & Dahle, K. (2008). Incremental validity of the Psychopathy checklist facet scores: Predicting release outcome in six samples. *Journal of Abnormal Psychology, 117,* 396–405.

Walters, G. D., White, T. W., & Denney, D. (1991). The Lifestyle Criminality Screening Form: Preliminary data. *Criminal Justice and Behavior, 18,* 406–418.

Weaver, C. M., Meyer, R. G., Van Nort, J., & Tristan, L. (2006). Two-, three-, and four-factor PCL-R models in applied sex offender risk assessments. *Assessment, 13,* 208–216.

Webster, C. D., Douglas, K. S., Eaves, D., & Hart, S. D. (1997). *HCR-20: Assessing Risk for Violence* (Version 2). Burnaby, BC, Canada: Mental Health, Law, and Policy Institute, Simon Fraser University.

Part I
Child and Juvenile Risk

3
Gender-Specific Childhood Risk Assessment Tools
Early Assessment Risk Lists for Boys (EARL-20B) and Girls (EARL-21G)

LEENA K. AUGIMERI, PIA ENEBRINK, MARGARET WALSH, and DEPENG JIANG

Introduction

Antisocial behavior during childhood is an important warning sign for continued behavior problems (for example, delinquency or conduct disorder) in adolescence and adulthood (Loeber & Farrington, 2001; Moffitt, Caspi, Harrington, & Milne, 2002), leading to substantial personal and familial suffering and societal costs. Children can engage in a range of antisocial behaviors; however, for the purposes of this chapter we are defining antisocial behavior as acts that would lead to criminal charges if the child were at the age of criminal liability. Some examples of antisocial behavior include: assault, aggression, fighting, physically attacking people, theft, cruelty to animals, lying, cheating, and serious violations of rules. However, since many children show variability and desistance from such behaviors over time (Lipman, Bennett, Racine, Mazumdar, & Offord, 1998), it can be difficult to predict which children will continue or discontinue with their antisocial behavior.

One way to enhance predictions is to concentrate on risk factors. Over the past two decades rigorous research has been conducted on risk factors contributing to antisocial behavior. As a result, there is a fairly comprehensive and documented understanding about early factors that place antisocial children at "risk" for engaging in future delinquency and later offending (Howell, 2003; Lahey, Moffit, & Caspi, 2003; Loeber, Burke, & Lahey, 2002; Loeber, Farrington, & Petechuk, 2003). Despite general consensus about which variables predict future aggression and violence, little has been done until recently by way of compiling and organizing this knowledge to help clinicians working with high-risk children in day-to-day practice. Lately, a number of structured professional judgment tools, utilized in risk assessment and based on descriptions of evidence-based risk factors for antisocial behaviors, have been developed for use with adults (e.g., HCR-20) (Webster, Douglas, Eaves, & Hart, 1997), and for youth (e.g., SAVRY) (Borum, Bartel, & Forth, 2002). These have helped advance the field and benefited correctional and forensic mental health systems of care (Bloom, Webster, Hucker, & De Freitas, 2007; Webster, Martin, Brink, Nicholls, & Middleton, 2004). However, prior to 1998, there were no assessment schemes available to identify specific domains of risk for antisocial children under the age of 12 (Augimeri, Koegl, Ferrante, & Slater, 2006b).

The ability to identify or predict which antisocial preadolescent child will continue to engage in such behavior in adolescence or adulthood represents one of the most important challenges in the field of developmental criminology. It is based on the tantalizing proposition that the careful identification of risk factors will lead to the development of effective prevention and intervention strategies for children (Augimeri, Webster, Koegl, & Levene, 1998). Addressing this gap in professional practice, researchers and practitioners at the Centre for Children Committing Offences (CCCO) housed at the Child Development Institute (CDI) in Toronto, Canada, were the first to develop a comprehensive psychosocial risk assessment framework specifically focused on young children with antisocial behavior problems and who may have also been in trouble with the law (Borum et al., 2002). The first assessment tool for boys, under the age of 12, appeared as a "consultation edition" in 1998 (Augimeri et al., 1998) and has since been updated to the Early Assessment Risk List for Boys, Version 2 (EARL-20B) (Augimeri, Koegl, Webster, & Levene, 2001). A parallel assessment tool for girls was also developed in 2001, the Early Assessment Risk List for Girls, Version 1 Consultation Edition (EARL-21G) (Levene et al., 2001).

Method of and Rationale for Development

Early identification and targeted interventions are considered key when helping troubled young children and their families and are equally important for the communities and service providers who bear responsibility for the healthy development of children. Given the focus of the CCCO at the CDI (that is, research, training, and dissemination of evidence-based practices pertaining to young children in conflict with the law), its work in the past decade focused on the development of a comprehensive and remarkably straightforward crime prevention strategy for dealing with these young at-risk children. This three-stage crime prevention strategy includes: (1) *police–community referral protocols* that navigate at-risk children through the system in a timely manner to appropriate service providers; (2) *structured clinical risk assessment* utilizing the EARLs that gauges the risk of future antisocial potential and treatment needs for targeted children; and (3) *gender-specific STOP NOW AND PLAN (SNAP®) programs* that are tailored to meet the clinical needs of aggressive and antisocial children and their families.

As service providers, researchers, and policy makers seem to have a good understanding of the importance of early interventions in supporting antisocial children at risk for future delinquency (Brestan & Eyberg, 1998; Farrington & Welsh, 2007; Frick, 1998), a structured, early assessment of risk tool would help to facilitate rational resource allocation according to identified risk and need. This early identification and intervention is especially relevant for aggressive and antisocial children, because the early age at first offense is one of the strongest and most robust predictors of reoffending (Loeber, Farrington, Stouthamer-Loeber et al., 2003). The "savings" associated with such early identification and intervention could be realized not only for the individual child, but also for family and community (Hoge & Andrews, 1996).

Recognizing that risk assessment is increasingly becoming a standard part of mental health practice (Monahan, 1996), the development of a comprehensive risk assessment scheme to help clinicians identify young children who are considered to be at risk for continued antisocial behavioral problems (see Augimeri, Koegl, Levene, & Webster, 2005) made imperative sense. In fact, the U.S. Office of Juvenile Justice and Delinquency Prevention Study Group on Serious and Violent Offenders recommended the development and validation of screening instruments to identify children at risk of becoming serious and violent offenders (Loeber & Farrington, 1998).

Early work by Loeber (1990, 1991) and CDI researchers (Day 1998; Day & Hunt, 1996) helped shape the CCCO's thinking about structured risk assessment as it pertained to young children (for a detailed history of the rationale for the development of the EARLs see Augimeri et al., 2005). The EARL-20B and EARL-21G assessment covers a wide range of variables related to children, their family, neighborhood, responsiveness to treatment, and other social factors (for example, poverty, negative peer influence) that have been shown in the scientific literature to be positively related to subsequent antisocial behavior. As previously indicated, even though there is no shortage of dependable information on this subject (see, for example, Burke, Loeber, Mutchka, & Lahey, 2002; Loeber & Farrington, 2001; Loeber & Stouthamer-Loeber, 1998), little had been done until now by way of harnessing this information and making it available to clinicians in a practical and usable way (Hrynkiw-Augimeri, 2005).

Description of Measure

The EARL-20B and EARL-21G are validated gender-sensitive structured professional judgment (SPJ) risk assessment tools. The SPJ model emerged from the actuarial and clinical debate that seems to pull the best from both approaches (see Webster, Hucker, & Bloom, 2006) because it is "systematic, consistent, and grounded in research" (Borum & Verhaagen, 2006, p. 75).

The EARL framework, modeled after an SPJ violence risk assessment instrument for use with adults in civil, forensic, and correctional settings (HCR-20; see Chapter 8, this volume), outlines empirically recognized risk processes that relate to the development and maintenance of aggressive and antisocial behavior problems among children. The EARL-20B and EARL-21G were developed with a threefold purpose: (1) to provide a platform for increasing clinicians' and researchers' general understanding of early childhood risk factors; (2) to offer structure that helps clinicians systematically identify and manage risks in order to plan appropriate treatment to improve clinical outcomes; and (3) as a result, to improve the reliability and validity in predicting the likelihood of antisocial children engaging in future delinquent behavior (Augimeri et al., 2005). Thus, the EARLs aim to balance clinical utility (e.g., service planning, resource allocation) with prediction and have been noted in the literature as "decision-enhancing" tools (Enebrink, Långström, & Gumpert, 2006a).

The EARLs are divided into three main categories: Family, Child, and Responsivity factors. Family items assess the extent to which the child has or has not been effectively nurtured, supported, supervised, and encouraged by its parents or caregivers. Assessors also must gauge the level of support and amount of stress the family is encountering, and the extent to which its members may or may not endorse or participate in antisocial activities. Under the Child items, the focus is on individual risk factors associated with the child and the extent to which he or she performs his or her social role and acts responsibly and sensibly. Also included under this domain is the consideration about the quality of the child's neighborhood. The third (two-item) category, Responsivity, focuses on the ability and willingness of both the child and family to engage in treatment and to benefit from planned interventions. Table 3.1 lists the items included the EARL-20B, Version 2 and EARL-21G, Version 1.

Each of the 20 EARL-20B and 21 EARL-21G items are rated zero (0), one (1), or two (2). A rating of 0 indicates that the characteristic or circumstance is not evident. A rating of 2 indicates that the characteristic or circumstance is present, and a rating of 1 indicates that there is some, but not complete, evidence for the factor. The scores of the EARL-20B and EARL-21G items can be added into a total summary, ranging from 0 to 40 and 0 to 42, respectively. A "Critical Risk" checkbox is included beside each item. These boxes were intended to denote risk items of particularly high concern to the clinician when conducting the assessment and are based on the specifics of the case, not on the opinion that a particular risk factor is applicable in all or most cases. Flagging critical risk items is important for both treatment planning and clinical risk management, as described further under next section. An evaluation of the total sum, risk factor pattern, and case-specific factors, and conducting an overall estimate of "low," "moderate," or "high" risk of antisocial behavior completes the assessment.

Interpreting Risk

The clinical challenge, of course, is to be able to predict which boys or girls will persist in their antisocial patterns, describe how these patterns may establish over time, and plan as well as implement interventions that can break the vicious circles of antisocial behavior.

The higher the total score (that is, a higher number of risk factors), the more likely a child is at risk for engaging in future antisocial behavior. This relationship is based on the presumption that scores on risk factors are additive. Such a connection generally holds (Hall, 2001), and with

Table 3.1 Items in the Early Assessment Risk List for Boys and Girls

Family (F) Items	Child (C) Items	Responsivity (R) Items
Household Circumstances	Developmental Problems	Family Responsivity
Caregiver Continuity	Onset of Behavioral Difficulties	Child Responsivity
Supports	Abuse/Neglect/Trauma	
Stressors	Hyperactivity/Impulsivity/ Attention Deficits (HIA)	
Parenting Style	Likeability	
Antisocial Values and Conduct	Peer Socialization	
Caregiver–Daughter Interaction*	Academic Performance	
	Neighborhood	
	Authority Contact+	
	Antisocial Attitudes	
	Antisocial Behavior	
	Coping Ability	
	Sexual Development*	

Source: Koegl, C. J., Augimeri, L. K., Ferrante, P., Walsh, M., & Slater, N. (2008). A Canadian programme for child delinquents. In R. Loeber, N. W. Slot, P. van der Laan, & M. Hoeve, (Eds.), *Tomorrow's criminals: The development of child delinquency and effective interventions* (pp. 285–300). Aldershot: Ashgate. (Reprinted with permission.)

+ Item specific to the EARL-20B.

* Item specific to the EARL-21G.

data averaged across many cases, this is usually true. However, risk factors are probably both cumulative and interactive (Monahan et al., 2001). It is therefore probably as important to focus on each child's individual presentations of items across the risk summary as the total score. No single risk factor can sufficiently predict future antisocial behavior, but it is possible that a single risk factor may play a disproportionate role in contributing to a particular child's overall level of risk. For example, a child could achieve a relatively low total EARL-20B or EARL-21G score yet display one category of behaviors (for example, antisocial friends, abuse–neglect–trauma) so salient to the child that he or she is actually at great risk for embarking on an antisocial trajectory. It is for this reason, and to assist with matching intervention resources to level of need, a "Critical Risk" checkbox is included beside each item. In this way, the EARL-20B and EARL-21G afford the opportunity to adapt assessment and treatment to meet the requirements of a particular case, a feature viewed as essential to evidence-based clinical practice (American Psychological Association, 2006).

The tool can be completed by a single clinician (with or without the parent) or by a clinical team. The assessor must carefully evaluate each of the items based on the information obtained through a structured interview process, case conference or, for research purposes, a case file review. To inform a structured approach to clinical judgment (see Borum, 1996), evaluators are expected to obtain and assess information from multiple agents (e.g., teachers, parents, child care givers, doctors) and multiple sources (e.g., clinical records, school reports, standardized tests) (American Academy of Child and Adolescent Psychiatry, 1997). This process ensures that the evaluator has at hand the most up-to-date and accurate information before rendering a clinical risk judgment and before suggesting or offering particular interventions and treatments.

This tool was designed for clinicians and professionals experienced in and knowledgeable about working with children who have serious antisocial behavior problems. It is vital that assessor(s) score the items exactly as described in the coding sections of the manual. As noted by Webster and Hucker (2007), a key principle of conducting risk assessments is that "risk assessments should lead to risk management" (p. 130), and the developers of the EARLs intend the tool to be used only by individuals who understand that principle. In addition, it should not be used in a strictly mechanical way to determine the availability, nature, or intensity of treatment using the individual or total scores. Training is highly recommended to gain a better understanding of the tool's utility in regard to assessing risk and using the completed EARL Summary Sheet as a "prescription" to determine effective clinical risk management plans. For a demonstration of this, see the case example at the end of the chapter.

Gender-Sensitive Approach to Risk Assessment

It is becoming increasingly recognized that both boys and girls present with serious antisocial behaviors that require intervention (Moffit, Caspi, Rutter, & Silva, 2001), and the presentation of these behaviors as well as future outcomes may vary partly due to gender issues. Because it is important to consider that childhood risk factors may not be the same or may operate differently for boys and girls across developmental stages (Moffit et al., 2001), separate assessment tools for boys and girls were developed. The intention with this approach was both to capture possible gender-specific risk processes and enhance treatment planning and evaluation for boys and girls. Most of the EARL-21G item headings parallel the EARL-20B headings, although the content of items and coding guidelines differ in as much as the research literature revealed gender differences in the manifestation and influence of individual risk factors. Two distinct items (*Caregiver–Daughter Interaction* and *Sexual Development*) were added, and one item was removed (*Authority Contact* was subsumed under *Antisocial Behavior*) to yield a 21-item tool for girls (refer to Table 3.1).

Reliability: EARL-20B

In moving the EARL-20B from a Version 1 to a Version 2, it was necessary to evolve the tool within a research context so that basic psychometric properties such as reliability could be established. To do this, our first study of the EARL-20B, Version 1, tool measured the basic inter-rater reliability through a prospective study of 21 boys and their families admitted into the SNAP Under 12 Outreach Project (SNAP ORP). The SNAP ORP is housed at the Child Development Institute (formerly known as the Earlscourt Child and Family Centre at the time of the study), an accredited, family-focused treatment centre for children under the age of 12 years exhibiting serious antisocial behavior problems (i.e., having police contact for engaging in these behaviors/activities). Results showed moderate-to-good inter-rater agreement based on the total score on pretreatment assessment (.64) to posttreatment assessment (.88) (Hrynkiw-Augimeri, 1998). Qualitative findings further suggested that the tool was especially helpful in providing clinicians "with a thorough assessment procedure, a guide to gear the treatment interventions, and a barometer to evaluate whether a child was still considered high-risk at post intervention" (Hrynkiw-Augimeri, 1998, p. 31).

As part of a more stringent evaluation, we tested the reliability and predictive validity of the EARL-20B (see below) through a follow-up of a large sample of SNAP ORP–treated children (Hrynkiw-Augimeri, 2005). Files of 379 boys admitted to the SNAP ORP between 1985 and 1999 were retrospectively coded using Version 1 of the EARL-20B. Each of three raters was randomly assigned 193 files to code. Of these, 100 were common (all three raters rated these files), and 93 were unique to each of the three raters. Raters were blind as to which files were common and all outcome data. Analyses revealed excellent agreement between the three raters on the total EARL-20B score for the 100 common files (intraclass correlations coefficient, ICC_1 = .82) as well as the Family items subscale (ICC_1 = .78). In addition, there was good agreement on the EARL-20B Child items (ICC_1 = .73) subscale and lower though moderately acceptable agreement on the Responsivity items (ICC_1 = .53) subscale. An examination of the individual items in the right hand column of Table 3.2 indicated a range of agreement from excellent to poor.

Overall, results indicate acceptable inter-rater reliability for the EARL-20B assessments, especially for the total EARL-20B score with values comparable to other structured professional judgment tools such as the SAVRY (.81) (Catchpole & Gretton, 2003), START (.87) (Nicholls, Brink, Webster, Desmarais, & Martin, 2006), and HCR-20 (.78) (McNeil, Gregory, Lam, Binder, & Sullivan, 2003).

Research conducted by others on the EARL-20B, Version 2, has yielded similarly encouraging findings. Researchers tested the inter-rater reliability of Version 2 of the EARL-20B with children referred to nine child and adolescent psychiatric units across Sweden (Enebrink, Långström, Hultén, & Gumpert, 2006b). Kappa statistics indicated good agreement for most of the individual EARL-20B items (mean = .62, range = .30 to .87; only two items were poor, between .30 and .40), whereas intraclass correlation coefficients for Total, Child, and Family subscale scores indicated excellent agreement (.90 to .92). The overall estimate of high, medium, or low risk for antisocial behavior received an acceptable κ-value of 0.48.

Table 3.2 EARL-20B Item, Subscale, and Total Scores: Descriptive Statistics and Inter-Rater Reliability

EARL-20 B Items	Descriptive Statistics *M (SD)*	Inter-Rater Reliability *ICC_1 (95% CI)*
Family Items	6.12 (2.71)	0.78 (0.71–0.84)
F1 Household Circumstances	1.06 (0.82)	0.61 (0.50–0.70)
F2 Caregiver Continuity	0.73 (0.75)	0.47 (0.35–0.58)
F3 Supports	0.81 (0.79)	0.53 (0.42–0.64)
F4 Stressors	1.49 (0.63)	0.48 (0.36–0.59)
F5 Parenting Style	1.39 (0.62)	0.60 (0.50–0.69)
F6 Antisocial Values and Conduct	0.65 (0.71)	0.61 (0.51–0.70)
Child Items	12.99 (3.77)	0.74 (0.66–0.81)
C1 Developmental Problems	0.28 (0.52)	0.54 (0.44–0.65)
C2 Onset of Behavioral Difficulties	1.60 (0.51)	0.60 (0.49–0.69)
C3 Trauma	0.88 (0.88)	0.63 (0.53–0.72)
C4 Impulsivity	0.77 (0.66)	0.62 (0.52–0.71)
C5 Likeability	0.43 (0.57)	0.46 (0.35–0.58)
C6 Peer Socialization	1.31 (0.69)	0.43 (0.31–0.55)
C7 School Functioning	1.39 (0.65)	0.61 (0.50–0.70)
C8 Structured Community Activities	1.13 (0.83)	0.53 (0.42–0.64)
C9 Police Contact	1.39 (0.83)	0.71 (0.62–0.78)
C10 Antisocial Attitudes	1.08 (0.69)	0.51 (0.39–0.62)
C11 Antisocial Behavior	1.68 (0.49)	0.17 (0.05–0.30)
C12 Coping Ability	1.04 (0.73)	0.52 (0.41–0.63)
Amenability Items	1.85 (1.22)	0.53 (0.42–0.64)
A1 Family Responsivity	1.08 (0.78)	0.51 (0.39–0.62)
A2 Child Treatability	0.77 (0.70)	0.44 (0.32–0.56)
Total Score	20.28 (6.13)	0.82 (0.75–0.87)

Note: For descriptive statistics N = 379 boys; for reliability analyses n = 100.

Reliability: EARL-21G

To date, a number of studies have been completed on the EARL-21G—all of which have produced similar positive findings to the EARL-20B in terms of the clinical utility, reliability, and validity of the tool. The first of these studies (Levene, Walsh, Augimeri, & Pepler, 2004) was a retrospective examination of the reliability and validity of the EARL-21G. Like the previously mentioned retrospective study for boys in the SNAP ORP, a search of criminal records for girls who had participated in the gender-sensitive sister program, SNAP Girls Connection (SNAP GC), was performed in order to determine long-term involvement in crime. Intraclass correlation coefficients were calculated for total scores derived from three coders who assessed 30 common files. Encouragingly, modest agreement between raters was found, with statistically significant positive Pearson correlations of .64, .65, and .84, of the EARL total sum scores and intraclass correlation coefficients of .67 (single measure) and .86 (average measure).

We subsequently repeated the inter-rater reliability coding exercise prospectively, using seven clinicians who rated 12 common case files (see Levene et al., 2004). In this study, a higher rate of agreement was achieved, with an overall Pearson correlation of .81 of total sum scoring, and intraclass correlation coefficients of .80 (single measure) and .96 (average measure) were obtained. All correlations were significant at or beyond the 0.01 level.

Further, a team of researchers and clinicians generated preadmission EARL-21G profiles for a total of 162 girls who received the SNAP GC (Yuile, 2007). Trained coders read each girl's case file using an EARL-21G manual to assign the risk ratings for each girl. All files were assessed using a detailed research codebook developed to specify the criteria outlined in each of the EARL-21G risk items (Levene et al., 2001). Inter-rater reliability was calculated by randomly selecting 47 common cases for all coders to read and code. Mean agreement on classifying girls into no (0), low (1), and high (2) risk categories for each of the 21 risk factors ranged from .34 to .88 (kappa) (Cohen, 1960) with an averaged item-level agreement on the individual items of .55. Landis and Koch (1977) suggest that kappa values from .41 to .60 are moderate, and that values above .60 are substantial. Reliability scores for four risk factors were too low (i.e., .36 to .40); those items most difficult to assess through the case reviews were Supports, Peer Socialization, Academic Performance, and Antisocial Attitudes. Therefore, to improve reliability, all risk factors were collapsed into two binary groups from a 3-point scale to a 2-point scale. Collapsing each risk factor also helped to define two groups of girls that would be meaningful for interpretation and statistically suitable for comparison (Yuile, 2007). For the majority of risk factors (i.e., seven Family risks and seven Child risks) collapsing allowed a comparison between girls rated high-risk (score of 2), with moderate- and low-risk girls (scores of 0 or 1). By collapsing this way, high-risk versus moderate- and low-risk, it provided two groups of girls, each with a sufficient sample size to make a valid comparison, because the number of girls at low risk (0) was too small to be a meaningful group. In contrast, the remaining five Child risks did not receive as many high-risk ratings, and so the distribution of scores was not adequate for collapsing into a low-/moderate-risk group (0 and 1) and a high-risk group (2). Consequently, the scores were collapsed into 0 (no risk) versus 1 and 2 (moderate to high risk). The inter-rater agreement on scores using this dichotomous classification reached an acceptable range (kappa .40 to .89; mean of .67).

Validity: EARL-20B

Concurrent Validity. Also of interest was the relationship between the Child Behavior Checklist (CBCL) (Achenbach & Rescorla, 2001) delinquency subscale scores at discharge rated by parents and the EARL-20B total score at admission rated by clinicians. The aim was to determine whether EARL-20B total scores were predictive, or more accurately *post*dictive (see Kropp & Hart, 2000), of the CBCL discharge delinquency score. There was a positive correlation between the CBCL Delinquency subscale scores at discharge and the EARL-20B total score, $r = .34$, $p < .001$. Two regression models were fitted to examine the relationship between the CBCL Delinquency subscale score at discharge and the EARL-20B total score. Model 1 examined the overall association without controlling for the other candidate factors (i.e., CBCL delinquency admission score, age, and treatment effects). Model 2 examined the relationship controlling the CBCL delinquency score at admission, age, and treatment effects (number of ORP sessions attended). The results of the two models are shown in Table 3.3.

Results indicated that the EARL-20B total scores postdicted the CBCL Delinquency subscale at discharge. These findings held after controlling for the admission CBCL delinquency subscale score, age, and treatment effects. The relatively low value for R^2 (.12) for Model 1 suggests that these results, though significant, leave much of the variance (88%) of CBCL delinquency discharge scores unexplained. Controlling for admission CBCL delinquency subscale score, age, and treatment effects in Model 2 increased the variance explained to 41%. Results from Model 2 also indicated that the effect of the number of ORP group sessions attended on the CBCL delinquency discharge score approached significance ($p = .10$) after controlling for delinquency admission score and EARL-20B total score.

In a prospective multicenter project in Sweden, parents of 76 clinic-referred boys completed questionnaires about child behavior problems and participated in a semistructured interview, yielding information about *Diagnostic and Statistical Manual of Mental Health Disorders,* 4th ed. (DSM-IV) diagnosis and EARL-20B risk factors (Enebrink et al., 2006a). The associations of the EARL-20B total sum to concurrently, separately completed parent-rated scales of antisocial behavior reflecting child reactive and proactive aggressive behavior and impulsivity/conduct problems were positively related to the EARL-20B with moderate to high correlation coefficients (*rs* 0.46 to 0.68) (Enebrink et al., 2006b).

Predictive Validity. The first follow-up (8 years) of a sample of 379 boys who participated in the SNAP ORP included a search of correctional records to determine whether each boy had subsequent antisocial behavior and, as a result, any evidence of criminal charges. In Canada, children under 12 are not held liable for criminal offenses. Therefore, the criterion for participation was that the child had to have reached the age of 12 years by the time the review of criminal records began. This way, all participants would have reached the age of potential criminal liability and would be eligible for youth or adult court contact.

Hrynkiw-Augimeri (2005) investigated whether boys with higher EARL-20B total scores were more likely to be found guilty of committing an offense in the future than boys with lower EARL-20B total scores. The mean EARL-20B total scores of boys who were found guilty of an offense were significantly higher than for those boys who were not found guilty of an offense, 21.62 ($SD = 5.94$) and 20.32 ($SD = 6.23$), respectively (t (377) = 2.07, $p < .05$).

Table 3.3 Results From Regression of CBCL Delinquency Discharge Score

Model	B	SEB	β	*t* Value	sr^2	pr^2
		Model 1				
EARL-20B Total score	0.56	0.10	0.34	5.49***		
		Model 2				
EARL-20B Total score	0.24	0.09	0.15	2.65**	0.17	0.14
CBCL Delinquency admission score	0.65	0.06	0.57	10.32***	0.57	0.53
Number of ORP group sessions	−0.22	0.14	−0.09	−1.63	−0.11	−0.08
Age at follow-up	−0.18	0.17	−0.06	−1.05	−0.07	−0.05

Note: *$p < .05$; **$p < .01$; ***$p < .001$.

To illustrate this relationship further, logistic regression analyses were conducted on the probability of being found guilty of an offense as a function of EARL-20B total scores. Two models were fitted to examine the relationship between the EARL-20B score and the probability of being found guilty of a future offense. Model 1 examined the relationship without considering raters' confidence level in their EARL-20B scores. Model 2 included the interaction between raters' confidence level and EARL-20B scores. The results of these analyses are shown in Table 3.4.

Again, results indicated that, as EARL-20B scores increased, the probability of being found guilty of a future offense rose significantly. On average, the estimated odds of being guilty of future offenses increased by 1.03 for each unit increase in EARL-20B scores. Figure 3.1 shows how the association between EARL-20B total scores and being found guilty of a future criminal offense was moderated by the raters' confidence level (determined by the amount and quality of information contained in the clinical file).

Results of receiver operating characteristic (ROC) analyses supported this finding, with higher total scores postdicting findings of guilt at levels greater than expected by chance, AUC = .56, *95% CI* = .51–.62, SE_{AUC} = .03, $p < .05$. We then considered the severity of outcomes for those 164 boys found guilty of an offense at follow-up. As expected, as EARL-20B total scores increased in magnitude, boys were more likely to be found guilty of committing more offenses, $r = .16$, $p < .05$, and the number of times the youth came before the courts to receive a disposition, $r = .18$, $p < .05$. These relationships held after controlling for length of follow-up. Using a median split on EARL-20B total scores to group boys into low (EARL-20B total scores = 0 to 21) and high (EARL-20B scores = 22 to 40) risk categories, a Chi-square analysis revealed that significantly more boys in the high-risk group were found guilty of an offense (49%) than boys in the low-risk group (38%), χ^2 (1) = 4.87, $p < .05$. Of the 164 boys who were found guilty of an offense, 88 were identified at high risk (having high EARL-20B scores, true positives), and 76 were not identified as being at risk (false negatives). This resulted in sensitivity (boys with future offense at follow-up and identified at risk by EARL-20B) of 54%. Of the 215 boys with no future offense, 123 were identified as being at low risk (true negatives), resulting in a specificity of 57%. Of the 180 boys identified at risk by high EARL-20B scores, 92 had no offense at follow-up (false positives), resulting in a *positive predictive value* (boys classified at high-risk with future offenses at follow-up) of 49%. Of the 199 children at low-risk by EARL-20B tool, 123 had no offense, resulting in a *negative predictive value* (boys classified at low-risk with no offenses at follow-up)

Table 3.4 Results From Logistic Regression Model of Being Found Guilty of an Offense

Model	B	SE	Wald	Odds Ratio	95% CI Lower	95% CI Upper
		Model 1				
EARL-20B Total score	0.03	0.02	3.86*	1.03	1.00	1.08
		Model 2				
EARL-20B Total score	0.03	0.04	0.65	0.97	0.89	1.05
Confidence level						
Medium vs. Low	–2.21	0.98	5.05*	0.11	–1.81	2.41
High vs. Low	–2.77	1.20	4.38*	0.06	–2.28	2.41
Confidence level × EARL-20B score						
Medium vs. Low	0.09	0.05	3.13	1.09	0.99	1.19
High vs. Low	0.11	0.05	3.99*	1.11	1.00	1.22

Note: *$p < .05$; **$p < .01$; ***$p < .001$.

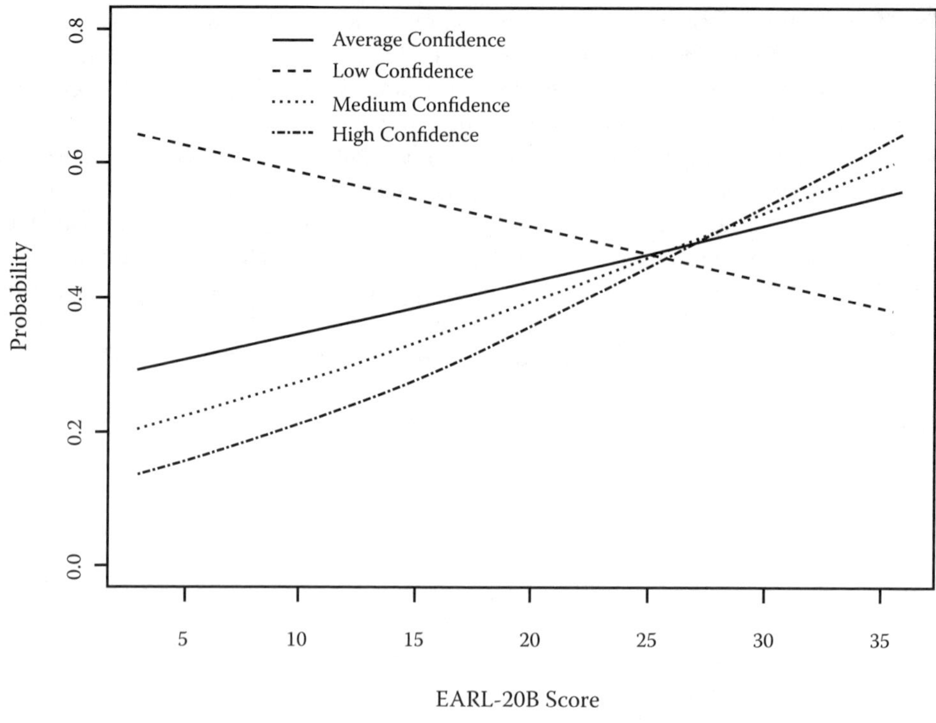

Figure 3.1 Predicted probability of future offense by EARL-20B score as a function of rater confidence.

of 62%. The above results demonstrate that the higher the total EARL-20B score, the more likely the boy would be found guilty of committing an offense.

An association between the EARL-20B and future offense is evident: the relationship became stronger as the raters became more confident in their assessments (that is, had better information available in the file). Table 3.4 demonstrates that, when raters had little or no confidence in their ratings, there was no significant association between the EARL-20B score and future offense. Given this finding, users of the EARLs should be cautious in regard to its clinical application; if a rater is not "confident" in the information being used to score the device (for example, lack of or discrepancy in the information) it is highly recommended that the rater not score the item in question until further information is available.

The predictive validity of the EARL-20B was also assessed prospectively by researchers, (Enebrink et al., 2006a) using a sample of 76 clinic-referred children. An examination of the EARL-20B total summary score and short-term risk (evaluated as low, medium, or high risk) showed moderately good predictive validity to parent/teacher ratings of reactive and proactive aggression and disruptive behaviors at the 6-month (Total score *r*s: .31–.53; short-term risk *r*s: .47–.58) and 30-month (Total score *r*s: .20–.38; short-term risk *r*s: .31–.50) follow-ups. EARL-20B-based estimates were also significantly related to a conduct disorder (CD) diagnosis at 30-month outcome (Odds Ratio total sum 1.33, 95% *CI* [1.11–1.59], short-term risk 6.67 [1.49–29.91], long-term risk 15.75 [2.18–113.56]). Furthermore, at baseline, clinicians at each clinic had been asked to fill in separate evaluations of the boys' risk. In general, these unstructured clinical evaluations were not as consistently associated with outcome.

To evaluate possible *incremental* validity of the EARL-20B over unstructured clinician evaluations and baseline CD, separate hierarchical linear regression analyses were performed.

EARL-20B-based predictors, particularly the EARL-20B short-term summary risk judgment, significantly increased the explained variance for aggression and conduct problems at the 30-month follow-up, compared to unstructured clinician evaluations and baseline CD, respectively (short-term summary risk rating added to clinician evaluations: ΔR^2: .06–.18; short-term summary risk rating added to baseline CD: ΔR^2 = .07–.17). The results of this longitudinal study suggest promising clinical utility of the risk judgment tool. As with research on other SPJ tools (SAVRY, see Chapter 4; SARA, Chapter 11; SVR-20/RSVP, Chapter 13; HCR-20, Chapter 8), it demonstrates that the summary risk ratings of low, moderate, and high risk that are intended to be used in clinical practice possess strong validity vis-à-vis outcomes.

Predictive Validity of Subscales

The 20 items in the EARL-20B were clustered into subscales using exploratory and confirmatory factorial analyses to test for construct and content validity, and to determine if the factors would fall or cluster under larger or different subscales than the already defined Family, Child, and Responsivity domains. We first conducted exploratory factor analysis (EFA) to extract latent factor structures that underlie the 20 items in the EARL-20B device and examine how these items cluster into common factors. Confirmatory factor analysis (CFA) was then used to clarify the factor structure that emerged from the EFA. Both EFA and CFA identified a three-factor structure for the EARL-20B. Three subscales of the EARL-20B were generated by summing their respective items. It has been proved the three subscales are good predictors of an antisocial or violent outcome (Hrynkiw-Augimeri, 2005).

As valid and reliable indices of risk, and based on their ability to predict antisocial conduct in the form of official youth and adult criminal convictions (Hrynkiw-Augimeri, 2005), these subscales were used as predictor variables. Figure 3.2 depicts the three-subscale structure of the EARL-20B, and the interrelationships between individual items (for complete details see Hrynkiw-Augimeri, 2005).

The overall plan of this evaluation was to estimate the effects of the SNAP ORP and examine factors associated with treatment effectiveness (risk profile of the child and treatment intensity). Treatment intensity was established by separating those who received one or more individual befriending sessions (labeled as *enhanced treatment*) from those who received no individual befriending sessions (labeled as *standard treatment*). We employed the growth mixture model approach to statistically classify boys to delinquency classes according to repeated measure CBCL delinquency scores collected over three time periods (pre- and posttreatment, and 6 months postdischarge). Growth mixture modeling uses both random effects and trajectory classes to represent individual difference in development, resulting in a very flexible repeated measure analysis (Muthen & Muthen, 2000). The growth mixture modeling uses all available information for analysis, even those with missing data at both post and follow-up assessment. A three-class model was used to include the three subscales (child, family, and biological) derived from the EFA/CFA analyses of the EARL-20B, as predictors of delinquency class membership and the predictor (*Standard* or *Enhanced* SNAP ORP) of delinquency change rate within each class using CBCL scores collected over three time periods (pre- and posttreatment, and 6 months postdischarge). Treatment intensity was used to explain variation in treatment effects within each delinquency class.

Of the 379 boys who received the SNAP ORP program (Standard or Enhanced), preprogram CBCL delinquency information was available for 319 cases, 193 cases had both pre- and post-CBCL scores, and there were 38 cases for which delinquency information was available for all three assessment points. To test the possibility that the small number of follow-up cases were biased in terms of problem severity and/or level of risk, we compared these boys with those who did not have a follow-up assessment and found that they were not different in terms of their

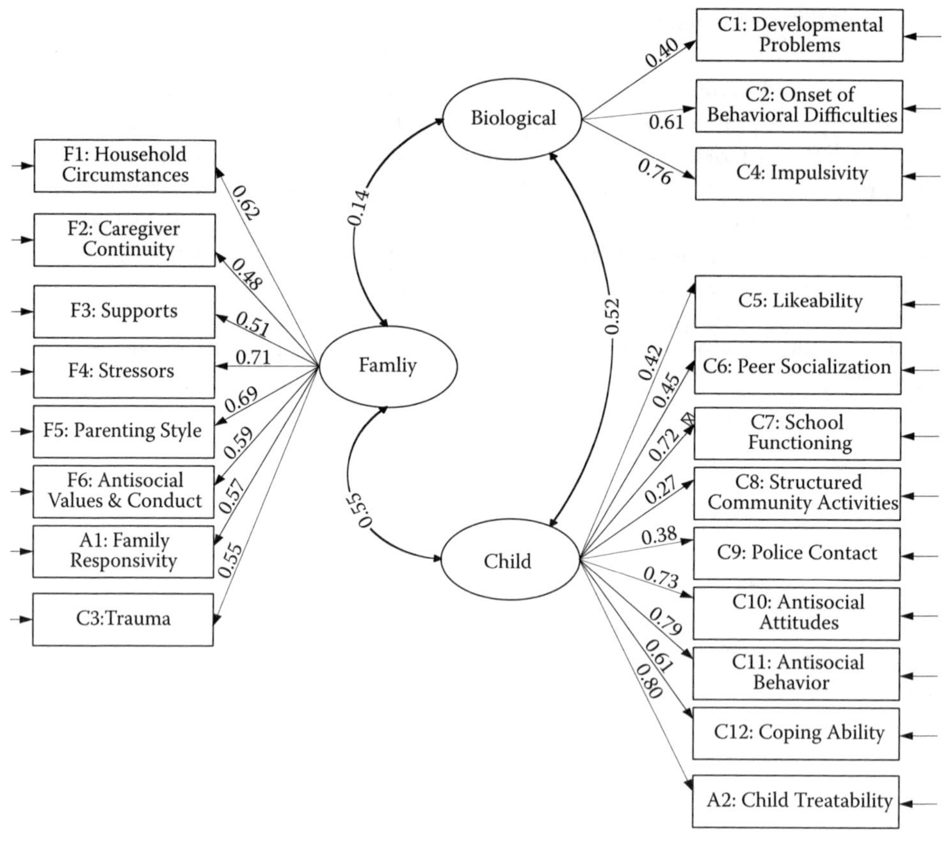

Figure 3.2 EARL-20B, version 1 subscales and intercorrelations.

pre-CBCL delinquency (means: 73.7 vs. 72.6, respectively; p = .45), and total EARL-20B scores (means: 21.6 vs. 20.9, respectively; p = .48). Table 3.5 displays the estimated results from the extended growth mixture model.

Results indicate that as the risk factor scores increase (child, family, and biological subscales of the EARL-20B), the probabilities of being in the high- and medium-delinquency classes increase, which provides support for the concurrent validity of the EARL-20B. In particular, the child and biological subscales had significant predictive effects on delinquency class membership, while the effect of the family subscale on class membership did not. SNAP ORP does not make significant difference in the treatment effect for the low-delinquency class boys (see full description of analysis and results, Augimeri, Jiang, Koegl, & Carey, 2006).

In terms of risk as assessed by the EARL-20B, results indicate that the tool, and in particular, the child and biological subscales, significantly distinguished between delinquency class (high vs. low, and medium vs. low). These factor-derived scales are not meant to substitute the Family, Child, and Responsivity domains within the EARL-20B manual, but are meant to further enhance clinical risk management decisions about the type and amount of services that are offered to children with conduct problems. Based on the pattern of results from the analysis, we know that children who score higher on the child and biological subscales of the EARL-20B are more likely to engage in delinquent behavior (that is, be a member of the high-delinquency class). If their measured level of CBCL delinquency places them in the high-risk class, it would

Table 3.5 Enhanced SNAP ORP Treatment Effects by Delinquency Class

Delinquency Class	Estimate (SE)+		SIG
High ($N = 37$)			
Initial level	82.6	(1.34)	***
Change following SNAP ORP	2.64	(1.99)	
Change regressed on enhanced SNAP ORP	−8.01	(2.34)	***
Moderate ($N = 219$)			
Initial level	74.5	(0.64)	***
Change following SNAP ORP	−3.96	(0.76)	***
Change regressed on enhanced SNAP ORP	−1.98	(1.00)	*
Low ($N = 63$)			
Initial level	60.9	(1.89)	***
Change following SNAP ORP	−2.24	(1.93)	
Change regressed on enhanced SNAP ORP	−1.76	(1.76)	
C Regressed on (High- vs. Low-Delinquency)			
Child subscale	0.60	(0.15)	***
Family subscale	0.17	(0.11)	
Biological subscale	0.89	(0.31)	**
C Regressed on (Medium- vs. Low-Delinquency)			
Child subscale	0.21	(0.07)	**
Family subscale	0.07	(0.07)	
Biological subscale	0.55	(0.22)	*

Note: Significance (SIG): ***$p < 0.001$; **$p < 0.01$; *$p< 0.05$.
+Estimates are estimated regression coefficients from growth mixture modeling.

be important, if not necessary, to offer these boys enhanced services such as individual befriending, school advocacy, academic tutoring, and individual family counseling.

Validity: EARL-21G

Predictive Validity. An investigation has been completed on the efficacy of the EARL-21G in predicting girls' convictions (Levene et al., 2001). Total scores derived for 67 SNAP GC case files were used to divide the sample at the median to compare the prevalence of offending between the bottom (mean = 12.7, range = 5 to 17) and top (mean = 22.3, range = 18 to 30) ends of the distribution. Official conviction data showed that, overall, only 18 out of 67 (27%) of the girls were found guilty of committing an offense at follow-up, and although higher EARL-21G scores were related to more offending (34% vs. 20%) the difference between the two groups failed to reach statistical significance.

To investigate the relationship between individual and overall risk scores, behavior problems, and responsiveness to treatment (Yuile, 2007), a team of researchers and clinicians generated preadmission EARL-21G profiles for 85 girls who received the SNAP GC (see Yuile, 2007, for detailed description of analysis and results). Trained coders read each girl's case file using an EARL-21G manual to assign the 21 Child, Family, and Responsivity risk ratings for each girl. All files were assessed using a detailed research codebook that enabled the raters to gather and record detailed information about the nature of each risk scored as present (low or high risk) for each girl (Levene et al., 2001). Behavior symptoms were assessed by teachers (74 of the 87 girls had at least one teacher assessment) and parents (85 had at least one parent assessment)

(Achenbach & Rescorla, 2001) at admission, posttreatment, and at 6-, 12-, and 18-month follow-up intervals. A mixed-model design (specifically a growth curve procedure) captured variation across individuals in initial levels of behavior and rates of change as accounted for by different levels of EARL-21G scores. This approach offers the benefit of examining girls' individual trajectories of behavioral change at each level of the risk factor (low and high risk), as opposed to relying on the mean of girls' scores.

For parent report, total risk scores were associated with changes in antisocial behaviors (conduct disorder and externalizing problems). The higher the total risk score, the smaller the treatment effects immediately following the intervention. No significant long-term treatment effects associated with level of risk were found. For teacher report, total risk was also associated with long-term change in rule-breaking behaviors. The higher the total risk score, the greater the SNAP GC treatment effects over time to 18 months follow-up.

Concurrent Validity. There were strong associations between girls' total risk scores and initial severity of behavior problems across parent- and teacher-reported behavior scales. The higher the total risk score, the higher the level of behavior problems. Table 3.6 displays the estimated results from the extended growth mixture model.

Limitations and Necessary Future Research

For the purposes of this chapter we want to identify two key limitations. Obviously this is not an exhaustive list, but our attempt to highlight what we see as important areas to consider: (1) Users need to understand the EARLs were originally developed for use with children engaging in antisocial behavior, under the age of 12, referred to a children's mental health center in a large multicultural city. The authors of the EARLs attempted to bring awareness to possible differences in cultural values, attitudes, and gender norms in the overview and coding sections of the manuals, (e.g., in relation to girls pubertal development, emerging sexuality, treatment responsivity, parenting style, and caregiver continuity). However, users should always demonstrate an awareness and knowledge of the cultural context influencing how information is gathered and understood during an EARL assessment. At this time, the EARLs have been translated into Swedish, Norwegian, Finnish, Dutch, and French (in process) and have been adapted for use in both urban and rural settings across Europe, Canada, the United States, and New Zealand. (2) At present, the EARL-20B and EARL-21G assessment framework focuses on a risk deficit and does not currently capture the presence of protective factors for boys and girls (see Stouthamer-Loeber, Loeber, Wei, Farrington, & Wikström, 2002). Stouthamer-Loeber and colleagues (2002) state that protective factors have been thought of as the "processes that interact with risk factors in reducing the probability of a negative outcome" (p. 112). A risk assessment tool may be more beneficial in its predictive utility when both risk and protective factors are identified and taken into account, given that other research has found that long-term antisocial outcomes are best predicted by using a combination of both risk and protective factors (Loeber, Pardini, Stouthamer, & Raine, 2007). It is also imperative that we, as authors, ensure that the EARLs undergo continual review and improvement, in light of new research findings, in order to keep them current and able to address relevant clinical issues, as well as ongoing evaluation of how the EARLs improve treatment planning and implementation.

Conclusion

The early prediction of juvenile delinquency represents an important challenge in the field. The challenge is the consideration of whether it is feasible or realistic to presume that delinquent behavior can be predicted accurately, especially in very young children. Researchers and clinicians have to deal with extremely short histories (maximum 11 years) and long follow-up periods

Table 3.6 Mixed-Model Results for Total Risk Score and SNAP GC Intervention Effects

		Initial Effect on Total Risk		Immediate Effect on Total Risk	Long-Term Effect on Total Risk
Aggression	Parent	0.60	***	0.19	−0.09
	Teacher	0.80	***	−0.03	−0.28
Conduct disorder	Parent	0.48	***	0.24 *	0.03
	Teacher	0.80	***	0.00	−0.35
Rule breaking	Parent	0.44	***	0.17	−0.01
	Teacher	0.68	***	0.08	−0.35 *
Externalizing problem	Parent	0.50	***	0.26 *	−0.10
	Teacher	0.79	***	−0.03	−0.23
Oppositional defiant disorder	Parent	0.35	**	0.15	−0.28
	Teacher	0.53	**	0.15	−0.28

Note: Predicting change in parent and teacher reports of girls' behaviors at admission, immediate postintervention, and long-term at 6, 12, and 18 months follow-up. EARL scores were centered by ground means. For every 1-point increase in EARL-21G total risk score, the behavior score changes by the amount indicated.

$^*p < 0.05$. $^{**}p < 0.01$. $^{***}p < 0.001$.

(until these children are considered youths or adults). From the point children are assessed to the time they become adolescents or adults, a multitude of factors can affect their life course. Therefore, the overarching goal of the EARL is not *only* to assess risk but to play a pivotal role in helping clinicians determine effective clinical risk management plans that may actually buffer risk and prevent these high-risk children from eventually entering the juvenile and/or adult justice systems. In light of our current findings (see Augimeri et al., 2006a), it may be imperative that long-term risk management plans are implemented for a percentage of high-risk children to ensure continued support and positive life outcomes. Age-appropriate tools such as the SAVRY (Borum et al., 2002) for adolescence and HCR-20 (Webster et al., 1997) for adults should be utilized when appropriate. Balancing clinical utility with prediction, the EARL-20B and EARL-21G join other devices designed to help professionals make practical day-to-day decisions about prioritizing treatment and understanding children on a case-by-case basis.

Case Example

(The following case example is provided to illustrate how the EARL-20B Summary Sheet is used and rated in order to ascertain an effective clinical risk management plan.)

Robbie is a six-year-old feisty, sad boy who physically looks like a "stout little man." He met all his developmental milestones on time (e.g., walked, talked, and was toilet trained) and is currently in a regular grade one class. Every day he is withdrawn from the classroom, so that he can receive remedial help for reading and math. He has been placed on waiting list for an Identification Placement Review Committee meeting. This process will determine if he will be placed in a specialized learning program and/or has psychosocial deficits. In addition, the teacher is extremely concerned about his explosive behavior and lack of attention. He is constantly getting into fights with peers and has had numerous altercations involving teachers and administrative staff—including the principal. When he gets angry he threatens others, is verbally abusive, and has major temper tantrums (dad reports that this kind of behavior began when he was just three or four years old). This has resulted in a number of in- and out-of-school suspensions. On a number of occasions he has described himself as being "out of control" and feeling very sad to the point of wanting to hurt himself when he is angry and upset. Given his difficult temperament, he is ostracized, bullied (as well as bullies), and isolated from other children. They find it hard to like him and he also indicates that "no one likes me." Adults also report that Robbie is an anxious, defiant boy who is difficult to engage, which makes it "hard to like him." He displays self-defeating thinking and has a misplaced sense of entitlement; however, he does know right from wrong and can be empathic.

Robbie has lived with his dad most of his life in a modest home in a neighborhood described as being "tough." This has been his home since he was a toddler. He lived with his biological mom for a short period of time when he was just over a year, when his parents separated. This arrangement fell apart, and Robbie was returned to his dad. He has little contact with his mother, given the strained relationship between his dad and mom. She has since remarried and has had four other children. Robbie talks about his mother fondly, but also indicates he resents her for leaving him behind. Dad reports that Robbie sometimes cries himself to sleep when he thinks about her. Dad is in his twenties and has indicated that he has "tried his best" with his son. He is able to acknowledge that Robbie has had to "grow up fast and raise himself" on many occasions, given he is always at work because finances are tight and has some issues of his own that he needs help with (e.g., he indicates he is a "social alcoholic" who also has relied on pain medication to deal with his health problems). Robbie's dad was also able to report that he has used punitive discipline (e.g., severe spanking) and on other occasions is very "easygoing" with his parenting as he lets Robbie do what he wants. He also indicated that he has neglected him on occasion, when he left him unattended when he went out or was "drunk." Dad acknowledges this behavior is not appropriate and has decided he needs to get help for himself and his son. This became evident for him when the police brought Robbie home after he was caught shoplifting at the local grocery store. The Children's Aid Society (child welfare) was also called when the police brought Robbie home late at night and no one was home. They referred the family to a local children's mental health center (Child Development Institute) for services. Dad was very responsive to this and indicated it was like a "call for help," because he felt his life was getting "out of control" and felt pretty isolated (even though he had a stable girlfriend who helped at times). He needed help to get things back on track in order to help his son and himself. Although Dad sees this as a big support, Robbie on the other hand is a bit more guarded about getting help.

SUMMARY DISCUSSION

The attached EARL-20B Summary Sheet is used to summarize all relevant information obtained from the various sources and informants in order to render a risk summary. EARL research has revealed that the more confident raters are in the information they have, the better the risk prediction (Hrynkiw-Augimeri, 2005). Although, there are no cutoff scores, Robbie's *Total Score* (27/40) may be considered high, given that the normal distribution of scores ranged from 3 to 36 with a mean of 20.9 and a median of 21 (SD = 6.1, n = 378) (Augimeri et al., 2001). In addition, to the total score, Robbie received a number of "2" ratings, especially under the *Child Items*. Although, it is important to pay attention to the Total Score, because the higher the score the greater the chance of future antisocial or violent behavior, assessors are also advised to focus their attention on the individual risk patterns and/or "clusters" of risk items. Evidence shows this may play a vital role in determining clinical risk management strategies and service duration (Augimeri et al., 2006a; Hrynkiw-Augimeri, 2005). The assessor also needs to determine which items (if any) are marked *Critical Risk*. This is used to red flag any items of particular concern and help the clinician to determine which clinical risk management strategies need to be dealt with immediately in order to diminish the levels of risk. In Robbie's case, a number of items were flagged as *Critical Risk*, and in the *Notes* section of the EARL-20B Summary Sheet, several clinical risk management strategies are focusing on these items. Once all the individual items, *Total Score*, and *Clinical Risk* ratings have been completed, the assessor than "takes a step back" from the rating scheme and determines an *Overall Clinical Judgment* rating. This allows assessors the discretion and clinical freedom to designate children as high, moderate, or low risk, regardless of the EARL-20B total score. In most cases, the *Total Score* and the *Overall Clinical Judgment* rating will correspond (if not, an assessor should specify the reasons for this discrepancy in the Notes section). In Robbie's case, a "High" risk rating was rendered.

The EARL-20B Version 2 Summary Sheet

(To be used in association with the EARL-20B, Version 2 Manual)

Child's Name or ID#: Robbie James (First name SURNAME) Date: 200801-10 (YYYY-MM-DD)

Assessor: L.A. Child's DOB: 200201-05 (YYYY-MM-DD) Age: 6

	Family Items	Rating (0-1-2)	Critical Risk
F1	**Household Circumstances** finances tight, modest	1	
F2	**Caregiver Continuity** dad (primary) - lived with bio-mom for a short period when he was 1 yr old	1	√
F3	**Supports** Child Development Institute, isolated (no extended family), Dad's partner	1	√
F4	**Stressors** dad's health problems, strained relationship w/ ex-wife, raising son on his own, dad feels "out of control"	2	
F5	**Parenting Style** punitive, lax, inconsistent, lacks nurturance, parents self	2	√
F6	**Antisocial Values and Conduct** dad (drinking & prescription drugs - pain medication)	1	√
	Child Items	**Rating (0-1-2)**	**Critical Risk**
C1	**Developmental Problems** met all developmental milestones on time	0	
C2	**Onset of Behavioral Difficulties** age 3 (serious temper tantrums)	2	
C3	**Abuse/Neglect/Trauma** neglect, abuse (severe spanking), abandonment issues	2	√
C4	**HIA (Hyperactivity/Impulsivity/Attention Deficits)** diagnosis attention problems, NO	1	√
C5	**Likeability** difficulty w/ adults, hard to engage, difficult temperament, feels "no one likes me"	2	√
C6	**Peer Socialization** ostracized, isolated, bullied, excluded	2	√
C7	**Academic Performance** grade 1, receiving w/drawl, struggling with math and reading	1	
C8	**Neighbourhood** lived in same neighborhood most of his life, tough	1	
C9	**Authority Contact** principals, teachers, police	2	
C10	**Antisocial Attitudes** self-defeating thinking, defiant, misplaced sense of entitlement, empathetic, knows right from wrong	1	
C11	**Antisocial Behaviour** problems - multiple settings, school suspensions, assault, threatens, swearing, stealing, bullies	2	
C12	**Coping Ability** depressive symptomotoly, feels out of control, anxious, self harm	2	√
	Responsivity Items	**Rating (0-1-2)**	**Critical Risk**
R1	**Family Responsivity** dad willing to get help, active, seems committed	0	√
R2	**Child Responsivity** interested but guarded	1	

Overall Clinical Judgment	LOW	MOD	HIGH
			√

TOTAL SCORE 27

Notes (Clinical Risk Management Plan): Robbie has experienced a lot of negative life circumstances. He is extremely angry and as a result is explosive at times and has major abandonment issues. Based on the EARL risk summary and the noted critical risk factors the following treatment recommendations are suggested: (1) Robbie attend the SNAP® Boys Groups – learn self control and problem solving strategies to help control his anger and deal more effectively with his problems; (2) dad attend the SNAP® Parent Group – learn effective parent management strategies; (3) connect Robbie to a structured community activity where he will have access to positive mentors and activities with children his age; (4) Robbie receive individual befriending with the SNAP® Group Leader to work on his individual goals, his academics and behavioral issues; (5) further assessment to investigate - depression, anxiety and attention issues; (6) connect dad to community supports to help him deal with alcohol, drug issues and (7) ensure dad and Robbie continue to be engaged in services.

The EARL-20B Summary Sheet provides an overall picture of "risk" and is used as a "prescription" to point to areas in need of good clinical risk management plan. As noted by Hart (2001), a "good" risk assessment procedure should: (1) yield consistent or replicable results; (2) be prescriptive; and (3) be transparent. The research presented above has demonstrated the reliability and validity of the tool. The EARL-20B Summary Sheet demonstrates how the device can be both "transparent" (in that the keywords listed beside each EARL item allow any person to see why the particular score was given) and "prescriptive" (in that *Critical Risk, Overall Clinical Judgment,* and *Total Score* help the assessor determine what level of clinical risk management is needed). It is the responsibility of assessors to use the EARL in the manner they were intended, so as to yield the best possible risk assessment.

References

Achenbach, T. M., & Rescorla, L. A. (2001). *Manual for the ASEBA school age forms and profile.* Burlington, VT: University of Vermont, Research Center for Children, Youth and Families.

American Academy of Child and Adolescent Psychiatry. (1997). Practice parameters for the assessment and treatment of children and youth with conduct disorder. *Journal of American Academy of Child and Adolescent Psychiatry, 36,* 122S–139S.

American Psychological Association Presidential Task Force on *Evidence-Based Practice.* (2006). Evidence-based practice in psychology. *American Psychologist,* 61, 271–285.

Augimeri, L. K., Jiang, D., Koegl, C. J., & Carey, J. (2006a). *Differential effects of the Under 12 Outreach Project (ORP) associated with client risk & treatment intensity.* Program Evaluation Report Submitted to the Centre of Excellence for Child and Youth Mental Health at CHEO.

Augimeri, L. K., Koegl, C. J., Ferrante, P., & Slater, N. (Fall 2006b). Why and how: Conducting effective clinical risk assessments with children with conduct problems. *Canada's Children, 12* (2), 24–27 (English); 28–32 (French).

Augimeri, L. K., Koegl, C. J., Levene, K. S., & Webster, C. D. (2005). Early Assessment Risk List for Boys and Girls (pp. 295–310). In T. Grisso, G. Vincent, & D. Seagrave (Eds.), *Mental health screening and assessment in juvenile justice.* New York: Guilford Press.

Augimeri, L. K., Koegl, C. J., Webster, C. D., & Levene, K. S. (2001). *Early Assessment Risk List for Boys: EARL-20B, Version 2.* Toronto, ON, Canada: Earlscourt Child and Family Centre.

Augimeri, L. K., Webster, C. D., Koegl, C. J, & Levene, K. S. (1998). *Early Assessment Risk List for Boys: EARL-20B, Version 1, Consultation edition.* Toronto, ON, Canada: Earlscourt Child and Family Centre.

Bloom, H., Webster, C., Hucker, S., & De Freitas, K. (2007). The Canadian contribution to violence risk assessment: History and implementations for current psychiatric practice. In H. Bloom & C. Webster (Eds.), *Essential writings in violence risk assessment and management* (pp. 77–92). Toronto, ON, Canada: Centre for Addiction and Mental Health.

Borum, R. (1996). Improving the clinical practice of violence risk assessment: Technology, guidelines and training. *American Psychologist, 51,* 945–956.

Borum, R., Bartel, P., & Forth, A. (2002). *Manual for the Structured Assessment of Violence Risk in Youth (SAVRY), Version 1 Consultation edition.* Florida: University of South Florida.

Borum, R., & Verhaagen, D. (2006). *Assessing and managing violence risk in juveniles.* New York: Guilford Press.

Brestan, E. V., & Eyberg, S. M. (1998). Effective psychosocial treatments of conduct-disordered children and adolescents: 29 years, 82 studies, and 5,272 kids. *Journal of Clinical Child Psychology, 27,* 180–189.

Burke, J. D., Loeber, R., Mutchka, J. S., & Lahey, B. B. (2002). A question for DSM-V: Which better predicts persistent conduct disorder—delinquent acts or conduct symptoms? *Criminal Behavior and Mental Health, 12,* 37–52.

Catchpole, R. E. H., & Gretton, H. M. (2003). The predictive validity of risk assessment with violent young offenders: A one-year examination of criminal outcome. *Criminal Justice and Behavior, 30,* 688–708.

Cohen, J. (1960). A coefficient of agreement for nominal scales. *Educational and Psychological Measurement, 20,* 37–46.

Day, D. M. (1998). Risk for court contact and predictors of an early age for a first court contact among a sample of high risk youths: A survival analysis approach. *Canadian Journal of Criminology, 40,* 421–443.

Day, D. M., & Hunt, A. C. (1996). A multivariate assessment of a risk model for juvenile delinquency with an under 12 offender sample. *Journal of Emotional and Behavioural Disorders, 4,* 66–72.

Enebrink, P., Långström, N., & Gumpert, C. H. (2006a). Predicting aggressive and disruptive behavior in referred 6- to 12-year-old boys: Prospective validation of the EARL-20B Risk/Needs Checklist. *Assessment, 13,* 356–367.

Enebrink, P., Långström, N., Hultén, A., & Gumpert, C. H. (2006b). Swedish validation of the Early Assessment Risk List for Boys (EARL-20B), a decision-aid for use with children presenting with conduct-disordered behavior. *Nordic Journal of Psychiatry, 60,* 468–446.

Farrington, D. P. & Welsh, B. C. (2007). *Saving children from a life of crime.* New York: Oxford University Press.

Frick, P. J. (1998). *Conduct disorders and severe antisocial behavior.* New York: Plenum.

Hart, S. D. (2001). Assessing and managing violence risk. In K. S. Douglas, C. D. Webster, S. H. Hart, D. Eaves and J. R. P. Ogloff (Eds.), *HCR-20 violence risk management companion guide* (pp. 13–26). Burnaby, British Columbia: Mental Health Law, and Policy Institute, Simon Fraser University.

Hall, H. V. (2001). Violence prediction and risk analysis: Empirical advances and guides. *Journal of Threat Assessment, 1,* 1–39.

Hoge, R. D., & Andrews, D. A. (1996). *Assessing the youthful offender: Issues and techniques.* New York: Plenum.

Howell, J. C. (2003). *Preventing & reducing juvenile delinquency: A comprehensive framework.* Thousand Oaks, CA: Sage.

Hrynkiw-Augimeri, L. K. (1998). *Assessing risk for violence in boys: A preliminary risk assessment study using the Early Assessment Risk List for Boys (EARL-20B).* Unpublished master's thesis, Ontario Institute for Studies in Education, University of Toronto, Ontario, Canada.

Hrynkiw-Augimeri, L. K. (2005). *Aggressive and antisocial young children: Risk prediction, assessment and management utilizing the Early Assessment Risk List for Boys (EARL-20B).* Unpublished doctorial dissertation, Ontario Institute for Studies in Education, University of Toronto, Ontario, Canada.

Kropp, P. R., & Hart, S. D. (2000). The spousal assault risk assessment (SARA) Guide: Reliability and validity in adult male offenders. *Law and Human Behavior, 24,* 101–118.

Lahey, B. B., Moffit, T. E., & Caspi, A. (2003). *Causes of conduct disorder and juvenile delinquency.* New York: Guilford Press.

Landis, R., & Koch, G. G. (March, 1977). The measurement of observer agreement for categorical data. *Biometrics, 33 (1),* 159–174.

Levene, K. S., Augimeri, L. K., Pepler, D., Walsh, M., Webster, C. D., & Koegl, C. J. (2001). *Early Assessment Risk List for Girls: EARL-21, Version 1, Consultation edition.* Toronto: Earlscourt Child and Family Centre.

Levene, K. S., Walsh, M. M., Augimeri, L. K., & Pepler, D. J. (2004). Linking identification and treatment of early risk factors for female delinquency. In M. M. Moretti, C. L. Odgers, & M. A. Jackson (Eds.), *Girls and aggression: Contributing factors and intervention principles* (pp. 147–163). New York: Kluwer Academic.

Lipman, E. L., Bennett, K. J., Racine, Y. A., Mazumdar, R., & Offord, D. R. (1998). What does early antisocial behaviour predict? A follow-up of 4- and 5-years olds from the Ontario Child Health Study. *Canadian Journal of Psychiatry, 43,* 605–613.

Loeber, R. (1990). Development and risk factors of juvenile antisocial behaviour and delinquency. *Clinical Psychology Review, 10,* 1–41.

Loeber, R. (1991). Antisocial behavior: More enduring than changeable? *Journal of the American Academy of Child and Adolescent Psychiatry, 30,* 393–397.

Loeber, R., Burke, J. D., & Lahey, B. B. (2002). What are adolescent antecedents to antisocial personality disorder? *Criminal Behaviour and Mental Health, 12,* 24–36.

Loeber, R., & Farrington, D. P. (Eds.). (1998). *Serious and violent juvenile offenders: Risk factors and successful interventions.* Thousand Oaks, CA: Sage.

Loeber, R., & Farrington, D. P. (Eds.). (2001). *Child delinquents: Development, interventions and service needs.* Thousand Oaks, CA: Sage.

Loeber, R., Farrington, D. P., & Petechuk, D. (2003, May). *Child delinquency: Early intervention and prevention.* Child Delinquency Bulletin Series. U.S. Department of Justice.

Loeber, R., Farrington, D. P., Stouthamer-Loeber, M., Moffit, T. E., Caspi, A., White, H. R., et al. (2003). The development of male offending: Key findings from fourteen years of the Pittsburgh Youth Study. In T. Thornberry & M. Krohn (Eds.), *Taking stock of delinquency: An overview of findings from contemporary longitudinal studies* (pp. 93–136). New York: Kluwer/Plenum.

Loeber, R., Pardini, D. A., Stouthamer-Loeber, M., & Raine, A. (2007). Do cognitive, physiological, and psychosocial risk & promotive factors predict desistance from delinquency in males? *Development & Psychopathology, 19,* 867–887.

Loeber, R. & Stouthamer-Loeber, M. (1998). Development of juvenile aggression and violence: Some common misconceptions and controversies. *American Psychologist, 53,* 242–259.

McNiel, D. E., Sandberg, D. A., & Binder, R. L. (1998). The relationship between confidence and accuracy in clinical assessment of psychiatric patients' potential for violence. *Law and Human Behavior, 22,* 655–669.

Moffitt, T. E., Caspi, A., Harrington, H., & Milne, B. J. (2002). Males on the life-course-persistent and adolescence-limited antisocial pathways: follow-up at age 26 years. *Development and Psychopathology, 14,* 179–207.

Moffitt, T. E., Caspi, A., Rutter, M., & Silva, P. A. (2001). *Sex differences in antisocial behavior: Conduct disorder, delinquency, and violence in the Dunedin longitudinal study.* Cambridge: Cambridge University Press.

Monahan, J. (1996). Violence prediction: The past twenty and the next twenty years. *Criminal Justice and Behavior, 23,* 107–120.

Monahan, J., Steadman, H. J., Silver, E., Appelbaum, P. S., Robbins, P. C., Mulvey, E. P., et al. (2001). *Rethinking risk assessment: The MacArthur study of mental disorder and violence.* New York: Oxford University Press.

Muthen, B., & Muthen, L. K. (2000). Integrating person-centered and variable-centered analyses: Growth mixture modeling with latent trajectory classes. *Alcoholism: Clinical & Experimental Research, 24(6),* 882–891.

Nicholls, T. L., Brink, J., Webster, C. D., Desmarais, S. L., & Martin, M.L. (2006). The Short-Term Assessment of Risk and Treatability (START): A prospective validation study in a forensic psychiatric sample. *Assessment, 13,* 313–327.

Stouthamer-Loeber, M., Loeber, R., Wei, E., Farrington, D. P., & Wikström, P.O. H. (2002). Risk and promotive effects in the explanation of persistent serious delinquency in boys. *Journal of Consulting and Clinical Psychology, 70,* 111–123.

Webster, C. D., & Hucker, S. J. (2007). *Violence risk assessment and management.* West Sussex, England: John Wiley & Sons Ltd.

Webster, C. D., & Hucker, S. J., & Bloom, H. (2006). Transcending the actuarial versus clinical polemic in assessing risk for violence. *Criminal Justice and Behavior, 29,* 659–665.

Webster, C. D., Martin, M. L., Brink, J., Nicholls, T. L., & Middleton, C. (2004). *Short-Term Assessment of Risk and Treatability (START).* Hamilton, ON, Canada: St. Joseph's Healthcare, Forensic Services.

Webster, C. D., Douglas, K. S., Eaves, D., & Hart, S. D. (1997). *HCR-20: Assessing Risk for Violence—Version 2.* Burnaby, BC: Mental Health, Law, and Policy Institute, Simon Fraser University.

Yuile, A. (2007). *Developmental pathways of aggressive girls: A gender-sensitive approach to risk assessment, intervention, and follow-up.* Unpublished doctoral dissertation, York University, Toronto, ON, Canada.

4
Structured Assessment of Violence Risk in Youth (SAVRY)

RANDY BORUM, HENNY LODEWIJKS, PATRICK A. BARTEL, and ADELLE E. FORTH

Description of Measure

The *Structured Assessment of Violence Risk in Youth* (SAVRY) (Bartel, Borum, & Forth, 2003; Borum, Bartel, & Forth, 2006) is a "structured professional judgment" (SPJ) tool for assessing violence risk in adolescents (between the approximate ages of 12 and 18). For purposes of using the instrument, violence is defined as "an act of physical battery sufficiently severe to cause injury that would require medical attention, a threat with a weapon in hand, or any act of forcible sexual assault." Risk itself is viewed as the product of dynamic and reciprocal interplay between factors that increase, and factors that decrease, the likelihood of violent offending in the developing young person over time (Borum & Verhaagen, 2006). Although designed specifically to assess risk of violence, several studies have found the SAVRY also to be effective in forecasting risk of general criminal or delinquent recidivism. It has been less successful for appraising risk of sexual offending specifically, but its performance has been comparable to that of other tools designed for juvenile sex offender assessment.

As with most SPJ risk tools, the SAVRY structures professionals' inquiries so that they consider risk factors that are empirically associated with violence, determine the applicability of each risk factor for a particular examinee, and classify each factor's severity and significance (Webster, Mueller, Isberner, & Fransson, 2002). The ultimate determination of a youth's overall level of violence risk is based on the examiner's professional judgment as informed by a systematic appraisal of relevant factors. In this way, the SPJ model draws on the strengths of both the clinical and actuarial (formula-driven) approaches to decision making and attempts to minimize their respective drawbacks (Borum & Douglas, 2003).

The SAVRY protocol is composed of 6 protective factors and 24 risk factors (see Table 4.1 for a list of SAVRY items). Risk factors are rationally divided into three categories: *Historical, Individual,* and *Social/Contextual.* The coding form also includes a section for listing "Additional Risk Factors" and "Additional Protective Factors" because the SAVRY is not exhaustive in identifying all potential risk and protective factors for any given individual. In the course of conducting a risk assessment or assessing patterns in past violent episodes, additional factors or situational variables may emerge that are important in understanding a particular juvenile's potential for future violence. In such situations, the evaluator should document and consider these additional factors in the final risk decisions.

Including protective factors is essential in the risk assessment process and is an important feature of the SAVRY. Protective factors are regarded differently than the simple absence of a risk factor. Indeed, protective factors are "conceptualized as variables that reflect involvement with and commitment to conventional society, that control against nonnormative activities, and that refer to activities incompatible with normative transgression" (Jessor, van den Bos, Vanderryn, Costa, and Turbin, 1995, p. 931). Although research on protective factors is more

Table 4.1 Items From the Structured Assessment of Violence Risk in Youth

Historical Risk Factors

- History of Violence
- History of Nonviolent Offending
- Early Initiation of Violence
- Past Supervision/Intervention Failures
- History of Self-Harm or Suicide Attempts
- Exposure to Violence in the Home
- Childhood History of Maltreatment
- Parental/Caregiver Criminality
- Early Caregiver Disruption
- Poor School Achievement

Social/Contextual Risk Factors

- Peer Delinquency
- Peer Rejection
- Stress and Poor Coping
- Poor Parental Management
- Lack of Personal/Social Support
- Community Disorganization

Individual/Clinical Risk Factors

- Negative Attitudes
- Risk Taking/Impulsivity
- Substance Use Difficulties
- Anger Management Problems
- Lack of Empathy/Remorse
- Attention Deficit/Hyperactivity Difficulties
- Poor Compliance
- Low Interest/Commitment to School

Protective Factors

- Prosocial Involvement
- Strong Social Support
- Strong Attachments and Bonds
- Positive Attitude Toward Intervention and Authority
- Strong Commitment to School
- Resilient Personality Traits

limited than research on risk factors, a number of studies have found them to have robust effects in understanding delinquency and problem behaviors, particularly their diminution or desistance (Jessor et al., 1995). For example, among three cohorts of adolescents, Lodewijks et al. (in press) found that protective factors added incremental utility beyond the risk factors in a regression model, that high-risk youth were much less likely to have protective factors than low-risk youth, and that that the combined effects of protective and risk factors explained desistance processes significantly better than either protective or risk factors alone.

The SAVRY is coded on the basis of reliable, available information. In most nonemergent circumstances it is helpful to include information from an interview with the examinee and a review of relevant and available records (for example, police or probation reports, mental health and social service records). The time required to gather this information will vary according to the complexity of the case. Once the information is gathered, however, it typically takes only 10 to 15 minutes to code all the SAVRY items.

Because the SAVRY does not use cutoff scores evaluators assign a code, but not a numerical score, for each item. Risk items have a three-level coding structure for severity (High, Moderate, or Low). For example, in coding the History of Violence item, a youth would be coded as "Low" if he had committed no prior acts of violence, "Moderate" if he was known to have committed one or two violent acts, and "High" if there were three or more. Protective factors are simply coded as present or absent.

The primary objective of the SAVRY is not to "quantify" risk, but to provide operational definitions for key (empirically and professionally supported) risk factors for examiners to *apply* across different assessments. Accordingly, when faced with uncertainty, how examiners decide to code any given risk item is less critical than how they assess that factor's association with violence. After carefully weighing the risk and protective factors relevant to a particular examinee, an evaluator must ultimately form an opinion or make a judgment about the nature and degree of the juvenile's risk for violence. As with other SPJ instruments, although the SAVRY is sufficiently flexible to accommodate varying styles of risk communication, the coding form prompts evaluators to make a final *summary risk rating* of Low, Moderate, or High. This summary risk rating is a professional judgment—not an actuarial or algorithmic one—based on the results of the entire SAVRY assessment of risk and protective factors.

Uses and Users

Fundamentally, the SAVRY is designed for use as an "aid" or a "guide" in professional risk assessments and intervention planning for violence risk management in youth. With its emphasis on dynamic factors, the SAVRY is designed also to be useful in intervention planning and monitoring of ongoing progress. This may include formulating clinical treatment plans, determining conditions of community supervision, or planning release and discharge. Those factors that contribute most strongly to increasing risk (that is, criminogenic factors) can be targeted for intervention, and protective factors may be enhanced or implemented to further the overall objective of reducing the risk of future violent behavior. The SAVRY requires a thoughtful, thorough professional assessment to ensure its effectiveness. The SAVRY's main purpose is simply to structure and guide the risk assessment process by increasing the evaluator's consistency and reliance on empirically supported factors, and to give greater transparency to the resulting risk judgment. That is, it is designed to support, rather than replace, professional judgments.

Beyond the general caveats of uses and user qualifications, one additional limitation is worth noting. The SAVRY was designed primarily to support assessments of general violence risk (potential for engaging in some violent act toward anyone during a specified time period), including assessments intended to prevent violent behavior through imposition of supervision or intervention (e.g., probation/community supervision). Assessments of *general violence risk* differ, however, from assessments of *targeted violence*, defined as circumstances where a youth comes to the official attention of a school, clinical, or juvenile justice professional because of a concern about the potential for acting violently toward an identified or identifiable person (Borum, Fein, Vossekuil, & Berglund, 1999; Borum & Reddy, 2001; Fein & Vossekuil, 1998; Fein, Vossekuil, & Holden, 1995). If, for example, a teenage boy is referred by his school administrator because other students heard him talking about "blowing up the school," the first-line objective is typically to appraise the likelihood that the boy is on a pathway toward engaging in a violent act toward the school or particular persons at the school, not just his risk for general violence. Targeted violence cases of "threat assessments" must rely more heavily on case-specific facts rather than general nomothetic risk factors. An evaluator could not reasonably assume or dismiss concerns of a targeted attack simply because the general violence risk factors were not present.

The SAVRY may be used by professionals in a variety of disciplines who conduct assessments and/or make intervention/supervision plans concerning violence risk in youth. Professionals who engage in these activities should, of course, be aware of and comply with all relevant laws, policies and ethical standards, including only practicing within their areas of competence. At a minimum, those who use the SAVRY should have expertise (that is, knowledge, training and experience) in child/adolescent development, youth violence and delinquency, and conducting individual assessments. In general, psychologists, psychiatrists, trained juvenile probation officers, and social workers with requisite expertise would be qualified to use the SAVRY. Professionals who meet the general user qualifications often can learn how to use the instrument by studying the manual and learning collaboratively with colleagues by comparing ratings and rationales to identify "weak spots" or rating biases. The SAVRY Manual does not require that a specified training course be completed, though some systems have adopted their own user guidelines. The State of Connecticut, for example, created its own "Train the Trainer" program to ensure consistency when they adopted the SAVRY for use in their juvenile detention facilities. Similarly, in The Netherlands—where SAVRY assessments are required before any leave is approved for youth residing in a correctional facility or institution—examiners must complete a two-day training program which reviews the instrument's theoretical and empirical underpinnings and includes three group-reviewed case studies to facilitate consistency and appropriate coding of the instrument. The SAVRY is designed for use primarily with adolescents between the ages of 12 and 18 years of age. It is possible to use the SAVRY when assessing people slightly younger or older than the target ages; however, because SAVRY item selection was based primarily on research with adolescents, its use outside that range requires a greater degree of caution. For young people who fall outside of the intended age range, it is recommended that evaluators also consider using one of the other age-appropriate SPJ risk protocols such as the HCR-20 (Webster, Douglas, Eaves, & Hart, 1997) for young adults or the EARL (Early Assessment Risk List) tools (Augimeri, Webster, Koegl, & Levene, 2001) for children under age 12.

Questions more commonly arise about upward rather than downward extension of the SAVRY, because many juvenile detention facilities can retain jurisdiction over youth through age 21 or longer. Although the HCR-20 has been researched extensively with adults, relatively few studies have focused on the early adult period between the ages of 18 and 22. Accordingly, some have found the SAVRY to be useful in this age range, particularly in cases where the young person still (or before incarceration) lives with his or her parents and is expected to return to their care.

The SAVRY may be used for assessing both male and female adolescents, because the preponderance of existing research suggests that many risk and protective factors operate similarly for both genders, though the sensitivity and rates of exposure for each may differ (Blum, Ireland, & Blum, 2003; Connor, Steingard, Anderson, & Melloni, 2003; Fergusson & Horwood, 2002; Huizinga et al., 1991; Moffitt et al., 2001-Dunedin; Pepler & Sedighdeilami, 1998-Canada; Rowe, Vazsonyi, & Flannery, 1995; Simourd & Andrews, 1994; Zahn et al., 2008). The SAVRY authors do understand and appreciate that a substantial proportion of existing research on violence risk factors has been conducted only on males. As data increasingly become available on gender-based differences on SAVRY-coded items, the authors remain open to the possibility of developing a modification for girls, but any such effort will be informed and guided by sound, convincing empirical research.

In the current SAVRY Manual, where known research indicates a particular risk factor may apply differently to males and females, this is noted in the specific item descriptions

(Bjorkvist, Lagerspetz, & Kaukianen, 1992; Rowe, Vazsonyi, & Flannery, 1995). Recent research from the Gender Aggression Project (GAP) (Moretti, Odgers, Jackson, & Repucci, 2004) indicates, for example, that trauma—particularly from sexual abuse—may bear a stronger causal relationship to violent behavior in girls than boys. Girls in the juvenile justice system, however, are twice as likely as boys to have been physically abused and four times more likely to have been sexually abused. Also, girls' risk, more so than that of boys, may be affected by caregiver disruption—along with its consequent impact on attachments—and early sexual maturation (Breslau, Davis, Andreski, & Peterson, 1991; Levene et al. 2001; Moretti & Odgers, 2006; Odgers & Moreti, 2002; Wall & Barth, 2005). This GAP research is consistent with findings from reviews conducted by the Girls Study Group, which found certain factors to be more sensitive to gender effects including: early puberty or developmental factors, sexual abuse/assault, depression/anxiety, cross-gender peer influence, and attachments/bonds to school and prosocial institutions (Zahn et al., 2008). These emergent findings should be given special consideration when using the SAVRY with female adolescents.

The SAVRY is used throughout the world, and the instrument and manual have official translations in the following languages: Dutch by Henny Lodewijks; Swedish by Niklas Langstrom; Finnish by Riittakerttu Kaltiala-Heino; Spanish and Catalan both by Ed Hilterman; German by Martin Rieger; and Norwegian by Geir Tafjord and Kirsten Rasmussen.

Method and Rationale for Development

Adolescence is the peak developmental risk period for initiating or participating in acts of serious violence (U.S. Department of Health and Human Services, 2001). Consequently, risk assessments are often requested in juvenile justice settings, schools, psychiatric emergency services, civil psychiatric hospitals, outpatient clinics, and other settings. Historically, most assessments were unstructured clinical assessments conducted by mental health practitioners. Through the 1990s, however, as risk assessment research and assessment technology emerged, the need for better methods and greater reliance on empirical research became strikingly apparent.

Though some advances had been made with adult risk assessment tools, reflected by many instruments covered in this book, specialized efforts were needed for adolescent evaluations to address developmental differences in the nature of risk, relevance of risk factors, and operation of risk factors (Borum & Grisso, 2007; Borum & Verhaagen, 2006; Hoge, 2001, 2002; Hoge & Andrews, 1996), all of which are critical determinants of youths' behavior (Griffin & Torbet, 2002; McCord, Widom, & Cowell, 2001; Rosado, 2000). Violence risk in adolescents differs from adults in a variety of important ways. The base rates or normative expectations are dissimilar. While adults and adolescents share some common risk factors, the mechanism and strength of the association often varies developmentally between adolescents and adults, and even between children and adolescents (Howell, 1997). Deviant peer influences, for example, are more robust risk factors in teens than in younger children. Conversely, parental and family risk factors weigh more heavily into risk for younger than older youth. Moreover, in risk assessments with juveniles, many personality-related factors are less stable than is typically seen with adults, and the explicit and implicit role of the examinee's degree of psychosocial maturity is more central (Borum, 2000, 2002, 2003b; Borum & Verhaagen, 2006).

In developing the SAVRY, our goal was to draw on the strengths of existing risk assessment technology and empirical findings with youth to create an instrument that would help structure and improve violence risk assessment practice—as well as risk management—with adolescents receiving treatment, monitoring, or preventive services from a variety of systems.

Our appraisal was that a successful assessment guide would need several key features, specifically it would need to be:

1. *Systematic*: Covering the primary domains of known risk and protective factors, with clear operational definitions provided for each.
2. *Empirically grounded*: Items need to be based on the best available research and guidelines for juvenile risk assessment practice.
3. *Developmentally informed*: Risk and protective factors have to be selected on the basis of how they operate with adolescents, as opposed to children or adults.
4. *Treatment-oriented*: The risk assessment should have direct implications for treatment, which includes considering dynamic factors that can be useful targets for intervention in risk reduction.
5. *Flexible*: Allowing consideration of idiographic or case-specific factors as well as those derived from research.
6. *Practical*: Using the guide should not require much additional time beyond what is needed to collect information in a competent assessment. It should be inexpensive, easy to learn, and not require diagnostic judgments.

In 2000, the authors compiled items from two youth violence assessment tool prototypes, which they had been working on independently, and evaluated them for inclusion in a combined final version. Risk items were selected primarily on the size and robustness of the empirical relationship between the factor and violence as identified through prior reviews, meta-analyses, and original studies with adolescent populations (e.g., Hann & Borek, 2001; Hawkins et al., 1998, 2000; Howell, 1997; Lipsey & Derzon, 1998). The research base on protective factors for violence in adolescents was much less extensive (U.S. Department of Health & Human Services, 2001); nevertheless, the authors selected those with the greatest promise and that were measurable in a psychosocial assessment. While all included items demonstrated some empirical link to violence, a few, such as Poor Compliance, remained despite a lack of robust research because of their clinical relevance. Next, the authors constructed operational coding definitions for each SAVRY item—drawing from definitions used in prior studies where possible—and developed criteria to anchor the levels of severity. For example, the coding scheme for History of Violence item distinguishes between having no known acts of violence, as operationally defined in the SAVRY Manual (Low), having one or two acts that meet those criteria (Moderate), and having three or more (High).

A pilot version of the items and coding criteria was circulated to several risk assessment professionals for comments and applied in a few preliminary studies where researchers provided feedback about item clarity and language. The items were then revised, tightened, and integrated into a "Consultation Edition" of the SAVRY Manual (Borum, Bartel & Forth, 2001) released in February 2002. The SAVRY was commercially published in 2006.

Between the initial "Consultation Edition" and commercial publication, the only substantive item change involved a factor first labeled as "Psychopathic Traits." In the initial coding criteria—as is true with some other SPJ instruments—the rating was linked directly to scores on the *Hare Psychopathy Checklist: Youth Version* (PCL-YV) (Forth, Kosson, & Hare, 2003). The authors subsequently revised the item and removed the PCL-YV from its coding for several reasons. First, the PCL:YV is a psychometric instrument designed to assess the construct of psychopathy. For applied risk assessment, however, we were mainly interested in assessing the relevant cluster of traits as a "risk marker" for violence, rather than the diagnostic construct per se in juveniles. Second, the user qualifications for the SAVRY (a risk assessment tool) are less stringent than for the PCL:YV. Third, connotations of the term *psychopathy* are uniformly negative, and the label itself is so powerful that any information about a youth as an individual may be lost once this language is applied (Boccaccini et al., 2008; Edens et al., 2005; Edens and Vincent, 2008; Murrie et al., 2005, 2007). Further, given that several SAVRY items overlapped substantially with PCL:YV items, we sought to construct an item that captured only the otherwise unaccounted variance in the cluster of personality/behavioral traits. The result was the creation of a new item labeled "Low Empathy/Remorse" to substitute for the "Psychopathic Traits" factor. We examined the empirical effect of this change and found that the SAVRY including a "Psychopathic Traits" factor and one substituting a "Low Empathy/Remorse" factor correlated almost perfectly ($r = .99$) for a community and offender sample. The new "Low Empathy/Remorse" item was then included in a second printing of the SAVRY Manual, designated as "Version 1.1" (Borum, Bartel, & Forth, 2001) and in the commercially published version.

Reliability

Internal Consistency

While the SAVRY and its component domains are not intended as formal "scales," for heuristic purposes, we analyzed the internal consistency of SAVRY Risk Total in our validation sample and found it to be .82 for the offenders and .84 for the community sample (Bartel, Forth & Borum, 2004).

Inter-Rater Reliability

The primary issue of reliability for SPJ instruments, including the SAVRY, is inter-rater reliability, which indicates the degree of agreement between two or more different raters coding the same case based on the same information. The intraclass correlation coefficient (ICC) is a commonly used index of inter-rater agreement. Fleiss (1986) suggests using the following critical values for describing single measure ICCs: ICC > .75 = excellent; ICC between .60 and .75 = good; ICC between .40 and .60 = moderate; ICC < .40 = poor. Approximately six studies have examined the SAVRY's inter-rater reliability (see Table 4.2), mostly revealing good to excellent agreement between raters, with ICCs ranging from .81 to .97 for the SAVRY Risk Total and .72 to .95 for the SAVRY Summary Risk Rating. The risk factor domains—historical, individual, social, and contextual—are aggregated conceptually and are not designed to possess the psychometric properties of a test scale; nevertheless, the domains do show good internal consistency. For example, in a sample of male and female incarcerated Dutch adolescents, the inter-rater reliability of the SAVRY domains ranged from good to excellent both for girls (ICC: Historical = .92, Social/Contextual = .80, Individual = .72, SAVRY Risk Total = .82, Protective = .73) and for boys (ICC: Historical = .77, Social/Contextual = .94, Individual = .88, SAVRY Risk Total = .86, Protective = .83).

Table 4.2 Inter-Rater Reliability of the SAVRY

Study	SAVRY Risk Total ICC	SAVRY Risk Judgment ICC
McEachran, 2001	.83	.72
Catchpole & Gretton, 2003	.81	.77
Dolan & Rennie, 2008	.97	.88
Lodewijks, Doreleijers, de Ruiter, & Borum, 2008	.81	.77
Meyers & Schmidt, 2008	.97	.95
Viljoen et al., 2008	.91	N/A

Validity

Assessing the validity of SPJ instruments requires a different approach than for traditional psychological tests. SPJ instruments are not numerically driven and are designed principally to improve human (professional) judgment by structuring the assessments. Traditional psychometric theory, however, conceptualizes validity as a function of classification accuracy, typically based on one or more cutoff scores. Also used is receiver operating characteristic (ROC) analysis, which measures predictive accuracy in terms of relative improvement over chance across all possible cutting scores, not just categorical classification based on one given cut point. Although ROC analyses have some advantages over traditional approaches as a measure of predictive validity—specifically, that the metric is less affected by criterion base rates—to the extent that AUCs are calculated for "scores," it is arguably an imprecise validity index for SPJ instruments as they are intended to be used in practice.

Nevertheless, validity data must be reported in metrics that users and psychometricians can understand, and that facilitate comparison of different tools or measures. For example, to allow for more traditional validity analyses, for research (not clinical) purposes, a variable called "SAVRY Risk Total" is sometimes used to represent the contribution of the instrument, independent of the summary risk judgment. The SAVRY Risk Total is calculated by transposing item ratings of Low, Moderate, and High to numerical values of 0, 1, and 2, respectively, and summing the values. To "quantify" the risk judgments, the Summary Risk Ratings (of Low, Moderate, and High) may be similarly transposed. In predictive validity studies, some researchers have reported offending rates for persons in each of the relative risk categories to demonstrate the degree of calibration between judged risk and actual recidivism.

Concurrent Validity

The concurrent validity of the SAVRY has been examined in relation to past violent/delinquent behavioral criteria and to both the *Youth Level of Service/Case Management Inventory* (YLS/CMI) (Hoge & Andrews, 2002; see Chapter 5, this volume) and the PCL:YV (Forth et al., 2003). In offender and community samples, the SAVRY Risk Total has shown correlations between .58 and .89 with the YLS/CMI and .70 and .78 with the PCL:YV (Borum, Bartel, & Forth, 2006, Welsh et al., 2008). The SAVRY protective domain correlates negatively with both of the other measures: –.46 and –.76 with the YLS/CMI and –.30 and –.64 with the PCL:YV. Because the YLS/CMI and PCL:YV measure only risk factors, this negative correlation is important for showing the discriminant validity of SAVRY's Protective Factors. Furthermore, in a study by Catchpole and Gretton (2003), the SAVRY Risk Judgment correlated .64 with the YLS/CMI summary classification and .68 with the PCL:YV Total score. Viljoen and colleagues (2008) also found significant correlations between the SAVRY Risk Total and scores on the Juvenile Sex Offender Assessment Protocol-II (J-SOAP-II) (r = .88) and the Juvenile Sexual Offense Recidivism Risk Assessment Tool- II (J-SORRAT-II) (r = .19). These correlations, along with additional research referenced below, indicate that, although the SAVRY shares variance with both these measures, it also possesses independent variance.

With regard to criterion-related concurrent validity, numerous studies using retrospective analysis and file review have revealed significant correlations between SAVRY scores and various measures of violence in juvenile justice and high-risk community-dwelling populations. In our two initial validation samples (Bartel et al., 2003), after we removed the "History of Violence" item to avoid, at a minimum, substantive criterion contamination, and hence possible validity inflation, SAVRY Total Risk scores were all significantly related to behavioral measures of institutional aggressive behavior (r = .40) and aggressive conduct disorder (CD) symptoms (r = .52), and protective factors were negatively related to both: r = –.31 for institutional aggression and $r = -.20$ for aggressive CD symptoms. Significant correlations have been found in other studies between SAVRY Risk Total scores and measures of violence among young male offenders in Canada ($r = .32$ in one study and $r = .25$ in another) (Catchpole & Gretton, 2003; Gretton & Abramowitz, 2002) and high-risk Native American Youth ($r = .56$ for the total sample, $r = .72$ for females, and $r = .50$ for males) (Fitch, 2002). SAVRY Summary Risk Ratings also correlated with community violence in studies by McEachran (2001) ($r = .67$) and Gretton and Abramowitz (2002) ($r = .35$).

Incremental Validity

The SAVRY also has demonstrated incremental (criterion) validity (or predictive power) beyond the YLS/CMI and the PCL-YV. Hierarchical regression analyses demonstrated that adding the SAVRY improved the predictive strength of a model including the YLS/CMI and the PCL:YV in predicting both institutional aggressive behavior and serious aggressive conduct disorder symptoms. The SAVRY also accounted for a larger proportion of the explained variance than either the YLS/CMI or the PCL-YV for predicting both Aggressive CD symptoms (SAVRY $\beta = .47$ vs. .07 for the YLS/CMI and .25 for PCL:YV) and institutional aggression (SAVRY $\beta = .26$ vs. .20 for the YLS/CMI vs. .07 for PCL:YV) (Bartel et al., 2003). Similarly, Welsh et al. (2008) reported that the SAVRY demonstrated strong incremental utility when added to predictive models initially including only the YLS/CMI and the PCL:YV in predicting both general recidivism and violent recidivism.

Predictive Validity

Using ROC analysis, which measures predictive accuracy in terms of relative improvement over chance, areas under the curve (AUCs) for the SAVRY Risk Total average about .74 to .80 across studies (See Table 4.3). Interestingly, as with the univariate comparisons, the examiner judgments (summary risk rating), not made on the basis of any cutting score, consistently perform as well as, and often better than, the linear combination of the scores themselves. For example, using ROC, McEachran (2001) reported an AUC for the SAVRY total score of .70, but the AUC for the SAVRY Summary Risk Rating was .89. While not all SAVRY studies have found that the Risk Rating is significantly superior to the Risk Total, this trend has been evident in research on other SPJ tools as well (see Chapter 1, Heilbrun, this volume, for a summary), and provides some of the first empirical evidence that clinical judgments—properly structured and based on sound assessments—can achieve levels of accuracy that rival that of any other known predictors while maintaining latitude for case-specific analysis.

Finally, a few investigators have examined the relationship between Summary Risk Ratings and actual recidivism. Catchpole and Gretton (2003) reported that youth classified as Low Risk had a 6% violent recidivism rate, while those rated as Moderate Risk and High Risk had rates of 14% and 40%, respectively. Those rated as High Risk also recidivated more quickly than Moderate or Low Risk rated youth.

Gammelgård, Weitzman-Henelius, and Kaltiala-Heino (2008) examined recidivism rates in a sample of SAVRY-assessed Finnish adolescents. Violent recidivism was reported for only 4% of those rated Low Risk, but 29% of those rated a Moderate Risk and 67% of the High Risk teens ($p < .001$). A corresponding logistic regression analysis adjusting the analyses for sex, age, diagnosis, service level, and time of follow-up, showed that the odds of violent recidivism also increased for each risk level. Compared to the Low Risk group, youth rated as Moderate Risk were nearly four times more likely, and youth rated as High Risk were nearly twenty-eight times more likely to violently reoffend.

Finally, Viljoen and colleagues studied the validity of the SAVRY and two sexual offense–specific risk instruments for juvenile offenders (Juvenile Sex Offender Assessment Protocol-II

Table 4.3 Studies of the Predictive Validity of the SAVRY on Institutional or Community Violent Recidivism

Study	Design	Strength of Association
Gammelgård, & Kaltiala-Heino (2007)	*Institutional violence* Retrospective study $N = 147$ (boys and girls)	Violent incidents: Risk Total, AUC = .71*
Gammelgård, Weitzman-Henelius, & Kaltiala-Heino (2008)	*Community violence* Retrospective study $N = 208$ (boys and girls)	Violent incidents: Risk Total, AUC = .71** Risk Total, OR = *27.85 (high-low)* Risk Total, OR = *3.83 (mod-low)*
Lodewijks, Doreleijers, de Ruiter, & Borum (2008)	*Institutional violence* Prospective study $N = 66$ (boys) Follow-up: 18 months	Violent incidents: Risk Total, AUC = .80*** Risk Rating, AUC = .86** Aggressive incidents: Risk Total, AUC = .73*
Catchpole & Gretton (2003)	*Community violence* Retrospective study $N = 66$ (90% boys) Follow-up: 12 months post-release	Violent recidivism: Risk Total, AUC = .73**
Dolan & Rennie (2008)	*Community violence* Prospective study $N = 99$ (boys) Follow-up: 6 months post-release	Violent recidivism: Risk Total, AUC = .64* Risk Rating, AUC = .64* General recidivism: Risk Total, AUC = .69* Risk Rating, AUC = .69*
Fitch (2002)	*Community violence* Retrospective study $N = 82$ (47 boys; 35 girls) Follow-up: 18 months	Males: Risk Total, $r = .50$** Females: Risk Total, $r = .72$*** Males and females: Risk Total, $r = 56$**
Gretton & Abramowitz (2002)	*Community violence* Retrospective study $N = 176$ (94% boys) Follow-up: 12 months	Violent recidivism: Risk Total, AUC = .67* Risk Rating, AUC = .74**
Hilterman (2007)	*Community violence* Prospective study $N = 85$ (72 boys; 13 girls) Follow-up: 10 to18 months	Violent recidivism: Risk Total, AUC = .78** Risk Rating, AUC = .74**
Lodewijks, de Ruiter, & Doreleijers (2008)	*Community violence* Prospective study $N = 82$ (47 boys; 35 girls) Follow-up: 18 months post-release	Violent recidivism: Risk Total, AUC = .76** (boys); AUG= .84* (girls) Risk Rating, AUC = .82*** (boys); AUG= .85*** (girls)
Lodewijks, Doreleijers, & de Ruiter (2008)	*Community violence* Retrospective study $N = 117$ (95% boys) Follow-up: 36 months	Violent recidivism: Risk Total, AUC = .65* Risk Rating, AUC = .71*

Table 4.3 Studies of the Predictive Validity of the SAVRY on Institutional or Community Violent Recidivism (continued)

Study	Design	Strength of Association	
McEachran (2001)	*Community violence* Retrospective study *N* = 108 (boys) Follow-up after release: 36 months	Violent recidivism: Risk Total, Risk Rating,	 AUC = .70* AUC = .89**
Meyers & Schmidt (2008)	*Community violence* Prospective study *N* = 121 Follow-up: 1 year and 3 years	*(Statistical significance levels not reported)* Violent recidivism: Risk Total (1 yr), Risk Total (3 yr), General recidivism: Risk Total (1 yr), Risk Total (3 yr), Nonviolent recidivism: Risk Total (1 yr), Risk Total (3 yr),	 AUC = .66 AUC = .77 AUC = .75 AUC = .76 AUC = .80 AUC = .68
Rieger, Stadtland, Freisleder, & Nedopil (2006)	*Community violence* Retrospective study *N* = 89 (boys) Follow-up: 12 months	Violent recidivism: Risk Total,	 AUC = .69*
Viljoen et al. (2008).	*Institutional Offending and Community Offending* Prospective study *N* = 169 boys adjudicated for sexual offenses Follow-up: 1 year in treatment 6.5 years in community	Sexual aggression during treatment: Risk Total, Risk Rating, Nonsexual aggression during treatment: Risk Total, Risk Rating, Sexual offense in community: Risk Total, Risk Rating, Serious nonsexual violent offense in community: Risk Total, Risk Rating, Any offense in community: Risk Total, Risk Rating,	 AUC = .52 AUC = .51 AUC = .69*** AUC = .59 AUC = .53 AUC = .51 AUC = .69* AUC = .56 AUC = .58 AUC = .50
Welsh et al. (2008)	*Community violence* Prospective study *N* = 133 Average follow-up: 35.8 months	*(Statistical significance levels not reported)* Violent recidivism: Risk Total General recidivism: Risk Total	 AUC = .81 AUC = .77

Note: AUC = Area Under the Curve. OR = Odds Ratio. *r* = Pearson correlation coefficient.
* $p < .05$, ** $p < .01$, *** $p < .001$ (two-tailed).

and the Juvenile Sexual Offense Recidivism Risk Assessment Tool- II) in a sample of 169 male juvenile sexual offenders. While none of the instruments showed a high degree of power in predicting sexual recidivism specifically (AUC between .51 and .54), in part due to low base rates of detected offenses), the SAVRY Risk Total performed modestly better than the others in forecasting serious nonsexual violent offending (SAVRY AUC = .69 vs. .63 for J-SOAP-II and .55 for J-SORRAT-II). The SAVRY Summary Risk Rating (AUC = .56) did no better than the others.

Limitations and Necessary Future Research

Results from the research conducted to date generally support the use of the SAVRY as a reliable and valid tool for assessing violence risk in adolescents. Most studies so far also seem to suggest that the SAVRY predicts general offending in youth as well as it does violent offending (e.g., Welsh et al., 2008). While the statistical tabulations of correlations, AUCs, and beta weights are commensurate with psychometric performance of other actuarial and SPJ risk assessment tools, we are far from approaching optimal prediction. Moreover, there remains an open question as to whether, and the extent to which, the examiner's Summary Risk Rating contributes to predictive accuracy beyond what can be achieved using the SAVRY Risk Total alone. This is significant because the SAVRY is designed as an SPJ instrument, not an actuarial one. Several studies using SPJ instruments—including a couple using the SAVRY—have found higher validity indices for the Summary Risk Rating than for the score. But at least an equal number of SAVRY studies have not found the rating to significantly outperform the total score. This certainly raises questions about how the SAVRY can be most effectively used.

Future Research

The next generation of SAVRY research should move beyond the broad question of whether it "works" to examine how, for whom, and under what circumstances it is more and less effective. Three areas should receive particular attention: age, gender, and race/ethnicity/culture. At least one study (Viljoen et al., 2008) has found that youth risk assessment instruments performed better with older adolescents than with younger ones. Perhaps some investigators should focus on the interstitial age ranges within the different SPJ violence risk tools and compare the effectiveness between them. Regarding gender, it is clear that research on the causes and correlates of violent offending in girls is moving forward, and that some discernible differences are emerging. Researchers examining the utility of the SAVRY should include girls in their studies whenever possible, and report results for boys and girls separately, so that we can further our efforts to refine our recommendations to SAVRY users. Third, better understanding how the SAVRY functions when assessing young people from different racial and ethnic groups will be an important issue for future investigations. As was true with gender, different rates of risk factor exposure and sensitivity to protective factors also may be important here (Chapman et al., 2006).

Finally, future studies might help to understand and refine the decision-making process in forming Summary Risk Ratings. It may be that there are clusters or "types" of high-risk cases, or that the risk rating might be made more reliably if additional structure or heuristics were provided. The feasibility and ultimate value of adding structure to the decision process is an empirical question, but given that the risk judgment is intended to be the primary product of a SAVRY-guided assessment, it certainly merits further investigation.

Case Example

Tarik is a 16-year-old male who has been incarcerated in a juvenile justice institution for the past 18 months after being adjudicated delinquent on charges of sexual battery and misdemeanor battery. He is the youngest of three brothers and has one younger half-brother. His psychosocial history reveals significant family disruption, particularly during his childhood years. As an infant, he was placed in foster care for two months and, at age two, was placed in a relative's care for three months. Tarik's father had a serious drug-dependence problem and regularly sold drugs as well. His father and mother had a conflict-laden relationship, characterized both by verbal and physical abuse, much of which occurred in the children's presence. His father was also physically abusive toward the boys. When Tarik was three years old, his mother took the children and fled to a women's shelter where they lived for a month. At age four, Tarik had a year-long, out-of-home residential placement. He returned home to find that his mother was in a new live-in relationship with a man who physically abused all of the children and who abused her in front of them. His biological father died in a car accident (under suspicious circumstances) when Tarik was six years old.

When he was eight, Tarik's mother sought mental health assistance because she was unable to handle his behavior problems at home. He was defiant and oppositional toward her and dismissive of authority, in general. He stole money and cigarettes and had frequent, and sometimes serious, fights with his younger half-brother. Tarik was placed in an alternative school for children with behavioral problems, which he attended until the age of 10. At this school he repeatedly threatened to harm other children (especially girls); he touched girls inappropriately without their permission and disregarded all attempts by teachers to correct or redirect his behavior. Outside school, Tarik spent his time with other boys "hanging around" and stealing bicycles. He was caught stealing bicycles at least four times, joyriding, and walking around with a fake gun. When Tarik was 11 years old, he threatened a boy with this gun.

At the age of 13, Tarik was placed in a residential treatment facility for children with behavioral problems where he remained for nearly two years. According to the psychologists in the facility, Tarik had an "uncontrollable hunger for attention," which led him to tell exciting (though untrue) stories to the other boys. Tarik manipulated other residents into doing his work, and he once ran away from the institution overnight. Records revealed that Tarik twice lured two different boys into his room, where he raped one and physically assaulted the other. Tarik says, however, that he does not think of himself as a rapist and therefore does not consider himself to be guilty. He stated that the victim wanted to have sex with him, and that he only had to "persuade him a little." He reportedly feels ashamed of what happened because he does not want people (especially his Turkish family members) to think he is gay.

Within the past year at the juvenile justice institution, treatment progress has been unremarkable. He is concerned only with the logistics of his detention (e.g., leave for the weekend), rather than meeting his treatment goals. He does not believe that the treatment setting is appropriate for him, because he does not regard himself as a sex offender. Staff clinicians report that Tarik is easily offended by others and that he denies and blames others for most of his problems. He tends to anger very easily and on multiple occasions has thrown furniture. He has frequent conflicts with other residents and with group leaders and has threatened both on multiple occasions, saying things like, "I'll stab you to death." He has shown an aptitude for sports, but becomes angry and upset whenever he loses. At school, he appears to be very motivated, and his academic performance is above average.

Both in the institution and in the community, Tarik has always tried to establish a dominant (and often manipulative) position among his peers, though he has never established any friendships. Many of the other youth resent and dislike him. When he has been on leave from the institution, Tarik has sought contact with the groups of delinquent boys he associated with when he was 9 years old. Tarik's mother remains very indulgent. He manipulates her easily, and she is unable to control his behavior.

Tarik's treatment team requested a formal risk assessment to assist them in deciding whether he could be "stepped down" from a closed institution to an open institution. The critical items are marked with respect to this aim. The general conclusion is that the probability of violent risk is still high. He needs aggression replacement training (ART) and functional family therapy (FFT) and needs to be more motivated for these treatment aims before being allowed to go to an open treatment facility.

The SAVRY was used as part of this assessment (see Table 4.4) to estimate the nature and degree of risk Tarik may pose, and—if necessary—to suggest ways to reduce his risk to facilitate his success in an open treatment setting. The risk assessment considered Tarik's relevant historical, social/contextual, and individual risk factors balanced against protective factors, and determined that, at the time of the examination, Tarik continued to pose a "high risk" for serious violence (i.e., physical battery) if moved to an open institutional treatment setting.

The basis for this judgment included Tarik's history of serious violence and delinquent behavior, negative early developmental events, problematic parental management, and strong cognitive and emotional skill deficiencies likely to predispose him to aggression. Six of the ten risk factors in the Historical domain—all "static" in nature—were rated as "High," with only two rated as "Low." Three of the six Social/Contextual risk factors were rated "High," predominantly indicating poor family management, lack of support, and poor coping skills. These factors, being more dynamic, led the evaluator to two recommendations: (1) that Tarik and his mother engage in functional family therapy to improve her management skills and ability to provide supervision, structure, and support, and (2) that further information be gathered about the nature of Tarik's intended community peer group and the possibility of prosocial mentoring models. Finally, Tarik was rated "High" on four

Table 4.4 Tarik's SAVRY Assessment

Historical Risk Factors	
History of Violence	High
History of Nonviolent Offending	High
Early Initiation of Violence	Moderate
Past Supervision/Intervention Failures	Moderate
History of Self-Harm or Suicide Attempts	Low
Exposure to Violence in the Home	High
Childhood History of Maltreatment	High
Parental/Caregiver Criminality	High
Early Caregiver Disruption	High
Poor School Achievement	Low
Social/Contextual Risk Factors	
Peer Delinquency	X (Insufficient Information)
Peer Rejection	Low
Stress and Poor Coping	High
Poor Parental Management	High
Lack of Personal/Social Support	High
Community Disorganization	X (Insufficient Information)
Individual/Clinical Risk Factors	
Negative Attitudes	High
Risk Taking/Impulsivity	Moderate
Substance Use Difficulties	Low
Anger Management Problems	High
Lack of Empathy/Remorse	High
Attention Deficit/Hyperactivity Difficulties	Low
Poor Compliance	High
Low Interest/Commitment to School	Low
Protective Factors	
Prosocial Involvement	Absent
Strong Social Support	Absent
Strong Attachments and Bonds	Absent
Positive Attitude Toward Intervention and Authority	Absent
Strong Commitment to School	Present
Resilient Personality Traits	Absent

of the eight Individual/Clinical risk factors, including those indicating difficulty in generating nonaggressive solutions to problems, controlling anger, feeling empathy and remorse, and engaging meaningfully in his treatment. To promote progress in these areas and diminish risk, the evaluator suggested that motivational interviewing strategies might be used to better engage Tarik in his risk reduction plan and to encourage him to set meaningful goals for himself. As his motivation shows signs of improvement, it was recommended that Tarik participate in aggression replacement therapy (ART). ART is a skill-driven, evidence-based program that focuses on nonaggressive conflict management skills, anger control, and enhanced "moral reasoning."

References

Bartel, P., Forth, A., & Borum, R. (2003). Development and concurrent validation of the Structured Assessment for Violence Risk in Youth (SAVRY). Unpublished manuscript.

Boccaccini, M. T., Murrie, D. C., Clark, J., & Cornell, D. G. (2008). Describing, diagnosing, and naming psychopathy: How do youth psychopathy labels influence jurors? *Behavioral Sciences and the Law, 26,* 487–510.

Borum, R. (1996). Improving the clinical practice of violence risk assessment: Technology, guidelines and training. *American Psychologist, 51,* 945–956.

Borum, R. (2000). Assessing violence risk among youth. *Journal of Clinical Psychology, 56,* 1263–1288.

Borum, R. (March, 2002). Why is assessing violence risk in juveniles different than in adults? Paper Presented at the Biennial Conference of the American Psychology-Law Society, Austin, TX.

Borum, R., Bartel, P., & Forth, A. (2005). Structured Assessment of Violence Risk in Youth (SAVRY). In T. Grisso, G. Vincent, & D. Seagrave (Eds.), *Mental health screening and assessment in juvenile justice* (pp. 311–323). New York: Guilford Press.

Borum, R., Bartel, P., & Forth, A. (2006). *Manual for the Structured Assessment for Violence Risk in Youth (SAVRY).* Odessa, FL: Psychological Assessment Resources.

Borum, R., & Douglas, K. (March, 2003). New directions in violence risk assessment. *Psychiatric Times, 20*(3), 102–103.

Borum, R. Fein, R., Vossekuil, B., & Berglund, J. (1999). Threat assessment: Defining an approach for evaluating risk of targeted violence. *Behavioral Sciences and the Law, 17,* 323–337.

Borum, R., & Grisso, T. (2006). Developmental issues in assessing violence risk in youth.

Borum, R., & Reddy, M. (2001). Assessing violence risk in Tarasoff situations: A fact-based model of inquiry. *Behavioral Sciences and the Law, 19,* 375–385.

Borum, R., & Verhaagen, D. (2006). *Assessing and managing violence risk in juveniles.* New York: Guilford Press.

Catchpole, R., & Gretton, H. (2003). The predictive validity of risk assessment with violent young offenders: A 1-year examination of criminal outcome. *Criminal Justice and Behavior, 30,* 688–708.

Chapman, J. F., Desai, R. A., Falzer, P. R., & Borum, R. (2006). Violence risk and race in a sample of youth in juvenile detention: The potential to reduce disproportionate minority confinement. *Youth Violence and Juvenile Justice, 4,* 170–184.

Dolan, M. C., & Rennie, C. E. (2008). The Structured Assessment of Violence Risk in Youth (SAVRY) as a predictor of recidivism in a U.K. cohort of adolescent offenders with conduct disorder. *Psychological Assessment, 20,* 35–46.

Edens, J. F., Cowell, L. H., Desforges, D. M., & Fernandez, K. (2005). The impact of mental health evidence on support for capital punishment: Are defendants labeled psychopathic considered more deserving of death? *Behavioral Sciences and the Law,* 23, 603–623.

Edens, J., & Vincent, G. M. (2008). Juvenile psychopathy: A clinical construct in need of restraint. *Journal of Forensic Psychology Practice, 8,* 186–197.

Fein, R. A., & Vossekuil, B. (1998). *Protective intelligence and threat assessment investigations: A guide for state and local law enforcement officials* (NIJ/OJP/DOJ Publication No. NCJ 170612). Washington, DC: U.S. Department of Justice.

Fein, R. A., Vossekuil, B., & Holden, G. A. (1995, September). Threat assessment: An approach to prevent targeted violence. *National Institute of Justice: Research in Action,* 1–7.

Fitch, D. (2002). Analysis of common risk factors for violent behavior in native American adolescents referred for residential treatment. Unpublished doctoral dissertation. University of Texas–Clear Lake.

Forth, A. E., Kosson, D. S., & Hare, R. D. (2003). *Hare Psychopathy Checklist–Revised: Youth Version.* Toronto: ON, Multi-Health Systems.

Gammelgård, M., Weitzman-Henelius, G., & Kaltiala-Heino, R. (2008). The predictive validity of the Structured Assessment of Violence Risk in Youth (SAVRY) among institutionalized adolescents. *Journal of Forensic Psychiatry and Psychology, 19,* 352–370.

Gretton, H., & Abramowitz, C. (March, 2002). SAVRY: Contribution of items and scales to clinical risk judgments and criminal outcomes. Paper presented at the Biennial Conference of the American Psychology and Law Society, Austin, TX.

Griffin, P., & Torbet, P. (2002). *Desktop guide to good juvenile probation practice.* National Center for Juvenile Justice, Pittsburgh, PA [producer]. Washington, DC: Office of Juvenile Justice and Delinquency Prevention.

Grisso, T. (1996). Society's retributive response to juvenile violence: A developmental perspective. *Law and Human Behavior, 20,* 229–247.

Hann, D. A., & Borek, N. (2001). *Taking stock of risk factors for child/youth externalizing behavior problems.* Bethesda, MD: National Institute of Mental Health.

Hawkins, J., Herrenkohl, T., Farrington, D., Brewer, D., Catalano, R., & Harachi, T. (1998). A review of predictors of youth violence. In R. Loeber & D. Farrington (Eds.), *Serious and violent juvenile offenders: Risk factors and successful interventions* (pp. 106–146). Thousand Oaks, CA: Sage.

Hawkins, J., Herrenkohl, T., Farrington, D., Brewer, D., Catalano, R., Harachi, T., & Cothern, L. (April, 2000). Predictors of youth violence. *Bulletin*, Washington, DC: Office of Juvenile Justice and Delinquency Prevention.

Hilterman, E. (2007, June). Use of SAVRY by clinicians and its relation with recidivism by juveniles in Catalonia, Spain. Paper presented at the meeting of the International Association of Forensic Mental Health Services, Montreal, QC, Canada.

Hoge, R. (2001). *The juvenile offender: Theory, research and applications.* Norwell, MA: Kluwer Plenum.

Hoge, R. (2002). Standardized instruments for assessing risk and need in youthful offenders. *Criminal Justice and Behavior, 29,* 380–396.

Hoge, R., & Andrews, D. (1996). *Assessing the youthful offender: Issues and techniques.* New York: Plenum.

Hoge, R & Andrews, D. (2002). *Youth Level of Service/Case Management Inventory.* Toronto, ON, Canada: Multi-Health Systems.

Howell, J. (1997). *Juvenile justice and youth violence.* Thousand Oaks, CA: Sage.

Lipsey, M., & Derzon, J. (1998). Predictors of violent or serious delinquency in adolescence and early adulthood: A synthesis of longitudinal research. In R. Loeber and D. P. Farrington (Eds.), *Serious and violent juvenile offenders: Risk factors and successful interventions,* (pp. 86–105). Thousand Oaks, CA: Sage Publications.

Lodewijks, H. P. B., Doreleijers, Th. A. H., & Ruiter, C. de (2008). SAVRY risk assessment in a Dutch sample of violent adolescents: Relation to sentencing and recidivism. *Criminal Justice and Behavior, 35,* 696–709.

Lodewijks, H. P. B., Doreleijers, Th. A. H., Ruiter, C. de, & Borum, R. (2008). Predictive validity of the Structured Assessment of Violence Risk in Youth (SAVRY) during residential treatment. *International Journal of Law and Psychiatry, 31,* 263–271.

Lodewijks, H. P. B., Ruiter, C. de, & Doreleijers, Th. A. H. (2008). Gender differences in risk assessment and violent outcome after juvenile residential treatment. *International Journal of Forensic Mental Health, 7,* 105–117.

Lodewijks, H. P. B., Ruiter, C. de, & Doreleijers, Th. A. H. (in press). The impact of protective factors in desistance from violent reoffending: A comparative study in three cohorts of adolescent offenders. *Journal of Interpersonal Violence.*

McCord, J., Widom, C. S., & Crowell, N. A. (Eds.) (2001). *Juvenile crime, juvenile justice.* Washington, DC: National Academy Press.

McEachran, A. (2001). The predictive validity of the PCL:YV and the SAVRY in a population of adolescent offenders. Unpublished master's thesis. Burnaby, British Columbia: Simon Fraser University.

Meyers, J., & Schmidt, F. (2008). Predictive validity of the Structured Assessment for Violence Risk in Youth (SAVRY) with juvenile offenders. *Criminal Justice and Behavior, 35,* 344–355.

Murrie, D. C., Boccaccini, M. T., McCoy, W., & Cornell, D. G. (2007). Diagnostic labeling in juvenile court: How do descriptions of psychopathy and conduct disorder influence judges? *Journal of Clinical Child and Adolescent Psychology*, 36, 1–14.

Murrie, D. C., Cornell, D. G., & McCoy, W. K. (2005). Psychopathy, conduct disorder, and stigma: Does diagnostic labeling influence juvenile probation officer recommendations? *Law and Human Behavior,* 29, 323–342.

Rieger, M., Stadtland, C., Freisleder, F. J., & Nedopil, N. (2006, June). The predictive validity of risk assessment instruments SAVRY and PCL: YV in a German sample of adolescent offenders. Paper presented to the 6th Annual International Association of Forensic Mental Health Services Conference, Amsterdam, The Netherlands.

Rosado. L. (Ed.) (2000). *Kids are different: How knowledge of adolescent development theory can aid decision-making in court.* Washington, DC: American Bar Association Juvenile Justice Center.

U.S. Department of Health and Human Services. (2001). *Youth violence: A report of the Surgeon General.* Rockville, MD: U.S. Department of Health and Human Services, Substance Abuse and Mental Health Services Administration, Center for Mental Health Services, National Institutes of Health, National Institute of Mental Health.

Viljoen, J., Scalora, M., Cuadra, L., Bader, S., Chavez, V., Ullman, D., & Lawrence, L. (2008). Assessing risk for violence in adolescents who have sexually offended: A comparison of the J-SOAP-II, J-SORRAT-II, and SAVRY. *Criminal Justice and Behavior, 35(1),* 5–23.

Welsh J., Schmidt F, McKinnon L, Chattha H., Meyers J. (2008). A comparative study of adolescent risk assessment instruments: predictive and incremental validity. *Assessment, 15,* 104–15.

Zahn, M. A., Brumbaugh, S., Steffensmeier, D., Feld, B. C., Morash, M., Chesney-Lind, M., Miller, J., Payne, A. A., Gottfredson, D. C., Kruttschnitt, C. (2008). Violence by teenage girls: Trends and context. Office of Justice Programs: Washington, DC. NCJ 218905.

5
Youth Level of Service/Case Management Inventory

ROBERT D. HOGE

The Youth Level of Service/Case Management Inventory (YLS/CMI) is designed to assist the professional in evaluating risk and needs in youthful offenders. The instrument is considered an actuarial risk/need assessment tool in that it is based on empirically derived content and yields quantitative estimates of risk and need levels. It may also be used like a structured professional judgment instrument to help guide clinical judgments about risk and needs. The format of the instrument is consistent with a considerable body of research summarized below that demonstrates the superiority of these approaches to unstructured clinical assessments.

The measure is useful in evaluating risk for both general and violent offending, and these risk assessments may be relevant in a variety of contexts, including pretrial diversion, detention, and disposition/sentencing. The measure is also designed to provide information about treatment need areas, and this can be important in case planning and management. The YLS/CMI is appropriate for use by a wide range of professionals, including psychologists, social workers, probation officers, and child care workers. Use of the instrument requires some background in child and adolescent psychology and specialized training in administering and interpreting the measure.

The YLS/CMI was originally developed using data collected from samples of Canadian juvenile offenders. However, the instrument has been successfully used with male and female youth from community and institutional settings, various ethnic groups (e.g., Canadian Aboriginal, African American), and in a variety of national contexts (e.g., United States, United Kingdom, Singapore, Croatia, Kenya).

Rationale for Development

The YLS/CMI is based on recent theories of the causes of criminal activity in youth (see Guerra, Williams, Tolan, & Modecki, 2008; Hoge, 2001) and on the considerable empirical research conducted on the causes and correlates of youth crime (see Heilbrun, Lee, & Cottle, 2005; Hoge, Guerra, & Boxer, 2008; Lipsey & Derzoni, 1998; Loeber & Dishion, 1983) (see Table 5.1 for a list of significant correlates of delinquent activity).

The nature of the links between the criminogenic factors and antisocial behavior is complicated, and the relevance of the factors to different gender, ethnic, and cultural groups not always well established. However, there is strong support for an association between these factors and delinquency.

A history of delinquent activity or conduct disorder, the first factor identified in Table 5.1, clearly constitutes a major predictor of future antisocial behavior. Youth demonstrating an established pattern of defiance and conduct problems are at the highest risk of continuing antisocial actions.

The second factor, and perhaps the most significant one, reflects the young person's attitudes, values, and beliefs regarding antisocial actions. These function as both direct and indirect determinants of behavior. When these attitudes and values are antisocial in nature, they are going to guide the individual to antisocial behaviors and serve as subsequent justifications for the actions.

Table 5.1 Major Risk/Need Factors

Proximal Factors
History of conduct disorder
Antisocial attitudes, values, and beliefs
Dysfunctional parenting
Dysfunctional behavior and personality traits
Poor school/vocational achievement
Antisocial peer associations
Substance abuse
Poor use of leisure time
Distal Factors
Criminal/psychiatric problems in family of origin
Family financial problems
Poor accommodations
Negative neighborhood environments

Aspects of the family environment, particularly those relating to parent–child relations, constitute another set of contributors. These generally impact indirectly on delinquent activity through their influence on the youth's attitudinal, personality, and behavioral dispositions. In other cases, though, the parent may have a more direct impact, for example, where lax supervision provides the youth with increased opportunities to engage in delinquent acts.

The fourth set of variables closely linked with youthful antisocial behavior reflects behavioral and personality attributes of the youth. Impulsivity, attentional problems, aggressivity, and addictive patterns of behavior are a few of these constructs. It is clear from research (and clinical experience) that a youth's engagement in a delinquent act in a particular situation reflects, to some extent, the more-or-less stable behavioral and personality attributes he or she brings to the situation.

Poor academic achievement, problems in school adjustment, and low educational aspirations have all been implicated in antisocial activities. The link between these variables and delinquent activity is complex, but it is clearly present.

Antisocial, procriminal associates constitute another type of variable that is closely linked with delinquency. These associates may include the youth's peers, parents, siblings, or others. Antisocial associates may impact the delinquent activity by influencing the youth's reactions to the immediate situation or, more indirectly, by fostering the adoption of antisocial attitudes and modes of behaviors.

Alcohol and/or drug use—delinquent behaviors themselves—are also linked with other types of delinquent activity. There may be direct links where, for example, a crime is committed to obtain the substance, or the effects may be more indirect where the use contributes to impulsive behaviors.

Finally, poor use of leisure time constitutes one of the important proximal factors. In many cases the youth simply has too much free time and engages in the antisocial behavior as a response to boredom.

These eight factors are identified as the most immediate or proximal correlates of juvenile antisocial behavior. A second set of factors (see Table 5.1) are considered more distal. They are important, but they tend to operate through their influence on the proximal factors, although the mechanisms of their influence is not always fully understood (Andrews & Bonta, 2006; Rutter, Giller, & Hagell, 1998). These include criminal or psychiatric problems in the family, financial or accommodation problems in the family, and negative neighborhood environments.

The application of this research on criminogenic factors to assessment and case planning with juvenile offenders depends on three key constructs (Andrews & Bonta, 2006; Andrews, Bonta, & Hoge, 1990). *Risk factors* refer to characteristics of the youth or his or her circumstances which increase the risk of antisocial behaviors. We can treat the criminogenic factors identified in Table 5.1 as the major risk factors.

Need factors refer to the subset of risk factors that can be changed through interventions and, if changed, reduce the chances of future antisocial behaviors. These are sometimes referred to as dynamic risk factors. To illustrate, a history of conduct disorder constitutes a risk factor; youths exhibiting such a history are at higher risk for delinquent behavior than those who do not. However, this is a static, historical variable and cannot be changed (although the probability of future antisocial behaviors can, of course, be reduced through effective interventions). Antisocial peer associations is another need or risk factor, but a dynamic one. That is, interventions which reduce these associations should reduce the youth's risk for reoffending (see Andrews & Bonta, 2006; Andrews et al., 1990; Hoge, 2001, for further discussions on these concepts).

The *responsivity factor,* the third relevant concept, refers to characteristics of the youth or his or her circumstances that, while not directly related to his or her delinquent activity, should be taken into account in case planning. Examples include reading ability, motivation to change, and emotional maturity. We can also include here strength or protective factors, such as the availability of a cooperative parent or an interest in sports.

The YLS/CMI is based on this work identifying the major criminogenic risk and need factors and on four principles of best practice (Andrews & Bonta, 2006; Andrews et al., 1990). The *assessment principle* states that interventions should be based on standardized assessments of risk, need, and responsivity because of their superiority to informal, clinical assessments in a variety of contexts (Bonta, 2002; Borum & Verhaagen, 2006; Grisso, 1998; Grove & Meehl, 1996).

The *risk principle of case classification* is based on the finding that effective programs provide more intensive services for high-risk cases and less intensive services for lower-risk cases. For example, in the case of probation, close and intensive monitoring should be reserved for offenders at greatest risk for continuing antisocial behavior. Similarly, lengthy and expensive treatment programs should involve those with high levels of need. The principle is important because limited resources should not be used with youth who do not require them. And overinvolvement of lower-risk youth in the juvenile justice system has been associated with their increased risk for reoffending (see, e.g., Dishion, McCord, & Poulin, 1999; Dodge, Dishion, & Lansford, 2006).

The *need principle of case classification* is based on the finding that effective programs target the specific needs of the youth; that is, they focus on eliminating or ameliorating those specific factors placing the youth at risk for antisocial behavior (Andrews et al., 1990). If the youth's delinquency relates to inadequate parenting and associations with antisocial peers, then interventions should focus on these areas of need. There are two considerations underlying this principle. First, by observing the principle we make maximum use of limited resources; we are going to provide services where they are most needed. Second, research discussed in the reviews and meta-analyses cited above demonstrates that interventions have their greatest impact when they focus on the needs of the individual. Unfortunately, many juvenile justice systems do not permit the necessary levels of individualization.

The *responsivity principle of case classification* states that the choice of interventions should reflect noncriminogenic factors that might also have a bearing on responses to interventions. For example, there is little point in placing a youth with limited reading skills in a cognitive behavior modification program requiring the reading of complicated material. Another illustration would involve a girl whose delinquent activities are clearly associated with drug abuse and her associations with an antisocial group of youth. However, she may also be suffering from depression and anxiety associated with past child abuse, and those conditions would have to be taken into account in planning an intervention, since they might interfere with the treatments provided for the peer group association and substance abuse risks.

We have also included strength or protective considerations as responsivity factors, and it is important to consider these in case planning. For example, if a cooperative parent is available, he or she should certainly be involved in the intervention. Similarly, a risk related to poor use of leisure time could be addressed where the youth has an interest in a particular sport.

Purposes of the Measure

The YLS/CMI is designed to aid the professional in assessing the youth's risk, need, and responsivity factors with the goal of insuring that the risk, need, and responsivity principles are observed in case planning. The instrument is particularly useful in informing correctional decisions regarding appropriate levels of security and supervision, and in planning interventions within community and institutional settings. It may also prove useful in early prevention programs where it is important to provide an early identification of risk and need factors.

Development of the instrument reflected several goals. First, we wanted to ensure that the measure included the full range of risk, need, and responsivity factors associated with delinquent behavior. Second, an effort was made to ensure a direct link between the risk/needs assessment and case planning to help ensure that the risk, need, and responsivity principles are observed. For this reason a case management component involving the identification of specific goals and means of achievement for the case is built directly into the instrument. A third goal was to incorporate a professional override feature to ensure that the final judgment about risk level and needs rests with the responsible professional, and that exceptional circumstances can be recognized. Generating support for the reliability and validity of the measure was the fourth goal, and the results of these efforts are described below. A fifth goal was to ensure that the instrument would be accepted as a useful and practical tool. To this end considerable consultation with probation officers, psychologists, and social workers was carried out before the final form of the instrument was developed. Finally, because the items in Part I are based largely on dynamic risk items, the instrument is also designed to assist in reviewing changes in risk/need levels over time.

Description of the YLS/CMI

The YLS/CMI User's Manual, Quick Score Forms, and supporting materials are available from Multi-Health Systems (Hoge & Andrews, 2002). The following is a description of the various sections of the measure.

Part I: Assessment of Risk and Needs

The 42 items in this section reflect the risk and need factors identified in the literature as most closely linked with general and violent youth crime. The eight domains of Part I are identified in Figure 5.1. Each domain is defined by a set of items that are correlates of juvenile offending.

The assessor indicates each item that describes the youth. An opportunity is also provided for indicating if a strength or protective factor is represented in a domain in recognition of the critical role played by these factors (Guerra et al., 2008). These are made at the same time as the risk assessment and are designed to reflect the presence of a positive factor that could be utilized in case planning. For example, we might record that there is an individual in the family who can represent a resource in case planning or that the youth shows a particular strength in an academic area.

Domains	Sample Items
1. Prior and Current Offenses	Three or more prior convictions
	Prior custody
2. Family Circumstances/Parenting	Inadequate supervision
	Poor relations (father-youth)
3. Education/Employment	Disruptive classroom behavior
	Truancy
4. Peer Relations	Some antisocial friends
	No/few positive friends
5. Substance Abuse	Chronic drug use
	Substance use linked to offenses
6. Leisure/Recreation	Limited organized activities
	No personal interests
7. Personality/Behavior	Physically aggressive
	Short attention span
8. Attitudes/Orientation	Antisocial/procriminal attitudes
	Callous, little concern for others

Figure 5.1 Domains and sample items for Part I of the Youth Level of Service/Case Management Inventory.

Part II: Summary of Risks and Needs

This section provides an opportunity to calculate risk/needs subtotals for each of the eight domains as well as an overall risk/needs score. The User's Manual also provides score ranges for low, moderate, high, and very high risk levels. These are based on a large sample of Canadian male and female juvenile offenders. Agencies are also advised for form their own normative scores. This is because the nature of the samples may differ, as well as policies regarding the treatment of offenders. Developing local norms ensures that the ranges are relevant to the agency or jurisdiction.

Part III: Assessment of Other Needs and Special Considerations

This section provides an opportunity to record information about issues that, while not directly related to the youth's delinquent activity, may have a bearing on development of an intervention plan. These include the responsivity factors discussed above.

Items are divided into two categories. The first includes circumstances relating to parenting and the family such as "drug/alcohol abuse," "financial/accommodation problems," and "cultural/ethnic" issues. The second includes characteristics of the youth such as "physical disability," "depressed," and "shy/withdrawn."

Part IV: Professional's Assessment of the Juvenile's General Risk/Need Level

An opportunity for a professional override is provided in this section to ensure that special or exceptional circumstances are accommodated, and final decisions regarding the treatment of the youth rests with the responsible professional. In cases where they do override the risk rating, professionals are to describe the basis for such. An example is the case where a youth scored at the moderate risk/need level, but, because of the recent death of a grandfather who was a key to holding the family together, the probation officer concluded that the level of risk should be elevated to high. The inclusion of this section is included to ensure that decisions are not dictated in a rigid way by a score from a single assessment instrument.

Part V: Contact Level

This section provides an opportunity to indicate the level of supervision appropriate in the particular case. This will normally reflect the overall level of risk/need recorded for the case. The categories are Administrative/Paper, Minimum Supervision, Medium Supervision, and Maximum Supervision.

Part VI: Case Management Plan

The final section is used to facilitate formulation of case plans. The professional first identifies a set of goals for the youth, which reflect the specific needs identified in Part I. If, for example, chronic alcohol use is identified as a need, then one goal should be to address the pattern of alcohol use. Next, the means for achieving the goal are identified in specific and concrete terms. For example, the means of achieving the reduction in alcohol use would be addressed by providing one-on-one counseling to the youth twice per week and ensuring attendance at AA meetings.

Scoring, Interpretation, and Implementation of the YLS/CMI

The YLS/CMI is designed for use by frontline staff members in juvenile justice and correctional settings. This includes psychologists, social workers, probation officers, and other youth workers. It is also useful with some modifications in school and mental health settings where the criminal history domain may not be relevant and where separate norms would have to be developed. Although professional training in a mental health area is not required for use of the measure, specialized training in administering, scoring, and interpreting the measure is necessary.

Scoring items on the YLS/CMI should be based on as broad a range of information as possible. A comprehensive interview with the youth and an examination of available file information will be the primary bases for scoring. An interview guide associated with the instrument is available. Interviews with collateral informants such as parents, teachers, probation officers, and others should be utilized when available. Reconciling contradictory information is left to the discretion of the professional completing the assessment.

When a more intensive psychological assessment of the youth has been conducted—for example, in cases in which serious psychological or developmental deficits are suspected, the test results can be used to inform YLS/CMI judgments (Hoge, 2008; Hoge & Andrews, 1996a). For example, the youth might be administered standardized intelligence, achievement, and personality tests. The results of these tests, along with the interview and file information, could be used as a basis for identifying risk/need factors through the YLS/CMI.

Total and domain scores from the YLS/CMI are designed to assist in case planning. Several guidelines can be offered for establishing the goals and means of achieving goals:

- The goals of the intervention should be directly relevant to the specific risks and needs of the youth as identified in Part I.
- The goals should be stated in concrete terms. For example, the goal might be to improve school performance and attendance over a four-week period.
- The means of achievement should also be stated in concrete terms. To illustrate, if the goal is improvement in school performance, then specific interventions should be indicated (e.g., enroll in a homework club, access tutorial help with reading, establish a token economy reward program).
- Goals and means of achievement should be timely. Young people do not think in terms of long-term events; it is important to be able to evaluate progress in achieving goals within fairly limited time frames.
- Goals should be realistic. Youth must make progress in meeting their needs, but there is no point in setting them up for failure.

- Progress on the goals should be reevaluated at periodic intervals; a case review version of the YLS/CMI is available.

Care should be taken in introducing an instrument such as the YLS/CMI into a juvenile justice or probation system. The following are some important implementation guidelines:

- A commitment to the use of standardized assessments should be included in the mission statement of the agency.
- All professionals in the system should be provided with an introduction to the YLS/CMI, including judges, prosecuting attorneys, police, and other relevant personnel. This does not require intensive training in the application of the measure, but it does involve familiarizing them with its purpose.
- The instrument should be introduced into the system in a rational manner that takes account of existing procedures. Efforts should be made to reduce redundancy in the assessment process.
- Comprehensive training should be provided to all professionals using the measure by a qualified trainer. The training should involve extensive practice with the measure and checks to ensure that adequate levels of inter-rater agreement are being achieved.
- A resource person should be available to answer questions about the use of the measure and to monitor quality control.
- Periodic retraining should be provided where needed.

Several cautions should be observed in using an instrument such as the YLS/CMI. First, the measure should only be used by individuals with training in scoring, interpreting, and applying the measure. Second, scores from the instrument should not be used in a rigid way in making decisions. For example, a total YLS/CMI score should not be used as a cutoff for determining a custody assignment. Final decisions about the youth should rest with the responsible professional and not a single assessment tool. Third, the use of the instrument as a basis for "net widening" should be guarded against. This problem may arise where youth with high risk/need scores are assigned severe dispositions regardless of other considerations.

Research With the YLS/CMI

The following illustrates some of the research that has been conducted with the YLS/CMI (additional information is provided in the *User's Manual*, (Hoge & Andrews, 2003).

Reliability

Several researchers have reported reliability data from research based on samples of adjudicated offenders. Rowe (2002) reported a coefficient alpha value of .91 for the total risk/need score and a mean coefficient alpha value of .72 for the eight subscales. Schmidt, Hoge, and Gomes (2005) obtained a mean coefficient alpha value of .69 for the subscales.

Poluchowicz, Jung, and Rawana (2000) reported an inter-rater agreement coefficient of .75 for the overall risk/need score based on 33 cases scored by two independent raters. These researchers also reported adequate inter-rater agreement for all subscales except Leisure/Recreation (*median* r = .70). Schmidt et al. (2005) reported inter-rater agreement ranging from .61 to .85 (*median* r = .76) based on 29 cases.

Construct Validity

Construct validity is supported in several studies reporting relations between YLS/CMI scores and measures of externalizing disorders. Perfect agreement is not expected in these cases

Table 5.2 Correlations of Total YLS/CMI Scores With Select Assessment Measures

	Total YLS/CMI Score
Parent CBCL–Total Problem Score	.46***
Parent CBCL–Externalizing Score	.54***
Parent CBCL–Internalizing Score	.34***
Youth CBCL–Total Problem Score	.46***
Youth CBCL–Externalizing Score	.53***
Youth CBCL–Internalizing Score	.32***
Parent SSRS Standard Problem Behavior Score	.50***
Jesness Asocial Index	.47***
PESQ Total Problem Severity Score	.47***

Source: Schmidt et al., 2005.

Note: *N*s range from 29 to 71,*** $p < .001$. CBCL = Child Behavior Checklist; SSRS = Social Skills Rating System; PESQ = Personal Experience Screening Questionnaire.

because the YLS/CMI represents a broader construct than the alternative measures. However, the analyses do bear on the ability of YLS/CMI scores to reflect a conduct disorder construct.

Schmidt et al. (2005) reported significant correlations between total Risk/Need scores from the YLS/CMI and parallel scores from the following parent and self-report measures of behavioral maladjustment: the child and parent versions of the Child Behavior Checklist (Achenbach & Rescorla, 2001), Jesness Asocial Index (Jesness, 2003), Social Skills Rating System (Gresham & Elliott, 1990), and Personal Experience Screening Questionnaire (Winters, 1991) (see Table 5.2).

Rowe (2002) also provided correlations between total YLS/CMI risk/need scores and scores from a variety of alternative indices of behavioral pathology: Total, Factor 1, and Factor 2 scores from the Psychopathy Checklist–Youth Version (Hare, Forth, & Kosson, 1994); the Childhood and Adolescent Taxon Scale (Quinsey, Harris, Rice, & Cormier, 2006); the Disruptive Behavior Disorder Rating Scales (Pelham, Gnagy, Greenslade, & Milich, 1992); and a conduct disorder symptom scale based on DSM-IV items. He reported statistically significant relations between YLS/CMI total scores and each of the alternative indices.

Concurrent Validity

Hoge and Andrews (1996b) examined the tool's concurrent validity by comparing YLS/CMI subscores across three disposition categories (probation, open custody, secure custody). As expected, risk/need scores increased linearly and significantly across those three disposition categories. Jung (1996) compared a group of adjudicated offenders with a sample of high school students who had had no involvement with the juvenile justice system. The delinquent group obtained significantly higher total and subscale scores than the nondelinquent group.

Predictive Validity

A number of researchers have presented correlations between YLS/CMI total and subscores and indices of general and violent reoffending based on prospective designs (see Table 5.3).

The reoffending indices in those cases are based on official records and reflect general recidivism. The correlation values support the predictive validity of the total scores and subscores. Separate analyses by gender were reported in two of the studies. Schmidt et al. (2005) found a significant correlation between total scores and reoffending for males but a nonsignificant correlation for a small sample of females. Rowe (2002) reported significant correlations between

Table 5.3 Sample Correlations Between YLS/CMI Total Scores and Subscores and Indices of Reoffending

YLS/CMI Subscore	Hoge & Andrews (1996)		Rowe (2002)		Schmidt et al. (2005)	
	r	*N*	*r*	*N*	*r*	*N*
Prior Convictions/Dispositions			.25**	408	.05	110
Family/Parenting	.27**	331	.18**	408	.30**	110
Education/Employment	.22**	331	.36**	408	.22*	110
Peer Relations	.14*	331	.35**	408	.30**	110
Substance Abuse	.12*	331	.14*	408	.18	110
Leisure/Recreation	.13*	331	.27**	408	.31**	110
Personality/Behavior	.21**	331	.32**	408	.23*	110
Attitudes/Orientation	.29**	331	.32**	408	.31**	110
Total YLS/CMI	.30**	331	.41***	408	.32**	110

Note: * = $p < .05$, ** = $p < .01$, *** = $p < .001$.

total YLS/CMI scores and indices of both general and violent reoffending for males, although for females the correlations were significant only for general reoffending.

Categorical analyses were reported in two studies. Jung and Rawana (1999) divided their sample into those who had and had not reoffended within six months following conclusion of their dispositions. The total YLS/CMI score was significantly higher for the recidivists (M = 15.74, SD = 8.01) than for the nonrecidivists (M = 9.22, SD = 7.46) ($F(1, 249) = 38.55$, $p < .001$; Cohen's $d = .88$). The researchers also compared the two groups' scores from the eight subscales and reported that the scores were significantly higher in each case for the reoffending group. YLS/CMI total scores and subscores were significantly predictive of reoffending for males and females and native and nonnative samples. Gossner and Wormith (2007) also reported significant predictive validity values for both genders and native and nonnative samples.

Costigan and Rawana (1999) analyzed data based on a follow-up of subjects of the Jung and Rawana (1999) study. They employed multivariate analyses in which youths were divided into three risk groups on the basis of YLS/CMI total scores and subsores (low, moderate, high). The mean number of new offenses differed as a function of the total score: Low Risk (M = 3.4, SD = 8.0), Moderate Risk (M = 5.5, SD = 5.4), and High Risk (M = 12.5, SD = 9.8). The differences were significant: $F(2,192) = 18.98$, $p < .001$. Mean reoffending rates also varied across three risk categories where calculated separately for each of the eight subscores. Risk scores were predictive of reoffending for both males and females and native and nonnative samples.

Several researchers have also calculated predictive accuracy analyses. Jung (1996; Jung & Rawana, 1999) used a linear discriminant analysis based on the eight YLS/CMI subscores to predict reoffending. The analysis yielded a 75.38% correct classification value (RIOC = 20.10%). Schmidt et al. (2005) reported an Accuracy Rate of 57% (RIOC = 14%) in the prediction of general offending and an Accuracy Rate of 56% (RIOC = 9%) in the prediction of serious reoffending. A similar result was reported for the prediction of violent reoffending by Catchpole and Gretton (2003). Rowe (2002) assessed the predictive power of total risk scores through survival analyses. Youths classified at high YLS/CMI risk levels recidivated at a significantly faster rate across time (Log rank = 60.50, $p < .001$).

Hoge and Andrews (1996b) examined the relationship between YLS/CMI scores and adjustment ratings made by probation officers subsequent to intake. This included ratings of compliance with probation conditions and overall adjustment while on probation. Both YLS/CMI total risk/need scores and subscores correlated significantly with the adjustment ratings; higher risk/ need scores were associated with lower levels of compliance and postdisposition adjustment (Prior and Current Offenses were not included in the analysis).

The predictive validity studies discussed above were all based on samples of Canadian youth. However, support for the predictive validity of the YLS/CMI has also been reported in research conducted with samples drawn from the United States (e.g., Flores, Travis, & Latessa, 2003; Holsinger, Lowenkamp, & Latessa, 2006; Shepherd, Green, & Omobien, 2005), Australia (e.g., Thompson & Putnins, 2003), and the United Kingdom (e.g., Marshall, Egan, English, and Jones, 2006).

Dynamic Validity

Rowe (2002) evaluated the predictive validity of YLS/CMI scores by analyzing associations between changes in YLS/CMI scores from intake to case termination and reoffending indices. Increased risk/need scores were associated with higher reoffending rates than lower risk/ need scores. In other words, changes (increases) in YLS/CMI scores were associated with future delinquent activity.

Case Studies

Two case studies will be presented for illustrative purposes, one representing a moderate risk/need case and the other a high risk/need case. Both are adapted from cases presented in the YLS/CMI User's Manual (Hoge & Andrews, 2002).

MODERATE-RISK CASE

Jack is a 14-year-old male convicted of three counts of breaking and entering and theft. The YLS/CMI was completed by the probation officer as part of the predisposition report prepared for the court. The instrument was completed based on data gathered by way of face-to-face interviews with Jack, his mother, and probation officer; telephone interviews with Jack's school principal and two of his teachers; and file review. Jack was friendly and cooperative during the interview, although reluctant to reveal some information.

Risk/Needs Scores (Parts I and II)

Jack has been convicted of three counts of breaking and entering and theft and has seven prior convictions for similar offenses. The value of the stolen items was generally not significant. He has served two periods of probation, with numerous infractions during those probation periods. He obtained a score of 3/5 on the Prior and Current Offenses/Disposition domain, placing him in the high risk/need range for this category.

Jack is an only child living with his mother, and there has been no contact with the biological father for some years. There is a positive bond between mother and youth, but the mother has a history of psychiatric and substance abuse problems, and an abusive common-law partner lived in the home until about two years ago. The mother appears to care about Jack, but her parenting practices have been very poor. Jack received a score of 5/6 on the Family Circumstances/Parenting domain, placing him in the high risk/need range for this category.

The youth has never presented as a behavior problem in school and has generally related well to teachers and peers. Although of apparently at least normal intelligence, his academic performance has generally been below average. Truancy has been a significant problem in the past. His score on the Education/Employment domain was 2/7, placing him in the moderate range.

Jack is generally described as a loner, with few friends. However, his most recent offenses were conducted while in the company of an antisocial peer, and he appears to have few prosocial acquaintances or friends. His score of 3/4 on the Peer Relations domain places him in the high risk/need range for this category.

There is no evidence of any form of substance abuse, and his score of 0 on the Substance Abuse domain places him in the low risk/need category.

Jack spends most of his time alone and does not seem to have any interest beyond playing video games. His score on the Leisure/Recreation items was 3/3, placing him in the high risk/need range.

None of the items on the Personality/Behavior domain (e.g., physically aggressive, poor frustration tolerance) was present, indicating a low score on this domain. A Strength was indicated in this case, because the youth presented as friendly and cooperative.

Two items indicating a lack of motivation for addressing his issues were present on the Attitudes/Orientation domain, indicating a moderate risk/need score for the subscale (2/5).

Jack's Overall Total Risk/Need score was 18, placing him in the moderate risk/need range. His standings on the individual domains were as follows:

- Current Offenses/Dispositions: 3/5 [moderate]
- Family Circumstances/Parenting: 5/6 [high]
- Education/Employment: 2/7 [moderate]
- Peer Relations: 3/4 [moderate]
- Prior and Substance Abuse: 0/5 [low]
- Leisure/Recreation: 3/3 [high]
- Personality/Behavior: 0/7 [low]
- Attitudes/Orientation: 2/5 [moderate]

Personality/Behavior was identified as a strength and protective factor.

Assessment of Other Needs and Special Considerations (Part III)

Items checked under Family/Parents included marital conflict, financial problems, and significant family trauma (relating to the recent death of the maternal grandfather). Items checked under Youth included underachievement, victim of neglect, shy/withdrawn, and poor social skills.

Your Assessment of the Juvenile's General Risk/Need Level (Part IV)

The probation officer agreed with the moderate overall risk/need score.

Contact Level (Part V)

Intensive probation supervision was recommended, along with consideration of out-of-home placement.

Case Management Plan (Part VI)

Three initial goals and corresponding interventions were recommended. The first goal was an increased involvement in external activities, and Jack was encouraged to continue to involvement in Boys and Girls Club activities and follow up an interest in sea cadets. The second goal was to improve school performance, and Jack was enrolled in a special after-school program for low-achieving students, which also involved some recreational activities. The final goal was to improve the coping and parenting skills of the mother. The means of achievement in this case was to encourage the mother, which was facilitated by encouraging Jack's mother to continue contact with a community mental health worker.

* * * *

HIGH-RISK CASE

Michael is a 17-year-old male convicted of several counts of assault. The YLS/CMI was completed by the probation officer as part of the predisposition report for the court. The instrument was completed based on a file review (prior probation and police reports), an interview with Michael's mother, a telephone interview with a previous principal of Michael, and a comprehensive interview with Michael. Michael was friendly and cooperative throughout the assessment process. His behavior while in detention was without problems.

Risk/Need Scores (Parts I and II)

Michael has been convicted of two counts of felony and one count of misdemeanor assaults stemming from two incidents in which Michael was among a group who forced themselves into homes and attacked residents. The accused and victims were known to one another, and no serious injuries resulted. Michael's criminal history includes convictions for robbery, burglary, disorderly conduct, and assaults. He has received one secure custody disposition and four probation dispositions. He has three violations for probation violations. Michael obtained a score of 5/5 on the Prior and Current Offenses/Disposition domain, placing him in the high risk/need range.

Michael lives with his mother and three siblings, and the family has had no contact with the father for some years. The family is cohesive, and the children and mother obviously care for one another. However, the mother has a history of substance abuse (although abstinent for some months) and a minor delinquency history. Although a caring person, the mother's parenting practices have been dysfunctional, and the children are essentially out of control. Michael obtained a score of 5/6 on the Family Circumstances/Parenting domain, placing him in the high risk/need range. A Strength was also indicated due to the mother's concern and commitment to addressing the family's problems.

Michael has recently been expelled from school for fighting with other students. His educational history reveals a pattern of low academic achievement and some behavior problems. Educational assessments indicate that he is at least of normal intelligence, and there are no obvious learning disabilities. Michael is out of school and making no efforts to find a job. His score on the Education/Employment domain was 5/7, placing him in the high risk/need range.

The youth has no prosocial friends and associates almost exclusively with a group of antisocial individuals, some of whom have minor involvement with the juvenile justice system. His score on the Peer Relations domain was 4/4, placing him in the high risk/need category.

There is some suspicion that Michael has been involved in a minor way in the drug trade, but no proof was available. He admits to occasional use of cannabis, but there is no evidence of other forms of substance abuse. His score on the Substance Abuse domain was 1/5, placing him in the moderate range.

Michael is not involved in any organized activities and does not participate in a positive way in any hobbies or sports. Mostly he just "hangs around" with his friends. He scored 3/3 on the Leisure/Recreation domain, placing him in the high risk/need category.

Michael has a history of verbal and physical assaults, and it is apparent that he has difficulty in controlling his emotions. He expresses little remorse for the victims of his assaults, feeling they deserved what they got. He obtained a score of 4/7 on the Personality/Behavior domain, placing him in the moderate risk/need category. On the other hand, the probation officer who dealt with Michael indicated that, in spite of all of his problems, he came across as a likeable youth and that adults who have dealt with him generally saw considerable potential for improvement. For this reason, a Strength was indicated.

Because of his antisocial attitudes, defiant behavior, and generally passive responses to prior helping efforts, Michael obtained a score of 3/5 on the Attitudes/Orientation domain placing him in the moderate range.

Michael's total YLS/CMI score was 31, placing him at the high end of the high risk/need range. His scores on the eight domains may be summarized as follows:

- Current Offenses/Dispositions: 5/5 [high]
- Family Circumstances/Parenting: 5/6 [high]
- Education/Employment: 5/7 [high]
- Peer Relations: 4/4 [high]
- Prior and Substance Abuse: 1/5 [moderate]
- Leisure/Recreation: 3/3 [high]
- Personality/Behavior: 4/7 [moderate]
- Attitudes/Orientation: 3/5 [moderate]

Strengths were indicated for Family Circumstances/Parenting and Personality/Behavior.

Assessment of Other Needs and Special Considerations (Part III)

Four items were checked under the Family/Parent category: chronic history of offenses, drug/alcohol abuse, financial/accommodation problems, and cultural/ethnic issues. Two items were checked in the Youth category: underachievement, and peers outside age range.

Your Assessment of the Juvenile's General Risk/Need Level (Part IV)

The probation officer in this case agreed with the high overall risk/need range.

Contact Level (Part V)

Maximum supervision was indicated as the appropriate contact level in this case.

Case Management Plan (Part VI)

The disposition in this case involved a custody sentence suspended conditionally upon attendance at and successful completion of a day treatment program for high-risk youth and young adults, accompanied by close probation supervision.

Three initial goals were identified. The first was to reduce Michael's anger level and help him develop anger management skills by way of counseling in the day treatment program and participation in an anger management program. The second goal was directed toward improvements in educational skills and attitudes, with the intervention involving counseling and attendance at the special education classes available in the program. The third goal was to improve the family situation through encouraging the mother's continued attendance at a drug counseling program and the family's participation in counseling available from Family Service Agency.

Conclusion

Valid and comprehensive intake assessments are critical for the delivery of effective services to the juvenile offender. The careful identification of risk and need factors is needed to guide decisions about appropriate levels of supervision and security, and about the interventions required to reduce the youth's risk for engaging in future antisocial activities. Research and clinical experience also support the importance of basing these assessments on standardized instruments. The YLS/CMI has been presented as an example of such an instrument.

The YLS/CMI has a number of strengths in addition to its value in assessing risk and need factors. For example, it can help to ensure consistency in the assessment of delinquent youth, since all professionals are basing their evaluation on the same factors. In the same sense the measure can facilitate communication among professionals, since all are using a similar terminology to describe the risk and need characteristics of the youth. Finally, use of an instrument of this type facilitates transparent and defensible decision making that is research based.

There are also advantages for management in the use of the YLS/CMI. For example, it can assist in systematically collecting a broad range of information about youth and the kinds of interventions they are provided. This information may be important in audits of agency activities and in advocating for funding. Where reassessments of YLS/CMI scores are conducted, information can be of value in evaluating the effectiveness of the agency's interventions. Finally, information collected with the instrument can assist in allocating resources within the agency. For example, work loads can be adjusted on the basis of the risk/need levels of the clients being dealt with by the worker.

There are, however, a number of areas in which further research is required. While some predictive validity studies using violent reoffending as the outcome variable have been reported, much of the research has focused on general indices of reoffending, and additional information about the prediction of violent offending is needed. As well, future research should focus on more specific indices of violent offending, taking into account the seriousness of the offense, the nature of the aggression, the circumstances of the action, and characteristics of the victim.

While data are available regarding the validity of the YLS/CMI for males and females and certain ethnic and minority groups, additional research is needed for ethnic and racial minority group members. Research is now under way examining the predictive validity of the scores for Hispanic American youth and young people in other cultures (for example, Singapore, Russia, Taiwan), and these results should be available shortly.

Information on links between the risk/need assessment, the type of intervention provided, and the impact of the intervention on changes in risk/need levels is also important. Can the conduct of an assessment based on the YLS/CMI actually lead to reductions in risk and needs?

References

Achenbach, T. M., & Rescorla, L. A. (2001). *Manual for the ASEBA School Age Forms and Profiles.* Burlington, VT: University of Vermont Research Center for Children Youth and Families.

Andrews, D. A., & Bonta, J. (2006). *The psychology of criminal conduct* (4th ed.). Florence, KY: Anderson.

Andrews, D. A., Bonta, J., & Hoge, R. D. (1990). Classification for effective rehabilitation: Rediscovering psychology. *Criminal Justice and Behavior, 17,* 19–52.

Bonta, J. (2002). Offender risk assessment: Guidelines for selection and use. *Criminal Justice and Behavior, 29,* 355–379.

Borum, R., & Verhaagen, D. (2006). *Assessing and managing violence risk in youth.* New York: Guilford Press.

Catchpole, R. E. H., & Gretton, H. M. (2003). The predictive validity of risk assessment with violent young offenders: A one-year examination of criminal outcome. *Criminal Justice and Behavior, 30,* 688–708.

Costigan, S., & Rawana, E. (1999, June). Critical evaluation of the long-term validity of the Risk/Need Assessment Form. Paper presented at the Annual Conference of the Canadian Psychological Association, Montreal, Quebec.

Dishion, T. J., McCord, J., & Poulin, F. (1999). When interventions harm: Peer groups and problem behavior. *American Psychologist, 54,* 755–764.

Dodge, K. A., Dishion, T. J., & Lansford, J. E. (Eds.). (2006) *Deviant peer influences in programs for youth.* New York: Guilford Press.

Flores, A. W., Travis, L. F., & Latessa, E. J. (2003). Case classification for juvenile corrections: An assessment of the Youth Level of Service/Case Management Inventory (YLS/CMI). Final Grant Report, National Institute of Justice, U. S. Department of Justice.

Gossner, D., & Wormith, J. S. (2007). The prediction of recidivism among young offenders in Saskatchewan. *Canadian Journal of Police and Security Services, 5,* 1–13.

Gresham, F. M., & Elliott, S. N. (1990). *Social Skills Rating Scale.* Bloomington, IN: Pearson.

Grisso, T. (1998). *Forensic evaluation of juveniles.* Sarasota, FL: Professional Resource Press.

Grove, W. M., & Meehl, P. E. (1996). Comparative efficiency of informal (subjective, impressionistic) and formal (mechanical, algorithmic) prediction procedures: The clinical-statistical controversy. *Psychology, Public Policy, and the Law, 2,* 293–323.

Guerra, N. G., Williams, K., Tolan, P., & Modecki, K. (2008). Theoretical and research advances in understanding the causes of juvenile offending. In R. D. Hoge, N. G. Guerra, & P. Boxer (Eds.), *Treating the juvenile offender.* New York: Guilford Press.

Hare, R. D., Forth, A., & Kosson, D. S. (1994). *The Psychopathy Checklist–Youth Version.* Toronto, ON: Multi-Health Systems.

Heilbrun, K., Lee, R., & Cottle, C. (2005). Risk factors and intervention outcomes: Meta-analyses of juvenile offending. In K. Heilbrun, N. Goldstein, & R. Redding (Eds.), *Juvenile delinquency: Prevention, assessment, and intervention* (pp. 111–133). New York: Oxford.

Hoge, R. D. (2001). *The juvenile offender: Theory, research, and applications.* Boston, MA: Kluwer.

Hoge, R. D. (2008). Assessment in juvenile justice systems. In R. D. Hoge, N. G. Guerra, & P. Boxer (Eds.), *Treating the juvenile offender.* New York: Guilford Press.

Hoge, R. D., & Andrews, D. A. (1996a). *Assessing the youthful offender: Issues and techniques.* New York, NY: Plenum Press.

Hoge, R. D., & Andrews, D. A. (1996b, August). Assessing risk and need factors in the youthful offender. Paper presented at the Annual Conference of the American Psychological Association, Toronto, Ontario.

Hoge, R. D., & Andrews, D. A. (2002). *Youth Level of Service/Case Management Inventory users' manual.* North Tonawanda, NY: Multi-Health Systems.

Hoge, R. D., Guerra, N. G., & Boxer, P. (Eds.). (2008) *Treating the juvenile offender.* New York: Guilford Press.

Holsinger, A. M., Lowenkamp, C. T., & Latessa, E. J. (2006). Predicting institutional misconduct using the Youth Level of Service/Case Management Inventory. *American Journal of Criminal Justice, 30,* 267–284.

Jesness, C. F. (2003). *Jesness Inventory–Revised.* Toronto, ON: Multi-Health Systems.

Jung, S. (1996). Critical evaluation of the validity of the Risk/Need Assessment with Aboriginal young offenders in Northwestern Ontario. Unpublished Master's thesis, Lakehead University, Thunder Bay, ON.

Jung, S., & Rawana, E. P. (1999). Risk-need assessment of juvenile offenders. *Criminal Justice and Behavior, 26,* 69–89.

Lipsey, M. W., & Derzon, J. H. (1998). Predictors of violent or serious delinquency in adolescence and early adulthood: A synthesis of longitudinal research. In R. Loeber & D. Farrington (Eds.), *Serious and violent juvenile offenders: Risk factors and successful interventions* (pp. 86–105). Thousand Oaks, CA: Sage.

Loeber, R., & Dishion, T. J. (1983). Early predictors of male delinquency: A review. *Psychological Bulletin, 94,* 68–99.

Marshall, J. Egan, V., English, M., & Jones, R. M. (2006). The relative validity of psychopathy versus risk/needs-based assessments in the prediction of adolescent offending behaviour. *Legal and Criminological Psychology, 14,* 197–210.

Pelham, W. E., Gnagy, E. M., Greenslade, K. E., & Milich, R. (1992). Teacher ratings of *DSM-III-R* symptoms for the disruptive behavior disorders. *Journal of the American Academy of Child and Adolescent Psychiatry, 31,* 210–218.

Poluchowicz, S., Jung, S., & Rawana, E. P. (2000, June). The inter-rater reliability of the Ministry Risk/Need Assessment Form for juvenile offenders. Paper presented at the Annual Conference of the Canadian Psychological Association, Montreal, Quebec.

Quinsey, V. L., Harris, G. T., Rice, M. E., & Cormier, C. A. (2006). *Violent offenders: Appraising and managing risk* (2nd ed.). Washington, DC: American Psychological Association.

Rowe, R. (2002). Predictors of criminal offending: Evaluating measures of risk/needs, psychopathy, and disruptive behavior disorders. Unpublished doctoral dissertation, Department of Psychology, Carleton University, Ottawa, ON.

Rutter, M., Giller, H., & Hagell, A. (1998). *Antisocial behavior by young people.* Cambridge, UK: Cambridge University Press.

Schmidt, F., Hoge, R. D., & Gomes, L. (2005). Reliability and validity analyses of the Youth Level of Service/Case Management Inventory. *Criminal Justice and Behavior, 32,* 329–344.

Shepherd, J. B., Green, K., & Omobien, E. O. (2005). Level of functioning and recidivism risk among adolescent offenders. *Adolescence, 40,* 23–32.

Thompson, A. P., & Putnins, A. L. (2003). Risk-need assessment in inventories for juvenile offenders in Australia. *Psychiatry, Psychology, and Law, 10,* 324–333.

Winters, K. C. (1991). *The Personal Experience Questionnaire.* Los Angeles, CA: Western Psychological Services.

Part II
Adult Risk

6
The Violence Risk Appraisal Guide and Sex Offender Risk Appraisal Guide for Violence Risk Assessment and the Ontario Domestic Assault Risk Assessment and Domestic Violence Risk Appraisal Guide for Wife Assault Risk Assessment

MARNIE E. RICE, GRANT T. HARRIS, and N. ZOE HILTON

In this chapter we describe a family of violence risk assessments developed using similar techniques. All this work is most fully presented in two books (Hilton, Harris, & Rice, 2008; Quinsey, Harris, Rice, & Cormier, 2006). Here, we first describe two actuarial instruments for the prediction of violent recidivism and then present an actuarial system for the prediction of wife assault recidivism. Among psychologists, the impetus for developing actuarial violence risk assessments began more than a half century ago with the recognition that actuarial methods are generally more accurate than clinical judgment, experience, and intuition (Meehl, 1954; see also Ægisdóttir et al., 2006; Grove & Meehl, 1996) and this is especially true for violence risk (Hanson & Morton-Bourgon, 2007; Hilton, Harris, & Rice, 2006).

The risk assessments described in this chapter contrast with most in this book in at least one of three principal ways. First, the present tools are all actuarial inasmuch as the items were selected based on their observed relationships with outcome in specific development samples, and they are accompanied by tables of measured recidivism rates (experience tables) and percentiles also based on large samples. Actuarial tools differ from certain others (e.g., raw total score on the SVR-20) that might use formulaic methods to yield a total, but did not use measured relationships in specific development samples to arrive at the formula and do not provide both experience/outcome tables and percentile norms, the defining properties of "actuarial."

Second, the present actuarial tools and many of the others are alike in relying on clinical skill to evaluate some items, but the present tools differ from most in advising no modification of the score based on clinical judgment. This supplementary clinical discretion has been recommended by developers of some instruments to lower practitioner resistance, incorporate rare or idiosyncratic risk factors, allow application to new samples, adjust for offender aging, give credit for putative progress in therapy, recalibrate for possible differences in base rates, accommodate fear of making an error, and accede to the idea that such review is a professional responsibility. Recommendations and claims aside, no evidence supports contentions that any alteration (based on clinical judgment) of actuarial scores, as defined above, results in more accurate decisions compared to actuarially derived scores alone. Indeed, because there is good reason to believe such revision generally results in decreased accuracy (see Grove & Meehl, 1996; Hanson & Morton-Bourgon, 2007; Harris & Rice, 2007a; Hilton & Simmons, 2001; Janus & Meehl, 1997;

Quinsey, Harris et al., 2006), we reversed our initial position which permitted small clinical adjustments to actuarial scores (c.f., Webster, Harris, Rice, Cormier, & Quinsey, 1994).

Third, the present violence risk assessments do not include items labeled "dynamic." Unfortunately, this term lacks a clear consensual meaning, such that identical constructs are called static in some assessments (e.g., sexual deviance in the Sex Offender Risk Appraisal Guide, SORAG) but dynamic in others (e.g., sexual deviance in the Violence Risk Scale–Sexual Offender Version, VRS-SO, Chapter 7 of this volume). The definition we adopt for a dynamic factor is one that can be shown to change and that, when changed, alters risk (Hanson & Harris 2000; Quinsey, Harris, Rice, & Cormier, 1998, 2006; Rice, in press; see also the "causal" dynamic risk factor in Douglas & Skeem, 2005). Furthermore, dynamic factors are of two types. "Stable" dynamic factors are ones that act much like static factors inasmuch as, once changed, they alter long-term risk, whereas "acute" or "fluctuating" dynamic factors are ones that must be measured very frequently because they change (and affect risk) during follow-up (Hanson & Harris, 2000; Quinsey, Harris et al., 2006). Returning to the above example of sexual deviance, empirical evaluations indicate that, while initial or one-time measures of sexual deviance predict recidivism among sex offenders, prerelease changed measures of sexual deviance do not (e.g., Rice, Quinsey, & Harris, 1991), and thus sexual deviance does not meet our definition of a dynamic risk factor. In fact, there have as yet been no empirical demonstrations that prerelease changes in any risk factors (including those produced by therapy) are actually dynamic as defined here (c.f., Hanson, Harris, Scott, & Helmus, 2007). That is, there have been no demonstrations that prerelease or posttreatment changes in such putatively dynamic variables make a statistically significant addition to the predictive accuracy for violence achieved by static items alone.* By contrast, within-subject fluctuations in various states (e.g., attitudes, moods, intoxication) have been reported to indicate the imminence of violence, especially among those whose static risk is high (Mulvey et al., 2006; Quinsey, Coleman, Jones, & Altrows, 1997; Quinsey, Jones, Book, & Barr, 2006; Skeem et al., 2006). Thus, there is some evidence that such acute or fluctuating dynamic variables aid in anticipating when a high-risk offender might violently recidivate, although work on incorporating these findings into formal assessment has not been completed. Actuarial systems incorporating fluctuating dynamic factors, when developed, will be useful for short-term, postrelease community management aimed at affecting when violent recidivism occurs, but not for making release decisions for long-term risk assessment about who is likely to be violent.

Our continuing research into improving actuarial risk assessment includes consideration of new actuarial items (and statistical interactions among them). No empirical results of our own or from other investigators have shown, however, that so-called later generations of risk assessments (inserting items expected to reflect prerelease changes in risk, or instructing users to arrive at a final assessment through the application of clinical judgment) have improved† on the predictive validity of actuarial violence risk assessments. Thus, the risk assessments we describe here remain purely actuarial and use static items alone.

* Olver, Wong, Nicholaichuk, and Gordon (2007) reported they found dynamic risk factors in a sample of sex offenders. However, careful reading of all of the methods and results (Olver, 2003) reveals that prerelease changes on putatively dynamic variables did not increase predictive accuracy beyond that achieved by static variables alone.

† As discussed later in this chapter, some clinical judgment schemes (either as raw sores or as trichotomous final judgments) have been reported to predict relevant outcomes (other chapters in this volume). The question relevant in this context of instrument design and improvement is why. We see no convincing evidence, with respect to the long-term risk of violent recidivism in forensic populations, that the predictive value of such schemes, compared to actuarial tools based on static items, depends on the incorporation of clinical judgment or any dynamic (by our definition) aspects of their items.

The Violence Risk Appraisal Guide (VRAG)

Description

The VRAG is an actuarial instrument that assesses the risk of violent recidivism among men apprehended for criminal violence (Harris, Rice, & Quinsey, 1993). Development, scoring, and validation have been described in detail elsewhere (Quinsey, Harris et al., 2006). Frequently updated information is available at www.mhcp-research.com/ragpage.htm. The 12 VRAG items and their range of scores are shown in Table 6.1. Each score has been associated with one of nine categories, each bearing a known likelihood of violent recidivism in seven years and increasing linearly from 0% in the lowest category to 100% in the highest. There are also norms for ten years of opportunity. Each VRAG score is associated with a particular percentile whereby the violence risk of an individual examinee is evaluated according to his standing relative to a large sample of violent offenders.

Whether intended for research or individual assessment, the recommended basis for scoring the VRAG is a comprehensive psychosocial history (see Quinsey, Harris et al., 2006). This history should address childhood conduct, family background, antisocial and criminal behavior, psychological problems, and details of all offenses. Adequate psychosocial histories include more than past and present psychiatric symptoms and should rely on collateral information (i.e., material gathered from friends, family, schools, correctional facilities, police, and the courts). Scoring the VRAG is not a clinical task in its typical sense, because it does not require contact between the assessor and the person being assessed. Nevertheless, compiling the required psychosocial history clearly requires clinical expertise.

Because such samples were used in its development or validation, the VRAG is appropriately used for men convicted of serious offenses and male mentally disordered offenders (Harris, Rice, & Cormier, 2002; Pham, Ducro, Marghem, & Réveillère, 2005; Snowden, Gray, Taylor, & MacCulloch, 2007; Thomson, 2005; Urbaniok, Noll, Grunewald, Steinbach, & Endrass, 2006; Yessine & Bonta, 2006), including sex offenders (Dempster, 1998; Harris et al., 2003; Rettenberger & Eher, 2007), where it has been reported to predict dichotomous violent recidivism, and its severity and rapidity, all with large effect sizes (Rice & Harris, 2005). It has also been shown to predict reported violence (where criminal charges have not necessarily been laid)

Table 6.1 Violence Risk Appraisal Guide Items and Ranges Indicating Relative Weights

Item	Score Range
1. Lived with both parents to age 16	5
2. Elementary school maladjustment	6
3. Alcohol problems	3
4. Never married	3
5. Nonviolent criminal history	5
6. Failure on prior conditional release	3
7. Age at index offense[a]	7
8. Victim injury[a]	4
9. Any female victim in index offense[a]	2
10. DSM-III Personality disorder	5
11. DSM-III Schizophrenia[a]	4
12. Psychopathy Checklist (Hare, 2003) score	17

Note: See Quinsey, Harris et al., 2006, for definitions, instructions, norms, and practice materials.

[a] Inversely scored item.

among both male and female civil psychiatric patients (Doyle, Dolan, & McGovern, 2002; Gray, Fitzgerald, Taylor, MacCulloch, & Snowden, 2007; Harris, Rice, & Camilleri, 2004). Although the rank ordering of likelihood of violence of examinees is highly replicable from population to population, the norms (but not percentile ranking) may be expected to vary depending on follow-up time (Harris & Rice, 2007a). Users should have training in scoring the Psychopathy Checklist–Revised (PCL-R) and should demonstrate that they can score the VRAG to acceptable levels of reliability.

Method of and Rationale for Development

Outcome Variable. Unlike nonactuarial risk assessments, the development of the VRAG was based directly on follow-up research in which the outcome variable was any new criminal charge for a violent offense (coded blind to all potential independent variables). In deciding what constituted violence, we included homicide, attempted homicide, kidnapping, forcible confinement, wounding, assault causing bodily harm, armed robbery, and rape. In our jurisdiction, a charge of assault or attempted murder can be laid even without physical contact between offender and victim, but very rarely, so assault was counted as violent recidivism. Moreover, although some sexual assaults rely on guile or abuse of trust rather than physical force, we counted all sexual assaults involving physical contact as violent. We did not count as violent such noncontact sex offenses as exhibitionism and voyeurism.

We operationalized violent recidivism as subsequent criminal charges even though not everyone charged was convicted. Certainly, both criminal charges and convictions are imperfect measures of actual violent conduct: In addition to wrongful arrest and conviction, not every violent crime is reported to the authorities; not all police investigations result in the identification of a perpetrator; not all identified perpetrators are apprehended and arrested; and some guilty perpetrators are not convicted. Our research indicated, however, that charges entailed less measurement error than convictions. A design feature of modern criminal justice systems is that false positive errors are much less preferable than all others—maximum accuracy of the outcome is of less concern than is avoiding false positives. In the empirical search for valid predictors of violence, our priority was different—the most accurate dependent variable. Although criminal charges appear to be an optimal measure, studies have also shown that criminal convictions, institutional records of aggression, and self-reported violence are generally predicted by the same variables, and, especially in this context, by VRAG scores.

Because most subjects in the VRAG development samples had been institutionalized, it was important that subsequent violence in other institutions, for which the offender might well have been charged had it occurred in the community, not be missed. Records of subsequent institutionalizations (both correctional and psychiatric) were examined, and those violent acts that would have resulted in criminal charges had the incident occurred outside an institution were also recorded; fewer than 10% of the violent reoffenses were based on this criterion. It was also important not to count those offenders who had no opportunity to be violent because they were held in secure custody or had died. Consequently, official records were examined to address those possibilities. Finally, for the purposes of VRAG construction, the outcome data were analyzed as dichotomous, so that the dependent variable in development analyses was at least one instance of violent recidivism. *Opportunity* was defined as release to the community, a minimum-security psychiatric hospital, or a halfway house. Three offenders who committed violent acts even though they did not technically have the opportunity to do so (e.g., by escaping from a secure facility and attacking a member of the public) were included as violent recidivists. On average, the development sample had 81.5 (SD = 60.6) months of opportunity to recidivate, defined as the duration between each subject's first opportunity and the study end date, or until his first violent reoffense (whichever occurred first). Time spent institutionalized for nonviolent offenses (or other reasons) was subtracted in the calculation of opportunity.

Independent Variables. The follow-up studies that formed the development research examined approximately 50 potential predictor variables for which there existed empirical support in the prediction of crime. Because many of the subjects had also been forensic patients, variables related to psychiatric history, distress, and diagnosis were also tested. Some variables were evaluated because clinicians attached importance to them (e.g., expressions of remorse, volunteering for treatment, whether the offender was regarded by clinicians as having "insight"). In VRAG development, the tested variables reflected these categories: childhood history (e.g., *DSM–III* conduct disorder items, elementary school maladjustment, education), adult adjustment (e.g., criminal history, psychiatric history, employment, marital status, social support, socioeconomic status), index offense characteristics (e.g., number and sex of victims, victim injuries, alcohol involvement), and assessment results obtained or obtainable early in the first postindex offense admission (e.g., IQ, MMPI scores, Level of Supervision Inventory, *DSM–III* diagnoses, PCL-R score) all coded (blind to outcome) to a high standard of inter-rater reliability from institutional records that included thorough psychosocial history information.

Construction Samples. The goal was an actuarial instrument for the prediction of violent recidivism among serious offenders for whom the courts, clinicians, and criminal justice officials were required to make predictive decisions—those who have already committed at least one serious antisocial act. Offenders with only minor offenses and citizens who have committed no offenses were not the population of interest. We compiled a heterogeneous sample of serious offenders from two previous studies (Rice, Harris, & Cormier, 1992; Rice, Harris, Lang, & Bell, 1990). Of these 685 men, 618 had an opportunity to recidivate, and there were few differences between these and the 67 without opportunity—those with opportunity had less serious index offenses (this variable was inversely related to violent recidivism), were less likely to have a female victim, and were more likely to have married. There was no reason to expect that the development subjects were less dangerous than the others or that they were unrepresentative. The only exception to this was that the released group included no mass murderers (men who had killed more than three people), although there were some in the unreleased group.

Analytic Strategy. Potential predictor variables without a significant bivariate relationship with violent recidivism were not considered further. A few variables were highly collinear (e.g., prior criminal charges and prior convictions for violent offenses); from such pairs, the variable with the lower correlation with violent recidivism was dropped. Then least-squares stepwise multiple regression selected variables that made independent and incremental contributions to the prediction of violent recidivism. Separate analyses were run for variables in each of the categories described above. In addition, the development sample was subdivided (e.g., randomly, treated vs. assessed only). Only variables selected by the regression analyses in a majority of such subsidiary analyses were eligible in a final regression analysis that considered all variables that had survived thus far. Variables selected by this step became the 12 VRAG items. Subsequent testing indicated that logistic and Cox proportional hazards regression would have selected substantially the same items as would the use of continuous measures of violent recidivism—the number, severity, and rapidity of violent reoffenses (Quinsey, Harris et al., 2006).

Although unitary item weights would have performed almost as well (Harris et al., 1993; see also Grove & Meehl, 1996), we decided that the small improvement afforded by differential weights could be worthwhile. The weights were derived not from the regression coefficients but using a simpler method described by Nuffield (1982) in which the weight is computed actuarially based on the item's base rate relationship with the dependent variable in the development sample. This computation is described in detail elsewhere (Harris et al., 1993; Quinsey, Harris et al., 2006) and meant that a score of zero could be recommended for missing items because that entailed adding the score for the overall base rate. Although we liked this continual reference to the base rate in determining weights and in scoring, it was a very conservative strategy, and now that more data are available to support its use, we now recommend prorating for missing items (Quinsey, Harris et al., 2006, pp. 164–165; see also: http://www.mhcp-research.com/bk2errors.htm). Briefly, the assessor first determines, on the basis of all the items that can be scored according to the manual, whether the assessee's score is positive (or negative). Then, the examinee is given the same proportion of positive (negative) points for the unscored items as obtained for the items that can be scored. Elsewhere (Appendices of Quinsey, Harris et al., 2006), we have provided an extensive manual for the VRAG including detailed scoring instructions, norms, answers to frequently asked questions, instructions for the compilation of suitable psychosocial histories, and practice case material.

Reliability and Psychometric Properties

As a direct consequence of the methods used to determine item weights, the mean VRAG score in the development sample was very close to zero (.91, *SD* = 12.9). The first evaluation of interrater reliability used the independent coding by two trained raters of 20 randomly selected subjects and yielded a Pearson correlation coefficient of .90. Reliability coefficients exceeding .90 have also been reported in several subsequent evaluations (e.g., Douglas, Yeomans, & Boer, 2005; Ducro & Pham, 2006; Harris et al., 2002, 2003) but are not guaranteed (e.g., Sjöstedt & Langström, 2002). In the development sample, the standard error of measurement was 4.1, roughly half the size of one VRAG category. The 95% confidence intervals for each category showed that confidence tended to decrease slightly as scores increased (Harris et al., 1993), but the standard error of measurement and the observed rates of violent recidivism (and confidence intervals) indicated that any single "true" score can be expected to differ from the obtained score by more than a single VRAG category with a probability of less than .05 (Harris et al., 1993). In this regard, we note that Hart, Michie, and Cooke (2007) claimed that VRAG scores are so imprecise as to be "virtually meaningless," a claim we have refuted elsewhere (Harris, Rice, & Quinsey, 2008) (www.mhcp-research.com/hmcrespond.htm).

Validity

The VRAG predicted violent recidivism (base rate = 31%) in the development sample with a high degree of accuracy—the area under the curve was .76. The original sample (plus additional subjects not previously released) was followed up with 10 years' mean opportunity (Rice & Harris, 1995). The base rate of violent recidivism was 43%, and the ROC area was .74 for the VRAG's prediction of violent recidivism. In 35 studies with nonoverlapping samples (http://www.mhcp-research.com/ragreps.htm), the VRAG's average ROC area is .72 for the prediction of violent recidivism—a large effect by conventional standards (Rice & Harris, 2005). Under optimal conditions (high reliability; not dropping, replacing, or modifying items; fixed and equal follow-up durations), the VRAG yields ROC areas of approximately .85 in predicting violent recidivism (Harris & Rice, 2003). As mentioned earlier, the VRAG has been shown to generalize (although sometimes with lower effect sizes) across violent outcomes (number of violent reoffenses, institutional violence, very serious violence, self-reported violence, general recidivism, overall severity of violent recidivism, rapidity of violent failure), follow-up times (12 weeks to 10 years), countries (8 in North America and Europe), offender populations (mentally disordered offenders, sexual aggressors, violent felons, developmentally delayed sex offenders, emergency psychiatric patients, wife assaulters, and juvenile offenders), all of which is extensively reviewed elsewhere (Quinsey, Harris et al., 2006) (see also: www.mhcp-research.com/ragreps.htm). Some data suggest the VRAG predicts violence among women (Harris et al., 2004) or in mixed-sex samples (Doyle & Dolan, 2006; Gray et al., 2007; McDermott et al., 2007; Thomson, 2005), but there are few studies on serious female offenders specifically. Replications of the VRAG have generally reported that obtained rates of violent recidivism matched the predicted rates for each category, if the average score of the sample is similar, the follow-up duration is approximately the same as for the norms, and the outcome is similar (Harris & Rice, 2007a).

In several evaluations, the VRAG has been more accurate than the final output of structured professional judgment schemes (Barbaree et al., 2001; Grann & Wedin, 2002; Gray et al., 2007; Hilton, Harris, Rice, Houghton, & Eke, 2008; Pham, 2004; Pham et al., 2005; Polvi, 2001; Sjöstedt & Langström, 2002), in many cases statistically significantly. Some of these studies used the total raw score on the structured professional judgment (SPJ) instrument (although that is not advised for individual decision making) as output rather than the recommended categorical judgment, and some of the comparisons involved outcomes other than generally violent recidivism or instruments not developed for violent recidivism specifically. We know of no report in which clinical intuition (structured or unstructured) statistically significantly outperformed the VRAG in the prediction of violent recidivism on the same cases. We regard this as consistent with our position that optimal long-term, prerelease violence risk assessment can currently be achieved by relying on a comprehensive set of static predictors without adjustment based on clinical judgment (c.f., Harris & Rice, 2003; Harris et al., 2002).

The Sex Offender Risk Appraisal Guide

Description and Development

We observed that sex offenders' known rates of violent recidivism were higher than expected based on their VRAG scores (Harris & Rice, 2007a; Rice & Harris, 1997), suggesting that separate norms might be required for men institutionalized for contact sex offenses against minors and coercive sexual assaults against women. We also reported that those personal variables associated with recidivism among such sex offenders were slightly different than among violent offenders without histories of sex offenses (Quinsey, Rice, & Harris, 1995; Rice, Harris, & Quinsey, 1990; Rice et al., 1991). As examples, phallometrically assessed sexual deviance has only been reported to predict recidivism among sex offenders; an index offense of homicide indicates lower-than-average risk only among violent nonsex offenders; and the relationship between recidivism and the age and sex of prior victims differs between sex offenders* and other violent offenders.

Consequently, the VRAG was modified to predict violent recidivism for sex offenders by dropping two items (female victim in the index offense and victim injury in the index offense, both scored inversely) that did not afford incremental value among sex offenders in particular, and by adding four that did (in decreasing order of weight: prior history of violent offenses, prior convictions for sex offenses, having an adult female or male child victim, and phallometrically assessed sexual deviance). Weights were computed and norms derived as in the VRAG using a development sample of 288 sex offenders from previous samples (Rice, Harris, Quinsey et al., 1990, 1991), where the outcome variable was the same as that employed in the development of the VRAG—at least one subsequent charge for a violent offense. Weights for all items were derived using the same method employed in the development of the VRAG (Nuffield, 1982). The result was the 14-item *Sex Offender Risk Appraisal Guide* (SORAG). The items and their range of scores are shown in Table 6.2. SORAG scores are associated with one of nine risk categories,

* It has been suggested that sex offenders require postactuarial discounts for having gotten older themselves (Barbaree, Blanchard, & Langton, 2003, 2007; Wollert, 2006). Our empirical analyses indicated that postactuarial adjustments for aging are invalid (Harris & Rice, 2007b) for sex offenders and serious offenders in general.

Table 6.2 Sex Offender Risk Appraisal Guide Items and Ranges Indicating Relative Weights

Item	Score Range
1. Lived with both parents to age 16	5
2. Elementary school maladjustment	6
3. Alcohol problems	3
4. Never married	3
5. Nonviolent criminal history	5
6. Violent criminal history	7
7. Convictions for prior sex offenses	6
8. History of sex offenses against girls only[a]	4
9. Failure on prior conditional release	3
10. Age at index offense[a]	7
11. DSM-III Personality Disorder	5
12. DSM-III Schizophrenia[a]	4
13. Phallometric test results	2
14. Psychopathy Checklist (Hare, 2003) score	17

Note: See Quinsey, Harris et al., 2006, for definitions, instructions, norms, and practice materials.

[a] Inversely scored item.

each with a known likelihood of violent recidivism in seven years and increasing linearly from 7% to 100%.

There are also norms for 10 years of opportunity. As for the VRAG, each SORAG score is also associated with a percentile rank. The base rate of violent recidivism in the development sample was 42% in seven years. Elsewhere (Quinsey, Harris et al., 2006, Appendices), we provided an extensive manual for the SORAG, which includes detailed scoring and coding instructions, norms for individual scores and the nine standard SORAG categories, answers to frequently asked questions, instructions for the compilation of suitable psychosocial histories, and practice case material. Also, as for the VRAG, the SORAG can be prorated as long as no more than four items are missing or scored by substitution.

Reliability and Validity

In construction, the inter-rater reliability of the SORAG was reported to be .90 (Quinsey, Harris et al., 2006), and similarly high reliability coefficients have been reported in subsequent replication studies (e.g., Ducro & Pham, 2006; Harris et al., 2003; Langton et al., 2007). In the development samples, SORAG scores had a mean of 8.90 (SD = 11.33) and a standard error of measurement of 3.58, and 9.99 (SD = 10.8) and very low standard error of measurement (.012) in a subsequent independent replication (Harris et al., 2003). That replication also reported a very close correspondence between observed rates of violent recidivism for the SORAG categories and those expected on the basis of the norms.

In development, the SORAG yielded an ROC area of .75 in predicting violent recidivism that was replicated (.73) in the subsequent independent evaluation (Harris et al., 2003), which also reported that SORAG scores significantly predicted the rapidity and severity of recidivism. In nine nonoverlapping samples of released sex offenders from four countries, SORAG scores have yielded a mean AUC area of .73 in predicting violent (including sexual) recidivism (www.mhcp-research.com/ragreps.htm). As with the VRAG, accuracy is enhanced by not dropping or replacing SORAG items, high reliability, and constant follow-up duration (Harris & Rice, 2003; Harris et al., 2003; Langton et al., 2007). The accuracy of SORAG scores in predicting violent recidivism has been reported to be improved neither by the addition of less accurate actuarial tools (Seto, 2005) nor by additional structured or unstructured clinical intuition (Barbaree et al., 2001; Johansen, 2007).

The Appropriate Outcome for Sex Offenders

Several actuarial systems and structured clinical judgment schemes for sex offenders have been developed using only those reoffenses that can be determined to have been sexually motivated solely from the name of the criminal charge (for example, rape, sexual assault, sexual battery, etc.). This approach, probably motivated by American statutes aimed specifically at protecting the public from sexually motivated violence (rather than from violent crime in general), ranks offenders quite differently from an approach based on officially detected violent recidivism overall (Barbaree, Langton, & Peacock, 2006; Harris et al., 2003). It is evident that research based on police "rap sheets" alone misses sex offenders' most serious sexually violent offenses (homicide, especially) and unnecessarily underestimates the rate of officially detected sexually violent recidivism (by inappropriately classifying all charges for assault, battery, kidnapping, abduction, and so on, as nonsexual). Among sex offenders, there is evidence that officially detected violent recidivism is a better index of officially detected sexually motivated violence than sexual recidivism recorded on police rap sheets alone (Rice, Harris, Lang, & Cormier, 2006). Thus, even if the only concern were sex offenders' risk of sexually motivated reoffending, we recommend actuarial assessment developed using officially detected violent recidivism overall.

The Ontario Domestic Assault Risk Assessment (ODARA)

Description

ODARA is a 13-item actuarial instrument that assesses the risk of violent recidivism against a female domestic partner, among men with a police record for such violence (Hilton et al., 2004). Development, scoring, and validation of the ODARA have been described in detail elsewhere (Hilton et al., 2009) including norms, scoring details, answers to frequently asked questions, and practice case material. The 13 equally weighted dichotomous ODARA items are presented in Table 6.3. An item is treated as missing when the available documentation indicates that it might be present but the information is incomplete or ambiguous, and the ODARA score may be prorated for up to five missing items, with some loss of predictive accuracy (Hilton et al., 2009). Similar to the VRAG and SORAG, ODARA scores are associated with one of seven categories, each with a known probability of wife assault recidivism in an average of 51 months, and increasing linearly from 5% in the lowest category to 70% in the highest. Norms also indicate the percentile rank for each ODARA score category (Hilton et al., 2004, 2009).

The ODARA differs from the other assessments in this chapter in that it was designed not to require a comprehensive psychosocial history. Created in collaboration with the Ontario Provincial Police primarily for police officers to use at the scene of a domestic call or during routine subsequent investigation, the ODARA was designed for efficient scoring based on information available to frontline users. The ODARA is also suitable for application in a structured interview by nurses, shelter counselors, or other victim service workers (Hilton, Harris, & Holder, 2008); however, it has not been validated without criminal record data.

Method of and Rationale for Development

Outcome Variable. The outcome variable was a subsequent physical assault against a female domestic partner evident either in narrative police reports (regardless of whether criminal charges were laid), or in criminal justice archives of charges and convictions. This approach was taken because the ODARA was expected to inform frontline police and clinical work before (or

Table 6.3 Ontario Domestic Assault Risk Assessment and Domestic Violence Risk Appraisal Guide Items and DVRAG Ranges Indicating Relative Weights

Item	DVRAG Range[a]
1. Prior domestic assaults in the police record	6
2. Prior nondomestic assaults in the police record	6
3. Prior incarceral sentence of at least 30 days	3
4. Failure on prior conditional release	3
5. Threat to harm or kill anyone else at the index incident	1
6. Confinement of partner at index incident	1
7. Victim concern about possible future domestic assaults	2
8. Number of children	2
9. Victim's biological children from a previous partner	3
10. Violence against nondomestic victims	8
11. Substance abuse score	4
12. Assault on victim when pregnant	5
13. Barriers to victim support	5
14. Psychopathy Checklist (Hare, 2003) score[b]	7

Note: See Hilton et al., 2009, for definitions, instructions, norms, and practice materials.
[a] All ODARA items are dichotomous.
[b] Not included in the ODARA.

in the absence of) the decision to arrest or charge. It was also expected to inform conditional release decisions by police and bail courts after the laying of charges but before possible conviction. In subsequent analyses, we found that ODARA scores also predicted subsequent criminal charges and conviction for wife assault recidivism (Hilton et al., 2009). In this sense, the ODARA is comparable to the Static-99 (this volume) constructed to predict only a specific kind of violence using readily obtained and empirically selected items.

The development subjects were followed up for a mean of 4.8 years. At-risk time was initially defined for each offender as the time between his index assault and the date police and criminal records were retrieved for follow-up, or until the date associated with his next instance of wife assault in the official record, regardless of any nonviolent or nondomestic offenses (mean = 4.3 years). Because we did not know how long an offender had spent in pretrial or sentenced custody for nondomestic offenses, we could not compute the duration of actual opportunity to recidivate, and all subjects who had no such opportunity were necessarily counted as nonrecidivists, a conservative approach that would underestimate the base rate of recidivism and attenuate predictive accuracy (Hilton & Harris, 2009).

In addition, offenders who committed even very serious violent reoffenses resulting in conviction were treated as nonrecidivists if the victim was not a female partner. In subsequent cross-validation, this restriction substantially reduced the predictive accuracy reported compared to that obtained when such nondomestic violent recidivists were dropped from the sample (Hilton & Harris, 2009).

Independent Variables. We examined all variables for which there was any existing empirical support in the prediction of violent or criminal recidivism, items from existing nonactuarial domestic violence risk assessments, and all information about the offender, victim, their relationship, and the index and prior domestic incidents that we could glean from the police records. We excluded from consideration, however, any variable that could not reasonably be obtained by front-line investigating police officers.

Construction Sample. The goal was an actuarial instrument that predicted violent recidivism against a female domestic partner. The construction sample comprised 589 cases extracted in reverse chronological order from a large police archive covering most areas of Ontario, a province inhabited by over a third of the population of Canada. All cases in which there was clear evidence that a man had committed a physical assault (or, rarely, threatened death with a weapon in hand) were included (Hilton et al., 2004). Because no cases meeting these criteria were excluded on the basis of location, age, ethnicity, or socioeconomic status, the resulting sample could be expected to be representative of the population of men with a police record for wife assault; subsequent cross-validation with cases selected from Ontario's largest urban region supported this claim (Hilton, Harris, Rice, Houghton, & Eke, 2008).

Analytic Strategy. Potential items not yielding statistically significant bivariate associations with the outcome variable were dropped from consideration at the first step. Then, logistic regression with dichotomous wife assault recidivism as the dependent variable, and setwise, stepwise selection of incrementally and independently valid predictor variables, was used in bootstrapped analyses (Hilton et al., 2004). Potential items were analyzed in six categories: index assault details, domestic offense history, nondomestic offense history, sociodemographic characteristics, relationship details, and victim reports. A final regression analysis selected the incremental and independent predictors from each set (Hilton et al., 2004).

Reliability, Psychometric Properties, and Validity

Mean ODARA score on construction was 2.89 ($SD = 2.14$, standard error of measurement = .48), and the intraclass correlations coefficient (ICC) for inter-rater reliability was ICC ≥ .90 among research coders. Subsequent tests of reliability and scoring accuracy with police officers and other frontline users from several disciplines replicated very high inter-rater reliabilities (ICC > .90) and average scoring errors of less than a half point after one day of training (Hilton et al., 2004; Hilton, Harris, Rice, Eke, & Lowe-Wetmore, 2007). ODARA norms, 95% confidence intervals, and low standard error of measurement indicate that cases have a probability of less than .05 of misclassification by more than one ODARA category (Hilton et al., 2004).

The ODARA predicted wife assault recidivism (base rate = 30%) with a large effect size (Rice & Harris, 2005): AUC was .77 on construction and .72 on cross-validation with 100 comparable cases (Hilton et al., 2004). In a new sample limited to 346 men with an in-depth correctional file, AUC was .65 (Hilton, Harris, Rice, Houghton, & Eke, 2008). In a third independent cross-validation limited to 391 men without such a record, AUC was .67, but up to .80 (and .74 on average) when using equal samples of wife assault recidivists and men with no violent reoffenses (Hilton & Harris, 2009). The latter two successful replications included new samples drawn from the same police archive as used for ODARA construction, but these were supplemented by several hundred drawn from similar archives (according to the same criteria) of metropolitan police services in Canada's largest city. The ODARA was associated with dichotomous wife assault recidivism, the number of recidivistic offenses during follow-up, their severity and seriousness, and an estimate of the rapidity of recidivism (Hilton et al., 2004, in press). We have reported that users make more proficient risk-related decisions when they have use of the ODARA score in their investigation (Hilton, Harris, & Rice, 2009).

The Domestic Violence Risk Appraisal Guide (DVRAG)

Description

DVRAG is a 14-item actuarial instrument that assesses a wife assaulter's risk of violent recidivism against a female domestic partner among men with a police record for such violence

(Hilton, Harris, Rice, Houghton, & Eke, 2008). It is intended for use only when there is sufficient correctional or clinical information to conduct an in-depth assessment similar to the VRAG and SORAG. The DVRAG items are shown in Table 6.3. Readers will note that these are the 13 ODARA items (now not dichotomous) plus the score on the PCL-R. Development, scoring, and validation of the DVRAG have been described in detail elsewhere (Hilton et al., 2009) including norms, scoring details, answers to frequently asked questions, and practice case material. The DVRAG can be used when as many as five items are missing and scored by prorating (Hilton et al., 2009). Each score has been associated with one of seven categories, each with a known likelihood of wife assault recidivism based on an average 5.1 year follow-up and increasing linearly from 14% in the lowest category to 100% in the highest. The DVRAG gives more discrimination at the higher end, and less at the lower end, than its frontline screening companion tool (the ODARA) from which it was derived.

Like the VRAG, SORAG, and ODARA, each DVRAG score is associated with a percentile so that the risk of an individual is evaluated in comparison to a large sample of wife assault offenders with a correctional history. Also, as with the VRAG and SORAG, a comprehensive psychosocial history is recommended for scoring the DVRAG, particularly for the PCL-R. Users should demonstrate they can score the DVRAG to an acceptable level of inter-rater reliability, and should either have training in scoring the PCL-R or have access to a reliable PCL-R score on the offender.

Development and Validation

The DVRAG was developed and cross-validated on cases from the ODARA research that had a correctional risk–needs assessment and had sufficiently complete information to permit reliable scoring of several nonactuarial, formal domestic violence risk assessments. The DVRAG development sample exhibited a higher base rate of wife assault recidivism (49%) than had the larger ODARA sample over an equivalent average follow-up.

Outcome Variables. Unlike the other assessments described in this chapter, the components of the DVRAG were selected on the basis of their association with several outcome variables: dichotomous wife assault recidivism, the number of such offenses, the number involving severe violence, the Cormier-Lang score (Quinsey, Harris et al., 2006) for the seriousness of subsequent criminal charges for wife assault, and the total victim injury caused in recidivistic wife assaults (Hilton, Harris, Rice et al., 2008).

Independent Variables. The principal analyses in the development of the DVRAG involved existing, published formal instruments for assessing the risk of domestic violence. The independent variables were scores on the ODARA (Hilton et al., 2004), the Spousal Assault Risk Assessment (SARA) (Kropp, Chapter 11, this volume), the Danger Assessment, (DA) (Campbell, 2007), and the Domestic Violence Screening Instrument (DVSI) (Williams & Houghton, 2004). In addition, we also considered the PCL-R (Hare, 2003) and a nine-item modification of the VRAG (ever married, female victim, and *DSM-III* schizophrenia were nearly invariant). Subsidiary analyses also evaluated the potential incremental predictive value of several variables pertaining to the perpetrator's history of childhood aggression and antisociality, and exposure to child abuse, neglect, and having witnessed domestic violence as a child.

Analytic Strategy. Because the ODARA is the only available actuarial tool for the frontline assessment of the risk of wife assault recidivism, the primary empirical question addressed in development of the DVRAG was, "Given that the police have already completed the ODARA, what additional formal clinical assessment can provide incremental value in assessing the risk of wife assault recidivism?" We anticipated that the result would be a coherent system of actuarial assessment in which frontline users would derive an optimal appraisal of risk given available resources, then that frontline assessment would inform and be refined by clinical information (for the purposes of sentencing, assigning to intervention, and making parole decisions, as examples) when additional assessment resources were provided to the case. Thus, the first analytic steps in the DVRAG development were identifying the best bivariate predictors of each of the five outcome variables reflecting the frequency and severity of wife assault recidivism. Then multivariate methods were used to identify which formal clinical assessments afforded the most independent and incremental value to the ODARA score in predicting those outcomes.

Despite the fact that it is not a formal risk assessment and not designed to measure domestic violence, the PCL-R was clearly the best additional assessment. PCL-R score was the best bivariate predictor of all but one of the outcome variables and made the only statistically significant independent and incremental improvement to the ODARA in four of the five outcomes. The DVRAG was established as the 13 ODARA items plus the PCL-R score. Subsidiary analyses with all five outcome variables indicated that no improvement to DVRAG accuracy was achieved by adding items reflecting the perpetrator's childhood history of antisociality, abuse, and neglect. Weights for all 14 DVRAG items were derived using the same method employed in the development of the VRAG and SORAG (Nuffield, 1982).

Reliability, Psychometric Properties, and Validity

Mean DVRAG score in the development sample was 2.9 (*SD* = 8.9). Inter-rater reliability on new correctional file cases was ICC = .90, and standard error of measurement = 2.2. An experienced forensic clinician achieved acceptable reliability even without explicit DVRAG training (Hilton, Harris, Rice et al., 2008). Again, as with all the actuarial assessments described in this chapter, the available data on the reliability and 95% confidence intervals for DVRAG categories imply that an individual's true DVRAG score has a probability less than .05 of being misclassified by more than one DVRAG category.

The DVRAG predicted dichotomous wife assault recidivism with an AUC = .71 in the development sample and .70 in a new sample (base rate = 41%) of 346 cases (the same sample as that reported above as the second ODARA cross-validation sample; Hilton, Harris, Rice et al., 2008). In this cross-validation, the DVRAG was significantly more accurate than the ODARA and all the other nonactuarial formal domestic violence assessments evaluated (SARA, DA, and DVSI). DVRAG score also significantly predicted the number of new assaults, their severity and seriousness, and victim injury (Pearson *r*s = .29 to .44 in cross-validation) (Hilton, Harris, Rice et al., 2008), almost always significantly more accurately than all the other formal, nonactuarial domestic violence risk assessments (Hilton, Harris, Rice et al., 2008). Analyses of the combined samples indicated that the PCL-R and nine-item version of the VRAG were better predictors of all five wife assault outcomes than were the three nonactuarial, formal domestic assault instruments (SARA, DA, and DVSI; Hilton, Harris, Rice et al., 2008).

Limitations and Future Research With ODARA and DVRAG

To date, there have been no replications of ODARA and DVRAG predictive accuracy by other researchers, although we know of research under way in Canada, the United States, and the United Kingdom. The literature indicates that actuarial violence risk assessments have generally been successfully replicated (Hanson & Morton-Bourgon, 2007). Although some ODARA items are potentially changeable, there have yet been no studies of the predictive accuracy of changed scores or any other dynamic variables in domestic violence risk assessment. We are currently examining the ODARA and DVRAG in a comparison-group follow-up study of inmates in a correctional treatment program for domestic violence. We have often been asked to examine the prediction of domestic assault recidivism by women, and several items on our existing instruments are obviously not applicable to violence against men, making this endeavor a likely step for future research.

Limitations and Future Directions: The Challenge of Actuarial Violence Risk Assessment

Developing and validating an actuarial assessment with a large effect in the assessment of violence risk does not guarantee its universal acceptance. After a decade and a half, we recognize several thorny issues that lie outside the comparatively straightforward matter of empirically measured ROC areas in follow-up studies. A few of these problems are technical. For example, if true base rates are very low (or very high), it can be argued (e.g., Vrieze & Grove, 2008, but also see Mossman, 2008) that the most appropriate decision is to treat all cases the same (e.g., release everyone), especially if the costs associated with false positive and false negative errors are regarded as equivalent (Harris & Rice, 2007a; Rice & Harris, 1995). An actuarial tool sharpens the focus on what is unknown (e.g., the true cost of misses vs. false alarms) in ways that reliance on clinical intuition evidently does not. Elsewhere we have addressed some of these technical and values issues (Harris & Rice, 2007a), for example, in showing there are more data upon which to estimate long-term base rates than some commentators have implied.

Other troubles pertain to blending technical and emotional concerns. As mentioned above, some have complained (Hart et al., 2007) that actuarial risk assessments are not "precise" enough to be used in high-stakes circumstances, recommended decision making be avoided altogether, and advised practitioners to examine their own beliefs about risk instead. Fear of making an error (though quite understandable) is independent of the evaluation of predictive effects. Most forensic practitioners cannot ethically refuse to make risk-related decisions by shifting responsibility to others, and when decisions must be made (e.g., some offenders must be released while others are detained), the only ethical, rational course is to use the largest predictive effects available (Grove & Meehl, 1996). As another example, we share some commentators' personal disagreement with aspects of statutes mandating preventative detention and incapacitation, but we disagree (Harris, Rice, & Quinsey, 2008) with misrepresenting empirical findings (for example, by asserting misleading standards for "accuracy") (Wollert, 2006).

More fundamentally, however, we have not always appreciated the profoundly counterintuitive nature of actuarial assessment (Harris, 2003). The undeniable fact that actuarial assessment is more accurate than clinical judgment guarantees that optimal risk assessment frequently forces practitioners to make decisions contrary to everything their own instincts, feelings, and experiences tell them. No doubt this is made even more difficult by an evolutionary history that has left each of us with an implicit (but powerfully influential) "theory of mind" facilitating human social interaction by providing serviceable causes and predictions for the conduct of others (Platek, Keenan, & Shackelford, 2007). Those who develop actuarial systems for insurance or weather forecasting need not surmount inherent theories-of-mortality or theories-of-meteorology. But optimal implementation of actuarial assessment in the prediction of human behavior surely faces resistance due to a specialized universal certainty that we know why people act the way they do and can use that knowledge to anticipate their actions. To some, actuarial assessment feels like naïve and mindless reliance on simplistic statistical algorithms, an irrational emotional response unaltered by overwhelming evidence that the feeling is misleading.

At first, it seemed reasonable to us that a concession allowing practitioners to insert a controlled amount of clinical intuition after the computation of an actuarial score (Webster et al., 1994) would overcome this resistance. Such an insertion had scant hope of increasing predictive effect sizes, but one might expect it to improve real decisions by moving practice part way from unaided clinical judgment toward some reliance on actuarial scores. Several things, however, discouraged us from continuing this recommendation, including the implication that we were guilty of a sort of actuarial hypocrisy (Janus & Meehl, 1997).

Foremost has been the use of actuarial tools in our own institution. Although they had been available for many years and clinicians had received much information and training in their use, release decisions by an independent tribunal were unrelated to actuarial scores, but were related to such invalid indicators as physical attractiveness and perceived insight (Hilton & Simmons, 2001; McKee, Harris, & Rice, 2007). This poor tribunal performance was directly attributable to suboptimal advice from forensic clinicians whose opinions were unrelated (or very weakly related) to actuarial scores. Consequently, clinical opinions rendered in everyday practice did not predict recidivism in follow-up research, although actuarial scores did. Apparently, forensic clinicians looked at actuarial scores but deviated from them so much and so often (based on the subsequent application of clinical intuition) that their advice to the tribunal was indistinguishable from that same clinical intuition. Avoidable violence and unnecessary detention both resulted from their deviations.

Instructions to incorporate clinical judgment in arriving at a final assessment are a feature of some actuarial systems (e.g., Classification of Violence Risk, COVR) (Monahan, Chapter 9, this volume), but more especially of nonactuarial schemes for the exercise of "professional discretion" (see chapters pertaining to the Early Assessment Risk List [EARL], Historical-Clinical-Risk Management 20 [HCR20], Risk for Sexual Violence Protocol [RSVP], and SARA in this volume). Others might disagree, but we regard this as ill conceived for several reasons: First, these instructions to insert clinical judgment were accompanied by no empirical support; indeed, these latter, nonactuarial schemes have usually been promulgated without accompanying specific empirical evidence as to reliability or validity. Second, subsequent findings indicate that the final "trichotomous" clinical assessments rendered by these nonactuarial schemes (only ratings of "low," "moderate," or "high" are encouraged) frequently suffer from low reliability (de Vogel, de Ruiter, van Beek, & Mead, 2004; Douglas et al., 2005, Kropp & Hart, 2000). Because the standard error of measurement is a function of reliability, ratings of "moderate" often cannot be reliably distinguished either from "low" or "high," severely limiting usefulness (Hilton, Carter, Harris, & Sharpe, 2008). Third, even among experienced forensic clinicians, such nonnumeric terms lack useful consensual meaning (even before application to real cases) and might do nothing to remedy biases known to plague clinical decision making (Hilton et al., 2009). Finally, we are aware of no evidence that using these nonactuarial schemes with the permission to insert idiosyncratically determined clinical intuition actually improves forensic practice.

The same could be said of purely actuarial systems—where is the evidence that they have actually improved practice? We believe we have obtained some evidence that the addition of actuarial scores to routine case material has improved the risk-related decision proficiency of forensic professionals (Hilton, Harris, Rawson, & Beach, 2005; Hilton, Harris, & Rice, 2007), but evidence is admittedly scarce. At this point, no one can promise that the introduction of any formal violence risk assessment (actuarial or nonactuarial) will improve real risk-related decisions. No one really knows what strategies in the application of available empirical evidence will ensure that avoidable violent recidivism and unnecessary restriction of offenders' freedom are simultaneously minimized. We seriously doubt, however, that giving permission to abdicate decision-making responsibility, recommendations to incorporate unspecified amounts of clinical intuition, nonspecific warnings to exercise caution, or advice to introspect on one's beliefs about violence represent any hope for practical progress. Our own approach has been an attempt to expand the formalization of all aspects (risk-related and risk-irrelevant) of the decision (McKee et al., 2007) so as to minimize the role of all informal judgment. We hope to evaluate such efforts in the future.

Appendix—Examples

Space limitations preclude exemplifying the comprehensive psychosocial evaluation that forms the basis for VRAG, SORAG, and DVRAG scoring. Full accounts of that process, guidelines, norms, and practice materials are presented elsewhere (Hilton et al., 2009; Quinsey, Harris et al., 2006). Here we present brief synopses, especially to illustrate recommended formats for reporting actuarial scores for individual cases. The details reflect true cases rendered anonymous.

EXAMPLE ONE: VRAG AND SORAG

(For brevity, we use the example of a sex offender for both the VRAG and SORAG. However, in practice we now recommend only the SORAG for sex offenders, because it has been normed specifically for them and because there are now enough studies to support its use).

Brief History

Pierre Cassbay was raised in foster homes from the age of one month until he was placed, at age three, with a well-to-do family. As a young child, he was bright and very knowledgeable for his age, but by age ten, it became obvious that he was disturbed—he was hyperactive and impulsive and frequently ran away from home. He was unpopular and spent his time in school daydreaming and destroying his pencils, rulers, and clothing. His foster mother moved him to a private school, but the problems continued. Pierre was institutionalized at age 12 when child welfare authorities became convinced he was too disturbed to remain with his foster mother, of whom he was very fond. In the institution, he was discovered several times leading other children in sex play. At age 15, he returned to his foster home, whereupon he was reported to be a reasonably well-behaved student with good grades. He continued to be hyperactive, had an unusual interest in the routes of streetcars and buses in his city, and was frequently bullied by other students. At age 17, he was apprehended by police after having taken a 10-year-old girl into the woods. No evidence of assault was found, and no charges were filed. Later that year, Pierre was charged with the murder of a four-year-old girl. He had taken the victim from her front yard to beneath a viaduct where he choked, brutally sexually assaulted, and then stomped her to death. Upon his arrest, he admitted to two unsolved sexual murders and over a hundred assaults on children aged 3 to 10. He was found not guilty by reason of insanity and sent to a maximum security forensic psychiatric hospital, where he spent most of the next thirty years. On a phallometric assessment, he exhibited a preference for young boys.

Actuarial Assessment

Mr. Cassbay's score on the VRAG, computed using clinical material gathered shortly after his admission, placed his risk of violent recidivism (defined as a subsequent criminal charge or equivalent for a violent offense) in a group of offenders that comprised the eighth, or second highest, of nine VRAG categories. Among male violent offenders in the studies described above, just 3% obtained higher VRAG scores, and approximately 82% in this category met the research criteria for having reoffended violently within an average of ten years of opportunity after release.

Mr. Cassbay's score on the Sex Offender Risk Appraisal Guide (SORAG), computed using clinical material gathered shortly after his admission, placed his risk of violent recidivism (defined as a subsequent criminal charge or equivalent for a violent offense) in a group of sex offenders that, as for the VRAG, comprised the eighth or second highest of nine categories. Among male sex offenders in the studies described above, only 4% obtained higher SORAG scores, and approximately 89% in this category met the criteria for having reoffended violently within an average of ten years of opportunity after release.

Follow-Up

Over his many years in the maximum security hospital, Pierre was consistently diagnosed with pedophilia and sometimes with schizophrenia and personality disorder. He was never prescribed neuroleptics. During this period, he was briefly discharged twice on a trial basis to less secure facilities. He returned both times because he was judged not to be ready for lesser security. At age 52, he had severe glaucoma and was legally blind. He was generally noted to be well behaved. The forensic tribunal that determined dispositions for such patients again decided it was time to move Pierre to lesser security. A few months after the transfer, he was granted escorted access to the community, at first with staff members, and then soon with a fellow patient he had known back at the maximum security hospital. On their first outing together, Pierre purchased knives and an axe from a hardware store and then he and his escort brutally murdered a young man who was also a patient of their current hospital. Pierre anally raped the victim who had previously rejected his sexual advances. Pierre and his accomplice were found not guilty by reason of insanity for this murder and returned to the maximum security hospital. In a subsequent follow-up study, Mr. Cassbay was recorded as having had one day of opportunity at the time of having met the criteria for violent recidivism.

EXAMPLE TWO: ODARA

Police Occurrence Report # 1184

Police were dispatched to 47 First Street, Nortown, at 20:14 hrs on October 15, 2006, in response to a call from a neighbor complaining about noise. Officers arrived at 20:31 hours and encountered a female person who was observed to have been crying. No one else was at the location. While Officer #6409 was interviewing the woman, her husband (the accused) returned. He has no previous record with police. Based on statements from both parties and witnesses, officers determined that, at approximately 20:00 hours, while playing checkers, the victim and the accused began to argue about household expenses. The argument became heated and had been going on for approximately 25 minutes when the accused became very agitated and attempted to leave the room. The victim claims she demanded that he stay to deal with the problem at which time he told her to, "Just shut up," and slapped her with an open hand across the face. He then left the residence on foot. Upon his return, the accused stated that he had gone to a friend's house. There was an odor of alcohol on his breath. He was cooperative with the investigation and was arrested and taken to the station without incident.

The victim reported she and the accused have been married for 18 years and currently reside together at 47 First Street. She stated that they argue regularly, but most of the time it does not become physical. When asked about prior occurrences, she stated that he has grabbed or pushed her but could not recall a specific occasion. She stated that he is not a violent person toward others and will walk away rather than fight. However, the victim stated that she is now worried that he will hit her again. The victim claimed that the accused drinks socially and will have several beers on the weekend, does not have a major drinking problem, but does tend to be more easily angered when drinking. She stated that the accused drank three beers during the evening and she was drinking ginger ale. Their only child is the victim's 20-year-old daughter from an earlier relationship.

Actuarial Assessment

Based on the police investigation, the accused received a score of 3 on the ODARA; positive items were: Accused has indicators of substance abuse, Victim was concerned about future violence; Victim has a biological child from a previous partner. This score comprises the fourth or middle of seven ODARA categories. Among wife assaulters in the studies described above, seven out of ten scored 3 or less on the ODARA, and 30% of those in this category committed another assault on a female partner that came to the attention of the police within an average of five years.

Follow-Up

On December 19, 2006, the accused pled guilty to domestic assault and received a sentence of three months' probation. The only subsequent police contact occurred nine months later, when officers were called to investigate neighbors' complaints about a loud argument. Both members of the couple admitted they were having an argument, but both denied there had been any assault or threats of physical violence. Officers' investigation revealed no evidence to the contrary. A warning was issued, and no further police action was taken.

Acknowledgment

The authors thank Vern Quinsey for decades of collaboration and wise mentorship, and helpful comments on an earlier draft.

References

Ægisdóttir, S., White, M. J., Spengler, P. M., Maugherman, A. S., Anderson, L. A., Cook, R. S., et al. (2006). The meta-analysis of clinical judgment project: Fifty-six years of accumulated research on clinical versus statistical prediction. *The Counseling Psychologist, 34,* 341–382.

Barbaree, H. E., Blanchard, R., & Langton, C. M. (2003). The development of sexual aggression through the life span: The effect of age on sexual arousal and recidivism among sex offenders. In R. A. Prentky, E. S. Janus, & M. C. Seto (Eds.), *Understanding and managing sexually coercive behavior* (pp. 59–71). Annals of the New York Academy of Sciences, Vol. 989. New York: New York Academy of Sciences.

Barbaree, H. E., Langton, C. M., & Blanchard, R. (2007). Predicting recidivism in sex offenders using the VRAG and SORAG: The contribution of age-at-release. *International Journal of Forensic Mental Health, 6,* 29–46.

Barbaree, H. E., Langton, C. M., & Peacock, E. J. (2006). Different actuarial risk measures produce different risk rankings for sexual offenders. *Sexual Abuse: A Journal of Research and Treatment, 18,* 423–440.

Barbaree, H. E., Seto, M. C., Langton, C. M., & Peacock. E. J. (2001). Evaluating the predictive accuracy of six risk assessment instruments for adult sex offenders. *Criminal Justice and Behavior, 28,* 490–521.

Campbell, J. C. (2007). Prediction of homicide of and by battered women. In J. C. Campbell (Ed.), *Assessing dangerousness: Violence by sexual offenders, batterers, and child abusers.* (2nd ed.) (pp. 85–104). New York: Springer.

de Vogel, V., de Ruiter, C., van Beek, D., & Mead, G. (2004). Predictive validity of the SVR-20 and Static-99 in a Dutch sample of treated sex offenders. *Law and Human Behavior, 28,* 235–251.

Dempster, R. J. (1998). *Prediction of sexually violent recidivism: A comparison of risk assessment instruments.* Unpublished Master's thesis, Department of Psychology, Simon Fraser University, Burnaby, BC, Canada.

Douglas, K. S., & Skeem, J. L. (2005). Violence risk assessment: Getting specific about being dynamic. *Psychology, Public Policy, and Law, 11,* 347–383.

Douglas, K., Yeomans, M., & Boer, D. F. (2005). Comparative validity analysis of multiple measures of violence risk in a sample of criminal offenders. *Criminal Justice and Behavior, 32,* 479–510.

Doyle, M., & Dolan, M. (2006). Predicting community violence from patients discharged from community mental health services. *British Journal of Psychiatry, 189,* 520–526.

Doyle, M., Dolan, M., & McGovern, J. (2002). The validity of North American risk assessment tools in predicting in-patient violent behaviour in England. *Legal and Criminological Psychology, 7,* 141–152.

Ducro, C., & Pham, T. (2006). Evaluation of the SORAG and the Static-99 on Belgian sex offenders committed to a forensic facility. *Sexual Abuse: A Journal of Research and Treatment, 18,* 15–25.

Grann, M., & Wedin, I. (2002). Risk factors for recidivism among spousal assault and spousal homicide offenders. *Psychology, Crime and Law, 8,* 5–23.

Gray, N. S., Fitzgerald, S., Taylor, J., MacCulloch, M. J., & Snowden, R. J. (2007). Predicting future reconviction in offenders with intellectual disabilities: The predictive efficacy of VRAG, PCL-SV and the HCR-20. *Psychological Assessment, 19,* 474–479.

Grove, W. M., & Meehl, P. E. (1996). Comparative efficiency of informal (subjective, impressionistic) and formal (mechanical, algorithmic) prediction procedures: The clinical–statistical controversy. *Psychology, Public Policy, and Law, 2,* 293–323.

Hanson, R. K., & Harris, A. J. R. (2000). Where should we intervene? Dynamic predictors of sexual offense recidivism. *Criminal Justice and behavior, 27,* 6–35.

Hanson, R. K., Harris, A. J. R., Scott, T., & Helmus, L. (2007). Assessing the risk of sexual offenders on community supervision: The Dynamic Supervision Project. Corrections Research User Report 2007-05. Ottawa, ON, Canada: Public Safety Canada.

Hanson, R. K., & Morton-Bourgon, K. E. (2007). *The accuracy of recidivism risk assessments for sexual offenders: A meta-analysis.* (Report No. 2007-01). Ottawa, ON, Canada: Public Safety and Emergency Preparedness.

Hare, R. D. (2003). *The Revised Psychopathy Checklist.* Toronto, ON, Canada: Multi-Health Systems.

Harris, G. T. (2003). Men in his category have a 50% likelihood, but which half is he in? *Sexual Abuse: A Journal of Research and Treatment, 15,* 389–393.

Harris, G. T., & Rice, M. E. (2003). Actuarial assessment of risk among sex offenders. *Annals of the New York Academy of Sciences, 989,* 198–210.

Harris, G. T., & Rice, M. E. (2007a). Characterizing the value of actuarial violence risk assessment. *Criminal Justice and Behavior, 34,* 1638–1656.

Harris, G. T., & Rice, M. E. (2007b). Adjusting actuarial violence risk assessments based on aging and the passage of time. *Criminal Justice and Behavior, 34,* 297–313.

Harris, G. T., Rice, M. E., & Camilleri, J. A. (2004). Applying a forensic actuarial assessment (the Violence Risk Appraisal Guide) to nonforensic patients. *Journal of Interpersonal Violence, 19,* 1063–1074.

Harris, G. T., Rice, M. E., & Cormier, C. A. (2002). Prospective replication of the Violence Risk Appraisal Guide in predicting violent recidivism among forensic patients. *Law and Human Behavior, 26,* 377–394.

Harris, G. T., Rice, M. E., & Quinsey, V. L. (1993). Violent recidivism of mentally disordered offenders: The development of a statistical prediction instrument. *Criminal Justice and Behavior, 20,* 315–335.

Harris, G. T., Rice, M. E., & Quinsey, V. L. (2008). Shall evidence-based risk assessment be abandoned? *British Journal of Psychiatry, 192,* 154.

Harris, G. T., Rice, M. E., Quinsey, V. L., Lalumière, M. L., Boer, D., & Lang, C. (2003). A multi-site comparison of actuarial risk instruments for sex offenders. *Psychological Assessment, 15,* 413–425.

Hart, S. D., Michie, C., & Cooke, D. J. (2007). Precision of actuarial risk assessment instruments. *British Journal of Psychiatry, 190* (suppl. 49), s60–s65.

Hilton, N. Z., Carter, A. M., Harris, G. T., & Sharpe, A. J. B. (2008). Does using non-numerical terms to describe risk aid violence risk communication? Clinician agreement and decision-making. *Journal of Interpersonal Violence, 23,* 171–188.

Hilton, N. Z., & Harris, G. T. (2009). How nonrecidivism affects predictive accuracy: Evidence from a cross-validation of the Ontario Domestic Assault Risk Assessment (ODARA). *Journal of Interpersonal Violence, 24,* 326–337.

Hilton, N. Z., Harris, G. T., & Holder, N. L. (2008). Actuarial violence risk assessment in hospital-based partner assault clinics. *Canadian Journal of Nursing Research, 40,* 56–70.

Hilton, N. Z., Harris, G. T., Rawson, K., & Beach, C. (2005). Communication of risk information to forensic decision-makers. *Criminal Justice and Behavior, 32,* 97–116.

Hilton, N. Z., Harris, G. T., & Rice, M. E. (2006). Sixty-six years of research on the clinical versus actuarial prediction of violence. *The Counseling Psychologist, 34,* 400–409.

Hilton, N. Z., Harris, G. T., & Rice, M. E. (2007). The effect of arrest on wife assault recidivism, controlling for pre-arrest risk. *Criminal Justice and Behavior, 34,* 1334–1344.

Hilton, N. Z., Harris, G. T., & Rice, M. E. (2009). *Risk assessment of domestically violent men: Tools for criminal justice, offender intervention, and victim services.* Washington, DC: American Psychological Association.

Hilton, N. Z., Harris, G. T., Rice, M. E., Eke, A. W., & Lowe-Wetmore, T. (2007). Training front-line users in the Ontario Domestic Assault Risk Assessment (ODARA), a tool for police domestic investigations. *Canadian Journal of Police and Security Services, 5,* 95–98.

Hilton, N. Z., Harris, G. T., Rice, M. E., Houghton, R. E., & Eke, A. W. (2008). An indepth actuarial assessment for wife assault recidivism: The *Domestic Violence Risk Appraisal Guide. Law and Human Behavior, 32,* 150–163.

Hilton, N. Z., Harris, G. T., Rice, M. E., Lang, C., Cormier, C. A., & Lines, K. J. (2004). A brief actuarial assessment for the prediction of wife assault recidivism: The Ontario Domestic Assault Risk Assessment. *Psychological Assessment, 16,* 267–275.

Hilton, N. Z., & Simmons, J. L. (2001). Actuarial and clinical risk assessment in decisions to release mentally disordered offenders from maximum security. *Law and Human Behavior, 25,* 393–408.

Janus, E. S., & Meehl, P. E. (1997). Assessing the legal standard for predictions of dangerousness in sex offender commitment proceedings. *Psychology, Public Policy and Law, 3,* 33–64.

Johansen, S. H. (2007). *Accuracy of predictions of sexual offense recidivism: A comparison of actuarial and clinical methods.* Dissertation Abstracts International: Section B. The Sciences and Engineering Vol. 68 (3-B) p. 1929.

Kropp, P. R., & Hart, S. D. (2000). The Spousal Assault Risk Assessment (SARA) Guide: Reliability and validity in adult male offenders. *Law and Human Behavior, 24,* 101–118.

Langton, C. M., Barbaree, H. E., Seto, M. C., Peacock, E. J., Harkins, L., & Hansen, K. T. (2007). Actuarial assessment of risk for reoffense among adult sex offenders. *Criminal Justice and Behavior, 34,* 37–59.

McDermott, B. E., Quanbeck, C. D., Scott, C. L., Edens, F., & Busse, D. (2007). Examining the role of static and dynamic risk factors in the prediction of in-patient violence. *Law and Human Behavior.*

McKee, S. A., Harris, G. T., & Rice, M. E. (2007). Improving forensic tribunal decisions: The role of the clinician. *Behavioral Sciences and the Law, 25,* 485–506.

Meehl, P. E. (1954). *Clinical vs. statistical prediction.* Minneapolis: University of Minnesota Press.

Mossman, D. (2008). Analyzing the performance of risk assessment instruments: A response to Vrieze and Grove (2007). *Law and Human Behavior, 32,* 279–291.

Mulvey, E. P., Odgers, C., Skeem, J., Gardner, W., Shcubert, C., & Lidz, C. (2006). Substance use and community violence: A test of the relation at the daily level. *Journal of Consulting and Clinical Psychology, 74,* 743–754.

Nuffield, J. (1982). *Parole decision-making in Canada: Research towards decision guidelines.* Ottawa, ON, Canada: Supply and Services Canada.

Olver, M. E. (2003). *The development and validation of the Violence Risk Scale: Sexual Offender Version (VRS:SO) and its relationship to psychopathy and treatment attrition.* Unpublished doctoral dissertation, Psychology Department, University of Saskatchewan, Saskatoon, SK, Canada.

Olver, M. E., Wong, S. C., Nicholaichuk, T., & Gordon, A. (2007). The validity and reliability of the Violence Risk Scale–Sexual Offender version: Assessing sex offender risk and evaluating therapeutic change. *Psychological Assessment, 19,* 318–329.

Pham, T. H. (2004). Assessing risk for violence in a Belgian forensic population: Concurrent and predictive validity of the Hare Psychopathy Checklist, the Violence Risk Assessment Guide (VRAG) and the Historical Clinical Risk-20 items (HCR-20). Unpublished manuscript.

Pham, T. H., Ducro, C., Marghem, B., & Réveillère, J. (2005). Evaluation du risque de récidivie au sein d'une population de délinquants incarceréré ou interné en Belgique francophone. *Annales Médico Psychologiques, 163,* 842–845.

Platek, S. M., Keenan, J. P., & Shackelford, T. K. (2007). *Evolutionary cognitive neuroscience.* Cambridge, MA: The MIT Press.

Polvi, N. H. (2001, February). *The relative efficacy of statistical versus clinical predictions of dangerousness.* Dissertation Abstracts International: Section B: Sciences and Engineering, 61 (7-B). Department of Psychology, Simon Fraser University, Burnaby, BC, Canada.

Quinsey, V. L., Coleman, G., Jones, B., & Altrows, I. F. (1997). Proximal antecedents of eloping and reoffending among mentally disordered offenders. *Journal of Interpersonal Violence, 12,* 794–813.

Quinsey, V. L., Harris, G. T., Rice, M. E. & Cormier, C. A. (1998). *Violent offenders: Appraising and managing risk.* Washington, DC: American Psychological Association.

Quinsey, V. L., Harris, G. T., Rice, M. E., & Cormier, C. A. (2006). *Violent offenders: Appraising and managing risk* (2nd Ed.). Washington, DC: American Psychological Association.

Quinsey, V. L., Jones, G. B., Book, A. S., & Barr, K. N. (2006). The dynamic prediction of antisocial behavior among forensic psychiatric patients: A prospective field study. *Journal of Interpersonal Violence, 21,* 1–27.

Quinsey, V. L., Rice, M. E., & Harris, G. T. (1995). The actuarial prediction of sexual recidivism. *Journal of Interpersonal Violence, 10,* 85–105.

Rettenberger, M., & Eher, R. (2007). Predicting reoffence in sexual offender subtypes: A prospective validation study of the German version of the Sex Offender Risk Appraisal Guide (SORAG). *Sexual Offender Treatment, 2,* 1–12.

Rice, M. E. (2008). Current status of violence risk assessment: Is there a role for clinical judgment? In G. Bourgon, R. K. Hanson, J. D. Pozzulo, K. E. Morton Bourgon, & C. L. Tanasichuk (Eds.). *Proceedings of the North American Correctional and Criminal Justice Psychology Conference.* Public Safety Canada User Report 2008-02. Public Safety Canada: Ottawa, ON. Available from: http://www.publicsafety.gc.ca/res/cor/rep/2008-02-naccjpc-eng.aspx.

Rice, M. E. & Harris, G. T. (1995). Violent recidivism: Assessing predictive validity. *Journal of Consulting and Clinical Psychology,* 63, 737–748.

Rice, M. E. & Harris, G. T. (1997). Cross validation and extension of the Violence Risk Appraisal Guide for child molesters and rapists. *Law and Human Behavior, 21,* 231–241.

Rice, M. E. & Harris, G. T. (2005). Comparing effect sizes in follow-up studies: ROC, Cohen's d and r. *Law and Human Behavior, 29,* 615–620.

Rice, M. E., Harris, G. T., & Cormier, C. A. (1992). Evaluation of a maximum security therapeutic community for psychopaths and other mentally disordered offenders. *Law and Human Behavior, 16,* 399–412.
Rice, M. E., Harris, G. T., Lang, C., & Bell, V. (1990). Recidivism among male insanity acquittees. *Journal of Psychiatry and Law, 18,* 379–403.
Rice, M. E., Harris, G. T., Lang, C., & Cormier, C. A. (2006). Violent sex offenses: How are they best measured from official records? *Law and Human Behavior, 30,* 525–541.
Rice, M. E., Harris, G. T., & Quinsey, V. L. (1990). A followup of rapists assessed in a maximum security psychiatric facility. *Journal of Interpersonal Violence, 5,* 435–448.
Rice, M. E., Quinsey, V. L., & Harris, G. T. (1991). Sexual recidivism among child molesters released from a maximum security psychiatric institution. *Journal of Consulting and Clinical Psychology, 59,* 381–386.
Seto, M. C. (2005). Is more better? Combining actuarial risk scales to predict recidivism among adult sex offenders. *Psychological Assessment, 17,* 156–167.
Sjöstedt, G., & Langström, N. (2002). Assessment of risk for criminal recidivism among rapists: A comparison of four different measures. *Psychology, Crime and Law, 8,* 25–40.
Skeem, J. L., Schubert, C., Odgers, C., Mulvey, E. P., Gardner, W., & Lidz, C. (2006). Psychiatric symptoms and community violence among high-risk patients: A test of the relationship at the weekly level. *Journal of Consulting and Clinical Psychology, 74,* 967–979.
Snowden, R. J., Gray, N., Taylor, J., & MacCulloch, M. J. (2007). Actuarial prediction of violent recidivism in mentally disordered offenders. *Psychological Medicine, 37,* 1539–1549.
Thomson, L. (2005, June). *Risk assessment in patients with schizophrenia in a high security hospital.* Forensic Psychiatry Research Society. University of Edinburgh, UK.
Urbaniok, F., Noll, T., Grunewald, S., Steinbach, J., & Endrass, J. (2006). Prediction of violent and sexual offences: A replication study of the VRAG in Switzerland. *Journal of Forensic Psychiatry and Psychology, 17,* 23–31.
Vrieze, S. I., & Grove, W. M. (2008). Predicting sex offender recidivism. I. Correcting for item overselection and accuracy overestimation in scale development. II. Sampling error-induced attenuation of predictive validity over base rate information. *Law and Human Behavior, 32,* 279–291.
Webster, C. D., Harris, G. T., Rice, M. E., Cormier, C. A., & Quinsey, V. L. (1994). *The Violence Prediction Scheme.* Toronto, ON, Canada: Centre of Criminology, University of Toronto.
Williams, K, R., & Houghton, A. B. (2004). Assessing the risk of domestic violence reoffending: A validation study. *Law and Human Behavior, 28,* 437–455.
Wollert, R. (2006). Low base rates limit expert certainty when current actuarials are used to identify sexually violent predators: An application of Baye's Theorem. *Psychology, Public Policy, and Law, 12,* 56–85.
Yessine, A. K., & Bonta, J. (2006). Tracking high-risk, violent offenders: An examination of the national flagging system. *Canadian Journal of Criminology and Criminal Justice, 48,* 573–607.

7
Two Treatment- and Change-Oriented Risk Assessment Tools

The Violence Risk Scale and Violence Risk Scale–Sexual Offender Version

STEPHEN C. P. WONG and MARK E. OLVER

For persons with entrenched patterns of violence, the assessment, prediction, and treatment/management of the violent behaviors are the three major links essential in their rehabilitation, the goal of which is to reduce their risk of violence and, consequently, societal violence. The underlying assumptions of this approach are that assessment, which identifies the causes of violence that are dynamic or changeable, in combination with interventions and treatments, can reduce the likelihood violence. There is now an extensive literature documenting the efficacy of behavioral interventions to reduce general and violent recidivism (see McGuire, 2008, for a recent review). It follows that violence risk assessment and prediction should be considered as no more than the prelude for a general violence reduction strategy.

If violence reduction is the goal of the assessment-prediction-treatment trilogy, then assessment and prediction of violence should be guided by the theoretical underpinnings of violence reduction treatment and should be integrated in their implementation to increase the likelihood of successful outcome (see Wong, Gordon, & Gu, 2007). The "what works" literature, a large body of literature that addresses the issues of effective correctional treatment, has identified the Risk-Need-Responsivity (RNR) (Andrews & Bonta, 2006) principles as useful guidelines for treatment designed to reduce the risk of recidivism. Treatment approaches, often referred to as correctional treatment, that follow the risk-need-responsivity principles are generally more effective in reducing the risk of recidivism in adult and young offenders than those that do not follow such principles (see Andrews & Bonta, 2003; Andrews, Zinger, Hoge, Bonta, Gendreau, & Cullen, 1990). Recent writings, including meta-analytic and other reviews, have identified the "... risk-need-responsivity framework (Andrews et al. 2003) [as] ... currently the best validated model" (McGuire, 2008, p. 2591) for reducing aggression and violence.

Briefly, the Risk principle, in addressing the question of "who" to treat, directs that the intensity of treatment should match the subjects' risk level (i.e., level of risk should be associated with a corresponding intensity of treatment). The Need principle, in addressing the question of "what" to treat, directs that the individual's criminogenic needs; that is, needs linked to violence or criminality, such as criminal attitudes, criminal associates, and so forth, must be identified for treatment. Improvements in criminogenic needs should result in violence risk reduction, whereas treatment of noncriminogenic needs will not reduce violence risk.

The Responsivity principle, in addressing the question of "how" to deliver treatment, directs that, to maximize treatment effectiveness, treatment delivery must accommodate the subject's idiosyncratic characteristics including their cognitive and intellectual abilities, learning styles, level of motivation and readiness for treatment, and cultural background. One of the most daunting responsivity factors in correctional treatment is to treat the seemingly unmotivated, noncompliant, and treatment-resistant offender, that is, dealing with the general issue of treatment readiness.

The Violence Risk Scale (VRS) (see Wong & Gordon, 2006) and the Violence Risk Scale–Sexual Offender version (VRS-SO) (see Olver, Wong, Nicholaichuk, & Gordon, 2007) integrate violence risk assessment and prediction with risk reduction treatment and the measurement of treatment change. These instruments also attend to the Risk, Need, and Responsivity Principles by addressing the "who," "what," and "how" questions of effective correctional treatment.

VRS/VRS-SO assessments inform treatment providers about "who" to treat by identifying the risk level of potential treatment candidates, secondly, "what" to treat by identifying dynamic or changeable risk predictors linked to violence as treatment targets, and "how" to treat by answering a key responsivity question, that is, the individual's readiness for treatment and the matching therapeutic approaches using a modified Stages of Change model (Prochaska, DiClemente, & Norcross, 1992). An additional function of the VRS/VRS-SO is that these tools can also measure treatment change using the Stages of Change model—linking, quantitatively, treatment change to changes in nonsexual violent or sexual recidivism. The VRS and the VRS-SO, which, obviously, can be used also as stand-alone risk assessment and prediction tools, share many common features including the rationale for their development, the use of static and dynamic risk predictors to identify criminogenic needs, and the Stages of Change model to quantify change and measure level of treatment readiness. To avoid duplication throughout the rest of this chapter, the areas of similarity between the two tools are indicated and discussed together where appropriate.

The Violence Risk Scale

The VRS is considered a conceptual actuarial risk assessment tool (Hanson & Morton-Bourgon, 2007) because the theoretical underpinnings of the tools and the risk predictors are derived primarily from the *Psychology of Criminal Conduct* (PCC) (see Andrews & Bonta, 1994, 1998, 2003, 2006), and the organization is based on a well-researched and validated model of correctional or risk reduction treatment: the Risk, Need and Responsivity Principles. The VRS/VRS-SO are actuarial in nature, because the computation of the total scores is based on clearly articulated scoring rubrics and the empirical validations of the tools are based on accepted practices in psychometrics.[1]

The Violence Risk Scale Static and Dynamic Variables

The VRS uses 6 static and 20 dynamic variables (see Table 7.1 for a listing of variables and brief item descriptions) for assessment. The five static variables, (1) *Age at First Violent Conviction,* (2) *Number of Young Offender Convictions,* (3) *Violence Throughout Lifespan,* (4) *Prior Release Failures or Escapes,* and (5) *Stability of Family Upbringing,* reflect the client's history or "track record" of violence and criminality and parallel what the PCC terms "antisocial behavioral history." The sixth VRS static variable, *Current Age,* reflects the well-established link between age and criminality (Hirschi & Gottfredson, 1983). Although age can change, it remains a VRS static factor because age-related changes obviously cannot be influenced by interventions.

The VRS dynamic variables are changeable or potentially changeable factors that can be affected by psychological, social, or physiological means, such as treatment. Changes in the dynamic factors (also referred to as variable risk factors, Kraemer, Kazdin, Offord, Kessler, Jensen, & Kupfer, 1997) should be linked to changes in recidivism. The antisocial attitude domain of the PCC is captured by seven VRS variables: *Criminal Attitude, Interpersonal Aggression, Weapon Use, Insight into Violence, Violence Cycle, Impulsivity,* and *Cognitive Distortion,* that identify different facets of criminal attitudes and other closely related issues that can be selectively targeted for treatment. The antisocial associate domain of the PCC is captured by the VRS *Criminal Peers*

Table 7.1 VRS Static and Dynamic Items and Brief Item Descriptions*

	Static Items
S1	Current age: Less than 30 years; 30–39; 40–44; 45 years and older
S2	Age at first violent conviction: <15 years; 15–19; 20–29; 30 years and older
S3	Number of young offender convictions: >2; 2; 1; 0
S4	Violence throughout lifespan: Pattern of violence beginning early; few incidents; 1 incident; no history
S5	Prior release failures: 1 or more escapes; breached twice; breached once; no failures
S6	Stability of family upbringing: very little stability; more stability but still inadequate; fairly stable; stable
	Dynamic Items
D1	Violent lifestyle: Overall lifestyle characterized by violence
D2	Criminal personality: Pressure of shallow effect and deceitful interpersonal behaviors
D3	Criminal attitudes: Does not believe in the importance of pro-social behavior and rules
D4	Work ethic: Does not use socially appropriate ways to support self financially
D5	Criminal peers: Violent behavior and negative peer influences are closely related
D6	Interpersonal aggression: Habitual use of violence or aggression in interpersonal interactions
D7	Emotional control: Lack of emotional regulation
D8	Violence during institutionalization: Prone to violent behaviors while in custody
D9	Weapon use: Significant association between possession or use of weapons and violence
D10	Insight into violence: Poor understanding of the precipitating factors of violence
D11	Mental disorder: Association between mental disorder and violent behavior
D12	Substance abuse: Substance abuse problems linked to violence
D13	Stability of relationships: Unable to maintain stable marital or common-law relationships
D14	Community support: Lack of positive support people, services, or plans in community
D15	Release to high-risk situation: Offender is planning or likely to be released to situations linked to violence
D16	Violence cycle: Recurring pattern of interpersonal, situational, and personal factors linked to violence
D17	Impulsivity: Typically does not consider consequences before reacting
D18	Cognitive distortions: Uses distorted thinking to justify or rationalize violent behavior
D19	Compliance with community supervision: Poor cooperation with community supervision
D20	Security level at release: Likely to be released from higher security institutions

Note: The authors thank Dr. Kathy Lewis for assembling this table.

* All items are rated on a four-point (3, 2, 1, 0) scale. Item descriptions are abbreviated examples of the originals and are not intended to be used for clinical or research purposes. Please consult the VRS rating manual (Wong & Gordon, 1999–2003) for more detailed descriptions, stages of change ratings, and scoring instructions.

variable. Antisocial personality of the PCC is captured by the VRS *Criminal Personality* variable *(Shallow Affect & Deceitful Interpersonal Interactions)*, which primarily reflects the Psychopathy Checklist–Revised (PCL-R) Factor 1 characteristics (Hare, 2003). The domains of home, school, work, and leisure of the PCC are captured by the VRS variables: *Violent Lifestyle, Work Ethic, Substance Abuse, Stability of Relationships with Significant Others, Community Support, Release to High Risk Situations,* and *Compliance with Community Supervision.*

Two VRS variables that are not found in either the PCC or among the risk factors suggested by Douglas and Skeem (2005) as potential dynamic factors to consider are *Violence During*

Institutionalization and *Security Level of Anticipated Release Institution*, both of which are well supported by empirical research (Duncan, Kennedy, & Patrick, 1995; Hann & Harman, 1992; Lattimore, Visher, & Linster, 1995; also see Wong & Gordon, 2006 for more detailed discussions). In sum, there is good theoretical support for the inclusion of all 26 static and dynamic variables in the VRS.

Ratings of the VRS/VRS-SO Static and Dynamic Variables. The VRS/VRS-SO static variables can predict recidivism, but remain unchanged regardless of treatment interventions. The VRS/VRS-SO dynamic and static variables are rated on 4-point Likert scales (0, 1, 2, or 3) based on a careful file review and a semistructured interview. For most variables, higher ratings indicate a closer link to violence in lifetime functioning. Higher ratings on the static variables indicate worse "track records" of criminality and early experiences. Dynamic variables closely linked to violence (rated 2 or 3) are appropriate targets for violence reduction treatment (the *Need principle*). The total VRS/VRS-SO score (the sum of static and dynamic variable ratings) indicates the level of violence risk; the higher the score, the higher the risk. Individuals with higher VRS/VRS-SO scores should be appropriate candidates for high-intensity intervention (the *Risk principle*). High VRS/VRS-SO scores also indicate that there are many problem areas linked to violence (sexual violence) and criminality. There are also guidelines in place to use Clinical Overrides to adjust risk appraisals under exceptional circumstances such as clear expression of an intention to commit an offense. Details about rating and scoring the VRS/VRS-SO are set forth in the VRS/VRS-SO Manuals (Wong & Gordon, 1999–2003; Wong, Olver, Nicholaichuk & Gordon, 2003; also see Wong & Gordon, 2006).

The VRS/VRS-SO uses a scheme based on a modified Transtheoretical Model of Charge to assess the individual's readiness for treatment and treatment change. Dynamic variables identified as treatment targets (rated 2 or 3) are also rated to determine the individual's stage of change (i.e., readiness for treatment) evidenced by the individual. The five stages of change are *Precontemplation, Contemplation, Preparation, Action,* and *Maintenance.* Those in the Precontemplation stage have neither insight nor intention to change in the foreseeable future, are often in denial, and externalize blame. Those in the Contemplation stage are "fence-sitters"; they acknowledge their problems but have shown no relevant behavioral change: "all talk, no walk." Those in the Preparation stage combine intentions to change with relevant behavioral changes to address problems. However, changes tend to be recent or quite unstable. Those in the Action stage actively and consistently modify their behaviors, attitudes, and environment to address their problems, overt behavioral changes are made, commitments are followed to completion, and energy is expended to change. In the Maintenance stage, relapse prevention techniques are used to consolidate, strengthen, and generalize the gains made in the Action stage to other challenging situations. The operationalizations of the Stages of Change are designed to measure the extent to which the positive coping skills and strategies that the individual has learned are stable, sustainable, and generalizable. Progression in treatment from a less-advanced to more-advanced stage of change for each treatment target is an indication of improvement, which should lead to risk reduction in that treatment target. Progression through the stages is translated into a quantitative measure of risk reduction for each treatment target.

For both VRS/VRS-SO, the pretreatment rating for each of the dynamic risk variables minus the change in risk based on the individual's progress through the stages provides the posttreatment level of risk. Progression from one stage to the next stage is set as equivalent to 0.5 points in the reduction in risk rating, with the exception of progressing from the precontemplation to the contemplation stage because no behavioral change is required and, therefore, no reduction in risk is registered. For example, a subject who progresses from the contemplation stage at the start of treatment to the action stage at the end of treatment has progressed through two stages, resulting in a 1-point reduction of the pretreatment VRS/VRS-SO rating of that particular dynamic variable. Each dynamic variable targeted for treatment is so rated to determine the total reduction in risk at the end of treatment.

Using the stages of change model to evaluate changes in risk has important advantages over simply rerating items at posttreatment. Some of the criteria for rating VRS/VRS-SO dynamic items are based in large part on behaviors that are typically observed in community settings, but not in controlled environments such as prisons or mental health facilities, which is especially the case for sex offenders (for example, access to potential child victims, child pornography, and so forth). Given this reality, where appropriate, the stages of change descriptions were developed to "capture offense-linked proxy behaviors that are relevant to treatment and are observable in (custodial) and/or treatment settings" so that therapists can evaluate the degree of change taking place by observing in-treatment behaviors (Olver et al., 2007, p. 321). The stages of change operationalization also describe how offenders change in therapy, in addition to evaluating the amount of change and potential risk reduction that has occurred.

Target Populations for the VRS

The VRS has been validated on adult male offenders in Canada (Burt, 2000, 2003; Gordon, 1998; Lewis, 2004; Wong & Burt, 2007; Wong & Gordon, 2006) with a substantial number of them being of aboriginal ancestry. The VRS has also been validated on adult male medium secured forensic psychiatry inpatients in the United Kingdom (Dolan & Fullam, 2007), in the Netherlands (de Vries Robbé, Weenink, & de Vogel, 2006), and in Canada (Wilde & Wong; 2000). Both the VRS and the VRS-SO currently are required assessment tools for participants of the Dangerous and Severe Personality Disorder (DSPD) (Home Office, Department of Health, 1999) program in the United Kingdom. The DSPD program has 287 purposefully created beds in two high-security hospitals and two prison settings. Extensive research and program evaluations efforts are under way for the DSPD program. The Correctional Service of Canada uses the VRS to assess risk and to measure treatment change in the Violence Prevention Program for high-risk violent federal offenders (Wong & Gordon, 2006, p. 281). The Irish Prison Service and the Victoria and Queensland Corrective Service in Australia also use the VRS as one of their primary assessment tools for their offenders.

The VRS has also been validated in a sample of 154 high-risk and personality-disordered offenders, many of whom had significant psychopathic characteristics (Lewis, Olver, & Wong, 2009). Research is under way to validate the VRS on female forensic samples as well. Based on available evidence, the VRS is appropriate for use in the assessment and prediction of risk for violent and nonviolent recidivism, to guide treatment planning and to measure risk change in male forensic samples, including those with significant psychopathic personality characteristics.

Most VRS dynamic items were selected and their description written to assess a certain construct such as criminal attitude. The rating of a dynamic item (0, 1, 2 or 3), in most cases, assesses the degree of association between the construct and violence. For example, the rating of the *Criminal Attitude* item assesses the degree of association between *Criminal Attitude* and violence, and so does the *Substance Abuse* item. The more items that are positively endorsed (rated 2 or 3), the more the individual's problem areas are associated with violence. As such, ratings of the VRS dynamic items can be used to assess the association of common criminogenic needs areas with violence simply based on face validity of the items. When the VRS/VRS-SO is used in this manner without aggregating the ratings and referring to normative empirical data such as base rate information, the user is essentially using a structured professional judgment approach to assess risk, that is, make a judgment of the risk level based on weighing the evidence provided by a number of risk predictors.

Reliability and Validity of the VRS

The VRS can be rated reliably; interclass correlations of .80 to over .90 have been obtained (see de Vries Robbé et al., 2006; Dolan & Fullam, 2007; Lewis et al., 2008; Wong & Gordon, 2006). Internal consistency as measured via Cronbach's alpha is .93, and the standard error of measurement for the VRS total score is .54 (Wong & Gordon, 2006). Concurrent validity assessed based on associations with other empirically validated risk assessment tools or schemes produced large correlations in the expected directions: with the Psychopathy Checklist–Revised (PCL-R), between .62 and .83; Level of Service Inventory–Revised (LSI-R), .83; General Statistical Information on Recidivism (GSIR), –.63); and Historical-Clinical-Risk Management 20 (HCR-20), between .83 and .84 (see de Vries Robbé et al., 2006; Dolan & Fullam, 2007; Lewis et al., 2009; Wong & Gordon, 2006).

Exploratory factor analysis produced three correlated factors, which accounted for 56% of the total variance (Wong & Gordon, 2006). Factor 1 included 2 static and 10 dynamic predictors (accounting for 41.7% of variance); it tends to measure attitudes and behaviors specific to interpersonal violence. Factor 3 consisted of 1 static and 9 dynamic predictors; it tends to measure a broad pattern of antisocial lifestyle. Factors 1 and 3 were quite highly correlated ($r = .55$) and are more closely linked to violent reconviction ($r = .38$ and .32 respectively; both $p < .001$), than Factor 2 (with 3 static and 1 dynamic predictor; $r = .13$; $p < .001$), which consisted of a combination of demographic static factors and certain dynamic factors (e.g., impulsivity) that tend to reflect young age and criminogenic need more typical for younger offenders (e.g., antisocial peers, impulsivity). Factors 1 and 3 are not as strongly correlated with Factor 2 ($r = .12$ and .20, respectively) as with each other. The results of the preliminary factor analyses suggested that Factors 1 and 3, which have most of the dynamic variables, have more in common with each other than with Factor 2, which has three of six static variables. These results provided some evidence for the separation of the static and dynamic predictors.

Predictive validity of the VRS has been assessed using violent and nonviolent criminal convictions as the criterion variable after release to the community with a mean follow-up time of 4.4 years ($n = 918$; Wong & Gordon, 2006). Pearson correlations and receiver operating characteristic (ROC) analyses produced values of .40 and .75 for violent reconviction, respectively, and .39 and .72 for nonviolent reconvictions, respectively. Similar predictive validities were obtained for 1-, 2-, and 3-year follow-ups. The normative sample was divided into high-, medium-, and low-risk groups using approximately 1 *SD* above and below the mean as cutoff scores. To control for time at risk, survival analyses of the three groups produced three clearly separated and significantly different survival functions, further evidence for the predictive validity of the VRS (Figure 7.1).

When divided into 5-point bins, there was an approximate linear relationship between VRS dynamic score intervals[2] and violent recidivism ($R^2 = 0.97$), indicating that there is a near proportionate increase in violence risk with each increase in VRS score interval. In other words, the more problems the offender experiences, as indicated by an increase in VRS score, the higher the likelihood of violent recidivism. A similar linear relationship between VRS total score and violent recidivism also was obtained ($R^2 = 0.84$; Wong & Gordon, 2006; see Figure 7.3).

Male forensic psychiatric inpatients in the United Kingdom ($n = 136$) with subsequent violent institutional behaviors against a person had significantly higher VRS scores than those who did not have such violent behaviors (Dolan & Fullam, 2007). In the same study, predictive validity assessed using ROC analyses produced identical areas under the curve (AUCs) of .71 for VRS and the HCR-20. In a sample of Dutch forensic psychiatric patients (de Vries Robbé et al., 2006; $n = 50$), correlations of the VRS scores with violent recidivism at $r = .48$ and AUC values of .78 were obtained after 9.4 years of follow-up in the community postrelease.

In a sample of 154 violence-prone offenders with a mean PCL-R score of 26 referred for violence reduction intervention (Lewis et al., 2009), the mean VRS score was 61.5, or about 1.2 *SD*

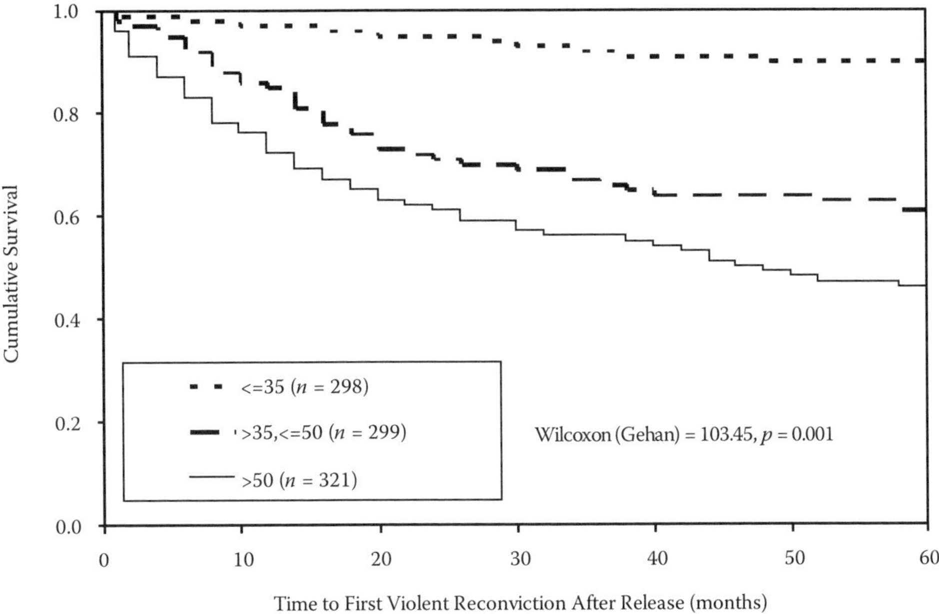

Figure 7.1 Survival analyses using low, medium, and high VRS groups. (Results adapted from Wong & Gordon, 2006. With permission.)

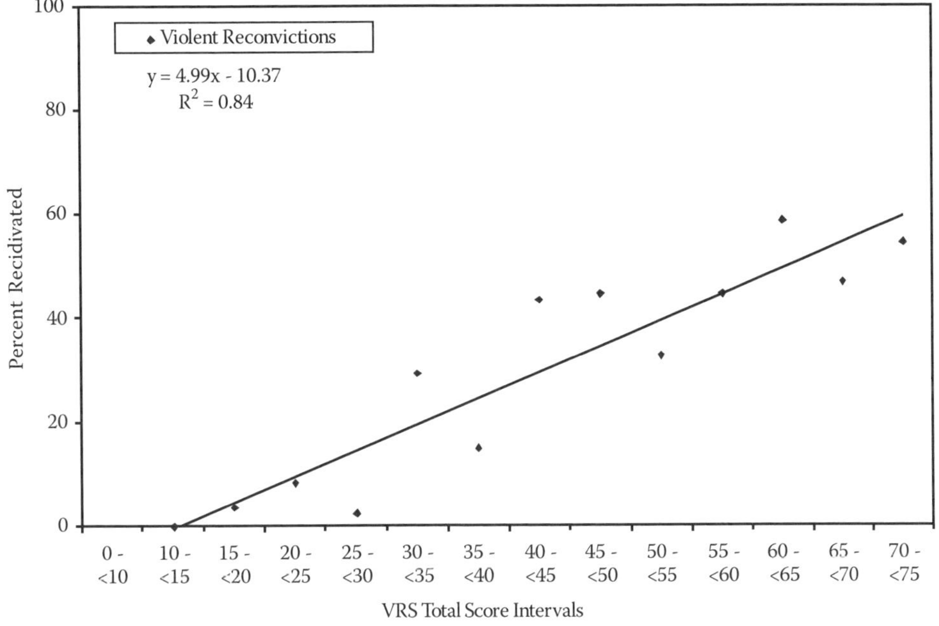

Figure 7.2 VRS total score intervals and the prediction of violent reconvictions. (Results adapted from Wong & Gordon, 2006. With permission.)

above the VRS mean score (41.9) of the normative sample. The findings provide evidence for construct validity for the VRS, given that a higher-risk sample with high psychopathy scores also demonstrated higher VRS scores. As in Wong and Gordon (2006), dynamic variables had higher correlations with violent than nonviolent reconvictions (the opposite trend was evident for static variables), but this difference was more pronounced in the above sample of high-risk/high-need offenders (Lewis et al., 2009) than in the lower-risk normative group (Wong & Gordon, 2006). The results suggest that the VRS dynamic variables appear to be better able to predict violence than nonviolence criminal behaviors even in a sample of high-risk personality-disordered offenders, thus offering support for the construct validity of the VRS as a measure of violence risk.

Linking Changes in the VRS Dynamic Variables to Treatment Outcome

The conditions required to evaluate the dynamic nature of putative dynamic variables have been clearly articulated by Kraemer et al. (1997). Variable dynamic variables are those that are simply changeable, but are not the target of interventions (for example, age). In contrast, causal dynamic variables are those that, when purposely manipulated, such as through a treatment program, produce predicted changes in outcomes such as reduction in recidivism. The cause-and-effect nature of the causal dynamic variables is important to establish for treatment purposes because the purpose of risk reduction treatment is to affect changes in the positive risk predictors with resulting reductions in criminal offending. The necessary and sufficient conditions to establish the causal nature of dynamic predictors are that the dynamic variables are measured in at least two time points to assess change, and that changes or reductions in the dynamic variables are linked to reductions in recidivism evaluated in a prospective follow-up design.

In a sample of 154 high-risk violent and personality-disordered male federal offenders who participated in a violence reduction treatment program for 8 to 10 months, VRS dynamic variables that were identified as treatment targets were rated on the stages of change pre- and posttreatment (at two time points) to assess treatment improvement (Lewis et al., 2009). The movements in the stage of change pre- and posttreatment were used to generate change scores for the participants who were prospectively followed up posttreatment for 6 years in the community. Significant negative correlations were obtained between VRS change scores and violent ($r = -.26$) but not with nonviolent recidivism. In other words, more treatment improvements (that is, more positive changes) were linked to lower rates of violent, but not nonviolent, recidivism. Four groups that demonstrated different degrees of treatment changes were created by dividing the magnitude of VRS change scores into quartiles, and violent recidivism was assessed using Cox regression survival analyses to control for static risk and different follow-up times. Groups with larger change scores showed lower rates of violent recidivism. The results suggest that the VRS dynamic variables can be used to assess treatment-mediated changes in risk for violence and can be considered as causal dynamic variables according to criteria set forth by Kramer et al. (1997). A caveat is that treatment change and recidivism, though causally linked, could be mediated by yet another unidentified intervening variable.

The VRS Screening Version

The VRS screening version (VRS-SV) was developed to serve as a screening tool for use in brief intake evaluations, or to determine those who may require a more in-depth assessment for other major decision-making purposes. The VRS-SV consists of 11 VRS predictors with 6 static (S1, S2, S3, S4, S5, S6) and 5 dynamic VRS predictors (D1, D6, D7, D8 and D17) that sample a representative range of the dynamic predictors. The sample ($n = 918$) used to validate the VRS-SV is the same as the VRS (see Wong & Gordon, 2006). ROC analyses used to assess the predictive validity of the VRS-SV produced AUCs of .74 for both violent and all reconvictions (with upper and lower bounds for 95% confidence intervals of .71 and .77 for both) with a mean follow-up time of 4.4 years. These results indicate that the VRS-SV is suitable for rapid assessments and screening purposes. Although assessments using the VRS-SV provide much less information about the subject than those employing the VRS, the predictive efficacy of the SV is almost indistinguishable from the VRS. As such, the SV is useful for identifying offenders' risk levels and associated treatment needs.

Sex Offender Risk Assessment: Instruments, Issues, and Practices

A substantial amount of work in the field of sex offender risk assessment and prediction has identified a number of key static predictors of sexual recidivism (e.g., Hanson and Bussière, 1998; Hanson, Steffy, & Gauthier, 1993; Quinsey, Rice, & Harris, 1995; Rice, Harris, & Quinsey, 1990). Predictors such as repeated convictions for new sex offenses and male victim gender are robust static predictors of sexual recidivism. Subsequent investigations (e.g., Beech, Friendship, Erikson, & Hanson, 2002; Hanson & Harris, 2000; Hudson, Wales, Bakker, & Ward, 2002; Olver, 2003) and meta-analyses (see Hanson and Morton-Bourgon's, 2004, updated meta-analysis of 95 sex offender recidivism studies) have identified dynamic predictors of sexual recidivism such as deviant sexual interests, antisocial orientation, intimacy deficits, and sex offender attitudes.

Sexual offender risk assessment tools consisting solely of static predictors typically combine the ratings of a number of historical or unchangeable predictors—such as past sexual or criminal convictions—in an actuarial manner to arrive at a score that correlates with future sexual offending. Examples of these static actuarial tools include the Sex Offender Risk Appraisal Guide (SORAG; Quinsey et al., 1995), Rapid Risk Assessment for Sexual Offense Recidivism (RRASOR) (Hanson, 1997), Static 99 (Hanson & Thornton, 1999), and the Static 2002 (Hanson & Thornton, 2003) among others. Static actuarial measures are fairly reliable to rate and have good levels of predictive accuracy (e.g., Hanson & Morton-Bourgon, 2007; Harris et al., 2003). However, because static risk assessment tools use past events to predict future events, they are not suitable for assessing the current functioning of the individual or informing important clinical or management activities such as treatment to reduce the risk for sexual recidivism, assessment of changes in risk, and community supervision of the individual. After all, reducing and managing recidivism risk should be the primary focus of risk assessment work, not recidivism prediction per se (see Douglas and Kropp, 2002; Wong et al., 2007; Wong & Hare, 2005).

The use of dynamic predictors to link risk assessment and treatment assumes that offender risk is not static, fixed, or immutable, but rather is dynamic and changeable and that positive changes can occur on treatment targets. Offenders can reduce their risk through appropriate treatment (see Andrews et al., 1990; Hanson et al., 2002) or simply with the passage of time through aging (e.g., Prentky, Janus, Barbaree, Schwartz, & Kafka, 2006). Instruments with dynamic variables can be used to identify appropriate intervention targets (i.e., criminogenic needs) and measure changes in risk with treatment. As well, dynamic variables can be used to assess changes in risk, be it positive or negative, with the passage of time or with some significant event in the person's life.

The Violence Risk Scale–Sexual Offender Version (VRS-SO)

The VRS-SO (Wong et al., 2003) integrates sex offender risk assessment and treatment planning, including the assessment of change, within a single instrument. The VRS-SO, modeled closely after the VRS, uses both static and dynamic variables to assess sexual recidivism risk, whereas dynamic variables are used to identify treatment targets and measure changes in risk as a result of treatment or other change agents.

Table 7.2 VRS-SO Static and Dynamic Items and Brief Item Descriptions

	Static Items
S1	Age at release: < age 25; 25–34; 35–44; 45 years and up
S2	Age at first sex offense: < age 20; 20–24; 25–34; 35 and up
S3	Sex offender type: Mixed offender; child molester; rapist; incest offender
S4	Prior sex offenses: 4 or more prior sexual charges/convictions; 2–3 prior; 1 prior; 0 prior
S5	Unrelated victims: 4 or more unrelated victims; 2–3 unrelated; 1 unrelated; 0 unrelated (all related)
S6	Victim gender: 2+ male victims; 1 male and 1 female/or 2+ female; 1 male victim only; 1 female victim only
S7	Prior sentencing dates: 11+ prior sentencing dates; 5–10 prior; 2–4 prior; 0–1 prior
	Dynamic Items
D1	Sexually deviant lifestyle: Lifestyle hobbies, interests, work, or relationships involve sexually deviant behaviors [SD]
D2	Sexual compulsivity: Strong sex drive and high frequency of sexual behavior and cognitions [SD]
D3	Offense planning: Victim grooming and premeditation involved in sexual offending [SD]
D4	Criminal personality: Interpersonal and emotional attributes conducive to criminal behavior (e.g., lack of remorse) [C]
D5	Cognitive distortions: Attitudes and distorted thinking supportive of sexual offending [TR]
D6	Interpersonal aggression: Physically and/or verbally aggressive behavior in interpersonal interactions [C]
D7	Emotional control: Tendency to overcontrol or undercontrol emotions linked to sexual offending [DNL]
D8	Insight: Poor understanding of causes of sexual offending and unwillingness to discuss/explore sexual offending [TR]
D9	Substance abuse: Substance use problems linked specifically to sexual offending [C]
D10	Community support: Lack of positive support people, services, or plans in community (or unwilling to use) [C]
D11	Release to high-risk situation: Offender seems likely or has shown pattern of returning to situations linked to sex offending [TR]
D12	Sexual offending cycle: Pattern of interpersonal, situational, and personal factors linked to sexual offending [SD]
D13	Impulsivity: Behavior displays tendency to "act first, think later" and lacks reflection or forethought [C]
D14	Compliance with community supervision: Poor attitude and/or cooperation with community supervision [C]
D15	Treatment compliance: Poor attitude and/or cooperation with sex offender treatment [TR]
D16	Deviant sexual preference: Interests or preferences for deviant sexual stimuli or behavior (e.g., children, violence) [SD]
D17	Intimacy deficits: Incapacity to form or maintain adult romantic relationships [DNL]

Source: Adapted from Olver, Wong, Nicholaichuk, and Gordon (2007). (With permission.)

Note: SD = loading on the Sexual Deviance factor; C = loading on the Criminality factor; TR = loading on the Treatment Responsivity factor; DNL = did not load.

* All items are rated on a four-point (0, 1, 2, 3) scale. Item descriptions are abbreviated examples of the originals and are not intended to be used for clinical or research purposes. Please consult the VRS-SO rating manual (Wong et al., 2003) for more detailed item descriptions, stages of change ratings, and scoring instructions.

The VRS-SO comprises 7 static and 17 dynamic items that are empirically, theoretically, or conceptually related to sexual recidivism risk (see Table 7.2). The static items were developed using statistical–actuarial procedures. A pool of 24 static variables identified from the literature were initially coded and correlated with sexual recidivism on approximately half of a randomly selected sample of medium- to high-risk treated sex offenders. Variables with the strongest univariate relationships to outcome were retained and rescaled to a 4-point format. The items were then cross-validated on the remainder of the sample. The dynamic component was developed through a detailed review of the sex offender prediction and treatment literature including meta-analytic reviews (Hanson & Bussière, 1998), individual studies identifying dynamic predictors (e.g., Hanson & Harris, 2000), and theoretical contributions from the relapse prevention literature (Pithers, 1990; Ward & Hudson, 1998) and the *Psychology of Criminal Conduct* (see editions by Andrews & Bonta, 1998, 2003, 2006).

VRS-SO total scores range from 0 to 72 and are organized into four risk categories: Low (0 to 20), Moderate–Low (21 to 30), Moderate–High (31 to 40), and High (41 to 72). As with the VRS, there are guidelines in place using Clinical Overrides to adjust risk appraisals under exceptional circumstances (e.g., clear expression of intent to sexually reoffend). Similarly, the VRS-SO assesses and measures change using a modified application of the transtheoretical model operationalized for each of the 17 dynamic items, with criminogenic items receiving such ratings pre- and posttreatment to arrive at a quantitative index of change.

Reliability, Validity, and Factor Structure of the VRS-SO

A growing body of research has examined the psychometric properties of the VRS-SO. Olver et al. (2007) conducted an exploratory factor analysis of the dynamic items (N = 321) and found 15 out of 17 items loaded on three oblique factors labeled Sexual Deviance, Criminality, and Treatment Responsivity (see Table 7.1). VRS-SO ratings were completed based on reviews of comprehensive clinical and institutional file information on a sample of 321 treated sex offenders by trained coders. Sexual Deviance taps a pattern of deviant sexual interests, preoccupations, and behavior, Criminality measures a general antisocial orientation such as impulsivity, aggressiveness, substance abuse, and criminal personality characteristics, and Treatment Responsivity assesses sex offender attitudes and cognitions, including insight and attitudes toward treatment. The highest correlations were observed between Treatment Responsivity × Criminality (r = .55), followed by Treatment Responsivity × Sexual Deviance (r = .38), and the smallest correlation with Criminality × Sexual Deviance (r = .18). Beggs and Grace (in press) conducted a confirmatory factor analysis of the dynamic items in a sample of 218 male adult child molesters who received treatment services from the Kia Marama program in New Zealand; roughly 20% of them were of Maori descent. The authors arrived at a four-factor solution, with the three original factors being reproduced quite closely (12 out of 15 items loading) and a fourth factor labeled Self-Management.

The VRS-SO can be rated reliably with intraclass correlations for dynamic item scores ranging from .74 to .95 (Beggs & Grace, in press; Beyko & Wong, 2005; Olver et al., 2007). Good internal consistency has been obtained for the dynamic items (α = .81) and scale total (α = .84) (Olver et al., 2007). Evidence for concurrent validity has been obtained with high correlations observed between the Static 99 and VRS-SO static items (r = .70 to .81). The dynamic factors are also correlated with content-relevant self-report measures, including Sexual Deviance and measures of sexual interests (r = .32), Criminality with anger/hostility (r = .18), and Treatment Responsivity with pro-offense attitudes (r = .34) (Beggs & Grace, in press).[3] Our validation research of the VRS-SO (Olver et al., 2007) on a heterogeneous sample of sex offenders found that there were differences in the dynamic factor scores among different types of sex offenders. For instance, rapists tended to score relatively high on the Criminality factor (M = 9.5 out of a maximum 18 points), while child molesters tended to score quite low ($M = 6.9$) on this factor yet quite high on Sexual Deviance ($M = 10.1$ out of a maximum 15 points, rapists $M = 4.8$). These results support the construct validity of the factors insofar as rapists tend to be more criminalized, and are less likely to have deviant preferences, than other types of sex offenders (Firestone, Bradford, Greenberg, & Serran, 2000; Looman & Marshall, 2005; Polaschek & King, 2002). Further research examining the relationship of the VRS-SO to different pathways of sexual offending also revealed that sex offenders with an impulsive, approach-oriented pathway to offending scored particularly high on the Criminality factor (Yates & Kingston, 2006).

Concurrent validity of the Sexual Deviance factor was demonstrated with phallometric assessments of deviant arousal (Canales and Olver, 2008). Significant correlations were obtained between Sexual Deviance factor scores and arousal to male child ($r = .26$) and female child pictorial stimuli ($r = .35$) but not adult heterosexual stimuli ($r = .04$); the latter also support the discriminant validity of the VRS-SO. The findings provide support for the construct validity of a psychometric assessment of sexual deviance with important practical implications. For instance, such assessments may be a substitute for phallometric testing if the latter is refused, unavailable, or impractical.

The predictive validity of the VRS-SO for sexual and nonsexual violent recidivism was examined in a sample of 321 treated sex offenders who were followed an average 10 years postrelease and had a 25% base rate of sexual offense recidivism (Olver et al., 2007). VRS-SO static, dynamic, and total scores, coded by raters blind to recidivism outcome, significantly predicted sexual recidivism, as did each of the three broad dynamic factors (see Table 7.3). Dynamic scores, assessed at one time point, also significantly added to the predictive efficacy of static measures as demonstrated by using Cox regression survival analysis to control for the contributions of either the total VRS-SO static scores: Wald (1) = 22.64, $p < .001$; dynamic item total, Wald (1) = 6.27, $p = .012$, or the Static 99: Wald (1) = 7.76, $p < .01$; dynamic item total, Wald (1) = 18.67, $p < .001$.

Of particular note is that, whereas the total static scores predicted both sexual and nonsexual violent recidivism, the total dynamic scores predicted sexual, but not nonsexual, recidivism. The latter was due primarily to the strong negative correlation between the Sexual Deviancy factor and nonsexual violent recidivism. The differential correlations between the three broad dynamic factors with sexual and nonsexual violent recidivism reflect the heterogeneity of sex offenders, that is, the potential different underlying causes of their risk for sexual or nonsexual violent recidivism. Child molesters who tend to be sexually deviant but less involved in general criminality, scored relatively higher on the Sexual Deviancy factor and lower on the Criminality factor; the opposite trend was observed among rapists (Olver et al., 2007). The three factors

Table 7.3 Predictive Accuracy of the VRS-SO Scale Components for Sexual and Nonsexual Violent Recidivism (N = 321)

	Sexual Recidivism			Nonsexual Violent Recidivism		
Measure	*r*	AUC	95% CI	*r*	AUC	95% CI
VRS-SO static	.36***	.74***	.68–.80	.17**	.60**	.53–.66
VRS-SO dynamic	.26***	.67***	.60–.74	.06	.55	.48–.61
VRS-SO total	.34***	.72***	.66–.78	.11*	.57*	.51–.64
Sexual deviance	.16**	.61**	.54–.68	−.25***	.35***	.29–.41
Criminality	.21***	.65***	.58–.72	.28***	.67***	.61–.73
Treatment responsivity	.15**	.59**	.52–.66	.15**	.60**	.53–.65

Source: Results adapted from Olver, Wong, Nicholaichuk, & Gordon, 2007. (With permission.)
Note: *** $p < .001$, ** $p < .01$, * $p < .05$.
* All measures except VRS-SO static are based on posttreatment ratings.

provide information useful in identifying the potential causes of sexual and nonsexual violent recidivism risk, and guiding the focus of sex offender risk reduction treatment.

Ranges on the VRS-SO total scores were used to create low, moderate–low, moderate–high, and high risk groups. Survival analysis conducted on the four groups showed that they were significantly different in their risk for sexual recidivism with higher risk groups showing higher rates of sexual recidivism (see Figure 7.3). Although labels of high, moderate, and low risk traditionally have been used to classify people according to their likelihood of engaging in some type of behavior, such labeling often creates problems insofar as the meaning of "high risk" or "low risk" often mean different things to different people. As a result, it is our view that it is preferable to link scores on a scale directly to risk for recidivism (see Wong & Gordon, 2006, p. 302 for further discussions).

VRS-SO posttreatment total scores, divided into seven 5-point bins, were plotted against sexual recidivism rates on follow-up. A regression analysis showed a very strong linear relationship (R^2= .97) (see Figure 7.4) between VRS-SO total score intervals and sexual reconviction rates. Increases in VRS-SO scores in 5-point intervals produced a near proportionate increase in risk for sexual recidivism; that is, an increase in the number of problem areas identified by the VRS-SO was associated with a proportionate increase in sexual recidivism risk. The procedure, when repeated for nonsexual violent recidivism using the 5-point intervals, demonstrated a linear though smaller relationship (R^2= .73) than for sexual recidivism, suggesting that the tool is more efficacious in predicting sexual than nonsexual recidivism, as expected.

Beggs and Grace (in press) conducted an independent validation study of the VRS-SO in a sample of 218 male adult treated child molesters who were followed for an average 4.5 years

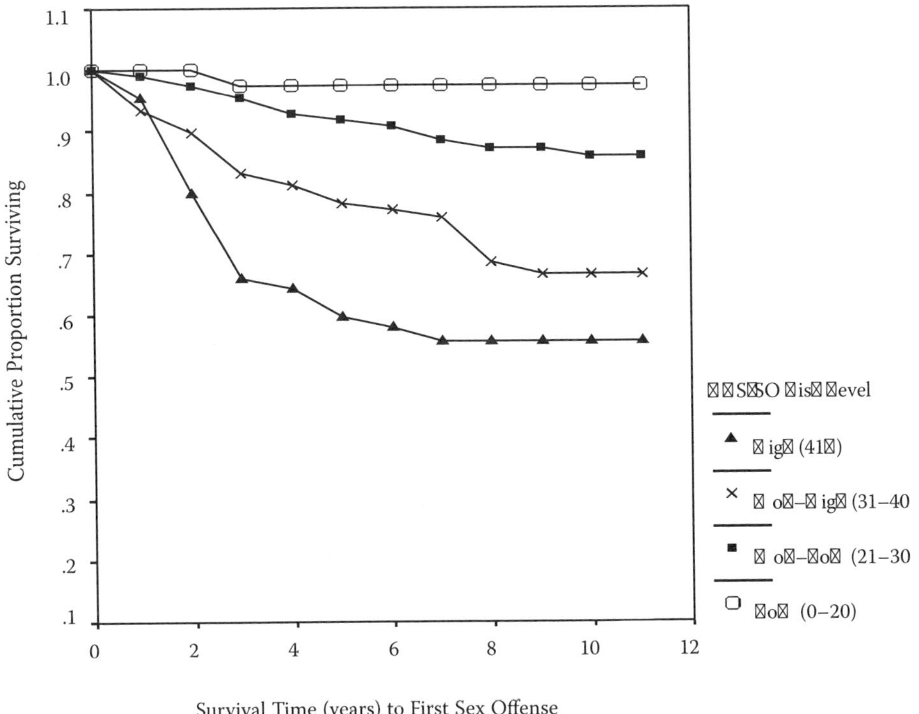

Figure 7.3 Survival analysis: Cumulative sexual recidivism failure rates as a function of VRS-SO risk level over a 10-year follow-up. (Adapted from Olver, Wong, Nicholaichuk, and Gordon, 2007. With permission.)

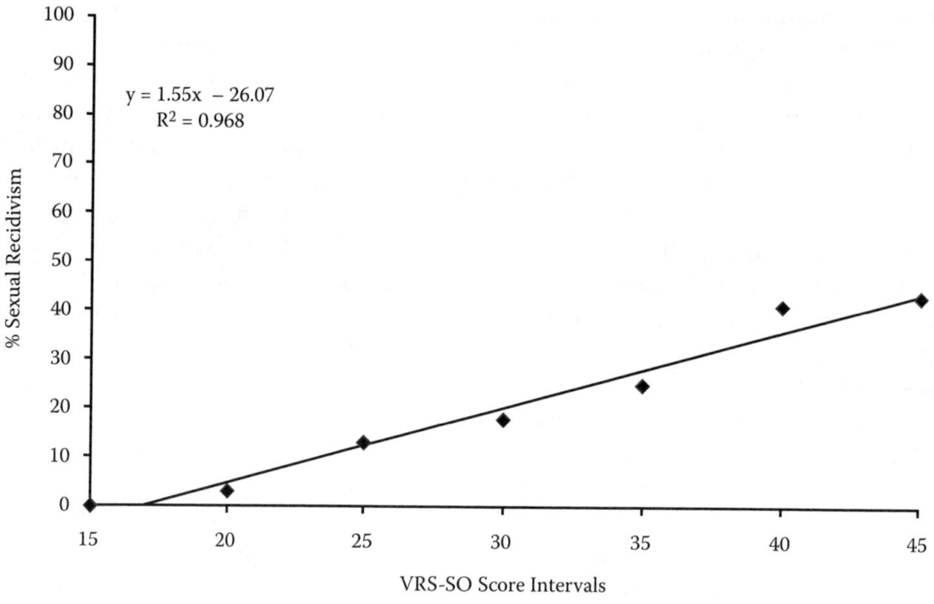

Figure 7.4 VRS-SO total score intervals and the prediction of sexual recidivism.

postrelease, 7.3% of whom were convicted for a new sex offense. The VRS-SO demonstrated strong predictive accuracy for sexual recidivism, with the dynamic items (posttreatment $r = .34$, AUC = .80) showing stronger prediction than the static component ($r = .17$, AUC = .67). Support was also obtained for the incremental validity of the dynamic items for sexual recidivism after controlling separately for the Static 99 and the VRS-SO static.

Linking Changes in the VRS-SO Dynamic Variables to Changes in Sexual Recidivism

Although incremental validity data may be informative, such analyses do not demonstrate that dynamic variables can change or that potential changes are meaningful. Incremental validity analyses only demonstrate that these attributes, which are measured at one time point and have shared variance with the static items, explain unique variance in outcome. As discussed earlier, to demonstrate the causal nature of dynamic predictors, positive changes in the dynamic variables (measured at two or more time points) should be linked to lower rates of recidivism. Given the shared variance between static and putatively dynamic items, controlling for static risk using statistical means should serve to isolate variance that is dynamic, changeable, and possibly linked to reductions in recidivism.

In their initial validation study of the VRS-SO, Olver et al. (2007) computed change scores from the dynamic items rated at two time points (pre- and posttreatment, about 6 months apart) and examined the relationship of change scores to sexual recidivism. Although zero-order correlations between change and sexual recidivism were modest when examined in the overall sample ($r = -.09$, $p = .10$), the relationship of change to recidivism was significant among actuarially high-risk offenders, defined by a Static 99 scores of 4 or higher ($r = -.15$, $p < .05$, $n = 204$), but not among actuarially low-risk offenders, defined by a Static 99 scores from 0 to 3 ($r = .01$, *ns*; $n = 117$). The results of Cox regression survival analysis further demonstrated change scores to be significantly associated with reductions in sexual recidivism ($e^B = 0.896$) after controlling for the VRS-SO static items. The results were replicated by Beggs (in press), who examined the relationship of VRS-SO change scores to recidivism rates of the treated sex offender sample referenced in Beggs and Grace (in press). Change scores were significantly negatively correlated with any new sexual conviction ($r = -.15$) and continued to predict reductions in sexual recidivism ($p < .06$) after controlling for Static 99 in Cox regression survival analysis.

The New Zealand Department of Corrections Community Probation and Psychological Services (see Wilson, 2008) conducted a pilot project of the Adult Sex Offender Treatment Programme, a high-intensity, prison-based, cognitive behavioral sex offender program, in a sample of 10 rapists. Selected for the pilot project as a result of having been deemed high risk, the sample had a mean Static 99 score of 7 and pretreatment VRS-SO dynamic score of 32. Offenders were rated pre- and posttreatment on the VRS-SO and completed over 285 hours of treatment over an 8-month program. Nine out of 10 offenders successfully completed the program and, on average, demonstrated 5.5 points of change (approximately two-thirds of a standard deviation) on the dynamic items, with a mean posttreatment dynamic score of 26.7. In total, two of the offenders were downgraded from high risk to moderate-high, and one offender was downgraded from moderate-high to moderate-low. While this is a small sample, the results provide additional support for changes on the dynamic items of the VRS-SO with treatment.

In sum, a growing body of research supports the notion that the dynamic variables on the VRS-SO can change, and that positive changes (i.e., improvement) on these variables are associated with reductions in sexual offending even after controlling for static risk. These findings, interpreted with caution as indicated in the discussion with the VRS, suggest that the VRS-SO dynamic predictors could be deemed "causal risk factors" using Kraemer et al.'s (1997, p. 341) criteria and terminology as outlined in the preceding discussion of the VRS. Although, Kraemer et al. (1997) concede that "when causal risk factors are identified for an outcome, questions may still remain about the mechanism or process by which those causal risk factors operate," identifying the relevant causal risk factors "might provide inspiration about where to look for the cause" (p. 341), whether this be completing sex offender treatment, enhancing community supports, aging, or others.

Practical Issues in the Clinical Use of the VRS-SO

This next section expands on the scale description, clinical use, and research on the VRS-SO, as described above. It provides an overview of specific practical issues in the clinical applications of the VRS-SO including the clinical use of the three broad dynamic factors, identifying offense-paralleling or "analogue" behaviors for rating the dynamic items and guiding treatment, the development of a screening version or short form of the VRS-SO, and potential use of the VRS-SO in special clinical–legal contexts.

Applications of the Broad Dynamic Factors. Factor analysis of the VRS-SO provides additional conceptual clarity regarding the risk dimensions underpinning the dynamic items and has practical utility as well. As reviewed above, we found conceptually meaningful differences in the risk dimensions among different of sex offender types: rapists tended to score higher on Criminality and lower on Sexual Deviance, and child molesters demonstrated the opposite pattern (Olver et al., 2007). In general, the risk dimension scores can be used to indicate differential treatment needs (for example, a sexually deviant vs. a generally nondeviant but criminalized rapist) to assist in case formulation and treatment planning. It follows that a rapist scoring high on the Sexual Deviance dimension should be considered for treatment that focuses on monitoring, changing, and controlling deviant fantasies and arousal such as through masturbatory reconditioning. On the other hand, a rapist with low scores on the Sexual Deviance dimension is unlikely to require much work in this area; to do so would be a misuse of treatment resources and unlikely to reduce the likelihood of reoffending. As such, use of VRS-SO dynamic item and risk dimension scores in treatment planning should make treatment more individualized, and would comply with good clinical and professional practice standards to use the least intrusive approach in treatment while increasing the efficacious use of treatment resources.

Offense-Paralleling or Analogue Behaviors. An important practical limitation in assessing risk among sex offenders is that, while in custody, their ability to access potential victims or engage in other sexually deviant behaviors (e.g., viewing child pornography) is limited. As such, offense-paralleling, analogue, or proxy behaviors have to be used to assess the continued presence of dynamic risk markers. Though the need to use offense-paralleling behaviors to assess sex offenders is more obvious, the same also applies to some criminogenic needs for nonsexual offenders, such as family violence or use of specific weapons.

The VRS-SO includes, where appropriate, offense-analogue and proxy behaviors in the rating descriptions of the items and the stage of change to assess risk and to evaluate change. Some behavioral analogues can occur in the community and can continue unabated within the institution, such as deviant sexual fantasies of children, violence, and coercive sex. Some sex offenders may indulge in inappropriate fantasies about staff and may even try to establish personal liaisons with them as a substitute for sexually deviant behaviors they practice in the community. Other offense analogue behaviors may include using child images available in shopping catalogues or magazines, engaging in lusty and sexually degrading talk, or developing indiscriminate casual homosexual liaisons. In sum, the VRS-SO makes use of many of these offense-analogue behaviors to assess the presence or absence of dynamic risk factors and treatment change.

The VRS-SO Screening Version

For reasons similar to the development of the VRS screening version, a screening version of the VRS-SO, the VRS-SO-SV has been developed which consists of all seven static items and six dynamic items.[5] The VRS-SO-SV was validated based on a randomly selected half of the original normative sample, then cross-validated on the remaining half. Correlations for the screening version with sexual reconviction (construction sample r = .40, validation sample r = .33) are comparable to that of the scale total (r = .34). The VRS-SO-SV appears to have predictive accuracy comparable to the full version, a finding that is similar to that of the VRS and its screening version. Also similar to the VRS-SV, the screening version of the VRS-SO can be used to identify risk levels of offenders, for example, for treatment and intervention planning purposes. The stages of change ratings are usually made only with the full scale for both the VRS and VRS-SO; the screening versions provide a quick appraisal of risk and are not meant to replace the full-length version.

Target Populations for the VRS-SO. The VRS-SO initial validation sample consisted of a range of treated male federal offenders varying from low to very high risk with a slightly negatively skewed distribution; the sample also consisted of a number of sex offenders of aboriginal descent. The validity of the tool has been examined using a separate sample (Beggs & Grace, in press) with very similar results, and as mentioned above, the VRS-SO is a required assessment measure for participants in the DSPD program in the United Kingdom.

The VRS-SO can be used to assess sex offenders ranging from low to high risk, although it is important to underscore its utility with offenders who are considered high risk, have entrenched deviant interests or serious track records of sexual violence, and who may present with personality disorders including psychopathy (e.g., see Olver & Wong, 2006; Olver et al., 2007). For instance, over three-quarters of the sex offenders in the VRS-SO validation sample had an intake psychiatric diagnosis of some form of personality disorder, and over half received a diagnosis of antisocial personality disorder or had antisocial personality traits (Olver & Wong, 2009b). The VRS-SO also predicts sexual recidivism among those with significant psychopathic characteristics (PCL-R scores > 25) (Olver & Wong, 2009). In sum, the VRS-SO can be used with adult sex offenders who may vary in their risk level (from low to high risk); who may have different victim preferences (from children to adult), different offending behaviors (from contact to noncontact offenses), and different personality disorders, including psychopathy.

The VRS-SO also has potential applicability within special sex offender evaluation contexts including Dangerous Offender (DO) evaluations in Canada, the DSPD program in the United Kingdom, and Sexually Violent Predator (SVP) evaluations in the United States. For these evaluations, the potential value of the VRS-SO to inform judgments regarding sexual offense risk is obvious. However, unlike static tools, the VRS-SO can also assess change in risk related to treatment and other intervening events, as is often required by law. For example, after the first seven years of their indeterminate sentences, the release eligibility of DOs in Canada must be assessed biannually (Canadian Criminal Code sec. 761.1). Participants in the DSPD program, which provides treatment to these high-risk and personality-disordered individuals to reduce their likelihood of reoffending violently, are also closely monitored to assess their treatment progress and possible changes in risk.

SVP legislation in the United States allows for indeterminate, involuntary institutionalization of sex offenders upon completion of their criminal sentences if they are deemed to be at high risk for sexual reoffending as the result of an underlying mental disorder typically quite broadly defined (see Prentky et al., 2006). The intention of SVP legislation is to detain offenders involuntarily for treatment purposes, ostensibly to reduce dangerousness and the risk for sexual violence. As with DO and DSPD examinees, the VRS-SO can be used not only in the predetention assessment to provide information concerning risk and treatment readiness, but also in postdetention assessment for purposes of identifying any treatment-related changes and reassessing for risk.

Research on the clinical application of the VRS-SO with persons adjudicated as DOs, DSPDs, and SVPs is clearly needed. The New Zealand pilot prison-based program for high-risk rapists may be seen as a proxy to similar special high-risk populations, the results of which demonstrated that movement on the risk variables can occur with intensive treatment, and this may translate into incremental reductions in risk level (e.g., from high to moderate-high and so on). Future investigative efforts would be well served to examine if such treatment-related changes in these and other special populations translate into reductions in sexual recidivism and dangerousness.

Conclusion

Risk assessment tools with dynamic predictors can assist in assessing the current functioning of the individual in areas that are amenable to change such that interventions designed to lower the individual's risk for violence could be delivered. The VRS and the VRS-SO were developed to integrate the assessment and treatment of violence guided by appropriate theoretically models of nonsexual or sexual violence assessment and intervention. Empirical evidence indicates that the VRS/VRS-SO can assess, significantly better than chance, the likelihood of future violence using a combination of static and dynamic predictors. The VRS/VRS-SO dynamic variables can be used to guide risk reduction treatment by identifying violence-linked dynamic variables as treatment targets and using a modified Stages of Change Model to identify the subject's readiness for change and to measure treatment changes that are linked to reduction in violent and sexual recidivism.

Case Illustration Using the VRS-SO

The following clinical case was developed to illustrate the use of the VRS-SO for risk assessment, treatment planning, and evaluating change. Although this case has been informed by previous cases, the details including the client's name, history, and treatment responses are fictitious and are intended for illustration purposes only.

Bill, a 36-year-old White man, was serving his first 4-year federal sentence for sexual assault against two teenage boys, aged 13 and 14 years. Bill came from a fairly affluent middle-class background with no reported abuse or neglect growing up. He first learned about sex through erotic magazines he hid around his home. Bill reported being sexually attracted to and had crushes on school-age boys. His first sexual experience occurred when he was about 13 with a neighborhood boy who was about 11. He was also involved in mutual fondling and oral sex with other neighborhood boys. Bill occasionally dated girls in high school, but these relationships were generally short-lived. In his 20s and early 30s, Bill reported living a marginalized existence, drinking heavily, frequently unemployed, and remaining sexually attracted to boys.

Bill received his first conviction for sexual interference at age 22, when he enticed an 11-year-old who was riding his bike home and performed fellatio on him. He complimented the victim, saying he had nice eyes, and, when the boy asked if he had a smoke, Bill invited him back to his home, noticing the boy was unsupervised. Bill used a similar modus operandi with other boys. Bill remained socially isolated, with the exception of the company of the estranged boys he would invite into his home. Here he would entice them with alcohol and soft drugs, and, should they appear willing, he would sexually assault them. Bill rationalized that he was pleasuring the victims because they occasionally ejaculated and they "freely" consented. Even following his fourth sexual conviction, Bill maintained that he had not harmed the victims because they "wanted it," and if anybody was to blame, it was the irresponsible parents who failed to provide proper supervision. When Bill was arrested, police found a cache of photos of naked boys on Bill's computer hard drive. After a short remand and trial, Bill was found guilty and sentenced to his current term of incarceration. He was recommended to complete sex offender treatment as part of his correctional plan.

Following his admission to treatment, Bill maintained a cautious and skeptical stance toward the prospect of treatment, stating that he simply wished to get it over with so that he could be granted parole and avoid being detained on long-term supervision after completing his sentence. In the pretreatment assessment, Bill reported that most of his sexual fantasies involved boys generally between the ages of 10 and 15, although he reported also having some attraction to young men. He reported masturbating almost daily to these fantasies and admitted to having more victims over the years than he had been convicted for. Despite his drug and alcohol use, Bill reported that he was seldom intoxicated during his sexual offenses; he generally used intoxicants to establish relationships with the victims before sexually assaulting them.

Bill's criminal record indicated three prior convictions for sexual offenses and two unadjudicated charges plus a probation infraction when he was found in the company of minors at a fast food restaurant, thus violating his probation order requiring him not to have unsupervised contact with this group. Bill had four prior sentencing occasions, with no convictions for any nonsexual offenses.

Bill denied that he has problems with aggression and anger; however, he reported a history of other emotional problems, including depression and anxiety. He also abused nonprescription medications. Although he reported having had some short-lived gay relationships, Bill never cohabitated with a lover for any meaningful period of time and was frequently lonely and socially withdrawn. Feeling inadequate and self-conscious, Bill reported that the victims filled an emptiness within him through their social contacts during which they would chat, play cards, and drink and "make me feel human again." Although Bill had some family members in the city, he reported that contacts were sporadic and that they drifted further apart as his legal problems grew.

Figure 7.5 presents the first page of a VRS-SO score sheet illustrating Bill's ratings on the static items pretreatment. Bill's item scores reflect the fact that he is a 36-year-old man serving a 4-year sentence, meaning that he will at most be 40 years old when he is released. He was charged for his first sex offense at age 22, is a child molester by virtue of the age of his victims, and has two stayed sexual charges and four prior sexually related convictions. Given that his probation violation seemed sexually motivated, it would be scored as a sex offense according to the VRS-SO scoring manual, and in total he would have six prior sexual offenses. Finally, Bill had more than four prior victims, all of whom were unrelated males, and he has four prior sentencing dates. All told, Bill's VRS-SO static score was 15.

Figure 7.6 presents the second page of Bill's VRS-SO score sheet with ratings on his dynamic items pre- and posttreatment. Bill's VRS-SO dynamic items profile at pretreatment (see left-hand side of the form) indicated that many dynamic items were criminogenic. For the sake of brevity, the scoring rationale for a few representative items on each factor is discussed in detail. First, all of the items on the sexual deviance

VRS:SO Score Sheet ©

Name: Bill　　Client #: ______

Pre-Treatment Rater: Dr. M. Olver　　Pre-Treatment Rating Date: 2007/01/15

Post-Treatment Rater: Dr. M. Olver　　Post-Treatment Rating Date: 2007/09/14

Static Factors

Risk Factor[1]		Codes	Score	I or N
S1	Age at Time of Release	Under 25 years 25 to 34 years 35 to 44 years 45 years or older	3 2 (1) 0	
S2	Age at First Sexual Offense	Under 20 years 20 to 24 years 25 to 34 years 35 years or older	3 (2) 1 0	
S3	Sex Offender Type	Mixed (both adult and child victims) Child molester (child victims only) Rapist (adult victims only) Incest (related victims predominantly)	3 (2) 1 0	
S4	Prior Sexual Offenses	4-4+ prior arrests/charges/convictions for a sexual offense 2-3 prior arrests/charges/convictions for a sexual offense 1 prior arrests/charge/conviction for a sexual offense No prior arrests/charges/convictions for a sexual offense	(3) 2 1 0	
S5	Unrelated Victims	4 or more unrelated victims 2-3 unrelated victims 1 unrelated victim No unrelated victims (related victims only)	(3) 2 1 0	
S6	Number and Gender of Victims	2 or more male victims & any number of female victims 2 or more female victims *or* 1 female and 1 male victim 1 male victim only 1 female victim only	(3) 2 1 0	
S7	Prior Sentencing Dates	11 or more prior sentencing occasions 5-10 prior sentencing occasions 2-4 prior sentencing occasions 0-1 prior sentencing occasions	3 2 (1) 0	
Total Static Factor Score		Before Treatment	15	
		After Treatment	15	

1 If it is necessary to omit a Static or Dynamic Factor, the rater should indicate whether the omission is because there is insufficient information (I) or because the item is not applicable (N).

1

Figure 7.5 VRS-SO static items score sheet and ratings for the case of Bill. (VRS-SO score sheet is copyrighted. Figure reprinted from Wong, Olver, and Stockdale, 2009, in press. With permission.)

factor were criminogenic for Bill (i.e., receiving a 2- or 3-point rating). For instance, given that Bill reported being sexually preoccupied with preteen boys, fantasized about this group predominantly, and had an under-age pornography collection, he received a score of 3 on the deviant sexual preference item. As well, because he masturbated and fantasized quite frequently, he received a score of 2 on sexual compulsivity; a higher reported frequency of sexual thoughts and behaviors would have generated a score of 3.

For Stage of Change:	Use These symbols to Indicate the Stage of Change:	# of Stages Changed:
P/C = Precontemplation/Contemplation	O = Pretreatment	No Change = 0
P = Preparation	X = Post-treatment	1 Stage = .5
A = Action		2 Stages = 1.0
M = Maintenance		3 Stages = 1.5

DYNAMIC FACTORS AND TOTAL SCORES

	RATINGS										
	Pre-Tx *(a)*	F 1[†]	F 2	F 3	Stage of Change[††]	# of Stages Changed x .5 *(b)*	Post-Tx *(a-b)*[†††]	F 1	F 2	F 3	I or N
D1 Sexually Deviant Life Style	0 1 2 (3)	3			(P)C X A M	1.5 1 (.5) 0	2.5	2.5			
D2 Sexual Compulsivity	0 1 (2) 3	2			(P)C X A M	1.5 1 (.5) 0	1.5	1.5			
D3 Offense Planning	0 1 2 (3)	3			P(C)X A M	1.5 1 (.5) 0	2.5	2.5			
D4 Criminal Personality	0 (1) 2 3		1		P/C P A M	1.5 1 .5 0	1		1		
D5 Cognitive Distortions	0 1 2 (3)			3	(P)X P A M	1.5 1 .5 (0)	3			3	
D6 Interpersonal Aggression	(0) 1 2 3		0		P/C P A M	1.5 1 .5 0	0		0		
D7 Emotional Control	0 1 (2) 3				P(C)X A M	1.5 1 (.5) 0	1.5				
D8 Insight	0 1 (2) 3			2	(P)C X A M	1.5 1 (.5) 0	1.5			1.5	
D9 Substance Abuse	0 (1) 2 3		1		P/C P A M	1.5 1 .5 0	1		1		
D10 Community Support	0 1 (2) 3		2		P(C)X A M	1.5 1 (.5) 0	1.5		1.5		
D11 Release to High-Risk Situations	0 1 (2) 3			2	(P)C X A M	1.5 1 (.5) 0	1.5			1.5	
D12 Sexual Offending Cycle	0 1 2 (3)	3			(P)C X A M	1.5 1 (.5) 0	2.5	2.5			
D13 Impulsivity	(0) 1 2 3		0		P/C P A M	1.5 1 .5 0	0		0		
D14 Compliance with Community Supervision	0 1 (2) 3		2		(P)X P A M	1.5 1 .5 (0)	2		2		
D15 Treatment Compliance	0 (1) 2 3			1	P/C P A M	1.5 1 .5 0	1			1	
D16 Deviant Sexual Preference	0 1 2 (3)	3			(P)C X A M	1.5 1 (.5) 0	2.5	2.5			
D17 Intimacy Deficits	0 1 2 (3)				(P)X P A M	1.5 1 .5 (0)	3				
Total Dynamic Factor Score →	Pre-Tx: 33	Factors: 1	2	3	**Total Dynamic Factor Score →**		Post-Tx: 28.5	Factors: 1	2	3	
Total Static Factor Score From Previous Page →	15	14	6	8	**Total Static Factor Score From Previous Page →**		15	11.5	5.5	7	
Total Static + Total Dynamic Factor Score →	48				**Total Static + Total Dynamic Factor Score →**		43.5				

Indicate if Clinical Override was used: Yes O No X

† *To calculate scores for Factors 1 (Sexual Deviancy), 2 (Criminality), & 3 (Treatment Responsivity): Place Pre-Tx score in the corresponding shaded box to the right (Note: D7 is excluded). Tally each column (F1, F2, F3) and enter total score in appropriate box.*

†† *For treatment purposes, specify whether the client is in Precontemplation or Contemplation stage by circling (O) or marking (X) the 'P' or 'C' stage for pre- and post treatment, respectively.*

††† *If there is a deterioration during treatment, 'b' score is added to 'a' score for the corresponding Dynamic Factor.*

Figure 7.6 VRS-SO dynamic items score sheet and stages of change ratings for the case of Bill. (VRS-SO score sheet is copyrighted. Figure reprinted from Wong, Olver, and Stockdale, 2009, in press. With permission.)

Bill had a mixture of high and low scores on items comprising the criminality and treatment responsivity factors. Bill received low scores on several criminality factor items: given that he had basically no concerns with physically or verbally aggressive interpersonal behavior and impulsivity, he received a score of 0 on interpersonal aggression and 0 on impulsivity. However, concerns remained regarding Bill's potential problems with community supervision. He received a score of 2 on compliance with community supervision, given his past probation violation in which he made contact with children. Although he had some contact with his family, by and large they were estranged, and having few meaningful supports in the community, Bill received a score of 2 on community support. Although he also abused substances, the use of substances did not seem to have a strong link to sexual offending. Rather, Bill's substance use seemed to be part of the grooming process, and as such, he received a score of 1 on substance abuse and a 3 on offense planning.

Finally, Bill's loneliness and lack of fulfilling intimate relationships coupled with an inability to regulate negative emotions (e.g., feelings of depression and inadequacy) suggested that intimacy deficits and, to a certain degree, emotional control were linked to his offending and were thus criminogenic (receiving ratings of 3 and 2 on these items, respectively). In terms of items on the treatment responsivity factor, Bill had clear attitudes and cognitions supportive of sexual offending (e.g., given that he viewed his victims as willing and justified his offending), thus receiving a score of 3 on cognitive distortions. Given that he was cooperative (although reluctant) with treatment and seemed to have some limited understanding of the issues and events contributing to his sexual offending (justifying his behavior), he received a score of 1 on treatment compliance and a 2 on insight.

After rating Bill's static and dynamic items pretreatment, he received a total score of 48, placing him in the high-risk range for sexual offense recidivism. On each of the items deemed criminogenic (i.e., 2- or 3-point rating), Bill was rated as being in the precontemplative or contemplative stage of change, given that he had yet to acknowledge his problems or was aware of his problems but reluctant to make changes. Stages of change ratings are only rated on criminogenic items—that is, those rated 2 or 3. For instance, given that Bill was very reluctant to change his deviant fantasies despite their maladaptive nature, he was rated as being in the precontemplative stage of change on deviant sexual preference. Moreover, although Bill knew he was depressed, anxious, and lonely and that such emotional states were linked to his sexual offending, he had yet to make any positive change in his emotional functioning at the outset of treatment, and as such, he was rated as being in the contemplative stage on emotional control.

CASE CONCEPTUALIZATION

The VRS-SO can be used to assist case conceptualization and treatment planning. The static items provide an empirical, history-based estimate of the offender's risk, reflect the extensiveness of past sexual and nonsexual misconduct, and should show no change with treatment. For Bill, the static variables indicated he is a sexual recidivist, boy-victim child molester who began his offense history rather young and who will be under 40 years of age at the time of his release—all of which are static variables that, in combination, seem to put him at significant risk to reoffend sexually. As well, most of the static variables cannot change, with the exception of additional convictions and passage of time (aging). The dynamic items, on the other hand, can be used to elucidate the various elements involved in the persistence and maintenance of sexual offending behavior (i.e., what makes him a multirecidivist, boy-victim child molester?). Specifically, dynamic items dubbed criminogenic can be used to create a dynamic risk profile of individual needs and, hence, areas that should be targeted for intervention. For instance, in Bill's case, he scored particularly high on items comprising the sexual deviance factor, indicating that deviant sexual interests, sexual preoccupations, extensive fantasy, grooming, a strong sex drive, and sexualized lifestyle appeared to play a significant role in his offending. In addition, linked to Bill's offending appeared to be certain items falling under the criminality factor, such as lack of community support, as well as the treatment responsivity factor, including cognitive distortions conducive to sexual offending, exposure to high-risk situations (and hence repeated victim access), and little insight about his offending behavior. Perpetuating Bill's offense cycle appeared to be his intimacy deficits, which could have served to exacerbate his pervasive feelings of loneliness, depression, and anxiety, during which he would seek sexual and emotional solace in the company of his victims.

TREATMENT PROGRAM

Treatment consisted of a 12-month, high-intensity inpatient sex offender program and a combination of group and individual therapy. Bill had the opportunity to disclose his offenses in group and benefit from the group's feedback by other treatment participants who also had sexual offenses. He completed a detailed crime cycle and learned about the cognitive, behavioral, and emotional dynamics of his sexual offending. Although at first rationalizing and minimizing his molestation of boys, the feedback and challenges he received from other group members, coupled with the constructive and accepting group environment and individual psychotherapy, gradually increased his acceptance of responsibility and accountability for his offending. Bill also completed a detailed relapse prevention plan that articulated his reoffense pathways, high-risk situations, and escape and avoidance strategies to circumvent relapse. In addition to these therapeutic interventions, Bill completed treatment modules that specifically addressed cognitive distortions and attitudes related to sexual offending, healthy relationships and attachments, assertiveness and social skills, victim empathy, and fantasies/healthy sexuality.

Bill underwent phallometric testing as part of his treatment, which confirmed his strong deviant arousal to preteen boys. Importantly, Bill also demonstrated arousal to young men. Bill underwent arousal control sessions, in which he was asked to allow himself to become aroused and then resort to mental strategies in an attempt to decrease his arousal. Although he was eventually able to do this, Bill, not unexpectedly, continued to show deviant arousal when he did not attempt to suppress it. During individual therapy, Bill was encouraged to monitor his fantasies and was counseled on the importance of masturbating to healthy sexual fantasies as a means of heightening healthy sexual interest and controlling deviant arousal. Bill also underwent covert sensitization in an attempt to reduce deviant arousal.

Bill made modest gains in a number of areas. Bill's fantasy monitoring records demonstrated a decrease in the frequency of deviant fantasies and an increase in appropriate adult male homosexual fantasies, and his frequency of masturbation decreased as well. In his work, Bill noticed that, whenever he experienced negative affect (loneliness, stress, or feeling overwhelmed), he would sometimes retreat into his fantasy world. Over the course of treatment, he became better at disclosing and discussing his feelings one on one and using other, more appropriate coping strategies. Bill was able to identify cognitive distortions he used to justify his sexual offending behavior and used some effective strategies to challenge them; however, he frequently struggled with relinquishing his justifications and at times dwelled on the physiological displays of sexual excitement shown by his victims during the abuse to excuse and minimize his offending behavior.

As such, the sincerity of Bill's buy-in to treatment was sometimes uncertain. At times, he needed to be reminded to complete homework assignments, and primarily during the early stages of the program, it was uncertain whether Bill was merely spouting program rhetoric or had actually internalized the material. For the most part, Bill did not seem to have substantial empathy for people or his victims, and he continued to struggle with accepting that his behavior was truly damaging to them. However, he did recognize that child sex offense legislation served a purpose and that he manipulated and exploited his young victims, albeit while making palliative comparisons (e.g., that he would never engage in intercourse with his victims, and all his victims had to do was decline his overtures, which they sometimes did). The covert sensitization work also prompted Bill to contemplate the potentially serious and costly outcomes of his behavior that he could face, some of which he had never considered (e.g., being adjudicated a dangerous offender upon recidivating).

Bill agreed to attend a maintenance outpatient sex offender program in the community following his release (imposed as a special condition by his case management team), although he expressed mild reluctance to follow through on this, given that he had already successfully completed a high-intensity treatment program and was not sure whether more treatment was necessary. Bill's case management team also worked hard to establish supports for him in the community, and he reestablished some contact with an older sister (providing her with a copy of his relapse prevention plan), who agreed to support him. In the course of his work on intimate relationships and attachments, the supportive treatment environment, and individual work, Bill began to develop an increasing level of trust. As such, an additional component of his release planning involved establishing links to the gay community so that Bill may have an opportunity to develop further healthy supports.

In summary, following the completion of treatment, Bill was judged to have made varying gains in all of his criminogenic need areas. However, Bill was judged only to have advanced to the preparation stage on several of his dynamic risk factors, given that his changes were relatively recent (i.e., made over the course of a 12-month treatment program), and he had not yet had any opportunity to practice his skills in real-world contexts. During times of emotional distress, Bill would occasionally lapse, although with continued support he would regain control. For instance, Bill reported reductions in the frequency of deviant fantasy and increases in the frequency of appropriate sexual fantasies (i.e., consenting adult homosexual fantasies); however, given that he would lapse into deviant fantasy on occasion and had not demonstrated greater consistency in his arousal control and appropriate fantasies, he was considered to have only progressed to the preparation stage. Similarly, although he could discuss painful feelings and emotions with treatment staff to "drain off negative affect," on occasion he had coped with negative feelings in treatment through social isolation and was again appraised to be in the preparation stage on emotional control.

As illustrated in Figure 7.6, at posttreatment, Bill's VRS-SO score changed by four points (roughly one-half of a standard deviation) as he moved to the preparation stage on eight of the criminogenic items. Although Bill continued to fall within the high-risk range (with a score of 44) at the end of treatment, he fell within the lower end of this risk category and had demonstrated some important changes. It is important to emphasize that, in many ways, this reflects the reality of a repeat sex offender, who can hardly be expected to be radically transformed after a 12-month program. This being said, a continued reduction in Bill's risk would be anticipated should he complete a maintenance sex offender group and continue to demonstrate sustained behavior change in his dynamic risk factors on return to the community. For Bill to move into action stages for most of the criminogenic factors, he must demonstrate sustained changes over a significant period of time. Moving into the maintenance stage would require the generalization of the changes to real-life situations and for Bill to have withstood significant challenges with little or no relapse.

Endnotes

1. A related but different classification of risk measures that incorporate dynamic items is structured professional judgment (SPJ), which involves systematically rating relevant risk variables from a guide or scheme and using professional judgment to combine this information into a risk appraisal (usually low, medium, or high), such as the HCR-20. In contrast to actuarial approaches, items are not summed to arrive at a risk total score.
2. The VRS dynamic scores were divided into 11 five-point bins. It should be noted that aggregating the percentage that recidivate within the five-point intervals can potentially reduce error variance within the intervals, thus artificially inflating the R^2 (see Wong & Gordon, 2006, p. 25). The R^2 values reflect the linearity of the five-point risk bins rather than the linearity of the VRS scores.
3. Sexual interests self-report measures consisted of Wilson Sexual Fantasy Questionnaire subscales (exploratory, intimate, impersonal, sadomasochistic); Anger-hostility self-report measures consisted of State Trait Anger Expression Inventory subscales (state, trait, expression, control); Pro-offense attitudes self-report measures consisted of Abel-Becker Cognition Scale, Burt rape Myth Acceptance, and Internal-External Locus of Control Scale (Allen, Grace, Rutherford, & Hudson, 2007).
4. Since static scores are derived from risk predictors that are linked to both sexual and nonsexual recidivism.
5. VRS-SO-SV dynamic items: Sexually Deviant Lifestyle, Deviant Sexual Preference, Interpersonal Aggression, Substance Abuse, Emotional Control, Cognitive Distortions.

References

Allen, M., Grace, R. C., Rutherford, B., & Hudson, S. M. (2007). Psychometric assessment of dynamic risk factors for child molesters. *Sexual Abuse: A Journal of Research and Treatment, 19,* 347–367.

Andrews, D. A., & Bonta, J. (1994, 1998, 2003, 2006). *The psychology of criminal conduct* (1st, 2nd, 3rd, 4th eds.). Cincinnati, OH: Anderson.

Andrews, D. A., Zinger, I., Hoge, R. D., Bonta, J., Gendreau, P., & Cullen, F. T. (1990). Does correctional treatment work? A clinically-relevant and psychologically informed meta-analysis. *Criminology, 28,* 369–404.

Beggs, S. M. (2008). Study 2. Measuring treatment outcome for child molesters: A comparative validity study. Unpublished doctoral dissertation. University of Canterbury, Christchurch, New Zealand.

Beggs, S. M., & Grace, R. C. (in press). Assessment of dynamic risk factors: An independent validation study of the Violence Risk Scale: Sexual Offender version. *Sexual Abuse: A Journal of Research and Treatment.*

Beech, A., Friendship, C. Erikson, M., & Hanson, R. K. (2002). The relationship between static and dynamic factors and reconviction in a sample of U.K. child abusers. *Sexual Abuse: A Journal of Research and Treatment, 14,* 155–167.

Beyko, M. J., & Wong, S. C. P. (2005). Predictors of treatment attrition as indicators for program improvement not offender shortcomings: A study of sex offender treatment attrition. *Sexual Abuse: A Journal of Research and Treatment, 17,* 375–389.

Burt, G. N. (2000). Predicting violent recidivism of treated violent offenders using the Psychopathy Checklist-Revised and the Violence Risk Scale. Unpublished master thesis. University of Saskatchewan, Saskatoon, SK, Canada.

Burt, G. N. (2003). Investigating characteristics of the non-recidivating psychopathic offender. Unpublished doctoral dissertation. University of Saskatchewan, Saskatoon, SK, Canada.

Canales, D., & Olver, M. (2008). *An examination of phallometric and psychometric measures of sexual deviance.* Poster presented at the 69th Annual Meeting of the Canadian Psychological Association, Halifax, NS, Canada.

de Vries Robbé, M.,Weenink, A., & de Vogel, V. (2006, June). *Dynamic risk assessment: A comparative study into risk assessment with the Violence Risk Scale (VRS) and the HCR-20.* Paper presented at the annual conference of the International Association of Forensic Mental Health Services, Amsterdam, The Netherlands.

Department of Justice Canada (2008). Section 761(1) of the Canadian Criminal Code. Retrieved from: http://laws.justice.gc.ca/en/C-46

Dolan, M., & Fullam, R. (2007). The validity of the Violence Risk Scale second edition (VRS-2) in a British forensic inpatient sample. *The Journal of Forensic Psychiatry & Psychology, 18,* 381–393.

Douglas, K. S., & Kropp, P. R. (2002). A prevention-based paradigm for violence risk assessment: Clinical and research applications. *Criminal Justice and Behavior, 29,* 617–658.

Douglas, K., & Skeem, J. (2005). Violence risk assessment: Getting specific about being dynamic. *Psychology, Public Policy, and Law, 11,* 347–383.

Duncan, R. D., Kennedy, W. A., & Patrick, C. J. (1995). Four-factor model of recidivism in male juvenile offenders. *Journal of Child Clinical Psychology, 24,* 250–257.

Firestone, P., Bradford, J. M., Greenberg, D. M., & Serran, G. A. (2000). The relationship between deviant sexual arousal and psychopathy in incest offenders, extrafamilial child molesters, and rapists. *Journal of the American Academy of Psychiatry and the Law, 28,* 303–308.

Gordon, A. (1998). *The reliability and validity of the Violence Risk Scale–Experimental Version 1.* Unpublished master's thesis, University of Saskatchewan, Saskatoon, Saskatchewan, Canada.

Gordon, A., & Wong, S. C. P. (in press). Offense analogue behaviours as indicator of criminogenic need and treatment progress. In Daffern, M., Jones, L., & Shine, J. (Eds.). *Offence paralleling behaviour: An individualized approach to offender assessment and treatment.* New York: Wiley.

Hann, R. G., & Harman, W. G. (1992). *Predicting violent risk for penitentiary inmates* (User Report No. 1992-08). Ottawa, ON, Canada: Department of the Solicitor General of Canada.

Hanson, R. K., (1997). *The development of a brief actuarial scale for sexual offense recidivism.* (User Report 97-04). Ottawa, ON, Canada: Department of the Solicitor General of Canada.

Hanson, R. K., & Bussière (1998). Predicting relapse: A meta-analysis of sexual offender recidivism studies. *Journal of Consulting and Clinical Psychology, 66,* 348–362.

Hanson, R. K., Gordon, A., Harris, A. J. R., Marques, J. K., Murphy, W., Quinsey, V. L., & Seto, M. C. (2002). First report of the Collaborative Data Outcome Project on the effectiveness of psychological treatment for sexual offenders. *Sexual Abuse: A Journal of Research and Treatment, 14,* 169–194.

Hanson, R. K., & Harris, A. J. R. (2000). Where should we intervene? Dynamic predictors of sexual offense recidivism. *Criminal Justice and Behavior, 27,* 6–35.

Hanson, R. K., & Morton-Bourgon, K. (2004). *Predictors of sexual recidivism: An updated meta-analysis.* (User Report 2004-02). Ottawa, ON, Canada: Public Safety and Emergency Preparedness Canada.

Hanson, R. K., & Morton-Bourgon, K. (2007). *The accuracy of recidivism risk assessments for sexual offenders.* (User Report 2007-01). Ottawa, ON, Canada: Public Safety and Emergency Preparedness Canada.

Hanson, R. K., Steffy, R. A., & Gauthier R. (1993). Long-term recidivism of sex offenders. *Journal of Consulting and Clinical Psychology, 61,* 646–652.

Hanson, R. K., & Thornton, D. (1999). *Static 99: Improving actuarial risk assessments for sex offenders.* (User Report 99-02). Ottawa, ON, Canada: Department of the Solicitor General of Canada.

Hanson, R. K., & Thornton, D. (2003). *Notes on the development of the Static-2002.* (User Report 2003-01). Ottawa, ON, Canada: Department of the Solicitor General of Canada.

Hare, R. D. (2003). *The Hare Psychopathy Checklist–Revised* (2nd ed.). Toronto, ON, Canada: Multi-Health Systems, Inc.

Harris, G. T., Rice, M. E., Quinsey, V. L., Lalumière, M. L., Boer, D. & Lang, C. (2003). A multi-site comparison of actuarial risk instruments for sex offenders. *Psychological Assessment, 15,* 413–425.

Hirschi, T., & Gottfredson, M. (1983). Age and the explanation of crime. *American Journal of Sociology, 89*(3), 552–584.

Home Office and Department of Health (1999). *Managing Dangerous People with Severe Personality Disorder: Proposal for Policy Development.* London: Department of Health.

Hudson, S. M., Wales, D. S., Bakker, L., & Ward, T. (2002). Dynamic risk factors: The Kia Marama evaluation. *Sexual Abuse: A Journal of Research and Treatment, 14,*103–119.

Kraemer, H. C., Kazdin, A. E., Offord, D. R., Kessler, R. C., Jensen, P. S., & Kupfer, D. J. (1997). Coming to terms with the terms of risk. *Archives of General Psychiatry, 54,* 337–343.

Lattimore, P. K., Visher, C., & Linster, R. L. (1995). Predicting arrest for violence among serious youthful offenders. *Journal of Research in Crime and Delinquency, 32,* 54–83.

Lewis, K. (2004). The relationship between the URICA and correctional treatment in a sample of violent male offenders. Unpublished doctoral dissertation. University of Saskatchewan, Saskatoon, SK, Canada.

Lewis, K., Olver, M. & Wong, S. C. P. (2008). The Violence Risk Scale: Validity, measurement of treatment changes and violent recidivism in a high risk and personality disordered sample of male offenders (unpublished manuscript).

Looman, J., & Marshall, W. L. (2005). Sexual arousal in rapists. *Criminal Justice and Behavior, 32,* 367–389.

McGuire, J. (2008). A review of effective interventions for reducing aggression and violence. *Philosophical Transactions of the Royal Society, 363* (1503), 2483–2622.

Olver, M. E. (2003). *The development and validation of the Violence Risk Scale: Sexual Offender Version (VRS:SO) and its relationship to psychopathy and treatment attrition.* Unpublished doctoral dissertation. University of Saskatchewan, Saskatoon, Saskatchewan, Canada.

Olver, M. E., & Wong, S. C. P. (2006). Psychopathy, sexual deviance, and recidivism among sex offenders. *Sexual Abuse: A Journal of Research and Treatment, 18,* 65–82.

Olver, M. E., & Wong, S. C. P. (2008). Predictors of sex offender treatment dropout: Implications for the responsivity principle (unpublished manuscript).

Olver, M. E., & Wong, S. C. P. (2009). Therapeutic responses of psychopathic sexual offenders: Treatment attrition, therapeutic change, and long-term recidivism. *Journal of Consulting and Clinical Psychology, 77,* 328–336.

Olver, M. E., Wong, S. C. P., Nicholaichuk, T., & Gordon, A. (2007). The validity and reliability of the Violence Risk Scale–Sexual Offender version: Assessing sex offender risk and evaluating therapeutic change. *Psychological Assessment, 19,* 318–329.

Pithers, W. D. (1990). Relapse prevention for sexual aggressors: A method for maintaining therapeutic gain and enhancing external supervision. In W. L. Marshall, D. R. Laws, & H. E. Barbaree (Eds.), *Handbook of sexual assault: Issues, theories, and treatment of the offender* (pp. 343–361). New York: Plenum Press.

Polaschek, D. L. L., & King, L. L. (2002). Rehabilitating rapists: Reconsidering the issues. *Australian Psychologist, 37,* 215–221

Prentky, R. A., Janus, E., Barbaree, H., Schwartz, B. K., & Kafka, M. P. (2006). Sexually violent predators in the courtroom: Science on trial. *Psychology, Public Policy, and Law, 12,* 357–393.

Prochaska, J. O., DiClemente, C. C., & Norcross, J. C. (1992). In search of how people change: Applications to the addictive behaviors. *American Psychologist, 47,* 1102–1114.

Quinsey, V. L., Rice M. E., & Harris, G. T. (1995). Actuarial prediction of sexual recidivism. *Journal of Interpersonal Violence, 10,* 85–105.

Rice, M. E., Harris, G. T., & Quinsey, V. L. (1990). A follow-up of rapists assessed in a maximum-security psychiatric facility. *Journal of Interpersonal Violence, 5,* 435–448.

Ward, T., & Hudson, S. M. (1998). A model of the relapse process in sex offenders. *Journal of Interpersonal Violence, 13,* 700–725.

Wilde, S., & Wong, S. (2000). The predictive and congruent validity of the Violence Risk Scale (Version 2) with mentally disordered offenders. Paper presented at the Annual Convention of the Canadian Psychological Association, Ottawa, ON, Canada.

Wilson, N. J. (2008). *New Zealand pilot prison based treatment of high risk rape offenders. Final report to Policy, Strategy, & Research.* New Zealand Department of Corrections.

Wong, S., & Burt, G. (2007). The heterogeneity of incarcerated psychopaths: Differences in risk, need, recidivism and management approaches. In H. Hervé & J. Yuille (Eds.), *The psychopath: Theory, research and practice,* Mahwah, NJ: Lawrence Erlbaum.

Wong, S. C. P., & Gordon, A. (1999–2003). *Violence Risk Scale.* Saskatoon, Canada: University of Saskatchewan, Department of Psychology.

Wong, S. C. P., & Hare, R. (2005). *Guidelines for a treatment program for psychopaths.* Toronto, ON: Multi-Health Systems.

Wong, S. C. P., & Gordon A. E. (2006). The validity and reliability of the Violence Risk Scale: A treatment-friendly violence risk assessment tool. *Psychology, Public Policy, and Law, 12(3),* 279–309.

Wong, S. C. P., Gordon, A., & Gu, D. (2007). Assessment and treatment of violence-prone forensic clients: An integrated approach. *British Journal of Psychiatry, 190 (Suppl.),* s66–s74.

Wong, S. C. P., Olver., M., Nicholaichuk, T., & Gordon, A. (2003). *Violence Risk Scale-Sex Offender Version.* Saskatoon, Canada: University of Saskatchewan, Department of Psychology.

Wong, S. C. P., Olver, M. E., & Stockdale, K. C. (2009). The utility of dynamic and static factors in risk assessment, prediction, and treatment. In J. T. Andrade (Ed.). *Handbook of violence risk assessment and treatment: New approaches for mental health professionals* (pp. 83–120). New York: Springer.

Yates, P. M., Kingston, D. A. (2006). The self-regulation model of sexual offending: The relationship between offense pathways and static and dynamic sexual offence risk. *Sexual Abuse: A Journal of Research and Treatment, 18,* 259–270.

8

Historical-Clinical-Risk Management-20 (HCR-20) Violence Risk Assessment Scheme

Rationale, Application, and Empirical Overview

KEVIN S. DOUGLAS and KIM A. REEVES

The *Historical-Clinical-Risk Management-20* (HCR-20) (Webster, Douglas, Eaves, & Hart, 1997) was one of the first violence risk assessment protocols developed under the *Structured Professional Judgment* (SPJ) model of risk assessment, a model that has now been subjected to more than 100 independent empirical studies (Guy, 2008). As described in the sections that follow, the HCR-20 is intended to provide a structured assessment of the risk factors that are present in a given case, the relevance of those risk factors for a given individual's violence risk, and what risk management strategies might be put into place in order to mitigate risk. The *HCR-20 Violence Risk Management Companion Guide* (Douglas, Webster, Hart, Eaves, & Ogloff, 2001) can be used in tandem with the HCR-20 to facilitate identification and conceptualization of risk management plans that link up with the more management-relevant HCR-20 risk factors (as described below). Given its SPJ approach, the HCR-20 differs both from the traditional, unstructured clinical approach to risk assessment and from the actuarial approach. However, as described later in this chapter, it shares features with both.

The HCR-20 has been translated into 16 languages and is used in a large number of correctional, forensic, and psychiatric agencies, systems, and institutions across North America, Europe, South America, Asia, and Australia. There have been more than 50 evaluations of its validity across approximately a dozen countries (Douglas, Guy, Reeves, & Weir, 2008; Guy, 2008). In this chapter, we describe the rationale for the development of the HCR-20, how to use it, its defining features, how its use differs from both unstructured clinical judgment and actuarial prediction, empirical evidence supporting its reliability and validity, and we present a sample case.

Description of Measure

Criterion Being Assessed

The HCR-20 is intended to facilitate assessments of risk for interpersonal violence, which is defined in the HCR-20 manual (Webster et al., 1997) as "actual, attempted, or threatened harm to a person or persons" (p. 24). Note that actual physical harm is not required—*threatened* or *attempted* harm fits the definition of violence. As written in the HCR-20 manual, "[t]hreats of harm must be clear and unambiguous threats (e.g., "I am going to kill you!"), rather than vague statements of hostility" (p. 24). To take an extreme example, if a person were to shoot a gun into a crowded room and strike no one, that is violence. There is simply no meaningful logical difference between attempted and completed violence in terms of the behavior and intention of the perpetrator, *other than* he or she failed. As such, it does not make sense to exclude attempts from the definition of violence.

Property damage or harm to animals is not considered violence, unless carried out in a manner that is intended to cause fear of harm in others (i.e., smashing a chair, or injuring an animal, while stating "this is what I want to do to you!"). Acts that cause primarily psychological harm count as violence, such as stalking, unlawful confinement, extortion, or kidnapping. All sexual assaults are considered violent, including those that do not cause physical harm (see Hart & Boer, Chapter 13, this volume). Including psychological harm in the definition of violence is consistent with legal principles. For instance, threats of violence, or acts that primarily cause psychological rather than physical injuries (i.e., kidnapping, extortion) can lead to legal responses such as arrest, prosecution, or involuntary civil commitment. In some countries such as Canada, "serious psychological harm" has been defined as constituting "serious bodily harm" so long as it "substantially interferes with the health or well-being of the complainant" (*R. v. McCraw,* 1991, p. 81). Further, including psychological harm in the definition of violence is consistent with the empirical reality that psychological damage can be as or more harmful than physical damage to a person. Acts in self-defense or the defense of others are not violence, so long as the degree of force used does not exceed that which is necessary to protect self or others. Acts that meet the definition of violence but are legally sanctioned (i.e., sports, military, law enforcement) are not considered violence unless they exceed the legal mandate that permits them.

As written in the HCR-20 manual:

> In a general sense, then, acts which are serious enough to result in criminal or civil sanctions, or for which the perpetrator could have been charged, should be considered violent, and those that are not as serious as this should not be considered violent (p. 25).

Type of Measure

The HCR-20 is an example of the SPJ approach to risk assessment. Described more fully in the "Method of and Rationale for Development" section, the SPJ approach attempts to retain the strengths associated with both clinical and actuarial approaches to decision making while limiting their weaknesses. Strengths of clinical decision making include a focus on an individual's characteristics and an orientation toward intervention and management. Strengths (though not defining features) of the actuarial approach include an emphasis on empirical support, operational coding of risk factors, reliability, and transparency of decision making. Weaknesses of unstructured clinical decision making include the potential for inconsistency between evaluators and within the same evaluator across evaluations, reliance on irrelevant factors, and omission of relevant factors. Weaknesses of actuarial decision making (at least as demonstrated in the violence risk assessment field) include overreliance on static (unchanging) risk factors that are less relevant to risk management than dynamic (changeable) risk factors, potential for limited generalizability across samples and settings, and potentially misleading reliance on final judgments characterized by numeric estimates of the probability of future violence in the individual case. These themes will be expanded on below, under "Method of and Rationale for Development" (for in-depth discussion of these topics, see Douglas, 2008; Douglas & Kropp, 2002; Douglas & Skeem, 2005; Hart, 1998; Heilbrun, Douglas, & Yasuhara, 2009; Heilbrun, Yasuhara, & Shah, Chapter 1, this volume; Mulvey & Lidz, 1995).

Description of Content and Items

Like most SPJ measures, the HCR-20 includes a professional manual consisting of several features: background of the specific risk assessment task that the HCR-20 was developed to address (i.e., risk for general violence in the case of the HCR-20; risk for sexual violence in the case of the SVR-20 or RSVP, see Hart & Boer, Chapter 13, this volume; risk for violence among adolescents in the case of the SAVRY, see Borum et al., Chapter 4, this volume; risk for antisocial behavior among children as in the case of the EARL-20-B and EARL-21-G, see Augimeri et al, Chapter 3, this volume; risk for spousal violence as in the case of the SARA, see Kropp & Gibas,

Historical (Past)	Clinical (Present)	Risk Management (Future)
H1. Previous Violence	C1. Lack of Insight	R1. Plans Lack Feasibility
H2. Young Age at First Violent Incident	C2. Negative Attitudes	R2. Exposure to Destabilizers
H3. Relationship Instability	C3. Active Symptoms of Major Mental Illness	R3. Lack of Personal Support
H4. Employment Problems	C4. Impulsivity	R4. Noncompliance with Remediation Attempts
H5. Substance Use Problems	C5. Unresponsive to Treatment	R5. Stress
H6. Major Mental Illness		
H7. Psychopathy		
H8. Early Maladjustment		
H9. Personality Disorder		
H10. Prior Supervision Failure		

Figure 8.1 HCR-20 scales and items. (Webster et al., 1997. *HCR-20: Assessing risk for violence,* Version 2. Burnaby, BC, Canada: Simon Fraser University. Reprinted with permission.)

Chapter 11, this volume); description of the measure; general information about violence risk assessment; research on the instrument; user qualifications; scope and purpose; definition of violence; administration principles; item definitions; item coding instructions; and instructions for reaching a final risk decision and informing risk management plans.

The HCR-20 scales and items are presented in Figure 8.1. The three HCR-20 scales are intended to cover past, present, and future. The Historical (H) Scale contains 10 items that cover important past risk factors, the five Clinical (C) Scale risk factors pertain to current or recent functioning, and the five Risk Management (R) Scale factors require ratings about future risk-relevant circumstances. There are 20 risk factors across these three scales—hence the name of the measure: HCR-20. Details about each of these three scales follow.

Historical Scale. The Historical (H) Scale is so named because it indexes a core set of important violence risk factors that may have occurred or transpired at some point in a person's history. It is important to note that these risk factors may very well, and likely often will, have crucial relevance for understanding a person's *current* and *future* risk for violence as well. For this reason, it is essential that evaluators not only diligently record the proper score for each risk factor, but consider the current and future relevance of each risk factor for a person's violence risk. Similarly, it would be a mistake to consider many of these risk factors to be static or unchanging. Whereas a person may always receive a high score on these items (i.e., a person with years of substance abuse) by virtue of the fact that the risk factor was present in the past, evaluators must consider the current and future relevance of each risk factor, as reflected by its current manifestation and course. Therefore, H scale risk factors need to be considered for risk management plans along with C scale and R scale risk factors.

There is no conceptual theme that ties the H scale risk factors together. They are united by temporal period and reflect a summary of what the current literature on violence indicates as core risk factors. However, it may be beneficial to consider these 10 risk factors as falling into several general categories: (1) problems in adjustment or living, (2) problems with mental health, and (3) past antisociality. *Problems in adjustment or living* are captured by H3 (Relationship Instability), H4 (Employment Problems), and H8 (Early Maladjustment). *Problems with mental health* include H5 (Substance Use Problems), H6 (Major Mental Illness), H7 (Psychopathy), and H9 (Personality Disorder). Finally, *past antisociality* is captured by H1 (Previous Violence), H2 (Young Age at First Violent Incident), and H10 (Prior Supervision Failure).

Clinical Scale. The Clinical (C) Scale captures *recent* and *current* functioning in important risk-relevant domains. Although most risk factors on the HCR-20 are potentially dynamic (including those on the Historical Scale), those on the C scale focus on phenomena that can change acutely. In some cases, change may be manifest over very short periods of time (e.g., hours or days), whereas in other cases, change may be more gradual (for example, months). There is direct evidence that the C scale items can change over time (Belfrage & Douglas, 2002; Douglas & Belfrage, 2001). This focus on *dynamic risk* is commensurate with an emerging emphasis in the risk assessment field to ensure that risk factors that are highly relevant to intervention and management are featured centrally within assessments (Andrews, Bonta, & Wormith, Chapter 10, this volume; Douglas, 2008; Douglas & Skeem, 2005; Dvoskin & Heilbrun, 2001; Mulvey & Lidz, 1995; Skeem & Mulvey, 2002). Therefore, C scale risk factors ideally should be reevaluated on a regular basis, a point we expand upon below. Corresponding ratings of risk level, and recommended or actual intervention and management strategies, should be adjusted accordingly.

Risk Management Scale. This section centers on forecasting how individuals will adjust to future circumstances. Although the Historical and Clinical Scales also are relevant to and should figure prominently in the development of risk management plans, the Risk Management (R) Scale is intended to focus evaluators' attention on development of appropriate future risk management plans, to speculate about what impediments to successful management might exist, and how to address such impediments.

The factors captured by the R scale items also can change over time (Belfrage & Douglas, 2002; Douglas & Belfrage, 2001). Therefore, as with the C scale, we recommend that the R scale items be reevaluated on a regular basis, consistent with the person's context. We would recommend that they are reevaluated or monitored whenever the C scale items are reevaluated, because changes in a person's recent functioning can have implications for his or her future functioning and the adequacy of plans.

Contexts and Populations in Which HCR-20 Is and Is Not Appropriate to Use

The HCR-20 is intended to be used with men and women age 18 and above. There is some leeway here; in some cases it may be appropriate to use the HCR-20 with younger persons (say, 16 or 17) if they have been living independently for some time. Similarly, it may make more sense in certain cases *not* to use the HCR-20 with a 19- or 20-year-old (a person living at home and dependent on parents, for instance). It will be up to the evaluator to judge whether the HCR-20 or something like the SAVRY (Borum et al., Chapter 4, this volume) is more appropriate in these cases on the cusp.

As stated in the HCR-20 manual, its use "should be restricted mainly to settings in which there is a high proportion of persons with histories of violence, and a strong suggestion of mental illness or severe personality disorder" (p. 5). The manual continues to explain that this would include forensic and civil mental health settings, and parole and other correctional settings. Research, described in detail later in this chapter, has been conducted and provides support for the use of the HCR-20 in samples of forensic psychiatric patients, civil psychiatric patients, offenders with mental disorders, and general correctional offenders, both for institutional and community violence. There have also been studies on the HCR-20 with young offenders.

More concretely, the HCR-20 can be used in the following settings and contexts: (1) release decision making (from correctional, psychiatric, or forensic facilities); (2) admission decision making (upon entry to correctional, psychiatric, or forensic facilities); (3) monitoring of risk while a person is incarcerated or institutionalized; and (4) monitoring of risk while a person is under a term of community supervision by correctional, forensic, or psychiatric authorities. The particular manner in which the HCR-20 can be used for such purposes will be described under the "Assessment Procedure: How to Use and Make Decisions with the HCR-20" section.

User Qualifications

The two minimal user qualifications for use of the HCR-20 are "expertise in conduct of individual assessments" (Webster et al., 1997, p. 17) and "expertise in the study of violence" (Webster et al., 1997, p. 17). The former includes training and experience in "interviewing; the administration and interpretation of standardized tests; and the diagnosis of mental disorder" (p. 18). The latter requires evaluators to "be familiar with the professional and research literatures on the nature, causes, and management of violence" (p. 18).

When used for clinical rather than research purposes, evaluators should have "a high level of expertise (e.g., graduate-level university courses or other specialized educational training, supervised field experience) and should have the requisite professional credentials (e.g., registered, licensed, or legally entitled to conduct individual assessments)" (Webster et al., p. 18). When used for research, raters may be well-trained graduate, medical, or even undergraduate students, so long as they are supervised by a person who is fully qualified to administer the HCR-20 under "clinical conditions."

Some items on the HCR-20 require an assessment of mental disorder. As stated in the HCR-20 manual:

> [U]sers who lack the requisite credentials to conduct psychodiagnostic assessments are not legally entitled to code these items, except in the following circumstances:
>
> - The items are coded in consultation with or under the supervision of accredited professionals.
> - The items are coded by referring to the results of existing psychodiagnostic assessments.
> - The items are coded provisionally, with a notation that the coding should be confirmed by an accredited professional.
> - The items are omitted altogether, with a notation concerning how their omission may have limited the final judgment of risk. (Webster et al., p. 18. Reprinted with permission.)

Note that the "requisite credentials" may vary across jurisdictions. It is possible for teams of professionals to complete the HCR-20. For instance, a psychiatrist or psychiatric nurse might complete ratings of items pertaining to major mental illness, a psychologist might contribute by assessing items pertaining to personality disorder and psychopathy, and a social worker or probation officer might complete items pertaining to social history and future plans. In this arrangement, it is important that a person with full qualifications oversee the compilation of ratings, and be responsible for finalizing and approving all final ratings and decisions stemming therefrom.

Method of and Rationale for Development

To understand why the HCR-20 (and other SPJ measures) was developed in the way it was, it is necessary to describe the choices available in the risk assessment field prior to the development of the SPJ model—unstructured clinical judgment and actuarial prediction. Of course, the "clinical versus actuarial" prediction issue has been discussed in the social, behavioral, and medical sciences for over 50 years (Meehl, 1954).

Unstructured clinical judgment is based primarily on professional opinion, intuition, and clinical experience. There is absolute discretion in selecting and conceptualizing risk factors, as well as how to integrate them to make decisions (Meehl, 1954). It is an informal and subjective method. Of course, clinical judgment is a crucial part of assessment and intervention. It is geared toward flexibility and relevance to the individual client or examinee. However, in terms of estimating future probabilities of events, or making predictions, there are numerous problems with this approach, as described below. As written by Grove and Meehl (1996), clinical prediction is an "informal, 'in the head,' impressionistic, subjective conclusion, reached (somehow) by a human clinical judge" (p. 294). In terms of *prediction,* "clinical" means that there are no replicable, specified rules for combining or integrating predictive factors. By contrast, the actuarial approach to prediction is "a formal method" that "uses an equation, a formula, a graph, or an actuarial table to arrive at a probability, or expected value, of some outcome" (Grove & Meehl, 1996, p. 294). That is, the defining feature of the term "actuarial" is the specification of replicable, routinized rules for combining or integrating predictive factors.

Both approaches have strengths and both have weaknesses, and the SPJ approach was developed to avoid the weaknesses of both, while trying to achieve the strengths of both. However, it is *not* a combined "clinical–actuarial" approach. Nor is it an "adjusted-actuarial" approach (that is, adjusting the numeric estimate of an actuarial prediction based on intuition or other non-actuarial means). There is no empirical support for the latter. The former is impossible, by definition. That is, the same single decision-making task cannot be both rule-bound and without rules; single decision tasks either are actuarial, or they are not, in which case they are clinical, as defined originally by Meehl (1954). It *would* technically be possible to construct a multistep decision-making *process* that includes both clinical and actuarial components. In fact, this is essentially the process recommended by Monahan et al. (2005; see also Monahan, Chapter 9, this volume) for using their Classification of Violence Risk (COVR), as well as by others (e.g., Doren, 2002). That is, an actuarial estimate is produced by the COVR and then used by a clinician as one piece of information in a discretionary judgment about whether to release or detain a psychiatric patient. Ultimately, such a multistep process is clinical, given that the clinician is left with the task of deciding how to integrate the actuarial estimate with other information.

Strengths and Weaknesses of Unstructured Clinical Discretion. Strengths of the clinical approach include responsivity and sensitivity to the individual case. This can enhance case conceptualization and working with people individually to derive risk management plans to reduce violence. Further, clinical decision making is highly flexible and widely applicable.

However, a purely unstructured clinical approach suffers serious weaknesses, given the absence of structure. This includes potentially low reliability, because different clinicians may combine or weight information differently for the same people. Further, decision-makers may not consider factors that actually relate to violent behavior, or consider other factors that do not relate to violence. Not only may there be inconsistency across raters, there also might be inconsistency within raters but across cases. As such, it is likely that such decisions will be of lower reliability and predictive validity than otherwise possible.

Because there are no rules for what risk factors to consider or how to use them in a risk assessment, and an evaluator does not specify such risk factors or how they were used, there is little transparency in unstructured clinical decision making, which is a problematic feature in legal settings, because it makes the later review of such decisions difficult. Hence, such decisions potentially jeopardize the rights of those about whom they are made, as well as thwart attempts at continuity of care. Other potential problems include susceptibility to decisional biases and heuristics. As such, we attempted to avoid these problems in the development of the HCR-20, as described in the sections that follow, yet retained some of the positive features of a clinical approach.

Strengths and Weaknesses of Actuarial Decision Making. A strength of actuarial prediction is that, being bound by combinatory rules, it facilitates inter-rater reliability and predictive validity, especially in comparison with unstructured approaches. In addition, because the rules used to combine items in order to reach risk decisions are specified *a priori,* actuarial predictions tend to be transparent, which is a benefit in legal contexts. In developing the HCR-20, we were interested in ensuring the features of reliability, validity, and transparency—just not through actuarial means, for reasons described next.

The predictive properties of most actuarial models used in the violence risk assessment field tend to be optimized within a development sample—often just a single sample is used, and the results are not cross-validated prior to use (Minnesota Sex Offender Screening Tool, MnSOST; Violence Risk Appraisal Guide, VRAG). That is, researchers measure some group of patients or offenders on some set of risk factors, observe who is and is not violent during some specified time window, and determine what risk factors are most strongly associated with violence in the extant sample. Typically, actuarial risk assessment instruments, such as those described in this book (VRAG; Sex Offender Risk Appraisal Guide, SORAG; COVR; Static-99; Level of Service Inventory-Revised, LSI-R), produce *estimated* probabilities of violence over some future time for persons who fall into certain score ranges on the test. Some, but not all, weight the individual risk factors on the risk assessment instrument according to their predictive validity in development (and, ideally, cross-validation) samples.

Although the promise of high reliability and accurate numeric estimates of individuals' probabilities of future violence is alluring, there are a number of vulnerabilities of the actuarial approach that, as of yet, have not consistently been demonstrated to have been overcome in the risk assessment field. Most actuarial procedures select risk factors because of demonstrated statistical associations with outcome (violence) within a given sample or samples. While such variables are related to violence in those samples, there is no guarantee that (1) they would have been so in other samples and (2) other risk factors would not have been associated with violence in other samples. Strict actuarial approaches (e.g., VRAG, see this volume) do not permit consideration of any variables that are not included on the instrument, which presumes that the original research that developed the instrument considered all potentially relevant risk factors, and all potentially relevant risk factors are in fact contained within the instrument. If actuarial procedures also weight variables, the presumption is that the same variables would have been weighted comparably in other samples, and that such weights apply equally to all persons in the development sample and any other sample in which the instrument is intended for use. Further, actuarial approaches presume that the observed probabilities of violence in development samples will apply to different samples.

The potential problems with this approach lie in the fact that actuarial approaches are *sample dependent.* That is, (1) the variables that are identified by whatever statistical procedures that are used to select them, (2) the weights given to such variables, and (3) the resulting observed probabilities of violence are all dependent on a myriad of sample-specific characteristics. Such characteristics include, but are not limited to, the variables chosen for study in the first place, the way in which such variables are defined and measured, the reliability of measurement, the demographics of participants, follow-up length, method used to detect violence, definition of violence, and the type of statistical procedures used. Given this sample dependence, any numeric estimates of risk for violence are subject to change if tested in new samples. This potential change has several possible implications: (1) estimates provided by actuarial instruments may, or may not, apply outside of development samples, and this cannot be known unless tested empirically; (2) the strength of prediction may diminish in new samples, to the extent that such new samples differ from the development sample (in fact, even if they are highly similar, predictive strength may diminish because the original estimates also capitalized on chance associations in the data). Hence, unless numeric estimates are demonstrated to be stable over numerous samples of intended application, it is risky to assume that they will in fact be stable. The basic problem here is a potential lack of robustness and generalizability of risk estimates.

We illustrate some of these problems. As a simple demonstration of the "if you don't measure it, it can't be on your instrument" problem, note that the Static-99, (see Chapter 12), one of the best validated sexual violence risk assessment measures, does not include "sexual deviation" as a risk factor, despite its strength in the empirical literature as a robust risk factor (Laws & O'Donohue, 2008). Other actuarial instruments fail to include risk factors that have broad support in the literature. For example, although the VRAG contains many common risk factors with a good deal of empirical support (i.e., psychopathy, alcohol use problems, separation from parents), there are a number of other risk factors (e.g., anger, previous violence, treatment noncompliance, stress) with empirical support across numerous samples that are not included for the simple reason that they either were not tested as candidate risk factors, or they were tested, but they failed to demonstrate independent statistical associations with violence *in the development sample.* This does not mean that such factors as sexual deviance or anger are irrelevant to violence, just that they were not included on some actuarial instruments because the authors either chose not to test them, they were not related to violence in the development research, or the data were not collected or available for review.

If actuarial instruments weight variables, the presumption is that the weights (1) strengthen the prediction and (2) apply equally to all people (that, say, alcohol problems are always 2.5 times more important than, say, child abuse, in determining future risk of violence). Grann and Långström (2007) tested the first assumption in a sample of 404 Swedish forensic psychiatric patients whom they followed in the community for approximately two years after forensic evaluation. They tested the accuracy of four types of weighting procedures (of the HCR-20 H scale) against unit weighting (all variables contributing equal weight to the predictive equation—the scoring option used for the HCR-20). Importantly, they first derived predictive algorithms on a subsample of cases and then tested the predictive accuracy of those algorithms in a new (cross-validation) subsample of cases. Such a procedure is vital to minimize the artificial inflation of predictive accuracy that many actuarial instruments enjoy because they are based on developmental samples, and not cross-validation samples (Harris, Rice, & Quinsey, 1993; Quinsey, Harris, Rice, & Cormier, 1998, 2006). Grann and Långström reported that the more complex the weighting procedure, the greater the diminishment in predictive accuracy upon cross-validation, with unit weighting achieving the strongest predictive accuracy. This finding confirms what Dawes (1979) asserted years ago—that unit weighting is just as accurate as cross-validated weighting procedures. He eloquently referred to this observation as the "robust beauty of improper [unweighted] linear models" (p. 571).

Blair, Marcus, and Boccaccini (2008) demonstrated the shrinkage that may occur upon cross-validation in a meta-analysis of the VRAG, SORAG, and Static-99. They coded correlational effect sizes for these instruments and then divided them into development samples and cross-validation samples. They further divided cross-validation samples into those conducted by the authors of the instruments and those conducted by independent authors unaffiliated with the instruments. They reported shrinkage for each instrument. For example, the effect size for the VRAG in its development sample was .44; it was .36 in cross-validation studies that included at least one of its authors; it was .30 for cross-validation studies that did not include any of its authors. For the SORAG, these estimates were .46, .35, and .29, respectively. For the Static-99, the development sample correlation was .33, and the independent cross-validation correlation was .27 (there were no cross-validations by the authors of the Static-99). Across all measures, development correlations shrank from .39 to .36 to .28.

The implication of such findings is that the numeric estimates of violence may not hold up upon cross-validation. The more precise the estimate (that is, point estimates such as "62%" as opposed to ranges of estimates), the greater the risk that it will not actually apply in new samples. Mills, Jones, and Kroner (2005), in a sample of 209 offenders, tested the robustness of LSI-R and VRAG estimates of recidivism by comparing the observed recidivism rates of reoffending (LSI-R) or violence (VRAG) to the estimates offered by each instrument, which were based on development samples. They reported that their data:

> . . . does not support the use of the initial validation probability bins of either instrument with our sample. The VRAG nine-bin system has the greater problem given the presence of probability reversals through the bins in conjunction with dissimilar probabilities associated with the bins. (p. 579)

In the study conducted by Mills et al. (2005), some of the VRAG bins associated with higher estimates of future violence compared to other (lower estimate) bins actually produced lower observed rates of violence. For instance, the ninth of nine VRAG bins produces an estimate of 100% probability of future violence, according to the authors (Quinsey et al., 2006). In Mills et al., the observed recidivism rate was just 33%. This observed rate of recidivism was in fact lower than the observed rates of recidivism in bins seven and eight, which, according to the VRAG, should be associated with lower, not higher, rates of future violence. What is the "correct" estimate of violence, then, for people who score in the ninth (or fifth, or second, etc.) bin of the VRAG? The answer is that there is no correct numeric estimate of future violence—such observed estimates are prone to bounce around across samples. Hence, it is possible or even likely that offering an ostensibly precise numeric estimate of recidivism will simply be misleading.

While it generally would be safe to assume that a person who scores higher on some actuarial instrument than another person would be at greater risk for violence, as demonstrated by meta-analytic linear associations of moderate magnitude between such instruments and violence (Blair et al., 2008), it is *not* safe to declare what the estimated numeric probability of violence of either person would be. In fact, it does not appear that risk assessment technology has yet advanced to a point where this is possible.

There are a couple of other potential limitations to some actuarial approaches. Many such approaches tend to be less relevant to risk management and treatment because they include mainly historical, static variables (an exception is the LS system, see Chapter 5 and Chapter 10, this volume), rather than dynamic risk factors that inform decisions about risk state as opposed to risk status (Douglas & Skeem, 2005). A corollary effect of this feature is that risk estimates can be unalterable, or "frozen in time." Regardless of changes in the risk management plan, or intervention successes, a person's risk will remain the same. Given that certain intervention approaches are effective in the reduction of crime and violence (Andrews & Bonta, 2004; Douglas, Nicholls, & Brink, 2009; Dowden & Andrews, 2000), such a static presumption is unfounded.

Rationale for Development of the HCR-20 (as an Instantiation of the SPJ Model). To combat the weakness of both the clinical and actuarial approaches, as outlined above, yet to try to incorporate their respective strengths, we aimed for the following characteristics in developing the HCR-20.

We used a *logical* or *rational* item selection method to foster generalizability and comprehensiveness of the risk factors on the HCR-20. This approach is in contrast to the empirical item selection approach used by most actuarial methods, the weaknesses of which were outlined above. Logical item selection involves a thorough review of scientific, theoretical, and professional literatures on some topic (here, violence) and the selection of risk factors with support across numerous samples and contexts. The goal is to avoid the omission of important risk factors or inclusion of unimportant risk factors because of chance associations in a development sample. In principle, because this approach is not sample dependent, risk factors should be generalizable across a variety of settings.

Also in contrast with actuarial approaches, the HCR-20 and other SPJ instruments do not use (1) score cutoffs to determine risk level, (2) numeric estimates of future risk for violence. In our view, such features of risk assessment instruments may perform well in development samples, but have great difficulty in achieving consistency upon cross-validation, as discussed above. Rather, as described in more detail below, the HCR-20 requires clinicians to arrive at a nonnumeric, categorical risk estimate of Low, Moderate, or High risk, based on (1) the presence of risk factors, (2) their relevance of risk in the instant case, and (3) the degree of management, supervision, or intervention required to mitigate risk. This feature differs sharply from actuarial approaches and has been criticized because it allows discretion at the risk decision stage (Quinsey et al., 2006). However, as described in the research section of this chapter, empirical evidence supports this feature of SPJ instruments.

The HCR-20 uses unit-weighting, rather than presuming that group-based statistically weighted and optimized risk factors will apply equally across samples and to all persons. Such an approach, as discussed above, actually may fare worse upon cross-validation compared to simple unit weighting (Grann & Långström, 2007). We do not assume that a given risk factor (say, substance use problems) will be equally important for all persons who have it. For some, it may be highly relevant to risk for violence. For others, it may not. We require users of the HCR-20 to determine for whom it is relevant, and for whom it is not. The rationale for this approach was to promote consideration by users of both the nomothetic level of analysis (risk factors supported through empirical studies of research samples) and the idiographic level (the relevance and manifestation of such nomothetically supported risk factors at the individual level).

The HCR-20, like other SPJ instruments, includes dynamic risk factors in order to facilitate the development of risk management plans. As described elsewhere (Douglas & Skeem, 2005; Skeem & Mulvey, 2002), estimating the risk level of a person may help in terms of determining the appropriate *intensity* of management, but it does little to determine the *type* of management that will reduce risk. For this reason, risk factors on the HCR-20 (particularly the C and R items) should be reevaluated, and management plans should be developed to mitigate them. Relevance to risk management and intervention is one of the strengths of the clinical approach that the HCR-20 attempted to incorporate.

However, as noted above, a purely unstructured approach is likely to produce lower reliability and validity than actuarial approaches, given that the latter have formal rules for the combination of risk factors. Therefore, we included a certain amount of structure into the HCR-20 in order to foster reliability and validity, features often associated with though not defining of the actuarial approach. Structure is found on the HCR-20 by the (1) inclusion of a fixed set of risk factors, (2) operational definitions of risk factors, (3) scoring or coding procedures for risk factors, and (4) direction for how to reach a final decision about risk based on consideration of the risk factors present and relevant in an individual case. These structural elements are described in more detail in the next section.

Assessment Procedure: How to Use and Make Decisions With the HCR-20

Administration Procedures

We recommend the following procedures and steps to complete an HCR-20 evaluation. Evaluators should gather information from as many sources as necessary in the context in which they work.

General categories of sources of information include: (1) relevant files and records; (2) interview with the examinee; (3) psychological testing and assessment procedures; (4) interviews with persons who have knowledge of the individual being evaluated; and (5) direct observation. The general principle we endorse is that evaluators should obtain as much relevant information as necessary to minimize the risk that important details about an examinee are missed.

Sources of Information. It is vital to secure as much file-based information as necessary in order to complete the HCR-20. This includes but is not limited to nursing notes, social histories, prior mental health evaluations, police reports, arrest records, vocational and educational evaluations, psychological test results, notes from past programming, treatment, or supervision experiences, and records detailing the examinee's adjustment while living in the community under supervision or in an institution.

We recommend, whenever possible, an interview of the person being evaluated. This is consistent with most ethical and practice codes of conduct pertaining to mental health and other human service professions. We do not have a standardized interview protocol, because our goal for the HCR-20 is that it can be integrated into existing practice regimes. The areas that should be covered in such an interview are similar to the areas that should be covered in a file review. An interview to complete the HCR-20 should not require evaluators to ask many more questions than they otherwise would in a comprehensive, thorough psychosocial interview intended to provide a full picture of an individual's history, risk factors, mental health status, past crime and violence, previous treatment and supervision experiences, current functioning, personality, and interpersonal relations. The interview is especially important for assessing current functioning captured by the Clinical Scale, as well as personality and attitudinal characteristics.

Formal psychological testing and assessment procedures will not be required in every case, or perhaps even in the majority of cases. One exception is the use of the Psychopathy Checklist–Revised (PCL-R) or Psychopathy Checklist-Revised: Screening Version (PCL:SV) for use in coding item H7 (Psychopathy). As discussed below, if evaluators must omit an item, including H7, they should state the limits that this might place on the accuracy and comprehensiveness of their evaluation. We leave it to the discretion of evaluators to decide whether such testing is required in a given case, and for what sorts of issues. Such testing could include, inter alia, intelligence and cognitive testing, including neuropsychological testing; semistructured assessment protocols for mental illness and personality disorder; personality assessment using broad-band personality measures; focused tests or assessments of individual constructs (i.e., insight; treatment motivation). We would recommend such testing for the purpose of completing the HCR-20 if, in the judgment of the evaluator, there was one or more areas on the HCR-20 that could not be completed without it.

Where possible and permissible, we recommend that evaluators conduct interviews, even by phone, with others who know the person who is being evaluated. Such third parties could be other professionals, friends, family, or coworkers. Of course, evaluators are expected to obtain any ethical or legal waivers to speak to third parties.

Although interviews clearly are an opportunity for observation, we recommend that, if possible, evaluators observe individuals in less formal contexts as well (that is, behavior on the ward; interaction with others). We realize that direct observation is only possible in certain contexts. We would encourage evaluators to take advantage of such possibility when it exists.

Evaluation Steps

We recommend the following steps be followed in an HCR-20 evaluation:

1. Gather as much information about the individual as is necessary using the five sources of information above. At a minimum, this should include an interview and review of case records.
2. Collate this information as it pertains to each of the HCR-20 risk factors. We recommend, when scoring HCR-20 risk factors, that evaluators consider the evidence both for and against the risk factors, so that the scoring and formulation process is as balanced as possible.
3. In addition to assigning scores of 0 (absent), 1 (possibly or partially present), or 2 (definitely present) to each risk factor, evaluators must engage in two further tasks in order to facilitate case formulation and risk management planning:
   a. Description of the *manifestation* of each risk factor that is present for the case at hand. It is important for evaluators to go beyond the mere noting of a risk factor, and to describe how that risk factor manifests in the individual being evaluated.
   b. Description of the *relevance* of each risk factor that is present to the risk of violence posed by the individual being evaluated. Even if many risk factors are present, evaluators should determine which are most concerning for an individual's risk for violence and, hence, most necessary to manage. In part, this can be done by consideration of the role that each risk factor has played in a person's previous violence.
4. Delineation of the treatment, supervision, or management strategies that logically flow from the risk factors that were identified, taking into account those that are considered most relevant to a person's risk for violence.
5. Determination of whether there are any items or other elements of the decision-making process that had to be omitted because of incomplete or conflicting information. If so, we strongly recommend revisiting those areas of the evaluation in order to maximize the chance that the evaluation is based on complete and valid information about an individual. If any risk factors cannot be coded and hence contribute to case formulation, evaluators should note whatever limits this missing information has on their judgments.
6. Determine whether reevaluation will be needed in the future and, if so, how soon.
7. Statement of whether the individual is considered to be Low, Moderate, or High risk. The complete meaning of these nonnumeric risk categories is described below. It is important to note that their meaning is *not* limited solely to the likelihood of future violence, although it has been inaccurately described as such by some critics (Quinsey et al., 2006).
   a. *High risk* should be applied to cases (1) with many relevant violent risk factors present, or (2) that require frequent, intensive, or highly restrictive supervision, monitoring, management, or intervention in order to stem violence risk. In general, evaluators should make a decision of High risk if they believe, based on the number and relevance of risk factors that are present, and the associated degree of intervention, supervision, monitoring, or management required to mitigate risk, that a person will likely be violent in the future if no appropriate risk management plans are enacted.
   b. *Low risk* should be reserved for cases (1) in which there are few relevant violent risk factors present, or (2) that require minimal or no supervision, monitoring, management, or intervention in order to stem violence risk.
   c. *Moderate risk* should be applied to cases which are neither high nor low risk, as defined above.

It is important to point out that the making of a rating of Low, Moderate, or High risk is almost peripheral to the main task at hand—identifying and managing risk factors. If using the *HCR-20,* it is *not* acceptable simply to score the items and provide a summary risk rating of Low, Moderate, or High risk. The summary risk rating is merely a shorthand way to note that the person is considered likely to be violent and in need of services. It is a vehicle through which evaluators express their judgments about case prioritization, that is, which persons have a high number of risk factors that require a high degree of intervention. The nature of such intervention must also be specified. The most important part of the risk assessment is to specify what those services are, and to try to put them into effect. As such, decisions of High risk and, to a lesser extent, Moderate or Low risk must be accompanied by (1) a rationale for the decision based on the evidence at hand (number and relevance of risk factors) and (2) the delineation of the risk management, supervision, monitoring, or intervention strategies required to mitigate risk.

We are aware that some evaluators would like both numeric cutoffs and associated numeric estimates of future violence. For reasons discussed above, we do not believe that the current state of the science permits either of these features in the risk assessment field, at least as applied to individuals rather than samples. Further, as reviewed below, the empirical evaluation of the SPJ system of nonnumeric categorical risk categories shows that they are as or more accurate in determining who will be violent in the future compared to actuarial approaches.

Team Evaluations

In some settings, responsibility for conducting assessments may be divided among several different professionals. For example, a psychologist or psychiatrist may assess major mental illness; a psychologist may assess personality or intellectual functioning; and a nurse, social worker, or probation officer may assess release plans. It is acceptable—and may even be desirable—for the HCR-20 to be completed on the basis of reports submitted by several independent professionals. However, a fully qualified user must assume responsibility for integrating the various components, and for making and documenting opinions.

Time Frame for Decisions About Risk for Violence

Historical Scale. The scoring time frame for all Historical items is lifetime, unless otherwise specified within the item. That is, has the risk factor been present *at any time in a person's life?* For example, if a person seriously abused substances 15 years ago but has been abstinent since, the evaluator would indicate that the risk factor is present. *However,* the evaluator might also indicate that the risk factor is not relevant to the person's current or future risk for violence, and it may play a small role in case conceptualization.

Although persons may always score high on H scale items by virtue of their past experiences or behaviors, evaluators should be aware that the coding of H scale items may need to be updated. This may occur if (1) a risk factor that previously was absent (or possibly/partially present) becomes present due to recent behavior (that is, if a person starts to abuse substances and had not done so in the past), or (2) a risk factor has been "dormant" for some time, in which case a score might be reduced from a score of 2 to a score of 1. H scale items can also be updated to correct past coding errors.

Clinical Scale. C scale risk factors ideally should be reevaluated on a regular basis. We recognize that some evaluators will be in a position to rate these risk factors only once. If other professionals then assume responsibility for the management of a person, we would recommend that these factors are reevaluated once the next evaluator has assumed responsibility for the case. In some situations, we realize, the C scale will be used for a single time-point evaluation because circumstances do not allow for reevaluation. If at all possible, however, these risk factors should be tracked over time, and corresponding ratings of risk level, and recommended or actual intervention and management strategies, should be adjusted accordingly.

The C items are intended to index recent and current functioning. However, there simply is no uniform evaluation window that can apply across settings. Indeed, for first-time evaluations, some clients may never have been evaluated previously, or if they have, evaluation results may not be known or available to the current evaluator. We offer some guiding principles to determine the best evaluation window:

1. If a person is being monitored regularly by a professional (i.e., through scheduled appointments), we recommend that the C scale items are updated at each appointment or session (be they weekly, monthly, biyearly). In such situations, the pertinent evaluation window should be the time since the person was last seen.
2. If a person is being evaluated for the first time by a particular professional, the evaluation window should be the previous six months. If the evaluator does not have information about the person that covers the past six months, then the evaluation window should cover as much of the past six months as possible, for as many of the risk factors as possible.

Evaluators also must decide what the time between reevaluations of the C scale items should be. As with the evaluation window, there is no single evaluation interval that makes sense in all contexts. We offer some guiding principles:

1. Higher-risk individuals should be reevaluated more frequently than lower-risk individuals. For higher-risk individuals, evaluators may decide that monthly, weekly, or in some cases, even daily, reevaluations are needed. For lower-risk individuals, evaluators may consider six months to be an appropriate reevaluation interval.
2. We recommend that reevaluation intervals not be longer than six months, if possible, unless a person has shown stable functioning and no violent behavior for at least twelve consecutive months. In such cases, annual reevaluations may be preferable.
3. Notwithstanding these general principles for determining the length of the evaluation interval, a reevaluation should take place under the following circumstances:
   a. There have been notable recent changes in a person's functioning.
   b. The person has engaged in recent violence.
   c. A transition is being considered or will occur (i.e., change in security or supervision level; release from institution).

In addition to rating whether the C items were present *at any time in the evaluation window,* evaluators can indicate whether the C item risk factors *currently* are present. This means that evaluators should not necessarily "take the average" of the risk factor across the evaluation period. For example, if during a six-month evaluation window a person had active symptoms of psychosis in the first month, but has not shown them since, that person should receive a score for the pertinent item, which indicates that the risk factor was present at some point during the evaluation window. The evaluator also should indicate that the risk factor is not *currently* present. By using this approach, the evaluator will know the *trajectory* of each risk factor over the evaluation window (increasing, decreasing, or stable). The evaluator may also choose to determine whether the risk factor has been fluctuating during the evaluation window, which will provide more information about the nature of the risk factor for a given person.

Risk Management Scale. Our recommendation for evaluation intervals for the R scale are similar to those for the C scale, as follows:

1. Higher-risk individuals should be reevaluated more frequently than lower-risk individuals. For higher-risk individuals, evaluators may decide that monthly, weekly, or, in some cases, even daily, reevaluations are needed. For lower-risk individuals, evaluators may consider six months to be an appropriate reevaluation interval.
2. We recommend that reevaluation intervals should not be longer than six months, if possible, unless a person has shown stable functioning and no violent behavior for at least twelve consecutive months. In such cases, annual reevaluations may be preferable.
3. Notwithstanding these general principles for determining the length of the evaluation interval, a reevaluation should take place under the following circumstances:
   a. There have been notable recent changes in a person's functioning.
   b. The person has engaged in recent violence.
   c. A transition is being considered or will occur (i.e., change in security or supervision level; release from institution).

Whereas for the C scale, evaluators must make ratings based on some logically defined recent period of time, for the R scale evaluators must make ratings based upon some logically defined *future* period of time. Essentially, evaluators should specify the approximate future time frame for which they are making their ratings. We recommend that this time period mirrors the evaluation interval. That is, if a high-risk person is being seen monthly by a professional, that professional should make R scale ratings for the month to come. If a person were more stable and being reevaluated semiannually or even annually, then the R scale ratings should project forward to cover what is foreseeable over the next six or twelve months.

Finally, R scale ratings can be completed for people who are residing within institutions and will be for some time, people for whom release is near, or people who already are residing in the community. Two types of R scale ratings can be made: *Institutional* ("In") or *Community* ("Out"). Under an "In" evaluation, evaluators rate the items for the period of institutionalization. For an "Out" evaluation conducted on people who currently are residing within an institution, evaluators rate the items based on discharge or release plans and planning, *as if the person were to be released right now.* That is, if the person were released right now, are his or her plans adequate to manage risk in the community? For persons residing in the community, evaluators should rate the items based on the assumption that they will continue to live in the community, unless other arrangements are known to the evaluator.

Overview of Research

Narrative (Douglas, Guy et al., 2008) and meta-analytic (Guy, 2008) reviews indicate that there have been over 50 studies on the HCR-20, and hence it would be impractical to review each of these individually. As such, we discuss the research on the HCR-20 using a "quasi-meta-analytic" approach. That is, for the most part, we report ranges and central tendencies of effect sizes across studies in any given research category (e.g., inter-rater reliability; predictive validity), and supplement this approach with discussion of representative individual studies.

Douglas and Kropp (2002) outlined an approach to the empirical evaluation of any SPJ measure. It is important first to establish inter-rater reliability and predictive validity of the ratings of risk factors. This demonstrates that the risk factors, as defined on a given instrument, can be agreed upon and, in turn, relate to violence (hence supporting their inclusion on SPJ instruments as risk factors). Second, it is important to test whether the judgments of evaluators who use SPJ instruments demonstrate both inter-rater reliability and predictive validity. This second feature of reliability and validity tests the nonactuarial judgments of risk that are required by SPJ instruments and are to be used in clinical practice. It is unique to SPJ instruments relative to actuarial instruments, since most actuarial instruments produce risk decisions purely on the basis of test results and do not permit evaluators to use their judgment in terms of offering risk estimates (although, as discussed above, proponents of some actuarial approaches advocate that actuarial tools be used in such a way). As such, our discussion of reliability and validity will provide a clear demarcation between numeric HCR-20 *scores,* and HCR-20 facilitated *judgments.*

Reliability

The most important type of reliability for the HCR-20 is inter-rater reliability. Structural reliability is of secondary importance, because the HCR-20 is not a measure of a psychological construct (e.g., depression; anger; psychopathy), and hence its items are not expected to "hang together" as should measures of psychological constructs. Nonetheless, there have been a few reports of internal consistency, which we review before focusing on inter-rater reliability.

Internal Consistency. Two studies have analyzed the internal consistency of the HCR-20. First, Belfrage (1998) investigated the Swedish translation of Version 1 of the HCR-20 (Webster, Eaves, Douglas, & Wintrup, 1995). Six clinicians scored the HCR-20 on the same 43 forensic patients and compared these scores to the patients' index offense and criminal records. Internal consistency, using Cronbach's alpha, for the HCR-20 total score was high at .95. Acceptably high alphas were obtained for the H, C, and R subscales, respectively (.96, .89, .85). In the second study of internal consistency of the HCR-20, Dunbar, Quinones, and Crevecoeur (2005) investigated Version 2 of the HCR-20 with 204 male offenders convicted of hate crimes in the United States. Similar to Belfrage (1998), all alpha coefficients were high (.94 for H; .90 for C; .95 for R).

Inter-Rater Reliability. The inter-rater reliability (IRR) of the HCR-20 has been investigated extensively. Most investigators have reported the IRR of the total or scale scores, with fewer having examined the IRR of the summary risk ratings of low, moderate, or high risk. We review these in turn. We also point out that studies have used different indices of IRR. Most have reported intraclass correlation coefficients (ICC), typically single measure. However, some studies have reported other indices (e.g., Pearson correlation coefficient; Kendall's tau). The reported ranges and central tendencies include all reliability coefficients, regardless of type.

Overall, across 36 studies (13 unpublished and 23 published) the IRR of the HCR-20 total numeric score is good to excellent.* For instance, across 25 studies, the median reliability coefficient for the HCR-20 total score is excellent, at .85.† Although IRR has ranged from .67 (Hildebrand, Hesper, Spreen, & Nijman, 2005) to .95 (McDermott, Edens, Quanbeck, Busse, & Scott, 2008), the majority of studies report IRR coefficients of .80 or greater. One study (de Vogel & de Ruiter, 2005) provided two reliability coefficients, one for males (ICC = .77) and one for females (ICC = .75).

* Cicchetti and Sparrow (1981), referring to κ and κ_w (which are equivalent to ICC) defined reliability indices below .40 as "poor," .40 to .59 as "fair," .60 to .74 as "good," and .75 or above as "excellent." These authors reported that these categories were consistent with those proposed by several other commentators. Landis and Koch (1977) offered the following scheme: below 0.00 (poor), .00 to .20 (slight), .21 to .40 (fair), .41 to .60 (moderate), .61 to .80 (substantial), and .81 to 1.00 (almost perfect).

† Some studies excluded the R subscale when coding the HCR-20 and hence reported the reliability of an "HC-15" composite. For instance, Grevatt, Thomas-Peter, and Hughes (2004) reported a Kendall's tau of .74 for this composite in a sample of 44 male forensic inpatients. Hill, Habermann, Klusmann, Berner, and Briken (2008) reported an intraclass coefficient (ICC) of .77 among a German sample of 166 male sexual homicide perpetrators.

For the H scale (24 studies), the median IRR value was .86, with a range from .58 (Dunbar et al., 2005) to .97 (Doyle & Dolan, 2006).* As with the HCR-20 total score, the majority of studies reported reliability coefficients of .80 or greater. IRR for the C scale is somewhat lower than for the Total or H scales, with a median across 20 studies of .74. The range extended from .55 (de Vogel & de Ruiter, 2005) to .95 (Howard, 2007), with the majority being .70 or greater. Across 19 studies, the median IRR coefficient for the R subscale was .68, with a range from .47 (Douglas, Ogloff, & Hart, 2003) to .98 (Howard, 2007). There was a split in the IRR coefficients, with a cluster between .51 and .69 and a second cluster between .81 and .98.

The lower reliabilities for the C and R subscales are most likely due to several factors. First, they likely require more judgment to score than the H scale items. Second, a significant proportion of studies do not rely upon mental health professionals as raters, who may be more adept at recognizing such factors such as insight or psychotic symptoms. Third, a number of studies have been "file only" studies, not including an interview. It is possible that without the benefit of an interview, ratings may suffer because there is (1) no chance for observation of current or recent functioning, and (2) no opportunity to tailor the assessment process to the type of information required to rate the HCR-20. Despite this, it is noted that the majority of studies report good or better IRR for these two subscales.

Although the summary risk rating (low, moderate, or high risk) is an important feature of the SPJ model, there are unfortunately few studies that have investigated its reliability. Because the summary risk rating essentially is a single item, its reliability can be expected to be lower than the reliability of a multi-item composite. The median IRR coefficient (ICC) is .65 across nine values (drawn from five studies), with a range of .41 (Douglas, Yeomans, & Boer, 2005) to .76 (de Vogel, de Ruiter, Hildebrand, Bos, & van de Ven, 2004). Because of the small number of investigations, each will be described in more depth. First, in a study of forensic psychiatric patients, de Vogel and de Ruiter (2005) coded the Dutch version of the HCR-20 (from file information only) on 42 female forensic psychiatric patients with personality disorders and a matched sample of 42 male forensic psychiatric patients. Good inter-rater reliability was observed for the summary risk rating (for 27 women, ICC = .74; for 28 men, ICC = .69). In a different study, de Vogel et al. (2004) reported ICC_1 values for five combinations of rater groups (researchers; treatment supervisors; group leaders) on a sample of 53 male and 7 female forensic psychiatric patients. ICC values ranged from .63 (between treatment supervisors and group leaders) to .76 (between two researchers). Intermediate values included .65, .65, and .68. de Vogel and de Ruiter (2006) later reported that there were no significant differences in the ratings of low, moderate, or high risk between researchers, treatment supervisors, and clinical "group leaders" (responsible for day-to-day provision of services) who independently rated the cases.

In another study, Douglas, Yeomans, and Boer (2005) coded the HCR-20 on 188 male offenders released from prison. The IRR of the HCR-20 structured final judgment ratings, based on 28 cases, was fair to moderate (ICC = .41). Even with the lower IRR, there were no "category errors," or cases rated high risk by one rater and low risk by the other. Most of the disagreements were between moderate- and high-risk ratings. Finally, Douglas, Ogloff, and Hart (2003) coded the HCR-20 on a random sample of 100 forensic psychiatric patients who were released into the community. The HCR-20 was coded independently by two masters-level clinicians based on the

* One study of reliability reported percentage agreement instead of traditional reliability coefficients. In a sample of male intellectually disabled offenders, independent raters coded the HCR-20 on 30 cases using clinical files (Lindsay et al., 2008). The reliability was calculated based on the number of agreed-upon ratings divided by the number of agreements plus disagreements, expressed as a percentage. For the H subscale, agreement was 89.4%, for the C subscale 93.1%, and for the R subscale the agreement was 82.7%.

clinical-legal files of participants at the time of discharge from the hospital. Percentage agreement on the 50 IRR cases for the summary risk ratings was 70% with no instances of category errors (ICC = .61).

Inter-Rater Reliability by Setting. As described above, the HCR-20 is used in a variety of settings,* and hence it is worthwhile to consider its reliability within those settings. Table 8.1 reports the median and range of reliability coefficients across different settings for the HCR-20 total and scale scores, along with the number of studies for each. Overall, across civil mental health, forensic mental health, corrections, and mixed samples, IRR for the HCR-20 total and H scale scores generally was excellent. There was more variability for the C and R scales, although IRR generally was strong for these subscales as well.

As shown in Table 8.1, the median IRR for the HCR-20 total score ranged from .79 (civil psychiatric) to .91 (corrections). For the H scale, it ranged from .83 (forensic psychiatric) to .94 (mixed samples). For the C scale, it ranged from .70 (civil psychiatric) to .83 (corrections). For the R scale, the median IRR ranged from .68 (mixed samples) to .90 (corrections). As mentioned above, there have been fewer studies of summary risk ratings. Reliabilities are generally lower than for the numeric scores; this is to be expected, given that it is a single item rating, rather than a multi-item scale.

Validity

In this section, we focus on the association between the HCR-20 and violence in terms of predictive validity. There have been other types of validity studied with the HCR-20, including its relationship with other risk assessment instruments, or its performance across different samples. However, the most important type of validity when it comes to risk assessment instruments is predictive validity. Hence, we will limit our discussion of validity research to this type of validity.

As with studies of the IRR of the HCR-20, the validity of this tool has been investigated extensively across a diversity of samples, settings, and countries. The HCR-20 was developed to assess risk for *general* violence, predominantly in populations where there is "a strong suggestion of mental illness or personality disorder" (Webster et al., 1997, p. 5). However, research on the HCR-20 has assessed its predictive validity with various violent outcomes including specific types of violence (e.g., sexual) and even nonviolent offenses (e.g., property crime, drug offenses). In a recent meta-analysis of 113 studies of the SPJ model, including 51 studies of the HCR-20 (Guy, 2008), the results indicated that effect sizes tended to be largest when SPJ instruments were used with the types of outcomes they were designed to be used with.

As with our review of the reliability of the HCR-20, we report the average validity effect sizes, rather than review dozens of studies individually. Study authors invariably use different types of effect sizes estimates, including correlation coefficients, odds ratios, and areas under the curve (AUCs) from receiver operating characteristic (ROC) analyses. Because the latter are most common in the risk assessment field, we converted other effect size estimates to AUCs for the purposes of this chapter. ROC analyses have been used commonly in the risk assessment field because they are less dependent on the base rate of the criterion variable in the sample (violence) than are other measures of association (e.g., correlation). AUC is an overall index of predictive

* Despite the fact that the HCR-20 was developed to assess general violence among adults, one study did investigate the use of the HCR-20 with adolescents. McEachern (2001) compared the HCR-20 and the SAVRY in a sample of 108 male juvenile offenders who were referred from court for inpatient psychiatric assessment (36 randomly selected nonrecidivists, 36 nonviolent recidivists, and 36 violent recidivists). This was a pseudo-prospective study conducted from comprehensive youth justice, police, mental health, medical, and social-demographic files. Inter-rater reliability, based on a subset of 36 files, was good (ICC_1 for Total, H, C, and R scores was .86, .88, .80, and .77, respectively).

Table 8.1 Median and Range of Inter-Rater Reliability Coefficients Across HCR-20 Studies

Setting	k*	HCR-20 Total *Mdn* [Range] (k)	H Scale *Mdn* [Range] (k)	C Scale *Mdn* [Range] (k)	R Scale *Mdn* [Range] (k)	SRR *Mdn* [Range] (k)
Forensic	21	.82 [.67–.95] (15)	.83 [.67–.94] (14)	.74 [.55–.94] (12)	.83 [.47–.94] (12)	.66 [.61–.76] (4)
Civil	3	.79 [.78–.80] (2)	.85 [.82–.87] (2)	.70 [.70] (1)	.81 [.81] (1)	—
Correctional	10	.91 [.67–.94] (7)	.90 [.58–.94] (5)	.83 [.58–.95] (6)	.90 [.58–.98] (5)	.41 [.41] (1)
Mixed	3	.90 [.90] (1)	.94 [.88–.97] (3)	.80 [.71–.89] (2)	.68 [.68] (1)	—

Studies include: Blum, 2004; Brown, 2004; Claix, Pham, & Willocq, 2002; Cooke, Michie, & Ryan, 2001; Côté, Hodgins, & Daigle, 2001; Dahle, 2006; Dernevik, 1998; Douglas, Ogloff, Nicholls, & Grant, 1999; Douglas, Ogloff, & Hart, 2003; Douglas, Yeomans, & Boer, 2005; Doyle & Dolan, 2006; Dunbar, 2003; Dunbar, Quinones, & Crevecoeur, 2005; Fujii, Tokioka, Lichton, & Hishinuma, 2005; Fujii, Lichton, & Tokioka, 2004; Gray, Snowden, MacCulloch, Phillips, Taylor, & MacCulloch, 2004; Gray, Fitzgerald, Taylor, MacCulloch, & Snowden, 2007; Grevatt, Thomas-Peter, & Hughes, 2004; Hildebrand, Hesper, Spreen, & Nijman, 2005; Hill, Habermann, Klusmann, Berner, & Briken, 2008; Howard, 2007; Kroner & Mills, 2001; MacPherson & Kevan, 2004; McDermott, Edens, Quanbeck, Busse & Scott, 2008; McNiel, Gregory, Lam, Binder, & Sullivan, 2003; Mills, Kroner, & Hemmati, 2007; Müller-Isberner, Sommer, Özokyay, & Freese, 1999; Pham, Claix, & Remy, 2000; Philipse, 2002; Polvi, 1999; Ross, Hart, & Webster, 1998; Strand, Belfrage, Fransson, & Levander, 1999; Warren, South, Burnette, Rogers, Friend, Bale, & Van Patten, 2005; Wintrup, 1996.

* Number of studies refers to the total number of studies within a given setting, rather than the number of studies that reported IRR data. Mixed samples include studies that combined data from more than one type of sample (correctional, civil mental health, forensic mental health). SRR = summary risk rating (low, moderate, high). For cells in which there is only one effect size summarized, that effect size also is reported as the median and range. *k* = number of studies.

accuracy, and can range from 0 (perfect negative prediction), to .50 (chance prediction), to 1.0 (perfect positive prediction). A given area represents the probability that a randomly chosen person who scores positive on the dependent measure (i.e., is actually violent) will fall above any given cutoff on the predictor measure, and that an actually nonviolent person will score below the cutoff (Mossman & Somoza, 1991). Another interpretation is that the AUC represents the probability that a violent person would score higher than a nonviolent person on the predictor. Although there are no formal categories, AUC values of approximately .65 to .70 may be considered moderate to large, and approximately .70 and above may be considered large (see, e.g., Douglas et al., 2005; Rice & Harris, 2005).

Overall, the results of predictive validity studies show that the association between the HCR-20 and violence is of moderate to large magnitude. The median AUC value for the HCR-20 total score across 42 studies is .69. This effect size is comparable to that for actuarial instruments designed to assess violence risk (.67) across 45 studies (Guy, 2008). Further, the effect size for the HCR-20 includes all studies, regardless of the type of outcome. As mentioned above, some studies have focused on the HCR-20's ability to predict specific types of violence (for example, sexual

Table 8.2 The Range of AUC Values for the HCR-20 Total, Subscales, and Summary Risk Rating

AUC	HCR-20 Total (k = 42)	H (k = 38)	C (k = 33)	R (k = 29)	SRR (k = 6)
.30–.39	1	1	1	0	0
.40–.49	2	3	5	3	0
.50–.59	14	14	18	12	0
.60–.69	36	34	29	27	3
.70–.79	29	25	20	18	5
.80–.89	15	6	1	2	2*
Total	97	83	74	62	10

Studies include: Allen & Howells, 2008; Cooke, Michie, & Ryan, 2001; de Vogel & de Ruiter, 2005; de Vogel & de Ruiter, 2006; de Vogel, de Ruiter, Hildebrand, Bos, & van de Ven, 2004; Dernevik, Grann, & Johansson, 2002; Dolan & Fullam, 2007; Dolan & Khawaja, 2004; Douglas, Ogloff, & Hart, 2003; Douglas, Ogloff, Nicholls, & Grant, 1999; Douglas, Yeomans, & Boer, 2005; Doyle & Dolan, 2006; Doyle, Dolan, & McGovern, 2002; Fujii, Tokioka, Lichton, & Hishinuma, 2005; Fujii, Lichton, & Tokioka, 2004; Grann, Belfrage, & Tengstrom, 2000; Grann, Sturidsson, Haggard-Grann, Hiscoke, Alm, & Dernevik, et al, 2005; Grann & Wedin, 2002; Gray, Hill, McGleish, Timmons, MacCulloch, & Snowden, 2003; Gray, Fitzgerald, Taylor, MacCulloch, & Snowden, 2007; Gray, Snowden, MacCulloch, Phillips, Taylor, & MacCulloch, 2004; Gray, Taylor, & Snowden, 2008; Grevatt, Thomas-Peter, & Hughes, 2004; Hartvig, Alfarnes, Skjonberg, Moger, & Ostberg, 2006; Kroner, & Mills, 2001; Lindsay, Hogue, Taylor, Steptoe, Mooney, O'Brien, et al., 2008; MacPherson, & Kevan, 2004; McDermott, Edens, Quanbeck, Busse, & Scott, 2008; McKenzie, & Curr, 2005; McNiel, Gregory, Lam, Binder, & Sullivan, 2003; Mills, Kroner, & Hemmati, 2007; Morrissey, Hogue, Mooney, Allen, Johnston, Hollin, Lindsay, & Taylor, 2007; Neves, & Gonçalves, 2008; Nicholls, 2001; Nicholls, Ogloff, & Douglas, 2004; Pham, Ducro, Marghem, & Réveillère, 2005; Philipse, 2002; Polvi, 1999; Ross, Hart, & Webster, 1998; Stadtland, & Nedopil, 2005; Stadtland, Hollweg, Kleindienst, Dietl, Reich, & Nedopil, 2005; Strand, Belfrage, Fransson, & Levander, 1999; Tengström, 2001; Tengstrom, Hodgins, Muller-Isberner, Jockel, Freese, & Ozokyay, et al., 2006; Urheim, Jakobsen, & Rasmussen, 2003; Warren, South, Burnette, Rogers, Friend, Bale, & Van Patten, 2005.

Note: k = number of studies. Values in the "Total" row are number of effect sizes, not number of studies.

* One AUC of .91.

assault) or nonviolent antisocial behavior. Guy (2008) reported that, when studies included outcomes that more closely conformed to the HCR-20 definition of violence, effect sizes tended to be higher. For example, studies that used the HCR-20 definition of violence, on average, produced a slightly higher weighted mean AUC of .73.

The median effect sizes for the H, C, and R scales are somewhat lower than for its total score, at .68, .62 and .65, respectively. Table 8.2 provides a breakdown of effect sizes as a function of scale and effect size range. The AUCs for the H scale ranged from .40 (Grevatt, Thomas-Peter, & Hughes, 2004) to .85 (Nicholls, Ogloff, & Douglas, 2004). For the C scale, the AUCs ranged from .46 (Nicholls et al., 2004) to .80 (de Vogel & de Ruiter, 2006). Finally, the range for R scale AUCs was from .48 (Nicholls, 2001) to .88 (de Vogel & de Ruiter, 2005). The AUCs for the HCR-20 have been broken down by setting as well (see Table 8.3 through Table 8.6).

Overall, the research indicates that the HCR-20 total and scale scores are associated with violence, with average effect sizes of moderate to moderate/large magnitude, comparable to actuarial risk assessment measures. This establishes that the risk factors, as defined, are associated with violence and, hence, ostensibly could serve as a basis for evaluators to make decisions about risk, a topic we turn to next.

Validity of Summary Risk Ratings. As described above, the summary risk ratings of low, moderate, or high risk are commonly used in the SPJ model to communicate concerns about

Table 8.3 The Range of AUC Values in Forensic Psychiatric Samples for the HCR-20 Total, Subscales, and Summary Risk Rating

AUCs	HCR-20 Total (k = 27)	H (k = 24)	C (k = 23)	R (k = 19)	SRR (k = 6)
.30–.39	1	1	0	0	0
.40–.49	0	1	4	1	0
.50–.59	9	8	9	10	0
.60–.69	20	18	15	19	2
.70–.79	16	8	12	4	3
.80–.89	8	4	1	1	2*
Total	54	40	41	35	7

Studies include: Allen & Howells, 2008; de Vogel & de Ruiter, 2005; de Vogel & de Ruiter, 2006; de Vogel, de Ruiter, Hildebrand, Bos, & van de Ven, 2004; Dernevik, Grann, & Johansson, 2002; Dolan & Fullam, 2007; Dolan & Khawaja, 2004; Douglas, Ogloff, & Hart, 2003; Fujii, Tokioka, Lichton, & Hishinuma, 2005; Fujii, Lichton, & Tokioka, 2004; Grann, Belfrage, & Tengstrom, 2000; Grann, Sturidsson, Haggard-Grann, Hiscoke, Alm, & Dernevik, et al, 2005; Gray, Hill, McGleish, Timmons, MacCulloch, & Snowden, 2003; Gray, Snowden, MacCulloch, Phillips, Taylor, & MacCulloch, 2004; Gray, Taylor, & Snowden, 2008; Gray, Fitzgerald, Taylor, MacCulloch, & Snowden, 2007; Grevatt, Thomas-Peter, & Hughes, 2004; Lindsay, Hogue, Taylor, Steptoe, Mooney, O'Brien, et al., 2008; MacPherson, & Kevan, 2004; McDermott, Edens, Quanbeck, Busse, & Scott, 2008; McKenzie, & Curr, 2005; Morrissey, Hogue, Mooney, Allen, Johnston, Hollin, Lindsay, & Taylor, 2007; Nicholls, 2001; Philipse, 2002; Polvi, 1999; Stadtland, & Nedopil, 2005; Strand, Belfrage, Fransson, & Levander, 1999; Tengström, 2001; Tengstrom, Hodgins, Muller-Isberner, Jockel, Freese, & Ozokyay, et al., 2006; Urheim, Jakobsen, & Rasmussen, 2003.

Note: k = number of studies. Values in the "Total" row are number of effect sizes, not number of studies.

* One AUC of .91.

Table 8.4 The Range of AUC Values in Civil Psychiatric Samples for the HCR-20 Total, Subscales, and Summary Risk Rating

AUCs	HCR-20 Total (k = 5)	H (k = 4)	C (k = 4)	R (k = 4)	SRR
.30–.39	0	0	0	0	0
.40–.49	0	0	1	0	0
.50–.59	1	4	5	1	0
.60–.69	9	11	13	1	0
.70–.79	11	9	1	12	0
.80–.89	4	2	0	0	0
Total	25	26	20	14	0

Studies include: Douglas, Ogloff, Nicholls, & Grant, 1999; Hartvig, Alfarnes, Skjonberg, Moger, & Ostberg, 2006; McNiel, Gregory, Lam, Binder, & Sullivan, 2003; Nicholls, Ogloff, & Douglas, 2004; Ross, Hart, & Webster, 1998.

Note: k = number of studies. Values in the "Total" row are number of effect sizes, not number of studies.

level of risk and degree of intervention required to mitigate that risk. This aspect of the HCR-20, and other SPJ tools, has been investigated less commonly than the numeric use of the instruments. Because this risk estimate is nonactuarial, it is perceived as controversial and criticized by some commentators (Quinsey et al., 2006; Rice et al., Chapter 6, this volume). Across all SPJ tools, however, there have been 16 studies of summary risk ratings, and evidence indicates that they are as or more strongly related to violence than is the numeric use of the instruments, or the use of actuarial instruments to which they have been compared, including the Static-99, the VRAG, and the SORAG (Guy, 2008; Heilbrun et al., 2009).

Table 8.5 The Range of AUC Values in Correctional Samples for the HCR-20 Total, Subscales, and Summary Risk Rating

AUCs	HCR-20 Total (*k* = 6)	H (*k* = 3)	C (*k* = 2)	R (*k* = 2)	SRR (*k* = 1)
.30–.39	0	0	0	0	0
.40–.49	0	0	0	0	0
.50–.59	2	0	0	0	0
.60–.69	5	4	0	0	0
.70–.79	3	2	2	1	1
.80–.89	3	0	0	1	0
Total	13	6	2	2	1

Studies include: Cooke, Michie, & Ryan, 2001; Douglas, Yeomans, & Boer, 2005; Kroner, & Mills, 2001; Mills, Kroner, & Hemmati, 2007; Neves, & Gonçalves, 2008; Warren, South, Burnette, Rogers, Friend, Bale, & Van Patten, 2005.

Note: *k* = number of studies. Values in the "Total" row are number of effect sizes, not number of studies.

Table 8.6 The Range of AUC Values in Mixed Samples for the HCR-20 Total, Subscales, and Summary Risk Rating

AUC	HCR-20 Total (*k* = 3)	H *k* = 5)	C (*k* = 2)	R (*k* = 2)	SRR
.30–.39	0	0	0	0	0
.40–.49	1	0	0	1	0
.50–.59	0	0	1	0	0
.60–.69	3	3	1	2	0
.70–.79	3	3	1	0	0
.80–.89	0	0	0	0	0
Total	7	6	3	3	0

Studies include: Doyle & Dolan, 2006; Doyle, Dolan, & McGovern, 2002; Grann & Wedin, 2002; Pham, Ducro, Marghem, & Réveillère, 2005; Stadtland, Hollweg, Kleindienst, Dietl, Reich, & Nedopil, 2005.

Note: *k* = number of studies. Values in the "Total" row are number of effect sizes, not number of studies.

Six studies have investigated the predictive accuracy of the HCR-20's summary risk ratings. In the first such study, Douglas et al. (2003) completed the HCR-20 for 100 randomly selected forensic psychiatric patients using clinical–legal files as they existed at the time of the patients' discharge to the community. Violent recidivism, detected through multiple file-based sources, was divided into three categories: any violence, physical violence, and non-physical violence. The HCR-20 summary risk ratings were statistically significant and of moderate to large size (any violence, AUC = .69; physical violence, AUC = .74; nonphysical violence, AUC = .68).

de Vogel and de Ruiter (2005; as described in detail above) coded the HCR-20 using file information of Dutch forensic psychiatric patients. For females, 15 cases were coded retrospectively (with inpatient violence as the criterion) and 27 cases prospectively (with postdischarge community violence as the criterion). For males, half were coded retrospectively, and half were coded prospectively (again, with inpatient and community violence as the respective criteria). The averaged predictive validity of the summary risk ratings across both community and inpatient violence were large for both men (AUC = .91) and women (AUC = .86).

In a second study of Dutch forensic psychiatric patients by de Vogel and de Ruiter (2006), the predictive validity of the HCR-20 was investigated prospectively in a sample of 127 males. Three groups of coders were compared: researchers, treatment supervisors, and group leaders.

In addition, a consensus score was obtained—after independent ratings were made, evaluators discussed each case for approximately one hour in order to reach agreement about the HCR-20 item scores, as well as the summary risk rating of low, moderate, or high risk. The outcome measure was again both inpatient and community violence recorded after a mean follow-up period of 21.5 months for inpatients and 15 months for those discharged into the community. The AUCs for violence for the HCR-20 summary risk ratings for the three groups of raters ranged from .64 to .77. However, the consensus rating was substantially higher, at .86. This finding of a larger AUC for consensus ratings provides some indication that, if possible, team-based risk assessments might provide more accurate risk estimates than individual risk ratings. The AUC for both verbal abuse (consensus AUC = .65) and verbal threat (consensus AUC = .71) were significant as well. In a third study by de Vogel and colleagues (2004), 120 forensic patients who were discharged from a forensic facility were followed in the community for an average of 73 months. The AUC for the SPJ judgment was .79.

Fujii, Lichton, and Tokioka (2004) studied the HCR-20 summary risk ratings in a sample of 169 forensic patients. The HCR-20 was administered during the first week of the patients' hospital admission. Episodes of inpatient violence (as defined in the HCR-20 manual) were recorded from hospital event records for a minimum of three months postadmission. The final risk judgment (in this study, high risk versus low/moderate risk) produced a significant AUC of .70.

Finally, HCR-20 summary risk ratings have been investigated in a correctional sample of 188 male offenders released from prison and followed for 6 to 11 years (Douglas et al., 2005). The HCR-20 was coded from extensive file information as it existed at the time of release. This study used a known-groups design, with 93 recidivistic participants being matched to 95 nonrecidivists. Reconviction and reimprisonment for a violent offense was the outcome variable, coded blind to HCR-20 ratings or group status. The AUC for the HCR-20 SPJ final judgment was large and significant (AUC = .79).

As with HCR-20 numeric scores, effect sizes for the summary risk rating tend to be higher when studies use the definition of violence contained in the HCR-20, rather than specialized forms of violence, or nonviolent antisocial behavior. Guy (2008) reported that the average AUC for the HCR-20 summary risk rating, regardless of type of outcome, was .70. However, when studies used the HCR-20 definition of violence, the average AUC was .76. For analyses involving physical violence only, it was .79.

It is possible to report the proportion of persons who are violent in any given sample as a function of estimated risk level. We have done so in Table 8.7. We caution that these percentages are not intended to represent numeric probability estimates that should be used in clinical practice. Rather, they are presented to indicate that, if evaluators choose to use the HCR-20 and its summary risk rating system, there is evidence that their judgments have some meaning.

Comparison of Summary Risk Ratings to Actuarial Ratings of Risk. The most basic test of the comparative validity of the summary risk ratings is a simple bivariate comparison between their predictive validity and the predictive validity of the HCR-20 numeric scores. If evaluators are using summary risk ratings as opposed to numeric scores to make their risk estimates, it is important that the summary risk ratings are at least as accurate as the numeric use of the HCR-20, if not more so. All six studies of the HCR-20 summary risk ratings permit this simple comparison. Comparing across nine sets of effect sizes from these six studies, seven favored the summary risk rating over the HCR-20 total score, in terms of the size of the AUC. For the two comparisons where the HCR-20 total score produced an AUC that was greater than that for the HCR-20 summary risk rating, it was greater by .03 and .04. For the seven comparisons that produced a larger AUC for the summary risk ratings compared to the HCR-20 total score, the differences tended to be small (.01., .01, .02, .03, .04), although two were more substantial (.09, .27).

Table 8.7 Percent Violent as a Function of HCR-20 Low, Moderate, and High Risk Ratings

Study	N	Setting	Risk Category Low % (n_v/n_t)	Moderate % (n_v/n_t)	High % (n_v/n_t)
de Vogel et al. (2004)	119	Forensic	0 (0/14)	15 (7/47)	62 (36/58)
de Vogel & de Ruiter (2005)					
Men	42	Forensic	0 (0/11)	8 (1/13)	78 (14/18)
Women	41	Forensic	0 (0/11)	14 (3/21)	77 (7/9)
de Vogel & de Ruiter (2006)	127	Forensic	0 (0/36)	8 (5/61)	64 (19/30)
Douglas et al. (2003)	100	Forensic	4 (1/23)	11 (7/64)	54 (7/13)
Douglas et al. (2005)	188	Corrections	19 (13/68)	59 (50/85)	86 (30/35)
Fujii et al. (2004)	169	Forensic		17 (22/127)	55 (18/33)

Note: n_v = number of participants who were violent within the estimated risk categories of low, moderate, or high risk; n_t = number of participants estimated to be low, moderate, or high risk; Fujii et al. (2004) collapsed the low and moderate risk categories for their analyses, which we report here. Values for de Vogel et al. (2004) calculated from raw data provided by Vivienne de Vogel.

On average, the AUC for the summary risk rating was greater than that for the HCR-20 total score by .064. The AUC for the summary risk rating was substantially larger than the HCR-20 H, C, and R scale scores in these studies, as these indices tend to be less strongly related to violence than the HCR-20 total score.

A more meaningful test of the comparative validity of the HCR-20 summary risk ratings and the HCR-20 numeric scores comes from multivariate rather than bivariate comparisons. Douglas et al. (2003) were the first study to report such an analysis, in the study described above of 100 forensic psychiatric patients. In Cox regression analyses, the H, C, and R scales were entered as the first block of predictors, with physical violence in the community as the outcome, and produced a significant model fit, $\chi^2 = 9.9$, $p < .05$. On the second block of predictors, the HCR-20 summary risk rating of low, moderate, and high risk was entered, producing a significant model improvement ($\Delta\chi^2 = 9.8$, $p < .01$) and final model ($\chi^2 = 20.07$, $p < .0001$). Importantly, *only* the summary risk ratings were significant in this final model, with an associated hazard ratio of 9.4, indicating that they increased the hazard of violence ninefold at each step of the predictor (i.e., from low to moderate risk, and from moderate to high risk).

de Vogel and de Ruiter (2006) reported the outcome of a similar analysis in their prospective study of 127 male Dutch forensic patients. They used Cox regression analyses with the HCR-20 subscales entered on the first block and the summary risk rating entered on the second block to determine if the final risk judgment added incremental validity to the subscale scores. Block one produced a significant model (χ^2 [3, $N = 127$] = 22.9, $p < .001$), and the HCR-20 summary risk ratings demonstrated incremental validity on block 2 as there was significant improvement to the model's fit upon their entry, $\Delta\chi^2$ (1, $N = 127$) = 6.8, $p < .01$. de Vogel et al. (2004) reported comparable findings from their other study of Dutch forensic patients.

Fujii et al. (2004) took a somewhat different approach, expanding the summary risk rating to five levels (low, low–moderate, moderate, moderate–high, and high). A stepwise regression demonstrated that the five-level summary risk rating added incremental validity over HCR-20 numeric scores (an increase in R^2 from .036 to .092), whereas the reverse was not true.

Finally, the HCR-20 summary risk ratings have been tested against *other* decision-making approaches, including unstructured clinical prediction, the PCL-R, PCL:SV, VRAG, and an actuarial instrument called the VORAS (Violent Offender Risk Assessment Scale) (Howells, Watt, Hall, & Baldwin, 1997). De Vogel et al. (2004), for instance, tested the summary risk rating against the HCR-20 numeric score, the PCL-R, as well as unstructured predictions of violence. Using Cox regression, they first entered the index of unstructured prediction, which produced a significant model fit. On the second block of predictors, they entered the PCL-R and HCR-20 total scores. This block also improved predictive accuracy, with the HCR-20 total scores accounting for the improvement to model fit. Finally, on block 3, they entered the HCR-20 summary risk ratings, which again produced a significant improvement to model fit, with both the summary risk ratings and the HCR-20 numeric score being significant individual predictors in the final model. The effect size (hazard ratio) for the summary risk ratings was 3.1, indicating that the hazard for violence tripled at each step of the predictor (from low to moderate risk, and from moderate to high risk).

Douglas et al. (2005) conducted a set of analyses using binary logistic regression that included the HCR-20 summary risk ratings, the VRAG's actuarial categorical system, and the VORAS. All variables were significant predictors of violent recidivism. However, the VORAS performed poorly, being inversely related to violence. As such, a second logistic regression model was tested that included only the HCR-20 summary risk ratings and the VRAG nine-level categorical system—the two indices intended to be used in practice. In the final model, both were significant predictors (odds ratio for the HCR-20 = 2.90, for the VRAG, 1.63). This result indicates that the nonactuarial HCR-20 summary risk rating and the actuarial VRAG risk estimate each offered unique predictive power.

Although only six studies have investigated the HCR-20 summary risk ratings, results support their utility, and are consistent with the 10 or so other studies of summary risk ratings of other SPJ instruments (Guy, 2008). In summary, all four studies that *directly* have tested the summary risk rating against the numeric use of the HCR-20 in multivariate analyses have shown that it adds incrementally to the numeric use of the instrument, often to the extent that the HCR-20 numeric score is no longer significant in the predictive model. Studies that have tested the summary risk ratings against other decision-making approaches (PCL-R; VORAS; VRAG; unstructured clinical prediction) have shown that it either is more strongly related to outcome than those other instruments, adds incrementally to them, or possesses unique predictive variance in the presence of them. This line of research is important, because the summary risk ratings are intended to be the basic method of communicating an evaluator's judgment about level of risk and anticipated degree of intervention. Further, the summary risk rating is nonactuarial and has been criticized by some on that basis (Quinsey et al., 2006; Rice et al., this volume). However, across six HCR-20 studies and ten other SPJ studies, results are consistent that summary risk ratings are as or more strongly related to violence than are numeric estimates of risk produced by SPJ instruments, or by other decision-making procedures, including actuarial ones.

Limitations and Necessary Future Research

Despite more than 50 empirical evaluations of the HCR-20, it has limitations, as do all risk assessment instruments. First we outline some of these limitations, and then discuss fruitful avenues for future research.

Limitations

Format of Risk Estimates. According to some commentators, the fact that the HCR-20 does not provide numeric estimates of future risk for violence (at least for clinical purposes) is a limitation of the HCR-20, and all SPJ instruments (Quinsey et al., 2006; see also Heilbrun et al., Chapter 1, this volume). We mention this criticism of the HCR-20 to acknowledge that it is considered a limitation by some. However, at the same time, we do not actually consider this a true limitation of the HCR-20, but rather a choice that we believe best reflects the state of the discipline. As discussed in detail above, although instruments that produce numeric estimates of risk for violence have the appearance of precision when it comes to estimating future risk for violence, research has to date failed to support the generalizability of such "precise" estimates upon cross-validation. Therefore, in our view a nonnumeric risk estimation system avoids this pitfall while, at the same time, provides guidance about relative risk, relevant risk factors, and the degree and nature of intervention, supervision, monitoring, and management required to mitigate risk.

Gender and Ethnicity. As with all existing risk assessment instruments, we do not yet know enough about the potential influence of gender and ethnicity on the utility of the HCR-20. Some have argued, for instance, that certain risk factors might be more important for women than men (Holtfreter & Cupp, 2007). Further, research indicates that some risk factors (i.e., psychopathy, as measured by the PCL-R), may manifest somewhat differently for people of different ethnic or racial backgrounds (Cooke, Kosson, & Michie, 2001).

Although we do consider further research on gender and ethnicity important and necessary, in our view the HCR-20 likely is robust across such demographic groups, for several reasons. First, because the HCR-20 items were neither selected from nor optimized statistically on a single sample, but rather chosen based on the broader literature, the potential for any of the risk factors to be dependent on *any* sample characteristic is lower than for instruments that did select and optimize risk factors and predictive algorithms based on single samples.

Second, research indicates that the HCR-20 performs comparably across genders and countries. The few studies of the HCR-20 with women do not provide any evidence that its predictive validity is lower than for men (de Vogel & de Ruiter, 2006; Nicholls et al., 2004; Strand & Belfrage, 2001). One study did indicate poor performance with a sample of women (Warren et al., 2005). However, this was a postdictive study in which the HCR-20 was used to "predict" past convictions of murder. Hence, it is of little relevance to the predictive validity of the HCR-20. Similarly, the HCR-20 has been evaluated in approximately 12 countries, with no discernible difference in predictive utility. In fact, in a meta-analysis of the larger SPJ literature (113 studies), Guy (2008) reported that neither gender nor country moderated the relationship between SPJ instruments and violence. Indeed, there was a nonsignificant ($p = .06$) trend for instruments to perform better for women than for men.

Because the HCR-20 (both its numeric scores and summary risk ratings made by researchers or clinicians) predicts violence at comparable levels across numerous countries, and because countries differ in terms of history, customs, sociopolitical leanings, ethnic mix, and laws, there is strong evidence for the robustness of the HCR-20 across ethnicities. However, there has been less research on its utility across ethnic groups *within* countries. Because the HCR-20 risk factors were neither selected nor optimized on any particular sample, however, there is reason to believe that it would be robust across different ethnic groups within countries. Fujii, Tokioka, Lichton, and Hishinuma (2005), in a sample of 169 forensic psychiatric patients, compared the frequency of HCR-20 risk factors and its predictive validity across 51 Asian American patients, 46 Euro-American patients, and 38 Native Hawaiian patients. Some risk factors were more prevalent than others across groups, and there were some differences in which risk factors were most predictive across groups. Although there were no significant differences in the predictive utility of the HCR-20 Total scores across groups, its performance was best among Native Hawaiians (AUC = .73) and worst among Asian Americans (AUC = .58). Because there was not a significant moderating effect for ethnicity, Fujii et al. concluded that their data indicated that the "HCR-20 has cross-cultural validity in Asian-American, Native-Hawaiian, and Euro-American samples" (p. 714).

We have two comments about the line of research pursued by Fujii et al. (2005). First, generally, it is an important line of research that can address whether the HCR-20, or any risk assessment instrument, performs comparably across different ethnic groups. Second, we would caution researchers to be somewhat wary about item-level tests that are based on single samples, because they are likely to be highly sample-specific. In fact, this is precisely the problem faced by actuarial instruments that select or weight single items based on single samples. There is no guarantee that any differences observed across ethnic (or any) groups at the item level are robust, and not due to sample peculiarities. For this reason, any differences in item-level frequency, reliability, or predictive validity should be (1) tested in large subgroups and (2) observed across multiple independent samples before firm conclusions can be drawn with confidence about reliable differences.

Nonetheless, we encourage evaluators to attend to any research on how certain risk factors may manifest differently across ethnic groups, particularly if there is research indicating differential predictive validity of such risk factors. In our view, the larger research on violence indicates that most risk factors (i.e., previous violence; substance use problems) are important regardless of ethnicity.

Similarly, we encourage evaluators to attend to how risk factors might manifest differently for men and women. Although we doubt that most risk factors will be relevant for one gender but not for the other, it is possible that certain risk factors might be more prevalent in one group versus another (i.e., childhood sexual abuse). It is also possible that there are "gendered" pathways to violence (Holtfreter & Cupp, 2007), and that the methods and expression of violence might vary across genders.

Because of the way that the HCR-20 is intended to be used, however, we consider such possible different manifestations of violence and violence risk factors across genders or ethnicities to be within the scope of the intended use of the HCR-20. That is, risk factors are unit-weighted, and evaluators are expected to describe both the individual manifestation of risk factors and their relevance for understanding violence, for the case at hand (that is, what does the risk factor *look like,* for this person, and how is it relevant to his or her risk for violence?).

Future Research

We encourage more research on all of the topics discussed under "Limitations," above. In addition, there are several other areas of research that could prove to be fruitful, both for further understanding of the HCR-20, and also for understanding about risk assessment in general.

Understanding the Effectiveness of Nonnumeric Categorical Risk Ratings. As reviewed above, research on the HCR-20 (and other SPJ instruments) indicates that its system of nonnumeric, categorical summary risk ratings performs as well as or better than the numeric (actuarial) use of the instrument, the PCL-R, and actuarial instruments such as the VRAG (and, in tests of other SPJ instruments, the Static-99). This finding has been robust across more than a dozen tests, across countries, and whether the research was conducted by individuals associated with the HCR-20 (or other SPJ instruments) or not. This finding is also potentially controversial, in that the categorical summary risk ratings, while based on a structured system, are not actuarial, but discretionary. The question arises, *why* do these discretionary judgments perform as well as or better than numeric/actuarial estimates? There is not a single study on point. We offer four possibilities that would make for interesting research studies.

First, it could be that the SPJ method of categorical risk ratings strikes an optimal balance between structure and discretion. Although structure is necessary to promote good decision making, it is possible that current actuarial risk assessment measures are overstructured. That is, they are fine-tuned as a function of development samples and may not fit as well when applied in different samples. Further, as part of their structure, most presume that all risk factors operate equally for all persons, rather than permitting a determination of which risk factors may be more or less important in individual cases. The SPJ model facilitates this latter aspect of decision making, and it could be that this relatively limited degree of discretion, couched within an otherwise structured decision-making process, improves accuracy.

Second, and related to applying discretion at the individual level, SPJ measures such as the HCR-20 may represent an effective method of bridging the nomothetic and idiographic levels of analysis. That is, SPJ measures include a standard, fixed list of risk factors that must be considered in every case. These factors have support in the broad empirical literature. However, there is not a presumption that each of these nomothetically supported risk factors apply equally at the idiographic or case level. Indeed, as with many phenomena in nature, the individual relevance of risk factors likely is normally distributed. Most statistical approaches that are used to develop or validate actuarial measures, however, are premised on group-based estimates (i.e., beta coefficients) that essentially average across all persons in a sample to determine the predictive strength of a variable for a *sample*, not for any given *person* within that sample. The SPJ approach embodied by the HCR-20, however, treats the scoring of nomothetically supported risk factors as a starting point in an individually based clinical assessment process. Additional aspects of this assessment process include explicating the individual manifestation and relevance of such risk factors for the given case at hand. In essence, this task is akin to determining where, in the distribution of a risk factor's potential relevance to violence, a person falls. This step is not represented in any actuarial measures that we are aware of, and may serve to optimize the relevance of nomothetic data at the idiographic level.

Third, the SPJ process may facilitate a task that even Meehl (1954)—the strongest, most persuasive, and most vocal advocate of the superiority of actuarial prediction over clinical prediction—conceded was likely better accomplished by people rather than algorithms: derivation of theory, and the recognition of configural relations or patterns. Many actuarial risk assessment instruments presume relatively simple relationships between risk factors and violence (a main-effect relationship where an increase in a risk factor elevates the odds of violence). Even actuarial instruments based on more complex statistical processes (that is, interactions between variables) ultimately presume a relatively simple relationship between risk factors and violence, and they do so, again, with the assumption that all risk factors in a predictive equation should be weighted equally for all persons.

The SPJ process encourages decision makers to build "individual theories" of violence for each person they evaluate. It may facilitate the identification of "configural relations" between a set of risk factors and violence, one in which risk factors might not only interact with one another, but may transact with one another, and with violence. It encourages decision makers to search for patterns amongst risk factors that may be of particular relevance for whether a person will be violent. Importantly, while guided by the nomothetic literature that essentially informs us that "the more risk factors present, the greater the risk," it does not presume that risk-relevant patterns or relations between risk factors will be uniform across individuals. In this way, it may be better suited to help clinicians *understand* the violence of individuals, rather than merely to predict it. It is geared toward identifying the most relevant, potentially causal, risk factors, and patterns among risk factors, *at the individual level.* This aspect of the SPJ model could be another reason that explains why the relatively basic judgments of low, moderate, and high risk are as or more accurate in forecasting future violence compared to other approaches.

Finally, it is possible that the risk judgments of low, moderate, or high risk simply permit the consideration of additional information above and beyond what is captured by the standard list of risk factors on SPJ instruments, or the actuarial instruments to which they sometimes have been compared. Indeed, SPJ measures encourage evaluators to consider whether any other risk-relevant information exists for any given case. Despite attempts to provide relatively comprehensive domain coverage of risk factors, it is always possible that there may be risk factors present for a given case that are not well represented amongst the standard risk factors contained in the instrument.

It has long been determined that a "fair test" between clinical and actuarial prediction can only be had if the two methods of prediction are based on the same information (Grove et al., 2000). We agree, but demur. The HCR-20 was never developed to inform the classic "actuarial versus clinical prediction" debate. Rather, it was developed to promote sound (reliable and valid) decisions about violence risk that also are relevant to risk reduction at the case level. At the same time, our goal was to ensure that it was no *less* valid than actuarial procedures, which it does not appear to be. As such, if it is effective because it permits the consideration of additional relevant information, so be it.

Reducing Violence. Ultimately, the point of assessing the risk for violence is to prevent future violence (Douglas & Kropp, 2002; Douglas & Skeem, 2005; Hart, 1998). The HCR-20 was developed in the manner it was in order to inform risk management and, hence, to reduce a person's risk for violence. However, this aspect of the HCR-20 has not yet received the research attention that it needs. That is, by using the HCR-20 to identify a person's key risk factors and to design optimal risk management plans, will the person be less likely to be violent in the future than if the HCR-20 were not used? To answer this question requires moving from risk assessment to intervention research, which we would encourage with enthusiasm.

There is indirect evidence to support the hypothesis that the appropriate use of the HCR-20 would reduce violence. Research based on a short version of the SARA (Spousal Assault Risk Assessment, an SPJ measure for spousal violence; see Chapter 11, this volume) used with police officers showed that, when officers rated cases as high risk, and also applied a commensurate degree of intervention (that is, a high level of appropriate interventions), future spousal violence was reduced in comparison to high-risk cases in which a commensurate degree of intervention was not enacted.

Version 3 of the HCR-20. The HCR-20 currently is under revision, and will be named HCR:V3 (Douglas, Hart, Webster, Belfrage, & Eaves, 2008). We are in the process of conducting beta testing, user feedback, and studies of its reliability and validity. The fundamental SPJ approach will be retained in HCR:V3, although there may be changes to items. New scoring options are being tested, as well. Evaluation of HCR:V3 will be an important research endeavor.

Case Example

Mr. Case is a 53-year-old Caucasian male who was first admitted to the Secure Forensic Hospital (SFH) on June 14, 1982, for a competency evaluation after he was charged with second degree murder. He was found competent to stand trial, but was readmitted to SFH on October 9, 1982, when he was found Not Guilty by Reason of Insanity (NGRI) for the same charge. Mr. Case has a Review Board hearing scheduled for next month to determine whether he should (1) be discharged without conditions; (2) discharged with conditions; or (3) not discharged.

A comprehensive violence risk assessment was conducted to inform the decision of the Review Board. The key questions addressed were: (1) What is the level of risk posed by Mr. Case, if he is released into the community? (2) What risk management strategies would mitigate this risk? The risk assessment included a lengthy interview with Mr. Case and a review of his institutional files. Given Mr. Case's lengthy forensic hospitalization, it was not considered necessary to conduct additional psychological testing. The Psychopathy Checklist–Revised (PCL-R) had recently been completed for Mr. Case by a psychologist with training on the instrument and was used to score HCR-20 Item H7 (Psychopathy) for the present assessment.

FAMILY HISTORY

Mr. Case was raised in Ohio by his natural parents and has one older brother. He had a good relationship with his parents and brother when younger, but fought frequently both verbally and physically with his brother starting at age 16. Mr. Case claims that the fights with his brother usually started as minor "sibling disagreements," but would quickly escalate into physical fights. He stated that both he and his brother are equally responsible for the fights. There is no evidence of substance abuse, domestic violence, or criminal activity by his parents. There is no evidence of any major problems during his childhood (up to the age of 16). However, Mr. Case reports that he often got in trouble for smoking (cigarettes) and staying out late before age 12. Starting at the age of 16, Mr. Case became heavily involved in drug use (see details below).

EDUCATIONAL HISTORY

Mr. Case did not enjoy school and did not do well academically, although before the seventh grade he attended regularly and had a good relationship with peers and teachers. Problems with peers started in the seventh grade. He was slow to mature and was picked on by much bigger students. He was involved in a few minor fights, usually as a result of him being bullied. He never caused a serious injury while in a fight, but was the victim of the occasional black eye. He failed seventh grade, and dropped out in ninth grade "to make money."

EMPLOYMENT HISTORY

After dropping out of school, he worked as a bike messenger for two months before quitting. He quit because he found the work too tiring (biking all day). Mr. Case estimates that he has had between 20 and 25 jobs and that he often became bored and quit after a couple of months. His longest job was for nine months as a dishwasher. He was fired twice for smoking marijuana at work. Mr. Case admits that he was not always a good worker—he would often show up late or miss shifts, and he started one fight with a coworker who he claims insulted him. The coworker received a laceration on his cheek.

Mr. Case had frequent periods of unemployment and typically relied on social assistance. His longest period of unemployment was approximately three years. During this time, Mr. Case hitchhiked his way to Mexico. He did not tell anyone he was leaving, but sent his mother a postcard when he was there. Because of his employment and financial problems, he spent months at a time living on the streets. During his times on the street, Mr. Case relied on his mother for financial support; he would call her and she would send him money. Prior to his admission to SFH, he moved between living with his mother and cheap hotels.

RELATIONSHIP HISTORY

Mr. Case has had five or six short romantic relationships. His longest relationship was for 2 to 3 months, 25 years ago, and he has never lived with a partner. He claims that relationships are not important to him, and he has not expressed any desire to have a relationship in the future.

Substance Abuse History

Mr. Case started using marijuana, hashish, and LSD when he was 16 years old. Over the next couple of years, Mr. Case used marijuana daily and hash and LSD every weekend and occasionally during the week. At age

19, he stopped using LSD, but started drinking alcohol more often. From the age of 19 to 25, Mr. Case drank alcohol five to six times per week, used marijuana daily, and used hashish three or four times a week. Often, Mr. Case used his social assistance money to pay for drugs. He reports that the drugs were psychologically addictive, and that he liked them because they allowed him "to dream." He claims that that he never did anything dangerous or reckless while using drugs, and there is no evidence to dispute this claim. He has not used LSD for over 25 years, but in the few years prior to his index offense he was drinking five or six days a week and was using marijuana several times per day.

MENTAL HEALTH HISTORY

Mr. Case first had first contact with a mental health professional at age 17 because of drug problems. He only met with his counselor on a few occasions before he stopped attending because he did not think that he had a drug problem.

At the age of 19, he was hospitalized for one month due to a "nervous breakdown." There are few details regarding what occurred to cause the nervous breakdown. He claims that his parents were causing him stress and, combined with his frequent drug and alcohol use, he suffered an emotional breakdown. He was hospitalized again at the age of 25 for two months when his parents were concerned about his frequent yelling at himself. Mr. Case states that he was hearing voices, and he was yelling at these voices to go away. During this hospitalization, staff reported that he was a cooperative patient and easy to manage. Mr. Case's next contact with a mental health professional occurred after his index offense (described below).

Mr. Case has received consistent diagnoses of paranoid schizophrenia and cannabis dependence disorder as a result of several psychodiagnostic assessments conducted over the course of his hospitalization.

CRIMINAL HISTORY

Mr. Case does not have any juvenile convictions or charges. However, he claims that he had some problems with the law before the age of 17, and that he also was charged with assault with a weapon and possession of a restricted weapon prior to his index offense. Mr. Case is unwilling to provide further information, and there are no available records of these alleged offenses because they occurred in Canada.

The index offense occurred May 15, 1982 (at the age of 27), when Mr. Case was living with a man he had met while living on the street. Mr. Case attacked and murdered his roommate while he slept by stabbing him multiple times with a screwdriver and hunting knife. The attack was so severe that the victim was nearly unrecognizable. After the attack, Mr. Case posed the body by laying the victim on his back and crossing his arms on his chest. Following the murder, he stole a number of the victim's possessions, some money, and his car and drove to St. Louis. He was arrested in St. Louis soon after, where the police found him in the victim's car with a bloodstained hunting knife and the victim's possessions (some of which were also bloodstained). When he was arrested, Mr. Case claimed that he did not commit the murder and that the victim gave him his possessions and car and said he would meet him in St. Louis. Mr. Case told the police that the victim was a witch, and that other witches may have done it. When the police confronted him about the bloodstained items, he told them that he did not know how they got there.

Mr. Case was charged with second degree murder, and on June 14, 1982, he was admitted to SFH for a competency evaluation. He was found competent to stand trial and released to court. On October 9, 1982, he was found NGRI for the murder and recommitted to SFH.

ADJUSTMENT AFTER HOSPITALIZATION

In Mr. Casc's 26 years at SFH he has been granted conditional discharges to semi-independent living eight times, but has never been able to last more than one year before returning to the hospital. His returns to the hospital were usually a result of his drug use or negative attitudes. He has had many positive drug tests for marijuana that have resulted in his involuntary return to full supervision. On other occasions, he simply did not seem happy while residing at these residences and asked to be returned to the hospital ward. On one occasion, six years ago, he used a knife to severely attack a coresident, whom he accused of being a witch who was trying to poison him. At the time, he had become noncompliant with medication and was using marijuana heavily. The victim needed 63 stitches about his head, face, and arms, and surgery to stop internal bleeding.

While residing at the hospital, Mr. Case has disobeyed rules on multiple occasions, such as leaving the hospital grounds without permission. On these occasions, he often returned to the downtown area overnight, where he would buy alcohol or marijuana, and voluntarily return to hospital the next day. On other occasions, he would simply return late from his day leaves. Mr. Case often seemed indifferent to having broken rules and reacts defensively when confronted by staff.

Mr. Case's last return to the hospital occurred in April 2005 for breaching his conditions (using alcohol and marijuana). He last went before the Review Board six months ago. The Review Board decided to continue his custody stay because they felt that he had not yet dealt with his substance abuse problems, that he failed to show consistent compliance with treatment and supervision, and that he was at high risk to reoffend as a result of this.

RECENT FUNCTIONING (PAST SIX MONTHS)

Since Mr. Case's last Review Board hearing, he has had a few problems. According to progress reports, he acknowledges that he has a mental illness that he needs treatment for. Mr. Case has stated that using drugs is bad for him, though he denies that his drug use might affect his mental illness, and he continues to use drugs. His privileges were suspended two months ago due to a positive drug screen. He has had four other positive drug screens since his last Review Board hearing.

Mr. Case appears to be compliant with his medications, and reports indicate that he is responding well. Recent staff reports have indicated that there have been occasional instances where he has delusional/disorganized thinking, odd movements, and has been smiling and laughing to himself, but that these behaviors have become less frequent in the past four months. In an interview two months ago, Mr. Case reported that when he takes drugs he "sees the wonders of the universe and can understand the mysteries of the world." He also reported that he "has met God and can enter the spirit world." His treatment team feels that his mental functioning is significantly affected by his substance use, and his continued use of marijuana has been his biggest problem.

Mr. Case claims that his treatment has been helpful, although he has not participated in the drug and alcohol program as recommended. Instead, he relies on a weekly meeting with his pastor for assistance. He states that this is the only person he trusts at the hospital. He often complains about the staff, states that he does not trust them, and feels that they are not "too together."

There has been the occasional minor conflict with other residents at the hospital, usually involving a verbal disagreement. The situation has not escalated, and according to staff reports, Mr. Case has handled these situations well. If he does feel angry, he often will take a short walk around the hospital grounds to calm himself down and/or speak with his pastor for advice. These two strategies have been effective for him according to treatment staff and his self-report.

For the past six months, Mr. Case has been working in the hospital recycling plant three days a week. His supervisor reports that he is a good worker: he is always on time, completes the tasks assigned to him, has only missed work due to legitimate reasons, and gets along well with his coworkers. On the days he does not work he often attends a drop-in center near the downtown area. At the moment, he is not permitted to attend this center because the hospital staff believe it is after these trips to the drop-in center, while he is still downtown, that he buys and uses drugs. His remaining leisure time is spent practicing yoga and reading books, mainly on the topic of Christianity.

RELEASE PLANS

Mr. Case currently has no plans as to where he would live if released. He also does not know where, or if, he will work. If he is required to find a new job, he is not sure of what type he would like and plans to rely solely on his disability benefits if he cannot find any employment that he wants. When asked about his treatment plan after release, he replies that his treatment will be up to his doctors. If it were up to him, he would not continue with treatment. When asked how he will keep himself safe, he states that he will "keep his house clean and mind his own business." If his symptoms start to worsen, he reports that he will seek help, but he did not explain from where he will get this help. He stated that, if the doctors recommend that he continue with his medications, he will, and he doesn't think he will have any problems with compliance. Mr. Case's treatment team has encouraged him to make more substantial plans for his release, but he has not yet complied.

Mr. Case is not concerned about facing any destabilizers. When asked specifically about the risk of using drugs and alcohol, he reports that he will quit drugs on his own, but cannot elaborate on any plan for this and says he will "play it by ear." His treatment team is concerned about his attitude toward his drug and alcohol use and has strongly suggested a community treatment program. Mr. Case has replied that, if the program is a required condition of his release, he will attend a program, but if it is only a "suggestion" he does not know if he will attend.

In terms of possible sources of personal support, both of his parents have passed away, and he has not been in touch with his brother since his mother's death ten years ago. He has made some friends while in the hospital, but he does not expect to keep in touch with them when released and no longer has friends in the community due to the length of time he has been hospitalized. His one source of support is his pastor. The treatment team is familiar with Mr. Case's pastor and believes that he will be a good source of support for Mr. Case.

Mr. Case does not expect to face any stressors when released. Although he does not have any plans for where he will live or how he will make money, he says that things will work themselves out. He feels that he handles stress well and that he will be able to handle any situation that he is faced with. Mr. Case does not feel that he is at risk to commit a new crime when he is released.

RISK ASSESSMENT

In order to inform my judgment of risk, I used the HCR-20 (Historical-Clinical-Risk Management 20) violence risk assessment instrument. The HCR-20 has been subjected to more than 50 empirical studies that, on average, indicate that it facilitates consistency in clinical evaluations of risk for violence, and that its risk factors and judgments of risk based upon them help evaluators to determine whether an individual poses a low, moderate, or high level of future risk for violence. This HCR-20 includes 20 risk factors to consider, along with standard instructions for how to rate them; I determined whether each of these risk factors was present for Mr. Case, and if so, how relevant it appeared to be for Mr. Case's risk of violence.

The HCR-20 includes 10 Historical risk factors—past events, experiences, or conditions that are known to increase the risk for violence. I determined that eight of these risk factors are definitely present for Mr. Case: previous violence (H1), young age at first violent incident (H2), relationship instability (H3), employment problems (H4), substance use problems (H5), major mental illness (H6), early maladjustment (H8), and prior supervision failure (H10). Two other risk factors from this scale were possibly or partially present: psychopathy (H7) and personality disorder (H9).

In terms of recent functioning, the HCR-20 includes five risk factors on its Clinical Scale that are intended to summarize a person's recent emotional, behavioral, and cognitive functioning. I determined whether these risk factors were present within the past six months—since Mr. Case's last Review Board hearing. I determined that three of the five risk factors definitely were present within the past six months: lack of insight (C1), active symptoms of major mental illness (C3), and unresponsive to treatment (C5). In addition, the other two risk factors were possibly or partially present: negative attitudes (C2) and impulsivity (C4).

The HCR-20 Risk Management Scale includes five risk factors that pertain to an individual's possible future living circumstances. I rated these risk factors as if Mr. Case were to be released into the community, rather than for continued hospitalization. That is, I determined, given Mr. Case's current release planning, whether the risk factors would be present if Mr. Case were released into the community by the Review Board next month. I used a six-month time frame for these ratings.

I determined that four of the five Risk Management risk factors were present for Mr. Case: plans lack feasibility (R1), exposure to destabilizers (R2), lack of personal support (R3), and noncompliance with remediation attempts (R4). One of the risk factors was possibly present—stress (R5).

Therefore, there are 15 of the HCR-20's 20 risk factors that definitely present for Mr. Case, and another 5 that are possibly or partially present. Some of these 15 present risk factors are especially relevant to understanding Mr. Case's risk for future violence, as follows.

There are several clusters of risk factors are of particular relevance and concern and also seem likely to influence and worsen one another. First, Mr. Case has paranoid schizophrenia (H6), and there is evidence of active psychotic symptoms within the past six months (C3). The murder that Mr. Case committed (H1) occurred when Mr. Case was experiencing psychosis, as did the more recent attack on a coresident; both appear to have been motivated by his psychotic symptoms. Second, Mr. Case has frequently been noncompliant with past supervision and risk management efforts (H10), has recently been noncompliant with supervision orders pertaining to drug use (C5), and has expressed considerable ambivalence about whether he will comply with treatment in the future (R4). Third, Mr. Case has a serious substance dependence disorder (H5) that he fails to acknowledge (C1) or seek treatment for (C5) and which appears to exacerbate his psychotic symptoms. Fourth, if Mr. Case were released from the hospital, especially without conditions, he likely would be exposed to situations and contexts (such as drug availability), which would destabilize his mental health (R2). In addition, he has not developed any coherent discharge plans (R1) that would provide him with stable housing, effective risk management and treatment, or reliable income.

There are two further areas of concern. First, Mr. Case has very little social support from friends, family, or a romantic partner (R3, H3). Such support can mitigate risk, but is limited for Mr. Case, other than his relationship with his pastor. Another potential risk-reducing opportunity—stable employment—also is missing (H4). Although he has worked effectively of late while in the institution, he has a clear record of employment problems when he has had the opportunity to work in the community, and he has no plans to work after release. The second main area of concern is Mr. Case's antisocial or psychopathic traits (H7, H9) and distrust of most professionals who work with him. This may make securing his agreement to start, comply with, and complete programming more challenging.

Given both the presence of a large number of risk factors and their relevance to Mr. Case's risk for violence, in my judgment Mr. Case is a high risk for violence. Furthermore, although history is not destined to repeat itself, consideration of H1 (previous violence) indicates the type of violence that might be of concern if Mr. Case were to act violently. That is, in my judgment Mr. Case is at high risk for violence that could cause serious injuries to others.

A judgment of high risk means that (1) there is a high likelihood that, if released soon with the current discharge plans, Mr. Case will act violently within the next six months; (2) Mr. Case should be considered high priority for the delivery of supervision and management resources; and (3) Mr. Case requires a high level or intensity of supervision and management in order to mitigate risk. While it is not possible to produce a meaningful numeric estimate of risk, there are numerous risk factors that have not been controlled, and for which there are no future risk management plans in place. I would recommend further efforts to engage Mr. Case in drug and alcohol treatment, and to increase his compliance with supervision and treatment efforts, perhaps through establishing a set of contingencies for compliance and noncompliance. It is also important to monitor his psychotic symptoms closely. It may also be worthwhile to foster Mr. Case's recent employment success and to assist him in finding employment and stable housing. If Mr. Case were to be released, I would recommend frequent (biweekly) monitoring and reevaluation of his risk factors.

CASE COMMENT

This case example provides an illustration of one potential application of the HCR-20, and one example of how to format an HCR-20 risk assessment report. Further, if this were an actual case report, evaluators might want to spend more time describing the details of risk management plans, which space limitations precluded us from doing. The important point that we were illustrating was that judgments of risk should be grounded in the case-specific evidence (e.g., the individual manifestation and relevance of HCR-20 risk factors, which themselves have nomothetic support), and that recommendations for risk management should be logically linked to the risk factors of most concern.

References

Allen, C., & Howells, K. (2008). *The implementation and evaluation of a structured professional judgment risk assessment tool within a high secure forensic hospital.* Paper presented at the annual conference of the International Association of Forensic Mental Health Services, Vienna, Austria.

Andrews, D. A., Bonta, J., & Wormith, J. (2004). *The Level of Service/Case Management Inventory user's manual.* North Tonawanda, NY: Multi-Health Systems.

Belfrage, H. (1998). Implementing the HCR-20 scheme for risk assessment in a forensic psychiatric hospital: Integrating research and clinical practice. *Journal of Forensic Psychiatry, 9,* 328–338.

Belfrage, H., & Douglas, K. S. (2002). Treatment effects on forensic psychiatric patients measured with the HCR-20 violence risk assessment scheme. *International Journal of Forensic Mental Health, 1,* 25–36.

Blair, P. R., Marcus, D. K., & Boccaccini, M. T. (2008). Is there an allegiance effect for assessment instruments? Actuarial risk assessment as an exemplar. *Clinical Psychology: Research and Practice, 15,* 346–360.

Blum, F. M. (2004). *Psychopathy, psychosis, drug abuse, and reoffense among conditionally released offenders.* Unpublished doctoral dissertation, University of Southern California, Los Angeles, CA.

Brown, L. K. (2004). *Assessing risk for elopement and breaches of conditional release in insanity acquittees.* Unpublished doctoral dissertation, Simon Fraser University, Burnaby, BC, Canada.

Cicchetti, D. V., & Sparrow, S. A. (1981). Developing criteria for establishing interrater reliability of specific items: Applications to assessment of adaptive behavior. *American Journal of Mental Deficiency, 86,* 127–137.

Claix, A., Pham, T., & Willocq, L. (2002, March). *Evaluation of the HCR-20 (historical-clinical-risk management) in a Belgian forensic population.* Poster presented at the annual conference of the international association of forensic mental health services, Munich, Germany.

Cooke, D. J., Kosson, D. S., & Michie, C. (2001). Psychopathy and ethnicity: Structural, item, and test generalizability of the Psychopathy Checklist—Revised (PCL-R) in Caucasian and African American participants. *Psychological Assessment, 13,* 531–542.

Cooke, D. J., & Michie, C., & Ryan, J. (2001). Evaluating Risk for Violence: A Preliminary Study of the HCR-20, PCL-R and VRAG in a Scottish Prison Sample. Scottish Prison Service occasional papers; no 5/200.

Côté, G., Hodgins, S., & Daigle, M. (2001). *Violent behaviour, PCL-R and HCR-20 among involuntary inpatients, forensic patients and severely mentally disordered inmates.* Paper presented at the First Annual Meeting of the International Association of Forensic Mental Health Services, Vancouver, British Columbia.

Dahle, K. (2006). Strengths and limitations of actuarial prediction of criminal reoffence in a German prison sample: A comparative study of LSI-R, HCR-20 and PCL-R. *International Journal of Law and Psychiatry, 29,* 431–442.

Dawes, R. M. (1979). The robust beauty of improper linear models in decision making. *American Psychologist, 34,* 571–582.

de Vogel, V., & de Ruiter, C. (2005). The HCR-20 in personality disordered female offenders: A comparison with a matched sample of males. *Clinical Psychology & Psychotherapy, 12,* 226–240.

de Vogel, V., & de Ruiter, C. (2006). Structured professional judgment of violence risk in forensic clinical practice: A prospective study into the predictive validity of the Dutch HCR-20. *Psychology, Crime & Law, 12,* 321–336.

de Vogel, V., de Ruiter, C., Hildebrand, M., Bos, B., & van de Ven, P. (2004). Type of discharge and risk of recidivism measured by the HCR-20: A retrospective study in a Dutch sample of treated forensic psychiatric patients. *International Journal of Forensic Mental Health, 3,* 149–165.

Dernevik, M. (1998). Preliminary findings on reliability and validity of the Historical-Clinical-Risk Assessment in a forensic psychiatric setting. *Psychology, Crime, and Law, 4,* 127–137.

Dernevik, M., Grann, M., & Johansson, S. (2002). Violent behaviour in forensic psychiatric patients: Risk assessment and different risk-management levels using the HCR-20. *Psychology, Crime & Law, 8,* 93–111.

Dolan, M., & Fullam, R. (2007). The validity of the Violence Risk Scale 2nd edition (VRS-2) in a British Forensic Inpatient Sample. *The Journal of Forensic Psychology and Psychiatry, 18,* 381–193.

Dolan, M., & Khawaja, A. (2004). The HCR-20 and post-discharge outcome in male patients discharged from medium security in the UK. *Aggressive Behavior, 30,* 469–483.

Doren, D. M. (2002). *Evaluating sex offenders: A manual for civil commitments and beyond.* Thousand Oaks, CA: Sage.

Douglas, K. S. (2008). The HCR-20 violence risk assessment scheme. In B. Cutler (Ed.), *Encyclopedia of psychology and law.* Thousand Oaks, CA: Sage.

Douglas, K. S., & Belfrage, H. (2001). Use of the HCR-20 in violence risk management: Implementation and clinical practice. In K. S. Douglas, C. D. Webster, S. D. Hart, D. Eaves, & J. R. P. Ogloff, (Eds.), *HCR-20: Violence risk management companion guide* (pp. 41–58). Burnaby, BC, Canada: Mental Health, Law, and Policy Institute, Simon Fraser University.

Douglas, K. S., Guy, L. S., Reeves, K. A., & Weir, J. (2008). *HCR-20 violence risk assessment scheme: Overview and annotated bibliography.* Retrieved April 5, 2009, from http://kdouglas.files.wordpress.com/2006/04/annotate10-24nov2008.pdf

Douglas, K. S., Hart, S. D., Webster, C. D., Belfrage, H., & Eaves, D. (2008). *HCR-20: Assessing Risk for Violence* (Version 3, Draft 1.0 Nov. 14, 2008). Burnaby, BC, Canada: Mental Health, Law, and Policy Institute, Simon Fraser University.

Douglas, K. S., & Kropp, P. R. (2002). A prevention-based paradigm for violence risk assessment: Clinical and research applications. *Criminal Justice and Behavior, 29,* 617–658.

Douglas, K. S., Nicholls, T. L., & Brink, J. (2009). Reducing the risk of violence among persons with mental illness: A critical analysis of treatment approaches. In P. M. Kleespies (Ed.), *Evaluating and managing behavioral emergencies: An evidence-based resource for the mental health practitioner* (pp. 351–376). Washington, DC: American Psychological Association.

Douglas, K. S., Ogloff, J. R. P., & Hart, S. D. (2003). Evaluation of a model of violence risk assessment among forensic psychiatric patients. *Psychiatric Services, 54,* 1372–1379.

Douglas, K. S., Ogloff, J. R. P., Nicholls, T. L., & Grant, I. (1999). Assessing risk for violence among psychiatric patients: The HCR-20 violence risk assessment scheme and the Psychopathy Checklist: Screening Version. *Journal of Consulting and Clinical Psychology, 67,* 917–930.

Douglas, K., S., & Skeem, J. L. (2005). Violence risk assessment: Getting specific about being dynamic. *Psychology, Public Policy, and Law, 11,* 347–383.

Douglas, K. S., Webster, C. D., Hart, S. D., Eaves, D., & Ogloff, J. R. P. (Eds.) (2001). HCR-20: *Violence risk management companion guide.* Burnaby, BC, Canada: Mental Health, Law, and Policy Institute, Simon Fraser University.

Douglas, K. S., Yeomans, M., & Boer, D. P. (2005). Comparative validity analysis of multiple measures of violence risk in a sample of criminal offenders. *Criminal Justice and Behavior, 32,* 479–510.

Dowden, C., & Andrews, D. A. (2000). Effective correctional treatment and violent reoffending: A meta-analysis. *Canadian Journal of Criminology, 42,* 449–467.

Doyle, M., & Dolan, M. (2006). Predicting community violence from patients discharged from community mental health services. *British Journal of Psychiatry, 189,* 520–526.

Doyle, M., Dolan, M., & McGovern, J. (2002). The validity of North American risk assessment tools in predicting in-patient violent behaviour in England. *Legal and Criminological Psychology, 7,* 141–152.

Dunbar, E. (2003). Symbolic, relational, and ideological signifiers of bias-motivated offenders: Toward a strategy of assessment. *American Journal of Orthopsychiatry, 73,* 203.

Dunbar, E., Quinones, J., & Crevecoeur, D. A. (2005). Assessment of hate crime offenders: The role of bias intent in examining violence risk. *Journal of Forensic Psychology Practice, 5,* 1–19.

Dvoskin, J. A., & Heilbrun, K. (2001). Risk assessment and release decision-making: Toward resolving the great debate. *Journal of the American Academy of Psychiatry and the Law, 29,* 6–10.

Fujii, D., Lichton, A., & Tokioka, A. (2004, August). *Structured professional judgment versus actuarial data in violence risk prediction using the Historical Clinical Risk Management-20.* Paper presented at the annual convention of the American Psychological Association, Honolulu, HI.

Fujii, D. E. M., Tokioka, A. B., Lichton, A. I., & Hishinuma, E. (2005). Ethnic differences in prediction of violence risk with the HCR-20 among psychiatric inpatients. *Psychiatric Services, 56,* 711–716.

Grann, M., Belfrage, H., & Tengstrom, A. (2000). Actuarial assessment of risk for violence: Predictive validity of the VRAG and the historical part of the HCR-20. *Criminal Justice and Behavior, 27,* 97–114.

Grann, M., & Långström, N. (2007). Actuarial assessment of violence risk: To weigh or not to weigh? *Criminal Justice and Behavior, 34,* 22–36.

Grann, M., Sturidsson, K., Haggard-Grann, U., Hiscoke, U. L., Alm, P., & Dernevik, M., et al. (2005). Methodological development: Structured outcome assessment and community risk monitoring (SORM). *International Journal of Law and Psychiatry, 28,* 442–456.

Grann, M., & Wedin, I. (2002). Risk factors for recidivism among spousal assault and spousal homicide offenders. *Psychology, Crime and Law, 8,* 5–23.

Gray, N. S., Fitzgerald, S., Taylor, J., MacCulloch, M. J., & Snowden, R. J. (2007). Predicting future reconviction in offenders with intellectual disabilities: The predictive efficacy of VRAG, PCL-SV and the HCR-20. *Psychological Assessment, 19,* 474–479.

Gray, N. S., Hill, C., McGleish, A., Timmons, D., MacCulloch, M. J., & Snowden, R. J. (2003). Prediction of violence and self-harm in mentally disordered offenders: A prospective study of the efficacy of HCR-20, PCL-R, and psychiatric symptomatology. *Journal of Consulting and Clinical Psychology, 71,* 443–451.

Gray, N. S., Snowden, R. J., MacCulloch, S., Phillips, H., Taylor, J., & MacCulloch, M. J. (2004). Relative efficacy of criminological, clinical, and personality measures of future risk of offending in mentally disordered offenders: A comparative study of HCR-20, PCL:SV, and OGRS. *Journal of Consulting and Clinical Psychology, 72,* 523–530.

Gray, N. S., Taylor, J., & Snowden, R. J. (2008) Predicting violent reconvictions using the HCR-20. *British Journal of Psychiatry: The Journal of Mental Science, 192,* 384–387.

Grevatt, M., Thomas-Peter, B., & Hughes, G. (2004). Violence, mental disorder and risk assessment: Can structured clinical assessments predict the short-term risk of inpatient violence? *Journal of Forensic Psychiatry & Psychology, 15,* 278–292.

Grove, W. M., & Meehl, P. E. (1996). Comparative efficiency of informal (subjective, impressionistic) and formal (mechanical, algorithmic) prediction procedures: The clinical-statistical controversy. *Psychology, Public Policy, and Law, 2,* 293–323.

Grove, W. M., Zald, D. H., Lebow, B. S., Snitz, B. E., & Nelson, C. (2000). Clinical versus mechanical prediction: A meta-analysis. *Psychological Assessment, 12,* 19–30.

Guy, L. S. (2008). *Performance indicators of the structured professional judgment approach for assessing risk for violence to others: A meta-analytic survey.* Unpublished dissertation, Simon Fraser University, Burnaby, BC, Canada.

Harris, G. T., Rice, M. E., & Quinsey, V. L. (1993). Violent recidivism of mentally disordered offenders: The development of a statistical prediction instrument. *Criminal Justice and Behavior, 20,* 315–335.

Hart, S. D. (1998). The role of psychopathy in assessing risk for violence: Conceptual and methodological issues. *Legal and Criminological Psychology, 3,* 121–137.

Hartvig, P., Alfarnes, S. A., Skjonberg, M., Moger, T. A., & Ostberg, B. (2006). Brief checklists for assessing violence risk among patients discharged from acute psychiatric facilities: A preliminary study. *Nordic Journal of Psychiatry, 60,* 243–248.

Heilbrun, K., Douglas, K. S, & Yasuhara, K. (2009). Controversies in violence risk assessment. In J. L. Skeem, K. S. Douglas, & S. O. Lilienfeld (Eds), *Psychological science in the courtroom: Controversies and consensus* (pp. 333–357). New York: Guilford Press.

Hildebrand, M., Hesper, B. L., Spreen, M. & Nijman, H. L.I. (2005). *De waarde van gestructureerde risicotaxatie en van de diagnose psychopathie: een onderzoek naar de betrouwbaarheid en predictieve validiteit van de HCR-20, HKT-30 en 195 PCL-R.* [The importance of structured risk assessment and of the diagnosis of psychopathy: A study into the reliability and predictive validity of the HCR-20, HKT-30 and PCL-R]. Utrecht, the Netherlands: Expertisecentrum Forensische Psychiatrie.

Hill, A., Habermann, N., Klusmann, D., Berner, W., & Briken, P. (2008). Criminal recidivism in sexual homicide perpetrators. *International Journal of Offender Therapy and Comparative Criminology, 52,* 5–20.

Holtfreter, K., & Cupp, R. (2007). Gender and risk assessment: The empirical status of the LSI-R for women. *Journal of Contemporary Criminal Justice, 23,* 363–382.

Howard, B. (2007). *Examining predictive validity of the Salient Factor Score and HCR-20 among behavior health court clientele: Comparing static and dynamic variables.* Unpublished doctoral dissertation, Pacific Graduate School of Psychology, Palo Alto, CA.

Howells, K., Watt, B., Hall, G., & Baldwin, S. (1997). Developing programmes for violent offenders. *Legal and Criminological Psychology, 2,* 117–128.

Kroner, D. G., & Mills, J. F. (2001). The accuracy of five risk appraisal instruments in predicting institutional misconduct and new convictions. *Criminal Justice and Behavior, 28,* 471–489.

Landis, J., & Koch, G. G. (1977). The measurement of observer agreement for categorical data. *Biometrics, 33,* 159–174.

Laws, D. R., & O'Donohue, W. T (Eds.). (2008). *Sexual deviance: Theory, assessment, and treatment* (2nd ed.). New York: Guilford Press.

Lindsay, W., Hogue, T., Taylor, J., Steptoe, L., Mooney, P., O'Brien, G., et al. (2008). Risk assessment in offenders with intellectual disability: A comparison across 201 three levels of security. *International Journal of Offender Therapy and Comparative Criminology, 52,* 90–111.

MacPherson, G. J. D., & Kevan, I. (2004). Predictive validity of the HCR-20 violence risk assessment scheme within a maximum security special hospital. *Issues in Forensic Psychology, 5,* 62–80.

McDermott, B. E., Edens, J. F., Quanbeck, C. D., Busse, D., & Scott, C. L. (2008). Examining the role of static and dynamic risk factors in the prediction of inpatient violence: Variable- and person-focused analyses. *Law and Human Behavior, 34,* 325–338.

McEachran, A. K. (2001). *The predictive validity of the PCL:YV and the SAVRY in a population of adolescent offenders.* Unpublished master's thesis, Simon Fraser University, Burnaby, BC, Canada.

McKenzie, B., & Curr, H. (2005). Predicting violence in a medium secure setting: A study using the historical and clinical scales of the HCR-20. *British Journal of Forensic Practice, 7,* 22–28.

McNiel, D. E., Gregory, A. L., Lam, J. N., Binder, R. L., & Sullivan, G. R. (2003). Utility of decision support tools for assessing acute risk of violence. *Journal of Consulting & Clinical Psychology, 71,* 945–953.

Meehl, P. E. (1954). *Clinical versus statistical prediction.* Minneapolis, MN: University of Minnesota Press.

Mills, J. F., Jones, M. N., & Kroner, D. G. (2005). An examination of the generalizability of the LSI-R and VRAG probability bins. *Criminal Justice and Behavior, 32,* 565–585.

Mills, J., Kroner, D., & Hemmati, T. (2007). The validity of violence risk estimates: An issue of item performance. *Psychological Services, 4,* 1–12.

Monahan, J., Steadman, H. J., Appelbaum, P. S., Grisso, T., Mulvey, E. P., Roth, L. H., Robbins, P. C., Banks, S., & Silver, S. (2005). *Classification of Violence Risk (COVR).* Lutz, FL: Psychological Assessment Resources.

Morrissey, C., Hogue, T., Mooney, P., Allen, C., Johnston, S., Hollin, C., Lindsay, W. R,. & Taylor, J. L. (2007). Predictive validity of the PCL-R in offenders with intellectual disability in a high secure hospital setting: Institutional aggression. *Journal of Forensic Psychiatry & Psychology, 18,* 1–15.

Mossman, D., & Somoza, E. (1991). ROC curves, test accuracy, and the description of diagnostic tests. *Journal of Neuropsychiatry and Clinical Neurosciences, 3,* 330–333.

Müller-Isberner, J. R., Sommer, J., Özokyay, K., & Freese, R. (1999, November). *Clinical use of the HCR-20 for predicting violence in a German forensic psychiatric hospital.* Paper presented at the International Conference on Risk Assessment and Management: Implications for Prevention of Violence, Vancouver, BC, Canada.

Mulvey, E. P., & Lidz, C. W. (1995). Conditional prediction: A model for research on dangerousness to others in a new era. *International Journal of Law and Psychiatry, 18,* 129–143.

Neves, A. C., & Gonçalves, R. A. (July, 2008). *Criminal recidivism and violation of conditional release: A comparative study of the LSI-R and the HCR-20 with Portuguese Probationers/parolees.* Poster presented at the annual conference of the International Association of Forensic Mental Health Services, Vienna, Austria.

Nicholls, T. L. (2001). *Violence risk assessments with female NCRMD acquittees: Validity of the HCR-20 and PCL-SV.* Unpublished doctoral dissertation, Simon Fraser University, Burnaby, BC, Canada.

Nicholls, T. L., Ogloff, J. R. P., & Douglas, K. S. (2004). Assessing risk for violence among female and male civil psychiatric patients: The HCR-20, PCL: SV, and McNiel & Binder's VSC. *Behavioral Sciences and the Law, 22,* 127–158.

Pham, T. H., Claix, A., & Remy, S. (2000, June). *Assessment of the HCR-20 in a Belgian prison sample.* Paper presented at the 4th European Congress on Personality Disorders. Paris, France.

Pham, T. H., Ducro, C., Marghem, B., & Réveillère, C. (2005). Évaluation du risque de récidive au sein d'une population de délinquants incarcérés ou internés en Belgique francophone [Prediction of recidivism among prison inmates and forensic patients in Belgium]. *Annales Médico-Psychologiques, 163,* 842–845.

Philipse, M. (2002, March). *Post-dictive validity of the HCR-20 in a Dutch forensic psychiatric sample.* Paper presented at the Annual Conference of the International Association of Forensic Mental Health Services, Munich, Germany.

Polvi, N. H. (1999). *The prediction of violence in pre-trial forensic patients: The relative efficacy of statistical versus clinical predictions of dangerousness.* Unpublished doctoral dissertation, Simon Fraser University, Burnaby, BC, Canada.

Quinsey, V. L., Harris, G. T., Rice, G. T., & Cormier, C. A. (1998). *Violent offenders: Appraising and managing risk.* Washington, DC: American Psychological Association.

Quinsey, V. L., Harris, G. T., Rice, G. T., & Cormier, C. A. (2006). *Violent offenders: Appraising and managing risk* (2nd ed.). Washington, DC: American Psychological Association.

R. v. McCraw, (1991). 3 S.C.R. 72.

Rice, M. E., & Harris, G. T. (2005). Comparing effect sizes in follow-up studies: ROC, Cohen's d and r. *Law and Human Behavior, 29,* 615–620.

Ross, D. J., Hart, S. D., & Webster, C. D. (1998). *Facts and fates: Prediction and management of hospital and community aggression using the HCR-20.* Port Coquitlam, British Columbia: Riverview Hospital.

Skeem, J., & Mulvey, E. (2002). Monitoring the violence potential of mentally disordered offenders being treated in the community. In A. Buchanan (Ed.), *Care of the mentally disordered offender in the community* (pp. 111–142). New York: Oxford Press.

Stadtland, C., Hollweg, M., Kleindienst, N., Dietl, J., Reich, U., & Nedopil, N. (2005). Risk assessment and prediction of violent and sexual recidivism in sex offenders: Long-term predictive validity of four risk assessment instruments. *Journal of Forensic Psychiatry & Psychology, 16,* 92–108.

Stadtland, C., & Nedopil, N. (2005). [Psychiatric disorders and the prognosis for criminal recidivism]. *Der Nervenarzt, 76,* 1402–1411.

Strand, S., & Belfrage, H. (2001). Comparison of HCR-20 scores in violent mentally disordered men and women: Gender differences and similarities. *Psychology, Crime and Law, 7,* 71–79.

Strand, S., Belfrage, H., Fransson, G., & Levander, S. (1999). Clinical and risk management factors in risk prediction of mentally disordered offenders—MORE important than historical data? A retrospective study of 40 mentally disordered offenders assessed with the HCR-20 violence risk assessment scheme. *Legal and Criminological Psychology, 4,* 67–76.

Tengström, A. (2001). Long-term predictive validity of historical factors in two risk assessment instruments in a group of violent offenders with schizophrenia. *Nordic Journal of Psychiatry, 55,* 243–249.

Tengström, A., Hodgins, S., Müller-Isberner, R., Jockel, D., Freese, R., & Ozokyay, K., et al. (2006). Predicting violent and antisocial behavior in hospital using the HCR-20: The effect of diagnoses on predictive accuracy. *International Journal of Forensic Mental Health, 5,* 39–53.

Urheim, R., Jakobsen, D., & Rasmussen, K. (2003, August). *Dimensions of inpatient aggressive behavior in a security ward: What is being "predicted"?* Paper presented at the 5th Nordic Symposium on Forensic Psychiatry, Ystad, Sweden.

Warren, J. I., South, S. C., Burnette, M. L., Rogers, A., Friend, R., Bale, R., Van Patten, I. (2005). Understanding the risk factors for violence and criminality in women: The concurrent validity of the PCL-R and HCR-20. *International Journal of Law and Psychiatry, 28,* 269–289.

Webster, C. D., Douglas, K., Eaves, D. & Hart, S. (1997). *HCR-20: Assessing risk for violence,* Version 2. Burnaby, BC, Canada: Simon Fraser University.

Webster, C. D., Eaves, D., Douglas, K. S., & Wintrup, A. (1995). *The HCR-20 scheme: The assessment of dangerousness and risk.* Burnaby, BC, Canada: Simon Fraser University and British Columbia Forensic Psychiatric Services Commission.

Wintrup, A. (1996). *Assessing risk of violence in mentally disordered offenders with the HCR-20. Unpublished master's thesis,* Simon Fraser University, Burnaby, BC, Canada.

9
The Classification of Violence Risk

JOHN MONAHAN

The Classification of Violence Risk (COVR) was developed with the goal of offering clinicians a structured tool to assist in their estimation of the risk of violence to others posed by an individual with a mental disorder. COVR is an interactive software program designed to estimate violence risk over the first several months after discharge from a mental health facility.

Description of the Measure

Using a laptop or desktop computer, COVR guides the evaluator through a brief chart review and a 5- to 10-minute interview with the patient. After the requested information has been entered, COVR generates a report that contains an empirically derived estimate of the patient's violence risk, including the confidence interval for that estimate and a list of the risk factors that COVR took into account to produce the estimate. Detailed descriptions of the research constructing and validating the software and the statistical model on which it rests can be found in Monahan et al. (2001), and Monahan, Steadman, Robbins et al. (2005).

COVR in Context

It may be useful to begin by situating COVR within the larger context of structured violence risk assessment (see Douglas, Ogloff, & Hart, 2003; Otto, 2000). This activity might usefully be seen as having three components (Monahan, 2006). In the first component—*selecting and measuring risk factors*—the mental health professional performing the assessment decides which risk factors to measure and how these risk factors should be measured. In unstructured (or clinical) risk assessment, risk factors are selected and measured based on the mental health professional's theoretical orientation and prior clinical experience, and may vary from case to case, as theory or experience dictate. In contrast, in all forms of structured risk assessment, decisions about which risk factors to measure and how to measure them are made in advance, before the actual risk assessment process begins. Explicit rules specify a risk factor's operational definition and quantification. In structured risk assessment, the mental health professional performing the assessment has no discretion regarding the selection or measurement of risk factors: these decisions are "structured" for him or her in advance by the appearance of specified variables, with instructions on how these variables are to be scored, on a formal risk assessment instrument.

The second component of violence risk assessment—*combining risk factors*—involves taking the person's individually measured risk factors (i.e., his or her "scores" on each of the risk factors) and assembling these risk factors into a single composite estimate of violence risk. In unstructured risk assessment, risk factors are assembled in an intuitive or holistic manner to generate a clinical opinion about violence risk. In some forms of structured risk assessment, risk factors are assembled into a composite estimate of risk by means of a mathematical process specified in advance. That process is sometimes as simple as adding the unweighted or weighted scores of the individual risk factors together to yield a total score, but it can involve more complex tree-based statistical procedures as well (see the section "Method of and Rationale for Development" later in this chapter).

In the final component of violence risk assessment—*generating a final risk estimate*—the mental health professional responsible for the risk estimate reviews the likelihood of violence produced by the first two components of the risk assessment process. In unstructured risk assessment, because the risk factors are already combined in an intuitive or holistic manner to generate a clinical opinion about violence risk, there is nothing to "review." The mental health professional's clinical opinion is his or her final estimate of violence risk. In some forms of structured risk assessment, however, the final risk estimate offered by the clinician may differ from the risk estimate produced by the first two (structured) components of the assessment process, based on additional (unstructured) information the clinician has gathered from interviews, significant others, and/or available records—information not included on the structured risk assessment instrument.

All forms of structured risk assessment specify in advance *at least* which risk factors are to be assessed and how those risk factors are to be measured (that is, the first component of the violence risk assessment process). Some tools (for example, the Historical-Clinical-Risk Management 20, HCR-20, see Chapter 8) structure *only* the choice and measurement of risk factors.* COVR goes on to *also* structure the manner in which the risk factors are combined to yield an estimate of risk (that is, the second component of the violence risk assessment process). But COVR allows the clinician to review this estimate, in the context of other (unstructured) available information, before issuing his or her final risk estimate. Still other tools (for example, the Violence Risk Appraisal Guide, VRAG, see Chapter 6) *completely structure* the violence risk assessment process. No clinical review is allowed: the structured risk estimate that is produced when the risk factors are combined is the final product of the risk assessment process. It is this final form of structured violence risk assessment that is properly termed "actuarial" (Meehl, 1954).

It is important to note that, in contrasting COVR with other structured violence risk assessment instruments (that is, VRAG and HCR-20) in the previous paragraph, I mean to contrast the instruments *used as their authors recommend they be used.* It is, of course, possible for a clinician to take any one of the three contrasted instruments and use it in a manner not envisioned by its authors. For example, one could administer COVR and accept as final the risk estimate that it generates, without subjecting that estimate to the recommended clinical review. Or one could administer VRAG and clinically review the resulting risk estimate, contrary to the admonition of its authors. Finally, despite the authors' explicit recommendations to the contrary, HCR-20 could be used clinically in the same manner that it is often used in research. That is, it is possible "to treat the HCR-20 as an actuarial scale and simply sum the numeric item codes to yield . . . total scores, ranging from 0 to 40" (Webster, Douglas, Eaves, & Hart, 1997, p. 21). There is nothing stopping a clinician from using one of these instruments in an "off-label" manner. But the clinician who did so would be ethically obligated to inform the recipient of any resulting risk communication that the estimate of violence risk it contained was generated by nonstandard procedures.

The MacArthur Violence Risk Assessment Study

The COVR software was constructed from data generated in the MacArthur Violence Risk Assessment Study (Steadman et al., 2000). In this research, 1,136 patients in acute psychiatric facilities in three states were assessed in the hospital on 106 potential risk factors for violent behavior. The inclusion criteria were: (1) civil admissions; (2) between the ages of 18 and 40 years; (3) English speaking; (4) of Caucasian, African American, or Hispanic ethnicity; and (5) a

* While the HCR-20 does not formally (i.e., mathematically) structure the way that risk factors are combined, it does provide less formal guidance to clinicians on how to aggregate risk factor scores into a summary risk estimate (see Webster et al., 1997, pp. 20–23).

Table 9.1 40 Risk Factors Included in COVR

Legal status	Motor impulsiveness
Major mental diagnosis and substance abuse	Parents fight with each other
Prior arrests—frequency	Valid attempt to kill self
Child abuse—seriousness	Sexual abuse before age 20
Diagnosis of schizophrenia, schizophreniform, schizoaffective	Marital status
	Threat/control override
Neurological screening—loss of consciousness	Prior hospitalization
Age	Thoughts of harming self
Anger reaction	Present at admission-suicide threat
Prior arrests—seriousness	Father's arrests
Employed full/part time	SIV—not frequent, not escalating, not while with target
Schedule of imagined violence (SIV)	
Father's drug use	Age at first hospitalization
Lived with father until age 15	Present at admission—depression
Alcohol abuse diagnosis	Years of education
Drug abuse diagnosis	Hallucinations
Gender	Functioning score
Child abuse—frequency	Primary diagnosis
Diagnosis of antisocial personality disorder	Present at admission—decompensation
Perceived coercion	Present at admission—substance abuse
Prior violence	Present at admission—personal problems

medical record diagnosis of schizophrenia, schizophreniform disorder, schizoaffective disorder, depression, dysthymia, mania, brief reactive psychosis, delusional disorder, alcohol or other drug abuse or dependence, or a personality disorder (Monahan et al., 2000).

Patients were followed for 20 weeks in the community after discharge from the hospital. Triangulated measures of violence to others included official police and hospital records, patient self-report, and the report of a collateral informant (most often, a family member) who knew the patient best in the community. The criterion measure of violence to others consisted of four acts: (1) any battery with physical injury, (2) the use of a weapon, (3) threats made with a weapon in hand, and (4) sexual assault.* (For a discussion of legal and ethical aspects of conducting this research, see Monahan, Appelbaum, Mulvey, Robbins, & Lidz, 1993.)

The COVR Software

COVR is capable of assessing those forty risk factors for violence (see Table 9.1) that emerged as most predictive of violence in the MacArthur Violence Risk Assessment Study. However, in any given administration COVR assesses only the number of risk factors necessary to classify a patient's violence risk, which may be considerably less than 40. Since COVR relies on a tree-based rather than a main-effects analytic strategy (see the section "Method of and Rationale for Development" later in this chapter), the same risk factors are not assessed for every patient. Among the risk factors assessed most frequently by the COVR, however, are the seriousness and frequency of prior arrests, young age, male gender, being unemployed, the seriousness and frequency of having been abused as a child, a diagnosis of antisocial personality disorder, the *lack of* a diagnosis of schizophrenia, whether the individual's father used drugs or left the home

* The complete data set for the MacArthur Violence Risk Assessment Study is available for reanalysis at: http://macarthur.virginia.edu

before the individual was 15 years old, substance abuse, impaired anger control, and violent fantasies (for the implications of these risk factors for reducing violence risk, and not merely assessing it, see Monahan & Appelbaum, 2000).

The COVR is designed to be administered by professionals in any of the mental health disciplines. To date, it has been validated for clinical use only on acute psychiatric patients being considered for discharge into the community (see below). If COVR is used with other populations, "caution rather than confidence is appropriate, at least until additional [validation] research has been conducted" (Monahan et al., 2001, p. 132).

Method of and Rationale for Development

The empirical development of COVR took place in seven stages over an 18-year period.

Stage One: Identifying Gaps in Methodology

When the MacArthur Violence Risk Assessment Study began in the mid-1980s, almost all existing studies of violence risk assessment suffered from one or more methodological problems. The studies (1) considered a constricted range of risk factors, often a few demographic variables or scores on a psychological test; (2) employed weak criterion measures of violence, usually relying solely on arrest; (3) studied a narrow segment of the patient population, typically males with a history of violence; and (4) were conducted at a single site (Monahan & Steadman, 1994a). Based upon this critical examination of existing work, the authors designed the MacArthur Violence Risk Assessment Study with the aim of overcoming the identified methodological obstacles (Monahan & Steadman, 1994b). To overcome the methodological problems found in existing studies, the MacArthur researchers (1) studied a large and diverse array of risk factors; (2) triangulated their outcome measurement of violence, adding patient self-report and the report of a collateral informant to data from official police and hospital records; (3) studied both men and women, regardless of whether they had a history of violence; and (4) conducted the study at three sites rather than at a single site.

Stage Two: Selecting Promising Risk Factors

Studies have suggested that a number of variables might be robust risk factors for violence among people with a mental disorder. The MacArthur research chose to assess risk factors in four domains: personal factors (e.g., demographic and personality variables), historical factors (e.g., past violence, mental disorder), contextual factors (e.g., social support, social networks), and clinical factors (e.g., diagnosis, specific symptoms). Next, the researchers chose what they believed to be the best of the existing measures of these variables, and they commissioned the development of a necessary measure where no adequate measure to assess a variable was available (e.g., the Novaco Anger Scale; Novaco, 1994).

Stage Three: Using Tree-Based Methods

The MacArthur researchers developed violence risk assessment models based on a "classification tree" method rather than on the usual linear regression method (Gardner, Lidz, Mulvey, & Shaw, 1996). A classification tree approach prioritizes an interactive and contingent model of violence—one that allows many different combinations of risk factors to classify an individual at a given level of risk (Breiman, Friedman, Olshen, & Stone, 1984). The particular questions to be asked in any assessment grounded in this approach depend on the answers given to prior questions. Factors that are relevant to the risk assessment of one individual may not be relevant to the risk assessment of another individual. This approach contrasts with a main-effects regression approach, in which a common set of questions is asked of everyone being assessed and every answer is weighted and summed to produce a score that can be used for predictive purposes.

Stage Four: Creating Different Cutoffs for High and Low Risk

Rather than relying on the standard single threshold for distinguishing among participants, the MacArthur researchers decided to employ two thresholds—one for identifying high-risk individuals and one for identifying low-risk individuals. The degree of risk presented by the intermediate "average-risk" group—those at neither high nor low risk—could not be statistically distinguished from the base rate of the sample as a whole.

Stage Five: Repeating the Classification Tree

To increase the predictive accuracy of the classification tree, those individuals designated as "average risk" were reanalyzed. That is, all of the participants who were not classified into groups designated as either "high" or "low" risk in the standard classification tree model were pooled together and reanalyzed. The reason for reanalyzing these data was to determine if the individuals who were not classified in the first iteration of the analysis might be different in some significant ways from the individuals who were so classified. This resulting classification tree model was referred to as an "iterative classification tree" (ICT) (Steadman et al., 2000). Using an iterative classification tree allowed the MacArthur researchers to classify many more patients as "high" or "low" risk than did using a main-effects regression approach (Monahan et al., 2001, p. 104).

Stage Six: Combining Multiple Risk Estimates

An important characteristic of the classification tree methodology is that variables entered initially into the tree carry more weight in determining the risk group to which an individual is assigned. Therefore, as a final step, the authors estimated several different risk assessment models in an attempt to obtain multiple risk assessments for each individual. That is, different risk factors were chosen to be the lead variable upon which a classification tree was constructed. This was done by choosing, from among the variables that statistically qualified for "lead variable" status, those that were not simply different indices of the same underlying variable, such as, for example, "alcohol use" and "alcohol diagnosis" would have been. The basic idea motivating the combination of multiple risk estimates was that individuals who scored in the high-risk category on many classification trees were more likely to be violent than individuals who scored in the high-risk category on fewer classification trees. Analogously, individuals who scored in the low-risk category on many classification trees were less likely to be violent than individuals who scored in the low-risk category on fewer classification trees (Banks et al., 2004). The result of this "multiple iterative classification tree" procedure was to place each patient into one of five groups whose rates of engaging in violence to others—as operationalized above—over the first several months after hospital discharge was 1%, 8%, 26%, 56%, or 76% (for discussions of how best to communicate violence risk estimates—as probabilities, as relative frequencies, or as categories (COVR allows users to choose any of these formats)—see Heilbrun et al., 2004; Monahan et al., 2002; Monahan and Steadman, 1996; Slovic, Monahan, & MacGregor, 2000).

Stage Seven: Developing the COVR Software

The multiple iterative classification tree models that were constructed had an impressive capacity to identify individuals with differing levels of violence risk. However, these models were also very computationally intensive and not suited to paper-and-pencil administration. As a result, the MacArthur researchers developed user-friendly software that could be employed to classify patients' violence risk.

Reliability

Reliability was addressed in the MacArthur Violence Risk Assessment Study by having each interviewer videotape five administrations of the risk assessment instrument and having those tapes blindly rescored by the other interviewers. This data set of 385 interviews yielded excellent kappa coefficients (alpha > .80) for all risk factors that appear in COVR (see Monahan et al., 2001, p. 149).

Validity

Of course, the successful construction of a structured risk assessment instrument does not answer the question of how well the instrument will perform when applied to new samples of individuals. As a rule, models constructed using procedures that rely on associations between variables in a particular sample are apt to lose predictive power when applied to new samples. This "shrinkage" is due to capitalization on chance associations in the original construction sample. Thus, it is essential to prospectively validate models on new samples to ensure that they maintain adequate levels of predictive power. Therefore, a prospective validation of the model of violence risk assessment was conducted (Monahan, Steadman, Robbins et al., 2005). In this research, supported by the National Institute of Mental Health, COVR software incorporating the multiple ICT procedure was administered to independent samples of acute inpatients (n = 157) and prospectively followed subsamples of discharged patients classified as at high or low violence risk.

Specifically, the COVR software was used to evaluate patients at two sites: Worcester, MA (a site in the construction study), and Philadelphia, PA (not a site in the construction study). The selection criteria for this validation study were slightly broader than those used in the MacArthur development study: (1) between ages 18 and 60 years; (2) of any race/ethnic background (that is, not limited to Caucasian, African American, and Hispanic); and (3) with any psychiatric diagnosis. Expanding the eligible sample in this fashion allowed us both to compare the validation results with the original sample on which the software had been developed and to test the validity of the software in assessing violence risk for a broader group of patients.

Laptop computers loaded with the COVR software were available at each facility. After informed consent had been given, chart and demographic information was entered, followed by patient assessment with the software. Patient self-report was relied upon for information not obtained from the chart, and probe questions were asked to clarify inconsistent answers. The software was administered by research interviewers (most often psychology graduate students). The average length of time to administer the software was less than 10 minutes.

Based on the original MacArthur analysis results, patients were assigned to (1) a high-risk category (equivalent to risk classes 4 and 5, the highest two risk classes in Banks et al., 2004), with an expected rate of violence of 63.6%; (2) a low-risk category (equivalent to risk class 1, the lowest risk class in Banks et al., 2004), with an expected rate of violence of 1.2%; or (3) an average-risk category (equivalent to risk classes 2 and 3, the intermediate risk classes in Banks et al., 2004), with an expected rate of violence of 15.6%. The patients' hospital clinicians were blind to the risk classification.

All of the high-risk individuals and a random sample of the low-risk individuals were selected for follow-up. Given limitations on resources, the need to maintain an adequate sample size in the groups that were followed, and because the primary aim of the study was to validate the high- and low-risk designations, patients assessed as neither high nor low risk of violence (that is, patients at average risk) were not followed up in the community. Patients who had been selected for follow-up were recontacted in the community and interviewed at 10 weeks and 20 weeks from the date of discharge.

Using the strict operational definition of violence from the original study, results indicated that 9% of the individuals classified by COVR at hospital baseline as at low risk of violence were found to be violent in the community within 20 weeks after discharge, compared to 35% of the individuals classified as at high risk of violence. When all individuals were blindly reclassified using the slightly more inclusive operational definition of violence (for example, including violence by a patient shortly after he or she was readmitted to a hospital), the rate of violence observed in the low-risk group remained at 9% but the rate of violence observed in the high-risk group rose to 49%.

Based on the findings of the original MacArthur study from which the COVR software has been developed, the rate of violence expected was 1.2% in the low-risk group and 63.6% in the high-risk group. The observed rates of violence that were obtained in this prospective sample of 9% and 49% for the low- and (recoded) high-risk groups, respectively, may reflect the shrinkage that can be expected whenever an actuarial instrument moves from construction to validation samples. It also could reflect a change in the base rate of violence from the previous samples to the new samples.

Limitations and Necessary Future Research

Research on at least two issues is crucial if COVR is to become a commonly used tool for violence risk assessment. First, can one assume that risk factors based on self-reported data are validly measured? Second, is clinical review of the COVR-generated risk estimate useful?

Can Patient Self-Report Be Believed?

In both the original research in which COVR's multiple iterative classification tree methodology was developed and in the subsequent research in which that methodology was validated, the MacArthur researchers operated under the protection of a Federal Confidentiality Certificate, and the patients studied were made aware of this protection (Monahan et al., 1993). The Certificate meant that most disclosures that the examinees made to the examiners were not discoverable in court and did not have to be reported to the police. In addition, in both the construction study and the validation study, the examinees were told that information from their police and hospital records was being collected, as well as information from interviewing a collateral informant who knew them well, to verify the information given by the examinee. Both of these components—the guarantee of confidentiality and the reliance on multiple information sources—may have encouraged examinees to provide more truthful information than they otherwise would have.

When COVR is used in the real world of clinical practice, of course, Federal Confidentiality Certificates will not be obtainable. However, police records will sometimes, and collateral informants will often, be available in clinical practice. The important question remains: will examinees be as forthcoming and honest in answering questions when COVR is used as a tool to make actual decisions on the nature, or length, or venue of their care as they were when COVR was being constructed or validated and the answers had no personal impact? What is the clinician to do when he or she has reason to doubt the truthfulness of an answer that a patient gives to a question that COVR presents?

Many examinees' answers, of course, cannot be "verified," because they relate to events in their interior lives (e.g., Does the patient really daydream often about harming someone?). Other answers are, in principle, capable of verification, but could be verified only with great difficulty in usual clinical situations (e.g., Was the patient's father actually arrested when the patient was a child?). Still other answers may be verifiable, to a greater or lesser degree, by recourse to data in the patient's existing hospital chart or outpatient record. What is the clinician to do when a patient's answer to a question posed by COVR is contradicted or called into question by other data sources? Consider the following examples.

- When asked about abusing alcohol, Patient A. answers in the negative, yet the chart indicates that, when he was admitted to the hospital on the previous evening, he had a blood alcohol level of .30.
- When asked about past arrests, Patient B. denies ever having been arrested, yet the file contains previous evaluations for competence to stand trial on numerous charges.
- When asked whether she was abused as a child, Patient C. answers "Never," but there is a notation in the chart that the patient's sister stated that the mother's boyfriend repeatedly sexually assaulted the patient when she was a girl.

Four courses of action are possible in situations involving conflicting information. First, the clinician could simply enter into the COVR the patient's answers as the patient reported them, even if the clinician were convinced that the patient was being untruthful.

Second, the clinician could enter into the COVR his or her best judgment as to the factually correct answer to the question asked. For example, the clinician could choose to credit the toxicology report, indicating recent alcohol abuse over the patient's self-reported denial of drinking, and enter "yes" to the appropriate alcohol abuse question.

Third, the clinician familiar with the contents of the chart could confront the patient when apparent discrepancies arise between chart information and the patient's answers. For example, the clinician could say to the patient who denied ever having been arrested, "I have a problem. You say you've never been arrested, but in your hospital record there's a competence report that says you were arrested for assault twice last year and once the year before. What about this?"

Finally, the clinician, on being convinced from information available in the record that the examinee was being untruthful in his or her answers, could simply terminate the administration of COVR and arrive at a risk estimate without the aid of this structured tool. For example, the clinician could base his or her clinical risk estimate entirely on information available in the chart or from other data sources that do not rely on the patient's problematic self-reports.

Which of these options is recommended? It is important to emphasize that COVR was constructed and validated using a variant of the third option described above. Although information obtained from a collateral informant was never revealed to the examinee, the examinee would be confronted on any apparent inconsistencies between his or her answers and information contained in the hospital chart.

The first option of simply entering into the program the examinee's answers as given, even if the clinician is convinced that the examinee is being untruthful, is clinically and ethically inappropriate. If the clinician does *not* clearly note the patient's apparent untruthfulness in the report that accompanies the COVR, the clinician would knowingly be basing a risk estimate on information that, in his or her best judgment, is invalid, without warning potential users of the estimate of its uncertain foundation. And if the clinician *does* clearly note the patient's apparent untruthfulness in the accompanying report, the clinician would, in effect, be telling the decision-maker to disregard the risk estimate that the clinician had just offered.

The second option of the clinician entering into the COVR his or her best judgment as to the factually correct answer to the question asked, rather than the answer that the patient provided, is problematic for two reasons. First, it makes no attempt to determine if there is an explanation for the apparent discrepancy that would indicate that the patient's account is actually correct (for example, someone else's toxicology laboratory slip was mistakenly placed in the patient's chart). Second, it varies from the procedures used to construct and validate the COVR, hence threatening the validity of the resulting estimate of risk. In the latter regard, to use clinician-generated answers rather than patient-generated answers raises the question of whether a clinician can accurately detect a patient's deception, when it occurs, without at the same time erroneously considering many true responses to be deceptive.

The recommendation of the COVR's authors is the third option—the examiner familiar with the contents of the chart should confront the patient when apparent discrepancies arise between the chart information and the patient's answers (Monahan, Steadman, Appelbaum et al., 2005, pp. 6–9). If the discrepancy is satisfactorily resolved, the clinician would then enter into the COVR the answer that the patient gives. If the discrepancy is not satisfactorily resolved (for example, if, after confrontation, the clinician still credits a recent toxicology report indicating alcohol abuse over the patient's denial), then the clinician would enter "missing" for that piece of data, rather than entering *either* the patient's self-report *or* the clinician's own judgment about the accurate scoring of this item, being sure to note this action in an accompanying report. The rationale of the MacArthur researchers for this recommendation is that COVR contains 10 classification tree models but can produce a reliable estimate of risk using only 5 models (Banks et al., 2004). As long as at least 5 models contain no missing data due to the clinician disbelieving a patient's answer (or due to any other reason), COVR will operate as designed. If more than 5 models contain missing data, COVR will not produce an estimate of risk, and the clinician will have to arrive at a risk estimate without the aid of this structured tool (that is, choose the fourth option, above).

Is Clinical Review of COVR Risk Estimate Useful?

In the view of its authors, the COVR software is useful in informing, but not replacing, clinical decision making regarding risk assessment. The authors recommended a two-phased violence risk assessment procedure in which a patient is first administered the COVR, and then the preliminary risk estimate generated by the COVR is reviewed by the clinician ultimately responsible for making the risk assessment in the context of additional information believed to be relevant and gathered from clinical interviews, significant others, and/or available records. This clinical review "would not revise or 'adjust' the actuarial risk score produced by the COVR" (Monahan, Steadman et al., 2005, p.11), but would likely be of a more qualitative nature (e.g., "higher than," or "lower than" the COVR estimate). The authors of the COVR believed it essential to allow for such a review, for two reasons (Monahan et al. 2001, pp. 130–135). The first reason had to do with possible limits on the generalizability of the validity of the software. For example, is the predictive validity of COVR generalizable to forensic patients, or to people outside the United States, or to people who are less than 18 years old, or to the emergency room assessments of persons who have not recently been hospitalized? The predictive validity of this instrument may well generalize widely. Yet there comes a point at which the sample to which a structured risk assessment instrument is applied differs so much from the sample on which the instrument was constructed and validated that one would be hard pressed to castigate the evaluator who took the structured risk estimate as advisory rather than conclusive. Research on the generalizability of COVR's predictive validity is a clear priority. Until a body of research on the generalizability of COVR to different populations has emerged, "the most useful estimates of risk generated [by COVR] are still those derived from the original MacArthur Study" (that is, likelihood of violence of 1%, 8%, 26%, 56%, or 76%) (Monahan, Steadman, Robbins et al., 2005, p. 815).

The second reason given for allowing a clinician the option to review a risk estimate produced by a structured tool is that the clinician may note the presence of rare risk or protective factors in a given case, and that these factors—precisely because they are rare—will not have been taken into account in the construction of the structured tool (Appelbaum, Robins, & Monahan, 2000). In the context of structured tools for assessing violence risk, the most frequently mentioned rare risk factor is a direct threat, that is, an apparently serious statement of intention to do violence to a named victim.

A careful study of (1) *how often*, when they review structured violence risk estimates, clinicians feel it necessary to modify those estimates; (2) *why* clinicians feel it necessary to revise the actuarial estimates, for example, the rare risk or protective factor that is believed to be important in assessing violence risk in a given case, but (because it is rare) is not measured by COVR; and (3) *how much* clinicians want to revise actuarial risk estimates, would be invaluable in this regard.

Case Examples

The COVR Professional Manual (Monahan, Steadman, Appelbaum et al., 2005) gives three case examples of the use of the COVR in clinical practice:

CASE EXAMPLE #1: HIGH RISK

Mr. Smith is a 27-year-old male salesman who has been hospitalized for the eighth time with a diagnosis of bipolar disorder. After 5 days in the hospital, he is being considered for discharge. Since an aggressive act toward Mr. Smith's wife while manic and intoxicated had precipitated his hospitalization, the clinician responsible for the discharge decision requests that COVR be administered. The next day, a COVR report is given to the responsible clinician that concludes: "The likelihood that Mr. Smith will commit a violent act toward another person in the next several months is estimated to be between 65% and 86%, with a best estimate of 76%." The report also lists the risk factors that were used to produce this estimate.

The clinician, after reviewing the COVR report and all the information in Mr. Smith's hospital chart, interviews Mr. Smith. The interview fails to uncover any unusual protective factors that would call into question the estimate of violence risk that COVR had produced. Moreover, it is clear that his manic state has not fully resolved. The clinician decides not to discharge Mr. Smith at the current time, but rather to continue a course of medication and anger management groups designed to lower his violence risk, and to recommend that Mr. Smith continue with anger management and intensive substance abuse treatment in the community when he is discharged. With the patient's consent, his wife is counseled about her risk should his symptoms recur and he start drinking again.

CASE EXAMPLE #2: LOW RISK

Ms. Jones is a 42-year-old female accountant who has been hospitalized for the first time for several days with a diagnosis of major depression. She is being considered for discharge. Since an ambiguous threat about a coworker had been noted by a nurse in her hospital chart, the clinician responsible for the discharge decision requests that COVR be administered. The next day, a COVR report, which is given to the responsible clinician, concludes: "The likelihood that Ms. Jones will commit a violent act toward another person in the next several months is estimated to be between zero and 2%, with a best estimate of 1%." The report also lists the risk factors that were used to produce this estimate.

The clinician, after reviewing the COVR report and all the information in Ms. Jones' hospital chart, interviews Ms Jones. The interview fails to uncover any unusual risk factors that would call into question the estimate of violence risk that COVR had produced, and Ms Jones explains the ambiguous comment, which turns out not actually to have been a threat, to the clinician's satisfaction. As she seems less depressed and is not suicidal, the clinician decides to discharge Ms. Jones at the current time and to follow up with routine care in the community.

CASE EXAMPLE #3: MODERATE RISK

Mr. Brown is a 21-year-old male security guard who has been hospitalized for several days with a diagnosis of borderline personality disorder with comorbid substance dependence, after getting into a shouting match with his girlfriend and cutting his arms. He is being considered for discharge. Since the chart indicates that Mr. Brown had been involuntarily committed on two prior occasions as "dangerous to others," the clinician responsible for the discharge decision requests that COVR be administered. The next day, a COVR report is given to the responsible clinician that concludes: "The likelihood that Mr. Brown will commit a violent act toward another person in the next several months is estimated to be between 20% and 32%, with a best estimate of 26%. The report also lists the risk factors that were used to produce this estimate.

The clinician, after reviewing the COVR report and all the information in Mr. Brown's hospital chart, interviews Mr. Brown. During the interview, Mr. Brown states his apparently serious intention to "teach a lesson she'll never forget" to his girlfriend, who has told him that he can't come back to live with her. He also responds affirmatively to a question about whether he has a firearm in the house. The clinician believes that this clinical information is indicative of a high risk of imminent violence. The clinician decides not to discharge Mr. Brown at the current time, but rather to continue a course of medication and psychotherapy designed to lower his violence risk. The clinician also decides to inform Mr. Brown's former girlfriend of the threat.

Conclusion

The three forms of structured risk assessment described above all specify in advance *at least* which risk factors are to be addressed and how those risk factors are to be measured. Some forms of structured violence risk assessment (e.g., the HCR-20, see Chapter 8) structure *only* the choice and measurement of risk factors. Other forms of violence risk assessment (e.g., COVR, described here) go on to *also* structure the manner in which the risk factors are combined to yield an estimate of risk. But COVR allows the clinician to review this estimate, in the context of other (unstructured) available information, before issuing his or her final risk estimate. Still other forms of violence risk assessment (e.g., VRAG, see Chapter 6) are *completely structured* (i.e., actuarial) tools. No clinical review is allowed; the structured risk estimate that is produced when the risk factors are combined is the final product of the risk assessment process.

COVR is the first violence risk assessment tool to be available solely in software format. Its acceptance in the field will depend largely on the findings of numerous independent research projects now ongoing in several countries attempting to replicate COVR's predictive validity and to generalize existing findings to other relevant populations, particularly to forensic ones.

References

Appelbaum, P., Robbins, P., & Monahan, J. (2000). Violence and delusions: Data from the MacArthur Violence Risk Assessment Study. *American Journal of Psychiatry, 157,* 566–572.

Banks, S., Robbins, P. C., Silver, E., Vesselinov, R., Steadman, H. J., Monahan, J., Mulvey, E., Appelbaum, P., Grisso, T., & Roth, L. H. (2004). A multiple-models approach to violence risk assessment among people with mental disorder. *Criminal Justice and Behavior, 31,* 324–340.

Breiman, L., Friedman, J., Olshen, R., & Stone, C. (1984). *Classification and regression trees.* Boca Raton, FL: CRC Press.

Douglas, K., Ogloff, J., & Hart, S. (2003). Evaluation of a model of violence risk assessment among forensic psychiatric patients. *Psychiatric Services, 54,* 1372–1379

Gardner, W., Lidz, C. W., Mulvey, E. P., & Shaw, E. C. (1996). A comparison of actuarial methods for identifying repetitively violent patients with mental illnesses. *Law and Human Behavior, 20,* 35–48.

Heilbrun, K., O'Neill, M. L., Stevens, T. N., Strohman, L. K., Bowman, Q., & Lo, Y-W. (2004). Assessing normative approaches to communicating violence risk: A national survey of psychologists. *Behavioral Sciences and the Law, 22,* 187–196.

Meehl, P. (1954). *Clinical versus statistical prediction.* Minneapolis: University of Minnesota Press.

Monahan, J. (2006). *Tarasoff* at thirty: How developments in science and policy shape the common law. *University of Cincinnati Law Review, 75,* 497–521.

Monahan, J., & Appelbaum, P. S. (2000). Reducing violence risk: Diagnostically based clues from the MacArthur Violence Risk Assessment Study. In S. Hodgins (Ed.), *Effective prevention of crime and violence among the mentally ill* (pp. 19–34). Dordrecht, The Netherlands: Kluwer Academic.

Monahan, J., Appelbaum, P., Mulvey, E., Robbins, P., & Lidz, C. (1993). Ethical and legal duties in conducting research on violence: Lessons from the MacArthur Risk Assessment Study. *Violence and Victims 8,* 387–396.

Monahan, J., Heilbrun, K., Silver, E., Nabors, E., Bone, J., & Slovic, P. (2002). Communicating violence risk: Frequency formats, vivid outcomes, and forensic settings. *International Journal of Forensic Mental Health, 1,* 121–126.

Monahan, J., & Steadman, H. J. (1994a). Toward a rejuvenation of risk assessment research. In J. Monahan & H. J. Steadman (Eds.), *Violence and mental disorder: Developments in risk assessment* (pp. 1–17). Chicago: University of Chicago Press.

Monahan, J., & Steadman, H. J. (Eds.). (1994b). *Violence and mental disorder: Developments in risk assessment.* Chicago: University of Chicago Press.

Monahan, J., & Steadman, H. J. (1996). Violent storms and violent people: How meteorology can inform risk communication in mental health law. *American Psychologist, 51,* 931–938.

Monahan, J., Steadman, H., Appelbaum, P., Grisso, T., Mulvey, E., Roth, L., Robbins, P., Banks, S., & Silver, E. (2005). *The Classification of Violence Risk.* Lutz, FL: Psychological Assessment Resources.

Monahan, J., Steadman, H. J., Appelbaum, P. S., Robbins, P. C., Mulvey, E. P., Silver, E., Roth, L., & Grisso, T. (2000). Developing a clinically useful actuarial tool for assessing violence risk. *British Journal of Psychiatry, 176,* 312–319.

Monahan, J, Steadman, H., Robbins, P., Appelbaum, P., Banks, S., Grisso, T., Heilbrun, K., Mulvey, E., Roth, L., & Silver, E. (2005). An actuarial model of violence risk assessment for persons with mental disorders. *Psychiatric Services, 56,* 810–815.

Monahan, J., Steadman, H. J., Silver, E., Appelbaum, P. S., Robbins, P. C., Mulvey, E. P., Roth, L., Grisso, T., & Banks, S. (2001). *Rethinking risk assessment: The MacArthur study of mental disorder and violence.* New York: Oxford University Press.

Novaco, R. (1994). Anger as a risk factor for violence among the mentally disordered. In J. Monahan and H. Steadman (Eds.), *Violence and mental disorder; Developments in risk assessment* (pp. 21–59). Chicago: University of Chicago Press.

Otto, R. (2000). Assessing and managing violence risk in outpatient settings. *Journal of Clinical Psychology 56,* 1239–1262.

Slovic, P., Monahan, J., & MacGregor, D. G. (2000). Violence risk assessment and risk communication: The effects of using actual cases, providing instruction, and employing probability versus frequency formats. *Law and Human Behavior, 24,* 271–296.

Steadman, H. J., Silver, E., Monahan, J., Appelbaum, P. S., Robbins, P. C., Mulvey, E. P., Grisso, T., Roth, L. and Banks, S. (2000). A classification tree approach to the development of actuarial violence risk assessment tools. *Law and Human Behavior, 24,* 83–100.

Webster C, Douglas K, Eaves D, and Hart, S. (1997). HCR-20: Assessing Risk for Violence (Version 2). Vancouver, Simon Fraser University.

10
The Level of Service (LS) Assessment of Adults and Older Adolescents

D. A. ANDREWS, JAMES BONTA, and J. STEPHEN WORMITH

The LS assessment instruments, from their beginning in the late 1970s (Andrews, 1982a), sought to (1) standardize and render transparent the information that guided the discretionary decisions of correctional professionals, (2) make that information a matter of record, (3) develop the capacity of professionals to assess risk of criminal recidivism, and (4) identify dynamic risk factors (or criminogenic needs). The standardization and transparency of these tools meets the ethical and legal standards for decision making in forensic contexts. Knowledge of level of risk assists in level of supervision decisions and assists with treatment and intervention planning. Knowledge of dynamic risk factors assists in the selection of intermediate targets of change for purposes of reducing reoffending in rehabilitation and crime prevention programming.

By the mid-1980s the risk-need (RN) model of correctional assessment and rehabilitation had become the risk-need-responsivity model (RNR) (Andrews, Bonta, & Hoge, 1990). From the beginning, a general social learning model of deviance was applied, and it is still known as the personal, interpersonal, and community-reinforcement perspective (PIC-R) (Andrews, 1982b). Thus, from the beginning, general cognitive social learning strategies were seen as universally applicable (general responsivity) with an appreciation for specific responsivity being developed in the 1980s and 1990s. By the late 1990s, the RNR model formally included principles having to do with systematic attention to staffing and management issues (Andrews, 2001; Bonta & Andrews, 2007).

The development of LS instruments and the RNR model continue to interact. Three major sources of LS content continue to be the opinions of correctional and forensic professionals, a broad and flexible theoretical perspective on human behavior (including criminal behavior), and the research literatures on the prediction of criminal behavior and crime prevention. The interactions among opinion, theory, research, and the RNR model will be evident throughout this overview of the instruments and their properties.

Today, the LS instruments are among the world's most widely used offender risk/need assessment tools. In America, 23 states and Puerto Rico use an LS instrument (Interstate Commission for Adult Offender Supervision, 2007), nine of thirteen Canadian jurisdictions use either the Level of Service Inventory–Revised (LSI-R) or Level of Service/Case Management Inventory (LS/CMI), and the use of LS instruments is evident in Australia, Singapore, Scotland, Ireland, the Isle of Jersey, and Croatia. In addition, use of an LS instrument is increasing in popularity in forensic psychiatric settings (Archer, Buffington-Vollum, Stredny, & Handel, 2006).

Description of LSI-R, LS/CMI, LS/RNR (Level of Service/Risk-Need-Responsivity), and LSI-R: SV (Level of Service Inventory–Revised: Screening Version)

The risk/need component of the LS instruments is actuarial based. Although the items were (rationally) selected based on evidence of their association with recidivism (and cross-validated with the original LSI construction sample), LS risk/need entails mechanical scoring with evidence-based contingency tables linking score categories with outcomes. The instruments were designed with reference to the prediction of general recidivism, although the underlying theory suggests wide-applicability across specific forms of rule violations, including violence.

Although the original LSI was designed for use with probationers and parolees (Andrews, 1982a), it has proven useful with other community corrections samples and within prisons, jails, and halfway houses, and forensic mental health clinics and hospitals. A youth version of this tool is available for those under the age of 16 (Hoge & Andrews, 2002; see Chapter 5 in the current volume). The LS instruments were not designed to assist in setting the severity of the criminal penalty on the basis of seriousness of the offense. That is, the LS instruments are not comprehensive surveys of the aggravating and mitigating factors that may be relevant at time of sentencing. In so far as risk, need, and responsivity considerations are relevant at time of sentencing, however, use of the LS is appropriate (Andrews & Dowden, 2007).

Detailed scoring manuals allow professionals with specific LS training to use the instrument even if they have not had prior formal training in psychological assessment. The publisher (Multi-Health Systems, MHS) maintains a list of Master Trainers who are qualified to train regular trainers and frontline users. LS validity estimates do increase with LS-focused training and experience (Lowenkamp, Latessa, & Holsinger, 2004).

The core instruments can be scored on the basis of interviews with the offender, interviews with collaterals (e.g., family member), reviews of files and official records, and in some settings, psychological test data (e.g., paper-and-pencil assessments of antisocial thinking). Some research projects have relied on paper-and-pencil questionnaire versions, computerized self-report versions, and reviews of case files and official records. The publisher of the LS materials offers computerized data entry and scoring, Web-based versions, and computerized record systems that amount to clinically relevant and psychologically informed management information systems. Agencies are also able to localize certain desired items in consultation with MHS (and typically the authors). A Software Developers Kit (SDK) allows larger organizations to embed LS tools in existing management information systems. SDK allows assessors to work within a single system with the option of prepopulated fields for reduced workload. Because it is all within their own system, agencies control the data and security around the data.

The Level of Service Inventory–Revised (LSI-R)

LSI-R (Andrews & Bonta, 1995) is a 54-item survey of indicators of risk/need distributed across ten subcomponents as outlined in Table 10.1. Each item is scored as risk indicator absent (0) or present (1), while a circled item number indicates insufficient information to score the item. Subcomponent scores are the simple sum of the number of items checked within that sub-component. The total LSI-R risk/need score is the sum of checked items.

Some of the dynamic items include a 4-item rating scale from "0" through "3," wherein "0" is a very unsatisfactory condition (very high risk), and "3" is a very satisfactory situation (very low risk). Zero and 1 ratings lead to a checked item, and ratings of 2 or 3 indicate that the item should not be checked. The descriptions for rating particular items greatly sharpen the construct that is being assessed. The ratings also facilitate more sensitive assessments of change than are possible with binary scoring.

The Level of Service/Case Management Inventory (LS/CMI)

In addition to providing a General Risk/Need score, the LS/CMI (Andrews, Bonta, & Wormith, 2004) assists in structuring an RNR-based service plan and service delivery and assessing case progress through to case closure. The multiple components are outlined in Table 10.2 along with selected items for some subcomponents.

Table 10.1 The Level of Service Inventory–Revised: A Sampling of the Items

	Criminal History (10 Items)
1	Any prior convictions, adult/number
5	Arrested under age 16
	Education/Employment (10)
12	Frequently unemployed
17	Suspended or expelled at least once
	Financial (2)
22	Reliance upon social assistance
	Family/Marital (4)
23	Dissatisfaction with marital or equivalent situation
26	Criminal, family/spouse
	Accommodation (3)
28	Three or more address changes, last year
	Leisure/Recreation (2)
30	No recent participation in an organized activity
	Companions (5)
33	Some criminal acquaintances
36	Few anticriminal friends
	Alcohol/Drug Problem (9)
37	Alcohol problem, ever
40	Drug problem, current
	Emotional/Personal (5)
47	Severe interference
50	Psychological assessment indicated
	Attitude/Orientation (4)
51	Supportive of crime
52	Unfavorable toward convention

Source: Andrews & Bonta (1995). *The Level of Service Inventory–Revised: User's Manual.* Multi-Health Systems, Sample Items. (Reproduced with permission of Multi-Health Systems, Inc.)

LS/CMI General Risk/Need is composed of eight subcomponents and a total of 43 items. Inspection of Table 10.2 reveals that seven of the subcomponents are based on the LSI-R. The eighth replaces Emotional/Personal with a concentration on the personality and behavioral elements of a propensity for antisocial conduct. It focuses on early and diverse patterns of misconduct, criminal thinking, generalized trouble, and indications that an assessment for psychopathy might be warranted. The LSI-R subtotals of Financial, Accommodation, and Emotional/Personal were dropped from the general risk need score, but are represented elsewhere in the LS/CMI.

The concept of offender strengths is formally represented by the opportunity to rate each of the eight subcomponents as an area of strength. A strength rating indicates that the area is

Table 10.2 Level of Service/Case Management Inventory (LS/CMI)

	Section 1: General Risk/Need Factors
1.1	**Criminal History (8 items)**
	1 Any prior youth dispositions or adult convictions
	5 Arrested or charged under age 16
1.2	**Education/Employment (9 items)**
	9 Currently unemployed
	13 Less than regular grade 12 or equivalent
1.3	**Family/Marital (4 items)**
	18 Dissatisfaction with marital or equivalent situation
	21 Criminal—Family/spouse
1.4	**Leisure/Recreation (2 items)**
	22 Absence of recent participation in an organized activity
1.5	**Companions (4 items)**
	25 Some criminal friends
	27 Few anticriminal friends
1.6	**Alcohol/Drug Problem (8 items)**
	30 Alcohol problem, currently
	31 Drug problem, currently
1.7	**Procriminal Attitude/Orientation (4 items)**
	36 Supportive of crime
	37 Unfavorable toward convention
1.8	**Antisocial Pattern (4 items)**
	41 Early and diverse antisocial behavior
	43 A pattern of generalized trouble
	Section 2: Specific Risk/Need Factors
2.1.	**Personal Problems with Criminogenic Potential (14 items)**
	2 Diagnosis of "psychopathy"
	6 Anger management deficits
	9 Poor social skills
2.2.	**History of Perpetration (21 items)**
	2 Sexual assault, extrafamilial, child/adolescent–female victim
	8 Physical assault (extrafamilial adult victim)
	18 Gang participation
	Section 3: Prison Experience–Institutional Factors (14 items)
	3 Last classification maximum
	7 Protective custody
	Section 4: Other Client Issues (21 items)
	1 Financial problems
	3 Accommodation problems
	5 Parenting concerns
	16 Victim of family violence
	Section 5: Special Responsivity Considerations (11 items)
	2 Women, gender specific
	3 Low intelligence

Table 10.2 Level of Service/Case Management Inventory (LS/CMI) (continued)

Section 9: Case Management Plan

Program Targets and Intervention Plan

Criminogenic Need	Goal	Intervention
1.		
2.		
3.		

Special Responsivity Considerations

Responsivity Issue	Proposed Approach to Address Issue
1.	
2.	
3.	

Section 10: Progress Record

Criminogenic Needs

Date	Criminogenic Need	Improvement	Deterioration	No Change

Source: Andrews, Bonta, & Wormith (2004). *Level of Service/Case Management Inventory: An Offender Assessment System: User's Manual.* Multi-Health Systems, Sample Items. (Copyright 2004, Multi-Health Systems, Inc. Reproduced with permission.)

Note: Item titles cannot be scored without reference to the formal criteria contained in the LS/CMI Manual.

one in which positive circumstances may be built upon in a case plan—for example, involving a significant other (friend, family member, school or work associate, recreational partner) in a directly supportive role in service delivery. Strength factors may also function in a protective fashion, reducing the criminogenic effects of other risk factors. The inclusion of strength notations is consistent with ongoing research on the role of strength factors, but they were introduced primarily on the strong opinions of LS users who want the case plan to reflect the totality of the person and not just risk factors. Health, mental health, and social concerns are expanded in Section 4, as are responsivity issues in Section 5. Additionally, there is a detailed review of personal problems with criminogenic potential (Section 2.1) and a detailed review of the variety of antisocial acts (Section 2.1).

Although developed in the next section of this chapter (Development: Rationale and Methods), a crucial point is that systematic surveys of current LS users revealed that they wanted to collect more information on which to base their judgments (in significant contrast to our early consultations with professionals who had no experience with structured assessment). This finding from our consultations with users underscores the value that experienced users now place on structured assessment. Many of our users were very aware of the value of gender-informed assessment, and that is apparent in LS/CMI.

The Level of Service/Risk-Need-Responsivity (LS/RNR)

Some potential users are overwhelmed by the apparent magnitude of LS/CMI and have requested an intermediate version between LSI-R and LS/CMI. LS/RNR (Andrews, Bonta, & Wormith, forthcoming) is a version composed of Sections 1, 2, and 5 of LS/CMI. Some users of LS/RNR will be with agencies that are satisfied with their existing case management approach.

The Level of Service Inventory–Revised: Screening Version (LSI-R: SV)

The eight-item LSI-R: SV (Andrews & Bonta, 1998) was introduced as a preliminary screening instrument for agencies faced with extremely large numbers of cases. Cases falling in the moderate- and/or high-risk categories are subject to a full LS assessment for purposes of program planning. The screening version has been the focus of less research than the other LSI instruments and is not a major focus of this chapter as a result.

Development: Rationale and Methods

The principles that guided the development of the LS instruments entailed a weighting of professional opinion, research evidence on prediction and effective treatment, the RNR model of assessment and treatment, and a comprehensive personality and cognitive social learning perspective on criminal conduct. The original LSI was developed in close consultation with Ottawa probation and parole officers and managers, senior personnel, and groups of officers and managers from across the province of Ontario. Development efforts raised the visibility of the Ottawa office in the province, and cooperation was high. It was the sixth pilot version of the LSI (LSI-VI) that was implemented province wide (Andrews, 1982a), and with minor revisions, it became LSI-R (Andrews & Bonta, 1995).

The input from the probation and parole officers was significant. The goal was to produce an instrument that made sense to them and fit with their skill sets and manner of working. The regular duties of all officers included the preparation of presentence reports for the courts, and officers routinely produced a narrative social-legal history based on interviews with cases and collaterals and reviews of official records. Thus, the subcomponents of the LSI fit very neatly with the domains and procedures officers were used to working with. The big change was a shift of emphasis toward specific indicators with documented empirical validity. The first version of the LSI was a 25-page interview schedule. Any reductions in that were viewed very positively, and LSI-VI, a single sheet, was an attractive alternative.

A professional override (discretion) has always been part of the LSI risk/need approach, and during development a monitoring of the overrides was helpful in uncovering information judged very valuable by the officers. For example, the items sampling the indicators of alcohol and drug abuse were added because substance abuse on the part of the offender was a frequent rationale for increasing supervision level. Forthcoming LS/CMI research will explore the incremental validity of overrides.

The research literature was reviewed with the following reports being notably valuable (Baird, Heinz, & Bemus, 1979; Barton & Jenkins, 1973; Glaser, 1964; Jenkins & Sanford, 1972; Waller, 1974). Additionally, the Research Branch of the Ontario ministry responsible for corrections had supported a number of projects with local and province-wide samples of offenders (Andrews & Kiessling, 1979; Gendreau, Grant, Leipciger, & Collins, 1979; Gendreau, Madden, & Leipciger, 1980; Madden, 1978; Renner, 1978; Rogers, 1981). Items were included in the first draft of the LS instrument if their predictive power was indicated by the results of one or more of the 11 studies cited immediately above. The specific wording was shaped by consistency with social learning and with "appropriateness" for the probation context. The final items in LSI-R additionally had empirical support from the first and second follow-up of the construction sample (Andrews, 1982a; Andrews & Robinson, 1984).

The late 1970s and early 1980s was a time of knowledge expansion in Ontario, combined with officers, managers, and policy people open to innovation. Resistance existed within the system, but a critical consensus was apparent on two sets of values: (1) implementing the least restrictive and least onerous of interpretations of the criminal penalty through structured discretion, and (2) risk-need–based rehabilitative programming.

The original three-level risk categorization for LSI-R reflected two considerations. First, discussions with probation officers and managers indicated a level of comfort with a three- or four-level designation of risk and with one that roughly divided the sample into equal numbers of cases. Second, we sought cutoff scores that fit the outcome data. A general rule was established wherein a new risk level was introduced when an increase of at least 5% in the recidivism rate from one score to the next was maintained for at least the next 4 score increments. That is, we wanted to be fairly certain, if the cutoff was 6, then the recidivism rates for those scoring 7, 8, etc. would be distinctly higher than that found at score 6 and below. A finer distinction was desired with LS/CMI, and a five-level risk/need was introduced. Again the specific cutoff scores were selected to reflect "real" dividing points in the outcome distribution. We also knew by the time of LS/CMI that approximately 50% of a probation sample would be Very Low Risk or Low Risk.

The route to LS/CMI was very similar to that followed with LSI-R, although the sophistication of the officers with regard to assessment was substantially greater than in the 1970s. The research and theoretical literature was much grander, the research had been subjected to considerable meta-analytic reviews, the movement toward some version of a general personality and cognitive social learning theory of crime was awash in criminology, and the RNR model had become more sophisticated. Consultations with teams of officers and managers from every geographic region of Ontario were arranged, and representatives of prisons were also involved. It was, we suppose, a series of focus groups aimed at improved assessment and treatment.

Yet there was consensus in regard to several issues of concern: the validity of the LSI-R with female offenders, with aboriginal offenders, violent offenders, sex offenders, and spouse abusers; the neglect of strengths; the neglect of noncriminogenic needs; and the ability of the LSI-R to predict violence. Some of our responses to these issues are evident in the additional subsections of LS/CMI. Others are evident in the studies reviewed in the validity section of this chapter with particular attention to validity with different types of offenders, females, ethnicity, mental status, and socioeconomic circumstances, and with different types of outcome measures.

In accord with the consultations and the research, Section 2.2 of LS/CMI directly reflects a concern with a violent past and with the variety of prior offenses. These were added to enhance validity in the prediction of violence and serious crime. Section 2.1 items, in conjunction with Section 1, now provide a near exhaustive set of criminogenic need areas. Section 4 surveys the noncriminogenic areas that may be important in case planning for motivational and/or humanitarian purposes.

An additional element in our approach to instrument development was our stance on item selection through multiple regression. With the exception of LSI-R: SV (our screening version), we were never looking for the minimum number of items required to predict recidivism. We were looking for predictive items that suggested not only risk level but the appropriate intermediate targets of change for purposes of reduced reoffending. An efficient predictive formula is not necessarily the most useful formula, the most predictive, or the least expensive. Less efficient formulas may be as predictive and yet much more useful in program planning. For LS/CMI, however the Emotional/Personal, Financial, and Accommodation sections of LSI-R were dropped from the General Risk/Need score because they offered little in the way of incremental value and were not highly correlated with recidivism. Thus, those issues are now represented in the social, health, and mental health set along with major concerns in work with women and minorities.

Factorial purity or multidimensionality was never a major concern in the development of the instrument. We are well aware that a single major factor underlies much of the predictive power of attitudes, associates, history, and problems in the domains of home, school, and work, but it was never our intention to produce a statistically pure measure. Once again, the multiple domains represent different potential targets of change, no matter that they may reflect the same underlying dimension of antisociality.

Reliability

The LS instruments have been submitted to reliability and related psychometric analyses in a variety of settings and jurisdictions. Types of analyses include the following: internal consistency, inter-rater and test-retest reliability. Three other forms of reliability—item-total, inter-subsection, and subsection-total correlations—all of which are measures of internal consistency, and standard errors of measurement, are provided in the LS manuals (Andrews & Bonta, 1995; Andrews et al., 2004).

Assessing the reliability of risk assessment instruments is more complex than for traditional, psychometric, paper-and-pencil scales, and considerable care must be taken in interpreting their findings. For example, interpreting test-retest reliability is complicated by the fact that any difference between two assessments of the same individual may be a result of true offender change, something that the LS products were designed explicitly to accomplish. As discussed later, these differences are important, because they may reflect changes in the client's degree of risk (possibly as a result of intervention) and may suggest a new direction or focus in the treatment and management of the offender. As such, this is no longer a question of reliability but of dynamic predictive validity. In addition, the LS instruments were developed primarily from a theoretical perspective, as compared to a psychometric scale construction approach. A minor exception was the LS/CMI, whereby a review of the psychometric properties of individual items guided the reduction of 54 items in the LSI-R to 43 items in the LS/CMI. Therefore, it is expected that psychometric characteristics such as the alpha coefficient may not be as high as found in traditional psychometric tools.

Internal Consistency

Internal consistency is typically measured by Cronbach's alpha, and the coefficient may be calculated for the complete instrument and its various subsections. Scales with fewer items will have lower alpha estimates, and this has commonly been found with the LS. The internal consistency of the LS has been examined in many different jurisdictions with a wide range of offender groups. The following is a brief review of internal consistency data found on the LSI-R and LS/CMI and is limited to findings from the total samples of these international studies. For alpha coefficients of offender subgroups, the reader is referred to the respective manuals (Andrews & Bonta, 1995; Andrews et al., 2004).

Alpha coefficients for the total LSI-R score and for subsections are presented in Table 10.3. Alphas for the total 54-item scale show some variability, ranging from .64 to .94, with a mean coefficient of .84. Alpha coefficients for the subsections vary considerably as evidenced by the mean coefficients. Criminal History, Education/Employment, and Alcohol/Drugs produced mean alphas of .75 or above, followed by Leisure/Recreation, Companions, Emotional/Personal, and Procriminal Attitudes, which were all above .60. The remaining subsections—Finance, Family/Marital, and Accommodation—had alphas of .46 or greater.

Alpha coefficients for the LS/CMI are listed in Table 10.4. Ten data sets were collected in Canada, while one came from the United States, consisting of data from nine different states. The Ontario and U.S. data sets comprise very large samples ($N = 76{,}496$ and $N = 42{,}384$, respectively, with alphas of .92 and .90 from Studies 6 and 7 in Table 10.4). The alpha coefficients for the complete 43-item scale were consistently high, ranging from .88 to .92, with an average of .89 (95% CI: .87 to .91). Some of the subsections had relatively high internal consistency, specifically Criminal History, with a mean alpha of .76, Education/Employment (.80), Companions (.71), and Alcohol/Drugs (.72). Others remained low, including Family/Marital (.44), Leisure/Recreation (.61), and Procriminal Attitudes (.65). As expected, the new subsection, Antisocial

Table 10.3 Internal Consistency as Measured by Cronbach's Alpha for the Total Score and Subsection Scores of LSI-R

Study	Total	CH	E/E	Fin	F/M	Acc	L/R	Co	A/DP	E/P	A/O
1	.82	.75	.74	.75	.74	.74	.74	.73	.75	.74	.76
2	.64	.62	.74	.07	.29	.06	.35	.45	.68	.38	.47
3	.71	.64	.67	.69	.67	.70	.67	.68	.71	.69	.71
4	.77	.68	.68	.71	.71	.71	.72	.70	.72	.73	.72
5	.79	.84	.81	.46	.52	.78	.67	.62	.86	.70	.66
6	.90	.83	.74	.36	.49	.54	.65	.69	.84	.69	.57
7	.90	.82	.56	.55	.28	.38	.59	.78	.80	.70	.45
8	.94	.81	.81	.53	.59	.61	.70	.59	.84	.69	.70
9	.84	.64	.82	.31	.55	.34	.69	.79	.67	.71	.98
10	.86	.74	.75	.43	.52	.44	.66	.70	.70	.70	.80
11	.88	.72	.80	.23	.49	.53	.60	.81	.81	.72	.68
12	.93	.84	.78	.39	.56	.63	.73	.46	.85	.58	.72
13	.89	.82	.79	.02	.24	.36	n.a.	.75	.82	.45	.60
Average	.84	.75	.75	.43	.52	.53	.65	.67	.78	.66	.68

Sources: 1 = Bonta, Motiuk, & Ker (1985); 2 = Andrews et al. (1983); 3 = Bonta & Motiuk (1985); 4 = Bonta & Motiuk (1986a); 5 = Wadel et al. (1981); 6 = Faulkner et al. (1992); 7 = Stevenson & Wormith (1987); 8 = Hollin, Palmer, & Clark (2003); 9 = Flores et al. (undated); 10 Lowenkamp & Latessa (undated); 11 = Holsinger et al. (undated); 12 = Palmer & Hollin (2007); 13 = Rettinger (1998).

Note: Total = Total LSI-R; CH = Criminal History; E/E = Education/Employment; Fin = Financial; F/M = Family/Marital; Acc = Accommodation; L/R = Leisure/ Recreation; Co = Companions; A/DP = Alcohol/Drug Problem; E/P = Emotional/Personal; A/O = Attitudes/Orientation; n.a. = not available.

Table 10.4 Internal Consistency as Measured by Cronbach's Alpha for the Total Score and Subsection Scores of LS/CMI

Study	Total	CH	E/E	F/M	L/R	Co	A/DP	PA/O	ASP
1	.89	.76	.87	.48	.71	.84	.46	.80	.67
2	.88	.74	.82	.39	.50	.51	.47	.78	.65
3	n.a.	.81	.82	.24	n.a.	.83	.81	.60	.60
4	.91	.80	.79	.32	.56	.67	.78	.47	.50
5	.87	.64	.78	.45	.46	.70	.78	.35	.48
6	.92	.86	.84	.39	.49	.63	.82	.62	.54
7	.90	.70	.75	.57	.67	.72	.84	.82	.51
8	.88	.78	.73	.69	.86	.77	.76	.76	.76
9	.86	.65	.76	.35	.45	.61	.87	.45	.43
10	n.a.	.73	.85	.52	.71	.62	.83	.67	.52
Average	.89	.75	.80	.44	.60	.69	74	.63	.57

Sources: 1 = Andrews (inmates; 1995); 2 = Andrews (probationers; 1995); 3 = Rettinger (1998); 4 = Girard (1999); 5 = Rowe (1996); 6 = Andrews, Bonta, & Wormith (Ontario: 2004); 7 = Andrews, Bonta, & Wormith (U.S.; 2004); 8 = Nowicki-Sroga (2003); 9 = Simourd (2004); 10 = Mills, Jones, & Kroner (2005).

Note: Total = Total LS/CMI; CH = Criminal History; E/E = Education/Employment; F/M = Family/ Marital; L/R = Leisure/ Recreation; Co = Companions; A/DP = Alcohol/Drug Problem; PA/O = Procriminal Attitudes/Orientation; ASP = Antisocial Pattern; n.a. = not available.

Pattern, with an average alpha of .59, produced low coefficients because, by design, it included items from all other subsections of the LS/CMI.

Inter-Rater Reliability and Test-Retest Reliability

A number of studies have examined "pure" inter-rater reliability with little (less than a month) or no interval between test administrations. For example, in their initial research, Andrews (1982a), Andrews and Robinson (1984), and Sparring (1982) reported correlations of .88, .92, and .87, respectively, for the LSI-R on a sample of Ontario probationers. Andrews and Robinson (1984) obtained retest reliabilities of .95 to .99 with the same assessor readministering the instrument within one month. Rettinger (1998) examined the inter-rater reliability of LSI-R scores from the files of 136 women offenders in Ontario. She obtained a correlation of .92 between raters for the total score. Thus, the mean inter-rater reliability of LSI-R total risk/need with short intervals is .92 (95% CI: .88 to .97, k = 6). Rettinger's subtotal inter-rater estimates ranged from .96 for Criminal History and .95 for Education/Employment to .68 for Family/Marital and .65 for Financial.

The extent to which total score reliability translates into assessor agreement on offender risk level from the LSI-R was 93% in Andrews (1982a). Austin, Coleman, Peyton, and Johnson (2003) reported that 79% of the prisoners were assigned to the same (high, medium, or low) risk level. Although more than two-thirds of the items had rates of less than 80%, follow-up training reduced the number of such items to 37%. Unfortunately, they did not report standard inter-rater reliability estimates for LSI total scores.

Researchers have also examined the simultaneous impact of two sources of variation, time and assessor, on reliability coefficients. Using different assessors at increasing test intervals, Andrews (1982a) obtained inter-rater reliability coefficients of .88, .87, and .80, at less than one month, one to two months, and greater than two months, respectively. In a naturalistic field study, Girard (1999) identified a sample of offenders in Ontario who had been administered the LS/CMI by two different assessors within an average time interval of 26 days. The repeated administrations were triggered by various events, including a relocation of the offender, a transition from institution to community, and a referral for programming or some administrative decision. The correlation between the two assessors for the total score was .88.

In a similar examination of test–retest, inter-rater reliability, Nowicka-Sroga (2004) examined the correlations of LSI-ORs administered in the field to offenders in Ontario between 16 and 19 years of age at different time intervals. Her overall correlation was an unimpressive .57, but this was explained with a reexamination of correlations by assessment interval. Assessments within six months of each other correlated .88, those between six months and a year correlated .62, those between one and two years correlated .56, and those between two to three years correlated .22.

Not surprisingly, Girard's (1999) subtotal reliabilities were quite varied, ranging from .91 for Criminal History, .88 for Alcohol and Drug Problems, and .75 for Education/Employment, to .68 for Companions and .55 for Antisocial Pattern, to .38 for Family/Marital, .26 for Leisure/Recreation, and .16 for Procriminal Attitudes. The former sections consist of more (at least eight) static or relatively stable items, while the latter subsections consist of fewer (two to four), more dynamic items.

Working from the same set of files and interview-based information, two trained but independent assessors produced highly correlated LS/CMI General Risk/Need scores (r = .92, n = 136; Rettinger, 1998; the same as previously noted for LSI-R). The mean inter-rater estimate with variable follow-up periods was .71 (95% CI: .52 to .91, k = 8). The follow-up periods varied from less than a month (scored .5 months) through to almost three years (scored 30 months). The correlation of inter-rater reliability estimate with length of the follow-up period was a very large

–.97. As will be shown in the validity section, LS-based assessments of change possess considerable predictive validity. Thus, the test-retest reliability coefficients of the LS must be interpreted with caution, particularly if the interval between assessments is more than a few weeks. In fact, the LS was designed to reflect client changes over time, and this validated characteristic now stands as one of its hallmarks.

Reliability Between LS Versions

Comparisons between the two versions of the LS instruments bear some resemblance to "parallel forms" reliability, although the LS/CMI is actually the successor to the LSI-R in that it incorporated a number of changes, most notably fewer items and subsections. However, these "parallel forms" analyses are relevant here for three reasons. First, this chapter focuses concurrently on the LSI-R and LS/CMI, so it is helpful to appreciate their comparability. In a related fashion, one may be interested in the generalizability of validity findings from one version of the instrument to the other, although further validation is always recommended following any changes to an instrument. Finally, practitioners may work with offenders who have been assessed with both versions, or they may be in the process of transitioning from one version to the other and want to make comparisons.

The purest measure of parallel forms reliability of the LS is reported by Rowe (1996). After administering both protocols to the same group of 340 male incarcerated offenders at the same time, he reported a correlation of .96 for the total score. The two versions have seven subsections in common (recall that the LS/CMI dropped Financial, Accommodation, and Emotional/Personal and added Antisocial Personality). Three of the seven subsections that appear on both measures had correlations of 1.00 because their items remained identical (Family/Marital, Leisure/Recreation, and Procriminal Attitude/Orientation). The other items, with minor changes to the number of items or directions for scoring, also had extremely high correlations, specifically Alcohol and Drug Problems (.99), Criminal History (.96), Companions (.95), and Education/Employment (.90).

Because an offender's score on all LS/CMI items can be taken either directly from his or her corresponding items on the LSI-R or can be deduced from some combination of items on the LSI-R (Andrews et al., 2004), LSI-R data sets that include item scores can be used to generate both LSI-R and LS/CMI scores. This provides one means of determining the comparability of the two versions of the LS. Although it is likely to generate particularly high correlations because the scores are determined from the same test administration, it is this analysis that is most relevant to the above noted reasons for making such comparisons. The most thorough examination was conducted by Andrews and his colleagues (2004), who amalgamated nine samples of more than 37,000 offenders from nine different jurisdictions in the United States. Results were presented separately for institution and community offenders and nicely replicated the pattern of findings reported by Rowe (1996). The correlations for total scores, by institutional and community offenders, respectively, were .97 and .98. As necessitated by the scoring protocol, correlations of 1.00 were produced for Family/Marital, Leisure/Recreation, and Procriminal Attitudes. These were followed by Alcohol and Drug Problems (1.00 and .99), Companions (.99), Education/Employment (.97 and .97), and Criminal History (.97).

Summary of Reliability

The internal consistency of the total score of both versions of the LS is high. However, the internal consistency of individual sections is quite variable. Test-retest reliability is high over the short term, but these correlations deteriorate over time because of the dynamic nature of the instrument. Our quest for high inter-rater reliability has been instructive. Caution must be exercised by any agency that introduces the LS, particularly if a large number of examiners are going to administer the instrument. To this end, staff training is crucial. We recommend authorizing or "accrediting" an LS assessor in a correctional agency only after he or she has conducted a number of assessments to some performance criterion (e.g., agreement with expert scoring). Secondly, training should be supplemented by periodic booster sessions and audit checks of practitioners' assessments. Finally, care must be taken to ensure that assessors understand and apply the scoring criteria in a consistent and equitable fashion and, when using a hard copy version of the instrument, to ensure they are calculating the scores correctly.

Validity

Construct Validity of LSI

The general personality and social cognitive model that underlies the LS instruments hypothesizes that there are individual differences in the propensity to engage in crime and that this propensity is partly determined by variations in risk/need factors as measured by the LS subcomponents. The validity of the general construct "propensity to engage in crime" and the subconstructs/facets as measured by the LS subcomponents can be tested in many different ways. Two approaches commonly used involve factor analysis and testing the convergent/divergent validities of the construct.

As we noted earlier, construct validity as assessed by factor analysis has never been a major concern in the development of the LS instruments. In fact, there are relatively few studies on the construct validity of the LS instruments, because predictive and external validity are the most important types of evidence for the use of any offender risk/need instrument.

Factor Analytic Evidence

Factor analysis is a statistical technique that identifies underlying unities among a set of variables and can assist in identifying the number of dimensions of the LS instruments. All of the factor analytic studies involved an exploratory technique closely associated with factor analysis (principal component analysis, using varimax rotation), and all, thus far, have been conducted on the LSI-R.

The first factor analysis of the LSI-R was conducted by Andrews, Bonta, Motiuk, and Robinson (1984) using a community sample of 598 probationers and an institutional sample of 152 male inmates. Three factors emerged for the probation sample and two factors for the inmate sample. The first factor for both samples received significant factor loadings from all of the LSI-R subcomponent scores, accounting for a substantial percentage of the variance in scores (75% and 83%). This led the authors to conclude that the LSI-R measured an underlying variable described as "generalized trouble" and supports the theoretical perspective that the LSI-R taps into a general construct of "propensity to engage in crime."

Similarly, the first factor that emerged from a small study of 61 probationers and inmates by Stevenson and Wormith (1987) also reflected a propensity to engage in crime (labeled "antisocial"). Loza and Simourd (1994) also found that the first factor yielded in their analysis of LSI-R scores on 161 male inmates was "Criminal Lifestyle" (accounted for 27% of the total variance), and the second factor was labeled "Emotional/Personal" (23% of the variance). In contrast to the previous findings, a large sample of 580 inmates (Bonta & Motiuk, 1986a) found that the first factor, accounting for 33.8% of the variance, was loaded by the Emotional/Personality subcomponent (factor loading of .74), and it was the second factor (13% of the variance) that reflected a troublesome, deviant lifestyle (e.g., Criminal History and Alcohol/Drugs had factor loadings exceeding .71).

Factor analytic studies have yielded either one-factor (Palmer & Hollin, 2007), two-factor (Andrews et al., 1984; Bonta & Motiuk, 1986a; Hollin, Palmer, & Clark, 2003; Loza & Simourd, 1994; Simourd & Malcolm, 1998), or three-factor solutions (Andrews et al., 1984; Bonta &

Motiuk, 1986b, Stevenson & Wormith, 1987). Both Bonta and Motiuk (1986b) and Stephenson and Wormith (1987) labeled the third factor as "subcultural" (significant loadings from the Companions subcomponent) and, therefore, highly related to the general construct of propensity to engage in crime. In summary, factor analytic studies of the LSI-R, whether they produce one, two, or three factors all have generated one factor that measures a propensity to engage in crime. This propensity is now better reflected in LS/CMI General Risk/Need with the addition of Antisocial Pattern and the movement of Emotional/Personal, Financial, and Accommodation items to Section 4. Perhaps it is time for a new commitment to understanding the factor structure of the LS instruments. For example, the editors of this collection have suggested a confirmatory as opposed to the exploratory approaches conducted to date.

Convergent–Divergent Validity

Evidence for a construct is provided when different measures of the same construct intercorrelate higher (convergent validity) than measures of a different construct (divergent validity). For example, if the LSI-R subcomponent Family/Marital measures difficulties in this domain, then the subcomponent score should correlate with an alternative measure of family and marital problems. At the same time, the subcomponent score should demonstrate a smaller correlation with a measures of dissimilar constructs, such as ties to offenders (divergent validity). Although analyses of both the convergent and divergent validities of a construct are recommended, most studies of the LS instruments provided only convergent validity evidence. Once again, all of the studies on the convergent validity of the LS instruments have been limited to the LSI-R.

The main results from studies on the convergent validity of the LSI-R subcomponents are presented in Table 10.5. Some studies (e.g., Andrews, 1982a) reported the simple correlations between the alternate measure and the LSI-R subcomponent even when more than one measure was available. In three cases (Andrews & Robinson, 1984; Bonta & Motiuk, 1985; Simourd & Malcolm, 1998) divergent validity information was also reported, and in these studies the convergent validity estimates exceeded the divergent validity estimate.

Predictive Validity

An offender risk/need assessment instrument is of limited value if scores on the instrument do not predict criminal behavior. Evidence of predictive validity is a *sine qua non* requirement for any assessment instrument that purports to measure the risk for reoffending.

When it comes to predictive validity, there are few offender assessment instruments that have been the subject of as much research as the LSI-R. Gendreau, Little, and Goggin (1996) conducted the first meta-analytic review of the predictive validity of the LSI-R in relation to any officially recorded general recidivism (arrest, conviction, or incarceration). The mean effect size (Pearson r), adjusted for sample size, was .33 for the LSI-R ($N = 4{,}579$). Although the effect size was not significantly greater than the effect sizes found for other commonly used instruments such as the Salient Factor Score or the Wisconsin Risk assessment instrument, Gendreau et al. (1996) nevertheless concluded, because of the fact that the LSI-R also measures criminogenic needs, that "of the available risk measures, the LSI-R is recommended" (p. 591).

In 2002, Gendreau, Goggin, and Smith once again examined the predictive validity of the LSI-R, but with the intention of comparing it to the Psychopathy Checklist–Revised (PCL-R) (Hare, 2003). Additional studies were gathered up to the year 2001, yielding 30 effect size estimates of general recidivism for the LSI-R (seven for the PCL-R) and nine effect size estimates of violent recidivism for the LSI-R. The adjusted mean effect size with respect to general recidivism for the LSI-R was .42 (CI of .39 to .45), and it was .28 (CI of .22 to .41) for the PCL-R. With respect to violent recidivism, the adjusted mean effect size was .29 (CI of .25 to .33) for the LSI-R, statistically indistinguishable from the PCL-R (adjusted mean effect size was .27, CI: .22 to .32).

Table 10.5 Convergent Validities of the LSI-R Subcomponents

Study	Sample	CH	EE	FM	COM	AD	EMO	ATT
Andrews, 1982a	91 probationers	r = .27–.28	r = .24–.41	r = .16–.22	r = .26		r = .16–.17	ns
Andrews et al., 1983; Andrews & Robinson, 1984; Andrews et al., 1986	192 probationers		MR = .36	r = .47	MR = .49	MR = .61	MR = .31	MR = .27
Bonta & Motiuk, 1985	75 inmates	MR = .66	MR = .58	MR = .56	r = .29	r = .34	MR = .67	
Motiuk, Motiuk, & Bonta, 1992	100 inmates		MR = .53	r = .39	r = .56	MR = .59	r = .33	MR = .60
Loza & Simourd, 1994	161 inmates	r = .70–.75	r = .30	r = .41	r = .46–.52	r = .49	r = .30	r = .38–.62
Simourd & Malcom, 1998	216 inmates	r = .76–.84	r = .20–.67	r = .17–.53	r = .39–.66	r = .13–.52	*ns*	r = .22

Notes: CH = Criminal History; EE = Employment/Education; FM = Family/Marital; COM = Companions; AD = Alcohol/Drug Problem; EMO = Emotional/Personal; ATT = Attitude/Orientation; Alternative measures for the LSI-R subcomponents Financial, Accommodations and Leisure/Recreation were unavailable. For the Emotional/Personal subcomponent, noncriminogenic needs (anxiety, self-esteem, etc.) were excluded; only criminogenic needs (e.g., self-control, sensation seeking, poor socialization) were used; MR = Multiple correlation; ns = not significant.

The most recent meta-analysis of the predictive validity of the LSI-R with general offenders comes from Mary Ann Campbell and her colleagues (Campbell, French, & Gendreau, in press), who collected studies of instruments intended to assess the risk for violent reoffending (the review period covered 1980 to 2006). Over 70 risk instruments were identified from the literature review; however, the meta-analysis was restricted to the most commonly used measures (i.e., LSI-R, PCL-R, Violence Risk Appraisal Guide [VRAG], and Historical-Clinical-Risk Management 20 [HCR-20]). Although all of the measures demonstrated satisfactory predictive validities, there were no differences in predictive accuracy among the measures. The mean effect size (unadjusted) for the LSI-R was .25 (k = 19; CI = .21 to .28). The mean Zr adjusted for sample size was .28 (CI: .25 to .31).

Finally, we would like to comment on the predictive validity of the LS/CMI, a "fourth-generation" assessment tool. Because the LS/CMI is relatively new, direct tests of its predictive validity are few (Girard & Wormith, 2004). However, given that the LS/CMI retains the risk/need assessment of the LSI-R, there is no reason not to believe that the predictive validity of the instrument will equal if not surpass the predictive validity estimates of the LSI-R (Andrews et al., 2004). Presently, the mean effect size for the LS/CMI for the prediction of general recidivism is .41 (k = 8) and .29 (k = 7) for violent recidivism, slightly better than what is found with the LSI-R (Andrews, Bonta, & Wormith, 2006).

In summary, meta-analytic reviews indicate that the validity of the LSI-R is equal to that of any other offender risk instrument, with respect to the prediction of both general and violent recidivism. It is also noteworthy that LSI-R scores predict institutional misconduct, making the instrument highly relevant to institutional classification decisions. A meta-analyses by Gendreau, Goggin, and Law (1997) found a mean effect size of $r = .22$ for the prediction of general institutional misconduct (k = 10, $N = 2{,}252$) while another meta-analysis (Campbell et al., in press) that focused on the LSI-R and *violent* misconduct reported an $r = .24$ (k = 5, $N = 650$).

Dynamic Predictive Validity

Approximately two-thirds of LS items are dynamic risk items. That is, they can change, and they are related to risk to reoffend. Dynamic risk factors predict criminal behavior as well as that accomplished by static risk factors (Gendreau et al., 1996; Mills, Kroner, & Hemmati, 2003). An important aspect of our interpretation of dynamic risk factors is that they can increase or decrease. Although some scholars have argued that criminal history is a dynamic risk factor because it is possible for criminal history to change (i.e., increase; Rice, 2007), our view of a truly dynamic risk factor is that it must be able to change in both directions. Thus, for example, employment is a dynamic risk factor (you can find a job or lose it), as is substance abuse (you can quit using drugs or you can begin using drugs), but not criminal history. Short-term changes in frequency and severity of criminal activity over time are not assessed with LS Criminal History.

Dynamic predictive validity is demonstrated when changes in total scores (made possible because of the many dynamic items comprising the instrument) predict changes in the probability of criminal behavior. The LSI-R is the only offender risk instrument that has any evidence of dynamic predictive validity. The first reports of dynamic predictive validity for the LSI-R come from two small studies by Andrews and Robinson (1984) and Motiuk, Bonta, and Andrews (1990). In the first study, 57 probationers were assessed at intake and six months later, while in the second study, 55 inmates were assessed and then reassessed approximately one year later. As shown in Table 10.6, offenders who changed in their risk level on retest showed expected changes in recidivism rates at follow-up (e.g., low-risk offenders who became high risk showed substantially higher recidivism rates than low-risk offenders who remained low risk upon reassessment).

Peter Raynor and his colleagues (Raynor, 2007; Raynor, Kynch, Roberts, & Merrington, 2000) and Thomas Arnold (2007) have conducted the largest tests of the dynamic predictive validity of the LSI-R. The periods between assessments averaged one year in the Raynor studies and 8.6 months in the study by Arnold. As can be seen from Table 10.6, support for the dynamic validity of the LSI-R is robust and replicable.

The dynamic feature of the LS instruments has two important benefits. First, it facilitates the monitoring of supervision and alerts correctional staff to the need to alter supervision requirements. For example, increases in risk scores may trigger more frequent and closer supervision by a probation officer, and decreases in scores may lead to fewer restrictions upon the offender. However, the most important benefit, as we noted in the beginning of this chapter, is that an LS instrument offers targets for service interventions. The subcomponents identify criminogenic needs that, when successfully addressed, reduce an offender's risk (i.e., adherence to the need principle). Of course, and in adherence to the risk principle, higher risk/need cases should be matched to more intensive levels of service.

External Validity

An important question with respect to validity is the extent to which an LS instrument generalizes beyond the original validation samples to other outcomes, settings, and offender samples. Meta-analytic studies reveal that the LSI-R and LS/CMI not only predict general offending but also violent offending and institutional misconduct. Other outcomes predicted by the LSI-R and LS/CMI scores include halfway house success (Bonta & Motiuk, 1985, 1987, 1990), parole violations (Bonta & Higginbottom, 1991; Bonta & Motiuk, 1990; Rowe, 1996), and partner abuse (Hanson & Wallace-Capretta, 2000). Recent research has demonstrated the validity of the LSI-R with samples from Singapore (Neo, Yen, Chng, Misir, & Goh, in press), the United Kingdom (Hollin & Palmer, 2006; Raynor, 2007, Raynor et al., 2000), Australia (Cumberland & Boyle, 1997), and Germany (Dahle, 2006). Studies have also shown the applicability of the instrument with Native offenders (Bonta, 1989; Holsinger, Lowenkamp, & Latessa, 2006) and mentally disordered offenders (Andrews, Dowden, & Rettinger, 2001; Harris, Rice, & Quinsey, 1993). There is even a promising study suggesting validity with sex offenders, but this study reports only convergent and concurrent validity (Simourd & Malcolm, 1998). Although much remains to be done with the LS instruments around the issue of ethnicity (Schlager & Simourd, 2007; Whiteacre, 2006), the evidence thus far has been quite positive. These replications and

Table 10.6 The Dynamic Predictive Validity of the LSI-R: Percent Recidivism (*n*)

			Reassessment Risk	
Study	***N***	**Intake Risk**	**Low**	**High**
Andrews & Robinson (1984)	57	Low	4.2 (24)	28.6 (7)
		High	0.0 (5)	57.1 (21)
Motiuk et al. (1990)	55	Low	0.0 (16)	33.3 (3)
		High	0.0 (3)	54.5 (33)
Raynor et al. (2000)	157	Low	26.2 (42)	54.8 (31)
England & Wales sample		High	55.3 (47)	78.4 (37)
Raynor (2007)	203	Low	29.0 (69)	59.0 (29)
Jersey sample		High	54.0 (84)	76.0 (21)
Arnold (2007)	1064	Low	13.0 (270)	26.0 (277)
		High	32.0 (378)	54.0 (139)

Note: Andrews & Robinson (1984) recoded into two risk categories from the original four.

widespread applicability are to be expected, because the LS instruments are based upon a general social learning theory. One area that has received considerable attention has been around the validity of the LSI-R and LS/CMI with female offenders.

Feminist scholars criticize risk assessment instruments that were largely developed on male offender samples for ignoring female-specific risk factors (Hardyman & Van Voorhis, 2004). The LS instruments have not been spared such criticism (Reisig, Holtfreter, & Morash, 2006). The original LSI-R validation study (Andrews, 1982a) had only 102 female offenders. Furthermore, the items forming the LSI-R were drawn from studies predominately comprised of male offenders. The search for empirically based, female-specific risk factors, however, has been fraught with controversy (Daigle, Cullen, & Wright, 2007). Moreover, with the LS/CMI now including potentially relevant female risk/need/responsivity factors, the criticism of ignoring female specific risk factors may be muted.

There are two, as yet unpublished, meta-analyses that provide evidence for the validity of the LSI-R with female offenders. The first by Goggin and Gendreau (2004) found an average effect size (r) of .41 (CI: .35 to .48, k = 14, N = 2,259). A second, larger meta-analysis was conducted by Lowenkamp and his colleagues (Lowenkamp, Smith, Latessa, & Cullen, 2007). They reviewed 25 studies that yielded 27 effect size estimates with 14,737 female offenders. This is a very recent literature with 63% of the data generated after 1999. The mean effect size was r = .35 (CI: .34 to .37), nearly identical to the effect size reported by Gendreau and colleagues for men (1996, 2002). In addition, some of the studies permitted a within-study gender analysis (k = 16). For males the mean effect size was .26 (CI: .25 to .27), and for females it was .27 (CI: .26 to .30).

The Risk Principle and the LS Instruments

The risk principle directs that intensive levels of services are to be reserved for medium- to high-risk offenders, while less intensive services are provided to low-risk offenders. The evidence for the risk principle now appears beyond question (Andrews & Bonta, 2006; Andrews & Dowden, 2006; Hanley, 2006; Lovins, Lowenkamp, Latessa, & Smith, 2007; Lowenkamp, Latessa, & Holsinger, 2006; Marlowe, Festinger, Lee, Dugosh, & Benasutti, 2006; Palmer, McGuire, Hatcher, Hounsome, Bilby, & Hollin, 2008). Risk in most studies, however, has been assessed by relatively simple measures (for example, a compilation of criminal history variables). There have been a few studies specifically testing the risk principle with the LSI-R as the measure of offender risk. Here, there is the expectation that use of the LSI-R to make decisions on assigning the appropriate level of service would result in lower rates of recidivism.

In the first test of the risk principle with the LSI-R, Andrews and Robinson (1984; Andrews et al., 1984) randomly assigned 190 probationers to either routine supervision or an augmented service (joint supervision by a professional probation officer coupled with a volunteer). High-risk offenders who received augmented services demonstrated lower recidivism rates than high-risk offenders receiving routine probation services (28% vs. 58%, respectively). Low-risk offenders receiving augmented services showed an increase in recidivism compared to their counterparts who received routine supervision (7% to 14%), although the latter differences were not statistically significant. This interaction effect between LSI-R risk level and service level has been replicated by the authors of the LSI-R (Bonta & Motiuk, 1987, 1990; Bonta, Wallace-Capretta, & Rooney, 2000; Motiuk & Bonta, 1991) and independent researchers (Bourgon & Armstrong, 2005).

What is notable about the Risk/Need-by-Service interaction is not only that higher-risk offenders benefit from enhanced services, but that lower-risk offenders are not subjected to unnecessary restrictions of liberty. In a number of studies, it was clearly demonstrated that application of the LSI-R would result in more appropriate levels of supervision than relying on routine classification procedures. For example, Bonta and Motiuk (1987, 1990) have shown that using the LSI-R to identify lower-risk inmates for placement in a correctional halfway house resulted in more inmates being diverted to community-based residential facilities. In another study (Bonta & Motiuk, 1992), use of the LSI-R to inform custodial security placement decisions was estimated to reduce rates of overclassification by 38%.

Summary of Validity

The concurrent, divergent, and most importantly, predictive validity of the LS instruments is well established. Additional studies on the factor structure of the instrument and evidence of convergent–divergent validity is welcomed. The evidence on predictive validity is substantial, and this research also expands on the many uses of the LS instruments (not the least of which is the prediction of violence, including violent institutional misconduct). Validity with many different offender samples (e.g., women, mentally disordered, racial minorities) has also been demonstrated. The evidence of dynamic predictive validity opens the door to the use of the instruments for case planning and monitoring. More work is needed (e.g., the predictive validity of the subcomponents, the role of assessing strengths and responsivity factors, predictive validity with sex offenders), and we are certain, especially with the recently developed LS/CMI, this research will come.

Limitations and Necessary Future Research

In summary, LSI-R and LS/CMI General Risk Need have yielded an impressive array of validity coefficients of considerable utility. In prediction of both general recidivism and violence, LS risk/need does as well or better than alternative assessment instruments. Unique to the LS instruments is the extensive evidence of dynamic predictive criterion validity, wherein changes in dynamic item scores are associated with shifts in reoffending rates. Also unique is the evidence of LSI-R Risk/Need-by-Service interaction. In brief, use of the LS renders decisions reliable, valid, and transparent. In the process, public protection is enhanced by assigning supervision and service according to risk/need, cost-effectiveness is enhanced by assigning low-risk cases to minimal supervision and service, as is implementation of the least restrictive and least costly interpretation of the penalty while respecting public protection.

Some limitations are specific to the LS products, while others are limitations of the field as a whole. Most notably, apart from LSI-R: SV, the LS instruments include many more items than are required to assess risk. Indeed, there is no need to conduct an LSI-R or LS/CMI assessment if all that is required is a one-time determination of level of risk. The need, responsivity, and other information is not required unless service planning is required. Generally, however, LSI-R: SV has been the focus of very little research, in particular in the prediction of violence (Daffern, Ogloff, Ferguson, & Thomson, 2005; Yessine & Bonta, 2006).

A specific hypothesis is that use of LS/CMI will enhance service planning and delivery that is in adherence with RNR and hence promote positive intermediate and ultimate outcomes. These research projects may be grand in design and implementation or designed on a smaller scale. The findings will contribute directly to understanding assessment issues but also to theories of criminal conduct and to the theory and practice of effective crime prevention. Intersite and interagency studies with LS/CMI will promote understanding of the contributions of broader social and cultural contexts to service planning and delivery and to outcomes. We have had a long-term interest in the interconnections among: (1) worker factors, (2) case factors, (3) service plans, (4) service delivery, (5) intermediate outcomes, and (6) ultimate outcome (Andrews & Kiessling, 1980; Hoge & Andrews, 1986). Agencies employing the LS/CMI have the opportunity to turn their service sites into field experiments. These data will provide quantitative estimates of the value of shifts in service and supervision.

LSI-R has been doing a decent job at predicting violence, but the evidence is mounting that specific attention to Section 2.1 and Section 2.2 of LS/CMI will enhance predictive validity through attention to a history of assault and anger management skill deficits (Barnoski, 2003; Girard & Wormith, 2004; Rettinger & Andrews, 2007).

According to available evidence, the predictive validity of LS risk/need is very robust across different types of people. However, some developmental and psychological criminologists and some feminist criminologists have suggested that age of onset and gender-specific pathways to crime are important moderators of the predictive validity of risk/need factors. Both deserve further exploration.

The interpersonal, familial, and marital factors may be less important predictors for persistent offenders with an early start to their careers than for late-starting offenders (Quinsey, Harris, Rice, & Cormier, 2006). It has been said that LS-type risk/need is irrelevant for female offenders following "gendered" pathways to crime (Reisig et al., 2006). "Gendered" pathways entail various combinations of early abuse, ongoing abuse, being harmed and being harmful, drug involvement, homelessness, and street crime, including the sex trade. Nongendered pathways entail economically motivated crime without the abuse history and pathology evident in gendered crime. One study of any officially recorded rule violations over a mean period of less than a year found that the recidivism of 155 women with a gendered pathway to crime was unpredictable by LSI-R scores, age, education, and minority status. Indeed, it could not be predicted by anything other than interoffender variation in the amount of time spent looking for it (that is, length of follow-up) (Reisig et al., 2006). The recidivism of the remaining 80 women was predicted by LSI-R scores. Rettinger and Andrews (2007) found that a strong LSI-recidivism link was maintained in over 100 different contexts, many of which are often called "gender specific." In view of the strong meta-analytic support for the predictive validity of LSI-R with female offenders (as shown in the validity section of this chapter with a total *N* exceeding 14,000) many female offenders must be following nongendered pathways to crime. Among many other considerations is the possibility that the as yet nonreplicated result of Reisig and colleagues is being overinterpreted.

We are in the process of compiling existing risk/need databanks in order to produce quantitative meta-analytic estimates of the relative, incremental, and moderator validities of LS general risk/need, age, gender, ethnicity, and gender-informed factors. We appreciate the importance of maximizing the applicability of risk/need assessments to all offenders, regardless of age, gender, and ethnicity, and strive to that end.

Case Example: An LS/CMI Assessment of a High-Risk/Need Offender

Michael Cooper is serving a sentence of three years for armed robbery, possession of a dangerous weapon, and escaping lawful custody. This is his fifth term of imprisonment. Mr. Cooper has reached his parole eligibility date, and he is under review for possible parole release. An assessment was requested to advise the parole board on Mr. Cooper's likelihood of completing his period of parole supervision without reoffending or violating the terms of his release and to identify services and strategies that would maximize his chances of success.

CRIMINAL HISTORY

Mr. Cooper has accumulated 24 prior convictions, including five previous assaults (all nonsexual), one of which occurred while in custody. His first arrest occurred at age 14 for shoplifting. Mr. Cooper has never been on probation or parole. His first offense as an adult was for assaulting a police officer, and he was sentenced to six months in jail. Police were called to a disturbance in a bar, and when they confronted a drunken Mr. Cooper, he swore at them and took a swing at one of the officers. Previous parole applications were always denied.

Mr. Cooper escaped from the minimum security camp to which he was transferred after serving half of his current prison term. He was working on a road gang and absconded when the supervising staff's attention was diverted. Mr. Cooper was apprehended a few hours later. Records indicate that Mr. Cooper has had 15 prior institutional misconducts ranging from possession of contraband (drugs) to assaulting staff. The assault on a staff member occurred when he was told to go to his cell following an argument with another inmate. Mr. Cooper pushed a correctional officer and warned that he knew where the officer lived, so he had better watch out. Following his escape and assault, Mr. Cooper was transferred to a maximum security facility where he is currently housed.

Repeated efforts were required to have Mr. Cooper attend an interview for his parole assessment. When he finally did attend an interview, he asked if the meeting would take long because he had to get to the gym for his workout. When asked to describe the present offenses, Mr. Cooper painted a picture of an innocent man who was wrongly convicted. He says that he and his friends were returning from a hunting trip when they were pulled over by the police. Apparently a local convenience store was robbed and the description of the suspects matched Mr. Cooper and his two friends. Arrest records and court transcripts are in conflict with this view. Both hidden camera and eyewitness evidence were used in the trial to confirm that Mr. Cooper and his friends were indeed the correct suspects. The witnesses testified that the perpetrators appeared to be under the influence of drugs, and that guns were used to threaten the clerk. Although the offenses were committed with two accomplices, there is no evidence that the crimes were part of gang activity or organized crime. The co-defendants were friends of Mr. Cooper, one of whom he had met while in prison, and the other was a long-time criminal associate.

EDUCATION/EMPLOYMENT

Mr. Cooper reported that he had numerous difficulties in school as he was growing up. He repeated grade 3, and he was placed into special education classes when he was 11 years old. Mr. Cooper remembered seeing the school psychologists for "tests," but could not elaborate any further. His difficulties in keeping up with the academic work and frustration over his poor reading skills ("I would get my 'b's and 'd's mixed up") led to numerous conflicts with other students, who teased him, and with teachers. Suspensions were frequent, and he finally left school when he was 16 years old and midway through grade 9.

After Mr. Cooper left school, which coincided with his leaving home, he lived either with friends or on the street. He supported himself by relying on the charity of others, committing crimes, or receiving welfare assistance. Mr. Cooper never worked for more than a few weeks at a time and either quit or was fired. He was not working prior to this term of imprisonment, and he has no employment offer upon release. As indicated by Mr. Cooper's employment history, he has no legitimate means of financial support. He has never worked long enough to establish a credit rating or save money. All his income appears to derive from illegitimate activities or from social assistance programs. He owes money to others for drugs and worries about meeting up with these individuals in the community.

FAMILY/MARITAL

At present, Mr. Cooper is single. He had a common-law partner prior to incarceration, and she left him shortly after sentencing. His third assault conviction occurred during a domestic dispute about his drug use. Mr. Cooper claims that he pushed his girlfriend out of the way in order to leave the apartment and meet his friends at a local bar. She fell and sustained bruises but was not injured otherwise. In Mr. Cooper's view, he treated her well, like all of his other girlfriends, and he denied feeling upset over her departure and said that "there are other fish in the sea." He is in no hurry to find a new girlfriend, and says that he wants to enjoy his bachelorhood when released.

Mr. Cooper receives weekly visits from his mother and sister. His older brother will visit about once a month, but he has not spoken with his younger brother for three months because of this brother's recent incarceration for theft charges. Mr. Cooper described his family as close knit and stated that he is always welcomed at his mother's home. However, he does not wish to impose on her, saying that she has had a difficult life with his father. His father was a violent man who would often beat her and sometimes the children. Mr. Cooper denied any sexual abuse from the father, and his closeness to his mother made up for the father's aloofness. Eventually, Mr. Cooper ran away from home because of this situation. The father was subsequently arrested and imprisoned, and died in prison from a drug overdose. Mr. Cooper reported that he could have returned home, but by then he had become used to living on his own. Although Mr. Cooper has not lived at home for many years, he still visits his mother and siblings regularly. They spend special occasions together, and during these gatherings an uncle (on his mother's side) and someone who he greatly admires usually attends. Mr. Cooper describes these gatherings as happy events filled with laughter and emotional warmth.

LEISURE/RECREATION

It comes as little surprise that Mr. Cooper shows little interest in legitimate activities. Quite the opposite, he expressed disdain about people who would spend all day "doing the 9 to 5" in order to make enough money to give to charities so that people like himself can get "food for free." When asked if he had ever participated in an organized activity such as the Kiwanis organization or a church group, he went into a long diatribe of what a waste of time it is to do something for no money. When asked to describe a typical day on the street, Mr. Cooper responded that it was all "sex, drugs, and rock and roll." Most of his spare time is spent with friends in bars, which is where his fourth assault charge took place. When a stranger would not give up a pool table to other waiting patrons, Mr. Cooper struck the man with a pool cue. No injuries were sustained, but the police were called.

COMPANIONS

Mr. Cooper began stealing when he was 14 years old, and after leaving home and school, he quickly established himself within a criminal social network. Never having worked, he has also never established any relationships with noncriminal individuals. Mr. Cooper further volunteered that he enjoys his life on the street and the excitement of crime. His friends are described as loyal associates who look after each other and help each other when in trouble.

ALCOHOL/DRUG PROBLEMS

After leaving home, Mr. Cooper soon took up drinking with the people he met. He reported that his alcohol use "got pretty bad," but that he left the drinking behind when he was introduced to cocaine. For Mr. Cooper, injecting cocaine is described as a wonderful sensation, and he was hooked right from the first time.

Much of Mr. Cooper's life appears to revolve around cocaine. He steals in order to buy the drug, which he uses on a daily basis when in the community. When imprisoned for the present offenses, Mr. Cooper had to be supervised in the prison hospital during detoxification. He had been rushed to hospitals on numerous occasions as a result of unintentional drug overdoses and advised by doctors that his cocaine abuse was affecting his heart. Despite feelings of paranoia when taking large amounts of cocaine, Mr. Cooper said that would continue taking the drug for the powerful rush it gives. He did admit that he cannot continue such a destructive path, but he felt he was still young and healthy enough to handle it, and that he will quit when he is older. Although none of his offenses have been for drug possession or trafficking, his fifth assault charge occurred in the residence of a known drug dealer. Mr. Cooper insists that he had simply accompanied some friends to the residence when a dispute broke out over "business," and neighbors heard the fracas and called the police. The resident claimed that he had been assaulted without provocation.

ATTITUDE/ORIENTATION

Throughout the interview Mr. Cooper expressed attitudes and values supportive of criminal behavior. He described his criminal friends in glowing terms and stated that victims of some of his crimes "had it coming to them," and most of the laws "that I supposedly broke are stupid." Prosocial activities were devalued and ridiculed. A good illustration is Mr. Cooper's views on volunteer organizations. As noted earlier, Mr. Cooper states that he was wrongly arrested and convicted, and his frequent institutional misconducts and reluctance to attend this preparole interview reflect a negative attitude toward following correctional rules. When asked how he would feel about reporting to a parole officer on a regular basis if paroled, Mr. Cooper answered that he saw no need to do this, since he should not have been imprisoned in the first place.

OTHER CLIENT (EXAMINEE) ISSUES

Mr. Cooper has not had a stable residence since leaving his mother's home. Between his frequent incarcerations, Mr. Cooper has lived either with friends, at hostels, or, in good weather, on the street. During his last release, he had lived in five different places. His friends are all known offenders, and the temporary shelters where he has lived are situated in neighborhoods with high levels of criminal activity.

Except for special education classes and the school psychologists, Mr. Cooper has never seen a mental health professional. Mr. Cooper described himself as an outgoing and energetic person who will not back down from a confrontation. He has no respect for people who try to exert their authority over him. He denied any feelings of nervousness, insomnia, or physical complaints. None of the drug overdoses were classified as suicide attempts, and he denies any hallucinations or delusions save when he injects too much cocaine.

In reviewing prison files and the results from the interview, it appears that Mr. Cooper has not formed any enduring emotional attachments to others. Despite what he reports about relationships with his mother and siblings, they appear transitory. He sees them only on special occasions or when he needs some money (his mother and younger sister have often loaned him money). He has had numerous relationships, but none have lasted more than a few months. When describing past assaults, Mr. Cooper showed no remorse over his actions and insists that either he was the "real" victim or the victim "deserved it." Further assessment into the possibility of a personality disorder may be warranted because it may have a bearing on how this examinee needs to be supervised and his responsiveness to treatment.

SUMMARY AND RECOMMENDATIONS

From all indications in Mr. Cooper's record and interview, there appears to be little motivation to change his criminal lifestyle. Mr. Cooper's score of 36 on the LS/CMI placed him in the "Very High" range for risk of reoffending (see Table 10.7). Within one year of release, 61% of offenders with similar scores were convicted for a new crime, leading to a custodial sentence (Andrews et al., 2004). Girard and Wormith (2004) reported that 83% of a sample of nonsex offenders in the Very High risk category was convicted of a new offense within 2.5 years of their release from custody. Moreover, almost half (48%) of them were convicted of a new violent offense compared to 24% for all nonsex offenders (the base rate). The assessment did not produce any information suggesting that his risk level should be overridden to a lower level (Table 10.7). Although there have not been any serious injuries as a result of Mr. Cooper's violent outbursts, he is considered to be at continued risk for both general and violent recidivism. The diversity of victims, locations, and circumstances of his violence suggest a generalized pattern of violent and property crime, most of which has been linked to his drug use and general antisocial lifestyle.

The results also indicate a number of areas that must be addressed if Mr. Cooper is to decrease his risk of both violent and nonviolent criminal behavior. He is severely addicted to cocaine, all his peers are criminal,

Table 10.7 A Risk/Need Profile (LS/CMI) of a High-Risk/Needs Offender (Michael Cooper)

Risk/Need	CH	E/E	F/M	L/R	Co	A/DP	PA/O	ASP	Total	R/N1	Override
Very High	8	**8–9**	4	—	**4**	7–8	**4**	**4**	**30+**	**Very High**	**Very High**
High	**6–7**	6–7	3	**2**	3	**5–6**	3	3	20–29	High	High
Medium	4–5	4–5	2	1	2	3–4	2	2	11–19	Medium	Medium
Low	2–3	2–3	**1**	—	1	1–2	1	1	5–10	Low	Low
Very Low	0–1	0–1	0	0	0	0	0	0	0–4	Very Low	Very Low

Source: Andrews, Bonta, & Wormith (2004). *Level of Service/Case Management Inventory: An Offender Assessment System: User's Manual.* Multi-Health Systems, Sample Items. (Copyright 2004, Multi-Health Systems, Inc. Reproduced with permission.)

Notes: CH = Criminal History; E/E = Education/Employment; F/M = Family/Marital; L/R = Leisure/Recreation; Co = Companions; A/DP = Alcohol/Drug Problem; PA/O = Procriminal Attitudes/Orientation; ASP = Antisocial Pattern; R/N1 = Score-based Risk/Need level; Override = Risk/Need level if override used; Examinee scores and categories are presented in **bold**.

he has no employment or academic skills, he has a low frustration tolerance, and he shows extremely supportive attitudes toward criminal behavior and negative attitudes toward prosocial behavior. Items that were flagged in the Specific Risk/Need Factors section of the LS/CMI for further attention include the following: clear problems of compliance; threat from third party; problem solving/self-management skill deficits; anger management deficits; intimidating/controlling; poor social skills; physical assault, extrafamilial (adult victim); physical assault, intrafamilial (partner victim); assault on an authority figure; and weapon use. The only strength in Mr. Cooper's profile is his positive relationship with his mother. At least, in her home he abstains from drug use, although it is difficult to ascertain how long he would be able to avoid drugs and violence by simply residing in her home. Nevertheless, Mr. Cooper's relationship with his mother can serve as a possible strength on which to build a case management plan.

Until Mr. Cooper accepts a willingness to try to cease using cocaine and abandon his violent and criminal lifestyle, an early release would not be recommended. While imprisoned, continued efforts should be made to engage Mr. Cooper in working in the prison industry and seeking psychological counseling to focus on his anger, drug abuse, and procriminal attitudes. When Mr. Cooper is released to the community either on parole or postrelease supervision, there are a number of suggestions for his community case management. Mr. Cooper should be required to reside at his mother's house. Apparently, this is one place where he does not use drugs. A referral to an intensive outpatient substance abuse program for offenders is strongly recommended. Participation in a weekly anger management program that targets aggressive behavior through social skills training and self-control is recommended. Intensive supervision commensurate with his degree of risk is also recommended.

References

American Educational Research Association, American Psychological Association, & National Council on Measurement in Education. (1999). *The standards for educational and psychological testing.* Washington, DC: American Educational Research Association.

Andrews, D. A. (1982a). *The Level of Supervision Inventory (LSI): The first follow-up.* Toronto, ON, Canada: Ontario Ministry of Correctional Services.

Andrews, D. A. (1982b). *A personal, interpersonal and community-reinforcement perspective on deviant behaviour (PIC-R).* Toronto, ON, Canada: Ontario Ministry of Correctional Services.

Andrews, D. A. (1995). The psychology of criminal conduct and effective treatment. In James McGuire (Ed.), *What works: Reducing re-offending* (pp. 35–62). Chichester: John Wiley & Sons.

Andrews, D. A. (2001). Principles of effective correctional programs. In L. L. Motiuk & R. C. Serin (Eds.), *Compendium 2000 on effective correctional programming* (pp. 9–17). Ottawa, ON, Canada: Correctional Services of Canada.

Andrews, D. A., & Bonta, J. (1995). *Level of Service Inventory–Revised.* Toronto, ON, Canada: Multi-Health Systems.

Andrews, D. A., & Bonta, J. (1998). *Level of Service Inventory–Revised: Screening Version.* Toronto, ON, Canada: Multi-Health Systems.

Andrews, D. A., & Bonta, J. (2006). *The psychology of criminal conduct* (4th ed.). Newark, NJ: LexisNexis/Matthew Bender.

Andrews, D. A., Bonta, J., & Hoge, R .D. (1990). Classification for effective rehabilitation: Rediscovering psychology. *Criminal Justice and Behavior, 17,* 19–52.

Andrews, D. A., Bonta, J., Motiuk, L. L., & Robinson, D. (1984). Some psychometrics of practical risk/needs assessment. Paper presented at the Annual Meeting of the American Psychological Association, Toronto, ON, Canada.

Andrews, D. A., Bonta, J., & Wormith, S. J. (2004). *The Level of Service/Case Management Inventory (LS/CMI).* Toronto, ON, Canada: Multi-Health Systems.

Andrews, D. A., Bonta, J., & Wormith, S. J. (2006). The recent past and near future of risk/need assessment. *Crime & Delinquency, 52, 7–27.*

Andrews, D. A., Bonta, J., & Wormith, S. J. (forthcoming). *The Level of Service/Risk-Need-Responsivity (LS/RNR).* Toronto, ON, Canada: Multi-Health Systems.

Andrews, D. A., & Dowden, C. (2006). Risk principle of case classification in correctional treatment. *International Journal of Offender Therapy and Comparative Criminology, 50,* 88–100.

Andrews, D. A., & Dowden, C. (2007). The Risk-Need-Responsivity model of assessment and human service in prevention and corrections: Crime-prevention jurisprudence. *Canadian Journal of Criminology and Criminal Justice, 50,* 439–464.

Andrews, D. A., Dowden, C., & Rettinger, J. L. (2001). Special populations within Canada. In J. A. Winterdyck (Ed.), *Corrections in Canada: Social reactions to crime* (pp. 170–212). Toronto, ON, Canada: Prentice Hall.

Andrews, D. A., & Kiessling, J. J. (1979). Volunteers and the one-to-one supervision of adult probationers. Toronto, ON, Canada: Ontario Ministry of Correctional Services.

Andrews, D. A., & Kiessling, J. J. (1980). Program structure and effective correctional practices: A summary of the CaVIC research. In R. R. Ross & P. Gendreau (Eds.), *Effective correctional treatment* (pp. 439–463). Toronto, ON, Canada: Butterworth.

Andrews, D. A., Kiessling, J. J., Mickus, S., & Robinson, D. (1986, June). Some convergent and divergent validities of the LSI. Paper presented to the annual meeting of the Canadian Psychological Association, Winnipeg, MB, Canada.

Andrews, D. A., & Robinson, D. (1984). *The Level of Supervision Inventory: Second report.* Toronto, ON, Canada: Ontario Ministry of Correctional Services.

Archer, R. P., Buffington-Vollum, J. K., Stredny, R. V., & Handel, R. W. (2006). A survey of psychological test use patterns among forensic psychologists. *Journal of Personality Assessment, 87,* 84–94.

Arnold, T. (2007). *Dynamic changes in the Level of Service Inventory–Revised (LSI-R) scores and the effects on prediction accuracy.* Master's dissertation, St. Cloud University, St. Cloud, MN.

Austin, J., Coleman, D., Peyton, J., & Johnson, K. D. (2003). *Reliability and validity of the LSI-R risk assessment instrument.* Washington, DC: The Institute of Crime, Justice and Corrections, George Washington University.

Baird, S. C., Heinz, R. C., & Bemus, B. J. (1979). The Wisconsin case classification and staff development project: A two-year follow-up report. Madison, WI: Wisconsin Division of Corrections.

Barnoski, R. (2003). *Washington's Offender Accountability Act: An analysis of the Department of Corrections' risk assessment.* Olympia, WA: Washington State Institute for Public Policy.

Barton, M. & Jenkins, W. L. (1973). *The maladaptive behavior record.* Felmore, AL: National Technical Information Services.

Bonta, J. (1989). Native inmates: Institutional response, risk, and needs. *Canadian Journal of Criminology, 31,* 49–62.

Bonta, J., & Andrews, D. A. (2007). *Risk-need-responsivity model for offender assessment and treatment.* (User Report No. 2007–06). Ottawa, ON, Canada: Public Safety Canada.

Bonta, J., & Higginbottom, S. (1991). Parole risk prediction: A pilot project. Paper presented at the 121st Congress of the American Corrections Association, Minneapolis, MN.

Bonta, J., & Motiuk, L. L. (1985). Utilization of an interview-based classification instrument: A study of correctional half-way houses. *Criminal Justice & Behavior, 12,* 333–352.

Bonta, J., & Motiuk, L. L. (1986a). Use of the Level of Supervision Inventory for assessing incarcerates. Paper presented at the 94th Annual Convention of the American Psychological Association, Washington, DC.

Bonta, J., Motiuk, L. L. (1986b). *The LSI in institutions: Toronto Jail, Hamilton-Wentworth Detention Centre, Ottawa-Carleton Detention Centre.* Report # 1. Toronto, ON, Canada: Ontario Ministry of Correctional Services.

Bonta, J., & Motiuk, L. L. (1987). The diversion of incarcerated offenders to correctional halfway houses. *Journal of Research in Crime and Delinquency, 24,* 302–323.

Bonta, J., & Motiuk, L. L. (1990). Classification to halfway houses: A quasi-experimental evaluation. *Criminology, 28,* 497–506.

Bonta, J., & Motiuk, L. L. (1992). Inmate classification. *Journal of Criminal Justice, 20,* 343–353.

Bonta, J., Motiuk, L. L., & Ker, K. (1985). *The Level of Supervision Inventory (LSI) among incarcerated offenders.* Report # 1. Toronto, ON, Canada: Ontario Ministry of Correctional Services.

Bonta, J., Wallace-Capretta, S., & Rooney, J. (2000). A quasi-experimental evaluation of an intensive rehabilitation supervision program. *Criminal Justice and Behavior,* 27, 312–329.

Bourgon, G., & Armstrong, B. (2005). Transferring the principles of effective treatment into a "real world" prison setting. *Criminal Justice and Behavior, 32,* 3–25.

Campbell, M. A., French, S., & Gendreau, P. (in press). The prediction of violence in adult offenders: A meta-analytic comparison of instruments and methods of assessment. *Criminal Justice and Behavior.*

Cumberland, A. K., & Boyle, G. J. (1997). Psychometric prediction of recidivism: Utility of the risk needs inventory. *Australian and New Zealand Journal of Criminology, 30,* 72–86.

Daffern, M., Ogloff, J. R. P., Ferguson, M., & Thomson, L. (2005). Assessing risk for aggression in a forensic psychiatric hospital using the Level of Service Inventory–Revised: Screening version. *International Journal of Forensic Mental Health, 4,* 201–206.

Dahle, K.-P. (2006). Strengths and limitations of actuarial prediction of criminal re-offence in a German prison sample: A comparative study of LSI-R, HCR-20 and PCL-R. *International Journal of Law and Psychiatry, 29,* 431–442.

Daigle, L. E., Cullen, F. T., & Wright, J. P. (2007). Gender differences in the predictors of juvenile delinquency: Assessing the generality-specificity debate. *Youth Violence and Juvenile Justice, 5,* 254–286.

Faulkner, P., Andrews, D. A., Wadel, D., & Hawkins, J. (1992). *Evaluation of a client-services management system.* Ottawa, ON, Canada: Solicitor General Canada.

Flores, A. W., Lowenkamp, C. T., & Latessa, E. J. (undated). *A profile of offenders in Coles and Cumberland Counties using the LSI-R.* Cincinnati, OH: University of Cincinnati.

Gendreau, P., Goggin, C., & Law, M. (1997). Predicting prison misconducts. *Criminal Justice and Behavior, 24,* 414–431.

Gendreau, P., Goggin, C., & Smith, P. (2002). Is the PCL-R really the "unparalleled" measure of offender risk? *Criminal Justice and Behavior, 29,* 397–426.

Gendreau, P., Grant, B. A., Leipciger, M., & Collins, C. (1979). Norms and recidivism rates for the MMPI and selected experimental scales on a Canadian delinquent sample. *Canadian Journal of Behavioral Science,* 11, 21–31.

Gendreau, P., T. Little, T., & Goggin, C. (1996). A meta-analysis of the predictors of adult offender recidivism: What works! *Criminology,* 34, 575–607.

Gendreau, P., Madden, P. G., & Leipciger, M. (1980). Predicting recidivism with social history information and a comparison of their predictive power with psychometric variables. *Canadian Journal of Criminology,* 22, 3–11.

Girard, L. (1999). *The Level of Supervision Inventory–Ontario Revision: Risk/need assessment and recidivism.* Unpublished doctoral dissertation. University of Ottawa , Ottawa, ON, Canada.

Girard, L., & Wormith, J. S. (2004). The predictive validity of the Level of Service Inventory-Ontario Revision on general and violent recidivism among various offender groups. *Criminal Justice and Behavior, 31,* 150–181.

Glaser, D. (1964). *The effectiveness of a prison and parole system.* Indianapolis, IN: Bobbs-Merril.

Goggin, C., & Gendreau, P. (2004). *The Empress' new clothes: The tale of a theory in spite of the data.* Unpublished manuscript available from the Centre for Criminal Justice Studies, University of New Brunswick, Saint John, NB, Canada.

Hanley, D. (2006). Appropriate services: Examining the case classification principle. *Journal of Offender Rehabilitation, 42,* 1–22.

Hanson, R. K., & Wallace-Capretta, S. (2000). *Predicting recidivism among male batterers* (User Report 2000-06). Ottawa, ON, Canada: Solicitor General Canada.

Hardyman, P. L., & Van Voorhis, P. (2004). *Developing gender-specific classification systems for women offenders.* Washington, DC: National Institute of Corrections.

Hare, R. D. (2003). *The Hare Psychopathy Checklist–Revised* (2nd ed.). Toronto, ON, Canada: Multi-Health Systems.

Harris, G. T., Rice, M. E., & Quinsey, V. L. (1993). Violent recidivism of mentally disordered offenders: The development of a statistical prediction instrument. *Criminal Justice and Behavior,* 20, 315–335.

Hoge, R. D., & Andrews, D. A. (1986). A model for conceptualizing interventions in social service. *Canadian Psychology, 27,* 332–341.

Hoge, R. D., & Andrews, D. A. (2002). *Youth Level of Service/Case Management Inventory: User's manual.* Tonowanda, ON, Canada: Multi-Health Systems.

Hollin, C. R., & Palmer, E. J. (2006). The Level of Service Inventory–Revised profile of English prisoners: Risk and reconviction analysis. *Criminal Justice and Behavior, 33,* 347–366.

Hollin, C. R., Palmer, E. J., & Clark, D. (2003). Level of Service Inventory–Revised profile of English prisoners: A needs analysis. *Criminal Justice and Behavior, 30,* 422–440.

Holsinger, A. M., Lowenkamp, C. T., & Latessa, E. J. (2006). Exploring the validity of the Level of Service Inventory–Revised with Native American offenders. *Journal of Criminal Justice, 34,* 331–337.

Holsinger, A. M., Lowenkamp, C. T., & Latessa, E. J. (undated). Ethnicity, gender and the Level of Service Inventory–Revised. Kansas City, MO: University of Missouri–Kansas City.

Interstate Commission for Adult Offender Supervision. (2007). *SO assessment information survey 4-2007.* available at http://www.interstatecompact.org/resources/surveys/survey_results/SexOffender_Assessment_042007.pdf.

Jenkins, W. D., & Sanford, W. L. (1972). *A manual for the use of the Environment Deprivation Scale in corrections: The prediction of criminal behavior.* Montgomery, AL: Rehabilitation Research Foundation.

Lovins, L. B., Lowenkamp, C. T., Latessa, E. J., & Smith, P. (2007). Application of the risk principle to female offenders. *Journal of Contemporary Criminal Justice, 23,* 383–398.

Lowenkamp, C. T., & Latessa, E. J. (undated). *A profile of offenders in Alaska using the LSI-R.* Cincinnati, OH: University of Cincinnati.

Lowenkamp, C. T., Latessa, E. J., & Holsinger, A. M. (2004). Empirical evidence on the importance of training and experience in using the Level of Service Inventory–Revised. *Topics in Community Corrections 2004.*

Lowenkamp, C. T., Latessa, E. J., & Holsinger, A. M. (2006). The risk principle in action: What have we learned from 13,676 offenders and 97 correctional programs? *Crime & Delinquency, 52,* 77–93.

Lowenkamp, C. T., Smith, P., Latessa, E. J., & Cullen, F. T. (2007). *Can 14,737 women be wrong?* Unpublished manuscript available from the Division of Criminal Justice, University of Cincinnati, OH.

Loza, W., & Simourd, D. J. (1994). Psychometric evaluation of the Level of Supervision Inventory (LSI) among male Canadian federal offenders. *Criminal Justice and Behavior, 21,* 468–480.

Madden, P. G. (1978). *Factors related to level of supervision among probationers in Ontario.* Toronto, ON, Canada: Ontario Ministry of Correctional Services.

Marlowe, D. B., Festinger, D. S., Lee, P. A., Dugosh, K. L., & Benasutti, K. M. (2006). Matching judicial supervision to clients' risk status in court. *Crime & Delinquency, 52,* 52–76.

Mills, J. F., Jones, M. N., & Kroner, D. G. (2005). An examination of the generalizability of the LSI-R and VRAG probability bins. *Criminal Justice and Behavior, 32,* 565–585.

Mills, J. F., Kroner, D. G., & Hemmati, T. (2003). Predicting violent behavior through a static-stable variable lens. *Criminal Justice and Behavior, 18,* 891–904.

Motiuk, L. L., & Bonta, J. (1991). Prediction and matching in corrections: an examination of the risk principle in case classification. Paper presented at the Annual Convention of the Canadian Psychological Association, Calgary, AB, Canada.

Motiuk, L. L., Bonta, J., & Andrews, D. A. (1990). Dynamic predictive criterion validity in offender assessment. Paper presented at the Annual convention of the Canadian Psychological Association, Ottawa, ON, Canada.

Motiuk, M., Motiuk, L. L., & Bonta, J. (1992). A comparison between self-report and interview-based inventories in offender classification. *Criminal Justice and Behavior, 19,* 143–159.

Neo, L. H., Yen, C. W., Chng, J., Misir, C., & Goh, K. (in press). The LSI-R: An appropriate risk/needs assessment instrument for incarcerated offenders in Singapore? *Psychology, Crime & Law.*

Nowicka-Sroga, M. (2004). *The Level of Supervision Inventory–Ontario Revision: A recidivism follow up study within a sample of young offenders.* Unpublished doctoral dissertation. University of Ottawa, Ottawa, ON, Canada.

Palmer, E. J., & Hollin, C. R. (2007). The Level of Service Inventory–Revised with English women prisoners: A needs and reconviction analysis. *Criminal Justice & Behavior, 34,* 971–984.

Palmer, E. J., McGuire, J., Hatcher, R. M., Hounsome, J. C., Bilby, C. A. L., & Hollin, C. R. (2008). The importance of appropriate allocation to offending behavior programs. *International Journal of Offender Therapy and Comparative Criminology, 52,* 206–221.

Quinsey, V. L., Harris, G. T., Rice, M. E., & Cormier, C. A. (2006). Violent offenders: Appraising and managing risk (2nd ed). Washington DC: American Psychological Association.

Raynor, P. (2007). Risk and need assessment in British probation: The contribution of the LSI-R. *Psychology, Crime, and Law, 13,* 125–138.

Raynor, P., Kynch, J., Roberts, C., & Merrington, S. (2000). *Risk and need assessment in probation services: an evaluation.* Home Office Research Study No. 211. London, England: Home Office.

Reisig, M. D., Holtfreter, K., & Morash, M. (2006). Assessing recidivism risk across female pathways to crime. *Justice Quarterly, 23,* 384–405.

Renner, J. C. (1978). *The adult probationer in Ontario.* Toronto, ON, Canada: Ontario Ministry of Correctional Services.

Rettinger, J. (1998). A *recidivism follow-up study to investigate risk and need within a sample of provincially sentenced women.* Unpublished doctoral dissertation. Carleton University, Ottawa, ON, Canada.

Rettinger, J., & Andrews, D. A. (2007). General and gender-specific risk-need in relation to adult female offender recidivism. Unpublished manuscript.

Rice, M. E. (2007). Current status of violence risk assessment: Is there a role for professional judgment? Invited address to the North American Correctional and Criminal Justice Psychology Conference, Ottawa, ON, Canada.

Rogers, S. (1981). *Factors related to recidivism among adult probationers in Ontario.* Toronto, ON, Canada: Ontario Ministry of Correctional Services.

Rowe, R. C. (1996). *Parole decision making in Ontario.* Toronto, ON, Canada: Ontario Ministry of the Solicitor General and Correctional Services.

Schlager, M. D., & Simourd, D. J. (2007). Validity of the Level of Service Inventory–Revised (LSI-R) among African American and Hispanic male offenders. *Criminal Justice and Behavior, 34,* 545–554.

Simourd, D. J. (2004). Use of dynamic risk/need assessment instruments among long term incarcerated offenders. *Criminal Justice and Behavior, 31,* 306–323.

Simourd, D. J., & Malcolm, P. B. (1998). Reliability and validity of the Level of Service Inventory–Revised among federally incarcerated sex offenders. *Journal of Interpersonal Violence, 13,* 261–274.

Sparring, M. (1982). *The Youth Service LSI.* Unpublished honours thesis. Department of Psychology, Carleton University, Ottawa, ON, Canada.

Stevenson, H. E., & Wormith, J. S. (1987). *Psychopathy and the Level of Supervision Inventory.* User Report #1987-25. Ottawa, ON, Canada: Solicitor General Canada.

Wadel, D., Hawkins, J., Andrews, D. A., Faulkner, P., Hoge, R. D., Rettinger, L. J., & Simourd, D. (1991). Assessment, evaluation, and program development in the voluntary sector. User Report #1991-14. Ottawa, ON, Canada: Solicitor General Canada.

Waller, I. (1974). *Men released from prison.* Toronto: University of Toronto Press.

Whiteacre, K. W. (2006). Testing the Level of Service Inventory–Revised (LSI-R) for racial/ethnic bias. *Criminal Justice Policy Review, 17,* 330–342.

Yessine, A. K., & Bonta, J. (2006). Tracking high-risk, violent offenders: An examination of the National Flagging System. *Canadian Journal of Criminology and Criminal Justice, 48,* 574–607.

11
The Spousal Assault Risk Assessment Guide (SARA)

P. RANDALL KROPP and ANDREA GIBAS

The Spousal Assault Risk Assessment Guide (SARA) (Kropp, Hart, Webster, & Eaves, 1994, 1995, 1999) is a structured professional judgment (SPJ) tool developed in the 1990s during a time of increased recognition of the social and economic tolls caused by spousal violence in our society. Since that time there has been a proliferation of research and commentaries on domestic violence risk assessment (Bennett Cattaneo & Goodman, 2005; Dutton & Kropp, 2000; Hilton & Harris, 2004; Kropp, 2004), and there is increasing evidence of the validity of a number of risk assessment tools including the SARA (Kropp & Hart, 2000), the Danger Assessment (DA) (Campbell, 1995; Campbell, Sharps, & Glass, 2001), the Domestic Violence Screening Instrument (DVSI) (Williams & Houghton, 2004), and the Ontario Domestic Assault Risk Assessment (ODARA) (Hilton et al., 2004). Within this growing field, SARA remains a popular risk assessment and case management tool for those working with perpetrators and victims of domestic violence. Indeed, SARA has now been translated into at least 10 languages and is being used in at least 15 countries on 5 continents. This chapter will review the content and development of the SARA, summarize existing reliability and validity studies, and conclude with a case study to illustrate its use.

Description of SARA

The SARA manual defines spousal assault as any actual, attempted, or threatened physical harm perpetrated by a man or woman against someone with whom he or she has, or has had, an intimate, sexual relationship. This definition is inclusive: it is not limited to acts that result in physical injury or death; it is not limited to relationships where the partners are or have been legally married; and it is not limited by the gender of the victim or perpetrator. Also, it is consistent with the observation that violence between intimate partners is pandemic in our societies regardless of the nature of their relationship. (Having said this, we recognize that male-to-female violence is especially prevalent and potentially lethal, so the majority of our comments in this chapter will refer to perpetrators as male, and victims as female.) In these ways it has a potentially wider application than some other risk assessment instruments that employ narrower definitions of spousal assault. For example, the DA is designed to assess risk for lethal violence only, and the ODARA cannot be used with dating or same-sex relationships, or with female perpetrators.

Development

Content. The first step was to undertake a careful review of the clinical and empirical literatures on risk for violence, with particular emphasis on spousal assault (Cooper, 1993). The risk factors originally identified in SARA continue to receive support in the clinical and professional literature (Bennett Cattaneo & Goodman, 2005; Dutton & Kropp, 2000; Hilton & Harris, 2004; Kropp, 2004; Kropp, Hart, & Belfrage, 2005; Riggs, Caulfied, & Street, 2002; Schumacher, Feldbau-Kohn, Slep, & Heyman, 2001). The authors of the SARA attempted to keep the list of factors relatively short and aimed at a moderate level of specificity (that is, at the level of traits, characteristics, or incidents, rather than the level of isolated or specific behavioral acts). The result was a list of twenty factors, referred to on SARA as items, grouped into the five content areas described below. A risk factor was included if any or all of the following conditions was satisfied: (1) there was compelling evidence in the empirical literature that the risk factor discriminated those who were violent toward spouses from those who were not; (2) there was evidence that the risk factor was associated with recidivistic spousal violence; or (3) the risk factor was included in other well-recognized professional guidelines for spousal violence risk assessment.

Criminal History Variables. Numerous studies indicate that a prior criminal record for violent offenses and conditional release violations unrelated to spousal assault are associated with an increased risk for violence in general and also, more specifically, for recidivistic spousal assault (Cadsky & Crawford, 1988; Campbell et al., 2003; Fagan, Stewart, & Hansen, 1983; Gondolf, 1988; Gondolf & White, 2001; Hanson & Wallace-Capretta, 2000; Hilton et al., 2004; Hilton & Harris, 2005; Jones & Gondolf, 2001; Saunders, 1992; Sonkin, 1987; Stuart & Campbell, 1989; Tweed & Dutton, 1998). The factors in this section cover past violence, as well as failure to abide by conditions imposed by the courts or criminal justice agencies. *Past assault of family members* refers to violence directed against members of the individual's family of origin or against his or her own children. It does not cover past spousal assaults, which are coded in a different section. *Past assault of strangers or acquaintances* refers to violence directed against people who are not biological or legal family members. *Past violation of conditional release or community supervision* refers to past failures to abide by the conditions of bail, recognizances, court orders, probation, and parole or mandatory supervision. It is irrelevant whether the conditions were imposed following an incident or allegation of spousal assault; any failure is considered a poor prognostic indicator.

Psychosocial Adjustment Variables. Two SARA items reflect the observation that recent or continuing social maladjustment is linked with violence. *Recent relationship problems* refers to separation from an intimate partner or severe conflict in the relationship within the past year (Bennett Cattaneo & Goodman, 2005; Campbell et al., 2001; Dutton & Kropp, 2000; Hilton et al., 2004; Hilton & Harris, 2005; Kennedy & Dutton, 1989; Kyriacou et al., 1999; Riggs et al., 2000; Williams & Houghton, 2004). *Recent employment problems* refers to unemployment and/or extremely unstable employment in the past year. It is unclear whether social maladjustment is the result of more chronic psychopathology or the cause of acute situational financial and interpersonal stress; regardless, these factors appear to be important predictors of violence (Carlson, Harris, & Holden, 1999; Dutton & Kropp, 2000; Hanson & Wallace-Capretta, 2000; Hilton & Harris, 2005; Hotaling & Sugarman, 1986; Kropp, 2004; Kyriacou et al., 1999; Riggs et al., 2000; Schumacher et al., 2001; Sherman et al., 1992; Stuart & Campbell, 1989; Williams & Houghton, 2004).

One item in this section, *victim of and/or witness to family violence as a child or adolescent,* is historical in nature and refers to maladjustment in the individual's family of origin. There is some debate about whether this factor is related to recidivism in spousal assaulters (see Bennett Cattaneo & Goodman, 2005), but it is likely an important factor in batterer treatment and may be causally related to the onset of spousal violence as a result of social learning mechanisms (Aldarando & Sugarman, 1996; Widom, 1989).

There is now a considerable body of evidence supporting the link between certain forms or symptoms of mental disorder and general and spousal violence (e.g., Dutton & Kropp, 2000; Hilton & Harris, 2005; Monahan & Steadman, 1994). This evidence provides the basis for four SARA items related to psychological adjustment: *recent substance abuse/dependence*

(Field, Caetano, & Nelson, 2004; Gondolf & White, 2001; Hanson & Wallace-Capretta, 2000; Hilton et al., 2004; Jones & Gondolf, 2001; Saunders, 1992; Stuart & Campbell, 1989; Williams & Houghton, 2004), *recent suicidal or homicidal ideation/intent* (Campbell, 1995; Campbell et al., 2003; Goldsmith, 1990; Saunders, 1992; Stuart & Campbell, 1989), *recent psychotic and/or manic symptoms* (Borum, Swartz, & Swanson, 1996; Douglas & Webster, 1999; Gondolf, 1988; Kessler et al., 2001; Magdol et al., 1997; Monahan et al., 2001; Schumacher et al., 2001), and *personality disorder with anger, impulsivity, or behavioral instability* (Dutton, 1995; Dutton & Kropp, 2000; Gondolf, 1998; Healy, Smith, & O'Sullivan, 1998; Hilton & Harris, 2005; Huss & Langhinrichsen-Rohling, 2000; Jones & Gondolf, 2001; Kessler et al., 2001; Magdol et al., 1997; Riggs et al., 2000; Schumacher et al., 2001). SARA does not assume that the mental disorder is responsible for or "causes" violent behavior (although it is recognized that symptoms of mental illness such as delusions can play a causal role). Rather, mental disorder is assumed to be associated with poor coping skills and increased social-interpersonal stress; thus, individuals with mental disorders may be prone to making and acting on bad decisions.

Spousal Assault History Variables. This section comprises seven items related to spousal assaults in the past. Risk factors based on the alleged or current offense are included in a different section, so that evaluators can more easily separate the quantum of perceived risk attributed to formally documented events (which are likely to be accepted as factual) versus that attributed to alleged events (which are likely to be contested).

The first four items concern the nature and extent of past spousal assaults. *Past physical assault* is an obvious risk factor, based on the axiom that past behavior predicts future behavior. Past assaults of intimate partners has received considerable support as a robust risk factor for spousal violence (Campbell et al., 2001; Dutton & Kropp, 2000; Fagan et al., 1983; Harrell & Smith, 1996; Healy et al., 1998; Hilton & Harris, 2005; Hilton et al., 2004; Riggs et al., 2000; Saunders & Browne, 2000; Sonkin, 1987; Williams & Houghton, 2004). *Past sexual assault/sexual jealousy* refers to physical assaults that are of a sexual nature or occur in the context of extreme sexual jealousy (Campbell et al., 2001; Goldsmith, 1990; Stuart & Campbell, 1989; Walker, 1989). *Past use of weapons and/or credible threats of death* refers to behavior that explicitly or implicitly threatens serious physical harm or death to an intimate partner (Campbell et al., 2003; Dutton & Kropp, 2000; Gondolf, 1988; Hart, 1992; Sonkin, 1987; Stuart & Campbell, 1989; Walker, 1989). *Recent escalation in frequency or severity of assault* refers to situations where the "trajectory" of violence seems to be escalating over time (Campbell, 1995; Campbell et al., 2003; Hart, 1992; Mahoney, Williams, & West, 2001; Sonkin, 1987; Stuart & Campbell, 1989; Weisz, Tolman, & Saunders, 2000).

The next three items of SARA concern behavior or attitudes that accompany assaultive behavior. *Past violation of "no-contact" orders* covers situations where an individual has failed to comply with the orders of a court or criminal justice agency that prohibit contact with victims of past spousal assaults (Andrews & Bonta, 2002; Hart, Kropp, & Hare, 1988; Hilton et al., 2004; Nuffield, 1982). Although it overlaps to some extent with the third item in the Criminal History section, we believed that such a violation is so directly relevant to spousal assault risk assessment that it deserved special attention. *Extreme minimization or denial of spousal assault history* may occur as part of a more general pattern of deflection of personal responsibility for criminal behavior, or it may be specific to past spousal assaults (Dutton, 1995, Gondolf & White, 2001; Hanson & Wallace-Capretta, 2000; Hilton & Harris, 2005; Shepard, Faulk, & Elliott, 2002; Sonkin, 1987). *Attitudes that support or condone wife assault* covers a wide range of beliefs or values—personal, social, religious, political, and cultural—that encourage patriarchy (i.e., male prerogative), misogyny, and the use of physical violence or intimidation to resolve conflicts and enforce control (Campbell et al., 2003; Daly & Wilson, 1998; Hanson & Wallace-Capretta, 2000; Murphy & O'Leary, 1989; Riggs et al., 2000; Schumacher et al., 2001; Sonkin, 1987).

Alleged (Current) Offense Variables. This section comprises three items, similar in content to those appearing in the previous section, that are scored solely on the basis of the alleged or current spousal violence offense: *Severe and/or sexual assault, use of weapons and/or credible threats of death*, and *violation of "no-contact" order.*

Other Considerations. The final section does not contain any specific items. It allows the evaluator to note risk factors not included in the SARA that are present in a particular case. An important example is the presence of stalking behavior, because this risk factor has received a great deal of attention in the literature in recent years in relation to spousal violence (Burgess et al., 1997; Douglas & Dutton, 2001; Kropp, Hart, & Lyon, 2002; Palarea, Zona, Lane, & Langhinrichsen-Rohling, 1999). Other examples of important risk factors include a history of disfiguring, torturing, or maiming intimate partners, a history of sexual sadism, and so forth. Such factors often have a rational or intuitive relevance to the nature and severity of risk, even though they have not been systematically evaluated in the empirical literature due to their rarity.

Applications

SARA was originally developed for use in the criminal justice system in four major contexts:

1. *Pretrial.* When someone is arrested for offenses related to spousal assault, the nature of the alleged acts or the defendant's history may raise the question of whether he should be denied pretrial release on the grounds that he poses an imminent risk of harm to identifiable persons (that is, his spouse, his children), or whether he should have pretrial release conditions that include no contact orders. Of note is that the use of pretrial risk assessments by police has increased in recent years, and this practice has received some attention in the literature (Belfrage, 2008; Hilton et al., 2004; Kropp, 2003; Kropp et al., 2005). Assessments prior to trial present some challenges due, often, to the inability of the evaluator to consider the most recent charges. Partly for this reason, the information regarding the "most recent offense" is partitioned so it can be excluded in pretrial evaluations.
2. *Presentence.* Risk assessments are sometimes requested when a defendant's case has proceeded to trial. If he has not yet been convicted, the results may assist judges who are considering the diversion or the conditional or unconditional discharge of the defendant. If he already has been convicted, the risk assessment findings may help judges to decide between alternative sentences (for example, probation versus incarceration) and to set or recommend monitoring, supervision, and treatment conditions in the community.
3. *Correctional Intake.* After conviction, risk assessments can be helpful to corrections staff who conduct "front-end" assessments in institutional or community settings. They can be used in the development of treatment plans, as well as to determine suitability or set conditions for conjugal visits, family visits, and temporary absences. For example, SARA is currently being used system-wide in the Correctional Service of Canada to assist in decisions of this nature.
4. *Correctional Discharge.* In the case of offenders who have been incarcerated, risk assessments prior to discharge can help corrections officials or parole boards to determine suitability or set conditions for conditional release, as well as assisting in the

development of a postrelease treatment or management plan. For a community-resident offender who is nearing the end of his supervisory period, a final risk assessment may indicate that correctional staff should communicate formal warnings to at-risk individuals in an effort to discharge any ethical and legal obligations before the case file is officially closed.

Although the immediate motivation for the development of SARA was to aid spousal assault risk assessments in the criminal justice system, the authors of SARA encourage three other potential uses:

1. *Civil Justice Matters.* There has been an increased recognition of family violence within the civil justice system. Spousal assault risk assessments now occur frequently in the context of separation/divorce and custody/access hearings. This is particularly important in light of the fact that many separations are precipitated by spousal violence, and that estrangement increases the risk for repeated and even escalated violence (e.g., Campbell et al., 2003; Dutton & Kropp, 2000; Hilton & Harris, 2005). In such situations, there is also often a concern about the risk of children witnessing future spousal violence.
2. *Warning Third Parties.* Virtually every jurisdiction in North America has statutory and/or common-law duties to warn or advise. These apply to mental health professionals, counselors, and social service providers (Dickens, 1985; Melton, Petrila, Poythress, & Slobogin, 2007). Generally, the duty to warn or advise comes about when the service provider has "reasonable and probable" or some such grounds to believe that an individual has the intent and the means to engage in behavior harmful to self or others. SARA can be used in situations where, during the course of voluntary or court-ordered assessment or treatment, a service provider is concerned that an individual poses an imminent risk of physical harm to his spouse and/or children. The presence of SARA factors would tend to support the existence of reasonable and probable grounds to warn others. Results obtained using SARA may act as an "independent check" of the professional judgment of service providers and may help them to explain to others the basis for their judgments.
3. *Quality Assurance and Critical Incident Review.* SARA can be used by mental health professionals, correctional staff, lawyers, and victim's advocates to check the thoroughness and quality of spousal assault risk assessments conducted by others, in two ways. First, did the evaluator fail to recognize or give adequate consideration to a risk factor that appears on the SARA? SARA is not exhaustive, in the sense that there are some specific factors not included in the instrument that may be associated with risk for violence. However, it does contain a basic or minimal set of factors that should be considered. Second, did the evaluator consider factors not included in the SARA? Although, as noted above, SARA is not exhaustive, it seems fair and reasonable that evaluators be asked to provide a clear rationale for basing their judgments on such factors.

Assessment Procedure

The authors of SARA suggest an assessment procedure based on multiple sources of information and multiple methods of data collection. This is based on the recognition that victims, offenders, and other collateral sources (e.g., children, neighbors) may tend to underreport violence (albeit for different reasons), but that their reports often provide crucial information that is otherwise difficult or impossible to obtain. Also, in many cases, structured assessment procedures (self-report inventories, semistructured interviews) are useful adjuncts to unstructured procedures ("clinical" interviews, reviews of police reports or other case history information). In general, the assessment should include (1) interviews with the accused and victim(s); (2) standardized measures of physical and emotional abuse; (3) standardized measures of drug and alcohol abuse; (4) review of collateral records, including police reports, victim statements, criminal records, and so forth; and (5) other assessments, as required. If the information is incomplete, the evaluator should postpone undertaking or completing the risk assessment until the missing information becomes available. If it is impossible to track down the missing information, the evaluator should proceed with the risk assessment and emphasize in the final report the ways in which conclusory opinions need to be limited.

Coding Judgments

The SARA is not "scored" in the manner of most psychological tests. Rather, the evaluator is called upon to make three kinds of judgments, which are coded on a summary form.

Presence of Individual Items. The presence of individual items is coded using a 3-point response format: 0 = *absent*, 1 = *subthreshold*, and 2 = *present*. The SARA manual presents detailed criteria for defining and coding each item. The presence of individual items is a relatively objective indicator of risk; in general, and especially in the absence of critical items (see below), risk can be expected to increase with the number of items coded present. Of course, completing SARA does require some degree of professional, subjective judgment on the part of the evaluator; however, it is important to remember that the items were selected on the basis of their demonstrated validity and that considerable pains have been taken to ensure that the coding of items is simple and clear.

Presence of Critical Items. Critical items are those that, given the circumstances in the case at hand, are sufficient on their own to compel the evaluator to conclude that the individual poses an imminent risk of harm. They are included in recognition of the fact that risk, as perceived by the evaluator, is not a simple linear function of the number of risk factors present in a case. This is why we do not simply sum the numerical scores on individual SARA items to yield a total "score"; it is conceivable that an evaluator could judge an individual to be at high risk for violence on the basis of a single critical item. Critical items are coded using a 2-point format: 0 = *absent*, 1 = *present*.

Summary Risk Judgments. Evaluators frequently are required to address two separate issues: imminent risk of harm to spouse (which generally is the issue that prompted the risk assessment) and imminent risk of harm to some other identifiable person (for example, the individual's children, other family members, or the new partner of an ex-spouse). With SARA, such risk is coded using a 3-point response format: 1 = *low*, 2 = *moderate*, and 3 = *high* (see the HCR-20 chapter for more detail about this format). If the individual is deemed to be at risk for harming "others," the evaluator must identify the potential victims. These summary risk judgments capture the evaluator's overall professional opinion in a straightforward manner that permits comparison with other evaluators.

Reviewing Percentile Distributions. In the 1999 version of the SARA manual (Kropp et al., 1999), an additional step was added to the SARA procedure. This involves contrasting the summary risk rating for imminent risk for spousal assault with percentile distributions for Total Scores and Number of Factors Present on the SARA. The evaluator can reference normative data for inmates ($N = 638$) or probationers ($N = 1{,}671$) who have committed spousal violence. A description of the normative data research is provided in a later section of this chapter (see also Kropp & Hart, 2000). Thus, *descriptive* cutoffs are provided that allow the evaluator to identify

Table 11.1 Summary of Studies Examining the Inter-Rater Reliability of the SARA

Study	Characteristics of the Sample	Administration of the SARA	Inter-Rater Reliability (ICC)			
			Total Score	Part 1 Total	Part 2 Total	Summary Risk
Kropp & Hart (2000)	86 male inmates	As recommended in SARA manual	.84	.68	.87	.63
Mowat-Léger (2001)	16 incarcerated male offenders in a correction and treatment center	As recommended in SARA manual	.99	.98	.93	
Grann & Wedin (2002)	18 males in forensic psychiatric setting; diagnosed with personality disorder	Not as recommended in SARA manual	.85	.88	.74	

offenders who possess a large number of risk factors relative to other offenders. If a discrepancy exists between the evaluator's professional judgment and the percentile ranking of the offender, the discrepancy must be explained. For example, if the evaluator believes the case to be a high risk, but the offender has a relatively low number of risk factors, the evaluator is asked to answer: "Why should a few risk factors be accorded so much weight?" This step represents a final cross-check of the evaluator's professional opinion.

Research

The first validation paper on SARA was published by Kropp & Hart (2000). Since that time, a number of studies have reported data on the psychometric properties of SARA. For the purpose of this review, we located a number of resources including five peer-reviewed journal articles, two government reports, one conference presentation, and one doctoral dissertation. Each of the studies is described and reviewed in detail below with particular reference to the reliability and validity of SARA. Summaries of the main findings from these studies are included in Tables 11.1, 11.2, and 11.3.

Our review revealed a number of methodological problems with many of the studies utilizing SARA, and the studies will be discussed in turn. However, a significant problem with many of the published studies was the apparent misapplication of SARA. In other words, many of the important validation studies of SARA did not administer the instrument according to the manual, excluded or approximated many of the SARA items due to inadequate information, or did not incorporate summary risk ratings (that is, the structured professional judgment method). These problems seriously limit the usefulness of the data and make interpretation of results difficult. Therefore, this review will discuss two categories of studies. First, we will discuss studies in which we believe the researchers used the *recommended administration* of SARA, that is, as it was intended to be used by the authors. We define "recommended" according to the detailed administration procedure provided in all versions of the SARA manual (i.e., Kropp et al., 1994, 1995, 1999) and the description provided in the previous section. Second, we will include studies that did not use the recommended administration of the SARA, rendering the integrity of the data in question. We chose to include this second group of studies because they are often cited in the literature and have been included in a recent meta-analysis of spousal violence risk assessment measures (Hanson, Helmus, & Bourgon, 2007). We suggest, however, that they be afforded less weight when considering the reliability and validity of SARA.

Table 11.2 Summary of Studies Examining the Predictive/Postdictive Validity of the SARA

Authors	Definition of Recidivism	Administration of the SARA	Statistic	Predictive/Postdictive Validity				
				Total	Part 1	Part 2	Summary Risk	Weighted Risk
Kropp & Hart (2000)	Offenders with history of spousal assault vs. nonhistory of spousal assault (n = 1010)	As recommended in SARA manual	t-tests (df), corrected for equal variance	27.04 (996.60)	11.11 (807.99)	35.24 (665.54)		
	Recidivistic vs. nonrecidivistic spousal assaulters (n = 102)		t-tests (df), corrected for equal variance	1.85 (100.00)	0.55 (100.00)	2.96 (98.19)		
			ROC–AUC				.70	
Williams & Houghton (2004)	Domestic violence recidivism in 6 months	As recommended in SARA manual	ROC–AUC	.65				.65
	Total recidivism		ROC–AUC	.70				.71
Cairns (2004)	Breach cases (n = 38)	As recommended in SARA manual	Odds ratio				H v. M/L = 2.5 M/H vs. L = 9.4	
Wong & Hisashima (2008)	Rearrest for DV-related offenses within 3 months	As recommended in SARA manual	Chi-square (using total number of risk factors dichotomized)	4.75				
Gibas, Kropp, Hart, & Stewart (2008)	Evidence from correctional records of new domestic violence offense	As recommended in SARA manual	Pearson's r	.31	.17	.31	.40	
Grann & Wedin (2002)	File review for reconviction of any spousal violence within a 10-year follow-up period	Not as recommended in SARA manual	ROC–AUC at 6 month follow-up	.52	.49	.54		

			ROC–AUC at 1 year	.59	.57	.57
			ROC–AUC at 2 years	.63	.58	.60
			ROC–AUC at 5 years	.65	.59	.62
Hilton et al. (2004)	Within a specific time frame (1997–2001), any violence against a female partner	Not as recommended in SARA manual	ROC–AUC	.64		
Heckert & Gondolf (2004)	Phone contact with the offender and his partner over 15 months to establish the following categories: repeat assault, one-time assault, threats of assault, controlling, or no assault	Not as recommended in SARA manual	ROC–AUC	.54		
			(cross-validation) ROC–AUC	.64		

Table 11.3 Summary of Studies Examining the Concurrent Validity of the SARA

Authors	Other Risk Assessment Instruments	Administration of the SARA	Concurrent Validity							
			Total	Part 1	Part 2	# of Factors	# Factors (Part 1)	# Factors (Part 2)	Summary Risk (Partner)	Summary Risk (Other)
Kropp & Hart (2000)	PCL:SV	As recommended in SARA manual	.43	.45	.30	.38	.39	.26	.34	
	GSIR		–.07	–.40	.15	–.07	–.31	.16	.01	
	VRAG		.29	.50	.08	.25	.53	.00	.11	
Williams & Houghton (2004)	DVSI	As recommended in SARA manual	.54						.57	.15
Mowat-Léger (2001)	ABI	As recommended in SARA manual	.46	.29	.48					
	IBWB		–.30	–.21	–.34					
	PCL: SV		.57	.59	.37					
	LSI-OR		.28	.55	.02					
Grann & Wedin (2002)	# of previous convictions	Not as recommended in SARA manual	.39	.55	.01 (n.s)					
	# of previous violent convictions		.29	.40	.04 (n.s)					
	PCL-R total		.59	.60	.28					
	H factor in HCR-20		.46	.65	.03 (n.s)					
	VRAG		.33	.49	–.01 (n.s)					
Hilton et al. (2004)	ODARA	Not as recommended in SARA manual	.60							

Note: n.s. = Not significant.

Finally, we will summarize the special case of a violence prevention study using the SARA on a police sample in Sweden.

Studies Using Recommended SARA Administration

Kropp and Hart (2000). The first systematic evaluation of the reliability and validity of SARA was reported by its authors. The study involved 2,681 male offenders (671 probationers and 1,010 inmates) in the Canadian criminal justice system. A variety of corrections (e.g., probation officers), mental health (e.g., treatment staff), and trained research staff (e.g., doctoral-level clinical psychology students) were responsible for providing SARA ratings for the sample. Inter-rater reliability was tested by having a doctoral student independently complete SARA from files on 86 cases previously assessed by corrections case managers. At the individual item level, intraclass correlation coefficients (ICC) ranged between 0.45 and 0.86 (*Mdn* ICC = 0.65). The inter-rater reliability ICC for the SARA total score was 0.84. The reliability was higher for Part 1 of SARA (i.e., related to criminal history and psychosocial adjustment; ICC = 0.87) than for Part 2 (i.e., related to spousal assault history; ICC = 0.68). The summary risk ratings (Low, Moderate, High) also demonstrated statistically significant inter-rater reliability (ICC = 0.63), even when dichotomized (Low/Moderate risk vs. High risk; ICC = 0.57). Last, inter-rater reliability for the SARA Critical Items was relatively low, but these items were also infrequently endorsed and had a restricted range.

Kropp and Hart also evaluated the concurrent validity and the criterion-group validity (i.e., known groups) of SARA. To test concurrent validity, SARA was compared to three general risk-related measures: the Psychopathy Checklist–Screening Version (PCL:SV) (Hart, Cox, & Hare, 1995), the General Statistical Information on Recidivism Scale (GSIR) (Nuffield, 1982), and the Violence Risk Appraisal Guide (VRAG) (Quinsey, Harris, Rice, & Cormier, 1998). The total SARA score ($r = 0.43$), Part 1 ($r = 0.45$), and Part 2 ($r = 0.30$) scores, respectively, exhibited moderate correlations with the PCL:SV. Both the GSIR ($r = -0.40$; note that a lower GSIR score indicates a higher level of risk) and VRAG ($r = 0.50$) correlated to a moderate and large degree with the general violence risk factors of the SARA (Part 1). Correlations with the spousal assault–specific items and summary risk ratings were not statistically significant. These results are evidence of the good convergent and discriminant validity of SARA when compared to validated measures of general violence risk.

Next, to assess for criterion-group validity, the authors compared inmates with ($n = 638$) and without ($n = 372$) a documented history of spousal violence. Group mean comparisons revealed significant differences across all 20 SARA risk factors. A similar pattern was noted for both the SARA continuous ratings and summary risk ratings: offenders with a history of spousal violence were rated higher than offenders without a documented history of spousal violence. Of the two parts of SARA, Part 2—Spousal Assault History—exhibited the greatest difference between offenders (spousal assault offenders: $M = 6.42$, $SD = 4.47$) and nonspousal assault offenders ($M = 0.12$, $SD = 0.51$), as would be expected due to the very nature of the items. Part 1 of SARA—Criminal History—demonstrated moderate to large differences between the two samples (spousal assault offenders: $M = 9.97$, $SD = 3.68$ and nonspousal assault offenders: $M = 7.38$, $SD = 3.50$).

In addition, group comparisons were made between recidivistic ($n = 52$) and nonrecidivistic ($n = 50$) spousal assaulters. Significant group differences were found between the groups using actuarial analogue measures of risk derived from SARA (i.e., the total score and number of factors present). Those individuals who were rated as high risk on SARA tended to be spousal assault recidivists, and those rated low risk to be nonrecidivists ($\chi^2_{(2, 102)} = 13.69$, $p = 0.001$). Sixty percent of the recidivists ($n = 31$) were rated high risk, while only 8% ($n = 4$) were rated as low risk. A similar pattern was found when the risk ratings were dichotomized into high versus moderate/low risk ($\chi^2_{(1, 102)} = 7.82$, $p = 0.005$). After controlling for treatment suitability, time at risk, and continuous (i.e., actuarial) scores on the SARA, the summary risk ratings continued to significantly differentiate between recidivist and nonrecidivist spousal assaulters. Receiver operating characteristic (ROC) analysis indicated that the area under the curve (AUC) for the SARA summary risk ratings was 0.70. Overall, the results suggest that SARA has an acceptable ability to discriminate between (1) those with and without a spousal assault history, and (2) recidivists and nonrecidivists. Regarding the latter finding, hierarchical logistic regression analyses indicated that structured professional judgment ratings of risk method outperformed the actuarial method in retrospectively predicting recidivism.

Williams and Houghton (2004). The authors used SARA in a study seeking a technique that would provide "the most valid and reliable method" of assessing risk for spousal violence (p. 439). The study focused primarily on the concurrent and predictive validity of the Domestic Violence Screening Instrument (DVSI) (Williams & Houghton, 2004), but SARA results were included for comparison purposes. The research was conducted with an overall sample of 1465 men arrested within a nine-month period in Colorado for committing an act of violence against female intimate partners. Approximately one-third of the sample had previously documented histories of spousal violence–related convictions or violations. SARA was administered post-adjudication by probation officers trained by staff that had attended a training workshop by the developers of the tool. The SARA ratings were completed on a subsample of 434 offenders, using all relevant sources of information (i.e., interview with the perpetrator and victim, and collection of collateral material), and summary risk ratings were made.

To determine the predictive validity of the two instruments (DVSI and SARA), the instruments were compared using ROC analysis. The total SARA scores and a weighted version of SARA,* which incorporated a summary risk rating (i.e., risk for violence against a partner), were used in the analyses. Separate ROC analyses were conducted to predict spousal violence–related recidivism and general recidivism. Both the SARA total scores (AUC = 0.65) and the weighted SARA scores (AUC = 0.65) predicted spousal violence recidivism significantly better than chance. The SARA total score and weighted SARA score AUCs were 0.70 and 0.71, respectively, when predicting general recidivism. The authors reported that the predictive accuracy of the DVSI was slightly less than that of SARA, but this difference was not statistically significant. It was also noted that the predictive accuracy of both the actuarial and structured judgment (i.e., summary risk ratings) components of SARA performed equally well.

Williams and Houghton also assessed the concurrent validity of SARA by correlating the total scores of the SARA and the DVSI. The level of agreement between the two instruments was moderate ($r = 0.54$). Additionally, when comparing the DVSI and the SARA summary risk ratings, the level of agreement was slightly greater ($r = 0.57$). As evidence of discriminant validity, the correlation between SARA summary risk ratings of violence toward others (i.e., nonintimate partners) and the DVSI was notably lower ($r = 0.15$).

Mowat-Léger (2001). This appears to be one of the first independent evaluations of the reliability and validity of SARA. The primary purpose of the research was to differentiate domestically violent and nonviolent men with respect to the risk factors commonly associated with spousal assault. Research participants included 154 incarcerated offenders at a correction and treatment center, of which 37 offenders were classified as family-only violent (FOV), 35 as stranger-only violent (SOV), 41 as generally violent (GV), and 41 as nonviolent (NV). SARA was rated using a

* The authors describe the weighted version as a cross-product computed between the total SARA scores and the summary risk rating of imminent risk of violence toward the partner.

semistructured interview with the offender and a file review. The ratings were conducted by the author of the study.

For the purpose of ascertaining inter-rater reliability of SARA, 16 offender interviews were recorded by the primary researcher. A second independent rater, a doctoral level psychologist, scored the SARA based on the audio recordings of the 16 interviews. The intraclass correlation coefficients ranged between 0.95 and 0.99 for all four sections of the SARA (e.g., 0.95 for Psychosocial Adjustment). Similarly, the SARA total, Part 1, and Part 2 scores had reported intraclass correlation coefficients greater than 0.90 (SARA total, ICC = 0.99; SARA Part 1, ICC = 0.98; SARA Part 2, ICC = 0.93). Within the sample under study, SARA exhibited impressive inter-rater reliability.

Mowat-Léger also examined known-group validity of SARA by testing whether SARA could differentiate between the four groups of offenders (FOV, SOV, GV, and NV). A between-subjects multivariate analysis of variance (MANOVA) was performed on three predictor variables: SARA total, Part 1, and Part 2 scores. The results were significant ($F_{(9, 360.34)} = 48.52$, $p < 0.001$), meaning that the SARA scores successfully differentiated between the four groups. The greatest contribution to the MANOVA was made by Part 2 of the SARA (Spousal Assault History). The FOV and GV groups had the greatest scores on SARA, followed by the SOV group, and lastly, the NV group. There did not appear to be a statistically significant difference between the FOV and GV groups in terms of Part 2 scores on SARA. This pattern also held for SARA total scores. With regard to Part 1 of SARA, the batterer group generated lower scores than the SOV and GV offenders. Overall, the FOV and GV groups presented as a higher risk for future violence against an intimate partner than either the SOV or NV groups, as assessed by the SARA.

In the course of her research, Mowat-Léger (2001) also examined the concurrent validity of SARA, when compared to two other domestic violence risk instruments—the Abusive Behavior Inventory (ABI) (Shepard & Campbell, 1992), and the Inventory of Beliefs about Wife Beating (IBWB) (Saunders, Lynch, Grayson, & Linz, 1987). The results indicate that the SARA total score was strongly and significantly correlated with the total score of the ABI ($r = 0.46$) and IBWB ($r = -0.30$),* and the two subscales of the ABI (Physical Abuse: $r = 0.59$ and Emotional Abuse: $r = 0.36$). Part 2 (Spousal Assault History) evidenced a stronger correlation with the domestic violence risk assessment instruments than Part 1 (Criminal History) of SARA (e.g., $r = 0.60$ vs. $r = 0.37$ for ABI physical abuse). Additional comparisons were conducted between SARA and conventional general risk for violence measures. The PCL:Screening Version (Hart, Cox, & Hare, 1995) and the Level of Service Inventory–Ontario Revision (LSI-OR) (Andrews, Bonta, & Wormith, 1995) were used as the general risk assessment instruments under comparison. Although all components of SARA were significantly correlated with the PCL:SV, Part 1 was particularly stronger ($r = 0.59$) than Part 2 ($r = 0.37$). A similar pattern was identified for Part 1 SARA scores and the LSI-OR ($r = 0.55$) compared to Part 2 of SARA ($r = 0.02$; nonsignificant). This result is to be expected, because Part 1 of SARA details the general criminal history of an offender and is not specific to spousal violence. Overall, the results of this research suggest that SARA exhibits convergent and divergent validity with measures of spousal violence and general recidivism.

Cairns (2004). SARA was included in a comprehensive evaluation of a domestic violence treatment program in Alberta, Canada. In this prospective research, 231 spousal assaulters were assessed on SARA using all available information, including an interview with the offender, at intake to the program. The concurrent validity of SARA was assessed by examining its relation to the Physical Abuse of Partner Scale (PAPS) (see Garner & Hudson, 2003), and Non-

* For the IBWB, individuals with attitudes that were more supportive of domestic violence scored higher on the SARA.

Physical Abuse of Partner Scale (NPAPS) (see Garner & Hudson, 2003). The PAPS and NPAPS are self-report measures of the level of physical and nonphysical abuse against an intimate partner. The authors reported that scores on both of these instruments administered pretreatment were elevated with increasing SARA risk level, but no test of statistical significant was provided. Predictive validity of SARA was measured by recording new breach of release conditions immediately before or during the treatment program. The average follow-up period was approximately 6 months duration. Of 39 documented breach cases considered, one (2.5%) was assessed as low risk on SARA, 17 (45.9%) at moderate risk, and 21 (55.3%) at high risk. These rates are in comparison to proportions of 17% low, 47% moderate, and 36% high risk in the total sample. Although Cairns did not report any measures of statistical significance in her report, it is possible to compute odds ratios based on these numbers. Thus, it appears that high-risk offenders were 2.5 times more likely to breach conditions than a combined low/moderate-risk group. Alternatively, moderate/high-risk offenders were 9.4 times more likely than low-risk offenders to breach conditions. The study lends further support for the concurrent and predictive validity of SARA.

Wong and Hisashima (2008). This study evaluated the use of the SARA and the DVSI by probation officers in the State of Hawaii between the years 2003 and 2007. During this time a total of 196 SARA assessments were completed on offenders. All probation officers had received training in the administration of SARA (many from the authors of the instrument), and the assessments were done in the field using multiple sources of information. However, summary risk ratings were not included in the report, and reasons for this were not given. The primary focus of this study was on predictive validity, and no inter-rater information was provided by the authors. To evaluate predictive validity, the authors grouped offenders into two categories of risk—low–medium (46%) and high (54%)—based on the percentile distributions provided in the 1999 manual (see Assessment Procedure section of this chapter). Cases were followed up for a minimum of three months and two types of recidivism were recorded: domestic violence recidivism (including violence, threatening, harassment, and restraining and protective order violations), and general recidivism (other crime).

Moderate correlations (Pearson's r) were found between the SARA and the DVSI ($r = .54, p < .01$) and the Level of Service Inventory–Revised ($r = .43, p < .01$), thereby demonstrating adequate concurrent validity. Predictive validity analyses revealed that 32% of the high risk SARA group and 17% of the low-moderate group were rearrested for domestic violence offenses ($\chi^2 = 4.75, p < .05$). Additionally, 66% of the high-risk SARA group and 45% of the low-moderate group were rearrested for general offenses ($\chi^2 = 8.45, p < .01$). Overall, the authors recommended the continued use of the SARA and the DVSI in Hawaii, with cautionary notes regarding the small sample size and the short follow-up period employed. This study is also the first that we know of that has independently validated the percentile distributions reported in the 1999 SARA manual.

Gibas, Kropp, Hart, & Stewart (2008). Gibas et al. followed 108 incarcerated male spousal assaulters after their release from prison. Each offender was assessed with SARA shortly before release to the community and categorized as low (27%), moderate (28%), or high (45%) risk. The minimum follow-up time in the community was six months. Summary risk ratings and spousal-related recidivism were strongly related ($\chi^2 = 18.7, p < .001$) with 8%, 17%, and 31% of the low-, moderate-, and high-risk groups, respectively, committing new spousal offenses during the follow-up period. Part 1 ($r = .17, p < .05$), Part 2 ($r = .33, p < .01$), and the SARA total scores ($r = .31, p < .01$) were also significantly associated with spousal-related recidivism. The strongest association, however, was between the summary risk ratings for spousal violence and spousal recidivism ($r = .40, p < .01$). The summary risk ratings also demonstrated incremental validity over the SARA total (actuarial) score and the Statistical Information on Recidivism (SIR) Scale score (an actuarial measure of general recidivism risk) in predicting new spousal offenses ($B = 1.37, p = .01$). (Note: The SIR score was not significantly related to spousal violence or general violence recidivism in this sample). The results of this study were similar to those reported by Kropp & Hart (2000), and lend further support for the use of structured professional judgment (vs. actuarial measures), and for the use of a specific measure of spousal violence risk (vs. those designed for predicting general recidivism).

Studies Not Using the Recommended SARA Administration

In some studies, usually with explicit acknowledgment by the authors, SARA has been used in a manner that does not conform to the recommended administration procedure. The studies are included in this review because they all purport to have used SARA, and their results are frequently cited in the literature. They may therefore provide some important information about the use of SARA, although we had difficulty interpreting the results due to the methodological problems. The reader is advised to interpret the results with some caution.

Grann and Wedin (2002). The first approximated SARA study was conducted as a retrospective file review in Sweden by Grann and Wedin (2002). A total sample of 88 cases of male offenders subjected to a forensic psychiatric evaluation was selected. The cases involved offenders who had been convicted of a violent spousal assault or homicide and, due to the nature of the psychiatric setting, had been clinically diagnosed with a personality disorder. The researchers examined inter-rater reliability and the concurrent and predictive validity of the SARA ratings,* as completed by a bachelors-level psychology student. Because of the retrospective, file-based design of the study, material required to complete SARA was sometimes unavailable and thus omitted. In particular, 4 of the 20 items (i.e., 20%) of the SARA were deemed difficult to rate reliably from file information: Past Assault of Strangers (31% omission rate), Past Assault of Family Members (39%), Attitudes That Support or Condone Violence (48%), and Victim/Witness of Family Violence (59%). Although the missing items were prorated (i.e., replaced with the expected mean), the measurement reliability of SARA was likely diluted as a result. Further, the authors noted that SARA was used as "an actuarial tool in the strict sense" (p. 10), and summary risk ratings were not applied. This procedure thus appeared to violate the fundamental assumption, stated in the SARA manual, that risk is not a simple function of the number of risk factors present.

Nonetheless, the study provides some useful information regarding the inter-rater reliability of the SARA when coded from file information. On a subsample of 18 randomly selected cases rated independently by a doctoral-level psychologist, the results indicated that the reliability of SARA was acceptable; at an individual-item level, Cohen's kappa ranged from between 0.30 to 1.00 (average kappa = 0.58). Intraclass correlation coefficients for the SARA total, Part 1, and Part 2 scores were statistically significant at 0.85, 0.88, and 0.74, respectively.

Using a retrospective design, postdictive validity of SARA was assessed in the 88 cases with a follow-up period of approximately 10 years (Grann & Wedin, 2001). Reconviction was documented for spousal violence only, and 28% of the sample reoffended within the timeframe under review (cumulatively, 15% recidivism at 6 months, 18% at 1 year, 24% within 2 years, and 25% within 5 years of those available individuals). Three SARA risk factors were identified as being important in influencing risk for partner violence recidivism: Past Violation of Conditional Release or Community Supervision, Personality Disorder with Anger, Impulsivity,

* The Canadian version, not the Swedish version, of the SARA was used in this research because the Swedish version was not yet available.

or Behavioral Instability, and Extreme Minimization or Denial of Spousal Assault History. ROC analyses were conducted using the SARA total, Part 1, and Part 2 scores for the four distinct postdetainment time periods (6 months, 1 year, 2 years, and 5 years). Inclusive of all time periods, the AUCs ranged from 0.49 to 0.65, representing minimal improvements over chance in predicting spousal violence recidivism. The authors commented that the "strictly actuarial" (i.e., without incorporation of the summary risk ratings) use of SARA did not significantly enhance the statistical prediction of spousal assault recidivism over chance, a finding that is consistent with that reported by the authors of the SARA (Kropp & Hart, 2000). Other general actuarial instruments fared better than SARA in predicting recidivism (e.g., PCL-R). However, the authors acknowledged that the results of the study were appreciably limited by the retrospective design, the questionable reliability of SARA due to its simulation, and the use of a small, but highly selective sample (i.e., male offenders diagnosed with a personality disorder who committed "hands-on" spousal violence only, with a higher prevalence of psychopathy and generally antisocial traits and behaviors).

To examine concurrent validity, Grann and Wedin compared SARA total scores with five measures of general violence recidivism. The SARA total score correlated significantly with all five measures: (1) number of previous convictions (r = 0.39); (2) number of previous violent convictions (r = 0.29); (3) ratings on the PCL-R (r = 0.59); (4) the Historical items of the HCR-20 (*Webster, Douglas, Eaves, & Hart, 1997; r* = 0.46); and (5) the VRAG (r = 0.33). The researcher's hypothesis that Part 1 of SARA would correlate more strongly with measures of general recidivism than Part 2 of SARA was substantiated (e.g., for the VRAG) (Part 1 of SARA, r = 0.49, and Part 2, r = −0.01). SARA thus exhibited both convergent (Part 1) and divergent (Part 2) validity with other established measures of general violence risk prediction.

Hilton, Harris, Rice, Lang, and Cormier (2004). Hilton and colleagues included SARA in their validation research of Ontario Domestic Assault Risk Assessment Guide (ODARA). The development sample data for the ODARA was obtained from the Ontario Provincial Police, and the sample was considered typically representative of aggressive spousal assaulters. Offenders were included in the study if they met the following criteria: evidence of a cohabitating intimate relationship and evidence of an intimate partner–related assault ("forceful physical contact by a man against a current or former wife or common law wife," p. 269).* A total of 589 offenders were included in the construction sample, and an additional 100 offenders were used in the cross-validation sample. The measures were coded by individuals with "extensive" risk assessment experience and graduate research assistants who were trained and closely supervised. Similar to the Grann and Wedin (2002) study, with only the reliance on file information, some items on the SARA could not be reliably coded. The authors (Hilton et al., 2004) noted that "the integrity of . . . SARA scores cannot be guaranteed because the interviews and clinical judgments recommended by their authors were not available" (p. 271).

In the timeframe under review (between 1997 and 2001), one-third of the subjects in the study recidivated violently against a female partner. To compare the predictive validity of actuarial and SPJ partner violence–specific instruments, ROC analyses were conducted.† The ROC area under the curve for the SARA was reported to be 0.64, which was less than the ODARA (AUC = 0.77), but greater than another risk assessment instrument, the Danger Assessment (AUC = 0.59). ROC analyses were repeated with a cross-validation sample (n = 100), but the

* The authors indicated that the offender need not have been arrested or charged for the index assault to be eligible (because the evidentiary requirements may be higher and earlier cases appeared less likely to be charged).

† The authors acknowledged that the integrity of SARA could not be guaranteed, but ROC analyses were conducted simply for comparison purposes (Hilton et al., 2004).

SARA total score was not significantly related to recidivism in that sample. Finally, the total score on the SARA was correlated with the ODARA ($r = 0.60$), suggesting evidence of concurrent validity between SARA and the newly developed actuarial instrument.

Heckert and Gondolf (2004). This study attempted to examine the incremental predictive power of female spousal violence victims' perceptions of risk for future violence over the use of conventional risk assessment instruments. In the course of examining this issue, SARA was used and its psychometric properties were evaluated. This retrospective study relied on a database from a multisite evaluation of batterer intervention systems. The sample was comprised of 840 men from four U.S. cities (Pittsburgh, Dallas, Houston, and Denver) most of whom (82%) were mandated by courts to attend domestic violence treatment. Three risk assessment instruments were used in the study (SARA, DA, and Kingston Screening Instrument for Domestic Violence [K-SID]) (Gelles & Tolman, 1998), and all were approximated by the researchers. The instruments were not used in actual clinical practice, but were derived from the researcher's comprehensive dataset. It was acknowledged that most potential risk factors were included in their dataset, so "reasonable proxies" of the instruments could be ascertained. However, only 10 items of the SARA were used as recommended by the authors of the tool, with 6 items of the SARA being "similar,"* and 4 were "unavailable" from the file information provided. The researchers contend that the data set "probably has less missing data than most 'real world' administrations of risk instruments" (p. 797). Alternatively, it could be argued that only 50% of the SARA items were reliably applied. Further, like the Grann and Wedin and Hilton et al. studies, summary risk ratings were not used, and an approximated actuarial score served as the only measure of risk.

To determine the effectiveness of the treatment programs, the male participants and their female partners (if available) were called separately every 3 months for a 15-month follow-up period. The purpose of the follow-up was to establish the presence of spousal assault and other forms of abuse (e.g., controlling behaviors, verbal abuse, and threats). This resulted in the men being categorized as "repeat reassaulters," "one-time reassaulters," "threatening reassault," "controlling behavior or verbal abuse," or "no abuse." To evaluate predictive validity, ROC analyses were conducted, with the researchers noting that different coding strategies (e.g., total scores, number of factors present) were used to optimize the predictions of the stimulated instruments. The approximated SARA total score demonstrated modest predictive capability (AUC = 0.64). The SARA AUC was better than the K-SID (AUC = 0.57), but less than that DA (AUC = 0.70) in predicting multiple outcomes. The addition of the victim's perception of her own risk and safety to SARA slightly increased predictive ability (AUC = 0.69 and 0.67, respectively).

A Special Case: Prevention-Based Research

Most risk assessment research has focused on the narrow question of the ability of various instruments to predict or postdict recidivism. However, it has been argued that the appropriate and relevant test of the SPJ approach is its ability to prevent future violence from taking place (Douglas & Kropp, 2002). SARA was tested in exactly this fashion on a large sample of individuals arrested for spousal violence in Sweden (Belfrage, 2008; Kropp, 2003). Swedish police officers assessed 430 male spousal assaulters prior to recommending release conditions. All officers were trained by one of the authors (HB) of the Swedish version of SARA. Offenders were followed for an average of 11 months, and new spousal-related violations were recorded. However, an innovation in the design of this study was that officers were asked to document their recommended "protective actions" using a structured menu of 19 interventions (e.g., no-contact order,

* The authors do not detail what "similar" means, in regard to finding risk factor proxies in their data set.

alarm system installed, contacting a shelter). It was thus possible to examine the effects of risk (as measured by SARA), intervention level, and the risk/intervention interaction on recidivism.

First, SARA risk level was significantly related to recidivism ($\chi^2 = 5.9$, $p < .05$), with moderate- and high-risk offenders reoffending at a higher rate (26%) than low-risk offenders (16%). However, it was apparent that the relationship between risk level and outcome may have been affected by the intervening protective actions taken. This was evident in the data, because the mean number of strategies for the low-, moderate-, and high-risk groups were 3.1, 4.1, and 5.0, respectively ($p < .05$). The risk groups also differed significantly, in the expected direction, in the percentage of cases assigned the following strategies: security discussion, no-contact order, alarm package, initiate a support person, contact safe house, and protect home. Logistic regression analysis revealed that both risk level ($B = 2.3$, $p = .002$; $OR = 9.8$) and intervention level ($B = 2.0$, $p = .02$; $OR = 6.7$) had significant main effects on recidivism. Additionally, a risk by intervention interaction effect was observed ($B = -1.2$, $p = .02$). Thus, it appeared that high levels of intervention were most effective with high-risk offenders. Low-risk offenders offended more frequently with high levels of intervention. This apparently paradoxical result was interpreted as being perfectly in line with the *risk principle* commonly cited in the corrections literature (Andrews & Bonta, 2002; Andrews & Dowden, 2006), whereby it is accepted that management resources are best spent on high-risk offenders and often counterproductive with lower-risk offenders. Overall, the result of this study offers preliminary evidence that SARA can play an important role in the prevention of violence.

Case Study

The following case study is presented to illustrate the use of SARA. For the purposes of this chapter, the report is condensed and briefer than what we would typically recommend in practice. However, it contains the essential elements of a SARA-based risk assessment evaluation.

REFERRAL INFORMATION

Mr. K. is currently before the court on bail for one count of threatening, contrary to Section 264.1 of the Criminal Code of Canada. The victim of the threatening is his wife, Sandra K. One of the conditions of his Recognizance of Bail order is that he attend this Forensic Psychiatric Outpatient Clinic for a spousal violence risk assessment. This report is based on a review of the following information: (1) copy of the police report; (2) 90-minute interview with Mr. K.; (3) 60-minute interview with Mr. K.'s wife, the victim; and (4) criminal record information on Mr. K. At the outset of the interview the purpose of the assessment and limits of confidentiality were explained to him. Mr. K. stated that he understood these issues as explained to him and consented to the interview.

BACKGROUND

Personal History

Mr. K.'s description of his childhood lacked detail, but he managed to communicate that he grew up in an environment of extreme neglect. He indicated that at age seven his mother left him "somewhere." He could not be specific about the circumstances but recalled feeling "scared." He indicated that this pattern of being passed from caretaker to caretaker (usually relatives and "babysitters") continued throughout his childhood. Mr. K. commented that he was physically abused as a child, but he could not recall who committed the assaults. He then tearfully described an experience occurring between ages eight and ten that involved being sodomized on several occasions by a babysitter. He added that this was the first time that he had ever disclosed this information.

This individual reported that he had difficulty in school, particularly with reading, and only completed grade seven. He believes that he was diagnosed with a learning disorder, but he could not be specific. He does not admit to committing a great deal of delinquent behavior as a child, but admitted to some shoplifting, fighting, and setting fire to outhouses. He stated that he was frequently truant and was eventually expelled for missing too much school. Mr. K. acknowledged that he has a juvenile criminal record, but could not be specific about offenses. He stated that he did spend some time in juvenile detention. Police records indicate that Mr. K. had five convictions as a juvenile for property offenses.

Mr. K. has been employed primarily through various labor positions, but has spent much of the past 10 years unemployed and collecting income assistance. He considers himself a reliable employee, although he admitted to having been fired on three occasions. He added that one of the dismissals was due to his drinking, which resulted in his arriving late. He explained that he was recently fired from work as a "mechanic's helper" because of his poor attendance. He is concerned about his financial situation and is currently in considerable debt due to a car loan, unpaid bills, and lack of employment.

Mr. K. described three long-term relationships with women (including his current relationship with Sandra), all of which involved frequent verbal fighting and verbal abuse on his part. He admitted to past physical assaults of female partners and mentioned that, on a couple of occasions, he has forced Sandra to have sex with him. He has one previous criminal conviction for assaulting Sandra. He has a four-year-old stepson with Sandra. According to Sandra their son has witnessed the domestic violence.

Current Offense and Criminality

Mr. K. was advised by counsel not to discuss the circumstances around the most recent offense. According to Sandra's statement to the police, the incident occurred five days ago, one day after Mr. K. was fired from his job. That evening he telephoned Sandra from a pub where he was drinking with friends. He asked her to join them at the pub, but she refused because it was too late to find a babysitter for her son. He began to verbally berate Sandra for being "a drag," "a sexual bore," and "caring more for that kid than for me." He then told her that he had been fired and that she should be there to support him. When she still refused, his anger began to escalate, and he began threatening her: "You're going to get it when I get home, I'm going to fucking kill you. . . . I thought you learned your lesson last time." Two of Mr. K.'s associates at the bar witnessed the threat. Before Mr. K. could return home Sandra phoned the police who arrested Mr. K. at the bar for threatening. He refused to take full responsibility for the incident, as he placed some of the blame on Sandra for what he described as "turning on him." Since his arrest for threatening, Mr. K. has complied with his release conditions.

According to the official criminal record Mr. K. has three prior convictions for assault, one against Sandra and the others against a previous intimate partner. There are no other violent offenses on record. Otherwise, he has 13 convictions for property offenses (theft and fraud), and three convictions for drug offenses (all for possession). He has violated a conditional release on one occasion by contacting Sandra by telephone, contrary to a no-contact order following his previous assault conviction. Mr. K. has never been convicted of using a weapon or threatening to use a weapon in past offenses, but Sandra indicated that he owns two hunting rifles and that he has threatened to use them against her in the past.

Mental Health History

Mr. K. denied experiencing any significant emotional or behavioral problems in the past. He stated that he has never seen a psychologist, psychiatrist, or any other mental health professional. He admitted to an extensive history of alcohol and drug abuse. He reported that he began drinking at approximately age 11, and began using cocaine at age 15. Both alcohol and cocaine have adversely affected virtually every aspect of his life (i.e., social, occupational, and familial functioning). His last alcohol and cocaine binge was five days ago.

On examination, Mr. K. looked his stated age of 32. He maintained an appropriate social presentation throughout the interview. Eye contact was appropriate, and there was no evidence of unusual behavior. Mr. K. periodically wept during the interview, usually when the content focused on his childhood or his current circumstances. He expressed concern about reconciling with Sandra, and admitted that he would probably "lose it" if he was sent to jail. With respect to his mood, he conceded that he feels sad and has had frequent thoughts about suicide. He also admitted feeling anxious if he is not active and complained that at such times thoughts will race through his head, causing discomfort. Mr. K. demonstrated little insight into his violent behavior. He attributed his past assaults to "drinking" and appeared to have some notion that he has "pent-up" feelings and anger. He indicated some interest in receiving treatment and believes that it would help to talk to other men "like him."

There did not appear to be any distortions either in the form or content of his thinking that would indicate the presence of a major mental disorder. His memory for recent and remote events was adequate. His attention and concentration also appeared to be within normal limits. He denied experiencing any hallucinations or delusions. However, he does appear to have some antisocial and borderline personality traits.

Summary of Sandra K.'s Statement

Mrs. K. described her husband as an extremely violent man. She noted that he has assaulted her physically, verbally, and sexually. She has observed that he seems to have an attitude of "ownership" with respect to his intimate partners and is extremely jealous. She also indicated that she has witnessed him assaulting his brothers, friends, and strangers (e.g., bar fights). Mrs. K. also described her husband's behavior as impulsive, often associated with alcohol or drug intake and withdrawal. She believes that any remorse for his actions is short lived. She also noted that the severity of her husband's violence appears to be increasing over time. She denied that weapons had ever been used in the assaults, but did report that he has threatened to use weapons "a few times" to manipulate her. Sandra explained that she has reached her limit and will be seeking a separation from Mr. K.

Risk Assessment and Management

To assist in formulating an opinion about risk in this case, I consulted the Spousal Assault Risk Assessment (SARA) Guide, a set of structured professional guidelines for assessing risk in domestic violence situations. Based on a review of SARA, it is clear that Mr. K. has a number of risk factors that have been identified in the empirical and professional literatures to be associated with repeated spousal violence. First, he has an established history of physical violence against family members and acquaintances, and he has violated conditions of release in the past. Second, he has a number of relevant psychosocial problems including a recent relationship separation, chronic employment instability, difficulties associated with childhood abuse, substance abuse, some suicidal ideation, and borderline and antisocial personality traits. Third, he has a chronic history of spousal violence that involves physical and sexual assaults, threats of violence, recent escalation in the seriousness of the violence, and a violation of a no-contact order. Finally, there appears to be some evidence of minimization and denial of his spousal violence and proprietary attitudes regarding the victim.

Overall, it is my opinion that Mr. K. represents a high risk for spousal violence in the future. The potential victims of this violence are Mrs. K. and any future intimate partners. It is also possible that Mr. K. could present a risk to any new intimate partners of Mrs. K. It is likely that future violence is imminent due to Mr. K.'s difficulty in accepting his recent marital separation. Further, based on his past pattern of violence and threats, it is plausible that the violence could be severe and involve weapons and sexual violence.

Mr. K.'s risk for violence must be managed through a combination of monitoring, supervision, treatment, and victim safety planning strategies. Therefore, those supervising Mr. K. should monitor for signs of further deterioration in his relationship, employment, and financial status, and mental state. It is recommended that frequent contacts be made with both Mr. and Mrs. K. to monitor his whereabouts and any attempts to contact the victim. Supervision strategies should include a no-contact order with Mrs. K. and an order not to attend her residence or workplace. He should also be prohibited from possessing weapons and consuming drugs or alcohol, and mandatory urinalysis could be considered. While on supervision in the community, electronic monitoring might also be a useful surveillance strategy. Regarding treatment, Mr. K. would benefit from attending a spousal violence treatment program and substance abuse counseling. Finally, it should be ensured that Mrs. K. has a victim safety plan in place. She should be informed of available victim services, the contact information for her local shelter, supportive counseling, and a review of security options at her home and workplace.

Conclusion

It appears that SARA remains a popular instrument for those conducting spousal violence risk assessments. Feedback from participants in the hundreds of workshops conducted by the authors of the SARA suggests that professionals appreciate the practical utility, flexibility, and discretion involved in the procedure. The authors of the SARA have also been developing administrative software and online training programs to further assist practitioners in providing reliable and time-efficient risk assessments. Practical considerations aside, it also apparent that empirical evidence regarding the reliability and validity of SARA is mounting, although we have noted in this chapter that much of the published research on SARA has been flawed by the misapplication of the instrument. Future validation research is needed that utilizes the recommended SARA procedures. Further, since SARA is designed to prevent violence, the most useful research will not necessarily investigate the predictive validity of SARA, but rather the association between SARA risk assessments, risk management strategies, and violence reduction. As noted, we currently are involved in such research and encourage others interested in this field to follow.

References

Aldarando, A., & Sugarman, D. B. (1996). Risk marker analysis of the cessation and persistence of wife assault. *Journal of Consulting and Clinical Psychology, 64,* 1010–1019.

Andrews, D. A., & Bonta, J. (2002). *The psychology of criminal conduct* (3rd ed.). Cincinnati, OH: Anderson.

Andrews, D. A., Bonta, J., & Wormith, J. S. (1995). *Level of Service Inventory–Ontario Revision (LSI-OR): Interview and scoring guide.* Toronto, ON, Canada: Ontario Ministry of the Solicitor General and Correctional Services.

Andrews, D., & Dowden, C. (2006). Risk principle of case classification in correctional treatment: A meta-analytic investigation. *International Journal of Offender Therapy and Comparative Criminology, 50,* 88–100

Belfrage, H. (2008). Police-based structured spousal violence risk assessment: The process of developing a police version of the SARA. In A. C. Baldry & F. W. Winkel (Eds.), *Intimate partner violence prevention and intervention: The risk assessment and management approach.* Hauppauge, NY: Nova Science.

Bennett Cattaneo, L., & Goodman, L. A. (2005). Risk factors for reabuse in intimate partner violence: A cross-disciplinary critical review. *Trauma, Violence and Abuse, 6,* 141–175.

Borum, R., Swartz, M., & Swanson, J. (1996). Assessing and managing violence risk in clinical practice. *Journal of Practicing Psychiatry and Behavioral Health, 4,* 205–215.

Burgess, A. W., Baker, T., Greening, D., Hartman, C. R., Burgess, A. G., Douglas, J. E., & Halloran, R. (1997). Stalking behaviors within domestic violence. *Journal of Family Violence, 12,* 389–403.

Cadsky, O., & Crawford, M. (1988). Establishing batterer typologies in a clinical sample of men who assault their female partners. Special Issue: Wife battering: A Canadian perspective. *Canadian Journal of Community Mental Health, 7,* 119–127.

Cairns, K. V. (2004). *Alberta Mental Health Board Domestic Violence Treatment Program Evaluation: Report to the Partnering Ministries Committee.* Edmonton, AB, Canada: Alberta Mental Health Board.

Campbell, J. C. (1995). Prediction of homicide of and by battered women. In J. C. Campbell (Ed.), *Assessing dangerousness: Violence by sexual offenders, batterers, and child abusers* (pp. 96–113). Thousand Oaks, CA: Sage.

Campbell, J. C., Sharps, P. & Glass, N. (2001). Risk assessment for intimate partner homicide. In G. F. Pinard and L. Pagani (Eds.), *Clinical Assessment of Dangerousness: Empirical Contributions* (pp. 137–157). New York: Cambridge University Press.

Campbell, J. C., Webster, D., Koziol-McLain, J., Block, C., Campbell, D., Curry, M. A., Gary, F., Glass, N., McFarlane, J., Sachs, C., Sharps, P., Ulrich, Y., Wilt, S. A., Manganello, J., Xu, X., Schollenberger, J., Frye, V., & Laughon, K. (2003). Risk factors for femicide in abusive relationships: Results from a multi-site case control study. *American Journal of Public Health, 93,* 1089–1097.

Carlson, M. J., Harris, S. D. & Holden, G. W. (1999). Protective orders and domestic violence: Risk factors for reabuse. *Journal of Family Violence, 14,* 205–226.

Cooper, M. (1993). *Assessing the risk of repeated violence among men arrested for wife assault: A review of the literature.* Vancouver, BC, Canada: British Columbia Institute on Family Violence.

Daly, M., & Wilson, M. (1998). An evolutionary psychological perspective on homicide. In M. D. Smith & M. Zahn (Eds.), *Homicide: A sourcebook of social research* (pp. 58–71). Thousand Oaks, CA: Sage.

Dickens, B. (1985). Prediction, professionalism, and public policy. In C. D. Webster, M. H. Ben-Aron, & S. J. Hucker (Eds.), *Dangerousness: Probability and prediction, psychiatry, and public policy* (pp. 177–207). New York: Cambridge University Press.

Dobash, R. E., Dobash, R. P., Cavanagh, K., & Lewis, R. (2001). *Homicide in Britain: Risk factors, situational contexts and lethal intentions. Research Bulletin No. 1.* Manchester, UK: University of Manchester.

Douglas, K. S. & Dutton, D. G. (2001). Assessing the link between stalking and domestic violence. *Aggression and Violent Behavior, 6,* 519–546.

Douglas, K. S., & Kropp, P. R. (2002). A prevention-based paradigm for violence risk assessment: Clinical and research applications. *Criminal Justice and Behavior, 29,* 617–658.

Douglas, K. S., & Webster, C. D. (1999). Predicting violence in mentally and personality disordered individuals. In R. Roesch, S. D. Hart, & J. R. P. Ogloff (Eds.). *Psychology and law: The state of the discipline* (pp. 175–239). New York: Plenum.

Dutton, D. G. (1995). *The domestic assault of women: Psychological and criminal justice perspectives* (Rev. Ed.). Vancouver, BC, Canada: UBC Press.

Dutton, D., & Kropp, P. R. (2000). A review of domestic violence risk instruments. *Trauma, Violence, and Abuse, 1,* 171–181.

Fagan, J. A., Stewart, D. K., & Hansen, K. V. (1983). Violent men or violent husbands? Background factors and situational correlates. In D. Finkelhor, R. J. Gelles, G. T. Hotaling, & M. A. Straus (Eds.), *The dark side of families: Current family violence research* (pp. 49–67). Newbury Park, CA: Sage

Field, C. A., Caetano, R., & Nelson, S. (2004). Alcohol and violence related cognitive risk factors associated with the perpetration of intimate partner violence. *Journal of Family Violence, 19,* 249–253.

Garner, J. W., & Hudson, W. W. (2003). *Conceptualizing and measuring "healthy marriages" for empirical research and evaluation studies: A compendium of measures—Part II.* Washington, DC: Child Trends.

Gelles, R. J., & Straus, M. A. (1988). *Intimate violence: The causes and consequences of abuse in the American family.* New York: Simon and Schuster.

Gelles, R., & Tolman, R. (1998). *The Kingston Screening Instrument for Domestic Violence (KSID).* Unpublished risk instrument, University of Rhode Island, Providence.

Gibas, A., Kropp, P. R., & Hart, S. D., & Stewart, L. (2008). *Validity of the SARA in a Canadian sample of incarcerated males.* Paper presented at the Annual Conference of the International Association of Forensic Mental Health Services, Vienna, Austria.

Goldsmith, H. R. (1990). Men who abuse their spouses: An approach to assessing future risk. *Journal of Offender Counseling, Services and Rehabilitation, 15,* 45–56.

Gondolf, E. W. (1988). Who are those guys? Toward a behavioral typology of batterers. *Violence and Victims, 3,* 187–203.

Gondolf, E. W. (1998). *Assessing woman battering in mental health services.* Thousand Oaks, CA: Sage Publications.

Gondolf, E. W. & White, R. J. (2001). Batterer program participants who repeatedly reassault: Psychopathic tendencies and other disorders. *Journal of Interpersonal Violence, 16,* 361–380.

Grann, M., & Wedin, I. (2002). Risk factors for recidivism among spousal assault and spousal homicide offenders. *Psychology, Crime, and Law, 8,* 5–23.

Hanson, R. K., Helmus, L., & Bourgon, G. (2007). *The Validity of Risk Assessments for Intimate Partner Violence: A Meta-Analysis.* Ottawa: Public Safety Canada.

Hanson, R. K., & Wallace-Capretta, S. (2000). Predicting recidivism among male batterers. User Report 2000-06. Ottawa, ON, Canada: Department of the Solicitor General of Canada.

Hare, R. D. (1991). *The Hare Psychopathy Checklist—Revised manual.* Toronto, ON, Canada: Multi-Health Systems.

Harrell, A., & Smith, B. (1996). Effects of restraining orders on domestic violence victims. In E. Buzawa & C. Buzawa (Eds.), *Do arrests and restraining orders work?* (pp. 214–242). Thousand Oaks, CA: Sage.

Hart, B. J. (1992). *Program standards for batterer intervention services.* Reading, PA: Pennsylvania Coalition Against Domestic Violence.

Hart, S. D. (1998). The role of psychopathy in assessing risk for violence. *Legal and Criminological Psychology, 3,* 121–137.

Hart, S. D., Cox, D. N., & Hare, R. D. (1995). *Manual for the Hare Psychopathy Checklist: Screening Version (PCL:SV).* Toronto: Multi-Health Systems, Inc.

Hart, S. D., Kropp, P. R., & Hare, R. D. (1988). Performance of male psychopaths following conditional release from prison. *Journal of Consulting and Clinical Psychology, 56,* 227–232.

Healy, K., Smith, C., & O'Sullivan, C. (1998). *Batterer intervention: Program approaches and criminal justice strategies* (NCJ 168638). Washington, DC: National Institute of Justice.

Heckert, D. A., & Gondolf, E. W. (2004). Battered women's perceptions of risk versus risk factors and instruments in predicting repeated reassault. *Journal of Interpersonal Violence, 19,* 778–800.

Hilton, N. Z., & Harris, G. T. (2004). Predicting wife assault: A critical review and implications for policy and practice. *Trauma, Violence, and Abuse, 6,* 3–23.

Hilton, N. Z., and Harris, G. T. (2005). Predicting wife assault: A critical review and implications for policy and practice. *Trauma, Violence, and Abuse, 6,* 3–23.

Hilton, N. Z., Harris, G. T., Rice, M. E., Lang, C., & Cormier, C. A. (2004). A brief actuarial assessment for the prediction of wife assault recidivism: The ODARA. *Psychological Assessment, 16,* 267–275.

Hotaling, G. T., & Sugarman, D. B. (1986). An analysis of risk markers in husband-to-wife violence: The current state of knowledge. *Violence and Victims, 1,* 101–124.

Huss, M. T., & Langhinrichsen-Rohling, J. (2000). Identification of the psychopathic batterer: The clinical, legal, and policy implications. *Aggression and Violent Behavior, 5,* 403–422.

Jones, A. S. & Gondolf, E. W. (2001). Time-varying risk factors for reassault among batterer program participants. *Journal of Family Violence, 16,* 345–359.

Kennedy, L. W., & Dutton, D. G. (1989). The incidence of wife assault in Alberta. *Canadian Journal of Behavioral Science, 21,* 40–54.

Kessler, R. C., Molnar, B. E., Feurer, I. D., & Appelbaum, M. (2001). Patterns and mental health predictors of domestic violence in the United States: Results from the National Comorbidity Survey. *International Journal of Law and Psychiatry, 24,* 487–508.

Kropp, P. R. (2003, April). *Validity of law enforcement officers evaluations of risk.* Paper presented at the 3rd Annual Conference of the International Association of Forensic Mental Health Services, Miami, FL.

Kropp, P. R. (2004). Some questions about spousal violence risk assessment. *Violence Against Women, 10(6),* 676–697.

Kropp, P. R., & Hart, S. D. (2000). The Spousal Assault Risk Assessment (SARA) Guide: Reliability and validity in adult male offenders. *Law and Human Behavior, 24,* 101–118.

Kropp, P. R., Hart, S. D., & Belfrage. (2005). *Brief Spousal Assault Form for the Evaluation of Risk (B-SAFER).* Vancouver, BC, Canada: ProActive ReSolutions Inc.

Kropp, P. R., Hart, S. D., & Lyon, D. R. (2002). Risk assessment of stalkers: Some problems and possible solutions. *Criminal Justice and Behavior, 29,* 590–616.

Kropp, R. P., Hart, S. D., Webster, C. D., & Eaves, D. (1994). *Manual for the Spousal Assault Risk Assessment Guide.* Vancouver, BC, Canada: The British Columbia Institute Against Family Violence.

Kropp, R. P., Hart, S. D., Webster, C. D., & Eaves, D. (1995). *Manual for the Spousal Assault Risk Assessment Guide* (2nd ed.). Vancouver, BC, Canada: The British Columbia Institute Against Family Violence.

Kropp, P. R., Hart, S. D., Webster, C. W., & Eaves, D. (1999). *Spousal Assault Risk Assessment: User's Guide.* Toronto, ON, Canada: Multi-Health Systems, Inc.

Kurz, D. (1993). Physical assaults by husbands: A major social problem. In R. J. Gelles & D. R. Loseke (Eds.), *Current controversies in family violence* (pp. 88–103). Newbury Park, CA: Sage.

Kyriacou, D. N., Anglin, D., Taliaferro, E., Stone, S., Tubb, T., Linden, J. A., Muelleman, R., Barton, E., & Kraus, J. F. (1999). Risk factors for injury to women from domestic violence. *New England Journal of Medicine, 341,* 1882–1898.

Magdol, L., Moffitt, T. E., Caspi, A., Newman, D. L., Fagan, J., & Silva, P. A. (1997). Gender differences in partner violence in a birth cohort of 21-year-olds: Bridging the gap between clinical and epidemiological approaches. *Journal of Consulting and Clinical Psychology, 65,* 68–78.

Mahoney, P., Williams, L. M., & West, C. M. (2001). Violence against women by intimate relationship partners. In C. M. Renzetti, J. L. Edleson, & R. Kennedy Bergen (Eds.), *Sourcebook on violence against women.* Thousand Oaks, CA: Sage.

Melton, G. B., Petrila, J., Poythress, N., & Slobogin, C. (2007). *Psychological evaluations for the courts: A handbook for attorneys and mental health professionals* (3rd ed.). New York: Guilford Press.

Monahan, J., & Steadman, H. J. (1994). *Violence and mental disorder: Developments in risk assessment.* Chicago: University of Chicago Press.

Monahan, J., Steadman, H. J., Silver, E., Appelbaum, P. S., Robbins, P. C., Mulvey, E. P., Roth, L. W., Grisso, T., & Banks, S. (2001). *Rethinking risk assessment: The MacArthur study of mental disorder and violence.* New York: Oxford University Press.

Mowat-Léger, V. (2001). *Risk factors for violence: A comparison of domestic batterers and other violent and non-violent offenders.* Unpublished doctoral dissertation, Carleton University, Ottawa, ON, Canada.

Murphy, C., & O'Leary, K. D. (1989). Psychological aggression predicts physical aggression in early marriage. *Journal of Consulting and Clinical Psychology, 56,* 24–33.

Nuffield, J. (1982). *Parole decision-making in Canada: Research towards decision guidelines.* Ottawa, ON, Canada: Ministry of Supplies and Services Canada.

Palarea, R. E., Zona, M. A., Lane, J. C., & Langhinrichsen-Rohling, J. (1999). The dangerous nature of intimate relationship stalking: Threats, violence, and associated risk factors. *Behavioral Sciences and the Law, 17,* 269–283.

Quinsey, V. L., Harris, G. T., Rice, G. T., & Cormier, C. A. (1998). *Violent offenders: Appraising and managing risk.* Washington, DC: American Psychological Association.

Riggs, D. S., Caulfield, M. B., & Street, A. E. (2000). Risk for domestic violence: Factors associated with perpetration and victimization. *Journal of Clinical Psychology, 56,* 1289–1316.

Saunders, D. G. (1992). A typology of men who batter women: Three types derived from cluster analysis. *American Journal of Orthopsychiatry, 62,* 264–275.

Saunders, D. G., & Browne, A. (2000). Intimate partner homicide. In R. T. Ammerman & M. Hersen (Eds.), *Case studies in family violence* (2nd ed.) (pp. 415–449). New York: Kluwer Academic.

Saunders D. G., Lynch A. B., Grayson M., & Linz D. (1987). The inventory of beliefs about wife beating: the construction and initial validation of a measure of beliefs and attitudes. *Violence and Victims, 2,* 39–57.

Schumacher, J. A., Feldbau-Kohn, S., Slep, A. M. S., & Heyman, R. E. (2001). Risk factors for male-to-female partner physical abuse. *Aggression and Violent Behavior, 6,* 281–352.

Shepard, M. F. & Campbell, J. A. (1992). The Abusive Behavior Inventory: A measure of psychological and physical abuse. *Journal of Interpersonal Violence, 7,* 291–305.

Shepard, M. F., Falk, D. R., & Elliott, B. A. (2002). Enhancing coordinated community responses to reduce recidivism in cases of domestic violence. *Journal of Interpersonal Violence, 17,* 551–569.

Sherman, L. W., Smith, D. A., Schmidt, J. D., and Rogan, D. P. (1992). Crime, punishment and the stake in conformity: Legal and informal control of domestic violence. *American Sociological Review, 57,* 680–690.

Sonkin, D. J. (1987). The assessment of court-mandated male batterers. In D. J. Sonkin (Ed.), *Domestic violence on trial: Psychological and legal dimensions of family violence* (pp. 174–196). New York: Springer.

Stuart, E. P., & Campbell, J. C. (1989). Assessment of patterns of dangerousness with battered women. *Issues in Mental Health Nursing, 10,* 245–260.

Tweed, R. G. & Dutton, D. G. (1998). A comparison of impulsive and instrumental subgroups of batterers. *Violence and Victims, 13,* 217–230.

Walker, L. E. (1989). Psychology and violence against women. *American Psychologist, 44,* 695–702.

Webster, C. D., Douglas, K. S., Eaves, D., & Hart, S. D. (1997). *HCR-20: Assessing risk for violence, version 2.* Burnaby, BC, Canada: Mental Health, Law, & Policy Institute, Simon Fraser University.

Weisz, A. N., Tolman, R. M., & Saunders, D. G. (2000). Assessing the risk of severe domestic violence: The importance of survivors' predictions. *Journal of Interpersonal Violence, 15,* 75–90.

Widom, C. S. (1989). The cycle of violence. *Science, 244,* 160–166.

Williams, K. & Houghton, A. B. (2004). Assessing the risk of domestic violence reoffending: A validation study. *Law and Human Behavior, 24,* 437–455.

Wong, T. & Hisashima, M. A. (2008). *Domestic violence exploratory study on the* DVSI *and* SARA, *State of Hawaii, 2003–2007.* Hawaii: Interagency Council on Intermediate Sanctions (Available at www.hawaii.gov/icis).

12
Static-99
An Actuarial Tool to Assess Risk of Sexual and Violent Recidivism Among Sexual Offenders

DANA ANDERSON and R. KARL HANSON

Introduction

In 1988, Joseph Fredericks raped and murdered 11-year-old Christopher Stephenson. In 1994, Jesse Timmedequas raped and murdered Megan Kanka in New Jersey. These horrific crimes were both committed by men who had previously been convicted of sexual offenses, prompting new, widespread legislative initiatives to address the risk of sexual offenders in the community ("Christopher's Law" in Ontario; "Megan's Law" across the United States). Fortunately, sexual murder is rare, and, contrary to popular opinion, only a minority of sexual offenders are known to commit another sexual offense after being caught. The observed recidivism rate is 10% to 15% after five years, increasing to approximately 20% after 10 years (Hanson & Bussière, 1998; Harris & Hanson, 2004) Even considering that many offenses go undetected, it is difficult to argue that all sexual offenders will inevitably reoffend. Some will and others will not.

This chapter will describe one approach to evaluating the recidivism risk of individual sexual offenders, namely, Static-99 (Hanson & Thornton, 1999, 2000). Static-99 is the most widely used measure for the assessment of risk of recidivism among sexual offenders in Canada and the United States (Archer, Buffington-Vollum, Stredny, & Handel, 2006) and is used in jurisdictions as diverse as Taiwan, Israel, Finland, and Singapore. It is commonly used for diverse purposes, including treatment planning (McGrath, Cumming, & Burchard, 2003), community supervision (Interstate Commission for Adult Offender Supervision, 2007), and civil commitment evaluations (Jackson & Hess, 2007).

The purpose of this chapter is to review the development and validation of Static-99 and its application in applied risk assessment. We describe how it could be used on its own, as well as integrated into comprehensive evaluations involving both static and dynamic (changeable) risk factors.

The Development of the Static-99

Rapid Risk Assessment for Sexual Offense Recidivism and Structured Anchored Clinical Judgment Scale

Static-99 was developed by R. Karl Hanson and David Thornton to assess sexual offenders for their risk of sexual and violent recidivism. It was created from the Rapid Risk Assessment for Sexual Offense Recidivism (RRASOR) (Hanson, 1997) and Thornton's Structured Anchored Clinical Judgment (SACJ-Min) scale (described in Grubin, 1998). The RRASOR was developed with the goal of creating "an easily administered scale that was likely to be valid for a range of settings" (p. 4). The RRASOR items were obtained from Hanson and Bussière's (1998) meta-analytic study of factors related to sexual offense recidivism. In that study, they found that the following easily scored factors were among those most strongly correlated with sexual reoffending: prior sex offenses, stranger victims (of sex offenses), prior offenses (of any type), age, never married, nonrelated victims (of sex offenses), and male victims (of sex offenses). After examining the variables' association with sexual recidivism using stepwise regression, Hanson (1997) retained four variables for the RRASOR: age (of offender), previous sex offenses, presence of unrelated victims of sexual crimes, and presence of male victims of sexual crimes. A rating of 0 or 1 was assigned to 3 of the 4 items, and a rating of 0 to 3 points was assigned to the item "prior sex offenses." The items were then cross-validated on another sample. The total possible score on the RRASOR ranges from 0 to 6. Hanson (1997) concluded that the RRASOR could reasonably be used as a screening tool,* but cautioned that certain important variables were neglected and that the RRASOR is not intended to be used in isolation. Many variables known to predict sexual reoffending, such as phallometrically assessed deviant sexual preferences and psychopathy, were not included in the RRASOR. The RRASOR was developed as a brief, efficient tool, based on items that were easily scored from commonly available records.

David Thornton's Structured Anchored Clinical Judgment Scale (Grubin, 1998; Hanson & Thornton, 2000) utilized a stepwise approach to assessing risk of sexual and violent recidivism. The first step is comprised of historical variables, where one point is awarded for each of the following items: current sexual offense, previous sex offense conviction, current nonsexual violent offense conviction, previous nonsexual violent offense conviction, and three or more previous convictions (of any type). The number of points at the first step determines risk level. The second step includes aggravating factors (male victims of sex offenses, stranger victims of sex offenses, noncontact sex offense, substance abuse, previously in care, never married, deviant sexual arousal, high [>25] score on the Psychopathy Checklist–Revised); the presence of two or more aggravating factors raises the risk level one category. The third stage of this risk assessment method includes variables related to current behavior and treatment completion. Only the items in the first two steps that were subject to cross-validation, referred to as the SACJ-Min, were included in the development of the Static-99.

Despite their similarity, exploratory analyses indicated that RRASOR and SACJ-Min both made incremental contributions to the prediction of sexual recidivism. Consequently, Hanson and Thornton decided to combine the two instruments by retaining 10 nonredundant items: age, intimate relationship history (ever lived with a lover for 2+ years), index (current) nonsexual violent offense conviction, prior nonsexual violent offense conviction, prior sexual offending, general criminal history (sentencing dates), noncontact sexual offense conviction, extrafamilial sex offense victim(s), stranger victim(s) of sex offenses, and male victim(s) of sex offenses (see Figure 12.1).

The items were selected based on their empirical relationships with recidivism, and not on the basis of construct validity. Nevertheless, perusal of the items suggested that they could be grouped into five general categories: sexual deviance, which is indicated by male victims, offender never having lived common-law (or been married) for 2 or more years, and the presence of noncontact sexual offense(s); range of potential victims, indicated by the presence of extrafamilial victims and stranger victims; persistence of sexual offending, indicated by prior sex offenses (and this item is given the highest weighting in the Static-99); antisociality, as indicated by nonsexual violence (index and prior), and number of previous sentencing dates; and age.

* Subsequent research has supported the use of the RRASOR as a reasonable screening tool (average d of .60, based on 11,031 offenders in 34 different studies; see Hanson & Morton-Bourgon, 2009). We do not recommend its use, however, given Static-99's superior predictive validity.

Construction Samples

The first three samples described below were used to develop the scale, and the fourth was used to explore the validity of the findings. Specifically, various combinations of RRASOR and SACJ-Min items were tested in the Pinel, Millbrook, and Oak Ridge samples. Several combinations of items yielded equivalent predictive accuracy, and the 10-item version selected was deemed simpler than the other options. The predictive accuracy of the 10-item version, now called Static-99, was then tested on a completely new sample from Her Majesty's Prison Service that was not part of the development process. Given that there was no shrinkage between the developmental samples and the cross-validation samples, all available offenders were combined to compute

Question Number	Risk Factor	Codes		Score
1	Young	Aged 25 or older		0
		Aged 18 — 24.99		1
2	Ever Lived With	Ever lived with lover for at least two years?		
		Yes		0
		No		1
3	Index Nonsexual Violence — Any Convictions?	No		0
		Yes		1
4	Prior Nonsexual Violence — Any Convictions?	No		0
		Yes		1
5	Prior Sex Offenses	Charges	Convictions	
		None	None	0
		1 to 2	1	1
		3 to 5	2 to 3	2
		6+	4+	3
6	Prior Sentencing Dates (excluding index)	3 or less		0
		4 or more		1
7	Any Convictions for Noncontact Sex Offenses	No		0
		Yes		1
8	Any Unrelated Victims	No		0
		Yes		1
9	Any Stranger Victims	No		0
		Yes		1
10	Any Male Victims	No		0
		Yes		1
	Total Score	Add up scores from individual risk factors		

	POINTS	Risk Category
Suggested Nominal Risk Categories	0,1	Low
	2,3	Moderate-Low
	4,5	Moderate-High
	6+	High

Figure 12.1 Static-99 tally sheet.

the recidivism rate tables. The Oak Ridge sample was not included in the recidivism rate calculations because the survival times (dates of reoffense) were not available for that sample. Recidivism was defined as reconviction data in the three samples used to construct the Static-99 recidivism rate tables in the manual (the use of reconviction data as the definition of recidivism is further discussed in the "Validity" section of this chapter). Institute Philippe Pinel is a maximum-security psychiatric facility near Montreal, Quebec, Canada. The sex offenders used in this study were released between 1978 and 1993. The average age at release for this sample was 36 years. Although many offenders in this sample would have undergone some level of treatment, it is assumed that treatment methods would be relatively ineffective, given the recent advances in treatment approaches with sex offenders, as well as improvements in identifying appropriate treatment targets (see, for example, Hanson & Harris, 1998). For our purposes, they have been considered mainly untreated.

Information regarding recidivism was obtained for 344 offenders, comprised of 70% child molesters. The average years of follow-up data in this sample was four. The case files of the offenders were reviewed to obtain information regarding the predictor variables (i.e., items on Static-99), and records from the Royal Canadian Mounted Police (R.C.M.P.), the federal police service in Canada, were obtained from 1994 to determine recidivism rates up to that time. Some information from the case files in this sample could not be obtained; therefore, some information was extrapolated, aggregated, or omitted, depending on what information was available (see Hanson & Thornton, 1999, for details). Fifteen percent of this sample had recidivated with a new sexual crime, and 21% had recidivated with a violent (including sexual) offense.

Millbrook Correctional Centre was a maximum-security provincial jail located in central-eastern Ontario, Canada. This sample, consisting of 191 child molesters, was comprised of admissions between 1958 and 1974 and followed for an average period of 23 years. The average age of these offenders at release was 33 years. Approximately half of the offenders completed a brief treatment program, which had no observable effect on recidivism rates (Hanson, Steffy, & Gauthier, 1993). Clinical and correctional files were used to obtain information on the predictor variables, but some coding of variables was omitted due to the lack of information on file. As with the sample above, recidivism information (i.e., the criterion variable) was obtained from records from the R.C.M.P. Thirty-five percent of these offenders had reoffended with a new sexual crime and 44% had reoffended with a violent (including sexual) offense.

There were 142 offenders drawn from the population at Oak Ridge Division of the Penetanguishene Mental Health Centre. Oak Ridge is a maximum-security psychiatric hospital north of Toronto, Ontario, Canada. This sample was comprised of approximately 49% child molesters who were referred for psychiatric assessments related to legal proceedings (e.g., fitness to stand trial) or who were referred to the facility by courts, other correctional facilities, or the mental health system. The offenders in this sample were referred to the Centre between 1972 and 1993. The average length of follow-up of the releases was 10 years. Information regarding new convictions was obtained from the R.C.M.P. records. As well, new sexual offense recidivism information, regardless of charges laid, was obtained from mental health records. As with the above samples, some coding of variables was omitted from some cases. The average age at release of this sample was 30 years. Within the follow-up period, 35% of this sample had reoffended with a new sexual crime and 57% had reoffended with any type of violent (including sexual) crime.

The fourth sample, used for the validation of Static-99, was comprised of 531 offenders, approximately 61% of whom were child molesters, released from Her Majesty's Prison Service in England and Wales in 1979. All offenders were tracked for a fixed follow-up period of 16 years. This is considered an untreated sample, and information for all of the predictor variables was available. The average age at release for this sample was 34 years. The sexual reoffending rate of this sample within the follow-up period was 25%, and 37% of this sample had reoffended with any type of violent (including sexual) crime.

Reliability

In psychological measurement, reliability of a test can defined as the extent to which the observed scores are attributable to the construct of interest ("true score") rather than measurement error. There are several different methods of indexing reliability, including internal consistency, rater agreement, or test-retest consistency. The Static-99 items were derived from empirical data and not from any particular theory that would suggest what the items were measuring. Consequently, the Static-99 items were not expected to "hang together," even though it is possible to interpret item content post hoc. For example, convictions for noncontact offenses and male victims can be considered indicators of sexual deviance; however, these items were not chosen specifically because of their relationship to sexual deviance but for their stand-alone association with the outcome variable of interest—recidivism. Consequently, internal consistency is not an appropriate measure of reliability for Static-99.

For the purpose of the reliability on Static-99, our concern is rater reliability, or the extent to which observers or raters of the Static-99 agree on the scores for the same cases. In both research studies and applied evaluations, the rater reliability has been high (see Harris, Phenix, Hanson, & Thornton, 2003). Barbaree, Seto, Langton, and Peacock (2001), for example, found a correlation of .90 for raters retrospectively coding files for research. When comparing 55 cases rated by independent evaluators for civil commitment hearings in California, Hanson (2001) found an average 91% of agreement on item ratings, an item kappa of .80, and an intraclass correlation for total scores of .87. With high-risk federal offenders in Canada, Looman (2006) found inter-rater reliability of .90 (n = 26) and G. T. Harris et al. (2003) found an intraclass correlation of .87 (n = 10). Hanson, Harris, Scott, and Helmus (2007) found high levels of agreement for the scores computed by trained probation officers in a prospective study (intraclass correlation of .91). Rater reliability in the .90 range means that raters will rarely disagree by more than one point (SD = 1.97; the 95% confidence interval for standard error of measurement is 1.22).

Although inter-rater reliability levels reported have been generally high, this is not always the case. In a recent study, Ducro and Pham (2006) found an oddly low intraclass correlation coefficient of .63. Consequently, it is important to outline some considerations and guidelines for maintaining acceptable levels of agreement between raters. First, it is imperative to have adequate records—particularly for criminal history. The less complete the records, the more raters are required to extrapolate. In the Ducro and Pham (2006) study, standardized criminal history records were not available, and the coders had to infer the criminal history variables from the not-so-clear accounts provided in the clinical records of patients at a forensic psychiatric facility.

Second, procedures are needed to ensure that competency in the scoring criteria is achieved and maintained. In most cases, this involves structured training along with formal procedures for quality assurance (for example, peer review, scoring "parties"). The Static-99 scoring manual is reasonably thorough, but there are many subtle distinctions that are easily confused or forgotten. Consequently, even experienced raters (including the authors) need to regularly review the manual to avoid rater drift. The level of reliability places a limit on the validity, or predictive accuracy, of the tool. If raters disagree on the scoring, then the instrument will not provide the maximum potential level of predictive accuracy within that sample.

Validity

As with reliability, different types of validity are relevant for different types of tests. As noted above, the items chosen for the Static-99 were not chosen to assess latent constructs, but were chosen based on each item's direct association with recidivism. Notwithstanding the way in which the items were chosen, some exploration of construct validity has been conducted for the items on the Static-99.

A general consensus is developing that the major factors contributing to recidivism among sexual offenders are sexual deviance and antisociality. Hanson and Bussière (1998) summarized the factors related to sexual recidivism based on the data from several studies included in their meta-analysis. Measures of sexual deviancy produced the strongest predictors of sexual offense recidivism, and to a lesser extent, criminal lifestyle variables also predicted sexual recidivism. The factors of antisocial lifestyle and sexual deviancy held as the grouping labels for variables predicting sexual recidivism in an updated meta-analysis (Hanson & Morton-Bourgon, 2004, 2005). Roberts, Doren, and Thornton (2002) examined the structure underlying the relationships among various actuarial risk assessment instrument items and concluded that the components assessed by the instruments (including Static-99) were an antisocial/violence component and a pedophilic deviance/sexual repetitiveness component. Similarly, Barbaree, Langton, and Peacock (2006b) found that most actuarial instrument items load onto factors representing criminality or sexual deviance (which was reflected in four factors representing different aspects of sexual deviance).

Regardless of the types of factors or underlying dimensions that appear to be assessed by the Static-99, evaluators should be most concerned with the tool's predictive accuracy. There have been at least 42 studies (n = 13,288) examining the extent to which Static-99 accurately rank orders the offenders in terms of relative risk to reoffend in independent replication studies (Hanson & Morton-Bourgon, 2007). On average, these studies found predictive accuracy (average d = .70, 95% confidence interval of .64 to .76) similar to that observed in the developmental samples (d = .78). The standardized mean difference (d), is the difference between the recidivists and the nonrecidivists compared to the extent to which individuals within each of those groups vary from each other. The value of d is approximately double that of the correlation coefficient calculated from the same data. Another common method of reporting predictive accuracy is the area under the receiver operating characteristic curve (AUC) (Rice & Harris, 2005). This statistic is equivalent to the common language effect size, and is interpreted as the probability that a randomly selected recidivist will have a higher score on a test than a randomly selected nonrecidivist. In the case of Static-99, the AUCs are typically around .70. Similar levels of predictive accuracy have been found for diverse samples from Canada (16 studies), the United States (10 studies), and the United Kingdom (10 studies) (see Hanson & Morton-Bourgon, 2007), as well as in other European countries (Bengtson & Långström, 2007; Ducro & Pham, 2006; Endrass, Urbaniok, Held, Vetter, & Rossegger, in press; Rettenberger & Eher, 2006; Sjöstedt & Långström, 2001).

The variability of findings across studies, however, is more than would be expected by chance. In some studies, the predictive accuracy is substantially higher than in the developmental samples (e.g., Thornton, 2002), and in some cases, substantially lower (e.g., Långström, 2004; Tough, 2001). The reason for this variation is not fully understood, and it could plausibly be related to artificial differences in research methods and data sources, as well as to real differences in the relative predictive accuracy across populations.

Although Static-99 has demonstrated a robust ability to rank order offenders across samples, it is also important to consider the stability of the predicted recidivism rates. Even when evaluators can confidently identify offenders ranked in the top 10% of risk, decision-makers would be interested to know whether the absolute recidivism rates of the high risk group is 5%, 50%, or 95%. Determining the real recidivism rates is a difficult issue, because not all offenses are detected. Stability in the observed rates, however, would provide some basis upon which to extrapolate.

There has been relatively little research examining the stability of the absolute recidivism rates, and the results remain equivocal. In the developmental samples, Static-99 was able to differentiate a group of high-risk offenders, whose observed long-term recidivism rate was approximately 50%, from low-risk offenders, who observed recidivism rate was approximately 10%. Doren (2004a) concluded that the 5-year recidivism percentages, or probability estimates, were reasonably well replicated in seven studies for both the RRASOR and Static-99, with the exception of a total Static-99 score of four. Doren's (2004a) analysis, however, did not fully consider the impact of variations in base rates and variations in the relative risk associated with different risk categories (Mossman, 2006). In a new collection of eight studies, Helmus (2007) found that higher risk offenders (i.e., those with a score of 6 or over) reoffended sexually at a lower rate after 5 and 10 years than what would be expected given the probability estimates in the Static-99 manual. Similarly, Nicholaichuk's (2001) observed rates of recidivism at 10 years were generally lower in the high-risk samples than those observed in the Static-99 construction samples.

The reasons for these differences are not known, although the differences that have been observed are all in the same direction: down; i.e., the observed rates in the recent studies are lower than the rates observed in the development samples. The differences could be due to treatment effects, because most of the offenders in the construction samples either received no treatment or would have received treatment that would be regarded by today's standards as ineffective. Another factor is improved community supervision (residency restrictions, surveillance officers, and so forth). Officers might be "catching" the offenders for minor, nonsexual offenses, prior to sexual recidivism. Regardless of the reasons for the differences, evaluators should be cautious when interpreting and presenting the absolute recidivism rates, because the factors influencing these rates are not fully known.

Evaluators considering the absolute recidivism rates of a specific offender must assess the extent to which he is part of a sample similar to the development samples. If the offender is from a sample that differs substantially on a variable (or variables) known to influence recidivism rates (e.g., offender has completed a credible sex offender treatment program), then the evaluator must either find studies with more appropriate probability estimates or revise the explicit statement made regarding probability of recidivism accordingly (e.g., note the limitations to the current research, describe other factors relevant to recidivism risk, and indicate relevant research that suggests the variable(s) in the particular case that are associated with recidivism and not accounted for by the particular instrument).

Further complicating this issue is that the recidivism estimates are based on the reconviction data in the normative samples. The extent to which the observed recidivism rates approximate the real recidivism rates is a matter of debate in the scientific community. Victimization surveys find that a small proportion of sexual offenses are reported to police, and police records show that a minority of reported sexual offenses result in arrest or conviction. When given conditions of trust, convicted sexual offenders indicate that for each conviction there were 6 to 8 other victims for whom they were never the subject of criminal justice intervention (Groth, Longo, & McFadin, 1982; Weinrott & Saylor, 1991). For some offenses, the detection rate could be expected to be much lower (Russell, 1983a, 1983b).

Evaluators need to remember, however, the distinction between undetected offenses and undetected offenders. Even if the detection rate per offense is low, offenders who commit many of these offenses are likely to get caught (and appear in recidivism statistics). Consequently, the observed short-term recidivism rates are likely to seriously underestimate the true short-term rates, whereas the observed long-term recidivism rates will get closer to the true long-term rates as the length of the follow-up increases. Even with lifetime follow-up and complete records, the observed rates will always underestimate the true rates. The amount of this underestimation is unknown.

Appropriate and Inappropriate Populations

The Static-99 was developed for use with adult males who have been charged with or convicted of an offense that has a sexual motivation. The offense need not be named a sexual offense (i.e., the name of the charge could be one that does not necessarily indicate a sexual offense), but the motivation for the offense must be sexual (e.g., "theft" of women's used shoes). Some official record for an arrest, charge, conviction, breach, etc. must exist in order to use the Static-99. Obtaining "knowledge" of a sexual offense without official records (e.g., self-report, polygraph data) is not sufficient to use the Static-99.

The victim or victims of the sexual offense must be children, nonconsenting adults or adolescents, or others incapable of providing consent, including corpses and animals. The Static-99 is not for use with sex offenders whose only sexual offending involves no specific victim (e.g., prostitution, possession of pornography, illegal but consensual sexual behavior, such as consenting sex between similar-aged peers), nor for men whose only offenses are related to nondisclosure of HIV status. The Static-99 has not been validated for use with females or juveniles; however, some exceptions for juveniles are noted in the manual (e.g., older juveniles whose offending patterns are "adult" in nature) (see A. J. R. Harris et al., 2003, for further explanation).

The Static-99 was developed on adult male offenders released from custody who were followed for a period of time at risk in the community. These men had not been in the community for a lengthy time period following the detection and sanctioning of the sexual offending. Therefore, the Static-99 is not for use with offenders who have more than 10 years of offense-free behavior while "at risk" (i.e., in a community setting). The criteria for being offense-free include no sexual or violent offense charges, and no more than brief periods of incarceration for any reason (see Appendix 1 in A. J. R. Harris et al., 2003).

The Static-99 has shown acceptable levels of validity with Canadian Aboriginal offenders, clergy, offenders with developmental disabilities, offenders with psychiatric disorders, and offenders who have been charged but not convicted of a sexual offense. At the present time, there is no research to indicate that the factors included in the Static-99 are invalid with any of these populations. Static-99 has been demonstrated to work as intended in Westernized democracies (for example, Canada, United States, Europe, Australia, New Zealand); however, it has rarely been studied in different legal systems, and the preliminary studies have found lower-than-expected predictive accuracy for non-European sexual offenders in Sweden (Långström, 2004) and child rapists in Japan (Watanabe, Yokota, Yoshimoto, Ihara, & Fujita, 2007). It is always desirable to conduct a validity study before routinely using Static-99 in a specific jurisdiction; such validity studies are essential, however, when considering implementation in countries with legal traditions substantially different than those typically found in Westernized democracies.

Some evaluators are tempted to use Static-99 for offenders who do not fit into its sampling frame because no other measures have been validated for these special populations (for example, Internet-only offenders, johns). Avoid the temptation. Even if it was possible to score Static-99 (which is not always clear), the probability estimates and nominal risk categories derived from the construction samples would be meaningless when applied to groups outside the intended sampling frame.

Strengths and Limitations

Strengths

The Static-99 is the most widely used actuarial tool to gauge long-term risk potential of sexual and violent recidivism among sexual offenders. We believe there are several reasons for the widespread acceptance and use of this tool: Static-99 provides an explicit list of risk factors and an empirically supported method of combining the risk factors into an overall evaluation; it is as accurate as other measures for the prediction of sexual recidivism; it is relatively easily scored;

and it is freely available. Static-99 and the accompanying manual are available free of charge through the Web site of the office of Public Safety Canada (www.ps.gc.ca). Any individual or organizational user who wishes to obtain a copy may download all the necessary forms and directions. The disadvantage of such free distribution, however, is that access to the materials is no guarantee that they will be used correctly. Training and quality assurance programs are recommended for all users.

Another reason for the widespread implementation is that it can be scored by those without advanced professional degrees using readily available information. In contrast, several of the other tools required judgments and diagnoses that can only be completed by psychologists or psychiatrists (e.g., major mental disorder, psychopathy) and relatively costly evaluation procedures (e.g., phallometric data). The scoring of the Static-99 is straightforward, once the scoring rules have been learned and practiced. Unlike instruments that rely on subjective ratings or that use complicated algorithms, the Static-99 has the appeal of simplicity. The rules for scoring are clearly presented such that organizations have the ability to conduct their own quality assurance tests and to determine the reliability of their staff's ratings.

The widespread usage of the test has also resulted in far more research data being collected on Static-99 than on any other measure commonly used with sexual offenders. This plethora of research results in narrower confidence intervals for the group estimates, which translate into increasingly more precise estimates of a test's validity, again increasing the evaluators' confidence in the results of the tool.

Limitations

One major limitation of Static-99 is its lack of demonstrated construct validity. Evaluators who use more than one actuarial instrument frequently find that the results of different instruments conflict (Barbaree, Langton, & Peacock, 2006a). One approach to resolving such disagreements is to attempt to explain the divergent results by suggesting that the instruments are assessing different aspects of risk (e.g., Doren, 2004b). The problem with such interpretations is that Static-99 was not intended to have construct validity, so it is difficult to tell what it is measuring. Further work is required to establish conceptually meaningful, actuarial risk tools (see Hanson & Thornton, 2003, for an example).

Static-99 is as accurate as any of the other available measures for the prediction of sexual recidivism (Hanson & Morton-Bourgon, 2007). By conventional standards, the effect size is medium to large (Rice & Harris, 2005). Given the serious consequences of individual risk decisions, however, there would be value in improving the level of predictive accuracy. It is unlikely that the accuracy can be substantially improved by including alternate combinations of similar static, criminal history variables (Hanson & Thornton, 2003; Helmus, 2007). Improvements in predictive accuracy will likely come from assessing a broader range of variables.

Although Static-99 can be used on its own, we recommend that comprehensive assessments consider other factors that are consistently related to sexual or violent offense recidivism. Static-99 neglects a range of factors that have been demonstrated to be predictive of sexual recidivism. Most notably absent are direct measures of sexual deviance, such as phallometric testing results. Furthermore, Static-99 does not incorporate any dynamic risk factors (criminogenic needs), even though research indicates that such factors account for variance in recidivism beyond that which is accounted for by the static factors on the Static-99 (e.g., Beech, Friendship, Erikson, & Hanson, 2002; Hanson et al., 2007; Olver, Wong, Nicholaichuk, & Gordon, 2007; Thornton, 2002). When factors are included using a structured, empirically based procedure, they can increase the accuracy of the overall risk evaluation. One empirically based method of including dynamic factors with Static-99 scores is described in the next section.

Another external factor not fully considered in Static-99 is advanced age (Hanson, 2006). Static-99 has one item distinguishing between offenders 18 to 24 (higher risk) and those 25 or older (lower risk). There is accumulating evidence, however, that further age differentiations may increase the accuracy of risk prediction (e.g., Barbaree & Blanchard, 2008; Hanson & Thornton, 2003). In particular, offenders over the age of 60 are consistently at lower risk to reoffend than would be suggested by their Static-99 scores (Hanson, 2006). Research has yet to establish the extent to which the observed reduction in recidivism rates is due to offenders improving as they get older (Barbaree & Blanchard, 2008) or the observation that older sex offenders are generally lower risk than younger sex offenders (Harris & Rice, 2007).

The Sex Offender Needs Assessment Rating (SONAR)

In order to identify dynamic risk factors contributing to recidivism among sexual offenders, Hanson and Harris (1998, 2000) conducted a retrospective study of offenders released on community supervision. They investigated the files of 201 recidivists and 209 nonrecidivists (all sex offenders). They coded the notes taken by the supervising officers prior to the reoffense for the recidivists, and for the same time period for the nonrecidivists, and they interviewed the supervising officers. Following the data collection, Hanson and Harris generated a list of domains that separated the recidivists from the nonrecidivists. Some of these domains were labeled "stable" dynamic risk factors, because these were areas of the offenders' lives that appeared to be chronically troubled (i.e., for a period of 6 months to a year) prior to the reoffense. These domains are best described as persistent patterns of thinking, feeling, and behaving, or the typical processes in an offender that are capable of change, albeit with concerted effort (such as with treatment or through interventions during supervision), and once truly changed, the changes would be expected to endure. Other domains were labeled "acute" dynamic risk factors, because these areas appeared to create problems immediately prior to the commission of the reoffense (that is, within one month of the reoffending). These areas would be considered rapidly changing environmental circumstances or, alternatively, sudden glitches in the otherwise persistent patterns of functioning. This list of stable and acute dynamic risk factors became the Sex Offender Needs Assessment Rating (SONAR) (Hanson & Harris, 2001).

The Stable-2000 and Acute-2000

Combining the SONAR research with the work of other projects in dynamic risk assessment (Sex Offender Treatment Evaluation Project, Beech et al., 2002; Structured Risk Assessment, Thornton, 2002), Hanson and Harris created a more comprehensive list of stable and dynamic risk factors and embarked on a prospective validation study of their new instruments: the Stable-2000 and the Acute-2000.

The prospective validation study involved supervision offices of numerous jurisdictions in Canada and in the United States. Data on the Static-99, Stable-2000, Acute-2000, and other demographic and offense characteristics were collected for approximately 1,000 sex offenders who were new offenders to the caseloads of the participating officers. The Static-99 was scored once, the Stable-2000 was scored every 6 months until the offender had reached the end of his or her supervision period, and the Acute-2000 was scored at every supervision meeting until the offender had reached the end of his or her supervision period.* The study began in 2001, and the results of the study were published in 2007 (see Hanson et al., 2007).

* The project included six female sexual offenders, one of whom reoffended with a nonsexual violent offense.

The Stable-2007 and Acute-2007

The data from the Dynamic Supervision Project (Hanson et al., 2007) found support for Stable-2000 and Acute-2000, but also suggested changes to the Stable and Acute measures were warranted. First, the attitudes section did not add predictive validity and hence was removed. The reason for the lack of incremental validity is unknown. In the Hanson and Morton-Bourgon (2004) meta-analysis, offense-supportive attitudes showed an overall positive association with recidivism, but the effect was only significant for offenders who had entered treatment. Attitudes showed no relationship to recidivism for offenders assessed in adversarial contexts. Consequently, it cannot be immediately assumed that attitudes are inconsequential until issues in the applied measurement of attitudes are resolved. Irrespective of the cause, the attitude section as it was presented in the Stable-2000 did not add value to the measure and was therefore removed.

Aside from the above major change, other minor changes were made to the scoring of some sections. One item (Emotional Identification with Children) proved valid for child molesters but not rapists, and hence the instructions for the Stable-2007 lead the assessor to score the item only for offenders with a child victim. Finally, the method for scoring the measure was simplified, and the interpretive needs categories were changed to empirically derived groupings.

The items on the Acute-2000 remained as they were; however, it appears that these acute factors were not as acute as initially assumed. The ratings on the acute variables did predict recidivism, but the most recent acute measures did not predict recidivism as well as the aggregated ratings on the acute over a longer period prior to the reoffending. This result suggests that ongoing expressions of problematic behavior, as opposed to sudden glitches, better distinguished recidivists from nonrecidivists. These findings led to further suggestions for the administration of the Acute-2007 during the course of supervision.

The study found that stable and acute evaluations incrementally improved the risk predictions above that provided by Static-99. For the prediction of sexual recidivism, the AUC was .77 for the Static-99 alone and .81 for the Static-99 and the Stable-2007 combined. For offenders in the highest and lowest risk categories of the Static-99, the Stable-2007 scores did not suggest major modifications to the risk level For example, offenders who scored low on the Static-99 but high on Stable-2007 would be considered in the overall moderate-low category. However, those who scored in the low-moderate and moderate-high risk categories of the Static-99 more closely approximated the recidivism rates in the adjacent nominal risk category when Stable-2007 scores were in the extreme end. That is, offenders who scored in the low-moderate range of the Static-99 (i.e., a 2 or 3) but scored in the high range of the Stable-2007 recidivated at rates expected of offenders in the moderate-high category, whereas offenders scoring in the same Static-99 risk category but scoring in the low range on the Stable-2007 reoffended at rates expected of those in the low risk categories. Similarly, those scoring in the moderate-high range on the Static-99 (i.e., a score of 4 or 5) with a score in the low range on Stable-2007 reoffended at rates expected of those in a moderate-low risk category. However, those scoring in the same nominal risk category of the Static-99 but scoring in the high range on the Stable-2007 reoffended at rates comparable to those in the high risk categories. Specific recidivism rates for these overall risk/priority categories are offered in the appendices of Hanson et al. (2007). The reader is cautioned, however, on the small numbers within some of these combinations of nominal risk category bins. For example, there were only three individuals who had a Static-99 score of 6 or over (i.e., high-risk category) along with a low score on the Stable-2007, and only one of these individuals recidivated with a new sexual crime (an exhibitionist). This study is important because it demonstrated that the Static-99 could be implemented in a reliable and valid manner by community supervision officers (Helmus & Hanson, 2007). Furthermore, the supervision officers could be taught a structured approach to evaluating risk factors that improves risk prediction while providing meaningful targets for intervention (see Hanson et al., 2007).

Questions and Future Directions

Selecting an Actuarial Measure

Determining which actuarial measure to use depends on the similarity of the individual offender being assessed to the groups of offenders from which the normative data were derived, the referral question, and the resources available.

If the primary interest is the prediction of general violent recidivism (sexual or nonsexual), the Violence Risk Appraisal Guide (VRAG) and the Sex Offender Risk Appraisal Guide (SORAG) (Quinsey, Harris, Rice, & Cormier, 2005) appear more accurate than Static-99 (Hanson & Morton-Bourgon, 2007). Both the VRAG and SORAG, however, require the administration of the Psychopathy Checklist–Revised, which involves higher user qualifications and greater expenditure of resources (cost, time, etc.).

For the prediction of sexual recidivism, Static-99 is as accurate as any of the available measures, and more accurate than its predecessor, the RRASOR (Hanson & Morton-Bourgon, 2007). Some evaluators continue to use the RRASOR in the belief that it provides a purer measure of sexual deviance, whereas Static-99 taps both sexual deviance and general criminality. Given that there are better methods of assessing the constructs associated with risk (e.g., Stable-2007, Hanson et al., 2007; Thornton's Structured Assessment of Risk and Need, HM Prison Service, 2005), we believe that the use of the RRASOR should be completely discontinued. In every case where the RRASOR would be appropriate, Static-99 provides a better assessment of risk. To the extent that it makes sense to interpret the underlying constructs, Static-99 addresses a wider range of risk factors (both antisociality and sexual deviance), and it has been replicated much more extensively than the RRASOR (that is, in more countries, with more diverse samples, with a greater number of cases overall). Using both Static-99 and RRASOR has the added risk of inflating the perception of consistency, given that the RRASOR results will appear to be an independent confirmation of the Static-99 findings even though they add no new information.

Do We Need to Know Absolute Recidivism Rates?

Projecting absolute recidivism rates is difficult given the observed fluctuations across studies, and the expectation that interventions and global policy initiatives should systematically reduce recidivism. In many contexts, highly accurate estimates of absolute recidivism rates are not needed. For the purpose of supervising a given caseload of sexual offenders released to the community, the prominent concern is rank ordering the offenders in terms of risk in order to determine how the resources might be allocated most efficiently.

In other contexts, however, providing accurate probability estimates is of paramount importance. For example, in cases where legal decisions are made based on some statutorily defined probability of reoffending (for example, dangerous offender sentences in Canada and civil commitment hearings in many jurisdictions of the United States), evaluators need to carefully consider the available evidence and determine which findings are most appropriate for estimating the risk for the individual at hand (although it is recognized that many statutes do not specify a numeric "probability of reoffending," and case law is not unanimous or consistent in this requirement).

This Offender Seems Like an Exception—Can I "Override" the Static-99?

It is not unusual for evaluators to encounter offenders whose scores on the Static-99 does not seem well matched to their initial perception of the risk. For example, an offender's score may fall into the low-risk range, but his offenses were particularly violent, or there are many victims who do not figure on the official record. We recommend against adjusting the Static-99 findings based on such ad hoc observations.

When Hanson et al. (2007) conducted their prospective validation study of the static and dynamic risk assessment instruments (Static-99, Stable-2000, and Acute-2000), they collected information on "overrides" to the Static-99. That is, they allowed supervising officers who scored the measures to indicate if they felt there were circumstances that justified an adjustment of the overall risk assessment category, and they were asked to record what circumstance(s) they would use to make such an adjustment. There was no agreement about when the overrides should be used, and when they were, the adjusted risk assessment resulted in a slight decrease in predictive accuracy over that provided by Static-99 alone. When, however, the Stable-2007 factors were used to adjust the nominal risk category provided by the Static-99 score, the predictive accuracy was increased. Therefore, the Static-99, as noted throughout this chapter, does not account for all important factors in estimating risk of recidivism. Nonetheless, adjustments to the nominal risk category can be made by incorporating empirically based risk factors, and the current research by Hanson et al. (2007) provides a structured and validated tool for incorporating dynamic risk factors into the overall assessment.

Case Example

The following example suggests a way in which information obtained from the Static-99 and Stable-2007 might be utilized within the context of a risk assessment for an incarcerated individual.

Mr. Dodgy is a 38-year-old male serving a sentence of 5 years for sexual assault with a weapon. The current offense was committed against a previous girlfriend whom he dated for 6 months. His criminal history dates back to age 18 years when he was convicted for break, enter, and theft. Mr. Dodgy has one previous charge for sexual assault, but he pled to assault, and the sexual assault charge was withdrawn. This offense occurred 3 years ago and was perpetrated against the same victim of the current offense. It appears that the previous offense led to the breakup of the relationship. Mr. Dodgy has also been convicted of criminal harassment against the same victim 1 year before the current offense. Mr. Dodgy's previous offenses include assault (mainly against males, with the exception of the one noted above), other property offenses, and one driving while impaired. Mr. Dodgy was married 10 years ago to another woman, but this marriage lasted for approximately 1 year. He states they separated and divorced due to his infidelity and drinking. He has no children, and he has never lived with any woman other than his previous wife. Mr. Dodgy is not currently involved in a relationship, but says he dates "a lot" and enjoys "playing the field." He stated he does not have much luck with longer-term relationships, as women often become "naggy, bitchy, and boring" when there are increases in the commitment. Mr. Dodgy admitted he did not feel comfortable discussing his thoughts on relationships with women because there are too many women in positions of power over him (e.g., his parole officer, most of the facilitators of programs, and the unit psychologist), and he did not believe this was fair in a male correctional facility. Mr. Dodgy reported no difficulties making friends, but stated he prefers to be alone most of the time. He said his relationship with family members is "satisfactory" and said he would spend time with two of the men from work, but notes that one has a significant problem with drugs and alcohol, is frequently out of money, and often approaches Mr. Dodgy for small loans to manage until he receives his next paycheck. Mr. Dodgy characterizes his relationship with the current victim as "poison" and says he realizes he cannot ever see or contact her again. He admits to the current offense, but states that "it was blown out of proportion in court." He pled guilty after a preliminary hearing. Mr. Dodgy has been steadily employed with a roofing company for the past 15 years, and he believes he will be able to return to work for the same company. The most recent community assessment report indicates that his employer is likely to give him a job upon release. He admits to having a drinking problem and states that "most roofers drink on the job and smoke a lot of pot." He denied the use of drugs, including prescription medication; however, file information revealed an institutional charge one month ago resulting from a urinalysis testing positive for THC.

The following paragraphs summarize the findings on the Static-99 and Stable-2007 for Mr. Dodgy within the context of the risk assessment report. The risk assessment was being completed during Mr. Dodgy's period of incarceration to assist with an upcoming hearing with the Parole Board.

. . . The STATIC-99 is an instrument designed to assist in the prediction of sexual and violent recidivism for sexual offenders. This risk assessment instrument was developed by Hanson and Thornton (1999) based on follow-up studies from Canada and the United Kingdom with a total sample size of 1,301 sexual offenders. The STATIC-99 consists of 10 items and produces estimates of future reoffense risk based upon the number of risk factors present in any one individual. The risk factors included are the presence of prior sexual offenses, having committed a current nonsexual violent offense, having a history of nonsexual violence, the number of previous sentencing dates, age less than 25 years old, having male victims, having never lived with a lover for two continuous years, having a history of noncontact sex offenses, having unrelated victims, and having stranger victims. Mr. Dodgy scored a 5 on the STATIC-99. Using the data provided by the normative samples, individuals with these characteristics, on average, sexually reoffended at a rate 33% over 5 years and at 38% over 10 years. The rate for any violent recidivism (including sexual) for individuals with these characteristics was, on average, 42% over 5 years and 48% over 10 years. Based upon the STATIC-99 score, this places Mr. Dodgy in the moderate-high (between the 62nd and the 88th percentile) risk category relative to other adult male sex offenders. This nominal risk level will be combined with the STABLE-2007 Needs score to form a combined risk assessment.

The STABLE-2007 was developed to assess change in intermediate-term risk status, assess treatment needs, and help predict recidivism in sexual offenders. Hanson and Harris (2000; Hanson, Harris, Scott, & Helmus, 2007) developed this risk assessment instrument based on a large prospective study from Canada and the states of Alaska and Iowa with a total sample size of 997 sexual offenders. The STABLE-2007 consists of 13 items and produces estimates of stable dynamic risk based upon the number of stable dynamic risk factors present in any one individual. The risk factors included are the nature of significant social influences, capacity for relationship stability, emotional identification with children, hostility toward women, general social rejection, lack of concern for others, impulsivity, poor problem solving skills, negative emotionality, sex drive and preoccupation, sex as coping, deviant sexual preference, and cooperation with supervision.

Mr. Dodgy scored a 14 out of a possible 24 points on the STABLE-2007, and this score places him as high needs on this assessment instrument. Men without a child sexual victim are scored out of 24 possible points. The STATIC-99 and the STABLE-2007 are then combined into a composite score. Mr. Dodgy scored as a moderate-high risk on the STATIC-99, and this score is combined with Mr. Dodgy's STABLE-2007 score of high needs to produce estimates of sexual, violent, or any criminal recidivism between 1 and 4 years in the community. The complete risk tables are shown in the paper referenced below (Appendices 8 & 9). Compared to other sex offenders on community supervision, men with similar characteristics to Mr. Dodgy on both the static and dynamic risk factors assessed by these instruments fell into the high nominal risk category for sexual recidivism, and men with the same risk profile as Mr. Dodgy were seen to recidivate sexually at a rate of 17.1% over 2 years and 22% over 4 years (Appendix 8). Men with the same risk profile as Mr. Dodgy reoffended violently at rates that indicate Mr. Dodgy falls into the high nominal risk category for violent recidivism, and men with the same risk profile as Mr. Dodgy were seen to recidivate violently at a rate of 25.6% over 2 years and 31.9% over 4 years (Appendix 9). It is noted for the reader that these rates of recidivism are based on the only sample to date examining the combination of the STATIC-99 and STABLE-2007 scores, and hence caution must be exercised when interpreting these rates as estimates of the probability of recidivism.

As well, the nominal risk categories noted above are predicated on recidivism estimates provided by the STATIC-99 and STABLE-2007, which are group estimates based upon charges, reconvictions, and breaches of conditional release derived from groups of individuals with these risk characteristics. As such, these estimates are based upon a group of offenders with the same risk profile as Mr. Dodgy. Mr. Dodgy's risk may be higher or lower than the estimated probabilities, depending on other risk factors not measured by these instruments. Given the documentation provided and the information provided by Mr. Dodgy in our current interview, there are no apparent factors known or suspected to be associated with recidivism in Mr. Dodgy's case that would warrant an adjustment to the risk levels indicated in this report. The specific factors presenting as a focus for intervention (i.e., those that are highlighted as problematic according to the STABLE-2007 evaluation)

> are negative social influences, difficulties maintaining intimate relationships, hostility toward women, sexual preoccupations, lifestyle impulsivity and lack of cooperation with supervision. . . .

Conclusion

The Static-99 has proven to be a useful means of categorizing offenders according to their risk of recidivism. Although it can be used on its own, the most useful assessments are those that use a structured, empirically based method for combining static risk factors with measures of criminogenic needs (dynamic risk factors). The Static-99 can help gauge the long-term potential for sexual and violent recidivism among men who have already been charged with or convicted for a sexually motivated offense that involves a targeted victim or group of victims. The Static-99 is not valid with every sex offender. Also, the Static-99 neglects factors that have been repeatedly associated with risk for sexual and violent recidivism, and in the context of providing a comprehensive risk assessment, such factors should be considered. Promising measures of dynamic risk factors are the Stable-2007 and Acute-2007, which accounted for variance in recidivism beyond that accounted for by the Static-99 in the Dynamic Supervision Project (Hanson et al., 2007). The assessor must be cognizant of the limitations to any tool being used to assist in the estimate of potential for recidivism and therefore must be aware of the extent to which the individual offender being assessed is similar to the groups of offenders for whom the test has been validated, and the assessor must evaluate whether the tool assists in answering the referral question (or the extent to which the tool contributes meaningful information to address the reason for the risk assessment being conducted).

> There are very few human beings who receive the truth, complete and staggering, by instant illumination. Most of them acquire it fragment by fragment, on a small scale, by successive developments, cellularly, like a laborious mosaic.
>
> **Anaïs Nin**

References

Archer, R. P., Buffington-Vollum, J. K., Stredny, R. V., & Handel, R. W. (2006). A survey of psychological test use patterns among forensic psychologists. *Journal of Personality Assessment, 87,* 84–94.

Barbaree, H. E., & Blanchard, R. (2008). Sexual deviance over the lifespan: Reductions in deviant sexual behavior in the aging sex offender. In D. R. Laws & W. T. O'Donohue, (Eds.). *Sexual deviance: Theory, assessment and treatment* (pp. 37–60). New York: Guilford Press.

Barbaree, H. E., Langton, C. M., & Peacock, E. J. (2006a). Different actuarial risk measures produce different risk rankings for sexual offenders. *Sexual Abuse: A Journal of Research and Treatment, 18,* 423–440.

Barbaree, H. E., Langton, C. M., & Peacock, E. J. (2006b). The factor structure of static actuarial items: Its relation to prediction. *Sexual Abuse: A Journal of Research and Treatment, 18,* 207–226.

Barbaree, H. E., Seto, M. C. Langton, C. M. & Peacock. E. J. (2001). Evaluating the predictive accuracy of six risk assessment instruments for adult sex offenders. *Criminal Justice and Behavior, 28,* 490–521.

Beech, A., Friendship, C., Erikson, M., & Hanson, R. K. (2002). The relationship between static and dynamic risk factors and reconviction in a sample of U.K. child abusers. *Sexual Abuse: A Journal of Research and Treatment, 14,* 155–167.

Bengtson, S., & Långström, N. (2007). Unguided clinical and actuarial assessment of re-offending risk: A direct comparison with sex offenders in Denmark. *Sexual Abuse: A Journal of Research and Treatment, 19,* 135–153.

Doren, D. M. (2004a). Stability of the interpretive risk percentages for the RRASOR and Static-99, *Sexual Abuse: A Journal of Research and Treatment, 16,* 25–36.

Doren, D. M. (2004b). Toward a multidimensional model for sexual recidivism risk. *Journal of Interpersonal Violence, 19,* 835–856.

Ducro, C., & Pham, T. (2006). Evaluation of the SORAG and the Static-99 on Belgian sex offenders committed to a forensic facility. *Sexual Abuse: A Journal of Research and Treatment, 18,* 15–26.

Endrass, J., Urbaniok, F., Held, L., Vetter, S., & Rossegger, A. (in press). The accuracy of the Static-99 in predicting recidivism in Switzerland. *International Journal of Offender Therapy and Comparative Criminology.*

Groth, N., Longo, R., & McFadin, J. B. (1982). Undetected recidivism among rapists and child molesters. *Crime & Delinquency, 28,* 450–58.

Grubin, D. (1998). *Sex offending against children: Understanding the risk.* Police Research Series Paper 99. London Home Office.

Hanson, R. K. (1997). The development of a brief actuarial risk scale for sexual offense recidivism. (User Report 97-04). Ottawa, ON, Canada: Department of the Solicitor General of Canada.

Hanson, R. K. (2001). *Note on the reliability of Static-99 as used by the California Department of Mental Health evaluators.* Unpublished report. Sacramento, CA: California Department of Mental Health.

Hanson, R. K. (2006). Does Static-99 predict recidivism among older sexual offenders? *Sexual Abuse: A Journal of Research and Treatment, 18,* 343–355.

Hanson, R. K., & Bussière, M. T. (1998). Predicting relapse: A meta-analysis of sexual offender recidivism studies. *Journal of Consulting and Clinical Psychology, 66*(2), 348–362.

Hanson, R. K., & Harris, A. J. R. (1998). *The Sex Offender Need Assessment Rating (SONAR): A method for measuring change in risk levels.* (User Report 2000-01). Ottawa, ON, Canada: Department of the Solicitor General of Canada.

Hanson, R. K., & Harris, A. J. R. (2000). Where should we intervene? Dynamic predictors of sexual offense recidivism. *Criminal Justice and Behavior, 27,* 6–35.

Hanson, R. K., & Harris, A. J. R. (2001). A structured approach to evaluating change among sexual offenders. *Sexual Abuse: A Journal of Research and Treatment, 13*(2), 105–122.

Hanson, R. K., Harris, A. J. R., Scott, T., & Helmus, L. (2007). Assessing the risk of sexual offenders on community supervision: The Dynamic Supervision Project. User Report, Corrections Research. Ottawa, ON, Canada: Public Safety Canada.

Hanson, R. K., & Morton-Bourgon, K. (2004). Predictors of sexual recidivism: An updated meta-analysis. Corrections User Report No. 2004-02. Ottawa, ON, Canada: Public Safety and Emergency Preparedness Canada.

Hanson, R. K., & Morton-Bourgon, K. E. (2005). The characteristics of persistent sexual offenders: A meta-analysis of recidivism studies. *Journal of Consulting and Clinical Psychology, 73,* 1154–1163.

Hanson, R. K., & Morton-Bourgon, K. E. (2007). *The accuracy of recidivism risk assessments for sexual offenders : A meta-analysis.* Corrections User Report No 2007-01. Ottawa, ON, Canada: Public Safety and Emergency Preparedness Canada.

Hanson, R. K., & Morton-Bourgon, K. E. (2009). The accuracy of recidivism risk assessments for sexual offenders: A meta-analysis of 118 prediction studies. *Psychological Assessment, 21*(1), 1–21.

Hanson, R. K., Steffy, R. A., & Gauthier, R. (1993). Long-term recidivism of child molesters. *Journal of Consulting and Clinical Psychology, 61,* 646–652.

Hanson, R. K., & Thornton, D. (1999). *Static-99: Improving actuarial risk assessments for sex offenders.* User Report 99-02. Ottawa, ON, Canada: Department of the Solicitor General of Canada.

Hanson, R. K., & Thornton, D. (2000). Improving risk assessments for sex offenders: A comparison of three actuarial scales. *Law and Human Behavior, 24(*1), 119–136.

Hanson, R. K., & Thornton, D. (2003). Notes on the development of Static-2002. User Report 2003-01. Ottawa, ON, Canada: Department of the Solicitor General of Canada.

Harris, A. J. R., & Hanson, R. K. (2004). Sex offender recidivism: A simple question. Corrections Users Report No. 2004-03. Ottawa, ON, Canada: Public Safety and Emergency Preparedness Canada.

Harris, A. J. R., Phenix, A., Hanson, R. K., & Thornton, D. (2003). Static-99 coding rules: Revised 2003. Ottawa, ON, Canada: Department of the Solicitor General of Canada.

Harris, G. T., & Rice, M. E. (2007). Adjusting actuarial violence risk assessments based on aging or the passage of time. *Criminal Justice and Behavior, 34,* 297–313.

Harris, G. T., Rice, M. E., Quinsey, V. L., Lalumiere, M. L., Boer, D., & Lang, C. (2003). A multi-site comparison of actuarial risk instruments for sex offenders. *Psychological Assessment, 15(3),* 413–425.

Helmus, L. (2007). A multi-site comparison of the validity and utility of the Static-99 and Static-2002 for risk assessment with sexual offenders. Unpublished B.A. thesis, Carleton University, Ottawa, ON, Canada.

Helmus, L. M. D., & Hanson, R. K. (2007). Predictive validity of the Static-99 and Static-2002 for sex offenders on community supervision. *Sexual Offender Treatment, 2,* 1–14.

HM Prison Service. (2005). *Structured Assessment of Risk and Need (Sexual Offenders): Manual, v. 2.* London: Offending Behaviour Programmes Unit, HM Prison Service.

Interstate Commission for Adult Offender Supervision. (2007). Sex offender assessment information survey. ICAOS Documents 4-2007. Lexington, KY.

Jackson, R. L., & Hess, D. T. (2007). Evaluation for civil commitment of sex offenders: A survey of experts. *Sexual Abuse: A Journal of Research and Treatment, 19,* 409–448.

Långström, N. (2004). Accuracy of actuarial procedures for assessment of sexual offender recidivism risk may vary across ethnicity. *Sexual Abuse: A Journal of Research and Treatment, 16,* 107–120.

Looman, J. A. (2006). Comparison of two risk assessment instruments for sexual offenders. *Sexual Abuse: A Journal of Research and Treatment, 18,* 193–206.

McGrath, R. J., Cumming, G. F., & Burchard, B. L. (2003). *Current practices and trends in sexual abuser management: The Safer Society 2002 Nationwide Survey.* Brandon, VT: Safer Society Foundation, Inc.

Mossman, D. (2006). Another look at interpreting risk categories. *Abuse: A Journal of Research and Treatment, 18,* 41–63.

Nicholaichuk, T. (2001, November). *The comparison of two standardized risk assessment instruments in a sample of Canadian Aboriginal sexual offenders.* Paper presented at the annual conference of the Association for the Treatment of Sexual Abusers, San Antonio, TX.

Olver, M., Wong, S. C. P., & Nicholaichuk, T. P., & Gordon, A. (2007). The validity and reliability of the Violence Risk Scale–Sexual Offender Version: Assessing sex offender risk and evaluating therapeutic change. *Psychological Assessment, 19,* 318–329.

Quinsey, V. L., Harris, G. T., Rice, M. E., & Cormier, C. (2005). *Violent offenders: Appraising and managing risk,* (2nd ed.). Washington, DC: American Psychological Association.

Rettenberger, M., & Eher, R. (2006). Actuarial assessment of sex offender recidivism risk: A validation of the German version of the Static-99. *Sexual Offender Treatment, 1*(3), 1–11.

Rice, M. E., & Harris, G. T. (2005). Comparing effect sizes in follow-up studies: ROC area, Cohen's *d,* and *r. Law and Human Behavior, 29,* 615–620.

Roberts, C. F., Doren, D. M., & Thornton, D. (2002). Dimensions associated with assessments of sex offender recidivism risk. *Criminal Justice and Behavior, 29,* 569–589.

Russell, D. E. H. (1983a). The incidence and prevalence of intrafamilial and extrafamilial sexual abuse of female children. *Child Abuse & Neglect, 7,* 133–146.

Russell, D. E. H. (1983b). The prevalence and incidence of forcible rape and attempted rape of females. *Victimology: An International Journal, 7,* 81–93.

Sjöstedt, G., & Långström, N. (2001). Actuarial assessment of sex offender recidivism risk: A cross-validation of the RRASOR and the Static-99 in Sweden. *Law and Human Behavior, 25,* 629–645.

Thornton, D. (2002). Constructing and testing a framework for dynamic risk assessment. *Sexual Abuse: A Journal of Research and Treatment, 14,* 139–153.

Tough, S. E. (2001). *Validation of two standardized risk assessments (RRASOR, 1997; Static-99, 1999) on a sample of adult males who are developmentally disabled with significant cognitive deficits.* Unpublished master's thesis, University of Toronto, Toronto, ON, Canada.

Watanabe, K., Yokota, K., Yoshimoto, K., Ihara, N., & Fujita, G. (2007). *Recidivism in child rapists: Identifying high risk factors.* Unpublished manuscript, obtained from National Research Institute of Police Science, Tokyo, Japan.

Weinrott, M. R., & Saylor, M. (1991). Self-report of crimes committed by sex offenders. *Journal of Interpersonal Violence, 6,* 286–300.

13
Structured Professional Judgment Guidelines for Sexual Violence Risk Assessment

The Sexual Violence Risk-20 (SVR-20) and Risk for Sexual Violence Protocol (RSVP)

STEPHEN D. HART and DOUGLAS P. BOER

In this chapter, we review two related sets of structured professional judgment guidelines for assessing risk for sexual violence, the *Sexual Violence Risk-20* (SVR-20) (Boer, Hart, Kropp, & Webster, 1997) and the *Risk for Sexual Violence Protocol* (RSVP) (Hart, Kropp, Laws, Klaver, Logan, & Watt, 2003). The manuals have proven to be very popular and are in wide use internationally. More than 5,000 copies of the original English editions have been distributed, and authorized translations are available in several languages including Dutch, French, German, Norwegian, Spanish, and Swedish.

The SVR-20 and RSVP are reviewed together here because they are very similar in content and, in fact, may be considered equivalent or parallel forms of the same guidelines. The primary difference between them is that the RSVP puts more emphasis on psychological risk factors and development of case management plans and so is better suited for evaluations conducted by sex offender specialists or for treatment purposes.

We begin the chapter with detailed descriptions of the nature and development of the SVR-20 and RSVP. Next, we review research conducted to date on the reliability and validity of risk judgments made using the SVR-20 and RSVP. This is followed by a discussion of limitations in the research supporting their use and, finally, a case presentation that illustrates their use. The chapter incorporates material from the manuals, as well as from previous reviews (Boer & Hart, 2008a, 2008b).

Nature

Purpose

The SVR-20 and RSVP are structured professional judgment (SPJ) guidelines for conducting comprehensive, management-oriented sexual violence risk assessments in therapeutic and forensic settings. They help users to reach decisions regarding two major issues: the risks people pose for perpetrating sexual violence, and the strategies that would most effectively manage those risks.

Definition of Sexual Violence

The SVR-20 and RSVP define sexual violence as the "actual, attempted, or threatened sexual contact with another person that is nonconsensual" (Hart et al., 2003, p. 2; see also Boer et al., 1997, p. 9). This definition is and includes a wide range of acts that would constitute violations of criminal law in most jurisdictions, although an act need not be criminal to fit the definition. It excludes some forms of unusual, problematic, or even illegal sexual behavior that do not involve sexual contact with other people or that are consensual (for example, sex with animals, sadomasochistic sex with a consenting partner).

Definition of Risk

The SVR-20 and RSVP conceptualize risk broadly in terms of the nature, severity, imminence, frequency, and likelihood of future sexual violence. This is in stark contrast to actuarial risk assessment instruments that define risk solely in terms of the probability of arrest or conviction for future sexual violence, such as the Minnesota Sex Offending Screening Tool–Revised (MnSOST-R) (Epperson, Kaul, & Hesselton, 1998), Rapid Risk Assessment for Sex Offense Recidivism (RRASOR) (Hanson, 1997), Risk Matrix 2000–Sex (RMS) (Thornton et al., 2003), and Static-99 and Static-2002 (Hanson & Thornton, 1999, 2003; see also Chapter 12, this volume). The SVR-20 and RSVP go beyond this, to think about what kinds of sexual violence a given person might commit, against what kinds of victims, in what kinds of circumstances, and with what consequences.

Intended Applications

The SVR-20 and RSVP are intended for use in a wide range of civil and criminal justice contexts. The primary intended use is to assist forward planning in individual cases by guiding clinical–forensic decisions about risk assessment and management. This includes pretrial and sentencing evaluations; correctional intake and discharge evaluations; postsentence civil commitment or "sexually violent predator" evaluations; duty to protect, community notification, and sex offender registration evaluations; and child protection or custody/access evaluations. A second use of the SVR-20 and RSVP is in backward-looking evaluations, where the guidelines are used to evaluate the quality of risk assessments completed by others. This includes quality assurance checks or case reviews, as well as reviews of critical incidents. A third use of the guidelines is for more general research, education, and training.

Target Populations

The SVR-20 and RSVP are intended for use primarily with men aged 18 and older who have a known or suspected history of sexual violence. This is because the scientific and professional literatures that served as the basis for constructing the guidelines focus primarily on this group.

The SVR-20 and RSVP also may be used with caution to guide evaluations of older male adolescents (aged 16 or 17) who appear to be starting a career of adult sex offending early, as well as adult women. Although the scientific research is relatively limited, it appears that many of the same risk factors for sexual violence identified in adult males also are relevant in both these groups.

Neither the SVR-20 nor the RSVP should be used to evaluate children or young adolescents (aged 15 and younger). Sexual misbehavior of children and young adolescents differs in important ways from the sexual violence committed by older adolescents and adults (e.g., is targeted primarily at same-aged victims, is less likely to involve physical coercion) and may also be related to different causal processes, such as delayed social maturation.

Cautions Regarding Use

The SVR-20 and RSVP cannot be used to determine whether someone has committed an act of sexual violence in the past. Nor can they be used to determine whether someone "fits the profile of a sex offender," given the heterogeneity of people who commit sexual violence. The risk factors are associated with risk of future sexual violence among individuals who are already known or suspected to have committed sexual violence.

The SVR-20 and RSVP should not be used to assess risk of nonsexual violence, other forms of violence such as spousal violence and stalking, or nonviolent criminal conduct. If there is any evidence that the individual being evaluated may be at risk of antisocial behavior other than sexual violence, users should document their opinions and consider expanding the scope of their risk assessments accordingly.

The SVR-20 and RSVP focus on the risks posed by the examinee, rather than on the risks posed to a specific potential victim. Victim-focused risk assessments—sometimes referred to as threat assessments, victim safety planning or victim lethality assessments—differ from perpetrator-focused risk assessments in important ways, including consideration of psychological, social, and environmental factors that may increase the victim's vulnerability to sexual violence (Krug, Dahlberg, Mercy, Zwi, & Lozano, 2002). Evaluators should contemplate expanding their risk assessments to include consideration of victim vulnerability factors in cases where any future sexual violence is likely to be targeted at a specific person.

By their very nature, SPJ guidelines like the SVR-20 and RSVP are neither exhaustive nor fixed. In any given evaluation, there may be case-specific factors that are crucial to professional judgments concerning risk. The existence or use of professional guidelines does not obviate the need to exercise professional judgment (Addis, 2002; American Psychological Association, 2002; Reed, McLaughlin, & Newman, 2002).

Also by their nature, SPJ guidelines like the SVR-20 and RSVP cannot be used to estimate the specific likelihood or absolute probability that an individual person will commit sexual violence in the future. (Indeed, making estimates of this sort with any reasonable degree of certainty probably lies beyond the ability of science; see Hájek & Hall, 2002; Hart, Michie, & Cooke, 2007; Henderson & Keiding, 2006.)

Finally, the SVR-20 and RSVP reflected the opinions and recommendations of the authors at the time they were written. They do not set out the official position or policy of any agency, organization, or professional group. Like all guidelines, they must be updated (e.g., American Psychological Association, 2002; Reed et al., 2002). The SVR-20 is currently being revised with an expected completion date of 2010, and the RSVP is scheduled for revision by 2013.

Examiner Qualifications

Proper use of SPJ guidelines requires professional skill and judgment. According to the manual, users of the SVR-20 should meet two general requirements. First, examiners should have a good understanding of sexual violence, including at least a basic familiarity with the professional and scientific literatures on its nature, causes, and management. Second, examiners should have training and experience in individual assessment, including interviewing and reviewing third party information; training and experience in the administration and interpretation of standardized tests can also be helpful. The RSVP has a heavier focus on psychological concepts. Its manual adds a third requirement, namely, examiners should have training and experience in the assessment and diagnosis of mental disorder. The degree of knowledge and expertise required depends on relevant laws, regulations, and policies, as well as the purpose for which the SVR-20 or RSVP is to be used (e.g., using them in actual evaluations obviously requires greater knowledge and expertise than does using them in education or training).

Many professionals who routinely conduct sexual violence risk assessments may not be qualified to assess or diagnose mental disorder (for example, probation officers, law enforcement officers). When coding the presence and relevance of risk factors related to mental disorder, they have four options. First, they can assess risk factors related to mental disorder in consultation with or under the supervision of qualified professionals. Second, they can assess risk factors related to mental disorder by referring to the results of psychodiagnostic evaluations conducted by qualified people. Third, they can assess risk factors related to mental disorder provisionally, document this, and discuss the importance of having their provisional assessments confirmed by qualified professionals. Finally, they can decide not to assess risk factors related to mental disorder, document this, and discuss how the incomplete assessment limits their opinions regarding risk.

The SVR-20 manual does not discuss training for users. The RSVP manual states that users do not need to complete any specific training program, but rather can accomplish adequate training in a number of different ways, including self-study, supervised practice, and attendance at lectures or workshops. It recommends about 16 to 32 hours of training that includes the following components: a review of the manual, with particular emphasis on basic information and administration issues; a review of any critical advances in knowledge regarding sexual violence or risk assessment subsequent to publication of the RSVP manual; completion of practice cases based on file review; and completion of actual cases under supervision of or in consultation with experienced colleagues.

Development

Nature of SPJ Guidelines

The SPJ approach uses guidelines to help evaluators exercise discretion when conducting risk assessments (Douglas & Kropp, 2002; Hart, 2001, 2008; see also Chapter 1, this volume). Most generally, guidelines are "pronouncements, statements, or declarations that suggest or recommend specific professional behavior, endeavor, or conduct" (American Psychological Association, 2002, p. 1052). They are recommendations for best practice—also known as clinical practice parameters and practice or consensus guidelines—based on consideration of the relevant scientific, professional, and legal literatures.

The development of guidelines is one of the primary methods used to promote best practice in health care professions (Reed et al., 2002). Consistent with recommendations for health care guidelines (e.g., American Psychological Association, 2002), development of the SVR-20 and RSVP was based in part on a systematic review of the existing scientific research. Also consistent with recommendations, their development took into consideration existing standards of practice, ethical codes, and relevant law (e.g., American Psychological Association, 2002). Accordingly, the SVR-20 and RSVP may be considered research products (Addis, 2002), and their use may be considered evidence-based, empirically guided, or empirically supported practice—that is, "the conscientious, explicit and judicious use of current best evidence in making decisions about the care of individual patients" (Sackett, Rosenberg, Gray, Haynes, & Richardson, 1996, p. 71). The SVR-20 and RSVP differ from some guidelines in two important ways. First, they reflect the opinions and recommendations of the authors, rather than the official position or policy of any agency, organization, or association. Second, the guidelines are not practice standards, as they are not binding on and do not restrict the practice of any professional groups.

In the most general sense, the SVR-20 and RSVP function as reference texts on sexual violence risk assessment, systematic reviews of the relevant scientific and professional literature. They also function as *aides mémoire* or memory aids for guiding practice in a general sense. Finally, when users follow the procedures outlined in the manuals, they function as psychological tests—that is, evaluative devices or procedures—according to commonly accepted definitions (e.g., American Educational Research Association, American Psychological Association, & National Council on Measurement in Education, 1999). Like all tests, the SVR-20 and RSVP attempt to structure the process of assessment. Unlike many psychological tests, however, they were not intended to quantify behavior in the form of scores that can be interpreted with respect to norms or other criteria. Similar tests have been developed for use in a wide range of psycholegal assessments and have been referred to as *forensic assessment instruments* or *forensically relevant assessment instruments* (Grisso, 1986, 2003; Heilbrun, 2001; Heilbrun, Rogers, & Otto, 2002).

Due to their broad conceptualization of risk and their focus on prevention, SPJ guidelines such as the SVR-20 and RSVP go beyond prediction-focused evaluations (i.e., the evaluation of factors associated with increased probability of future violence) and may be considered "management-focused," "risk-need-responsivity," or "fourth-generation" risk assessment instruments (Andrews & Bonta, 2006; Andrews, Bonta, & Wormith, 2006).

Literature Review

As noted previously, the SVR-20 and RSVP guidelines were based on a systematic review of the scientific and professional literatures on sexual violence. The literature reviewed included a wide range of empirical reports, reviews, and guidelines that were published in journals and books or as reports available from government agencies. The administration procedures in the SVR-20 and RSVP were based primarily on publications from the professional literature: reviews and guidelines published in journal articles, books, or as agency reports. In contrast, the risk factors in the SVR-20 and RSVP were drawn from the scientific literature—empirical reports published in journals—as well as from other sources.

The literature reviews were broad in scope. We began by identifying articles and book chapters on sexual violence or sexual offending that contained information relevant to risk assessment and management from computerized databases in medicine (primarily psychiatry) and social science (primarily psychology and criminology). We excluded publications that were not available in English or focused solely on sexual misbehavior in children or adolescents. Next, we inspected the reference lists of the remaining publications to identify additional studies of potential relevance. The literature reviews we conducted were greatly assisted by narrative and meta-analytic reviews previously published by others (e.g., Hall, 1990; Hanson & Bussière, 1998; Krug et al., 2002; McGrath, 1991).

Our review of relevant material had two major goals. The first was to identify the types and sources of information generally considered important for conducting a comprehensive assessment of risk for sexual violence. The second was to synthesize a list of risk factors. We attempted to identify individual risk factors that were (1) supported by scientific research, (2) consistent with theory and professional recommendations, and (3) legally acceptable, that is, consistent with human or civil rights. (Some examples of legally unacceptable factors include ascribed factors such as age, sex, and race; reliance on such factors may be considered problematic or even a violation of constitutional or human rights.) We also attempted to make sure the list or set of factors was (1) reasonably comprehensive, (2) not unduly long, and (3) couched in the basic language of practitioners, that is, neither too general nor too specific.

The reviews for the SVR-20 and RSVP covered different literatures, because the publication of the SVR-20 predated that of the RSVP by six years. The relevant literature grew considerably during this period (that is, 1997–2003). The lists of risk factors developed for the manuals also differed somewhat because, as noted previously, the SVR-20 was developed for general use by a wide range of professionals, whereas the RSVP was intended primarily for use by sex offender specialists in management- and treatment-oriented evaluations.

Underlying Principles

The SPJ approach to violence risk assessment is based on at least three general principles (e.g., Hart, 2008). The first principle is *prevention.* The SPJ approach views the goal of violence risk assessment as the prevention of future violence, rather than the accurate prediction of violence. The prediction approach assumes that every person has a propensity for (that is, specific probability of) future violence that is static and unchanging, if nature takes its course. In contrast, the SPJ approach assumes that it is possible to modify people's thought processes and living circumstances in many different ways to influence their decisions whether or not to engage in violence.

The second principle is *structure.* The SPJ approach assumes that structure is helpful, or even essential, for organizing the work of the many professionals who share responsibility for assessing and managing sexual violence risk. Structure, in the form of manuals and worksheets, reduces the cognitive burden on professionals, allowing them to focus their thoughts on critical information and activities. Synthesizing complex information in this way facilitates analysis and, in particular, discourages reliance on potentially unhelpful cognitive heuristics (e.g., affect, anchoring, availability, representativeness) and encourages professionals to use their cognitive strengths (e.g., pattern recognition). Finally, it enhances accountability, something that also motivates people to analyze information with more effort and accuracy.

The third principle is *flexibility.* The SPJ approach assumes that the exercise of professional discretion is necessary, appropriate, and (potentially) helpful when making risk assessment and management. Although the scientific literature provides guidance concerning what may be important considerations *on average* when making decisions, it cannot be used to determine what should be done *in a given case.* According to the SPJ approach, risk assessments should be individualized (i.e., take into account the totality of circumstances in the case at hand), contextualized (i.e., take into account the examinee's current and potential future living circumstances), and dynamic (i.e., take into account changes over time in risk factors and the overall risks posed). There is no way that risk assessments of this sort can be made using fixed and explicit algorithms developed *a priori,* that is, before the case was even referred.

Format

SVR-20. The SVR-20 administration procedures are outlined in the test manual. Subsequent to the publication of the manual, worksheets were developed to help users.

Administration of the SVR-20 focuses on structuring three steps of the risk assessment process. First, users code the presence of 20 individual risk factors from 3 domains (see Table 13.1), as well as any additional case-specific risk factors, based on an interview with the examinee, interviews with relevant collateral informants, and a review of relevant records . Presence is coded using a 3-point ordinal rating scale according to the examiner's certainty that the risk factors are or have been present at some time in the past (*Absent, Possibly or partially present,* or *Present*). The presence rating for a risk factor can also be omitted, when there is insufficient information upon which to base a judgment.

Next, for each risk factor coded as present (*Yes*), users indicate whether there has been any recent change in the status of that factor. Examiners specify the time frame for "recent change," which is flexible. Recent changes are also coded on a three-point ordinal scale (*Exacerbation, No change,* or *Amelioration*). The ratings of recent change are intended to help users identify risk factors that may be the highest priority targets for various management strategies.

Finally, users make a final or summary rating of risk for sexual violence using a 3-point ordinal scale (*Low, Moderate,* or *High*), which is intended to reflect the degree of effort or level of intervention required in the case. A judgment of low risk indicates that the individual is not in need of any special intervention or supervision strategies designed to manage violence risk, and that there is no need to monitor the individual closely for changes in risk. A judgment of moderate risk indicates that a risk management plan should be developed for the individual, which typically would involve (at a minimum) systematic reassessment of risk. A judgment of high risk indicates an urgent need to develop a risk management plan for the individual, which typically would involve (at a minimum) advising staff, increasing supervision levels, placing the individual on a high-priority list for available treatment resources, scheduling regular reassessments, or even an emergency response (for example, hospitalization, suspension of conditional release).

Table 13.1 Risk Factors in the SVR-20

Domain		Risk Factor
Psychosocial adjustment	1.	Sexual deviation
	2.	Victim of child abuse
	3.	Psychopathy
	4.	Major mental illness
	5.	Substance use problems
	6.	Suicidal/homicidal ideation
	7.	Relationship problems
	8.	Employment problems
	9.	Past nonsexual violent offenses
	10.	Past nonviolent offenses
	11	Past supervision failure
History of sexual offenses	12.	High density
	13.	Multiple types
	14.	Physical harm
	15.	Weapons/threats
	16.	Escalation in frequency or severity
	17.	Extreme minimization/denial
	18.	Attitudes that support or condone
Future plans	19.	Lacks realistic plans
	20.	Negative attitude toward intervention

Source: Boer, D. P., Hart, S. D., Kropp, P. R., & Webster, C. D. (1997). *Manual for the Sexual Violence Risk–20: Professional Guidelines for Assessing Risk of Sexual Violence.* Burnaby, BC, Canada: Mental Health, Law, & Policy Institute, Simon Fraser University. (Reprinted with permission.)
Note: SVR-20 = Sexual Violence Risk-20 (Boer et al., 1997).

RSVP. The RSVP administration procedures are outlined in the test manual. The manual also contains supplementary materials to assist users, including a detailed *Worksheet.*

Administration of the RSVP is more detailed and complex than that of the SVR-20, comprising six steps. In Step 1, examiners gather case information, guided by a number of recommendations presented in the manual. The manual also contains a *Checklist of Information Sources* developed for quality assurance purposes.

In Step 2, users code the presence of 22 individual risk factors from five domains (see Table 13.2), as well as any additional case-specific risk factors. Presence ratings are made for two timeframes: more than one year prior to the evaluation ("past") and within the year prior to the evaluation ("recent"). Presence ratings for each timeframe are made using the same three-point ordinal scale as the SVR-20 (*Absent, Possibly or partially present,* or *Present*), which may be omitted when there is insufficient information.

In Step 3, users determine the relevance of the individual risk factors. "Relevant" risk factors are those the examiner believes are functionally (i.e., causally) related to the examinee's perpetration of sexual violence in the future, or are likely to substantially impair the effectiveness of risk management strategies designed to prevent future sexual violence. Relevance ratings are using a 3-point ordinal scale (*Not relevant, Possibly or partially relevant,* or *Relevant*).

In Step 4, users identify and describe the most likely scenarios of future sexual violence. They conjecture about what might happen in the future in light of information about the examinee's sexual violence history gathered in Step 1, risk factors identified as present and relevant in Steps

Table 13.2 Risk Factors in the RSVP

Domain		Risk Factor
History of sexual violence	1.	Chronicity of sexual violence
	2.	Diversity of sexual violence
	3.	Escalation of sexual violence
	4.	Physical coercion in sexual violence
	5.	Psychological coercion in sexual violence
Psychological adjustment	6.	Extreme minimization or denial of sexual violence
	7.	Attitudes that support or condone sexual violence
	8.	Problems with self-awareness
	9.	Problems with stress or coping
	10.	Problems resulting from child abuse
Mental disorder	11.	Sexual deviance
	12.	Psychopathic personality disorder
	13.	Major mental illness
	14.	Problems with substance use
	15.	Violent or suicidal ideation
Social adjustment	16.	Problems with intimate relationships
	17.	Problems with nonintimate relationships
	18.	Problems with employment
	19.	Nonsexual criminality
Manageability	20.	Problems with planning
	21.	Problems with treatment
	22.	Problems with supervision

Source: Hart, S. D., Kropp, P. R., Laws, D. R., Klaver, J., Logan, C., & Watt, K. A. (2003). *The Risk for Sexual Violence Protocol (RSVP): Structured Professional Guidelines for Assessing Risk of Sexual Violence.* Burnaby, BC, Canada: Mental Health, Law & Policy Institute, Simon Fraser University. (Reprinted with permission.)
Note: RSVP = Risk for Sexual Violence Protocol (Hart et al., 2003).

2 and 3, and probable living circumstances in the future. These descriptions of "possible futures" or "feared outcomes" are referred to as *scenarios,* short narratives designed to simplify complex forecasts in a way that facilitates planning. Examiners are encouraged to develop multiple scenarios, then "prune" those that are implausible in light of the facts of the case at hand or more general knowledge about sexual violence. The remaining plausible scenarios form the basis for the development of risk management strategies. The procedures used in this step of the RSVP were derived from more general scenario-planning methodology, which has been used successfully for many years in other fields to plan under situations of great or unbounded uncertainty (Ringland, 1998; Schwartz, 1990; van der Heijden, 1994).

In Step 5, users develop strategies for managing sexual violence risk in light of the relevant risk factors and scenarios of risk. The development of strategies is based on consideration of the sexual violence that might occur under each scenario, as well as relevance of individual risk factors. To ensure the risk management strategies are comprehensive, users are encouraged to consider four general categories: monitoring, treatment, supervision, and victim safety planning. Within each category, users identify specific strategies and then are encouraged to consider in explicit and specific terms how these strategies should be implemented in the case at hand (i.e., to move from strategies to tactics). The development of good risk management plans in Step 5 depends strongly and directly on the quality of the scenarios developed in Step 4.

In Step 6, users document their judgments regarding overall risk in the case. This facilitates clear communication and is also very important for liability management (i.e., protecting the examiner from allegations of negligence or misconduct; Monahan, 1993). Examiners are encouraged to make judgments concerning case prioritization (similar to the summary risk ratings of the SVR-20), risk of serious physical harm, any indication of other risks the examinee may pose, any immediate actions taken or required, and critical dates or triggers for case review.

Inter-Rater Reliability

Below, we summarize the findings of studies that have evaluated the inter-rater reliability of risk judgments made using the SVR-20 and RSVP. For each set of guidelines, publications and conference presentations are reviewed in chronological order, oldest to newest. We have attempted to eliminate redundancy by reviewing only a single paper or poster when multiple disseminations were based on the same dataset. Except where noted otherwise, we index inter-rater reliability using single-rater intraclass correlation coefficients, often abbreviated ICC1, calculated for absolute agreement using a mixed effects model. ICC1 is most appropriate for true continuous variables, but can also be used with ordinal categorical variables and is mathematically equivalent to another popular index, weighted kappa or K_W. Following Fleiss (1981), we interpreted ICC1 coefficients as follows: <.39 = poor, .40 to .59 = fair, .50 to .74 = good, and >.75 = excellent.

SVR-20

Sjöstedt and Långström (2003) evaluated inter-rater reliability between two independent raters in two subsamples of 15 cases each, randomly selected from a larger sample of 51 adult male rapists who underwent presentence forensic psychiatric evaluations in Sweden between 1988 and 1990. SVR-20 ratings were made on the basis of file information. Presence ratings for individual risk factors had generally poor to fair inter-rater reliability in the first subsample of 15 people, average Cohen's $\kappa = .36$. The authors speculated this may have been due to variation among raters in experience, and they repeated the analyses in a second set of 15 people after additional training. Inter-rater reliability for presence ratings increased; Cohen's κ ranged from .08 to 1.00, with $M = .51$ and $Mdn = .57$. In the second subsample, the inter-rater reliability of summary ratings of risk for sexual violence was fair, Cohen's $\kappa = .50$.

de Vogel, de Ruiter, van Beek, and Mead (2004) evaluated agreement between two independent raters in a subsample of 30 cases, randomly selected from a larger sample of adult male sex offenders admitted to a Dutch forensic psychiatric hospital between 1974 and 1996. SVR-20 ratings were made on the basis of file information. Inter-rater reliability was fair or better for 18 of 20 individual risk factors. Two risk factors had poor inter-rater reliability: Sexual deviance, ICC1 = .38; and Relationship problems, ICC1 =.29. According to the authors, the low reliability for Sexual deviance ratings was due to lack of clinical experience for one of three clinicians who made ratings; inter-rater reliability was good for the two experienced clinicians, ICC1 = .68. Also according to the authors, the low reliability of ratings for Relationship problems was due to lack of variance. Presence ratings for individual risk factors were also recoded and summed to create Total and Section scores. Inter-rater reliability for Total scores was excellent, ICC1 =.75; and for Section scores it was good to excellent, ICC1 = .74 for Psychosocial adjustment, ICC1 = .74 for Sexual offenses, and ICC1 = .78 for Future plans. Finally, inter-rater reliability of the summary rating of risk for sexual violence was fair, ICC1 = .48; in 2 of 30 cases (6.7%), one rater judged "high risk" whereas another rater judged "low risk."

Hildebrand, de Ruiter, and de Vogel (2004) evaluated the inter-rater reliability between two independent raters for a single SVR-20 risk factor, Sexual deviance, in a subsample of 24 cases randomly selected from a larger sample of 94 adult male rapists admitted to a Dutch forensic psychiatric hospital. Ratings were made on the basis of file information. Presence ratings were dichotomized, *Absent* versus *Possibly/Partially Present* or *Present.* The inter-rater reliability of the dichotomized ratings was fair, Cohen's κ = .59. Raters agreed on the presence or absence of sexual deviance in 19 of the 24 cases (79%).

Zanatta (2005) evaluated inter-rater reliability between independent raters in a subsample of 15 cases, randomly selected from a larger sample of 164 adult male sex offenders in Canada, 82 offenders who had received indeterminate sentences as Dangerous Offenders, and a control group of 82 repeat sex offenders. SVR-20 ratings were based on file information. Presence ratings were recoded and summed to create summary scores for the Psychosocial adjustment and Sexual offenses sections. The inter-rater reliability of the both section scores was excellent, ICC1 = .87.

Rettenberger and Eher (2007) evaluated inter-rater reliability between two independent raters in a subsample of 10 cases, randomly selected from a larger sample of 254 adult male sex offenders admitted to the Austrian federal correctional system in 2002 or 2003. SVR-20 ratings were made on the basis of file information. Presence ratings were recoded and summed to create Total scores. The inter-rater reliability of Total scores was excellent, ICC1 = .84.

Pérez Ramírez, Redondo Illescas, Martínez García, García Forero, and Andrés Pueyo (2008) evaluated agreement between two independent raters in 30 adult male offenders, randomly selected from a larger sample of a subsample of 163 sex offenders in Spain. SVR-20 ratings were made on the basis of file information. They reported that inter-rater reliability for ratings of the presence of individual risk factors, indexed using κ, was good to excellent, ranging from 0.73 to 1.00 with a mean of 0.95.

Barbaree, Langton, Blanchard, and Boer (2008), following on Langton (2003), evaluated agreement between two independent raters in a subsample of 63 cases, randomly selected from a larger sample of adult sex offenders who completed prison-based treatment in Canada. SVR-20 ratings were made on the basis of file information. Raters coded the presence for all individual risk factors for 99.5% of the subsample. Presence ratings were recoded and summed to create Total scores. The inter-rater reliability of Total scores was Spearman Rho = 0.75, interpreted by the authors as "moderate-high."

Watt and Jackson (2008) evaluated inter-rater reliability between two independent raters in a sample of 90 adult male sex offenders who had completed a community-based sex offender treatment program in Canada. SVR-20 ratings were based on file reviews. To maximize the reliability and validity of ratings, raters met after completing each series of 5 to 10 cases to review and discuss their ratings before coding the next series of cases. For individual risk factors, the inter-rater reliability of presence ratings was generally excellent, ranging from ICC1 = .62 to .96, with M = .83 and Mdn = .88. Presence ratings were recoded and summed to create Total and Section scores. The inter-rater reliability of Total scores was excellent, ICC1 = .93; the reliability of section scores was also excellent, ICC1 = .95 for Psychosocial adjustment, .89 for Sexual offenses, and .77 for Future plans.

Hill, Habermann, Klusmann, Berner, and Briken (2008) evaluated inter-rater reliability between two independent raters in a sample of 166 adult male sexual homicide offenders in Germany. SVR-20 ratings were based on forensic psychiatric reports, except one risk factor—Lacks realistic plans—could not be coded. Presence ratings for individual risk factors were recoded and summed to create Total scores. The inter-rater reliability of Total scores was excellent, ICC1 = .87.

RSVP

Hart (2003) evaluated the inter-rater reliability in a sample of 50 high-risk adult male sex offenders who were under community supervision in Canada. RSVP ratings were made by two independent raters based on file information. For individual risk factors, inter-rater reliability was calculated for presence ratings, both past and recent, as well as for relevance ratings. Inter-rater reliability for presence-past ratings was generally excellent, ranging from ICC1 = .58 to .97, with *Mdn* = .91. For presence-recent ratings, one risk factor could not be evaluated due to lack of variance; inter-rater reliability for the remaining 21 risk factors ranged from .62 to 1.00, with *Mdn* = .87. For relevance ratings, inter-rater reliability ranged from .65 to .95, with *Mdn* = .88. Item-level ratings were recoded and summed to create Total and Domain scores. For presence-past ratings, the inter-rater reliability of summary scores was excellent: ICC1 = .99 for Total, .93 for Sexual Violence History, .92 for Psychological Adjustment, .96 for Mental Disorder, .96 for Social Adjustment, and .98 for Manageability. For presence-recent ratings, the inter-rater reliability of summary scores was excellent: ICC1 = .96 for Total, .93 for Sexual Violence History, .90 for Psychological Adjustment, .96 for Mental Disorder, .87 for Social Adjustment, and .90 for Manageability. For relevance ratings, the inter-rater reliability of summary scores was excellent: ICC1 = .98 for Total, .93 for Sexual Violence History, .90 for Psychological Adjustment, .95 for Mental Disorder, .85 for Social Adjustment, and .93 for Manageability. Finally, the inter-rater reliability of conclusory opinions was good: for Case Prioritization, ICC1 = .68.

Watt, Hart, Wilson, Guy, and Douglas (2006) evaluated inter-rater reliability in a sample of 50 high-risk adult male sex offenders who were under community supervision in Canada. RSVP ratings were made by two independent raters based on file information. For individual risk factors, inter-rater reliability was calculated for presence ratings, both past and recent, as well as for relevance ratings. Inter-rater reliability for presence-past ratings was generally excellent, ranging from ICC1 = .58 to .97, with *Mdn* = .91. For presence-recent ratings, one risk factor could not be evaluated due to lack of variance; inter-rater reliability for the remaining 21 risk factors ranged from .62 to 1.00, with *Mdn* = .87. For relevance ratings, inter-rater reliability ranged from .65 to .95, with *Mdn* = .88. Item-level ratings were recoded and summed to create Total and Domain scores. For presence-past ratings, the inter-rater reliability of summary scores was excellent: ICC1 = .99 for Total, .93 for Sexual Violence History, .92 for Psychological Adjustment, .96 for Mental Disorder, .96 for Social Adjustment, and .98 for Manageability. For presence-recent ratings, the inter-rater reliability of summary scores was excellent: ICC1 = .96 for Total, .93 for Sexual Violence History, .90 for Psychological Adjustment, .96 for Mental Disorder, .87 for Social Adjustment, and .90 for Manageability. For relevance ratings, the inter-rater reliability of summary scores was excellent: ICC1 = .98 for Total, .93 for Sexual Violence History, .90 for Psychological Adjustment, .95 for Mental Disorder, .85 for Social Adjustment, and .93 for Manageability. Finally, the inter-rater reliability of conclusory opinions was excellent: For Case Prioritization, ICC1 = .92.

Watt and Jackson (2008) evaluated inter-rater reliability in a sample of 90 adult male sex offenders who had completed a community-based sex offender treatment program in Canada. RSVP ratings were made by two independent raters based on file information. To maximize the reliability and validity of ratings, raters met after completing each series of 5 to 10 cases to review and discuss their ratings before coding the next series of cases. For individual risk factors, inter-rater reliability was calculated for presence ratings, both past and recent, as well as for relevance ratings. Inter-rater reliability for presence-past ratings was generally good to excellent, ranging from ICC1 = .58 to .95, with *Mdn* = .68. For presence-recent ratings, three risk factors could not be evaluated due to lack of variance; inter-rater reliability for the remaining 19 risk factors was generally good to excellent, ranging from .32 to .83, with *Mdn* = .69. For relevance ratings, inter-rater reliability ranged from .62 to .92, with *Mdn* = .84. Item-level ratings were recoded and summed to create Total and Domain scores. For presence-past ratings, the inter-rater reliability of summary scores was excellent: ICC1 = .95 for Total, .91 for Sexual Violence History, .75 for Psychological Adjustment, .88 for Mental Disorder, .88 for Social Adjustment, and .92 for Manageability. For presence-recent ratings, the inter-rater reliability of summary scores was good to excellent: ICC1 = .85 for Total, .65 for Sexual Violence History, .79 for Psychological Adjustment, .68 for Mental Disorder, .87 for Social Adjustment, and .86 for Manageability. For relevance ratings, the inter-rater reliability of summary scores was good to excellent: ICC1 = .91 for Total, .90 for Sexual Violence History, .72 for Psychological Adjustment, .80 for Mental Disorder, .85 for Social Adjustment, and .89 for Manageability. Finally, the inter-rater reliability of conclusory opinions was excellent: For Case Prioritization, ICC1 = .75; for Risk for Serious Physical Harm, .85; and for Immediate Action Required, .81.

Validity

In this section we review research on the validity of risk judgments made using the SVR-20 and RSVP. Studies are organized according to three basic facets of validity: content-, criterion-, and more general construct-related validity. With respect to content-related validity, the primary evidence comes from the literature reviews on which the SVR-20 and RSVP were based, as discussed previously. Also, the RSVP manual presents tables that summarize the overlap of its content with those of other professional recommendations and guidelines, as well as several actuarial risk assessment instruments. Further evidence of the content-related validity comes from empirical research on the ability of the individual risk factors of the SVR-20 and RSVP to discriminate between known groups of sex offenders.

Criterion-related validity incorporates both concurrent and predictive validity. With respect to concurrent validity, because the SVR-20 and RSVP were designed to guide comprehensive assessment of risk factors for sexual violence and guide case management decisions, including decisions regarding which cases should be targeted for high-intensity management, it is reasonable to expect that ratings made using both guidelines should correlate moderately with scores on actuarial risk assessment instruments for sexual violence, such as the RRASOR, MnSOST-R, STATIC-99, and STATIC-2002. They should also correlate moderately with scores on instruments designed to assess risk for general (that is, nonsexual) violence in sexual offenders, including actuarial tests such as the Violent and Sex Offender Risk Appraisal Guides (VRAG and SORAG) (Quinsey, Harris, Rice, & Cormier, 1998, 2006; see also Chapter 6) and SPJ guidelines such as the Historical-Clinical-Risk Management-20 (HCR-20) (Webster, Douglas, Eaves, & Hart, 1997; see also Chapter 8). With respect to predictive validity, the critical issue is the extent to which ratings of risk for sexual violence made using the SVR-20 and RSVP, either in the form of scores (i.e., item ratings recoded into numeric form and summed) or global ratings (i.e., summary risk ratings on the SVR-20 and case prioritization ratings on the RSVP), are associated with recidivism. (It is possible to use the SVR-20 or RSVP to examine prediction of first-time sexual offending. For example, some police agencies use the guides to evaluate risk in cases where the examinee has no history of sexual offending. But research on this issue requires tremendous resources and, to the best of our knowledge, has not yet been undertaken.) Studies of construct-related validity are those that examined the correlates of the SVR-20 or RSVP with respect to theoretically relevant variables other than other risk assessment instruments or recidivism.

In each section that follows, we review publications and conference presentations in chronological order, oldest to newest, separately for the SVR-20 and RSVP. We have attempted to eliminate redundancy by reviewing only a single paper or poster when multiple disseminations were based on the same dataset.

Content-Related Validity

Dempster and Hart (2002), following on Dempster (1998), studied a sample of 95 adult males who were released into the community upon completion of sentences for serious sexual offenses. The SVR-20 was coded on the basis of prerelease correctional files, blind to case outcome. Based on review of police reports and criminal records at the end of a follow-up periods lasting several years, the offenders were divided into three groups: 42 nonrecidivists, 29 nonsexual violent recidivists, and 24 sexually violent recidivists. Dempster and Hart (2002) calculated the correlation between lifetime presence ratings for the 20 individual risk factors and recidivism, coded dichotomously (0 = *No*, 1 = *Yes*). The correlations between SVR-20 items and nonsexual violence ranged from –.12 to .48, with *Mdn* = .24; 18 of 20 correlations were positive in sign, and 11 of 20 were both positive and statistically significant ($p < .05$). The correlations with sexual violence ranged from –.06 to .50, with *Mdn* = .23; 18 of 20 correlations were positive in sign, and 9 of 20 were both positive and statistically significant ($p < .05$). The item with the lowest validity was Item 6 (Major mental illness), which was correlated –.05 with nonsexual violence and –.06 with sexual violence; this primarily due to the fact that very few of the offenders suffered from serious psychopathology aside from substance use or personality disorders.

Lennings (2003) studied 27 males, aged 16 to 68, charged with sexual offenses. He completed the SVR-20 on the basis of complete clinical evaluations. He divided the sample into two groups: 18 who were convicted or pleaded guilty, and 9 who were not found guilty (including one whose charges were dismissed due to health reasons). He then compared the lifetime presence ratings of offenders in the two groups. Despite the small sample size, the offenders who were convicted or pleaded guilty had presence ratings that were significantly higher ($p < .05$) than those of the offenders not found guilty on 9 of 20 items; none of the items had presence ratings that were significantly lower on offenders not found guilty.

McPherson (2003) studied a sample of 40 sexual offenders assessed or treated at a forensic psychiatric outpatient clinic. The SVR-20 was coded on the basis of clinic records. All were convicted of noncontact offenses, completed assessment and treatment, and then reoffended. Based on the nature of their new sexual offenses, they were divided into two groups: 20 committed a second sexual offense that also was noncontact, whereas the other 20 escalated to commit contact sexual offenses. McPherson analyzed the lifetime presence ratings and found that offenders who escalated had significantly higher ($p < .05$) ratings on 10 of 20 individual risk factors; none of the items had presence ratings that were significantly lower in offenders who escalated.

Hart and Jackson (2008) examined the association between RSVP ratings and recidivism in a sample of 90 adult male sex offenders who had completed a community-based sex offender treatment program in Canada. The RSVP was coded on the basis of file information. The base rate of recidivism, defined as police investigation of new sexual or sexually motivated offenses during a follow-up period that averaged about 4 years, was 18%. Hart and Jackson examined the correlation between the ratings for the 22 individual risk factors and recidivism. For presence-past ratings, the correlations ranged from ranged from –.08 to .29, with *Mdn* = .12; 20 of 22 correlations were positive in sign, and 6 of 22 were both positive and statistically significant ($p < .05$). For presence-recent ratings, the correlations ranged from ranged from –.13 to .27, with *Mdn* = .17; 20 of 22 correlations were positive in sign, and 8 of 22 were both positive and statistically significant ($p < .05$). Finally, for relevance ratings, the correlations ranged from –.07 to .27, with *Mdn* = .12; 17 of 22 correlations were positive in sign, and 6 of 22 were both positive and statistically significant ($p < .05$).

Criterion-Related Validity

Concurrent Validity: SVR-20 versus RSVP. The SVR-20 and RSVP are very similar in terms of development and content, and it is reasonable to expect that ratings made using the two guidelines will be highly correlated. Jackson and Healey (2008) examined this issue in a sample of 90 adult male sex offenders who had completed a community-based sex offender treatment program in Canada. The SVR-20 and RSVP were coded by two independent raters on the basis of file information. The raters made consensus ratings after completing their independent ratings. They analyzed the concurrent validity between lifetime presence ratings for risk factors made using the two guidelines—that is, "presence" ratings for the SVR-20, maximum of "past" and "recent" ratings for the RSVP. Jackson and Healey recoded the presence ratings into numeric scores and then summed individual item ratings into total scores, as well as domain scores. The SVR-20 risk factors were subdivided into four specific domains: Psychological adjustment, Items 1–6; Social adjustment, Items 7–11; Sexual offenses, Items 12–18; and Manageability, Items 19–20. The RSVP risk factors were divided into the five domains. The correlation between total scores for lifetime presence ratings on the SVR-20 and RSVP was r = .97. With respect to domains, SVR-20 Psychological adjustment scores correlated r = .57 with RSVP Psychological Adjustment scores and r = .92 with RSVP Mental disorder scores; Social adjustment scores correlated r = .83; SVR-20 Sexual offenses scores correlated r = .81 with RSVP sexual violence history scores; and Manageability scores correlated r = .78. These results support the view that the SVR-20 and RSVP are essentially equivalent or parallel forms.

Concurrent Validity: SVR-20. Langton (2003) studied 468 adult male sex offenders, the same sample subsequently studied by Barbaree et al. (2008). The SVR-20 was coded from institutional files. Lifetime presence ratings for individual risk factors on the SVR-20 were recoded into numeric scores and summed to yield total scores. Langton also examined the correlation between Total lifetime presence scores on the SVR-20 and total scores on actuarial risk assessment instruments. The correlations with tests of risk for sexual violence were as follows: RRASOR, $r = .20$; STATIC-99, $r = .36$; and MnSOST-R, $r = .46$. The correlations with tests of risk for general (i.e., nonsexual) violence were as follows: VRAG, $r = .53$; and SORAG, $r = .58$.

Zanatta (2005) studied 82 adult male sex offenders given indeterminate sentences under Canadian criminal law and compared them to a group of 82 adult male sex offenders who received determinate sentences. The SVR-20 was coded on the basis of institutional records. Lifetime presence ratings for individual risk factors on the SVR-20 were recoded into numeric scores and summed to yield total scores, which in turn were correlated $r = .71$ with total scores on the VRAG and $r = .72$ with total scores on the SORAG.

Dietiker, Dittmann, and Graf (2007) studied 64 sex offenders in Switzerland. They coded the SVR-20 on the basis of institutional records. Ratings on the SVR-20 were numerically recoded and summed to create total scores. Total scores on SVR-20 were strongly associated with expert clinical ratings of sexual violence risk, AUC = .89, as well as with numerical total scores on the HCR-20, $rho = .85, p < .001$.

Rettenberger and Eher (2007) studied 254 adult male sex offenders in Austria. They coded the SVR-20 based on institutional files. Lifetime presence ratings for individual risk factors on the SVR-20 were recoded into numeric scores and summed to yield total scores, which correlated $r = .78$ with total scores on the SORAG.

Concurrent Validity: RSVP. Kropp (2001) studied two samples of sex offenders, including a subsample of 53 offenders from the larger sample collected by Dempster (1998) and a subsample of 39 from Klaver, Watt, Kropp, and Hart (2002) and Hart (2003). The RSVP was coded on the basis of institutional files in both samples. "Past" and "recent" presence ratings on the RSVP were recoded into numeric scores, combined, and summed to yield total scores. MnSOST-R total scores correlated $r = .41$ with case prioritization ratings and $r = .53$ with total scores. STATIC-99 total scores correlated $r = .50$ with case prioritization ratings and $r = .53$ with total scores. SORAG total scores correlated $r = .33$ with case prioritization ratings and $r = .63$ with total scores.

Klaver et al. (2002) and Hart (2003) studied 50 adult male sex offenders at an outpatient forensic psychiatric clinic. The RSVP was coded on the basis of institutional records. "Past" and "recent" presence ratings on the RSVP were recoded into numeric scores, combined, and summed to yield total scores. STATIC-99 total scores correlated $r = .31$ with presence ratings and $r = .41$ with case prioritization ratings on the RSVP. MnSOST-R total scores correlated $r = .51$ with presence ratings and $r = .50$ with case prioritization ratings on the RSVP. SORAG total scores correlated $r = .45$ with presence ratings and $r = .46$ with case prioritization ratings on the RSVP.

Watt et al. (2006) studied 50 high-risk adult male sex offenders who were under community supervision in Canada. The RSVP was coded on the basis of institutional files. Presence and relevance ratings for individual risk factors on the RSVP were recoded into numeric scores and summed to yield total scores. STATIC-99 total scores correlated $r = .73$ with "past" presence ratings, $r = .69$ with "recent" presence ratings, $r = .77$ with relevance ratings, and $r = .77$ with case prioritization ratings on the RSVP. VRAG total scores correlated $r = .80$ with "past" presence ratings, $r = .76$ with "recent" presence ratings, $r = .82$ with relevance ratings, and $r = .65$ with case prioritization ratings on the RSVP.

Jackson and Healey (2008) studied 90 adult male sex offenders who had completed a community-based sex offender treatment program in Canada. The RSVP was coded on the basis of institutional records. Presence ("past" and "recent") and relevance ratings were recoded into numeric scores and summed to create total scores. Actuarial risk assessment instruments were scored from the same files, blind to RSVP ratings. STATIC-99 total scores correlated $r = .50$ and .51, respectively, with "past" and "recent" presence ratings; $r = .51$ with relevance ratings; $r = .71$ with case prioritization ratings; $r = .22$ with ratings of risk for serious physical harm; and $r = .61$ with ratings of risk for imminent sexual violence. STATIC-2002 total scores correlated $r = .55$ and .49, respectively, with "past" and "recent" presence ratings; $r = .53$ with relevance ratings; $r = .68$ with case prioritization ratings; $r = .17$ with ratings of risk for serious physical harm; and $r = .55$ with ratings of risk for imminent sexual violence. Finally, SORAG total scores correlated $r = .71$ and .68, respectively, with "past" and "recent" presence ratings; $r = .71$ with relevance ratings; $r = .67$ with case prioritization ratings; $r = .44$ with ratings of risk for serious physical harm; and $r = .46$ with ratings of risk for imminent sexual violence.

Predictive Validity: SVR-20. Using a retrospective case-control design, Dempster (1998) studied a sample of 95 adult males in Canada who were released to the community following incarceration for serious sexual offenses. Based on review of official records (police reports and criminal records) at the end of a follow-up period lasting several years, the offenders were divided into three groups: 42 nonrecidivists, 29 nonsexual violent recidivists, and 24 sexually violent recidivists. The SVR-20 was coded from files. Dempster examined both summary risk ratings and then numerically recoded items and summed them to yield total scores. According to relative operating characteristic (ROC) analyses, both SVR-20 summary risk ratings and total scores significantly discriminated between sexually violent recidivists and nonrecidivists, AUC = .77 and .74, respectively, $p < .001$. Summary risk ratings significantly discriminated between sexually violent and nonsexually violent recidivists, AUC = .68, $p < .05$, but total scores did not, AUC = .55, *n.s.* The predictive validity of the SVR-20 was equal or superior to that of other risk assessment instruments, including the RRASOR, SORAG, and VRAG. Finally, incremental validity analyses indicated that summary risk ratings had unique predictive power with respect to recidivism, even after controlling for numerical risk scores on the SVR-20.

Sjöstedt and Långström (2003) studied 51 adult male rapists who underwent presentence forensic psychiatric evaluations in Sweden between 1988 and 1990. The SVR-20 was coded on the basis of file information. In addition to summary risk ratings on the SVR-20, presence ratings for items were numerically recoded and summed to yield total and domain scores. Recidivism (new convictions for sexually violent offenses) was coded from official records during a follow-up period that averaged about 9.5 years after release. The base rate of recidivism was 20%. According to ROC analyses, neither the SVR-20 summary risk ratings nor the total and domain scores significantly predicted recidivism, all $.47 \leq \text{AUC} \leq .56$. VRAG scores also were not significantly predictive of recidivism, AUC = .58, but RRASOR total scores were, AUC = .71. According to correlational analyses, none of the risk assessment measures was significantly predictive of recidivism.

de Vogel et al. (2004) studied 122 adult male sex offenders admitted to a forensic psychiatric hospital in the Netherlands. Dutch translations of the SVR-20 and STATIC-99 were completed on the basis of file information. In addition to summary risk ratings on the SVR-20, presence ratings were numerically recoded and summed to yield domain and total scores. Using a retrospective design, they coded recidivism (new convictions for sexually violent offenses) from official records during an average follow-up period of about 11.5 years. The base rate of recidivism was 39%. ROC analyses indicated that the SVR had good predictive validity: for summary risk ratings, AUC = .83; for total scores, AUC = .80; and for scores on the Psychosocial adjustment, Sexual offenses, and Future plans sections, AUC = .68, .79, and .76, respectively. In comparison, the predictive validity of total scores on the STATIC-99 was not significantly lower, AUC = .71. Finally, incremental validity analyses indicated that summary risk ratings had some unique predictive power with respect to recidivism, even after controlling for numerical risk scores on the SVR-20.

Craig, Browne, Beech, and Stringer (2006) evaluated the predictive validity of several risk assessment measures, including the SVR-20, STATIC-99, and RMS, in a sample of 85 sexual offenders in the United Kingdom. The risk assessment measures were coded from files; SVR-20 ratings were recoded into numeric form and summed. Using a retrospective design, they determined recidivism (reconviction for new sexual offenses) over a follow-up period that averaged about 8.5 years. The base rate of recidivism was estimated to be 7% at 2 years, 12% at 5 years, and 18% at 10 years after release. According to ROC analyses, none of the risk assessment measures, including SVR-20 total scores, significantly predicted sexually violent recidivism at 2, 5, or 10 years after release in the group of sexual offenders, with AUCs ranging from .46 to .68.

Stadtland et al. (2005, 2006) studied 134 treated sex offenders in Germany, all adult males. The SVR-20 was coded on the basis of institutional files. Using a retrospective follow-up design, they examined the association between the risk assessment instruments and recidivism. Recidivism was defined as new convictions for sexually or nonsexually violent offenses during a postrelease follow-up period lasting an average of 9 years. SVR-20 ratings—available for 119 men who successfully completed treatment—were recoded numerically and summed to yield total and domain scores. The rate of recidivism among 67 offenders with SVR-20 total scores of 20 or lower was 16% (n = 11); the rate among 52 offenders with scores of 21 or higher was 38% (n = 20). According to Kaplan-Meier survival analyses, the difference between these two groups in recidivism as a function of time was statistically significant, Log rank and Breslow tests both $p < .001$. According to ROC analyses, the area under the curve (AUC) for SVR-20 total scores was .68; the AUCs for the Psychosocial adjustment, Sexual offenses, and Future plans domains were .68, .59, and .54, respectively. The predictive validity of the SVR-20 was slightly lower than that of STATIC-99 total scores (AUC = .72 for treatment completers), and slightly higher than that of HCR-20 numeric total scores (AUC = .65) and Psychopathy Checklist–Revised (PCL-R) total scores (AUC = .64); however, none of the differences were statistically significant.

Barbaree et al. (2008), following on Langton (2003), evaluated the predictive validity of the SVR-20 in 468 adult sex offenders who completed a prison-based sex offender treatment program in Canada. SVR-20 ratings were made on the basis of file information. Presence ratings were recoded numerically and summed to create total scores. Using a retrospective design, they coded recidivism, defined as any new conviction for a sexual or violent offense during a follow-up that averaged 5.1 years after release. According to ROC analyses, the SVR-20 significantly predicted recidivism, AUC = .63.

Hill et al. (2008) examined the association between SVR-20 ratings and recidivism in 166 adult male sexual homicide offenders in Germany. SVR-20 ratings were based on forensic psychiatric reports; one risk factor—Lacks realistic plans—could not be coded. Recidivism was defined as new convictions for sexually violent offenses, according to official records, during a lengthy follow-up period. The estimated base rate of recidivism at 20 years after release was 24%. Presence ratings for individual risk factors were recoded and summed to create Total scores. The scores were dichotomized into two groups, low (≤24) and high (≥25). SVR-20 scores were not significantly associated with recidivism; the rate of sexually violent recidivism in both the low and high groups was 24%. Similarly, total scores on the STATIC-99 were not significantly associated with recidivism.

Pérez Ramírez et al. (2008) studied 163 adult male offenders in Spain. The SVR-20 was coded on the basis of file information. Presence ratings were recoded numerically and summed to create total scores. Using a retrospective design, they coded recidivism from official records; the base rate of new sexual offenses was 15% over a follow-up that averaged about 5 years. ROC analyses indicated that SVR-20 total scores had a statistically significant association with recidivism, AUC = .83, $p < .001$.

Recently, Hanson and Morton-Bourgon (2009) conducted a meta-analysis of the predictive validity of sexual violence risk assessment instruments. They included many of the studies discussed here, as well as data from two unpublished studies (Thornton & Knight, 2006; Witte, Di Placido, & Wong, 2001). They calculated average effect sizes, indexed using Cohen's *d*, for SVR-20 summary risk ratings (based on data from three studies) and numeric total scores (based on data from 10 studies). The average effect sizes were large for both summary risk ratings and total scores, $M = 1.11$ and 0.68, respectively. In comparison, the average effect size for empirically derived actuarial risk instruments (based on data from 81 studies) was $M = 0.67$.

Predictive Validity: RSVP. Kropp (2001) studied a subsample of 53 offenders from the larger sample collected by Dempster (1998) that included 15 sexually violent recidivists and 38 nonrecidivists or nonsexually violent recidivists. The RSVP was coded from files; "past" and "recent" presence ratings on the RSVP were recoded into numeric scores, combined, and summed to yield total scores. RSVP case prioritization ratings were significantly correlated with sexually violent recidivism, $r = .40$, $p < .05$; the correlation between total scores and sexually violent recidivism was not significant, $r = .23$. In comparison, total scores on the MnSOST-R, STATIC-99, and SORAG were correlated, $r = .18$, .30, and .33, with sexually violent recidivism; the latter two correlations were statistically significant, $p < .05$. Turning to case prioritization ratings, 8 of 15 offenders (53%) rated as high priority were sexually violent recidivists, compared to 5 of 20 offenders (20%) rated as moderate priority and 2 of 19 offenders (11%) rated as low priority.

Hart and Jackson (2008) examined the association between RSVP ratings and recidivism in a sample of 90 adult male sex offenders who had completed a community-based sex offender treatment program in Canada. The RSVP was coded on the basis of clinical records. The base rate of recidivism (police investigation of new sexual or sexually motivated offenses during a follow-up period that averaged about 4 years) was 18%. Focusing first on case prioritization ratings made using the RSVP, most offenders were rated as low priority ($n = 42$) or moderate priority ($n = 36$); only 12 were rated as high priority. The recidivism rate in the low, moderate, and high priority groups was 9%, 17%, and 50%, respectively, a statistically significant association, χ^2 (2, $N = 90$) = 10.39, $p = .006$. Relative to the low-priority group, the odds of recidivism was

1.90 times higher in the moderate-priority group and 9.50 times in the high-priority group; the latter difference was statistically significant, χ^2 (1, $N = 54$) = 9.95, $p = .002$. Correlational analyses indicated that the predictive validity RSVP case prioritization ratings ($r = .31$) was at least as high as that of other risk assessment instruments, including the SVR-20 ($r = .28$ with presence scores), STATIC-99 ($r = .29$), STATIC-2002 ($r = .24$), and SORAG ($r = .30$). Finally, incremental validity analyses indicated that case prioritization ratings had some unique predictive power with respect to recidivism, even after controlling for numerical risk scores on the RSVP.

Construct-Related Validity

Several researchers have used the SVR-20 in studies whose primary focus was not the assessment and management of risk for sexual violence; instead, the guidelines were used to better understand specific risk factors, specific groups of sex offenders, or causes of sexual offending.

Three studies evaluated specific risk factors for sexual violence. Hildebrand et al. (2004) and Jackson, Read, and Hart (2008) used Item 1 of the SVR-20 to evaluate sexual deviance as a risk factor for recidivistic sexual violence. They found that sexual deviance was essentially uncorrelated with measures of psychopathic personality disorder and also had nonredundant predictive validity with respect to sexually violent recidivism. Nunes et al. (2007), in their reanalysis of studies that examined minimization and denial as a risk factor for sexual violence, included one study that used Item 17 of the SVR-20.

Several studies have used the SVR-20 to compare specific groups of sexual offenders in terms of individual risk factors or overall risk. For example, Craig, Browne, and Stringer (2004) compared sex offenders on probation with those referred to a secure forensic psychiatric hospital. They found no difference between the two groups with respect to total scores on the SVR-20. Zanatta (2005) examined sex offenders who received special indeterminate sentences. He found that sex offenders who received indeterminate sentences had higher risk scores on the SVR-20 than did repeat sex offenders who received determinate sentences. Ujeyl, Habermann, Briken, Berner, and Hill (2008) compared sexual homicide perpetrators incarcerated in prison to those detained in a secure forensic hospital. They found that those detained in forensic hospital had significantly higher risk scores on the SVR-20 than did those sentenced to prison terms.

Two studies have used the SVR-20 in research on the neurobiology of sexual offenders. Schiltz et al. (2007) examined structural differences between the brains of pedophiles and matched controls. Walter et al. (2007) examined functional differences. In both studies, the SVR-20 was used simply to describe participants, rather than as a variable in the primary statistical analyses.

Limitations of Supporting Research

Problems With Existing Research

There are several common problems with the research reviewed above. First, researchers made ratings on the basis of file information. It is difficult or even impossible to code some risk factors when institutional records are limited in nature and scope. The reliability of many risk factors, and in particular those related to mental health and future plans, may be misestimated (under- or overestimated) in the absence of an interview with the examinee.

A second common problem is that some researchers relied on untrained or inexperienced people to make ratings of risk factors. Although the risk factors in the guidelines are written in plain language, it is not a simple matter for people to make judgments about such things as sexual deviance, psychopathy, or the chronicity of an offender's history of sexual violence.

Third, some researchers coded only lifetime presence ratings on the SVR-20, failing to code recent change for individual risk factors or summary risk ratings. This may be due in part to reliance on restricted case history information and untrained or inexperienced raters. But the SVR-20 and RSVP specifically warn against "adding up the numbers" to make decisions regarding overall risk, which is contrary to the principles of the SPJ approach. Despite the fact that numeric total scores on the SVR-20 appear to perform as well as actuarial risk assessment instruments, there is also growing evidence that summary risk ratings or case prioritization ratings have even greater validity than do linear combinations of numerically recoded risk factors (e.g., Heilbrun, Douglas, & Yasuhara, 2009; see also Heilbrun, Yasuhara, & Shah, Chapter 1, this volume).

Finally, researchers have examined predictive validity exclusively using studies that follow up (or follow back) sex offenders over a lengthy period of time using a cohort or case control design. Such designs make it is impossible to code changes over time in risk factors or overall risk, or to control for potentially efficacious interventions, changes in life circumstances, and so forth. The result is that these studies likely underestimate the validity of all risk assessment instruments, including the SVR-20 and RSVP.

Needed Research

We recommend that researchers rate the SVR-20 and RSVP using clinical interviews and complete clinical records; use raters who are trained using the guidelines or experienced evaluating sex offenders; make complete ratings, not just ratings of the lifetime presence of individual risk factors; and evaluate predictive validity using prospective longitudinal designs that include repeated assessment of risk factors, as well as theoretically relevant mediating and confounding factors. But our "wish list" is more extensive (see also Hart, 2001; Hart et al., 2003).

A priority for future research is to examine how evaluators make summary risk ratings or case prioritization ratings. This could be examined using "talk-aloud" methods, in which evaluators—or teams of evaluators—discuss a risk assessment, encouraged by researchers to speak their thoughts out loud without censoring. The discussions could be taped, transcribed, and analyzed using various qualitative methods. Research of this sort may shed light on why global risk judgments sometimes outperform actuarial instruments in terms of predictive validity, which in turn may help us to better structure global judgments and better understand the importance of various risk factors.

A second priority is to examine how evaluators using the SVR-20 make case management decisions. Talk-aloud research may be helpful here, as well. The inter-rater reliability of case management decisions also is worthy of investigation.

Third, research should examine the utility of the scenario planning methods used in the RSVP. It is important to investigate the reliability and validity of the scenarios generated by evaluators, as well as how these scenarios guide the development of case management plans. It may also be helpful to determine whether alternative planning or case formulation methods may be more useful in some respects than are scenario planning methods.

Fourth, researchers may wish to examine the acceptability of (i.e., "consumer satisfaction" with) risk assessments conducted using the SVR-20 and RSVP. For example, do consumers of risk assessments—including courts, parole boards, correctional officers, health care providers, and sex offenders—understand and appreciate the findings? Are there ways to improve the acceptability of the risk assessments?

Finally, and most important, researchers should determine whether systematic implementation of the SVR-20 or RSVP leads to a reduction in future sexual violence. This can be done using a variety of quasi-experimental and experimental prospective research designs, although ideally researchers would compare implementation of the SPJ guidelines either to "business as usual" (i.e., risk assessments as they are currently conducted) or to the implementation of other means of structuring risk decisions, such as actuarial risk assessment instruments. One problem with this kind of research is that the statistical power required to detect between-group differences in postrelease recidivism rates will require both large sample sizes and a long follow-up.

Case Example

Below, we present a more detailed version of a case presented elsewhere (Hart & Kropp, 2008). Key details have been omitted or changed to protect the privacy of people involved.

OVERVIEW

Mr. V, an 84-year-old man, was the subject of a comprehensive sexual violence risk assessment. The purpose of the risk assessment was to help determine whether Mr. V, 4 years after his commitment as a sexually violent predator, continued to meet statutory criteria for civil commitment or should be granted a conditional or unconditional discharge.

PSYCHOSOCIAL HISTORY

Sexual Offenses

Mr. V had a history of 6 sexual offenses that involved noncoercive sexual touching and oral sex with and by prepubescent boys, aged 10 to 12. In each instance, Mr. V approached the boys, who were previously unknown to him, in public places and offered them money to engage in sex. The offenses occurred over an extended period of time: The first offense occurred when Mr. V was about 46 years old, and the most recent offense occurred when he was about 72 years old. Upon his release from prison at the age of 80, he was civilly committed as a sexually violent predator.

Past Functioning

Mr. V's development and social adjustment were positive until he reached the age of 46. His childrearing experiences were unremarkable, with the exception of unwanted sexual touching by his brother for a brief period of time when he was about 7 years old. He had no problems at school or work. He graduated from high school and completed 2 years of college. He served in the military during World War II and received an honorable discharge. He operated a successful business for many years. His social attitudes and orientation were prosocial, and he had no problems with the law. He had a stable marriage for many years and together with his wife raised four children, despite the fact that his wife had serious physical and emotional health concerns until her death when he was 46 years old. He was actively involved in a local church. Finally, during this period of his life, Mr. V had no serious problems related to physical or mental health.

Mr. V's psychosocial adjustment decreased markedly following his wife's death, when he was 46 years old. The most obvious change was that he developed a paraphilic disorder. Specifically, he became sexually interested in and sought out sexual contact with boys. As noted above, this resulted in convictions for sexual offenses on three occasions, each time as a result of sexual contact with boys aged about 10 or 11 years old. Although Mr. V consistently minimized his personal responsibility for sexual contact with boys in a highly defensive manner, it was clear from available evidence that he had experienced thoughts and urges involving sex with boys and, in fact, had masturbated to such thoughts on many occasions. Based on his history, Mr. V received a diagnosis of pedophilia. Concurrent with the onset of his paraphilia and subsequent convictions, Mr. V. had serious employment and financial problems, as well as problems with his personal relationships, including the dissolutions of a second marriage and strained relationships with his children.

Recent Functioning

Mr. V's adjustment following his civil commitment as a sexually violent predator, when he was about 80 years old, was generally positive. There is no indication that he exhibited serious behavior problems, including problems related to sexual behavior. He participated actively in treatment, including related activities such as polygraphic evaluations, and made progress (albeit limited) in some areas.

Mr. V's physical health was generally good, given his advanced age. He suffered from mild heart disease. His mobility was mildly restricted. He had an enlarged prostate gland. He reported a significant decline in sexual appetite, functioning, and behavior over the previous 5 years, and in particular during the previous 3 years (e.g., said he did not masturbate, did not experience sexual urges, was no longer able to achieve an erection).

Mr. V's mental health also was generally good. He exhibited mild symptoms of dysthymia (e.g., periods of feeling distressed and irritable). He also exhibited some signs of mild cognitive impairment, which likely reflected normal aging, but also may have reflected the early stages of dementia. He did not exhibit signs or report symptoms of paraphilia over the previous 5 years, and in particular during the previous 3 years (e.g., reported he no longer had sexual fantasies, urges, or behavior involving sexual contact with boys).

Mr. V's self-reported decline in sexual functioning and appetite were consistent with reports by institutional staff: Mr. V was not observed masturbating in his room, engaging in sexual talk or sexual activity with other patients, or attempting to acquire or make pornographic materials. Mr. V's reports also were consistent with the results of medical testing, which indicated that he was suffering from heart disease and prostate problems that would likely cause erectile difficulties, and with the results of polygraphic interviews, which indicated that he was not lying about his decreased sexual functioning and behavior.

Plans for the Future

Mr. V developed plans for his released from civil commitment that were reasonably detailed, feasible, and confirmed by collateral informants. He intended to seek accommodation at an approved facility, where the management had experience housing registered sex offenders. He arranged for volunteer and other activities, on a limited scale, that would allow him to make appropriate use of public transit (e.g., not on routes or at times where he was likely to encounter unaccompanied minors). He also made arrangements for financial support and plans for developing positive social relationships.

ANALYSIS USING THE SVR-20

There was evidence that six risk factors were definitely present in Mr. V's case by history: 1 (Sexual deviation), 2 (Victim of child abuse), 7 (Relationship problems), 8 (Employment problems), 17 (Extreme minimization and denial), and 18 (Attitudes that support or condone offending). There was also possible or partial evidence of two other risk factors: 12 (High density offenses) and 20 (Negative attitude toward intervention). But in each of these areas, Mr. V had demonstrated some capacity for good adjustment over extended periods of time, that is, up until the age of about 46.

In terms of recent change, there was evidence that 4 of Mr. V's risk factors had improved to some extent over the previous 12 years, including: 1 (Sexual deviation), 17 (Extreme minimization and denial), 18 (Attitudes that support or condone), and 20 (Negative attitude toward intervention).

The only additional (case-specific) risk factor that seemed relevant in this case was Mr. V's physical health problems, something that was deemed a potential risk-reducing factor by the evaluator. That is, if Mr. V's health and mobility problems continued or even worsened, they could impair both his desire and his ability to perpetrate sexual violence,

With respect to the summary risk rating, given the overall pattern of risk factors, both in terms of lifetime presence and recent change, the evaluator considered Mr. V to pose a low risk for future sexual violence. It seemed as though little effort or intervention would be required to prevent further offending in Mr. V's case, at least relative to other cases.

ANALYSIS USING THE RSVP

In Mr. V's case, there was evidence that eight RSVP risk factors were definitely present at some point in the past: 1 (Chronicity of sexual violence), 5 (Psychological coercion in sexual violence), 6 (Extreme minimization or denial of sexual violence), 7 (Attitudes that support or condone sexual violence), 8 (Problems with self-awareness), 11 (Sexual deviance), 16 (Problems with intimate relationships), and 18 (Problems with employment). There was possible or partial evidence of an additional 2 risk factors: 10 (Problems resulting from child abuse) and 21 (Problems with treatment). Again, in each of these areas, Mr. V had demonstrated some capacity for good adjustment over extended periods of time, that is, up until the age of about 46. The remaining risk factors appeared to be absent.

In terms of recent presence, there was definite evidence of one risk factor during the past year, namely, 16 (Problems with intimate relationships). In addition, there was possible or partial evidence of another four risk factors during the past year: 6 (Extreme minimization or denial of sexual violence), 7 (Attitudes that support or condone sexual violence), 8 (Problems with self-awareness), and 21 (Problems with treatment).

In terms of future relevance, the evaluator considered two items to be particularly important to consideration of the risks posed by Mr. V: 1 (Chronicity of sexual violence) and 5 (Psychological coercion in sexual violence). The evaluator considered another two risk factors to be definitely important to consideration of the management of the risks posed by Mr. V: 8 (Problems with self-awareness) and 21 (Problems with treatment). Furthermore, Mr. V's intact interpersonal skills and his general prosocial attitudes and orientation—considered under Items 17 (Problems with nonintimate relationships) and 19 (nonsexual criminality)—appeared to the evaluator to be relevant as areas of personal strength (i.e., resource or protective factors). The evaluator's formulation of Mr. V's past sexual offending was that the death of his first wife led to loneliness and a blockage of his normal or appropriate sexual outlets, which in turn allowed his underlying paraphilia—until that point, managed by a combination of internal and external controls (e.g., adequate self-regulation, active engagement in conventional social relationships and activities)—to emerge. In the rare circumstances when he was alone with children who resembled his preferred sexual stimulus, and when unobserved by other adults, he experienced a strong desire to have sex with boys, projected this sexual desire onto them (i.e., convinced himself that the boys wanted to have sex with him, rather than vice versa), and opportunistically sought to engage them in sex.

The evaluator developed two primary scenarios of future sexual violence. In the first, a "repeat" scenario, Mr. V is released into the community and has good initial adjustment, but becomes increasingly lonely, misses emotional and physical contact with others, begins to visit locations frequented by young boys (such as parks or schoolyards), and eventually tries to convince a young boy to have sex with him. In this scenario, the primary motivation is to reduce feelings of loneliness. The most likely victims are young boys, aged 10 to 12, strangers targeted in an opportunistic manner. The nature of the sexual activity is likely to be noncoercive sexual touching. There is some chance of an escalation to threats of psychological or physical harm, but the likelihood of serious physical harm seems remote, given the absence of any relevant history of such violence and Mr. V's declining physical health. The risk of the scenario seems chronic or long term, rather than acute or imminent; possible warning signs of escalating risk include increasing complaints of dysthymia or loneliness and increasing time spent outside in outdoor activities (i.e., not in his residence). In the second scenario, a "twist" scenario, Mr. V's mild cognitive impairment worsens progressively over the months following his release, his behavior becomes increasingly disinhibited, and he tries to sexually touch another person—probably a young boy aged 10 to 12, but possibly a male or female of any age, once again strangers targeted opportunistically. In this scenario, the primary motivation is sexual gratification; it is not so much that Mr. V's urge to engage in sex is strong, but rather that he is so disinhibited he acts out on even mild urges. If his behavior is disorganized by dementia, the chances of physical harm to victims may be even lower than in the first scenario. The risk appears to be distant or remote rather than acute or imminent; warning signs of increasing risk include noticeable worsening of cognitive functions (e.g., declining memory, impaired abstract thinking) and seriously disinhibited behavior (e.g., walking around naked, making grossly inappropriate sexual comments). The evaluator did not perceive any other plausible scenarios of future violence, such as alternative "twist" scenarios (e.g., obscene phone calls to young boys) or "escalation" scenarios (e.g., rape of an adult female, sexual homicide of a young boy). In contrast, the evaluator found it easy to develop an "improvement" or "desistence" scenario in which Mr. V is released, his decline in sexual appetite and function continues, and he develops a routine of activities that help him fulfill his personal needs in an appropriate manner. In this scenario, Mr. V does not experience any desire for contact—sexual or otherwise—with young boys, or develops coping strategies that are sufficient to control any minor or fleeting urges he experiences.

Based on these scenarios, the evaluator made detailed recommendations for case management plans. Briefly, these included developing strategies for: (1) caregivers and supervisors to monitor Mr. V's mood and social contacts, his cognitive functioning, and any evidence of disinhibited sexual behavior; (2) restricting Mr. V's residence and travel to limit his contact with children, whether intentional or accidental; and (3) increasing Mr. V's involvement in appropriate activities that included daily social contact with age-appropriate peers.

Finally, the evaluator reached a number of conclusory opinions to assist communication of the findings of the risk assessment. The rating of case prioritization was "low," because the evaluator believed it was feasible to develop and implement the case management plan with little effort and good chance of success. The rating of risk for serious physical harm also was "low," because the evaluator did not perceive any grounds to believe Mr. V would escalate to any sort of physical violence, let alone life-threatening violence. The rating of immediate action required was "low" or "no," because the evaluator did not see any special management activities that would require implementation prior to or immediately upon release. The rating of "other risks indicated" was "no," because the evaluator did not perceive Mr. V to pose a risk for some form of violence, such as intimate partner violence, bank robbery, assault of staff or fellow residents, and so forth. Finally, in terms of date for case review, the evaluator recommended that, if Mr. V was released, his risk should be reassessed within a month, and immediate reassessment should be triggered by any sign that Mr. V's sexual appetite or functioning are, in fact, still active.

Discussion

This brief case example illustrates some of the key features of the SVR-20 and RSVP. The most important lesson to be learned is that both sets of guidelines help evaluators attend to important risk factors for sexual violence, reach opinions regarding the risks for sexual violence posed by an individual, and develop case management plans to prevent the person from perpetrating future sexual violence. The SVR-20 and RSVP do this in somewhat different ways—the SVR-20 is simpler, but provides less structure than does the RSVP—but neither relies on quantification, reference to norms, or specific probability estimates that the person will commit sexual violence. The decisions made using the guidelines can be framed, justified, and challenged in narrative terms. They are grounded in the scientific literature, but not cloaked in a mantle of science that makes them invisible or inaccessible to people who are not statisticians. They are, admittedly, educated guesses—better than ignorant guesses, but guesses nonetheless. Yet they have great potential utility for guiding action in a manner that is both reasoned and reasonable. We believe this is the best science can offer to decision makers at this time, given the inchoate state of our knowledge about sexual violence.

References

Addis, M. E. (2002). Methods for disseminating research products and increasing evidence-based practice: Promises, obstacles, and future directions. *Clinical Psychology: Science and Practice, 9,* 367–378.

American Educational Research Association, American Psychological Association, & National Council on Measurement in Education. (1999). *Standards for educational and psychological testing.* Washington, DC: American Psychological Association.

American Psychological Association. (2002). Criteria for practice guideline development and evaluation. *American Psychologist, 57,* 1048–1051.

Andrews, D. A., & Bonta, J. (2006). *The psychology of criminal conduct* (4th ed.). Cincinnati, OH: Anderson.

Andrews, D. A., Bonta, J., & Wormith, S. J. (2006). The recent past and near future of risk and/or need assessment. *Crime & Delinquency, 52,* 7–27.

Barbaree, H. E., Langton, C. M., Blanchard, R., & Boer, D. P. (2008). Predicting recidivism in sex offenders using the SVR-20: The contribution of age-at-release. *International Journal of Forensic Mental Health, 7,* 47–64.

Boer, D. P., & Hart, S. D. (2008a). Sexual Violence Risk-20 (SVR-20). In B. L. Cutler (Ed.), *Encyclopedia of psychology and law* (pp. 743–744). Thousand Oaks, CA: Sage.

Boer, D. P., & Hart, S. D. (2008b). Sex offender risk assessment: Research, evaluation, 'best-practice' recommendations and future directions. In J. Ireland, C. Ireland, & P. Birch (Eds.), *Violent and sexual offenders* (pp. 27–42). Exeter, UK: Willan.

Boer, D. P., Hart, S. D., Kropp, P. R., & Webster, C. D. (2007). *Manual for the Sexual Violence Risk-20: Professional guidelines for assessing risk of sexual violence.* Vancouver, BC, Canada: British Columbia Institute on Family Violence and Mental Health, Law, and Policy Institute, Simon Fraser University.

Craig, L. A., Browne, K. D., Beech, A., & Stringer, I. (2006). Differences in personality and risk characteristics in sex, violent and general offenders. *Criminal Behaviour and Mental Health, 16,* 183–194.

Craig, L. A., Browne, K. D., & Stringer, I. (2004). Comparing sex offender risk assessment measures on a UK sample. *International Journal of Offender Therapy and Comparative Criminology, 48,* 7–27.

Dempster, R. J. (1998). *Prediction of sexually violent recidivism: A comparison of risk assessment instruments.* Unpublished Masters thesis, Department of Psychology, Simon Fraser University, Burnaby, BC, Canada.

Dempster, R. J., & Hart, S. D. (2002). The relative utility of fixed and variable risk factors in discriminating sexual recidivists and nonrecidivists. *Sexual Abuse: A Journal of Research and Treatment, 41,* 121–138.

de Vogel, V., de Ruiter, C., van Beek, D., & Mead, G. (2004). Predictive validity of the SVR-20 and Static-99 in a Dutch sample of treated sex offenders. *Law and Human Behavior, 28,* 235–251.

Dietiker, J., Dittmann, V., & Graf, M. (2007). Gutachterliche Risikoeinschätzung bei Sexualstraftätern Anwendbarkeit von PCL-SV, HCR-20+3 und SVR-20 [Risk assessment of sex offenders in a German-speaking sample: Applicability of PCL-SV, HCR-20+3, and SVR-20]. *Nervenarzt, 78,* 53–61.

Douglas, K. S., & Kropp, P. R. (2002). A prevention-based paradigm for violence risk assessment: Clinical and research applications. *Criminal Justice and Behavior, 29,* 617–658.

Epperson, D. L., Kaul, J. D., & Hesselton, D. (1998). *Final report on the development of the Minnesota Sex Offending Screening Tool-Revised (MnSOST-R).* St. Paul: Minnesota Department of Corrections.

Fleiss, J. L. (1981). *Statistical methods for rates and proportions* (2nd ed.). New York: Wiley.

Grisso, T. (1986). *Evaluating competencies: Forensic assessments and instruments.* New York: Plenum.

Grisso, T. (2003). *Evaluating competencies: Forensic assessments and instruments* (2nd ed.). New York: Kluwer Academic/Plenum Publishers.

Hájek, A., & Hall, N. (2002). Induction and probability. In P. Machamer & M. Silberstein (Eds.), *The Blackwell Guide to the philosophy of science* (pp. 149–172). London: Blackwell.

Hall, G. C. N. (1990). Prediction of sexual aggression. *Clinical Psychology Review, 10,* 229–245.

Hanson, R. K. (1997). *The development of a brief actuarial scale for sexual offense recidivism.* Ottawa, ON, Canada: Public Works and Government Services Canada.

Hanson, R. K., & Bussière, M. T. (1998). Predicting relapse: A meta-analysis of sexual offender recidivism studies. *Journal of Consulting and Clinical Psychology, 66,* 348–362.

Hanson, R. K., & Morton-Bourgon, K. E. (2009). The accuracy of recidivism risk assessments for sexual offenders: A meta-analysis. *Psychological Assessment, 21,* 1–21.

Hanson, R. K., & Thornton, D. M. (1999). *Static-99: Improving actuarial risk assessment for sexual offenders.* Ottawa, ON, Canada: Solicitor General of Canada (Corrections Research User Report 1999-02).

Hanson, R. K., & Thornton, D. (2003). *Notes on the development of Static-2002.* Ottawa, ON, Canada: Solicitor General of Canada (Corrections Research User Report 2003-01).

Hart, S. D. (2001). Assessing and managing violence risk. In K. S. Douglas, C. D. Webster, S. D. Hart, D. Eaves, & J. R. P. Ogloff (Eds.), *HCR-20 violence risk management companion guide* (pp. 13–25). Burnaby, BC, Canada: Mental Health, Law, & Policy Institute, Simon Fraser University, and Department of Mental Health Law and Policy, Florida Mental Health Institute, University of South Florida.

Hart, S. D. (2003, April). *Assessing risk for sexual violence: The Risk for Sexual Violence Protocol (RSVP).* Paper presented at the Annual Meeting of the International Association of Forensic Mental Health Services, Miami, FL.

Hart, S. D. (2008, July). *The structured professional judgment approach to violence risk assessment: Core principles.* Paper presented at the annual meeting of the International Association of Forensic Mental Health Services, Vienna, Austria.

Hart, S. D., & Jackson, K. (2008, July). *The predictive validity of the Risk for Sexual Violence Protocol (RSVP).* Paper presented at the annual meeting of the International Association of Forensic Mental Health Services, Vienna, Austria.

Hart, S. D., & Kropp, P. R. (2008). Sexual deviance and the law. In D. R. Laws & W. O'Donohue (Eds.), *Sexual deviance* (2nd ed.), (pp. 557–570). New York: Guilford Press.

Hart, S. D., Kropp, P. R., Laws, D. R., Klaver, J., Logan, C., & Watt, K. A. (2003). *The Risk for Sexual Violence Protocol (RSVP): Structured professional guidelines for assessing risk of sexual violence.* Burnaby, BC, Canada: Mental Health, Law, and Policy Institute, Simon Fraser University.

Hart, S. D., Michie, C., & Cooke, D. J. (2007). Precision of actuarial risk assessment instruments: Evaluating the 'margins of error' of group v. individual predictions of violence. *British Journal of Psychiatry, 190,* 60–65.

Heilbrun, K. S. (2001). *Principles of forensic mental health assessment.* New York: Kluwer Academic/Plenum Publishers.

Heilbrun, K. S., Douglas, K. S., & Yasuhara, K. (2009). Violence risk assessment: Core controversies. In J. Skeem, K. S. Douglas, & S. Lilienfeld (Eds.), *Psychological science in the courtroom: Controversies and consensus* (pp. 333–357). New York: Guilford Press.

Heilbrun, K. S., Rogers, R., & Otto, R. K. (2002). Forensic assessment: Current status and future directions. In J. R. P. Ogloff (Ed.), *Taking psychology and law into the twenty-first century* (pp. 37–59). New York: Kluwer Academic/Plenum Publishers.

Henderson, R., & Keiding, N. (2005). Individual survival time prediction using statistical models. *Journal of Medical Ethics, 31,* 703–706.

Hildebrand, M., de Ruiter, C., & de Vogel, V. (2004). Psychopathy and sexual deviance in treated rapists: Association with sexual and nonsexual recidivism. *Sexual Abuse: A Journal of Research and Treatment, 16,* 1–24.

Hill, A., Habermann, N., Klusmann, D., Berner, W., & Briken, P. (2008). Criminal recidivism in sexual homicide perpetrators. *International Journal of Offender Therapy and Comparative Criminology, 52,* 5–20.

Jackson, K., & Healey, J. (2008, July). *Concurrent validity of the RSVP vis-à-vis the SVR-20, Static-99, Static-2002, and SORAG.* Paper presented at the annual meeting of the International Association of Forensic Mental Health Services, Vienna, Austria.

Jackson, K., Read, J. D., & Hart, S. D. (2008, March). *The co-occurrence of psychopathy and sexual deviance as risk factors for sexual violence.* Paper presented at the annual meeting of the American Psychology–Law Society, Jacksonville, FL.

Klaver, J., Watt, K., Kropp, P. R., & Hart, S. D. (2002, August). *Actuarial assessment of risk for sexual violence.* Paper presented at the annual meeting of the American Psychological Association, Chicago, IL.

Kropp, P. R. (2001, April). *The Risk for Sexual Violence Protocol (RSVP).* Paper presented at the founding conference of the International Association of Forensic Mental Health Services, Vancouver, BC, Canada.

Krug, E. G., Dahlberg, L. L., Mercy, J. A., Zwi, A. B., & Lozano, R. (Eds.). (2002). *World report on violence and health.* Geneva: World Health Organization.

Langton, C. M. (2003). *Contrasting approaches to risk assessment with adult male sexual offenders: An evaluation of recidivism prediction schemes and the utility of supplementary clinical information for enhancing predictive accuracy.* Unpublished doctoral dissertation, Institute of Medical Science, University of Toronto, ON, Canada.

Lennings, C. J. (2003). The use of the SVR-20 in a forensic sample: A research note. *International Journal of Forensic Psychology, 1,* 147–153.

McGrath, R. J. (1991). Sex offender risk assessment and disposition planning: A review of empirical and clinical findings. *International Journal of Offender Therapy and Comparative Criminology, 35,* 328–350.

McPherson, G. J. D. (2003). Predicting escalation in sexually violent recidivism: Use of the SVR-20 and PCL: SV to predict outcome with non-contact recidivists and contact recidivists. *Journal of Forensic Psychiatry & Psychology, 14,* 615–627.

Monahan, J. (1993). Limiting therapist exposure to Tarasoff liability: Guidelines for risk containment. *American Psychologist, 48,* 242–250.

Nunes, K. L., Hanson, R. K., Firestone, P., Moulden, H. M., Greenberg, D. M., & Bradford, J. M. (2007). Denial predicts recidivism for some sexual offenders. *Sex Abuse, 19,* 91–105.

Pérez Ramírez, M., Redondo Illescas, S., Martínez García, M., García Forero, C., & Andrés Pueyo, A. (2008). Predicción de riesgo de reincidencia en agresores sexuales. *Psicothema, 20,* 205–210.

Quinsey, V. L., Harris, G. T., Rice, M. E., & Cormier, C. A. (1998). *Violent offenders: Appraising and managing risk.* Washington, DC: American Psychological Association.

Quinsey, V. L., Harris, G. T., Rice, M. E., & Cormier, C. A. (2006). *Violent offenders: Appraising and managing risk* (2nd ed.). Washington, DC: American Psychological Association.

Reed, G. M., McLaughlin, C. J., & Newman, R. (2002). American Psychological Association policy in context: The development and evaluation of guidelines for professional practice. *American Psychologist, 57,* 1041–1047.

Rettenberger, M., & Eher, R. (2007). Predicting reoffence in sexual offender subtypes: A prospective validation study of the German version of the Sexual Offender Risk Appraisal Guide (SORAG). *Sexual Offender Treatment, 2,* 1–12.

Ringland, G. (1998). *Scenario planning: Managing for the future.* Chichester, UK: Wiley.

Sackett, D. L., Rosenberg, W. M. C., Gray, J. A. M., Haynes, R. B., & Richardson, W. S. (1996). Evidence-based medicine: What it is and isn't. *British Medical Journal, 312,* 71–72.

Schiltz, K., Witzel, J., Northoff, G., Kathrin Zierhut, K., Gubka, U., Fellmann, H., Kaufmann, J., Tempelmann, C., Wiebking, C., & Bogerts, B. (2007). Brain pathology in pedophilic offenders: Evidence of volume reduction in the right amygdala and related diencephalic structures. *Archives of General Psychiatry, 64,* 737–746.

Schwartz, P. (1990). *The art of the long view.* New York: Doubleday.

Sjöstedt, G., & Långström, N. (2003). Assessment of risk for criminal recidivism among rapists: A comparison of four different measures. *Psychology, Crime & Law, 8,* 25–40.

Stadtland, C., Hollweg, M., Kleindienst, N., Dietl, N., Reich, U., & Nedopil, N. (2005). Risk assessment and prediction of violent and sexual recidivism in sex offenders: Long-term predictive validity of four risk assessment instruments. *Journal of Forensic Psychiatry & Psychology, 16,* 92–108.

Stadtland, C., Hollweg, M., Kleindienst, N., Dietl, N., Reich, U., & Nedopil, N. (2006). Rückfallprognosen bei Sexualstraftätern—Vergleich der prädiktiven Validität von Prognoseinstrumenten. *Nervenarzt, 77,* 587–595.

Thornton, D., & Knight, R. (2006). [Actuarial risk scales for sexual offenders referred to Bridgewater Treatment Center: 5 year follow-up]. Unpublished raw data.

Thornton, D., Mann, R., Webster, S., Blud, L., Travers, R., Friendship, C., & Erikson, M. (2003). Distinguishing and combining risks for sexual and violent recidivism. In R. Prentky, E. Janus, M. Seto, & A. W. Burgess (Vol. Eds.), *Annals of the New York Academy of Science: Vol. 989. Understanding and managing sexually coercive behavior* (pp. 225–235). New York: New York Academy of Science.

Ujeyl, M., Habermann, N., Briken, P., Berner, W., & Hill, A. (2008). Sexuelle Tötungsdelikte: Vergleich von Tätern im Straf- und im Maßregelvollzug [Comparison of sexual murderers in forensic psychiatric hospitals and in prison]. *Nervenarzt, 79,* 587–593.

van der Heijden, K. (1994). Probabilistic planning and scenario planning. In G. Wright & P. Ayton (Eds.), *Subjective probability* (pp. 549–572). Chichester, UK: Wiley.

Walter, M., Witzel, J., Wiebking, C., Gubka, U., Rote, M., Schiltz, K., Bermpohl, F., Tempelmann, C., Bogerts, B., Heinze, H. J., & Northoff, G. (2007). Pedophilia is linked to reduced activation in hypothalamus and lateral prefrontal cortex during visual erotic stimulation. *Biological Psychiatry, 62,* 698–701.

Watt, K. A., Hart, S. D., Wilson, C., Guy, L., & Douglas, K. S. D. (2006, March). *An evaluation of the Risk for Sexual Violence Protocol (RSVP) in high risk offenders: Interrater reliability and concurrent validity.* Paper presented at the annual meeting of the American Psychology–Law Society, St. Petersburg, FL.

Watt, K. A., & Jackson, K. (2008, July). *Interrater and structural reliabilities of the Risk for Sexual Violence Protocol (RSVP).* Paper presented at the annual meeting of the International Association of Forensic Mental Health Services, Vienna, Austria.

Webster, C. D., Douglas, K. S., Eaves, D., & Hart, S. D. (1997). *HCR-20: Assessing risk for violence,* version 2. Burnaby, BC, Canada: Simon Fraser University.

Witte, T., Di Placido, C., & Wong, S. (2001). *How dangerous are dangerous sex offenders? An estimation of recidivism and level of risk using a matched control group.* Saskatoon, SK, Canada: Regional Psychiatric Centre.

Zanatta, R. (2005). *Risk of violence and sexual recidivism: A comparison of Dangerous Offenders and repetitive sexual offenders.* Unpublished doctoral dissertation, Department of Psychology, Simon Fraser University, Burnaby, BC, Canada.

Author Index

A

Abramowitz, C., 71, 72
Achenbach, T. M., 49, 56, 88
Addis, M. E., 271, 272
Ægisdóttir, S., 5, 8, 99
Aldarando, A., 228
Alexander, W., 11
Allen, M., 143
Alterman, A. I., 25
Altrows, I. F., 100
Andershed, H., 25
Anderson, J. J., 66
Anderson, L. A., 99
Andrés Pueyo, A., 278, 285
Andrews, D. A., 2, 8, 10, 13, 28, 33, 44, 66, 67, 70, 82, 83, 84, 87, 88, 89, 90, 121, 122, 129, 150, 155, 199, 200, 201, 203, 204, 206, 208, 209, 210, 211, 212, 213, 214, 215, 216, 217, 220, 229, 239, 244, 273
Anglin, D., 228
Anthony, C., 27, 29, 30, 69
Appelbaum, P. S., 3, 10, 31, 46, 187, 188, 189, 191, 192, 193, 195, 196
Archer, R. P., 199, 251
Armstrong, B., 215
Arnold, T., 214
Augimeri, L. K., 43, 44, 45, 46, 49, 54, 55, 57, 58, 66, 67, 148
Austin, J., 208

B

Bader, S., 69, 70, 71, 73, 74
Baird, S. C., 204
Baker, T., 230
Bakker, L., 129
Baldwin, S., 171
Bale, R., 172
Banks, S., 3, 10, 31, 46, 187, 189, 191, 192, 195, 196
Barbaree, H. E., 105, 106, 107, 129, 137, 255, 256, 259, 260, 278, 284–285
Barnoski, R., 217
Barr, K. N., 100
Bartel, P., 13, 43, 44, 57, 63, 68, 70, 71
Barton, E., 228
Barton, M., 204
Beach, C., 113
Beech, A., 129, 259, 260, 284
Beggs, S. M., 131, 133, 134, 135, 136
Belfrage, H., 150, 162, 172, 175, 227, 230, 243
Bell, V., 103
Bemus, B. J., 204
Benasutti, K. M., 215
Bengtson, S., 256
Bennet Cattaneo, L., 227
Bennett, K. J., 43
Bennett Cattaneo, L., 228
Benning, S. D., 20
Berglund, J., 65
Bermpohl, F., 286
Berner, W., 162, 278, 285, 286
Bernfeld, G. A., 22
Bernstein, I., 24
Beyko, M. J., 131
Bilby, C. A. L., 215
Binder, R. L., 48
Birhle, S., 20
Birket-Smith, M., 19
Blair, P. R., 154, 155
Blanchard, R., 105, 260, 278, 284–285
Block, C., 228, 229, 230, 231
Bloom, H., 43, 45
Blud, L., 270
Blum, J., 66
Blum, R. W., 66
Boccacini, M. T., 23, 25, 26, 69, 154, 155
Boer, D. P., 12, 13, 22, 25, 32, 101, 104, 107, 113, 129, 148, 163, 169, 170, 171, 269, 275, 278, 284–285
Bogerts, B., 286
Bone, J., 191
Bonta, J., 2, 7, 8, 9, 10, 28, 35, 82, 83, 101, 121, 122, 129, 150, 155, 199, 200, 201, 203, 204, 206, 209, 210, 211, 212, 213, 214, 215, 216, 220, 229, 239, 244, 273
Book, A. S., 20, 24, 26, 100
Borek, N., 68
Borum, R., 13, 43, 44, 46, 57, 63, 65, 67, 68, 69, 70, 71, 72, 74, 83, 148, 150, 229
Bos, B., 163, 170
Bourgon, G., 215, 233
Bowman, Q., 191
Boxer, P., 81
Boyle, G. J., 214
Bradford, J. M., 132, 286
Breiman, L., 190
Brestan, E. V., 44
Brewer, D., 68
Briken, P., 162, 278, 285, 286
Brink, J., 43, 48, 155
Brown, S. L., 20
Browne, A., 229

Browne, K. D., 229, 284, 286
Brumbauch, S., 66, 67
Buffington-Vollum, J. K., 29, 69, 199, 251
Burchard, B. L., 251
Burgess, A. G., 230
Burgess, A. W., 230
Burke, J. D., 43
Burnette, M. L., 172
Burt, G. N., 125
Busse, D., 30, 104, 162
Bussière, M. T., 129, 131, 251, 256, 273

C

Cacciola, J. S., 25
Cadsky, O., 228
Caetano, R., 229
Cahill, M. A., 28, 29
Cairns, K. V., 234, 239–240
Cale, E., 25
Camilleri, J. A., 102, 104
Camp, J., 20
Campbell, D., 228, 229, 230, 231
Campbell, J. A., 239
Campbell, J. C., 110, 227, 228, 229, 230, 231
Campbell, J. S., 22, 24, 26, 27, 28, 30, 31, 33
Campbell, M. A., 28, 213
Canales, D., 132
Carey, J., 54, 57, 58
Carlson, M. J., 228
Carter, A. M., 113, 114
Caspi, A., 43, 44, 47
Catalano, R., 68
Catchpole, R. E. H., 12, 13, 28, 29, 48, 69, 70, 71, 72, 89
Cauffman, E., 21, 30
Caulfield, M. B., 227, 228, 229, 230
Chapman, J. F., 74
Chattha, H., 12, 70, 71, 73, 74
Chavez, V., 69, 70, 71, 73, 74
Chesney-Lind, M., 66, 67
Chng, J., 214
Cicchetti, D. V., 162
Clark, D., 21, 22, 210
Clark, H. J., 20, 24, 26
Clark, J., 69
Cleckley, H., 19, 20, 22, 27
Coggin, C., 22
Cohen, G., 5, 8
Cohen, I. M., 28, 49
Coleman, D., 208
Coleman, G., 100
Collins, C., 204
Colwell, L. H., 20
Connor, D. E., 66
Conroy, M. A., 35
Cook, R. S., 5, 8, 99
Cook, T. G., 25
Cooke, D. J., 4, 10, 20, 21, 22, 23, 104, 112, 172, 271
Cormier, C. A., 8, 21, 22, 88, 99, 100, 101, 103, 104, 105, 106, 107, 109, 110, 112, 114, 154, 155, 156, 158, 167, 171, 172, 217, 227, 228, 229, 230, 235, 236, 237, 242–243, 262, 280
Cornell, D. G., 69
Corrado, R. R., 28
Costa, P. T., 33, 63, 64
Costigan, S., 89
Cothern, L., 68
Cottle, C., 81
Cowell, L. H., 69
Cox, D. N., 19, 237, 239
Craig, L. A., 284, 286
Crawford, M., 228
Crevrecoeur, D. A., 162, 163
Crowell, N. A., 67
Cruise, K. R., 30
Cuadra, L., 69, 70, 71, 73, 74
Cullen, F. T., 121, 129, 215
Cumberland, A. K., 214
Cumming, G. F., 251
Cunningham, M. D., 29
Cupp, R., 172, 173
Curry, M. A., 228, 229, 230, 231

D

Daffern, M., 4, 216
Dahlberg, L. L., 271, 273
Dahle, K. P., 13, 32, 214
Daly, M., 230
Darkstone Research Group, 23–24
Dawes, R., 11, 154
Day, D. M., 44
De Freitas, K., 43
de Ruiter, C., 12, 13, 26, 69, 72, 113, 162, 163, 166, 168, 170, 171, 172, 277, 284, 286
de Vogel, V., 12, 13, 113, 125, 126, 162, 163, 166, 168, 169, 170, 171, 172, 277, 284, 286
de Vries-Robbé, M., 125, 126
DeCosta, J., 27, 29
DeCoster, J., 10
DeMatteo, D., 20, 22, 23, 34, 35
Dempster, R. J., 101, 280–281, 282, 284
Denney, D., 10, 32
Derzon, J. H., 68, 81
Desai, R. A., 74
Desforges, D. M., 69
Desmarais, S. L., 48
Di Placido, C., 285
Dickens, B., 231
DiClemente, C. C., 122
Dietiker, J., 282
Dietl, N., 284
Dishion, T. J., 81, 83
Dittman, V., 282
Dodge, K. A., 83

Dolan, M. C., 33, 69, 72, 102, 104, 125, 126, 163
Doreleijers, Th. A. H., 64, 69, 72
Doren, D. M., 152, 256, 257, 259
Douglas, J. E., 230
Douglas, K. S., 8, 11, 12, 13, 20, 22, 27, 29, 30, 31, 32, 33, 34, 43, 57, 63, 66, 104, 113, 123, 129, 147, 148, 150, 151, 155, 156, 161, 162, 163, 164, 166, 167, 168, 169, 170, 171, 172, 175, 187, 188, 229, 230, 242, 243, 272, 279, 280, 284, 287
Dowden, C., 155, 200, 214, 215, 244
Doyle, M., 33, 102, 104, 163
Drugge, J., 25
Ducro, C., 101, 104, 105, 106, 255, 256
Dugosh, K. L., 215
Dunbar, E., 162, 163
Duncan, R. D., 124
Duncan, S. A., 21, 29
Dutton, D. G., 227, 228, 229, 230, 231
Dvoskin, J. A., 150

E

Earle, J., 25
Eaves, D., 22, 43, 57, 66, 147, 148, 151, 162, 164, 175, 188, 227, 232, 233, 242, 280
Edens, J. F., 20, 21, 22, 23, 25, 26, 27, 28, 29, 30, 31, 32, 33, 34, 35, 69, 104, 162
Egan, V., 90
Eher, R., 101, 256, 278, 282
Eke, A. W., 105, 109, 110, 111
Elliott, S. N., 88, 229
Endrass, J., 101, 256
Enebrink, P., 12, 45, 48, 50, 52
English, M., 90
Epperson, D. L., 11, 270
Epstein, M. E., 33
Erikson, M., 129, 259, 260, 270
Eyberg, S. M., 44

F

Fagan, J. A., 228, 229
Falk, D. R., 229
Falzer, P. R., 74
Farrington, D. P., 43, 44, 56, 68
Fein, R., 65
Feld, B. C., 66, 67
Feldbau-Kohn, S., 227, 228, 230
Ferguson, M., 216
Fergusson, F., 66
Ferrante, P., 43, 46
Festinger, D. S., 215
Field, C. A., 229
Firestone, P., 132, 286
Fitch, D., 71, 72
Fitzgerald, S., 102, 104, 105
Flannnery, D. J., 66, 67
Flores, A. W., 90
Forth, A. E., 13, 20, 21, 22, 24, 26, 30, 43, 44, 57, 63, 68, 70, 71, 88
Fransson, G., 63
Freisleder, F. J., 73
French, D., 213
Frick, P. J., 33, 44
Friedman, J., 190
Friend, R., 172
Friendship, C., 129, 259, 260, 270
Frye, V., 228, 229, 230, 231
Fujii D. E. M., 169, 170, 172, 173
Fujita, G., 258
Fullam, R., 125, 126

G

Gacono, C., 25
Gagnon, N., 22, 34
Gammelgård, M., 71, 72
García Forero, C., 278, 285
Gardner, W., 8, 100, 190
Garner, J. W., 239, 240
Gary, F., 228, 229, 230, 231
Gauthier, R., 129, 254
Gelles, R. J., 243
Gendreau, P., 10, 22, 27, 28, 121, 129, 204, 211, 213, 215
Geyer, M. D., 29
Gibas, A., 148, 234, 240–241
Giller, H., 82
Girard, L., 208, 213, 217
Glaser, D., 204
Glass, N., 227, 228, 229, 230, 231
Glover, A. J. J., 22
Gnagy, E. M., 88
Goggin, C., 10, 27, 28, 211, 213, 215
Goh, K., 214
Goldman, R., 11
Goldsmith, H. R., 229
Gomes, L., 87, 88, 89
Gondolf, E. W., 228, 229, 235, 243
Goodman, L. A., 227, 228
Gordon, A. E., 100, 121, 122, 123, 124, 125, 126, 127, 128, 129, 130, 131, 132, 133, 134, 135, 136, 143, 259
Gore, K., 11
Gossner, D., 89
Gottfredson, D. C., 66, 67
Grace, R. C., 131, 133, 135, 136, 143
Graf, M., 282
Grann, M., 11, 31, 32, 105, 156, 233, 234–235, 236, 241–242, 243
Grant, B. A., 204
Grant, I., 22
Grant, L., 32
Gray, N. S., 21, 101, 102, 104, 105, 272
Grayson, M., 239

Green, K., 90
Greenberg, D. M., 132, 286
Greening, D., 230
Greenslade, K. E., 88
Gregory, A. L., 48
Gresham, F. M., 88
Gretton, H. M., 12, 13, 28, 29, 48, 69, 70, 71, 72, 89
Grevatt, M., 162, 166
Griffin, P., 67
Grisso, T., 3, 10, 31, 46, 67, 83, 187, 188, 189, 191, 192, 195, 196, 272
Groth, N., 257
Grove, W., 5, 8
Grove, W. M., 83, 99, 103, 112, 152
Grubin, D., 251, 252
Grunewald, S., 101
Gu, D., 121
Guay, J., 21
Gubka, U., 286
Guerra, N. G., 81, 84
Gumpert, C., 12, 45, 48, 52
Gumpert, C. H., 50
Guy, L. S., 20, 27, 29, 30, 147, 161, 165, 166, 167, 169, 171, 172, 279, 284

H

Habermann, N., 162, 278, 285, 286
Hagell, A., 82
Hájek, A., 271
Hakstian, A. R., 20
Hall, G., 171
Hall, J. R., 20, 271, 273
Hall, S. V., 45
Halloran, R., 230
Handel, R. W., 199, 251
Hanley, D., 215
Hann, D. A., 68
Hann, R. G., 124
Hansen, K. T., 106
Hansen, K. V., 228, 229
Hanson, K., 7, 9
Hanson, R. K., 99, 100, 111, 122, 129, 131, 214, 228, 229, 230, 233, 251, 252, 254, 255, 256, 258, 259, 260, 261, 262, 263, 270, 273, 285, 286
Harachi, T., 68
Hardyman, P. L., 215
Hare, R. D., 10, 13, 19, 20, 21, 22, 23, 24, 25, 26, 27, 28, 29, 31, 33, 35, 68, 88, 106, 123, 129, 211, 229, 237, 239
Harkins, L., 106
Harman, W. G., 124
Harpur, T. J., 20
Harrell, A., 229
Harrington, H., 43
Harris, A. J. R., 100, 129, 251, 254, 255, 258, 259, 260, 261, 262, 263
Harris, G. T., 8, 11, 21, 22, 88, 99, 100, 101, 102, 103, 104, 105, 106, 107, 108, 109, 110, 111, 112, 113, 114, 129, 131, 154, 155, 156, 158, 165, 167, 171, 172, 214, 217, 227, 228, 229, 230, 231, 235, 236, 237, 242–243, 255, 256, 259, 260, 262, 280
Harris, S. D., 228
Harrison, K., 20, 22
Hart, S. D., 10, 12, 19, 20, 21, 22, 26, 28, 30, 32, 43, 49, 57, 58, 66, 104, 112, 113, 147, 148, 151, 163, 164, 168, 170, 175, 187, 188, 227, 229, 230, 232, 233, 234, 236, 237–238, 239, 240–241, 242, 269, 271, 272, 273, 275, 276, 278–279, 280–281, 283, 284, 285–286, 287, 288
Hartman, C. R., 230
Hatcher, R. M., 215
Hawkins, J., 68
Haynes, R. B., 272
Healey, J., 281–282, 284
Healy, K., 229
Heckert, D. A., 235, 243
Heilbrun, K., 2, 3, 5, 6, 7, 8, 10, 11, 14, 20, 35, 71, 81, 148, 150, 167, 172, 187, 191, 192, 195, 272, 287
Heinz, R. C., 204
Heinze, H. J., 286
Held, L., 256
Helmus, L., 100, 233, 255, 257, 259, 260, 261, 262, 263
Hemmati, T., 22, 213
Hemphill, J. F., 22, 28, 31
Henderson, R., 271
Herrenkohl, T., 68
Hesper, B. L., 162
Hess, D. T., 251
Hesselton, D., 270
Heyman, R. E., 227, 228, 230
Higginbottom, S., 214
Hildebrand, M., 26, 162, 163, 170, 277, 286
Hill, A., 162, 278, 285, 286
Hilterman, E., 67, 68, 72
Hilton, N. Z., 99, 105, 107, 108, 109, 110, 111, 113, 114, 227, 228, 229, 230, 231, 235, 236, 242–243
Hirschi, T., 122
Hisashima, M. A., 234, 240
Hishinuma, E., 172, 173
Hodgkins, S., 31
Hoeve, M., 46
Hogan, M., 24, 26
Hoge, R. D., 2, 13, 44, 67, 70, 81, 83, 84, 87, 88, 89, 90, 121, 129, 199, 200, 216
Hogue, T., 163
Holden, G. A., 65
Holden, G. W., 228
Holder, N. L., 107
Hollin, C. R., 210, 214, 215

Hollweg, M., 284
Holsinger, A. M., 90, 200, 214, 215
Holtfreter, K., 172, 173, 215, 217
Horwood, L., 66
Hotaling, G. T., 228
Houghton, R. E., 105, 109, 110, 111, 227, 228, 229, 234, 236, 238
Hounsome, J. C., 215
Howard, B., 163
Howell, J. C., 43, 67, 68
Howells, K., 171
Hrynkiw-Augimeri, L. K., 44, 47, 50, 53, 58
Hucker, S., 43, 45, 47
Hudson, S. M., 129, 131, 143, 239, 240
Hughes, G., 162, 166
Hultén, A., 48, 50
Hunt, A. C., 44
Huot, S., 11
Hutton, H., 25

I

Ihara, N., 258
Ireland, M., 66
Ishikawa, S. S., 20

J

Jackson, K., 278, 279–280, 281–282, 284, 285–286
Jackson, R. L., 21, 251
Janke, C., 23, 25, 26
Janus, E. S., 99, 113, 129, 137
Jenkins, W. D., 204
Jenkins, W. L., 204
Jensen, P. S., 122, 128, 135
Jesness, C. F., 88
Jiang, D., 54, 57, 58
Johannson, P., 25
Johansen, S. H., 107
Johnson, J. T., 23, 25, 26
Johnson, K. D., 208
Johnstone, L., 4
Jones, A. S., 228, 229
Jones, G. B., 100
Jones, M. N., 155
Jones, R. M., 90
Jones, S., 21
Jung, S., 87, 88, 89

K

Kafka, M. P., 129, 137
Kaltiala-Heino, R., 67, 71, 72
Karpman, B., 19, 25
Kaul, J., 11, 270
Kazdin, A. E., 122, 128, 135
Keenan, J. P., 112
Keiding, N., 271
Keilen, A., 29, 69
Kennealy, P., 21, 23, 25
Kennedy, L. W., 228
Kennedy, W. A., 124
Kerr, M., 25
Kessler, R. C., 122, 128, 135
Kiessling, J. J., 204, 212, 216
King, L. L., 132
Kingston, D. A., 132
Klaver, J., 22, 269, 276, 283, 287
Kleindienst, N., 284
Klusmann, D., 162, 278, 285
Knight, R. A., 21, 32, 285
Koch, G. G., 49, 162
Koegl, C. J., 43, 44, 45, 46, 49, 54, 55, 57, 58, 66, 67
Kosson, D. S., 13, 20, 21, 22, 24, 26, 68, 88, 172
Koziol-McLain, J., 228, 229, 230, 231
Kraemer, H. C., 122, 128, 135
Kraus, J. F., 228
Kroner, D. G., 11, 22, 25, 155, 213
Kropp, P. R., 12, 22, 49, 110, 113, 129, 148, 161, 175, 227, 228, 229, 230, 231, 232, 233, 234, 236, 237–238, 240–241, 242, 243, 269, 272, 275, 276, 282, 283, 285, 287, 288
Krug, E. G., 271, 273
Kruttschnitt, C., 66, 67
Kullgren, G., 31
Kupfer, D. J., 122, 128, 135
Kynch, J., 214
Kyriacou, D. N., 228

L

Lacasse, L., 20
Lahey, B. B., 43, 44
Lalumière, M. L., 101, 104, 107, 129
Lam, J. N., 48
Lampropoulos, G. K., 5, 8
Landis, J., 162
Landis, R., 49
Lane, J. C., 230
Lang, C., 101, 103, 104, 107, 109, 110, 129, 227, 228, 229, 230, 235, 236, 242–243
Langhinrichsen-Rohling, J., 230
Långström, N., 11, 12, 31, 45, 48, 50, 52, 67, 104, 105, 156, 256, 258, 277, 284–285
Langton, C. M., 105, 106, 107, 255, 256, 259, 278, 282, 284–285
Lansford, J. E., 83
Latessa, E. J., 90, 200, 214, 215
Lattimore, P. K., 124
Laughon, K., 228, 229, 230, 231
Law, M., 7, 9, 213
Lawrence, L., 69, 70, 71, 73, 74
Laws, D. R., 22, 154, 269, 276, 287
Lebow, B., 5, 8, 175
Lee, P. A., 215
Lee, R., 81

Leipciger, M., 204
Leistico, A. M., 10, 22, 27, 29
Lencz, T., 20
Lennings, C. J., 281
Levene, K. S., 44, 45, 49, 55, 58, 66, 67
Lewis, K., 123, 125, 126, 128
Lichton, A. I., 169, 170, 172, 173
Lidz, C., 193
Lidz, W., 8, 100, 148, 150, 188, 190
Lilienfeld, S. O., 19, 21, 25
Linden, J. A., 228
Lindsay, W. R., 163
Lines, K. J., 107, 109, 110
Linster, R. L., 124
Linz, D., 239
Lipman, E. L., 43
Lipsey, M. W., 68, 81
Little, T., 211, 213
Lodewijks, H. P. B., 64, 67, 69, 72
Loeber, R., 43, 44, 46, 56, 81
Logan, C., 22, 269, 276, 287
Longo, R., 257
Looman, J., 132
Louden, J., 25
Lovins, L. B., 215
Low, Y. -W., 191
Lowenkamp, C. T., 90, 200, 214, 215
Lowe-Wetmore, T., 109
Loza, W., 210, 212
Lozano, R., 271, 273
Lykken, D. T., 20, 25
Lynam, D. R., 33
Lynch, A. B., 239
Lyon, D. R., 230

M

MacCulloch, M. J., 101, 102, 104, 105
MacGregor, D. G., 191
Madden, P. G., 204
Maden, T., 22
Mahoney, P., 229
Mailloux, D. L., 30
Malcolm, P. B., 210, 211, 212, 214
Manganello, J., 228, 229, 230, 231
Mann, R., 270
Marcus, D. K., 21, 154, 155
Marczyk, G., 20, 35
Marghem, B., 101, 105
Marlowe, D. B., 215
Marques, J. K., 129
Marshall, J., 90
Marshall, W. L., 132
Martin, M. L., 43, 48
Martínez García, M., 278, 285
Maugherman, L. A., 5, 8, 99
Mazumdar, R., 43
McCord, J., 67, 83
McCoy, W. K., 69
McCrae, R. R., 33
McDermott, B. E., 30, 104, 162
McEachran, A., 69, 71, 73, 164
McFadin, J. B., 257
McFarlane, J., 228, 229, 230, 231
McGovern, J., 102
McGowan, M., 12
McGrath, R. J., 251, 273
McGuire, J., 121, 215
McKay, J. R., 25
McKee, S. A., 113
McKinnon, L., 12, 70, 71, 73, 74
McLaughlin, C. J., 271, 272
McNiel, D. E., 48
McPherson, G. J. D., 281
Mead, G., 12, 13, 113, 163, 169, 170, 171, 277, 284
Meehl, P. E., 83, 99, 103, 112, 113, 151, 152, 174, 188
Meeks, M., 26
Melloni, R. H., Jr., 66
Melton, G., 1, 6, 231
Mercy, J. A., 271, 273
Merrington, S., 214
Messick, S., 34
Meyer, R. G., 21
Meyers, J., 12, 69, 70, 71, 73, 74
Michie, C., 10, 20, 21, 22, 104, 112, 172, 271
Mickus, S., 212
Middleton, C., 43
Milich, R., 88
Miller, J. D., 21, 33, 66, 67
Millon, T., 19
Mills, J. F., 11, 22, 25, 155, 213
Milne, B. J., 43
Misir, C., 214
Mitchell-Perez, K., 21
Modecki, K., 81, 84
Moffit, T. E., 43, 44, 47
Monahan, J., 3, 10, 31, 33, 44, 46, 152, 187, 188, 189, 191, 192, 193, 195, 196, 228, 277
Mooney, P., 163
Morash, M., 66, 67, 215, 217
Morton-Bourgon, K., 99, 111, 122, 252, 256, 259, 261, 262, 285
Mossman, D., 5, 9, 11, 112, 165, 257
Motiuk, L. L., 206, 210, 211, 212, 213, 214, 215, 216
Motiuk, M., 212
Moulden, H. M., 286
Mowat-Léger, V., 233, 236, 238–239
Muelleman, R., 228
Müller-Isberner, J. R., 63
Mulvey, E. P., 3, 8, 21, 31, 33, 100, 148, 150, 156, 187, 188, 189, 190, 191, 192, 193, 195, 196
Murphy, C., 230
Murphy, W., 129
Murrie, D. C., 23, 25, 26, 35, 69
Murry, F., 24, 26
Mutchka, J. S., 44

Muthen, B., 53
Muthen, L. K., 53

N

Nabors, E., 191
Nedopil, N., 73, 284
Nelson, C., 5, 8, 175, 229
Neo, L. H., 214
Neumann, C. S., 20, 21, 22
Newman, D. L., 271, 272
Nicholaichuk, T., 100, 122, 124, 125, 129, 130, 131, 132, 133, 134, 135, 136, 257, 259
Nicholls, T. L., 22, 32, 43, 48, 155, 166, 172
Nichols, C. N., 5, 8
Nicholson, D. E., 22
Nijman, H. L. I., 162
Noll, T., 101
Norcross, J. C., 122
Northoff, G., 286
Novaco, R., 190
Nowicka-Sroga, M., 208
Nuffield, J., 103, 105, 111, 229, 237
Nunes, K. L., 286
Nunnaly, J., 24

O

O'Brien, G., 163
O'Donohue, W. T., 154
O'Leary, K. D., 230
O'Neill, M. L., 191
O'Sullivan, C., 229
Odgers, C., 8, 67, 100
Offord, D. R., 43, 122, 128, 135
Ogloff, J. R. P., 4, 12, 22, 32, 147, 163, 166, 168, 170, 172, 187, 216
Olshen, R., 190
Olver, M. E., 100, 122, 124, 125, 129, 130, 131, 132, 133, 134, 135, 136, 137, 139, 140, 259
Omobien, E. O., 90
Otto, R., 6, 187, 271

P

Palarea, R. E., 230
Palmer, E. J., 210, 214, 215
Pardini, D. A., 56
Patrick, C. J., 20, 124
Payne, A. A., 66, 67
Peacock, E. J., 105, 106, 107, 255, 256, 259
Pelham, W. E., 88
Pepler, D. J., 44, 49, 55, 66, 67
Pérez Ramírez, M., 278, 285
Petechuk, D., 43
Petrila, J., 1, 6, 23, 29, 35, 231
Peyton, J., 208
Pham, T. H., 101, 104, 105, 106, 255, 256
Phenix, A., 255, 258, 259
Pithers, W. D., 131
Platek, S. M., 112
Polaschek, D. L. L., 132
Poluchowicz, S., 87
Polvi, N. H., 105
Porter, S., 25, 28
Poulin, F., 83
Poythress, N., 1, 6, 21, 25, 27, 33, 231
Prentky, R. A., 129, 137
Prochaska, J. O., 122
Pulos, S., 24, 26
Putnins, A. L., 90

Q

Quanbeck, C. E., 30, 104, 162
Quinones, J., 162, 163
Quinsey, V. L., 8, 21, 22, 88, 99, 100, 101, 103, 104, 105, 106, 107, 110, 112, 114, 129, 154, 155, 156, 158, 167, 171, 172, 214, 217, 237, 262, 280

R

Racine, Y. A., 43
Raine, A., 20, 56
Rasmussen, K., 67
Rawana, E. P., 87, 89
Rawson, K., 113
Raynor, P., 214
Read, J. D., 286
Reddon, J., 11
Reddy, M., 65
Redondo Illescas, S., 278, 285
Reed, G. M., 271, 272
Reeves, K. A., 147, 161
Reich, U., 284
Reidy, T. J., 29
Reiger, M., 67, 73
Reisig, M. D., 215, 217
Rennie, C. E., 33, 69, 72
Rescorla, L. A., 49, 56, 88
Rettenberger, M., 101, 256, 278, 282
Rettinger, J., 208, 214, 217
Révillère, J., 101, 105
Rice, M. E., 8, 11, 21, 22, 88, 99, 100, 101, 102, 103, 104, 105, 106, 107, 108, 109, 110, 111, 112, 113, 114, 129, 154, 155, 156, 158, 165, 167, 171, 172, 213, 214, 217, 227, 228, 229, 230, 235, 236, 237, 242–243, 256, 259, 260, 262, 280
Richardson, W. S., 272
Riggs, D. S., 227, 228, 229, 230
Ringland, G., 276
Robbins, P. C., 3, 10, 31, 46, 187, 188, 189, 191, 192, 193, 195, 196
Roberts, C. F., 214, 256
Robinson, D., 204, 206, 208, 210, 211, 212, 213, 215

Rogan, D. P., 228
Rogers, A., 172
Rogers, R., 6, 10, 20, 21, 22, 28, 272
Rooney, J., 215
Rosado, L., 67
Rosenberg, W. M. C., 272
Roskamp, P., 29, 69
Rosseger, A., 256
Rote, M., 286
Roth, L. H., 3, 10, 31, 46, 187, 188, 189, 191, 192, 195, 196
Rowe, D. C., 66, 67, 214
Rowe, R., 87, 88, 89, 90, 209
Ruiter, C. de, 64
Ruscio, J., 21
Rush, J. D., 5, 8
Russell, D. E. H., 257
Rutherford, B., 143
Rutherford, M. J., 25
Rutter, M., 47, 82
Ryan, J., 22

S

Sachs, C., 228, 229, 230, 231
Sackett, D. L., 272
Salekin, R. T., 10, 20, 27, 28, 29
Sandberg, D. A., 48
Sanford, W. L., 204
Santor, D., 28
Saunders, D. G., 228, 229, 239
Saylor, M., 257
Scalora, M., 69, 70, 71, 73, 74
Schiltz, K., 286
Schlager, M. D., 214
Schmidt, F., 12, 69, 70, 71, 73, 74, 87, 88, 89
Schmidt, J. D., 228
Schollenberger, J., 228, 229, 230, 231
Schubert, C., 8, 100
Schumacher, J. A., 227, 228, 230
Schwartz, B. K., 129, 137
Schwartz, P., 276
Scott, C. L., 30, 104, 162, 255, 260, 261, 262, 263
Scott, T., 100
Sedighdeilami, F., 66
Serin, R. C., 21
Serran, G. A., 132
Seto, M. C., 105, 106, 107, 129, 255
Sewell, K., 21, 28
Shackelford, T. K., 112
Shah, S., 148, 287
Sharpe, A. J. B., 113, 114
Sharps, P., 227, 228, 229, 230, 231
Shaw, E. C., 190
Shepard, M. F., 229, 239
Shepherd, J. B., 90
Sherman, L. W., 228
Silva, P. A., 47
Silver, E., 3, 4, 10, 31, 46, 187, 188, 189, 191, 192, 195, 196
Simmons, J. L., 99, 113
Simonsen, E., 19
Simourd, D. J., 66, 210, 211, 212, 214
Sjöstedt, G., 12, 104, 105, 256, 277, 284–285
Skeem, J. L., 8, 20, 21, 22, 23, 25, 27, 30, 31, 32, 33, 100, 123, 148, 150, 155, 156, 175
Slater, N., 43, 46
Slep, A. M. S., 227, 228, 230
Slobogin, C., 1, 6, 231
Slot, N. W., 46
Slovic, P., 191
Smith, B., 229
Smith, C., 229
Smith, D. A., 228
Smith, P., 10, 22, 27, 28, 211, 215
Snitz, B., 5, 8
Snowden, R. J., 21, 101, 102, 104, 105
Somoza, E., 165
Sonkin, D. J., 228, 229, 230
South, S. C., 172
Sparring, M., 208
Sparrow, S. A., 162
Spengler, P. M., 5, 8, 99
Spreen, M., 162
Stadtland, C., 73, 284
Steadman, H. J., 3, 4, 10, 31, 46, 187, 188, 189, 191, 192, 195, 196, 228
Steffensmeier, D., 66, 67
Steffy, R. A., 129, 254
Steinbach, J., 101
Steingard, R. J., 66
Steptoe, L., 163
Stevens, T. N., 191
Stevenson, H. E., 210, 211
Stewart, D. K., 228, 229
Stewart, L., 234, 240–241
Stockdale, K. C., 129, 139, 140
Stone, C., 190
Stone, S., 228
Stouthamer-Loeber, M., 44, 56
Strand, S., 172
Stredny, R. V., 199, 251
Street, A. E., 227, 228, 229, 230
Stringer, I., 284, 286
Strohman, L. K., 191
Stuart, E. P., 228, 229
Sugarman, D. B., 228
Sullivan, G. R., 48
Swanson, J., 229
Swartz, M., 229

T

Tafjord, G., 67

Taliaferro, E., 228
Taylor, J., 21, 101, 102, 104, 105, 163
Tempelmann, C., 286
Tengstrom, A., 31
Thomas-Peter, B., 162, 166
Thompson, A. P., 90
Thomson, L., 101, 104
Thornton, D., 129, 251, 252, 254, 255, 256, 258, 259, 260, 262, 270, 285
Tiemann, J., 33
Tokioka, A. B., 169, 170, 172, 173
Tolan, P., 81, 84
Tolman, R. M., 229, 243
Torbet, P., 67
Tough, S. E., 256
Travers, R., 270
Travis, L. F., 90
Tristan, L., 21
Tubb, T., 228
Turner, D., 26
Tweed, R. G., 228
Tyrer, P., 22

U

Ujeyl, M., 286
Ullman, D., 69, 70, 71, 73, 74
Ulrich, Y., 228, 229, 230, 231
Urbaniok, F., 101, 256

V

van Beek, D., 12, 13, 113, 163, 169, 170, 171, 277, 284
van der Heijden, K., 276
van der Laan, P., 46
van de Ven, P., 163, 170
Van Nort, J., 21
Van Patten, I., 172
Van Voohris, P., 215
Vazsonyi, A. T., 66, 67
Verhaagen, D., 63, 67, 83
Vesselinov, R., 191, 192
Vetter, S., 256
Viljoen, J., 69, 70, 71, 73, 74
Vincent, G. M., 20, 22, 23, 26, 27, 28, 30, 31, 69
Visher, C., 124
Vitacco, M. J., 20, 21, 22
Vossekuil, B., 65
Vrieze, S. I., 112

W

Wales, D. S., 129
Walker, B. S., 5, 8
Walker, L. E., 229
Wallace-Capretta, S., 214, 215, 228, 229, 230
Waller, I., 204
Walsh, M. M., 44, 46, 49, 55, 67
Walsh, T., 22, 23, 34
Walsh, Z., 22, 23, 34
Walter, M., 286
Walters, G. D., 10, 21, 27, 28, 29, 30, 32
Ward, T., 129, 131
Warren, J. I., 172
Watanabe, K., 258
Watt, B., 171
Watt, K. A., 22, 269, 276, 278, 279–280, 283, 284, 287
Weaver, C. M., 21
Webster, C. D., 22, 43, 44, 45, 47, 48, 49, 55, 57, 58, 63, 66, 67, 100, 112, 147, 148, 151, 162, 164, 175, 188, 227, 229, 232, 233, 242, 269, 270, 275, 280
Webster, D., 228, 229, 230, 231
Wedin, I., 105, 233, 234–235, 236, 241–242, 243
Weenink, A., 125, 126
Wei, E., 56
Weinrott, M. R., 257
Weir, J. M., 22, 27, 28, 33, 147, 161
Weisz, A. N., 229
Weitzmann-Henelius, G., 71, 72
Welsh, B. C., 44
Welsh, J., 12, 70, 71, 73, 74
West, C. M., 229
White, H. R., 44
White, M. J., 5, 8, 99
White, R. J., 228, 229
White, T. W., 10, 21, 32, 229
Whiteacre, K. W., 214
Widom, C. S., 67
Wiebking, C., 286
Wikström, P. O. H., 56
Wilde, S., 125
Williams, K., 81, 84, 110, 227, 228, 229, 234, 236, 238
Williams, L. M., 229
Wilson, C., 279, 284
Wilson, M., 230
Wilson, N. J., 135
Wilt, S. A., 228, 229, 230, 231
Winters, K. C., 88
Wintrup, A., 162
Witte, T., 285
Witzel, J., 286
Wollert, R., 105, 112
Wong, S. C. P., 28, 31, 100, 121, 122, 123, 124, 125, 126, 127, 128, 129, 130, 131, 132, 133, 134, 135, 136, 137, 139, 140, 143, 259, 285
Wong, T., 234, 240
Woodworth, M., 25
Wormith, J. S., 2, 89, 150, 200, 203, 209, 210, 211, 213, 217, 220, 239, 273
Wozniak, E., 4

X

Xu, X., 228, 229, 230, 231

Y

Yasuhara, K., 8, 11, 148, 167, 287
Yates, P. M., 132
Yen, C. W., 214
Yeomans, M., 12, 13, 32, 104, 113, 163, 169, 170, 171
Yessine, A. K., 101, 216
Yokota, K., 258
Yoshimoto, K., 258
Yuile, A., 49, 55

Z

Zahn, M. A., 66, 67
Zald, D., 5, 8
Zanatta, R., 278, 286
Zinger, I., 121, 129
Zona, M. A., 230
Zwi, A. B., 271, 273

Subject Index

A

Abusive Behavior Inventory (ABI), 239
Accuracy
comparison of approaches, 10–11
Action, stages of change, 124
Actuarial assessment instruments, 99–115
adjusted actuarial debate, 6n.
case example, 114–115
clinical discretion in scoring, 99–100
clinical override, 100–101
adjusted actuarial debate, 6n., 11, 14
reasons for prohibition, 112–113
defined, 5, 6
DVRAG, 109–111
dynamic factors, 100
features of, 7, 8
HCR-20 summary risk ratings versus, 171
limitations and future research directions, 112–113
ODARA, 107–109, 115
with PCL, 22, 35
predictive validity, 8–11
comparative, 10–11
versus SPJ, 12–13
predictors of recidivism, 9
RSVP correlation, 283
SORAG, 105–107, 114–115
Static-99; *See* Static-99
static versus dynamic risk factor classification, 101
strengths and weaknesses of, 148, 153–155
SVR-20 correlation, 282
VRAG, 101–105, 114–115
Acute 2000, 260
Acute 2007, 261–262
Acute dynamic factors, 100
Adjusted actuarial scoring, 6n., 11
Adjustment ratings, YLS/CMI scores and, 89–90
Adolescents/juveniles/youth; *See also* Structured Assessment of Violence Risk in Youth
actuarial versus SPJ approaches, comparative predictive performance, 13
level of service assessment instruments; *See also* Level of service assessment instruments
LSI youth version, 200
YLS/CMI; *See* Youth Level of Service/Case Management Inventory
PCL
predictive utility versus other instruments, 33
research needs, 34
PCL:YV, 21, 26, 28, 30–31
populations, 3
psychopathic trait stability, 21
Affective characteristics
PCL, predictive utility versus other factors, 32
psychopathy models, 20–21
Age
PCL key factors, 34
populations, 3
SAVRY future research, 74
Aggression replacement therapy (ART), 77
Aggressive behavior
EARLs, 50, 57
SAVRY predictive validity, 71
SAVRY Total Risk scores and, 70
Aggressive conduct disorder, 70
Anamnestic assessment, 2, 4
defined, 6
features of, 7, 8
predictive validity, 13–14
Antisocial characteristics, psychopathy model factor structure, 20
Antisocial conduct
Early Assessment Risk Lists, 43, 45
EARL-20B validity studies, 50
predictive utility, 57
PCL predictive utility versus other factors, 32
PCL predictive validity, 27–29
psychopathy and, 22–23
YLS/CMI, 81, 82
Antisocial personality
predictors of recidivism, 9, 10
sex offenders in VRS-SO validation sample, 136
Antisocial Personality Disorder (APD), 20
Antisocial Process Screening Device (APSD), 33
Attitudes, values, and beliefs
and antisocial behavior, 81
and domestic violence, 229–230
YLS/CMI, 85
YLS/CMI subscore correlations, 89

B

Base rates of violence, populations, 3
Behavior
anamnestic assessment, 6
assessment parameters, 4
EARL-20B validity studies, 50
PCL key factors, 34

SAVRY, 68–69, 70
stages of change, 124
YLS/CMI, 82, 85, 89

C

Case classification, risk/need/responsivity principles, 83–84
Case conference, EARLs, 46
Case file review, EARLs, 46
Case management plan, YLS/CMI, 86–87
Case planning, YLS/CMI, 84
Case prioritization ratings, SPJ approaches, 287
Causal risk factors, VRS-SO, 135
Centre for Children Committing Offences (CCCO), 43
Change, theoretical models, 124–125
Change-oriented tools; *See* Violence Risk Scale and Violence Risk Scale–Sexual Offender Version
Changes in risk state
SPJ research issues, 286–287
tools for assessment, 8
VRS-SO applications, 137
YLS/CMI, 84
Child Behavior Checklist (CBCL), 49–50, 53–55, 88
Child Development Institute (CDI), 43
Child factors, EARLs, 45, 46
Child molesters/pedophiles; *See also* Sexual deviance
neurobiology study, 286
RSVP case study, 289–291
Stable 2007 and Acute 2007, 261
Static-99
applications, 258
case example, 263–265
validation, 254–255
VRS-SO predictive utility, 133–134, 135
Childhood and Adolescent Taxon Scale, 88
Childhood Psychopathy Scale (CPS), 33
Children, 43; *See* Early Assessment Risk Lists
populations, 3
Civil commitment, 2
Classification of Violence Risk (COVR), 113, 187–197
case example, 196–197
description of measure, 187–190
context, 187–188
MacArthur Violence Risk Assessment Study, 188–189
risk factor list, 189
software program, 189–190
development method and rationale, 190–192
limitations and future research, 193–196
clinical review of risk estimate, utility of, 195–196
patient self-report, 193–195
predictive performance, comparative, 10
reliability, 192
validity, 192–193
Clinical contexts
contexts of risk assessment, 2
defined, 1
Clinical judgment
and actuarial assessment
actuarial score modification, 99–100, 196
override of actuarial risk levels, 6n., 11
reasons for excluding, 112–113
Static-99 override, 262–263
broken leg exceptions, 14
LSI override feature, 204
SARA applications, 231
unstructured; *See* Unstructured clinical judgment
YLS/CMI professional override feature, 84, 85
Clinical predictions, comparative accuracy, 6
Clinical review of risk estimates, utility of, 195–196
Clinical risk factors, SAVRY, 64, 76
Clinical scale, HCR-20, 149, 150
AUC value range, 166, 167, 168
inter-rater reliability, 165
scoring time frame, 159–160
Coding
EARLs, 56
RSVP, 275
SAVRY, 64–65, 68
SPJ approaches, 12
SVR-20, 274
Collateral observer reports
assessment parameters, 3, 4
LS assessment data, 200, 204
Combination of data
COVR development, 191
SPJ approaches, 12
Community factors
at-risk children, 44
EARLs, 45, 46
YLS/CMI, 82
Community misconduct, PCL predictive validity, 29–31
Community recidivism, PCL predictive validity, 27–29
Community settings
HCR-20 scoring, 161
populations, 3
YLS/CMI, 81
Community violence
at-risk children, 44
PCL predictive utility, 35
PCL predictive utility versus other instruments, 32–33
SAVRY predictive validity, 72, 73
Conduct disorder rating scale, 88
Conduct disorders (CD)

EARLs, 57
EARL-20B predictors, 52–53
EARL-21G, 56
SAVRY correlations, 68–69
SAVRY predictive validity, 71
SAVRY Total Risk scores and, 70
YLS/CMI, 81
Conduct problems, EARL-20B validity studies, 50
Congruence, factors to be considered in risk assessment, 6–7
Contemplation, stages of change, 124
Context
factors to be considered in risk assessment, 1–2, 4, 6
Static-99 use, 251
Contextual risk factors; *See* Social/contextual risk factors
COVR; *See* Classification of Violence Risk
Criminal history; *See* Historical variables/risk factors
Criminogenic factors, YLS/CMI, 81, 82, 83
Criminogenic needs, RNR model, 2
Cross-validation, 153–154
Cultural factors; *See also* Ethnicity/race/culture

D

Danger Assessment (DA), 227, 243
Dangerous and severe personality disorder (DSPD), 22, 125
Dangerous offender (DO) evaluations, 137
Darkstone Research Group, 23
Data collection, role of clinical judgment, 6
Data interpretation, role of clinical judgment, 6
Data selection, SPJ approaches, 12
Defiance, YLS/CMI, 81
Delinquency subscale, CBCL, 49–50
Demographics, and psychopathy measures, 20
PCL key factors, 34
PCL predictive performance, 10
PCL predictive utility versus other factors, 31
Detection rates, sex offenders, 257
Developmental differences in nature of risk factors, SAVRY, 67, 68
Deviance
sexual; *See* Sexual deviance
social, psychopathy model factor structure, 20
Diagnostic and Statistical Manual of Mental Disorders (DSM)
conduct disorder rating scale, 88
and EARL-20B risk factors, 50
psychopathy, 19
Disruptive Behavior Disorder Rating Scale, 88
Documentation of judgment, RSVP, 277
Domestic violence; *See* SARA
contexts of risk assessment, 2
DVRAG, 109–111
HCR-20 utility, 175
LS external validity, 214
ODARA, 107–109, 115
Domestic Violence Risk Appraisal Guide (DVRAG), 109–112
actuarial systems, 109–111
description, 109–110
development and validation, 110–111
limitations and future research, 111–112
reliability, psychometric properties, and validity, 111
Domestic Violence Screening Instrument (DVSI), 227, 238, 240
DVRAG; *See* Domestic Violence Risk Appraisal Guide
Dynamic risk factors/variables
and actuarial assessment, 100
anamnestic assessment and, 6
LSI-R dynamic predictive validity, 213–214
sex offenders, 129
VRS, 122–124
VRS-SO, 129, 130, 131, 143n.
applications, 135–136
causal risk factors, 135
linking to treatment outcomes, 128
YLS/CMI, 84

E

EARL-20B and EARL-21G; *See* Early Assessment Risk Lists
Early Assessment Risk Lists (EARL-20B and EARL-21G), 43–60, 113
administration and interpretation, 45–47
case example, 57–60
description of measure, 45
gender-sensitive approach, 47–49
reliability, EARL-20B, 47–48
reliability, EARL-21G, 49
limitations and future research, 56–57
method and development rationale, 44
validity, EARL-20B, 49–53
concurrent, 49–50
predictive, 50–53
validity, EARL-21G, 55–56, 57
concurrent, 56, 57
predictive, 55–56
validity, of subscales, 53–56
Education, YLS/CMI, 85
Employment, YLS/CMI, 85
Ethnicity/race/culture
EARLs, 56
HCR-20 limitations, 172–173
LS external validity, 214
PCL key factors, 34
and psychopathy measures, 28, 29
SAVRY future research, 74
YLS/CMI, 81, 89, 94

F

Factor structure, psychopathy models, 20–21
Factors in risk assessment; *See* Risk assessment, factors to be considered
Family factors
  at-risk children, 44
  EARLs, 45, 46
  YLS/CMI, 82, 85, 89
First-time sexual offending, prediction of, 280
Five Factor Model of personality, 33
Flexibility, SPJ principles, 274
Fluctuating dynamic factors, 100
Forensic assessment instruments, 272
Fourth-generation risk assessment instruments, 273
Future violence scenarios, 275–276

G

Gender
  EARLs, 56
  HCR-20 limitations, 172–173
  LS instruments and, 215, 217
  male victim gender of sex offender as predictor, 129; *See also* Sexual deviance
  populations, 3
  and psychopathy measures, 20, 28, 29, 34
  SAVRY future research, 74
  SAVRY predictive validity, 72
  SAVRY reliability, 68–69
  SAVRY utility, 66–67
  YLS/CMI, 81, 89, 94
Gender Aggression Project (GAP), 67
Gender-specific risks; *See* EARL-20B and EARL-21G
General Statistical Information on Recidivism (GSIR), 11, 237
General violence risk assessments, SAVRY caveats, 65
Goals, YLS/CMI, 86–87
Growth mixture model approach, EARL subscale predictive validity, 53
GSIR (General Statistical Information on Recidivism), 11, 237

H

Hare Psychopathy Checklist; *See* Psychopathy Checklist measures
HCR-20; *See* Historical-Clinical-Risk Management-20
Historical-Clinical-Risk Management-20 (HCR-20), 113, 147–180
  case example, 175–180
  correlations/comparisons with other instruments
    COVR, 188
    EARL-20B inter-rater reliability comparison, 48
    LSI-R validity, 213
    PCL predictive utility, 32–33
    SARA, 242
    SVR-20 predictive validity, 284
  description of content and items, 148–151
    clinical scale, 150
    contexts, settings, populations (in) appropriate for use, 150–151
    historical scale, 149–150
  description of measure, 147–156
    administration procedures, 156–157
    criterion being assessed, 147–148
    method and rationale for development, 151–152
    rationale for development, 155–156
    sources of information, 157
    strengths and weaknesses of actuarial decision making, 153–155
    strengths and weaknesses of unstructured clinical discretion, 152
    user qualifications, 151
  evaluation steps, 157–159
  future areas of research, 173–175
  limitations, 171–173
  older juveniles, 66
  predictive performance, comparative, 13
  research overview, 161–171
  research overview, reliability, 162–164
    internal consistency, 162
    inter-rater reliability, 162–164
  research overview, validity, 164–171
    predictive, 13
    summary risk ratings, 166–169
    summary risk ratings versus actuarial ratings of risk, 169–171
  revised version, 175
  risk assessment test battery, 35
  risk factors, 12n.
  team evaluations, 159
  time frame for decisions about risk for violence, 159–161
    clinical scale, 159–160
    historical scale, 159
    risk management scale, 160–161
  weighting of risk factors, 11
Historical scale, HCR-20, 149–150
  AUC value range, 166, 167, 168
  inter-rater reliability, 165
  scoring time frame, 159
Historical variables/risk factors
  delinquency prediction, 56–57
  and domestic violence, 228, 229–230
  as dynamic risk factor, 213
  PCL predictive utility versus other factors, 31
  predictors of recidivism, 9, 10
  psychopathy models, factor structure, 21

SAVRY, 63, 64, 76
YLS/CMI, 85, 89

I

Identification of risk factors, 4
Idiopathic subtype, psychopathy, 19
Impulsivity, EARL-20B validity studies, 50
Individual applicability, actuarial measures, 11
Individual/individualized risk factors
assessment approaches, 8, 14
EARLs, 45
SAVRY, 63, 64, 76, 77
Information sources, SARA assessment, 231–232
Insanity acquitees, populations, 3
Insanity acquittal, 2
Institutional misconduct
LS external validity, 214
PCL predictive utility, 35
PCL predictive validity, 29–31
SAVRY predictive validity, 71, 72, 73
SAVRY Total Risk scores and, 70
Institutional settings; *See also* Settings
HCR-20 scoring, 161
YLS/CMI, 81
Interpersonal characteristics
PCL predictive utility versus other factors, 32
psychopathy models, factor structure, 20–21
Interpretation of data, adjusted actuarial debate, 6n.
Interventions
assessment tool features, 8
and increased risk with low-risk spousal assault offenders, 244
populations, 3
Intervention targets, anamnestic assessment and, 6
Interviews
with HCR-20, 157
LS assessment data, 200
role of clinical judgment, 6
SARA assessment, 231, 232
SAVRY coding, 64
SPJ approaches, 286
Inventory of Beliefs about Wife Beating (IBWB), 239
Iterative classification tree (ICT), 191

J

Jesness Asocial Index, 88
JSORRAT (Juvenile Sexual Offense Recidivism Risk Assessment Tool-II), 70, 73–74
Juvenile justice setting, YLS/CMI caveats, 87
Juveniles; *See* Adolescents/juveniles/youth
Juvenile Sex Offender Assessment Protocol-II (JSOAP), 70, 71, 74
Juvenile Sexual Offense Recidivism Risk Assessment Tool-II (JSORRAT), 70, 73–74

K

Kingston Screening Instrument for Domestic Violence (K-SID), 243

L

Legal contexts, 2
defined, 1
populations, 3
SARA development for use in, 230–231
Leisure activity, YLS/CMI, 82, 84, 85, 89
Level of risk, parameters in risk assessment, 4
Level of service (LS) assessment instruments, 199–221
correlations/comparisons with other instruments
PCL predictive utility, 32
PCL-R, 10, 28
SARA, 239
description, 199–204
LS/CMI, 200–203
LSI-R, 200, 201
LSI-R:SV, 204
LS-RNR, 203
development method and rationale, 204–205
limitations and future research needs, 216–217
LS/CMI, 205
reliability, 206, 207
Violence Risk Scale, 8
LSI measures, 2
LSI-OR (Ontario Revision), 239
LSI-R, 205
PCL predictive utility versus, 32
predictive performance, comparative, 11
reliability, 207
strengths and weaknesses of actuarial decision making, 153, 155
LSI-R:SV, 205
predictive performance, comparative, 13
reliability, 206–210
internal consistency, 206–208
inter-rater and test-retest reliability, 208–209
validity, 210–216
construct, LSI, 210
convergent-divergent, 211, 212
dynamic predictive, 213–214
external, 214–215
factor analytic evidence, 210–211
predictive, 211, 213
risk principle and, 215–216
summary, 216

youth; *See* Youth Level of Service/Case Management Inventory
Level of supervision category, YLS/CMI, 86
Liability issues, RSVP, 277
Lifestyle
PCL predictive utility versus other factors, 32
psychopathy models, factor structure, 20–21
Lifestyle Criminality Screening Form (LCSF), 10, 32
Local norms, YLS/CMI, 85
Location
populations, 3
setting/context of assessment, 4
Long-term follow-up, PCL research needs, 34
LS; *See* Level of service assessment instruments

M

MacArthur Violence Risk Assessment Study, 10, 193
COVR, 188–189, 190, 191–192, 193, 195; *See also* Classification of Violence Risk
PCL:SV, 31, 32
Maintenance, stages of change, 124
Management-focused risk assessment instruments, 273
Management of risk; *See* Risk management
Mental health courts, 2
Mental health status
PCL-R and, 27
populations, 3
SPJ research problems, 286
Mentally disordered populations
COVR predictive ability with, 10
and domestic violence, 229
LS external validity, 214
predictors of recidivism, 9
SVR-20 and RSVP examiner qualifications, 271–272
Minnesota Sex Offender Screening Tool (MnSOST), 153
Minnesota Sex Offender Screening Tool–Revised (MnSOST-R), 270
clinical override, effects on accuracy, 11
RSVP correlation, 282, 283
RSVP predictive validity, 285
SVR-20 correlation, 282
Mixed model design, based on EARL-21G scores, 56, 57
Mixed model results, EARLs, 57

N

National contexts/jurisdictions, 81
HCR-20 applications, 147
LS external validity, 214
LS instrument use, 199
Static-99 use, 251
VRS/VRS-SO use, 125
YLS/CMI research needs, 94
YLS/CMI utility, 81
Need principle of case classification, 83
Needs; *See also* Risk/needs/responsivity model
RNR definitions, 2
YLS/CMI, 83
Neuroticism Extraversion Openness–Five Factor Inventory (NEO-FFI), 33
Non-Physical Abuse of Partner Scale (NPAPS), 239–240
Normative scores, YLS/CMI, 85
Not guilty by reason of insanity, 2, 3

O

Obligation to warn, 1, 231
ODARA, 107–109, 115, 227
SARA comparisons with, 242–243
Official records, assessment parameters, 3, 4
Ontario Domestic Assault Risk Assessment (ODARA), 107–109, 227
case example, 115
description, 107
limitations and future research, 111–112
method and rationale for development, 107–109
reliability, psychometric properties, and validity, 109
Oppositional defiant disorder, 57
Outcomes
assessment parameters, 3
definitions and measurement of, 10
Override feature
LSI, 204
Static-99, 262–263
YLS/CMI, 84, 85

P

Parameters
factors to be considered in risk assessment, 3–4, 6
Partner violence; *See* Domestic violence
PCL:SV, PCL predictive utility versus, 32
Peer relations
YLS/CMI, 85
YLS/CMI subscore correlations, 89
Personal Experience Screening Questionnaire (PESQ), 88
Personality disorders
dangerous and severe personality disorder (DSPD), 22
VRS and VRS-SO assessment, 125
PCL predictive utility versus other factors, 31

sex offenders in VRS-SO validation sample, 136
Personality variables
Five Factor Model of personality, 33
PCL predictive utility versus other factors, 31
predictors of recidivism, 9, 10
psychopathy, 22
SAVRY, 68–69
YLS/CMI, 82, 85
YLS/CMI subscore correlations, 89
Physical Abuse of Partner Scale (PAPS), 239, 240
Planning
EARLs and, 57
YLS/CMI, 84, 86–87
Police-community referral protocols, at-risk children, 44
Populations
factors to be considered in risk assessment, 3, 6
Precontemplation, stages of change, 124
Prediction
comparison of approaches, 10–11
versus risk management, 2
Preparation, stages of change, 124
Prevention
at-risk children, 44
SPJ principles, 273
Prior offenses; *See* Historical variables/risk factors
Probation setting, YLS/CMI caveats, 87
Probative value, PCL, 35
Professional override
LS assessment data, 204
YLS/CMI, 84, 85
Protect, obligation to, 1
Protectees, threats to, 2
Protective factors
clinical review of risk estimates, 195–196
EARLs and, 56
parameters in risk assessment, 4
SAVRY, 63–64, 76
future research, 74
Total Risk scores and, 70
YLS/CMI, as responsivity factors, 84
Psychology of Criminal Conduct (PCC), 122–123
Psychopathy
predictors of recidivism, 10
SAVRY items, 69
Psychopathy Checklist (PCL) measures, 19–35
actuarial measure selection, 262
applications and settings, 22–23
correlations/comparisons with other instruments
HCR-20, 157, 171
LSI-R validity, 211, 213
SARA versus PCL:SV, 237, 239
SAVRY versus PCL:YV, 68–69, 70, 71
SVR-20 predictive validity, 284
VRS-SO validation sample, 136–137
YLS/CMI versus PCL:YV, 88
definitions and concepts of psychopathy, 19
examiner qualifications, 23–24
instruments, 19–21
PCL-R and PCL:SV, 20–21
PCL:YV, 21
juveniles
SAVRY versus PCL:YV, 68–69, 70, 71
YLS/CMI versus PCL:YV, 88
PCL:YV, 21, 33
SAVRY versus PCL:YV, 68–69, 70, 71
YLS/CMI versus PCL:YV, 88
predictive performance, comparative, 10, 11, 13
reliability, 24–26
internal consistency, 24–25
inter-rater, 25–26
risk factors, 12n.
sex offenders
PCL-R versus, 252
SARA versus PCL:SV, 237, 239
in VRS-SO validation sample, 136–137
subtypes, psychopathy, 19, 25, 27
utility, 33–35
validity, incremental, 31–33
psychopathy versus other risk assessment instruments, 32–33
psychopathy versus other risk factors, 31–32
validity, predictive, 26–31
community misconduct, 29–31
community recidivism, 27–29
Psychosocial adjustment, and domestic violence, 228–229
Purpose of instrument
factors to be considered in risk assessment, 2–3, 6

R

Race; *See* Ethnicity/race/culture
Rapid Risk Assessment for Sexual Offense Recidivism (RRASOR), 129, 251–252, 257, 262, 270
RSVP correlation, 283
SVR-20 correlation, 282
SVR-20 predictive validity, 283, 284
Rating scale, SVR-20, 274
Recidivism; *See also specific instruments*
GSIR, 11, 237
JSORRAT, 70, 73–74
PCL predictive validity, 27–29
RRASOR; *See* Rapid Risk Assessment for Sexual Offense Recidivism
sex offenders, 101–105, 107
Static-99; *See* Static-99
Records
assessment parameters, 3, 4
LS assessment data, 200
role of clinical judgment, 6
SARA assessment, 231–232

SAVRY coding, 64–65
Records review, EARLs, 46
Recurring influences, parameters in risk assessment, 4
Reduction in violence, SPJ research needs, 287
Reports, assessment parameters, 3
Responsivity
at-risk children, 44
case classification, 83–84
defined, 121–122
EARL factors, 45, 46
RNR definitions, 2
YLS/CMI, defined, 83
Risk assessment, factors to be considered, 1–14
approaches (actuarial, SCJ, anamnestic), 5–6, 7–14
definitions, 5–6
predictors of recidivism among mentally disordered offenders, 9
context, 1–2
parameters, 3–4
populations, 3
predictive validity of approaches, 8–14
actuarial, 8–11
actuarial versus SPJ, 12–13
anamnestic, 13–14
structured professional judgment, 11–12
purpose, 2–3
Risk categories, HCR-20, 158–159
Risk factors
clinical review of risk estimates, 195–196
identification of, 4
populations, 3
RSVP, 275, 276
SPJ research issues, 286
SVR-20, 274, 275
SVR-20 and RSVP, 282
weighting, effects on accuracy, 11
YLS/CMI, defined, 83
Risk levels
cutoffs, 191
LSI-R, 204–205
parameters in risk assessment, 4
spousal violence, intervention effects, 244
Risk management
actuarial approach weaknesses, 148
change and treatment-oriented assessment tools; *See* Violence Risk Scale and Violence Risk Scale–Sexual Offender Version
EARLs and, 57
prediction versus, 2
risk assessment leading to, 47
RSVP, 276
Risk management scale
HCR-20, 149, 150
HCR-20 AUC value range, 166, 167, 168
HCR-20 inter-rater reliability, 165
HCR-20 scoring time frame, 160–161
Risk Matrix 2000-Sex (RMS), 270
SVR-20 predictive validity, 284
Risk/needs/responsivity (RNR) model
definitions, 2, 121–122
LS assessment instruments, 199–200
LS instruments, 204
tools for assessment, 8
YLS/CMI case classification, 83–84
Risk/needs/responsivity risk assessment instruments, 273
Risk principle
defined, 121
and LS instruments, 215–216
spousal violence, 244
Risk principle of case classification, 83
RNR; *See* Risk/needs/responsivity model
RRASOR; *See* Rapid Risk Assessment for Sexual Offense Recidivism
RSVP; *See* Sexual Violence Risk-20 and Risk for Sexual Violence Protocol
Rule breaking
EARL-21G, 56
EARLs, 57

S

Salient Factor Score, 211
Sample dependence, actuarial approach weaknesses, 153–154
SARA; *See* Spousal Assault Risk Assessment Guide
SAVRY; *See* Structured Assessment of Violence Risk in Youth
Scenario planning methods, research needs, 287
Scenarios, future violence, RSVP, 275–276
School/workplace contexts
defined, 1
populations, 3
Scoring
actuarial measures, and individual applicability, 11
adjusted actuarial debate, 6n.
PCL, 21
Self-reporting
assessment parameters, 3, 4
evaluation of, 193–195
Service level assessment, 215–216; *See also* Level of service assessment instruments
Settings
contexts of risk assessment, 4
factors to be considered in risk assessment, 1–2
HCR-20 applications, 147
HCR-20 inter-rater reliability, 164, 165
HCR-20 scoring, 161
HCR-20 validity, 166, 167
and PCL predictive performance, 10
populations, 3

YLS/CMI caveats, 87
Sex Offender Needs Assessment Rating (SONAR), 260
Sex Offender Risk Appraisal Guide (SORAG), 100, 105–107, 114–115, 129, 153
actuarial measure selection, 262
appropriate outcome for sex offenders, 107
case example, 114–115
correlations/comparisons with other instruments
HCR-20 validity, 167
RSVP correlation, 282, 283
RSVP predictive validity, 285, 286
SVR-20 correlation, 282
SVR-20 predictive validity, 283
description and development, 105–106
PCL incorporation into, 22
reliability and validity, 106–107
risk assessment test battery, 35
strengths and weaknesses of actuarial decision making, 154
Sex offenders
actuarial assessment tools
clinical override, effects on accuracy, 11
SORAG, 105–107, 114–115
versus SPJ approaches, comparative predictive performance, 13
juvenile, SAVRY validity, 71, 74
LS external validity, 214
PCL incorporation into assessment tools, 22
populations, 3
Static-99; *See* Static-99
static and dynamic risk factors, 100
VRS-SO, 129–143
application of broad dynamic factors, 135–136
dynamic variable changes and recidivism, 134–135
practical issues in clinical use, 135
reliability, validity, and factor structure, 131–134
static and dynamic variables, 129, 130, 131
Sexual deviance, 154
LS/CMI, 202
risk factor classification, 100
RRASOR and, 262
RSVP, 276
SORAG, 100, 105
SPJ case history, 288–291
SPJ limitations, 286
Static-99, 254, 256, 258, 261
case study, 263–265
development, 255, 256
limitations, 259
SVR-20, 277–278, 286, 289
VRAG-SO, 105, 114–115
VRS-SO, 125
applications of broad dynamic factors, 135
case example, 137–143
factor structure, 131, 132
offense-paralleling or analogue behaviors, 136
predictors or recidivism, 129, 130
Sexually Violent Predator (SVP) evaluations, VRS-SO applications, 137
Sexual Violence Risk-20 (SVR-20) and Risk for Sexual Violence Protocol (RSVP), 99, 113, 269–291
case example, 288–291
description, 269–272
applications, 270
cautions regarding use, 270–271
definition of risk, 270
definition of sexual violence, 269–270
examiner qualifications, 271–272
purpose, 269
target populations, 270
development, 272–277
format, 274–277
literature review, 273
nature of SPJ guidelines, 272–273
underlying principles of SPJ, 273–274
inter-rater reliability, 277–280
RSVP, 278–280
SVR-20, 277–278
predictive performance, comparative, 13
research, 286–287
existing studies, problems with, 286–287
needed, 287
RSVP risk assessment test battery, 35
utility of instruments, 291
validity, 280–286
concurrent, RSVP, 282–283
concurrent, SVR-20, 282
concurrent, SVR-20 versus RSVP, 281–282
construct-related, 286
content-related, 280–281
criterion-related, 281–286
predictive, RSVP, 285–286
predictive, SVR-20, 283–285
Short-Term Assessment of Risk and Treatability (START), 48
Shrinkage, actuarial measures, 10, 154
Situational variables, factors to be considered in risk assessment, 4
SNAP program, 44
under 12 outreach program ORP, 47, 49, 53, 55
Girls Connection (GC), 49, 55, 56, 57
Social/contextual risk factors, SAVRY, 63, 64, 76
Social deviance, psychopathy models, factor structure, 20
Social factors, at-risk children, 44
Social learning theory, LS instruments, 215
Social Skills Rating System (SSRS), 88
Software
COVR, 191–192

LS instruments, 200
SONAR (Sex Offender Needs Assessment Rating), 260
SORAG; *See* Sex Offender Risk Appraisal Guide
SPJ; *See* Structured professional judgment
Spousal Assault Risk Assessment (SARA) Guide, 113, 175, 227–247
assessment procedure, 231–233
coding judgments, 232–233
sources of information, 231–232
case study, 244–246
description of measure, 227–231
applications, 230–231
development, 227–230
future research needs, 246–247
research, 233–243
concurrent validity study summaries, 236
predictive/postdictive validity study summaries, 234–235
prevention-based, 243–244
research, studies not using recommended administration, 241–243
Grann and Wedin (2002), 241–242
Heckert and Gondolf (2004), 243
Hilton, Harris, Rice, Lang, and Cormier (2004), 242–243
research, studies using recommended administration, 237–241
Cairns (2004), 239–240
Gibas, Kropp, Hart, and Stewart (2008), 240–241
Kropp and Hart (2000), 237–238
Mowat-Léger (2001), 238–239
Williams and Houghton (2004), 238
Wong and Hisashima (2008), 240
Spousal violence; *See* Domestic violence
Stable 2000 and Acute 2000, 260
Stable 2007 and Acute 2007, 261–262
Stable dynamic factors, 100
Stages of change model, 124–125
START (Short-Term Assessment of Risk and Treatability), 48
Static-2002, 129, 270
RSVP correlation, 283
RSVP predictive validity, 286
Static-99, 153, 251–265, 270
case example, 263–265
correlations/comparisons with other instruments
HCR-20 validity comparisons, 167
RSVP correlation, 282, 283
RSVP predictive validity, 285, 286
SVR-20 correlation, 282
SVR-20 predictive validity, 284, 285
VRS-SO, 131
development, 251–255
construction samples, 253–255
RRASOR and SACJ-Min, 251–252
tally sheet, 253
limitations, 259–260
populations, appropriate and inappropriate, 258
questions and future directions, 262–263
reliability, 255
SONAR (Sex Offender Needs Assessment Rating), 260
Stable 2000 and Acute 2000, 260
Stable 2007 and Acute 2007, 261–262
strengths, 258–259
strengths and weaknesses of actuarial decision making, 154
validity, 255–257
Static risk factors/variables
actuarial approaches, 148
HCR-20, 148
sex offenders, 129
stable dynamic factors and, 100
VRS/VRS-SO, 122–124, 130, 131
STOP NOW AND PLAN (SNAP) programs, 44
Strengths; *See* Protective factors
Structure, SPJ principles, 274
Structured Anchored Clinical Judgment (SACJ-Min) scale, 251, 252
Structured Assessment of Risk and Need, 262
Structured Assessment of Violence Risk in Youth (SAVRY), 63–77, 150
case example, 74–77
description, 63–67
coding, 64–65
objective, 65
risk factors and predictive factors, 63–64
uses and users, 65–67
EARL-20B inter-rater reliability comparison, 48
high-risk children, 57
limitations and future research needs, 74
method, rationale for development, 67–69
PCL predictive utility versus, 33
predictive performance, comparative, 13
reliability, 69
setting/context of assessment, 67
validity, 70–74
concurrent, 70–71
incremental, 71
predictive, 71–74
Structured clinical risk assessment; *See* EARL-20B and EARL-21G
Structured interviews, EARLs, 46
Structured professional judgment (SPJ), 143n.
actuarial assessment versus, 12–13
defined, 5–6
features of, 7, 8

predictive validity, 11–13
Structured professional judgment tools
at-risk children; *See* EARL-20B and EARL-21G
and changes in risk status, 8
HCR-20; *See* Historical-Clinical-Risk Management-20
risk assessment test battery, 35
SARA; *See* SARA
SAVRY; *See* Structured Assessment of Violence Risk in Youth
SVR and RSVP; *See* Sexual Violence Risk-20 and Risk for Sexual Violence Protocol
Substance abuse
PCL predictive utility versus other factors, 31
predictors of recidivism, 9
SARA assessment, 232
YLS/CMI, 82, 85
YLS/CMI subscore correlations, 89
Summary Risk Rating, SAVRY, 74
Summary Risk Rating, SPJ instruments, 287
Supervision level category, YLS/CMI, 86
SVR-20; *See* Sexual Violence Risk-20 and Risk for Sexual Violence Protocol
Symptomatic subtype, psychopathy, 19

T

Tarassoff-type obligation, 1
Targeted interventions, anamnestic assessment and, 6
Targeted violence risk assessments, SAVRY caveats, 65–66
Taxometric studies, PCL, 21
Team evaluations, HCR-20, 159
Terrorism, contexts of risk assessment, 2
Threat assessments, 271
Time frame
PCL key factors, 34
PCL research needs, 34
Time interval between assessments, LS inter-rater and test-retest reliability, 208–209
Transtheoretical Model of Change, 124–125
Treatment-oriented tools; *See* Violence Risk Scale and Violence Risk Scale–Sexual Offender Version
Tree-based methods, COVR development, 190–191, 192

U

Unstructured clinical discretion, strengths and weaknesses of, 152
Unstructured clinical judgment, 151–152
EARL-20B validity studies, 52–53
strengths and weaknesses of, 6, 152
weaknesses of, 148
Unstructured clinical prediction, HCR-20 summary risk ratings versus, 171

V

Validity of approaches
actuarial, 8–11
actuarial versus SPJ, 12–13
anamnestic, 13–14
predictors of recidivism among mentally disordered offenders, 9
structured professional judgment, 11–12
Victim safety planning/victim lethality assessments, 271
Violence Risk Appraisal Guide (VRAG), 101–105, 114–115, 153
actuarial measure selection, 262
analytic strategy, 103–104
case example, 114–115
construction samples, 103
correlations with other instruments
COVR, 188
HCR-20 summary risk ratings, 171
HCR-20 validity, 167
LSI-R validity, 213
PCL predictive utility, 32
RSVP, 283
SARA, 237, 242
SVR-20, 282
SVR-20 predictive validity, 283, 284
independent variables, 103
method and rationale for development, 102
PCL incorporation into, 22
predictive performance, comparative, 11, 13
reliability, 104
risk assessment test battery, 35
risk factors, 12n.
strengths and weaknesses of actuarial decision making, 154, 155
validity, 104–105
Violence risk assessment considerations; *See* Risk assessment, factors to be considered
Violence Risk Scale (VRS) and Violence Risk Scale –Sexual Offender Version (VRS-SO), 121–144
risk-need-responsibility principle, 121–122
screening versions, 136–137
VRS, 122–129
dynamic variable changes, linkage to treatment outcomes, 128
reliability and validity, 126–128
screening versions, 128–129
static and dynamic variables, 122–125
target populations, 125
VRS-SO, 100, 129–143
application of broad dynamic factors, 135–136

dynamic variable changes and recidivism, 134–135
practical issues in clinical use, 135
reliability, validity, and factor structure, 131–134
static and dynamic variables, 129, 130, 131
VRS-SO case illustration, 137–143
case conceptualization, 141
treatment program, 141–143
Violent Offender Risk Assessment Scale (VORAS), HCR-20 summary risk ratings versus, 171
Violent recidivism
sex offenders, 107
VRAG, 101–105
VRAG; *See* Violence Risk Appraisal Guide
VRS; *See* Violence Risk Scale and Violence Risk Scale–Sexual Offender Version

W

Warn, obligation to, 1, 231
Weighting, risk factors, 11, 153, 154
Wilson Sexual Fantasy Questionnaire subscales, 143n.
Wisconsin Risk assessment instrument, 211
Workplace contexts, 1, 3

Y

YLS/CMI; *See* Youth Level of Service/Case Management Inventory
Youth; *See* Adolescents/juveniles/youth
Youth Level of Service/Case Management Inventory (YLS/CMI), 81–94
applications and administration, 81
case studies, 90–93
high-risk case, 91–93
moderate risk case, 90–91
correlations with other instruments
PCL predictive utility, 33
SAVRY concurrent validity studies, 70
SAVRY predictive power comparisons, 71
description, 84–86
predictive performance, comparative, 13
purpose and goals of measure, 84
rationale for development, 81–84
research with, 87–90
concurrent validity, 88
construct validity, 87–88
dynamic validity, 90
predictive validity, 88–90, 93–94
reliability, 87
scoring, interpretation, implementation, 86–87
strengths, limitations, future research needs, 93–94